Business Marketing

Connecting Strategy, Relationships, and Learning

THE IRWIN/MCGRAW-HILL SERIES IN MARKETING

Business Marketing
Connecting Strategy, Relationships, and Learning

F. Robert Dwyer
University of Cincinnati

John F. Tanner, Jr.
Baylor University

Irwin McGraw-Hill

Boston   Burr Ridge, IL   Dubuque, IA   Madison, WI   New York   San Francisco   St. Louis
Bangkok   Bogotá   Caracas   Lisbon   London   Madrid
Mexico City   Milan   New Delhi   Seoul   Singapore   Sydney   Taipei   Toronto

Irwin/McGraw-Hill

A Division of The **McGraw·Hill** Companies

BUSINESS MARKETING: Connecting Strategy, Relationships, and Learning

This book is printed on acid-free paper.

1 2 3 4 5 6 7 8 9 0 DOW/DOW 9 3 2 1 0 9 8

ISBN 0–256–22133–2

Vice president/Editorial director: *Michael W. Junior*
Publisher: *Gary Burke*
Executive editor: *Stephen M. Patterson*
Senior developmental editor: *Nancy Barbour*
Senior marketing manager: *Colleen J. Suljic*
Project manager: *Amy Hill*
Designer: *Keith McPherson*
Senior photo research coordinator: *Keri Johnson*
Photo researcher: *Michael J. Hruby & Associates*
Production supervisor: *Lori Koetters*
Supplement coordinator: *Jennifer L. Frazier*
Compositor: *Shepherd, Incorporated*
Typeface: *10.5/12 Adobe Garamond*
Printer: *R. R. Donnelley & Sons Company*

Library of Congress Cataloging-in-Publication Data
Dwyer, F. Robert.
    Business marketing / F. Robert Dwyer, John Tanner.
        p.   cm. -- (The Irwin/McGraw-Hill series in marketing)
    Includes bibliographical references and index.
    ISBN 0–256–22133–2
    1. Marketing.   I. Tanner, John F.   II. Title.   III. Series.
HF5415.D92   1999   98–21676
    658.8--dc21

http://www.mhhe.com

About the Authors

About the Authors

F. Robert Dwyer

Dr. Dwyer received his MBA and PhD from the University of Minnesota and earned his bachelor's degree at Michigan State University. Prior to his academic career, he worked in a marketing position at Honeywell.

He is the Joseph S. Stern Professor of Marketing at the University of Cincinnati (UC) and currently serves as marketing department head and director of the Direct Marketing Policy Center. A member of the faculty at the University of Cincinnati since 1978, Dr. Dwyer also served on the faculty at Northwestern University's Kellogg Graduate School of Management and at the University of Arizona. His primary teaching areas include marketing channels, marketing strategy, and direct marketing. He brings a blend of rigor, interaction, relevance, and enthusiasm to the classroom that has resulted in two teaching awards at the University of Cincinnati. In 1991 he was named the Robert B. Clarke Direct Marketing Educator of the Year by the Direct Marketing Educational Foundation.

Professor Dwyer has published scores of articles in leading academic journals on the development and management of buyer–seller relationships. His most cited work is the *Journal of Marketing* article "Developing Buyer–Seller Relationships" which he wrote with business marketing expert Paul Schurr and noted Korean scholar Sejo Oh. He also boasts of his 1995 Best Article of the Year Award from the *Journal of Business-to-Business Marketing,* "Environment, Structure and Performance in Interfirm Exchange," co-authored with University of Kentucky professor Bob Dahlstrom (his former student) and gifted colleague Murali Chandrashekaran.

Dr. Dwyer serves on the editorial review boards of the *Journal of Marketing, Journal of Interactive Marketing,* and *Journal of Business-to-Business Marketing,* among others. He has chaired the national conferences of the American Marketing Association and the Society of Franchising as well as the Direct Marketing Symposium, predecessor for today's Direct Marketing Educators' Conference.

Dedicated to the development of knowledge and the formation of human character even outside of the classroom, Dr. Dwyer is active in youth soccer, co-founder of the boys' club Millennium Falcon$_{24k}$, faculty advisor to the UC Students for Life, and co-founder and board vice president of the private independent school Royalmont Academy. His consulting clients include many Cincinnati-area companies and he has provided marketing and strategy training for executives at Lee Enterprises, Steelcraft, Hoxworth Blood Center, the Ssangyong Group, and other companies.

John F. Tanner, Jr.

At Baylor University, Dr. Tanner is the associate dean for the Hankamer School of Business Undergraduate Programs, research director of the Center for Professional Selling, and associate professor of marketing. He earned his PhD from the University of Georgia. Prior to entering academia, Dr. Tanner spent eight years in industry with Rockwell International and Xerox Corporation as both salesperson and marketing manager.

Dr. Tanner has received several awards for teaching effectiveness and research. Co-author of several other textbooks, including *Selling: Building Partnerships,* he also wrote the Center for Exhibition Industry Research's *Faculty Guide to Trade Shows,* an instructor's manual for incorporating trade shows into marketing and small business curricula, which is available free to any interested college faculty; just drop him an email with a postal address to jeff_tanner@baylor.edu.

Grants from the Center for Exhibition Industry Research, the Institute for the Study of Business Markets, University Research Council, the Wollongong Group, and others have supported his research efforts. Dr. Tanner has published over 30 articles in *Journal of Marketing, Journal of Business Research, Journal of Personal Selling and Sales Management,* international journals, and other publications. He serves on the review boards of several journals, including *Journal of Marketing Education, Journal of Personal Selling and Sales Management,* and *Journal of Marketing Theory & Practice.*

Dr. Tanner writes two monthly columns: one on sales and sales management topics for *Sales and Marketing Strategies & News* and another on trade show issues for *Ideas: the Magazine for Exhibit Managers.* He has also published over 50 articles in various trade publications like *Business Marketing, Sales Managers' Bulletin,* and *American Salesman.*

A state-licensed soccer coach, Dr. Tanner coaches three youth soccer teams and is working on his national coaching license. In addition, he serves local youth through the McLennan County Abstinence Collaboration.

Dedication

To T.K.C., Kathy, Chris, Mike, Matt, Dan, and John

Bob Dwyer

To those most precious: My God, my wife, my children and my parents.

Jeff Tanner

Contents in Brief

Part IV

Investing for Value in Customers and Yourself

Contents

Chapter 4   **Organizational Buyer Behavior**   90

Part II

Foundations for Creating Value

Chapter 7   Weaving Marketing into the Fabric of the Firm   184

Part III

Business Marketing Programming

Chapter 13 Sales and Sales Management 368

Chapter 14 Pricing and Negotiating for Value 400

Part IV

Investing for Value in Customers and Yourself

Preface

Welcome to what we hope is the first of many editions of *Business Marketing: Connecting Strategy, Relationships and Learning.* In the time that we've spent putting this together for you, the rapid change of business marketing has confirmed for us the need for this type of textbook.

You'll find that each chapter opens with an introduction to a firm and its activities in a particular area of business marketing. What you may not realize is that of the 17 firms, one changed its name, another went through a rough financial time but is now doing well, another sold off several divisions . . . well, you get the picture. Just keeping the company names straight has been a chore.

But has business marketing really changed? Do we really need another textbook?

We think so. Some of the greatest changes that require a fresh approach throughout a text (and not just a chapter or a reading) are

- The importance of global relationships.

- Keeping customers enthusiastic about doing business with you.

- Recognizing and managing the many types of customers (including distributors and other channel members).

- Recognizing and managing the many types of suppliers.

- Marketing's changing role in the learning organization and the competitive advantages gained with organizational learning.

- Integrating marketing communications and how it differs for business marketers.

These are just a few reasons why you'll find that this text is not the typical business marketing book. Chapters like "Weaving Marketing into the Fabric of the Firm" and the focus on current customers in "Marketing Opportunities" represent innovations in a business marketing text, yet they're representative of business practice. However, this is a theory-driven text blended with practice at a level that makes the text accessible yet useful for upper-level or graduate courses.

Our Philosophy

Naming this textbook was fun—oh sure, *Business Marketing* was easy. The challenge came in communicating how this book differs from other business marketing texts.

Connecting was chosen because it is only through connecting that marketing works. Connecting new knowledge with developed knowledge is the essence of learning, and learning is the essence of being market-driven. Connecting knowledge to people and people to knowledge is the essence of relationships. All of these connections are made in the context of marketing strategy. Truly, this book represents a unique approach to business marketing.

Relationship marketing is not a buzzword or a set of sales techniques, nor is it a business fad to be quickly adopted and then dropped just as quickly. Nor does relationship marketing operate as an exclusive organizational philosophy or strategy. We believe that relationship marketing is a strategic choice, enabled by technology, driven by global competition, capable of being taught. Hence, we have created a true relationship marketing text and teaching package.

Critical to this strategic choice is the organization's ability to learn—hence our emphasis on learning organizations. Some may say that learning organization theory is not marketing—yet being market-driven requires an understanding of learning organizations and making learning happen.

As we've said, this text is theory-driven, but at the same time, we've worked hard to make it as how-to as possible. Theory will guide people facing changing markets; the how-to will help them get started. Our assumption is that students have had principles of marketing and now plan to enter the field of business marketing after they graduate. Therefore, we want them to hit the ground running but capable of adapting to the changes that are bound to occur.

Another objective is to integrate this course with others. You'll find some material in this book that is unusual for a marketing text, but it is here because we hear from all sides that we have to break down the silos in academia. Readers should come away from this book with an understanding of the importance of not only other marketing courses, but also areas such as accounting and finance. Business marketers don't operate in a vacuum, so we've tried to sensitize them to the needs and contributions of others.

A textbook is really only a part of the experience. We welcome your feedback regarding the package. We hope you'll share with us your victories and your concerns when teaching business marketing.

Teaching Features

There are a number of features unique to this text. For example, each chapter begins with an **opening vignette,** a focus on a firm or industry that illustrates the importance of the material in the chapter. Then, throughout the chapter, reference is made to that firm or industry. This running example highlights the importance of the opening vignette, increasing readership and helping each chapter come alive.

Each opening vignette is followed by action-oriented **learning objectives.** While an excellent test bank has been developed using these objectives, we hope you will also find them useful in preparing essay and short-answer questions. Research indicates that students who use these are more able to identify important points as they read, increasing their learning, so we've taken great care in creating meaningful learning objectives.

Another related feature is the **Business 2 Business** box. Each chapter has two of these boxes, which are designed to encourage reflective learning. Most are tied to the opening vignette, and each one will cause students to pause and reflect on the material they have just read. Not just a discussion question, a Business 2 Business box provides additional detail and orients students to a deep consideration of how business marketing principles are applied.

Two **From the Field** boxes are included in each chapter, one of which focuses on an international issue or practice. These short stories illustrate key concepts as they've been applied by firms as big as IBM and as small as Freeman Exhibit Company. Our students tell us that these detailed examples are interesting and fun to read as well as helpful in keying on what is important in the chapter. Many From the Fields are original to this text, as we've conducted interviews and researched companies in order to create a feature that truly adds value to the student.

Key terms can be found at the end of each chapter. Each key term is in bold print in the chapter's sentence in which you find its definition. Further, each key term can also be found in what is probably the most comprehensive **glossary** of any business marketing text. We've made a significant effort to include both academic terms and the jargon of the field. Students familiar with these terms will enter the field speaking the language of business marketing.

Each chapter has at least 10 **discussion questions,** which can be used in class or as homework. You'll find questions that apply concepts, integrate material from earlier chapters, or require deep analysis of principles as well as questions that simply review the chapter. This variety of question types means that any reader, whether professor or student, can use these discussion questions for both in-class use and study.

An **Internet exercise** is also offered for each chapter. These exercises are, for the most part, designed to encourage students to further explore concepts presented in the chapter within the context of the focus firm. For example, students are expected to find and evaluate press releases about Intel, the focus firm of the advertising, publicity, and trade show chapter. These exercises will increase students' familiarity with the web while also encouraging them to conduct company research, applying concepts from the chapter.

Two **cases** also follow each chapter. Cases are designed for homework and class discussion focusing on the immediate chapter. You'll notice that many have data that require analysis, but the level of analysis is not as rigorous as with a longer case. Students will, however, have to carefully formulate their responses, synthesizing the concepts of each chapter with application.

Additional readings are provided for upper-level courses. These readings represent recent research papers that provide relevant detail to the concepts covered in the chapter. Professors may want to assign these when using the book at the graduate or senior level, whereas undergraduate students can use these to begin research on term papers.

Comprehensive cases can be found at the end of the book. These full-length cases are designed to integrate material across several chapters, and some are **video cases,** making use of video introductions to the written case. Many of these cases are new, some written especially for this text. Because we've developed an innovative text that deals with issues such as marketing's role in the learning organization, it was often impossible to locate cases that fit, so we created new ones. We also found a number of colleagues who shared our concerns about existing cases and wrote their own, which they've contributed to this text. As a result, you'll enjoy a number of cases involving global marketing issues presented within the context of typical marketing issues such as marketing communications planning.

Some professors are afraid of using a new text because it hasn't been field tested. That shouldn't be a problem with this text. While many cases are newly published, all have been used by the case authors and they've given us excellent case notes. You'll find these and other teaching tools in the **Instructor's Manual.** Both of us have taught classes using this text and we've incorporated our years of experience in developing course outlines, lecture suggestions, class exercises, question answers, and transparencies (many of which are not from exhibits in the book). We are passionate about teaching quality, and believe you'll find many useful ideas in the *Instructor's Manual.*

Irwin/McGraw-Hill hired the best test question writers (not Bob and Jeff!) in the business to create the **Test Bank**. Questions are tied directly to the learning objectives and the material covered in the discussion questions. Key terms are also an important element covered in the test questions.

One of the most exciting features about this package, and certainly one that has been fun to put together, is the **videotape library**. After pressuring our contacts in the field to provide us with videotape that isn't a part of other text packages, we've managed to locate some outstanding videos. You'll also find the video cases in this library.

Acknowledgments

Bringing a textbook to the market is not a solitary endeavor. To have a really good package requires the support and input of a lot of people, and we've been blessed with an excellent team. You'll notice an international flavor to this reviewer list. That was a purposeful move in order to ensure the global applicability of the book. The reviewers for this text were outstanding, and we'd like to acknowledge their contributions:

Jeffrey Blodgett, University of Mississippi

Brett Boyle, DePaul University

Robert Dahlstrom, University of Kentucky

Altan Erdem, University of Houston, Clear Lake

David Faulds, University of Louisville

Don Glover, Metro State University

Amjad Hadjikhani, Uppsala University, Sweden

Suzanne Hertz, Stockholm School of Economics, Sweden

Frank Johnson, University of Western Sydney, Australia

Vaughn Judd, Auburn University at Montgomery

Karl Mann, Tennessee Technical University

Ron Michaels, University of Central Florida

Jakki Mohr, University of Montana

Alfred Quinton, The College of New Jersey

Mary Lou Roberts, University of Massachusetts, Boston

Steven Thrasher, Pacific Lutheran University

David Urban, Virginia Commonwealth University

Elizabeth Wilson Woodside, Louisiana State University

Other faculty around the world gave us their cases. These wonderful people put a lot of time and effort into making these cases outstanding teaching tools. In appreciation of their gifts to the book, we thank

Sven Gibson, Baylor University

Mauricio Gonzales, ITESM, Mexico

Tom Leigh, University of Georgia

Faye McIntyre, Rockhurst College

Ralph Oliva, Penn State University

Jacqueline Pels, University Torcuato Di Tella, Argentina

Lou Pelton, University of North Texas

Some colleagues deserve a special thank-you. Thanks to Jim Comer, B.J. Zirger, Larry Chonko, and Mary Anne Raymond—colleagues with good examples and research with flesh and bones to hang on the data skeleton. Thanks also to Dave Wilson and the Institute for the Study of Business Markets for sparking research and interest in this field.

Thanks to Constantine Polychroniou—and his students—for testing most of the draft chapters in his business marketing class. We'd also like to thank our students who also served as guinea pigs as we taught the course using drafts.

Thanks to Bob Dahlstrom for encouraging us to showcase all the vistas in business marketing—not just steel and chemicals, but financial and marketing services, franchising, nonprofit customers, foodstuffs, and more.

With the number of original From the Fields and opening vignettes, we've had to rely on the assistance of many practitioners. Without their help, the book would not be nearly as exciting, so we would like to thank them here:

Courtney Chamberlain and Steve Sind, Center for Exhibition Industry Research

Howard Gardner III, Florida Furniture Industries

Jim Gudmens, First Data Corp.

Pete Jones, Hydrotech

Bernie Joyce, Martiny & Company

Tim Keane, Retail Target Market Systems

Richard Langlotz, Minolta Business Systems

Joe McGrath, Xerox, The Document Company

Laurie Spar and Dick Montesi, Direct Marketing Educational Foundation

Lester Wells, Bradburn Company

The creative support and encouragement from the Irwin/McGraw-Hill staff has been exemplary. We really appreciate the support of Steve Patterson and the staff assembled for this project. Nancy Barbour, as always, has been a joy to work with and we particularly want to thank her for keeping us on time and for serving as a friendly sounding board. Kudos too to Mike Hruby who found most of the photographs, Amy Hill, and Lori Koetters, who coordinated the production of the book, and Nick Childers of Arthur Scott Productions, who put the video together.

A number of people helped us with the manuscript preparation, including Cindy Lawless, Clint Dudley, Susan Seago, Amy Hereford, Elizabeth Vaughn, Dorynda Westbrook, and Patty Herbst. In addition, we've received helpful comments from our students who have used the text. They deserve our thanks, as do others who prefer to remain anonymous.

Bob Dwyer
Dwyerfr@email.uc.edu

Jeff Tanner
jeff_tanner@baylor.edu

Business Marketing
Connecting Strategy, Relationships, and Learning

Part I

Business Markets and Business Marketing

Congratulations! You have opened the book—really the door—to the dynamic world of business marketing. Get ready to explore a world that is brand new to most students.

We have organized *Business Marketing* into four parts. Briefly, Part I orients you to some of the unique phenomena and players in business markets. Part II delves into the world of strategic scanning, planning, and spanning in a business context in order to deliver superior value to customers. Part III covers the key areas of business marketing programming, from product development and channel management to the integration of advertising, trade shows, personal selling, and more into a fitting communication strategy. Part IV closes the book with critical concepts for evaluating and controlling marketing efforts, retaining customers, and thriving in tomorrow's global, technological, and professional environments.

Has Nestlé ever sent a specialist to your home to help you make the perfect iced tea for your weekend barbecue? In business markets, a seller's personnel sometimes work directly with the customer. They help the customer define specifications and test new products; plan delivery schedules; train production, sales, and service personnel; and, inevitably, "fight fires." In fact, exchange of personnel is just one means that buyer and seller in business markets *relate*. Part I provides the spectrum of buyer–seller relationships in business markets and addresses key motivations and challenges for their longevity.

Part I also distinguishes the business market from the more familiar consumer market in terms of its magnitude and volatility. More than a limited exposure to the varied relationships between organizations, we bet you have not purchased $40,000 of Steelcase furniture or received a bid from Service Master to maintain your apartment, nor have you received an invitation to stop by the Westvaco (envelopes) booth at the Promotion Management Association's Trade Show and Convention. Thus, Part I previews important distinctions on the concentration of participants, the types of products and customers, and formal and social dimensions of the purchasing process.

So let's get down to business. Part I introduces the fundamental character of business markets and the nature of decision making and purchasing by organizational customers—the very foundation for the strategic thinking we take up in Part II.

Chapter 1

Introduction to Business Marketing

BASF

What is BASF? You may own a videotape or cassette made by BASF, but most of its products are not available directly to consumers. From its advertising campaigns, it appears that it doesn't exactly make anything (actually it makes chemicals), but it does make snowboards stronger, mattresses softer, boots drier, houses livelier, and carpets longer lasting. Can you go out and buy a BASF product to make your carpet longer lasting? No. So why does it advertise on TV? Who is its audience? ●

Its advertising is directed at the women and men who purchase products for their companies and to those people who design products such as snowboards, mattresses, and carpets. The purpose of the television ads is to create the image that BASF creates value in those products. BASF hopes that when its salespeople call on the buyers for snowboard, mattress, and carpet manufacturers, those buyers will recognize the BASF name, remember what BASF does, and let the salesperson in. ●

BASF further supports its salespeople with direct mail, advertising in trade publications, and exhibits at trade shows that continue the same theme of making things better. All of these marketing efforts are aimed at reaching the persons responsible for deciding what the final product (be it a mattress, snowboard, or carpet), will be, how it will be designed to compete, and the bundle of benefits it will provide. ●

The German company has annual revenues greater than 50 billion deutschemarks, with 20 percent of its business in North America. The company operates six divisions: oil and gas, agricultural products, plastics and fibers, chemicals, dyes and finishing products, and consumer products. As you can see, most of its products are intended for commercial users. ●

BASF says, "We don't make a lot of the products you buy; we make a lot of the products you buy *better*." ●

Visit BASF's home page: **www.basf.com** ●

Learning Objectives

As you can see from the BASF story, you've probably encountered business-to-business marketing (or just business marketing, for short) without actually realizing it. Students are more familiar with consumer marketing, because they are the targets of consumer marketing. But the opportunities for careers in marketing are particularly attractive for students who enter business marketing (the marketing of products and services to other businesses). In this chapter, we introduce business marketing.

After reading it, you should be able to

● Define and explain the nature of business marketing.
● Illustrate the different types of business markets and how they differ from consumer markets.
● Discuss the nature of demand for business products and services.
● Explain the different approaches to business marketing, as typified in the relationships between buyers and sellers.

Business marketing is not the same as marketing to consumers. As you will see in this chapter, there are many differences that make business marketing unique and stimulating. At the same time, you will find what you learned in previous marketing courses to be helpful as you advance through this course.

Exhibit 1–1
Distribution of
Salt

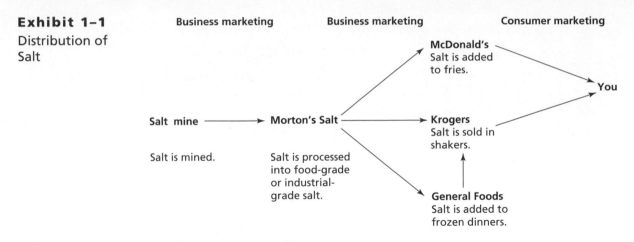

The Importance of Business Markets

How much salt does the average household in the United States use each year? Total food-grade salt sales for the United States are 1.33 million pounds annually. Consumption in the household, however, is 7–8 grams per day per person, which only equates to 824 thousand pounds. Why the difference? The consumption figure doesn't count the amount of salt that is in processed foods (such as frozen dinners) or foods we purchase in restaurants. Businesses purchase and use over 500,000 pounds of food-grade salt per year, or almost 40 percent of total salt sales, for such purposes as making pickles, breakfast cereals, and other food products.[1] Add to this amount the volume of industrial-grade salt (for such uses as chemical processes and salting frozen roads) and the industrial purchases of salt tower over consumer purchases.

To look at the magnitude of industrial purchases a little differently, consider that General Motors spends more than $50 billion per year on products and services—more than the gross national product of Portugal or Greece. General Motors employs over 1,350 purchasing agents, who *each* spend over $31 million annually! There are few consumers with that kind of spending power!

Most students, when they think of marketing, consider the marketing aimed at influencing their personal purchasing, which is marketing to consumers. Consumer purchases, however, represent a smaller dollar value than business purchases. While marketing to consumers may be more obvious, more students will enter business marketing after graduation than consumer marketing.

Business marketing is marketing products or services to other companies, government bodies, institutions (such as hospitals), and other organizations. McDonald's and other companies buy products, such as salt, and services to use in the production of their product. Exhibit 1–1 illustrates a few of the possibilities for food-grade salt. Morton Salt also sells salt to food processors like General Foods (which use it in the food products they make) and to retailers (which sell salt to you). With the exception of the purchase you make, all of the buying and selling in the exhibit involves business marketing.

Business marketing also includes the marketing of products and services that facilitate their operations. For example, McDonald's purchases paper to run through its copiers. Copies facilitate McDonald's real business, which is making hamburgers and fries. Marketing to government agencies and institutions (which also buy salt for cafeterias and other such uses) such as your college or university is also business marketing.

Why Study Business Marketing?

Business marketing is an exciting area of study. Students may be more familiar with consumer marketing; after all, everyone is a consumer. Business marketing, however, is new to most students. It is not the same as consumer marketing, and there are several compelling reasons for studying business marketing.

Marketing Majors Begin in Business Marketing

Are you a marketing major? More marketing majors find jobs with businesses that sell products or services to other businesses rather than with businesses that sell to consumers. For that reason alone, it seems worthwhile to study business marketing.

Indeed, the majority of business school graduates—whether in accounting, finance, logistics, management, production, real estate, or quantitative methods—will find themselves working at firms doing business with other organizations. Many companies have awakened to the fact that they must be market-driven if they are to survive. Being market-driven means that customer satisfaction and operational efficiency are the order of the day for every department and individual employee or associate. Market-driven means that at many organizations, individuals with complementary expertise and skills work in teams to constantly strive to serve organizational customers better, to innovate, and to develop means to approach new institutional markets. This book prepares you to make positive contributions to such teams in the business marketing environment.

But be careful. Students must not be motivated only for career and profit promise. You must develop your knowledge and intellect to realize your full human potential. Every person applies a part of that potential to participate in the political and economic life of society. A course in business marketing gives valuable insight into human nature and the workings of economic systems.

Magnitude of Business Marketing

One reason that more marketing majors begin their careers in business marketing than in consumer marketing, is because of the magnitude of business marketing. Purchases by organizations such as companies, government agencies, and institutions account for more than half of the economic activity in industrialized countries such as the United States, Canada, and France, making business marketing an important activity. As mentioned earlier, few consumers have the purchasing power of an organization. Understanding how organizations buy is important to marketers who want to capitalize on the size of the business market.

Business Marketing Is Unique

There would be no point in having a separate business marketing class if business marketing were the same as marketing to consumers. If one type of marketing fit all situations, then only one set of classes would be required. The way organizations buy is radically different from the way consumers purchase products and services, which results in different marketing requirements. Let's examine some ways in which business marketing is unique.

How Business Marketing Is Unique

Business marketing is unique in that channels of distribution are shorter and more direct, there is more emphasis on personal selling and negotiation, and complex buying processes result in unique promotional strategies. Relationships are also different between buyer and

---

1–1

FROM THE FIELD
Quest for the Baldrige Award Reshapes CRI

The Malcolm Baldrige award was established by Congress in 1987 to enhance U.S. competitiveness by promoting quality awareness. Since its establishment, only 28 companies have won the award. CRI's Baldrige award in 1997 is the first made to a service firm. CRI is a custom marketing research company that helps clients develop new products in consumer, medical, and service industries.

What makes the CRI experience different is that CRI's quality ratings went up as the number of customers went down. As Beth Rounds, senior vice president for business development, says, "We saw the Baldrige . . . as an opportunity for us to formalize the way we do business; that it would give us a framework for running our business." That framework included focusing on large accounts, and developing long-term relationships.

"When we made a commitment to working with fewer longer-term clients, it weeded out many companies that didn't fit our strategy," according to Rounds. "We certainly didn't tell them to go away, but we discussed our partnering philosophy, how we wanted to approach the business, and let them decide what was best to do."

For clients that didn't fit, CRI referred them to competitors. In 1988, the company had 138 clients. Nine years later, at the time of the Baldrige award, the number had fallen to 67. But don't worry about CRI. Revenue doubled during the same time period!

Source: Laurie Freeman, "Quest for Baldrige Reshapes CRI," *Business Marketing,* March 1997, p. 52.

---

seller when both are organizations than when one is an individual consumer. Because relationships are so important (indeed, relationship marketing is a major theme of this book), we'll discuss it first.

Buyer-Seller Relationships

In consumer markets, there are few industries where close personal relationships exist between buyer and seller. Perhaps in those instances where personal selling is the most important element of the marketing mix and where customer service is also important, relationships between buyer and seller may exist. These situations, however, are rare.

In business marketing, situations where strong personal and business relationships grow between buyer and seller are not as rare. The strategic importance of many purchases is too great for companies to always shop around when making a purchase; they need to make absolutely sure that the product fits their needs and that it will be available when needed at the right cost. Therefore, many companies enter into long-term contracts, build relationships that enable buyers and sellers to plan jointly, and work to secure the future for both companies. From the Field 1–1 describes how one company became more relationship-oriented, doubling revenue in the process.

As another example, all new Ford cars and trucks have Firestone tires. The importance of the Ford account to Firestone is great. For Firestone, it makes sense to build as strong a relationship as possible with the decision makers at Ford. Ford and Firestone plan new tire products together, because the cost of those new products will

Exhibit 1–2   The Relationship Continuum

Transactional Marketing	Relationship Marketing
Purpose of marketing is to make a sale.	Purpose of marketing is to create a customer.
Sale is result and the measure of success.	Sale is beginning of relationship; profit is measure of success.
Business is defined by its products and factories.	Business is defined by its customer relationships.
Price is determined by competitive market forces; price is an input.	Price is determined by negotiation and joint decision making; price is an outcome.
Communications are aimed at aggregates of customers.	Communications are targeted and tailored to individuals.
Marketer is valued for its products and prices.	Marketer is valued for its present and future problem-solving capability.
Objective: to make the next sale; find the next customer.	Objective: to satisfy the customer you have by delivering superior value.

SOURCE: Adapted from Frederick E. Webster, Jr., at Special Session on "Relationship Marketing," at the 1993 American Marketing Association Educators' Conference (August), Boston, Massachusetts.

impact the cost of new Ford cars and trucks, and because the quality of those tires will impact perceptions of Ford's quality. These joint efforts represent a partnership between the two firms.

Types of Business Relationships

Not all buyer–seller relationships in business marketing are partnerships like the one between Ford and Firestone. There are **transactional relationships**, situations where buyers and sellers interact with only selfish consideration, without thought of the possibility of future interaction. Think of relationships as falling somewhere along a continuum. At one end is the purely transactional relationship.

At the other end of the business relationship continuum is the partnership, which many writers liken to a marriage. As we see in Exhibit 1–2, a **partnership** is a relationship characterized by mutual commitment, high trust, and common goals. Achieving partnership status is a marketing objective for many marketing organizations. With partnership status come opportunities to develop new business, a chance to gain access to valuable information, and many other benefits. With partnership status, though, comes greater responsibility for the customer as well as the seller. While not all business relationships are partnerships, there is more emphasis placed on relationship quality and management in business marketing.

In addition to the end points of the continuum, it is helpful to categorize relationships on two other dimensions: the social dimension and the contractual dimension. **Social relationship** is the term we will use to describe a trading association supported principally by social bonds and habit; the organic dimension is the degree to which social bonds are part of the relationship. The "glue" holding together a social relationship includes interpersonal attraction, similarity in background or culture, a track record of successful cooperation, efficient communication, and general satisfaction. The transactional exchange just illustrated could evolve into a social relationship if the representative of the maintenance company becomes friends with the representative of the tool rental firm.

The social bonds and the positively reinforced interactions that support the social relationship are important to most business relationships. Sometimes trading parties need more assurance than friendship that the relationship can be sustained and that the other party will always be motivated to perform up to established standards; these assurances usually involve some type of contract. Contracts provide safeguards, so the relationships are called **safeguarded relationships**. Businesses use a variety of devices to safeguard relationships. They use contracts with large penalties for termination—often with detailed procedures for resolving conflicts. They also use the equivalent of hostages or pledges. For example, Comacho Packaging may license a packaging technology from Brik-Pak and put up $100,000 plus pay a royalty of 15 percent to Brik-Pak. Comacho would then sell the packaging technology for Brik-Pak in a particular market. If Comacho failed to meet sales goals or had quality problems, it would forfeit the $100,000. Brik-Pak, on the other hand, would lose the royalty if it terminates the agreement.

Corporate relationships are exchanges safeguarded by ownership or vertical integration, and represent the extreme of the contractual dimension. A university assures itself of sustained access to printing services by having its own printing operation. A medical equipment manufacturer may acquire a wholesaler to provide the selling and distribution services it requires. In each example, the trading relation becomes circumscribed by an employment relationship. Generally, employees work within a set of explicit rules and under an authority structure that is difficult—but not impossible—to duplicate in contracts between independent organizations.

Shorter Distribution Channels

In most cases, distribution channels do not include anyone between the manufacturer and the customer who uses the product, or user. Many manufacturers sell directly to the user, which reflects a large difference between business marketing and consumer marketing, as you can see in Exhibit 1–3. (Note that in some consumer situations, such as with Allstate Insurance or Burpee Seeds, there are direct channels, but companies with direct channels are much fewer there than in business marketing.) In situations where industrial distributors are used, there are still fewer steps between the consumer and manufacturer.

Shorter channels contribute to the closer relationship between manufacturer and buyer. Buyers can have more direct input into the product planning process. Direct relationships between various functional areas within both companies can result; for example, the accounts payable department of the buyer may talk directly with the billing department of the seller if problems arise.

Exhibit 1–3

Business Marketing Channels Are Much More Direct than Consumer Marketing Channels

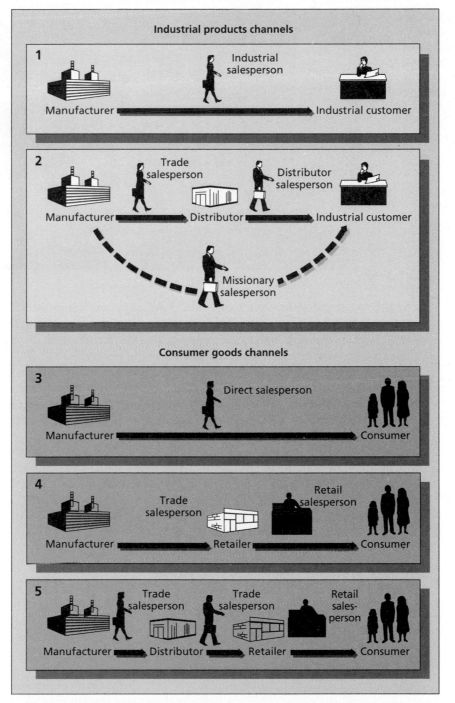

SOURCE: Barton A. Weitz, Stephen B. Castleberry, and John F. Tanner, Jr. *Selling: Building Partnerships.* Second edition. Burr Ridge, IL: Irwin/McGraw-Hill, 1995.

Emphasis on Personal Selling

Stronger relationships and shorter channels are two reasons why there is a greater emphasis on personal selling in business marketing. Direct communication between buyer and seller also increases the need for strong personal selling, because someone is needed to

Trade shows are like temporary industrial shopping malls, a unique element in the business marketing mix.
© Einzig Photographers Inc.

coordinate that communication. Salespeople are the members of the organization responsible for coordinating their company's efforts at satisfying their customers. That responsibility is greater when the organization is concerned about creating and maintaining partnerships with its customers.

Complex buying procedures involving many members of the buying organization also require personal selling. Only through personally getting to know each individual and coordinating the sales–purchase process can a business be successful. Multiple personal relationships can strengthen organizational relationships, and these relationships are the responsibility of the salesperson.

A customer's size and a direct channel also influence business marketing by increasing the importance of negotiation. Large orders sold directly by the manufacturer to the user or OEM (original equipment manufacturer) buyer increase the likelihood of negotiation because changes can be made to the product and price. There is greater flexibility in the seller's offering, increasing the potential for negotiating the final deal and adding to the importance of personal selling.

Unique Promotional Strategies

The complex buying process and inclusion of several people from different functional areas impact the business marketing promotional strategies, too. In a family, for example, the person who determines the budget is likely to be the person who makes the purchase and decides what is needed. When an organization makes a purchase, however, personnel from several different departments will determine together what the organization needs.

Each different department may have a separate set of needs and interests, which may influence how marketers promote their products. For example, BASF's carpet fiber may be advertised as a low-cost product to the finance department of carpet manufacturers. BASF's advertising to carpet manufacturers' marketing departments, however, would focus on how carpet companies' customers want longer-lasting carpet made with BASF's fiber.

Additionally, consumers can go to shopping malls for their purchases. Few business shopping malls exist, so trade shows or expositions are created. These shows last for a few

Exhibit 1–4
Types of
Customers

Companies That Consume	**Institutions**
Original equipment manufacturers	Hospitals
Users	Schools, colleges, and universities
Government Agencies	**Resellers**
Country	Wholesalers
State	Brokers
Local	Industrial distributors

days, and bring together buyers from all over the world. As you can see, business marketers engage in many unique promotional activities that are different from what you see as a consumer.

Business marketing is unique, with stronger buyer–seller relationships, shorter channels of distribution, a greater emphasis on personal selling, and unique promotional strategies. Another factor that makes business marketing different from marketing to consumers is that the buyers are different. In the next section, we explore the types of buyers for business products and services.

Business Markets

There are numerous differences between purchasing by organizations and purchasing by consumers. Many of the differences are due to the fact that consumers purchase for personal consumption, and in most cases individuals within organizations do not. They purchase to satisfy needs of the organization. Other factors, too influence the nature of business buying, making it different. These factors are the types of customers, the types of products they buy, the size and location of customers; the complex processes and rigorous standards of purchasing, the nature of business relationships, and the nature of demand. It is important to understand these differences so that you can appreciate the special challenges facing business marketers and so that you can better apply what you have already learned about marketing.

Types of Business Customers

There are four types of business customers, as illustrated in Exhibit 1–4: firms that consume the product or service (such as original equipment manufacturers), government agencies, institutions, and firms that purchase and resell the product. This book focuses on the first three—those organizations that purchase for consumption. We will discuss those firms that purchase and resell products, but we focus on industrial distributors that distribute products consumed by other organizations, rather than wholesalers and retailers of consumer products.

Original Equipment Manufacturers
When a company purchases a product or service to be included in its own final product, the company is called an **original equipment manufacturer (OEM)**. For example, General Motors may buy gauges for installation in the dashboards of its automobiles. In this instance, General Motors is an OEM.

GM is representative of all types of customers, as it buys to manufacture products, as well as buying products for resale through their dealer network.

Ingersoll-Rand automotive parts; Roger Ball/The Stock Market.

Users

When GM purchases copier paper from Xerox, General Motors is considered a **user**, or the business equivalent of the final consumer. General Motors is also a user of market research purchased from service bureaus such as Donnelly and JD Power as well as other services such as accounting and computer services. When GM purchases machine tools used to assemble cars, GM is still considered a user, even though the tools are used in the manufacturing process. Since the tools and research are not part of the final product, GM is considered a user to manufacturers of tools, research, and other such products or services.

Government Agencies

In the United States, the government is the largest single purchaser of products and services, buying more than $300 billion worth each year. The federal government is also the country's largest single landlord, renting and maintaining more property than any other individual organization. As such, the government buys and uses many products.

In this and other countries, the government may be the only customer for some products. In all countries, the government is probably the only buyer of tanks and other armored weapon systems. In the United States, companies can own their own telephone system for internal use. On the other hand, in some countries, all telephone systems must be leased from the government. The government, then, is the only customer for telephone switching equipment.

The purchasing processes used by the government can be frustrating and complex, particularly since the government seeks to accomplish social objectives through purchasing. Policies designed to encourage the growth of minority- or women-owned businesses as well as small businesses are examples of social objective policies that influence government purchasing.

The government goes to great lengths to find and support these businesses, as illustrated in From the Field 1–2, "Me Tarzan—You Buyer?" Once the qualifications for designation as minority- or women-owned or small business are met, however, such companies can grow significantly if they are successful in selling to the government.

The federal government is not the only government customer. State governments also purchase goods and services, as do local institutions. In addition to buying such products as copiers, buildings, and roads, they also buy salt, both for applying to roads and for use in jails, employee cafeterias, and other uses!

1–2

FROM THE FIELD
Me Tarzan—You Buyer?

Trade shows are typically thought of as a marketing jungle, with seller Tarzans trying to carry off buyer Janes. The General Services Administration (GSA), however, is different. As the country's largest landlord, GSA has a captive market: the U.S. government. GSA isn't looking for buyers. So why does it exhibit at trade shows?

Alicia Astrich, marketing communications specialist for the GSA's Office of Business Development, explains, "We use trade shows to attract potential suppliers, to inform suppliers, and to strengthen our relationship with suppliers. Our job is really to act as a consultant for the government, and to find the best suppliers who will actually provide the product or service."

The government has many programs designed to assist small and disadvantaged businesses that might otherwise pass the government by. These programs, such as the Mandatory Source Program, Subcontracting Program, Minority Bank Deposit Program, and Rural Area Business

Program, need promotion in order to achieve the goals set by Congress. "Our objectives are twofold," notes Astrich. First, the GSA wants to make suppliers aware of procurement programs and opportunities. The emphasis here is on identifying new suppliers as well as making current suppliers aware of new opportunities.

The second objective is to strengthen relationships with current suppliers. Being government, business is often conducted at arm's length. "At the same time, however, we want to be open to suggestions for service improvement, cost containment, and other ideas our suppliers might have," says Aldrich. Shows offer an excellent forum for such discussions and strengthen relationships with suppliers. "We need strategic partnerships, just as any profit-based organization does, and for the same reasons. We find our exhibiting at shows helps us identify potential partners and develop stronger relationships."

Source: John F. Tanner Jr., "Me Tarzan, You Buyer?" *ideas* (September 1995), pp. 4–5.

Institutions

Institutions include organizations such as schools (kindergarten through twelfth-grade systems as well as colleges and universities), hospitals and nursing homes, churches, and charitable organizations. Some of these organizations may use purchasing procedures similar to those utilized by government agencies, while others may follow less standardized procedures. Hospitals, nursing homes, and psychiatric and substance abuse centers make purchases related to the medical services they provide, and may use criteria similar to those used by OEMs in making these purchases. Churches purchase products and services for use to facilitate the services they provide, with criteria and buying processes that may vary widely from church to church. Because of the special purchasing needs of institutions, many firms have special divisions or sales forces for these markets. Xerox, for instance, offers educational and medical institutions the same prices as government agencies (the lowest that Xerox offers) and has special salespeople for institutional markets.

Industrial Distributors

Industrial distributors are those organizations that supply industrial companies with products and services. For example, Brazos Valley Equipment supplies farmers and ranchers with John Deere tractors, harvesters, and other farm implements. Waco Hotel and Motel Supply provides central Texas hotels and motels with janitorial, office, pool, and restaurant supplies and just about anything else anyone needs to run a hotel or motel. C.M. Tanner Wholesale Grocery in Carrollton, Georgia, delivers produce, meats, and other groceries to institutions including West Georgia State College. These distributors provide services similar to those delivered by wholesalers and retailers of consumer goods; they make large purchases of certain products, and then sell smaller quantities of individual products—within a wide assortment of products—to industrial users or OEMs.

Types of Products

Products are generally classified on the basis of the type of organization purchasing the products and for what purpose. Whether the product is part of the organization's final product or facilitates the organization's activities is the primary difference in determining product type. Because the buying organization has its own customers with their own demand for quality, doing a superior job of buying products that become part of the final product can be a competitive advantage. Therefore, understanding the types of products bought and sold in business markets is important.

Products used in the final product include raw and manufactured materials, component parts or OEM parts, and assemblies. **Raw materials**, or materials processed only to the point required for economic handling and distribution, are also sold to OEMs for use in the products they manufacture. Gold and silver, for example, are purchased by companies such as AT&T for use in the manufacture of telecommunications equipment. Raw materials are often further processed into manufactured materials, such as steel. Iron is the raw material that is then processed into steel. GM may buy sheet steel, which is called a **manufactured material** because the material, which has been transformed from the raw material, requires further processing before GM can use it; the sheets must be cut to the proper size and so forth. If BASF supplied its carpet treatment product to GM for application to carpets in cars and trucks, the BASF product would be considered a manufactured material.

Component parts, or **OEM parts**, are parts assembled into the final product without further transformation. In some instances, a company may purchase OEM parts and assemble these to make a component for installation into the final product by another company. The component may then be called a subassembly or assembly. For example, Gates Controls may purchase plastic casing (a component part) from Plastech and parts from Metric Devices, and then assemble these into a tachometer that is sold to GM. GM would then put the tachometer into its cars or trucks. GM may refer to the part as an assembly.

Other products are facilitating products; they facilitate the company's achievement of its objectives but are not part of the final product. Hand tools, such as sanders, routers, portable saws, and other light tools, are called **accessory equipment**. Office equipment, such as personal computers and desktop printers, would also fit in the accessory equipment category.

Capital equipment, also called installations, refers to large equipment used in the production process that requires significant financial investment. Capital equipment would include overhead cranes, blast furnaces, industrial robots, and other manufacturing equipment as well as forklifts, road graters, and other heavy construction machinery.

The difference between accessory and capital equipment is important when it comes to marketing the equipment to users. Capital equipment is much more expensive, and its purchase may involve more members of the organization than purchase of accessory equipment. Marketing requirements are different as more members of the organization must be reached by marketing efforts.

Exhibit 1–5

Customer and Product Types IBM is an example of a company that buys all types of products from all types of companies, and sells many types of products to different types of companies.

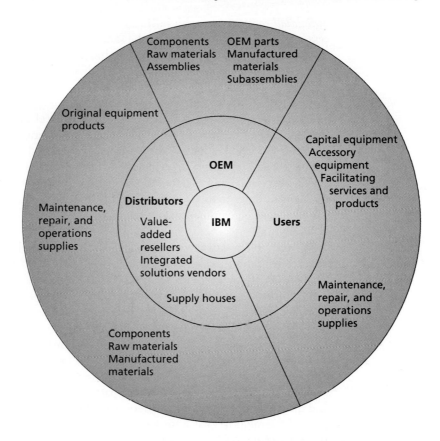

Products sold to users for use in the company's operations are often labeled **MRO** items **(maintenance, repair, and operations products)**. Operating supplies would include the copier paper mentioned earlier. Another term is **facilitating supplies** or **facilitating services**, because they support company efforts but are not part of the final product. Banking services, marketing research services, advertising services, and transportation services also fall into this category.

Maintenance products or services include janitorial products, painting contractors who paint the buildings, plumbing services, and heating and air conditioning services. The term *repair products and services* usually refers to repair of the manufacturing equipment and tools rather than repairs to the facility.

For example, GM purchases MRO items to maintain its plants and equipment. At the same time, GM buys OEM parts for use in its cars. GM will purchase both, but the classification system enables us to recognize the different decision processes used for each and the different marketing requirements brought about by those processes, which we will discuss in later chapters. Exhibit 1–5 is a matrix that illustrates which types of customers purchase which types of products.

Size and Location of Customers

Size and location of customers create unique challenges for business marketers that are not faced by those who market directly to consumers. As we indicated earlier, General Motors purchases $50 billion in products and services per year. There are no individual consumers with that kind of purchasing power. *Business customers are larger than individual consumers* so each business customer is more important to the financial success of the business marketer. At the same time, *there are fewer individual business customers.* For example, if a company's product is components used in new cars, there are only a few manufacturers to sell to. One dissatisfied customer can have a significant impact on the firm.

Business customers are also *more likely to be geographically concentrated.* Industries tend to arise around key resources. For example, steel manufacturing requires iron ore, limestone, energy, access to labor, and access to customers. Through the mid-20th century, the Great Lakes and major river systems enabled Chicago, Cleveland, and Pittsburgh to access ore from the Minnesota Iron Range; coal from the Dakotas, Kentucky, and Pennsylvania; and major steel markets in Detroit and the eastern seaboard. Breakthroughs in water transport and scale economies in production have made steel an internationally traded commodity, but the early steel industry was located near those sources of supply.

For technology-driven companies, a key "raw material" is personnel, so some industries form around pockets of qualified personnel. For example, the "silicon prairie" (Richardson, Texas, a suburb of Dallas) is the U.S. home of many global telecommunications companies, including Nortel (formerly Northern Telecom) from Canada, Alcatel from France, and Ericsson from Sweden. New companies locate in the silicon prairie because of the availability of engineers with telecommunications experience.

Geographic concentration has an influence on marketing to these organizations. Firms that supply telecommunications companies also locate in the silicon prairie, which lowers their costs of serving these accounts. Whereas Coca-Cola has to be concerned with consumer access to Cokes in even remote parts of the country, electronics wholesalers may find most of their telecommunications market located in one metropolitan area.

At the same time that business markets tend to be geographically concentrated, they are also *globally oriented.* Because customers are fewer in number and tend to be larger and geographically concentrated in various parts of the globe, competition for business tends to be more global. Also, the large-scale operations and transportation systems that made steel an internationally traded commodity have made other markets more global. Cement is another example of an industry that was once regionally competitive. Constrained by rail and truck transportation, cement companies located near their major markets and competed in a limited geographic area. Today's specialized ships enable cheap water transport to complement production-scale economies. Cement companies are now more global, with CEMEX headquartered in Mexico being the world's largest producer.

Consider again the silicon prairie. Its importance at the advent of the hand-held calculator was quite high, as Texas Instruments was a leader in developing both the silicon prairie and calculators. Initial product success hinged principally on the sophistication of the integrated circuitry. Now that the market has matured and circuitry is quite standard, efficient assembly is critical for success. Offshore assembly is now the norm; marketers of calculator parts may sell to assemblers in China one year, in Costa Rica the next.

Note that these generalizations about geographic concentration and global orientation do not hold for all business marketers. Xerox, for example, sells to all types of businesses and is less concerned with geographic concentration than with global orientation. Xerox must provide the same level of service for the products it sells in the most remote parts of the country as in urban centers. Xerox copiers can be found on U.S. Navy submarines, in oil fields, and on ranches and farms, as well as in offices of companies large and small. While there are more copier users in New York City than in Bismarck, North Dakota, companies like Xerox face many of the distribution and marketing challenges that consumer products companies must overcome.

Business marketers are more likely to conduct business globally and face global competition than are consumer marketers.
James Willis/Tony Stone Images.

Purchasing Standards and Processes

What fraction of any five-year-old's Christmas presents survived to New Year's Day? What percentage of new car buyers applied spreadsheet models to compare purchasing against leasing? Was the Smith family's decision to vacation in Disney World a result of Dad's formal proposal being stronger than Mom's proposal for the Alaskan cruise? These questions invite you to consider some key distinctions between household and organizational buying. These distinctions preview material covered later in the text.

Strict Standards

When college roommates find that last week's reheated spaghetti tastes foul, they toss the stuff and call for a pizza. But if the food served on Delta flight 34J to Salt Lake City is foul, no pizza can substitute. Frequent flyers are apt to fume. They may spend their company's travel budget on United next time. When a power company must brown out or purchase auxiliary power because a bad expansion joint has left a boiler out of commission, you can bet both purchasing agent and vendor will get called on the carpet.

As you can see, business buyers apply strict performance standards to their purchases. Professional purchasers and multiperson buying teams have formal responsibility for product and vendor evaluation. Inputs often must conform to design specifications, cost constraints, delivery windows, and the like. A host of organizational mechanisms support the application of such strict standards.

Purchasing Processes

The larger number of people involved in organizational purchasing contrasts sharply with typical household buying. Within families, purchasing roles are more flexible, often arising from implicit negotiation, expertise, and habit. While in both cases, someone may purchase a product for use by someone else, the sheer size and complexity of organizations and the number of people involved often lead to a more complex purchasing process.

Furthermore, many organizational controls are in place to assist professional purchasers—and evaluate them. Comprehensive vendor scoring systems are commonplace. Quality inspection at origin, cost accounting systems, and cash flow management have only crude equivalents among consumers. For example, almost every home owner you know has probably complained about inadequate closet space. But do they calculate the "warehousing" costs of their golf clubs, camping gear, and heirlooms? Do they measure inventory carrying costs (e.g., spoilage, opportunity cost of money) on toilet paper or apples by the case? Even before you take up the chapters on purchasing and distribution, you can well anticipate these important distinctions in business purchasing.

The Nature of Demand

Demand for business products does not always operate in the same fashion as demand for consumer goods. In part, the nature of demand in business markets is due to the types of products sold, varying for raw materials, component parts, and so forth. Understanding demand is important for business marketers because decisions concerning which markets to serve, what business to be in, and where to invest company resources are based on projections of demand. Two concepts, derived demand and joint demand, are useful in understanding how demand for business products can be determined.

Derived Demand

When business analysts and economists focus on consumer spending and consumer confidence, they are looking for indicators that affect the entire economy. Consumer and government spending ultimately drives all of the economy. Business marketers must recognize that the demand for their products and services is **derived demand**; that is, demand for their products and services is derived from the demand for their customers' products and services (whose demand may also be derived). Ultimately, most demand is derived from consumer demand, the exception being demand derived from government purchases such as arms sales.

In the salt example at the beginning of this chapter, it is easy to see how Morton Salt can predict salt sales based on the predictions of sales for institutional foods, meals purchased outside the home, and home purchases. The demand for salt is derived from the demand for, among other things, fast food. Similarly, the demand for BASF's carpet treatment product is derived from the demand for buildings, vehicles, and other products that use carpets as well as the demand for remodeling existing facilities and homes.

For suppliers to manufacturers of consumer products, the issue of derived demand may not be too great. In this situation, there is virtually a one-to-one relationship; for every consumer product purchased, there is a one-to-one relationship with the supplier of a component of that product. If we made bottle caps and sold them to Coca-Cola, for example, then the demand for bottle caps would be the equivalent of the unit demand for bottled Cokes.

As we move further away from the consumer market, however, derived demand can cause wide swings in demand, called **volatility**. For example, assume we make a machine that processes salt and makes it ready for human consumption. Morton Salt will decide

Exhibit 1–6
Volatility of
Derived Demand

Time Period	Demand for Salt	Machines Needed to Handle Demand	Worn-Out Machines	Machines Available	New Purchases
1	100%	50			
2	95	47	10	40	7
3	105	52	7	40	12
4	100	50	12	40	10

At the beginning of Period 1, 50 machines are required based on forecast of sales. At the end of the year, 10 are worn out but 7 are purchased because only 47 are needed. Over year 2, 7 machines wear out, but 52 are needed so 10 are purchased.

how many of our machines to purchase based on the need for salt. Assume that in a year of steady sales, Morton Salt will purchase 10 machines to replace those that are old and worn out. In year one, salt demand goes down 5 percent, and Morton Salt may decide that it can get by with purchasing only seven new machines. In year 2, demand goes up 10 percent. How many will Morton Salt now replace? If demand of 100 percent equals 50 machines, 95 percent demand equals approximately 47 machines, while 105 percent demand means roughly 52 machines (52.5 to be exact). Based on a replacement rate of 20 percent, as illustrated in Exhibit 1–6, demand for our machines went from 7 to 12 to 10. Demand for our machine went up almost 50 percent, then down 20 percent, as compared to the change in salt demand of 5 percent to 10 percent. Derived demand can cause wide swings, or volatility, in the demand for industrial products.

Demand elasticity is also affected by derived demand. **Demand elasticity** is the percentage change in sales relative to the percentage change in price. In a consumer market, demand elasticity means that as price goes up, consumers will look for alternatives or do without and sales will go down. In many business markets, doing without is not an option. Morton Salt may choose to do without our salt processing machines, but if the price of raw salt went up, Morton Salt would have little option but to pay the higher price. So for products without substitutes, there is **inelastic demand**—it is not affected greatly by price.

On the other hand, there are many more substitutes for some industrial products than for consumer goods. When assembling a product, a manufacturer can choose between rivets, nuts and bolts, adhesives, and other forms of fasteners. When there are many substitutes and the choice of one or the other has no visible impact on the final product, demand will be more price elastic, or more affected by price.

Price elasticity is also driven by derived demand. If consumer demand is inelastic, so will demand for components be relatively unaffected by price. Conversely, if consumer demand is driven by price, suppliers for components will find their customers very price conscious.

Because of the importance of the concept of derived demand, business marketers are always paying close attention to consumer demand forecasts and reports. You may notice the importance paid by the news media to two types of consumer demand: that of new housing (often reported in terms of new housing starts) and that of new cars. The demand for so many industrial products and supplies is derived from the demand for housing and cars that they are important bellwethers of the economy as a whole.

Joint Demand

Joint demand, in contrast to derived demand, is a relatively simple concept to understand. **Joint demand** refers to situations where two products are used together and are demanded together. One example is Apple software. The demand for Apple software

---

1–2

BUSINESS 2 BUSINESS
BASF and Derived Demand

Consider the demand for BASF's product for making fabrics brighter and longer lasting. From what products would demand be derived? Is this situation more or less volatile for the marketing manager than with the carpet treatment product? Why? How would this influence the way you market these products?

---

exists as long as the demand for Apple computers exist. One cannot operate without the other. Should the entire world migrate to Windows, Mac-based programs would no longer be in demand. In one way, you could consider the demand for Mac-based software to be derived from that for Macintosh computers, but then the demand for Mac computers is based on the demand for the Mac software. Devoted Mac users base their devotion on the software, which takes advantage of hardware provided by the Mac.

Joint demand can create especially difficult marketing challenges for technology-based products because the company is dependent on the technology. If a better technology comes along and the company cannot make use of it, the company may lose out as demand for the technology it uses goes down. For example, there are many ways to receive a television signal: via a cable (which can be one of several types of wire, such as coaxial), via satellite, or via broadcast received by a regular antenna. Commercial networks that rely on only one form of delivery (i.e., broadcast to regular antennae) are finding that the demand for their product offerings is negatively affected by the decrease in demand for broadcast delivery systems, or the technology they depend on.

Similarly, in the computer-aided design (CAD) market, the demand for computers capable of operating CAD software is a function of the demand for newer CAD programs and vice versa. The difference between joint demand and derived demand is that with joint demand, the demand for both products is somewhat simultaneous because both products or services are consumed at the same time. With derived demand, the end product is consumed much further downstream by a consumer several steps or more away from the producer.

The Entire System

So far in this chapter, we've used two companies as running examples: GM and BASF. Let's put it all together and examine the flow of goods and services that go into one car. Exhibit 1–7 illustrates this flow.

At the beginning are the suppliers of raw materials. The plastic, steel and other metals, rubber, and glass used in automobiles are manufactured materials derived from such raw materials as petroleum, iron ore, and sand. A mining company may sell the raw material to a mill that produces the manufactured material. The mill may then sell the material to a contract manufacturer, which creates the component part for GM. For example, sheet metal may be stamped into hoods for Chevy Luminas.

Another company may supply gauges to GM. These gauges are assemblies composed of parts purchased from other manufacturers. BASF supplies manufactured materials, such as a carpet treatment product to make the carpet last longer and a velour treatment product

Exhibit 1–7
The Entire System

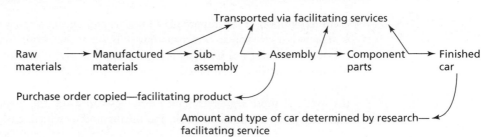

to make the seats last longer. GM assembles and paints the cars, using robots to spray each car with the correct amount of paint. The robots are capital equipment. Colors are chosen through marketing research, which determines which shades will sell best. That research, as is the transportation of the cars to GM's customers, is a facilitating service.

Each purchase order is copied on a Xerox copier (accessory equipment). At the end of each day, all offices are cleaned by the personnel of local janitorial companies, an MRO service. All of this is necessary so that GM can serve its customers. GM's customers include government agencies such as the armed services, which buy cars for staff transportation; institutions such as universities, which purchase vans to transport students on field and athletic trips; rental car companies; fleet users, such as BASF whose salespeople drive company cars to visit their customers; and retail dealers, which resell their cars to you and other consumers. With all these customers to satisfy, it is no wonder that GM purchases over $50 billion each year in goods and services!

As you have seen, quite a few purchases must be made before GM can build a car, Shaw Industries can make a carpet, or McDonald's can salt your fries. Each of those purchases is part of a marketing process conducted by vendors such as BASF and Morton Salt. In this section, we examine the marketing process that is the subject of the rest of the book.

Understanding the Market

Many organizations begin with a vision—the reason why the organization was created. Usually, that reason for being is based upon some general need or set of needs that has been identified in the market, and the organization is created to satisfy that need. Simply recognizing the need, however, is not enough. It wasn't until Chester Carlson invented xerography, the process that makes Xerox copying possible, that the Xerox Corporation was possible. The means to fulfill the need must also exist. When the recognition of a need and the means to satisfy it come together, an organization or business can be created.

The vision also reflects the stage of the organization. Organizations operating under the partnering philosophy would have a far different vision than those operating in the production era. Most firms, though, are at least in the marketing stage and recognize the importance of satisfying the customer.

Thus, the business marketing process often begins with an understanding of the buyer, what the buyer wants, and how that buyer makes decisions. This understanding is then combined with technology, or what a company can do, and the vision is created. Both Kodak and IBM were offered xerographic technology; both turned it down as it did not fit their vision. Another Rochester, New York, company, the Haloid Supply Co., recognized the value of Carlson's invention and renamed itself Xerox.

In recognition of the importance of understanding the market, the first part of the book is designed to give you an understanding of business marketing in general. The second part continues to build this understanding through a study of organizational buying behavior, or why organizations buy. Based on this understanding, you can then appreciate how marketers evaluate markets, targeting only certain segments, and creating offerings that meet the needs of those segments. These offerings constitute the marketing mix, which is the topic of the third part of the book, and the method by which marketing creates value.

The Marketing Mix Creates Value

The marketing mix consists of the usual four Ps you probably learned in principles of marketing. The four Ps—product, place, price, and promotion—are based on the utilities, or general benefits, provided by marketing, which are having the product the buyer wants, where the buyer wants it, at the right price, and letting the buyer know about it.

The four Ps illustrate that marketing is a process of creating value. Through marketing, we know just what to do with that iron ore that was dug out of the ground so someone can use it. When the iron ore is turned into steel, and the steel into a building material so that a factory can be built so that fish can be turned into fish sticks so you can eat tonight, value is created. Knowing that it needs to be done is the realm of marketing. How it is done is through the application of steelmaking technology using marketing information.

Polaroid, for example, developed its own process of making copies using regular paper in the early 1980s. Polaroid management, however, decided that there was not enough incremental value in its process, or competitive advantage, so the company never manufactured any copiers past prototypes. A **competitive advantage** is something that provides incremental value when compared to other offerings. The advantage can be gained through any of the four basic values of price, product, place, or promotion, either alone or in combination.

When BASF says that it doesn't make the carpet, it makes the carpet last longer, the company is describing the value it adds to the process of bringing you carpet. If it did not provide value, it would not be part of the process. Refer back to Exhibit 1–7 illustrating the complete system. That diagram illustrates what is called a **value chain** or system of value creation. Each organization adds its value to whatever it is that the system is creating, in this case a mode of transportation.

Therefore, the third part of this book discusses the process of creating value. The section begins with a chapter covering the processes relating to developing an overall strategy, and is followed by chapters concerning product development, channels of distribution, and integrated marketing communications. Two chapters examine portions of the communications mix, first advertising and trade shows, and then selling and sales management. A chapter on pricing rounds out this section.

Marketing Is an Integrative Process

The final part of the book reflects the integrative nature of business marketing. You should already have glimpsed that a high degree of interaction and cooperation is needed among members of a value chain. Each member is both buyer and seller to other members of the chain, which often results in a different form of relationship between buyer and seller than in consumer markets.

Customer retention and relationship building are important elements of success in today's business marketing environment. For relationships to be strong, the entire organization must be dedicated to solving the needs and satisfying the wants of each business partner. Careful internal integration and coordination are needed in relationship building strategies. This part of the book should integrate much of what you have learned in the prior chapters.

Summary

Business marketing is an important element in the economies of industrialized nations, accounting for more than half of the economy. Business marketing includes marketing to companies that buy products in order to make other products or to facilitate their companies' operations; marketing to government agencies, including state and local governments; marketing to institutions such as universities and hospitals; and marketing to resellers, including retailers, and industrial distributors.

Most marketing majors will begin their career in business marketing. Understanding business marketing is also important because of the magnitude of business marketing and because it is different from marketing to consumers.

Business marketing differs from consumer marketing in the types of customers served, their relative sizes and locations, the nature of buyer–seller relationships, and the nature of business demand. Organizations that consume products as part of their normal operations include OEMs, which use products as part of their own products. They buy raw materials, manufactured materials, assemblies, and component parts, which all become part of their final product.

Users are those organizations that use a product in their operations but not as part of their own product. Users use accessory equipment, capital equipment, MRO items, facilitating services and supplies, and other products. The government is an important user of products and services. Governments work to achieve political and social objectives through set-asides, technology subsidies, target zone development policies, and more. Institutions such as universities, churches, and hospitals also use products and services.

Business marketers are more likely to find their buyers geographically concentrated, but are also more likely to serve global markets and face global competition. Business buyers are larger than individual consumers, giving each business buyer more power in relation to the seller.

At the same time, relationships between buyers and sellers tend to be stronger in business marketing. While some business relationships are transactional, many companies seek partnership status with their customers.

Demand for business products operates differently than does consumer demand. Business product demand is derived from the demand for consumer products. As a result, business marketing demand can be quite volatile.

These factors make business marketing different from marketing to consumers. Channels of distribution are shorter, and there is a greater emphasis on personal selling. Relationships must be carefully managed. At the same time, unique promotion strategies such as trade shows are part of the business marketing mix.

Key Terms

accessory equipment

business marketing

capital equipment

competitive advantage

component parts

corporate relationships

demand elasticity

derived demand

facilitating services (or supplies)

inelastic demand

joint demand

maintenance, repair, and operations products (MRO)

manufactured material	**raw materials**	**transactional**
OEM parts	**safeguarded**	**relationship**
original equipment	**relationships**	**user**
manufacturer (OEM)	**social relationship**	**value chain**
partnership		**volatility**

Discussion Questions

1. Suppose that your company manufactures power tools used in sawmills to turn trees into lumber. Demand for what consumer goods would influence the demand for your power tools? Would overall demand for your products be likely to be more or less volatile than that for the salt production equipment discussed in the chapter? Why?

2. Identify three television advertisements you see regularly that appear to target a business market. What benefits are they trying to sell? How does their advertising differ from beer commercials, car commercials, and other consumer ads? Why do you think there is a difference?

3. How would marketing long-distance services to businesses be the same as marketing to consumers? How would it be different? Why?

4. Across the top of the page, list each type of product (such as OEM product). Then list a product that would fit each category. Try to use products not mentioned as examples in the chapter. Use BASF as your buying company.

5. How can derived demand cause volatility when, at the same time, distribution channels are short and tend to be direct in business marketing?

6. Assume you work for Shaw Industries, a carpet and flooring manufacturer. How would your marketing be different for the university market, the GSA (the General Services Administration of the federal government), and commercial real estate developers?

7. What is the relationship between price and value? How does marketing provide value? What are the types of value that marketing provides?

8. One business marketing student said, "All this stuff on relationships just means that it is who you know that counts. The good old boy network is what is important." Based on what you've read in this chapter, how would you respond to that statement?

9. Not all firms have moved into the partnering era. What might inhibit a firm's ability to shift from one operating philosophy to another? What might enhance that ability? What value would there be in moving earlier than competitors?

10. How would the firm's approach to doing business influence the way the firm implements the business marketing process?

Internet Exercise

Go to the BASF home page (**www.basf.com**) and answer the following questions:

1. Go to the *BASF Corporation* (North America) page, then to *Our Businesses,* where you should find a list of products offered. What products does it make?

2. Go to the *plasticizer* page. Describe its customers for plasticizers based on what you can learn from the home page. Who would buy those products? What position would they hold in what types of companies? What types of companies (based on Exhibit 1–5) are the customers for plasticizers? What type of product (based on the exhibit) is a plasticizer?

Cases

Case 1.1 Ferguson Industries

Gabe Ferguson needed a loan. Business was great this year for the family business, a company that made small fans used to cool personal computers. With business going so well, Gabe wanted to expand plant capacity by 25 percent. Unfortunately, the bank with which he had done business for over two decades was reluctant to provide him with the loan.

As Jaime Trevino, president of the local North Crest Bank branch, explained, "I know sales are great this year. But last year, sales were barely at break-even and three years ago, you lost 10 percent when you lost the Apple account. As it is, you still have four customers accounting for 75 percent of your business. I think you need more steady growth."

"But Jaime, without more plant capacity, I won't be able to get that steady growth," Gabe complained.

"Gabe, let's look at ways you can get steadier sales first. Then if the expansion is still warranted, we'll make the loan."

1. Why would sales vary so greatly for Gabe's company?

2. How can Ferguson Industries stabilize sales?

Case 1.2 Magnusson Manufacturing

Magnusson Manufacturing is a European maker of computer-automated manufacturing software. The company would like to enter the U.S. market, but has had difficulty. It exhibited its products at COMDEX, the large computer trade show, and at AASC, an engineering show, but few orders were taken.

Sven Gibson, marketing manager, was considering another approach. He felt that the company should hire and train four U.S. citizens to sell the products. Most of the companies that would use Magnusson software were located either in the Detroit–Chicago area, in a region including New York City to Baltimore, on the west coast, or in Houston. He felt the company could follow up on leads identified at the trade shows and make more sales by putting a rep in each area.

1. What are some alternatives that Sven should consider?

2. Discuss the factors that should affect the decision, paying particular attention to the factors influencing the types of organizations Magnusson should sell to or through.

Additional Readings

File, Karen Maru, "Is There a Trillion Dollar Family Business Market?" *Industrial Marketing Management* 24 (1995) pp. 247–255.

Webster, Frederick E., Jr., "Relationship Marketing," presentation, American Marketing Association Educators' Conference, 1993.

Chapter 2

The Character of Business Marketing

McDONALD'S

The golden arches dot our highways and may encircle your campus. They bring expectations of tidy restrooms en route to your spring-break destination and guarantee smiles when you order Happy Meals for two muddy midfielders. But, can you picture McDonald's in China? It is happening. Bringing Big Macs to one billion Chinese is no simple task.●

Robert Ma directs purchasing for McDonald's China Development Company. His job is to supply fresh produce daily to McDonald's' 44 Chinese restaurants, which are expected to grow to 300 by the year 2000. That means finding and transporting the right raw materials, minimizing spoilage, and delivering on time. Typically farmers bring their goods by tractor or donkey cart to meet trucks at specified collection points. Potatoes then go to a processing plant near Beijing, and then, by trucks, to the restaurants. Mr. Ma uses the state-run trains for long hauls, booking space far in advance. Still he must sometimes use a standby network of trucks when local transport is overbooked or inadequate. Mr. Ma has even gone so far as to fly in lettuce from the United States when flooding and hail overwhelmed the Chinese suppliers.●

Importantly, Mr. Ma also supports farmers to grow produce to McDonald's' standards. Seed selection and cultivation techniques come from McDonald's. Even abundant produce may not fit the bill. For example, China is number two in world potato production, but its spuds are too small for McDonald's' notorious long, thin fries. The solution: Work 10 years with Beijing area farmers to cultivate the refined, big tubers needed in any Value Meal.[1]●

Visit the McDonald's web site at **http://www.mcdonalds.com**●

Learning Objectives

This chapter aims to broaden your exposure to the realm of business marketing, introduce a bigger lineup of players in the field, and preview some of their roles for firms and the larger economy. We will emphasize the key marketing challenge of coordinating work that creates value. We begin with a brief review of the amazing performance of markets. For technically complex and specialized products, markets may need tweaking. Buyers and sellers complement their reliance on the price mechanism with a host of other means for coordinating action. As you might guess, the chapter discusses business relationships—long-run exchange between firms. We examine the motivations for relationships and how they develop. We also consider the special challenges of managing and sustaining business relationships. The closing section of the chapter underscores the connections each relationship has to a larger network of organizations. We want you to strive to examine any marketing problem within its broad context, the web of participants in value creation.

After reading this chapter, you should be able to

- Describe the effectiveness of price for coordinating business transactions to create value.

- Explain how value is determined in exchange.

- Identify conditions that impair the performance of pure markets to coordinate business exchange.

- Summarize the range of buyer and seller motivations to develop and maintain an exchange relationship.

- Describe a relationship development process for parties able to gradually deepen their interdependence.

- Identify three complementary mechanisms for coordinating business transactions.

- Describe the network of participants in the value chain.

- Illustrate the marketing efforts one firm might take with each member of the network.

Prices coordinate supply and demand for standard office supplies and equipment.
Both images courtesy Office Depot.

The Magic of Markets

It might have Waldo or your school logo on it. Maybe it's yellow with some green printing or teeth marks. In a matter of seconds you could put your hands on a pencil. It probably sold for less than $.25 whether purchased singly or by the box. But where did it come from? Did the Regional Bureau of Pencils contract for all inputs and schedule productions for the holidays or back-to-school rush? No. Did you solicit bids for contract production of your pencil? Of course not. This handy tool of business came from the market.

Markets Coordinate

Often taken for granted, markets provide a most amazing mechanism for meeting individual and organizational needs and allocating productive resources within a society. Office Depot knows that nearly every business needs pencils. Thus, it buys them by the gross from Dixon Ticonderoga or another supplier without a moment of thought about how a pencil might come into being. Similarly, anticipating summer orders from Office Depot, Dixon Ticonderoga orders more dowels and gum erasers, perhaps without any detailed knowledge of their origins. Let's look briefly at the work that almost magically gets done to yield a tool to sketch a budget, mark a board for cutting, or fill in bubbles on an answer sheet.

Detailed in a remarkable little story, "I Pencil: My Family Tree as Told to Leonard E. Read,"[2] pencil manufacturing involves the participation of scores of businesses, including thousands of individuals in many distinct steps. Indeed, the pencil boldly asserts in this story that "not a single person . . . knows how to make me." First, straight grain cedar is cut from forests in the Pacific northwest by loggers using saws, trucks and other gear. Then it is cut into slats, and the material is transported to the pencil manufacturer. Here is added the lead center, really graphite, possibly mined in Ceylon. The eraser or "plug" is made by reacting Indonesian rape seed oil with sulfur chloride. And so it goes on.

No single person could measure up to this task of pencil making. Markets coordinate nearly all the work necessary to give you or the Boeing Corporation pencils that do their job. The following sections review the fundamental elements and mechanisms of markets. We briefly see how they work to improve productivity, quality, and living standards.

Buyers Gauge Value

First of all, the buyer—you or Boeing—determined the value of the pencil when paying for it. Circumstances play a role in what buyers are willing to pay. Boeing's purchasing department may stock the supply cabinet with pencils ordered at $1.40 per box. Yet a forgetful industrial psychologist from Kansas City, staying in Minneapolis to give an assessment test to employees at Honeywell, might well pay $1 each for pencils from the hotel where she's staying. Nothing in the pencil has changed its worth. Clearly, the value of one pencil is less to a party who has several than to a party who has none. The buyer's circumstances play a great role in determining the value of any product or service.

Sellers Opt In or Out

Of course, the seller has a role in valuation. If costs of delivering a pencil are higher than what potential users are willing to pay, why make or deliver them? As producers reduce the number of shifts or lines devoted to pencil production, in time pencil supplies will shrink. When buyers find that pencils are more difficult to come by, seller promotions and discounting will be less common and, in effect, buyers will tend to bid up the price. But notice that costs do not make for value. Would a hand-crafted pencil made from hickory wood find buyers at $7.50 each? It seems doubtful. Would your bookstore sales clerk convince you that the $5 pencil was a real bargain because it cost $6 for UPS overnight delivery? Of course not.

Price coordinates the activities of the various businesses, from loggers to retail clerks. A boost in demand may tax current supplies. Price increases can slow purchases until new supplies arrive. Input prices will rise the same way, prompting input suppliers to hike the wages of loggers (to draw more to the forests) and graphite miners. On the other hand, a pencil glut will prompt deep discounting and eventually rollbacks in production and production capacity in various stages of manufacture. In this amazing system, prices serve as both signals and outcomes.

Marketers in this type of business environment must be attuned to changes in demand and sharpen their firm's attention to quality, particularly the quality aspects valued by end users. The system rewards efficient sellers with profits, and penalizes flabby sellers with weak profits or even losses. Thus, sellers should always strive for economy and take precautions against becoming complacent. Competitive intelligence and adaptability are advised too.

Beyond Market Coordination

Let's now consider situations where the market may fail. This sounds ominous, doesn't it? Actually, in today's world of commercial trading, the prevalence of transactional exchange—sometimes also called *spot markets* or *discrete markets*—is severely limited by technical complexity, exacting buyer standards, and a variety of dependencies between buyer and seller that arise from the initial exchange. In this complex and dynamic environment, price (the market) must be complemented with other mechanisms for coordinating work between two parties. Otherwise exchange will not take place, or exchange will prove unsatisfactory, even highly frustrating, for at least one of the parties. Some examples will clarify how markets can fail.

Countless products need mechanical fasteners in their assembly. Markets work extremely well for the provision of standard rivets, screws, staples, and bolts. Nearly 10,000 distributors carry the lines of scores of fastener producers in order to serve over 180,000 original equipment manufacturers. A manufacturing company using tens of thousands of standard fasteners will have its purchasing agents seek to obtain the best delivered price. Indeed, a handful of potential suppliers can vie for the order, and a savvy purchasing agent will often make each order a bidding contest. The low-price supplier in March has no advantage in April's reorder and may very well be replaced by a vendor with a price difference of just pennies per case.

As you can see, transactional exchange works quite well to keep suppliers on their toes, ever striving to offer the lowest price. Although there may be an adversarial character to the interaction (a consequence of short-run self-interest and the impersonal mechanism of the market), buyers benefit from low-cost inputs. And they don't have to needle underperforming suppliers to get proper service. Buyers work at arm's length from vendors and simply order from another source the next time around.

But transactional exchange has a limited range of effectiveness. Many products have a level of complexity and significance in the creation of value that are poorly served by transactional exchange. The purchasing agent seeking the lowest delivered price on standard fasteners might really do a disservice for the firm by not properly accounting for costs of defects, late delivery, inventory costs, ordering costs, and so on. In short, the benefits of transactional exchange might be improved upon by using additional means to coordinate activities between customers and suppliers. We can illustrate this more concretely with more examples. Obviously, some product designs—for functional or aesthetic reasons—require special fastening (e.g., tiny clips or large, light-weight, reverse-threaded bolts). Few distributors carry these items, at least not at inventory levels apt to satisfy start-up production levels. Possibly, the design calls for fasteners that do not yet exist.

Supply Management

If you are thinking that a company needing special fasteners ought to take its distributor to lunch, you have a sense for what many are calling **reverse marketing**, proactive management of the supply function. Much like McDonald's orchestrating the supply situation in China in our opening vignette, the OEM's purchasing function wants to clue the distributor in to its new fastener needs, hoping the distributor will be willing to build inventory or arrange to have the specialty supplies drop shipped on a schedule. Thus, *information sharing* and *joint planning* can be used to coordinate work in situations where markets need a little push or lubrication.

In the last two decades, the strategic role of purchasing (discussed in Chapter 3) has taken on new significance at many companies. Part of this interest stems from the global nature of competition in today's business markets. Indeed, companies formerly isolated from other players in the industry by cultural or geographic divides now find aggressive and creative rivals for market share. This has precipitated two related thrusts in business: (1) a press for accountability and effectiveness in marketing efforts (discussed in Part II),

Exhibit 2–1
Profit Impact
from Marketing
and Purchasing

Income Statements	Base Case		Case A: Marketing Impact		Case B: Purchasing Impact	
	$ (000)	%	$ (000)	%	$ (000)	%
Net revenue	$12,000	100%	$13,200	100%	$12,000	100%
Cost of good sold	$9,000	75%	$9,900	75%	$8,100	68%
Gross profit	$3,000	25%	$3,300	25%	$3,900	32%
Promotion	$1,000	8%	$1,200	9%	$1,000	8%
General and admin.	$1,500	13%	$1,500	11%	$1,700	14%
Net earnings	$500	4%	$600	5%	$1,200	10%

and (2) an invigorated quest for operational efficiency, the elimination of any waste. *Often the profit impact from purchasing and logistical efficiencies outweighs that from market penetration.*

Efficiency Gains

To illustrate, Exhibit 2–1 shows the impact on profits from two different business efforts. Case A shows a 10 percent sales increase over the base case as a result of a $200,000 promotional effort. Gross profits also surge 10 percent to $3.3 million. And netting out the program costs, net earnings before taxes show a 20 percent gain.

Case B shows the results of a $200,000 expenditure to improve purchasing processes—perhaps collaboration in production planning and quality control. Later in the book we detail the purchasing and collaboration process, but for now let's presume that as a result, supplier costs are trimmed, prices are reduced, defects are nearly eliminated, and the need for rework processes are all but forgotten. Consequently, costs of goods sold (COGS) are decreased by 10 percent from the base case. With sales unaffected, gross profits jump 30 percent and net earnings climb to $1.2 million—a 140 percent bump from the base case and *twice* the impact of the promotion program. A 10 percent COGS shavings can be tough to come by, but the payoffs of efficiency due to strategic purchasing management can be striking. Successful suppliers look beyond the receiving dock to recognize how they can support the efficiency and effectiveness goals of their customers.

In this vein, notice that Case B hints at a comprehensive approach to efficiency. That is, rather than simply negotiating for lower and lower prices on inputs, as we would see in transactional exchange, many buying firms—with the help of their suppliers—are looking at the bigger picture. It takes a bit of analysis to answer the questions: Is a $4.19 part a better buy than another at $4.65 if defects average 0.1 percent in the former and .01 percent in the latter? What if the former comes in monthly shipments by rail car versus skids deployed on the shop floor as needed, just-in-time, for the latter? Clearly, acquisition costs don't tell the whole story on efficiency.

Effectiveness Payoffs

We must emphasize that there is more to the story than efficiency. Savvy buyers are using their suppliers to make *market share gains.* A case in point is Brown–Forman Beverage Company's collaboration with Inland Container of Louisville, Kentucky, which

makes corrugated containers.[3] Don Harris, Inland's account executive, spends three days a week in a Brown–Forman office. He gets involved in the design process from the idea stage. Recently, Harris helped design a packaging and shipping container for Tropical Freezes, a frozen drink sold at retail in pliable plastic pouches. Harris came up with a solution that protected the pouches from being crushed, made them in the optimum size, and made the product safe from accidental damage caused by retailers cutting open a case. Thus, Inland's role in making the product secure and convenient for retailers enhanced the product's strength in the market.

We illustrate the nature of business markets by taking the fastener case a little further. Akin to Mr. Ma trying to get farmers in China to grow the right kind of potatoes for McDonald's, consider a design calling for a brand new fastener, a tension-spring clip, for Hewlett–Packard's (HP's) new laser printer. HP must find a supplier with both interest in and capabilities for making the tiny parts. HP might send specifications to candidate suppliers and invite bids, but what assurance does it have that the low-priced supplier will be able to deliver reliably or provide zero defects? What assurances will suppliers need in order to invest in the capability to supply HP? Will HP be vulnerable to price gouging at renewal time? These are just a few of the issues pertinent to buyers and sellers in business markets if they are interested in making a relationship work for an extended period.

Relationship Management

Buyer interest in maintaining a high-performance relationship often has its counterpart on the supply side. That is, the supplier may be attracted by the promise of recurring purchases due to their volume and relative certainty. But the supplier has valid concerns about set-up, administrative costs, long-run payoffs, and vulnerability. Does it make sense to assign a team to prepare a bid? How much managerial attention will this customer require? Will the company need to dedicate personnel or production systems to this account? Can the company work with the other firm's people? How much training is involved? Will it compromise operations with current customers? What is the long-run promise of this particular account? In what competitive position does this put the company at renewal?

Exhibit 2–2
The Realm of
Buyer–Seller
Relationships

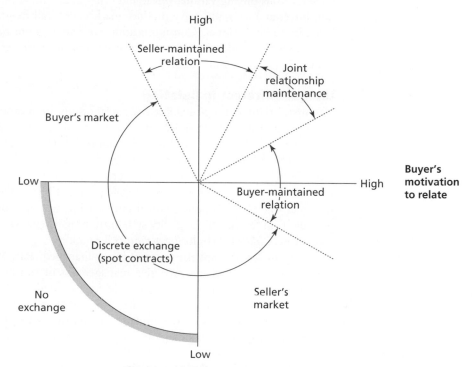

SOURCE: Adapted from F. Robert Dwyer, Paul H. Schurr, and Sejo Oh, "Developing Buyer–Seller Relationships." Used with permission from the *Journal of Marketing,* published by the American Marketing Association, vol. 52 (April 1987), p. 15.

A Map of Motives to Relate

Obviously, the stakes of both buyer and seller must be considered as factors of the exchange environment.[4] Exhibit 2–2 is a useful summary of our discussion to this point. It depicts each party's range of motivations for forging and sustaining a trading relationship. The horizontal axis represents the possibilities for a buyer. The buyer can be highly motivated to establish and maintain a relationship with a sole source supplier or a small set of vendors. Alternatively, the buyer may have little interest in a relationship or even a transaction.

The vertical axis shows that a seller has a similar range of stakes in a relationship. This surprises some readers. Doesn't a selling firm want to do business with all comers? The answer is no. Some business marketers choose not to sell to government agencies because the paper work is too thick and the margins too thin. A business consultant in the Midwest declined business opportunities with a prospective client because the expected follow-up business was inadequate in light of the anticipated service burdens. Potential customers in a particular region or business sector may be bypassed to avoid head-to-head competition with a specific rival firm. Suffice it to say that sellers have motives to build and maintain relationships that vary from one prospect or customer to another.

Spotting Transactional Exchange

Our discussion of pencils and standard fasteners in the opening section of the chapter actually previewed the lower left sector of Exhibit 2–2. What are essentially transactional relationships or **spot exchanges**, money traded for easily measured commodities, include

General Mills buying various wheat and other grains on commodities markets, a restaurant buyer at a cash-and-carry produce market, or a rail freight service offering standard box cars to any shipper. Communication content is quite narrow between transacting parties, and their identity is hardly relevant. Trading terms are simple and clear. Performance is practically immediate.

Unequal Interest in Relating

The upper right sector of Exhibit 2–2's relationship map captures our immediate discussion of relationships. Here, at least one party is motivated to build and keep a relationship.

In the upper sector we find the situation typified by today's mainframe computer industry. The value of any system depends on the depth and quality of ongoing support given by the vendor. Users are hardly locked in, as they might have been a decade ago. Open architectures, used systems, and plug-compatibles make relationship management the chief role of the supplier. For instance, if Digital Equipment Corporation does not provide its users with high-quality system training, upgrades, trouble shooting, and software installations, it risks losing accounts for good.

The right sector maps the realm of buyer-managed relationships. The chapter's opening vignette described the proactive management of supply to McDonald's in China. Another example, Korea's LGS (formerly Lucky Gold Star) runs its highly automated VCR assembly plant using components from suppliers it established with capital equipment, training, and personnel. Similarly, Toyota shares its production schedules and orchestrates a giant network of suppliers in its Toyota City complex.

Joint Interest in a Relationship

Between these two lopsided cases of seller-managed and buyer-managed relationships is an area where buyers and sellers have *mutual* stakes in a sustained trading relationship. A **strategic partnership** results when both parties have keen interests in maintaining an ongoing exchange. The strategic essence of the partnership rests on the significance of the resources and long-run consequences of the efforts. Thus, a three-year contract for a single supplier of lubricants to provide for all factory needs is apt to be regarded as less strategic than a joint R&D effort on new pollution controls.

Many of the strategic partnerships that characterize business markets have been sparked by the "quality revolution," a management process of renewed dedication to customer satisfaction and efficiency. Leaders in the quality movement—Xerox, Procter & Gamble, Dana Commercial Credit Corporation, and others—evidence an all-hands effort at continuous improvement in the systems of business: social (teamwork, creativity, motivation, etc.), technical (tool, machines, analytic techniques), and management (information flow, policies, adaptation of the other systems). Quite fittingly, suppliers have been brought into this process. From the Field 2–1 sketches supplier involvement at a Malcolm Baldrige Award winner.

Key Managerial Implications of Relationships

Many companies have found it necessary to reduce the number of suppliers as they expand their involvement with source firms. When buyer and seller share forecasts and plans, they usually find they can reduce inventories. Buyer participation in the vendor's production setup and quality control processes eliminates the costly process of coping with defective inputs (rework, reorders, and scrap). This sort of managerial attention by the buyer could be spread too thin if given to several competing suppliers.

Reducing the number of suppliers, of course, reduces the number of competitive bidders and thereby dampens the power of the marketplace to affect prices. But often the parties can establish a commodity index or some standardized costing method to cope

2–1

FROM THE FIELD
ADAC Laboratories

ADAC Laboratories is a 1996 winner of the Malcolm Baldrige National Quality Award and a Silicon Valley–based manufacturer of high technology health care products. Established in 1970, ADAC Laboratories designs, manufactures, markets, and supports products for nuclear medicine imaging, radiation therapy planning, and managing health care information. About 85 percent of its $250 million in revenues come from diagnostic imaging cameras. Exports have steadily increased to $65 million.

In 1993, it instituted a new approach for increasing customer satisfaction by eliminating a body of executives called the Quality Council, replacing it with two weekly meetings open to all employees, customers, and suppliers. At these meetings numerous employees present data on key measures of customer satisfaction, quality, productivity, and operational and financial performance. At the same time, a corporate planning process was instituted to focus on key business drivers and align plans and continuous improvement efforts. Significant investments were made in information systems tracking design defects and customer support calls.

The results of the program include the trimming of operational expenses from 40 to 26 percent of revenue. Significant gains in supplier performance have also been achieved. In 1992, ADAC instituted a program to certify is suppliers. By the end of 1996, over 80 percent of nearly 5,000 different parts received at ADAC came from certified suppliers. The number of purchased parts rejected in assembly have decreased 70 percent and defect rates, as measured at final inspection, have fallen by 40 percent. As a result of this, the volume of service calls in the first 30 days after installation has been cut in half and customer retention rates have increased from 70 to 93 percent.[5]

with this hazard. At the same time, when the buyer consolidates purchases, it often obtains a volume-justified price break from the supplier. Furthermore, with fewer suppliers, buyers often experience reduced variation on key part characteristics and service. This reduced variation enables higher uniformity and quality control in buyer operations.

On a related front, OEM buyers have worked with suppliers of component parts and materials to eliminate costly inventories and frequent handling costs by establishing just-in-time (JIT) relationships. Chapter 3 will address JIT as a purchasing strategy. Here we introduce its relationship character. A **JIT relationship** "requires the supplier to produce and deliver to the OEM precisely the necessary quantities at the necessary time, with the objective that products produced by the supplier conform to performance specification every time."[6] Unfortunately, some of the early JIT relationships were underachievers because buyers simply used their purchasing muscle to push inventories up the supply chain; no system efficiencies resulted. Others represented a simplistic attempt to mimic Japanese systems without thorough examination of the distance and climatic challenges posed for stockless throughput. Indeed, maybe the inefficiencies of a safety stock are more desirable than risking all-night truck driving on black ice or worse.

An assessment of JIT by suppliers to U.S. automakers showed evidence of missed opportunities. Fully 30 percent of the suppliers see JIT as merely an upstream shift of inventories, and only half the suppliers get stable delivery schedules from their customers.[7]

Clearly, the terms *relationship* and *strategic partnership* often convey trendy images or managerial intentions more than actions. In a depth interview with a marketing executive at a leading manufacturing company, one of the authors asked some of the standard questions used to assess a firm's intentions to forge relationships. The executive indicated his degree of agreement or disagreement to items such as "We expect our relationship with our supplier to last a long time" and "This company is (not) just another supplier." Intentions were good. Then the interview got to specific activities: Do you share market forecasts with your supplier? (No.) Do you involve this supplier in your production process? (No.) It went on like this. Good intentions and platitudes are not enough to make a relationship work.[8]

Developing Relationships

Because we have already introduced the notion of motivations to sustain a relationship, we should elaborate on what it means when a relationship works. We can then consider the process by which relationships develop.

High-Performance Criteria

As you might guess, managers want their relationships to be profitable. But the particular routes to profitability for trading partners don't strictly coincide with each other. To better understand the nature of business markets, let's look at the preferences of sellers and buyers.

Sellers   Sellers want substantial and reliable purchase volumes at adequate margins. And they want account management expenses, promotions, and other allocated costs to leave a large portion of the gross profit intact. A little cost accounting and historical comparison can reveal the profitability of newly established customer relationships. For example, a steel service center will strive to carry the specialty wires, I-beams, and alloys needed by manufacturers in its trade area. Its salespeople make regular calls and quotes, perhaps to attain a 40 percent share of State Fabricating's (SF's) purchases. If the steel service center can negotiate a contract supplying 80 percent of SF's needs at a price break of 10 percent, it can compute the incremental gross profit and add, say, 15 percent of the inventory reduction from knowing SF's production schedule, and the cost of 10 sales calls per year. It would then deduct the equivalent of 25 percent of the full cost of an inside salesperson now dedicated to the SF account. A similar analysis can gauge the profitability of other accounts or customer groups.

Buyers   Buyers often turn to supply partnerships motivated by evident inefficiencies in the production process—costly safety stocks, high return rates, numerous reorders, or long lead times. These forces have prompted purchasing directors to seek suppliers that will work collaboratively to eliminate waste and improve system economies. In the beginning of such a relationship, any efficiency gains can be measured against historical data. Continuing our example from the previous paragraph, as State Fabricators moves to a JIT system from its steel supplier, the regional steel service center, SF can determine its own inventory reduction savings, productivity gains from decreased line shutdowns, and labor savings in its purchasing operation.

Designing New Standards

After three or four years of JIT service from the steel supplier, the usefulness of historical data has waned for both parties. There is no obvious new performance yardstick. In this situation, partners rely on two broad types of assessments: internal and external.

Exhibit 2–3

Sales Agent Performance for the Gamma Corporation

Agencies	No. of Reps	Estimated Market Size	Gamma Sales	Gamma %	Competitive Intensity Index[1]
Webster (Milwaukee–Madison)	3	$16,500	$2,800	17%	4
Batham (Rochester)	2	15,200	$1,600	11	5
Smalz (Phoenix)	4	17,100	$4,800	28	3
Lincoln (Durham)	3	16,800	$2,320	14	3
Maxington (Peoria)	3	15,900	$3,240	20	4
Average	3	16,300	$2,952	18	4

[1]5 – high, 1 – low.

Internal Assessments   Some companies do periodic supplier evaluations, combining data on internal operations with assessments from their own managers on supplier professionalism, responsiveness, quality, technical capability, and vision. Hewlett–Packard, for example, evaluates its suppliers on technology, quality, responsiveness, delivery, and cost. The last two dimensions have gotten the focus of supplier attention since the ratings were instituted in 1985, largely because they are objectively measurable. That most suppliers have improved their on-time delivery by 20 to 30 percent, some even by 50 percent, supports the adage that what gets measured is what gets done.

Likewise, sellers track key accounts against sales and profitability objectives, reorders, inventory and service burdens, and promise of future business. It is possible to do the cost accounting to result in a simplified income statement for each key account or group of accounts.

External Measures   Sometimes a company can evaluate relationships on a relative basis against external norms provided by trade associations or consulting companies. Large firms may even produce their own profiles using supply relationships with various company operations. In this case each particular relationship can be compared to an external standard or profile derived from other relationships. It is not uncommon for electronics manufacturers to compare the performance of their independent sales agents across the country.

Although agencies are autonomous businesses and are paid a standard commission on sales, most participate in manufacturer training programs and may purchase demonstration equipment. Terminations and start-ups are far from costless. Cooperation between the manufacturer and agent enhances marketing effectiveness. Thus, comparing sales and market penetration rates between agents in similar markets helps the manufacturer to identify and analyze high-performance agency relationships.

We can see how external measures can be applied in an example. Exhibit 2–3 reveals that the Smalz agency in Phoenix is a high performer. Its market is less competitive than Batham's in Rochester, but the comparative data also reveal Batham's use of what appears to be an undersized sales force. Gamma might now effectively press Batham to add selling resources. Models such as these can be critical to the evaluation and direction of sustained business relationships.

Higher Standards

When buyers or sellers in business markets are asked what makes a good relationship, they always punctuate with more than dollar signs. They want integrity, fairness, loyalty, flexibility, consideration in partner's strategy, partner's participation in their own strategies, and compliance with established administrative procedures. Most companies have internal value systems that support these behaviors in contractual relations. They stand behind the product and honor commitments. With perhaps millions of business transactions conducted each week, these nonlegal sanctions seem to work reasonably well. Sellers who shirk obligations, misrepresent their abilities, and issue empty promises stand to lose accounts. Their tarnished reputation limits their ability to gain new ones. Buyers who are rigid in their demands and foreclose supply partners from planning impair their own productivity. Good suppliers in some industries have chosen not to deal with such customers. Others simply pull back on their inputs to the relationship, performing at minimum levels to retain the account or milk it of its waning value.

So what's the relative importance of profits and propriety in business relationships? An executive who had terminated a well-known supplier summarized his decision: "It was not so much what they failed to do for us, but what they tried to do to us that led us to quit." Indeed, commercial trading cannot be sustained in the absence of virtue.

Fortunately, many forces in the business environment induce good conduct. The potential for repeat business and the reputational ripples through the market from each excellent—or awful—exchange provide simple but powerful sanctions for ethical behavior and cooperation in relationships. As this behavior is reinforced, reciprocated, reinforced again, and so on, businesses often deepen their relationship.

Hydrotech, a Cincinnati-based distributor of hydraulics, proved instrumental in machine tool development at Cincinnati Milacron in the late 1980s. Hydrotech developed expertise in new hydraulics from Europe and—based on deep knowledge of Milacron's product line—was able to help Milacron improve the hydraulic systems in its tools. Since then, Hydrotech's involvement in applications engineering at Milacron has expanded, particularly to its plastic molding machines. The next section explores a provocative model for the development of such buyer–seller relationships.

A Model of Relationship Development

Many metaphors have been used in business and research to bring understanding to the complex phenomena of buyer–seller relationships. Indeed, the utility of a metaphor is in what it simply reveals about something very complicated. This book's authors have seen and heard metaphors of gardening, chemical bonding, child rearing, the symphony, and more. They have their place, but we have found the metaphor of courtship and marriage to more effectively illuminate facets of business relationships. The language of business marketers reflects this. You may have heard them talk about "getting better acquainted," "courting a prospect," "setting up house with XYZ," or "tying the knot." Theodore Levitt has offered a concise and illustrative observation:

> *The relationship between a seller and a buyer seldom ends when a sale is made. Increasingly, the relationship intensifies after the sale and helps determine the buyer's choice the next time around. Such dynamics are found particularly with services and products dealt in a stream of transactions between seller and buyer—financial services, consulting, general contracting, military and space equipment, and capital goods.*
>
> *The sale, then, merely consummates the courtship, at which point the marriage begins. . . . The quality of the marriage determines whether there will be continued or expanded business, or troubles and divorce.[9]*

This section of the chapter develops the marriage metaphor using business examples to illustrate concepts and implications from research on interpersonal relationships. Exhibit 2–4 complements our discussion, showing buyer and seller in four stages of relationship development.

Exhibit 2–4
The Relationship Development Process

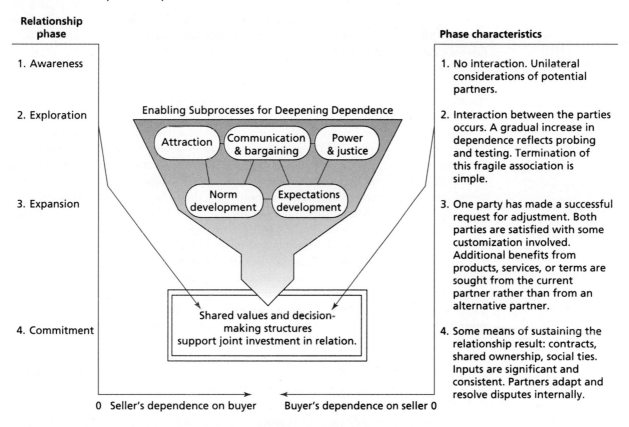

Relationship phase

1. Awareness

2. Exploration

3. Expansion

4. Commitment

Enabling Subprocesses for Deepening Dependence

Attraction

Communication & bargaining

Power & justice

Norm development

Expectations development

Shared values and decision-making structures support joint investment in relation.

0   Seller's dependence on buyer   Buyer's dependence on seller 0

Phase characteristics

1. No interaction. Unilateral considerations of potential partners.

2. Interaction between the parties occurs. A gradual increase in dependence reflects probing and testing. Termination of this fragile association is simple.

3. One party has made a successful request for adjustment. Both parties are satisfied with some customization involved. Additional benefits from products, services, or terms are sought from the current partner rather than from an alternative partner.

4. Some means of sustaining the relationship result: contracts, shared ownership, social ties. Inputs are significant and consistent. Partners adapt and resolve disputes internally.

SOURCE: Adapted from F. Robert Dwyer, Paul H. Schurr, and Sejo Oh, "Developing Buyer–Seller Relationships." Used with permission from the *Journal of Marketing,* published by the American Marketing Association, vol. 52 (April 1987), p. 21.

Awareness

In the **awareness stage**, buyer and seller independently consider the other as an exchange partner. Supplier advertisements and trade show exhibits might be noticed by the prospective buyer. At the same time, the supplier may collect information about product specifications, buying process, and the like at the prospective customer. This stage may last indefinitely, or the parties may move to the next stage of the process by engaging each other in some form of interaction.

Exploration

In the **exploration stage**, we find the parties probing and testing each other. The prospective buyer may attend a seminar given by the supplier. The supplier may make several sales calls. Even initial purchases can take place in this stage. They are part of a trial process. In the exploration phase, a relationship is very fragile. The parties have not significantly invested in the exchange. Neither party depends highly on the other. The association is easily terminated. But in this stage, the interplay of five enabling processes supports the developing relationship.

Attraction

Attraction is the degree to which the interaction between buyer and seller yields them net payoffs in excess of some minimum level. The payoffs are tangible and intangible rewards from the association, less economic and social costs. Practically, this can be illustrated by the buyer's purchasing director and a supplier's sales manager sharing college memories and striking a friendship at a Big Ten Alumni picnic in Atlanta. Atop these social rewards from the association the buyer looks for quality, technical know-how, a fair price, and logistical service. The supplier looks for steady orders at a fair margin plus a chance to satisfy additional needs within the buying organization. Both want minimal order costs, delays, and foul-ups.

In a fascinating case study in the automotive industry, business professors James Comer and B. J. Zirger (1995) detail the relationship development stages between an auto manufacturer, dubbed Zenith, and a supplier of vibration dampeners, labeled Alta.[10] Mechanical systems and road use in automobiles cause harmful vibrations that, unless dampened, cause mechanical stress and limit durability. Vibration dampers typically consist of a metal inner ring and outer rings separated by a ring made of a complex rubber compound. The product is not technically sophisticated, but a large number of variables in the design—width, thickness, metal and rubber composition, fit to other designs in the automobile—complicate product development.

The attraction between Zenith and Alta was triggered by the emergence of a new paradigm in the industry. Cost containment and reengineering in the late 1980s and early 1990s prompted automakers to examine long-standing supply relationships and explore value-added opportunities from engaging suppliers in product development. Suppliers, which had often dealt exclusively with a single automaker and simply priced dampers on the basis of blueprints received, began to send sales reps to engineers at prospect accounts. Their job was to find out what the prospective customer was working on and what problems it was facing, and then to develop credibility as a provider of solutions.

In the case study, Alta's salesperson responsible for new account development invited Zenith officials, primarily product engineers, to Alta's plant to demonstrate abilities, introduce the highly competent personnel, and ask for an opportunity to compete for an upcoming damper project. A few months later, Zenith had some problems with its current supplier's damper and engineers suggested blueprints be sent to Alta for a bid. Alta received the prints and gave them number one priority by assigning top-flight people to a bid management team.

Communication and Bargaining

In the development of relationships, communication and bargaining are the processes by which the parties rearrange the distribution of their obligations, rewards, and costs. Parties to most budding relationships hesitate to clearly state their needs, preferences, or goals. They talk around the issues or provide only vague hints of what they are after in the exchange. Not until they develop a level of comfort and familiarity do they begin to make disclosures. These disclosures will probably require **reciprocation**—a similar action returned by the other—if the association is to grow into a productive relationship.

Behavioral scientists tell us that there are dramatic effects on a relationship when parties bargain. After all, for parties to "take the trouble, go to the bother, and expend the psychic and physical energies necessary to negotiate," the partners must see some potential for a rewarding association.[11] See if this principle applies to your own social relationships. Asking your third-time date to meet you promptly might be a bold request. It could fracture the fragile relationship or it could lead to an accommodation that signals your date's interest in sustaining the association too. Likewise, a buyer who asks for delivery between 3:00 and 3:30 AM from a supplier whose delivery runs begin at 4:00 AM risks forgoing service from this supplier. Should the supplier arrange to make 3:00 AM deliveries, the exchange relationship may start to crystalize or even expand.

In the case of vibration dampers, Alta used a multifunctional team to provide a set of cost estimates for the design provided by Zenith. Purchasing people at Alta contacted paint, material, and component suppliers, while manufacturing identified assembly time, tooling, scrap, and so on. Tech center personnel determined that more computer-controlled machining equipment would be needed for the job. After four weeks Alta sent Zenith a preliminary bid that met specifications for Zenith and profitability requirements at Alta. Moreover, Alta recommended some design changes to improve performance.

Power and Justice

Adjustment in an exchange is a critical facet of relationship development. Concessions sought or granted in the bargaining process result from the just or unjust application of power. **Power**—an ability of one organization, Alpha, to get another organization, Beta, to do what it would not do otherwise—derives from Beta's dependence on Alpha for valued resources that are not easily obtained elsewhere. These valued resources can take many forms: status, economic rewards, expertise, and applied or ended punishments. **Justice**—the rendering of what is merited or due—results from the fair and respectful use of power. Evenhandedness and honesty characterize the just use of power. In contrast, the unjust application of power attempts to control another's actions against its will or without its understanding or in the absence of fault.

Akin to the significance of bargaining for marking progress, the successful (just) exercise of power sparks the transition from an exploratory relationship to one heading into the expansion phase. The premium dog food manufacturer IAMS enjoyed a strong market position among kennel owners. When it sought to penetrate the consumer market, it paid each kennel owner $5 per name for every new owner of a dog purchased from its kennel. Thus, instead of having to comply with some new requirement to obtain IAMS products or credit terms, kennels were delighted by the advent of a new profit center and a foundation for new kinds of cooperation with the IAMS company. It was the just application of power that established this basis for additional joint efforts between IAMS and kennel owners.

Zenith engineers reviewed Alta's bid for about three months before ultimately giving tentative acceptance. This meant that Zenith was willing to continue to work with Alta. Prices were in a reasonable range, and the redesign proposal was worthy of further examination and collaboration. This was a milestone in the developing relation, a platform for deeper cooperation.

Norms Development

Business relationships are forged to accomplish tasks and attain goals sought by each party. Simply put, there is work to be done. **Norms** are standards of behavior for the parties, the guidelines by which the parties interact. Some norms exist prior to and are brought to the exploratory phase. For example, buyer and sales rep share many elements when asked to outline a "script" for different types of sales calls.[12] Such scripts have less commonality when the parties come from different cultures or professions. As the parties interact, they customize their patterns of interaction. Practically, this means they may teach each other the language of their respective companies, meet with a negotiated frequency, communicate by mutually agreeable—even automated—channels, and begin to organize evaluation, planning, and decision-making tasks.

Zenith and Alta relied on common norms of exchange in their initial interactions. Professional courtesies, the language of automotive engineers, plant tour protocol, and the conveyance of blueprints inviting bids are general norms that enabled the two firms to begin to collaborate. The preliminary acceptance launches an opportunity for more customization of their patterns of interaction: frequency and locale of meetings, prototype development schedules, and product testing procedures.

Expectations

As the parties interact and explore the potential for ongoing exchange, they develop expectations. Foremost among expectations is **trust**, "the belief that a party's word or promise is reliable and a party will fulfill his or her obligations in an exchange relationship."[13] The trusting party derives confidence from a belief that the other party is consistent, honest, fair, responsible, and helpful. These expectations can be shaped in part by the other party's image advertising and reputation in the industry.

Based on industry reputation and limited interaction, Alta expected Zenith to give it a fair opportunity for its business and it risked four weeks of team effort in the preparation of a serious bid. On the other end, Zenith regarded Alta as a credible potential supplier, sent its personnel to Alta's plant, and took a risk itself by disclosing its designs. Neither Zenith nor Alta saw large investments yet, only small exposures to risk for the promise of cooperation and higher payoffs. Positive outcomes from these occasions of vulnerability build trust.

We should look for direct experience to play a key role in the migration of the relationship past the exploration phase. The relationship must be solidified in the expansion phase, to be taken up next, and satisfy the critical prerequisites for the commitment phase!

Expansion

In the **expansion stage** the association moves from one of testing and probing to one of enlarging rewards and the scope of exchange. Account development, cross-selling, and up-selling are manifestations of the expansion phase. Consider the experience of TMSS, a company providing consulting and administrative services in select fields. It is not uncommon for an advertising agency or financial service firm to use TMSS initially for mail, courier, and distribution services. Clients may then turn to TMSS for printing and reproduction services, later desktop publishing and creative services, and finally perhaps file and document management. As a client increasingly **outsources** or spins off internal functions to an outside provider, TMSS may realize a higher and higher proportion of its business from this particular client. Both firms find their dependence on the other has escalated. From the Field 2–2 illustrates an expansion in a novel purchasing arrangement.

The essence of the expansion phase is increasing dependence between the exchange partners. For Alta and Zenith the expansion is manifested in their interactions following their agreement on two critical documents: the "Presource Agreement" and a "Release to Tool." The former precipitated the formation of a development team consisting of representatives from various areas of Alta's manufacturing, purchasing, and technical centers, along with fixed and floating representatives from Zenith as well as Alta's suppliers. Weekly meetings alternated between Zenith's and Alta's facilities as the changes were made to damper designs as a result of ways that Alta and its suppliers knew to cut costs. Some of the lower-cost approaches involved redesign of other engine components. The ripple effect of such collaboration clearly reflected the growing interdependence of the two companies.

The "Release to Tool" agreement was a consequence of testing several hundred prototypes at Zenith's facility over the course of more than a year. But the words of the agreement—

2–2

FROM THE FIELD
A New JIT Relationship

The BOSE Corporation is a leading manufacturer of high fidelity audio speakers, systems, and components. In 1990, BOSE's director of purchasing and logistics, Lance Dixon, conceived of a new form of structuring relationships with suppliers. Dubbed JIT II, Dixon's system involved placing vendor representatives in the BOSE plants and empowering them to authorize BOSE purchase orders. The system uses the vendor professional, called an "inplant," to replace the traditional buyer and salesperson. The inplant develops intimate knowledge of customer needs, performs concurrent engineering with customer engineers, determines order quantities, manages inventories, uses customer computers, and is generally regarded as a customer employee, although paid by the vendor.

The JIT II program at BOSE has been highly successful. Now many other companies have looked to Dixon and BOSE to see how they might apply it in their procurement process. For example, Honeywell visited with Dixon and several inplant representatives at BOSE to see if JIT II principles might be applied in its operation. Honeywell had already initiated corporatewide pooled purchasing and promoted strategic supplier relationships to increase quality, shorten lead times, and improve delivery, but this was still a far cry from the supplier intimacy of JIT II.

Now Honeywell's Home and Building Control Strategic Materials and Procurement group has several on-site suppliers involved in planning, forecasting, scheduling, placing orders, working with design engineers, expediting deliveries, and consulting with users—sometimes on cross-functional teams. Other Honeywell facilities have set up similar arrangements for purchasing printing services, raw materials, packaging, and trucking services.

Honeywell sees payoffs beyond the reassignment of buyers and expediters. It sees reduced cycle times for designs, lower cost designs, parts consolidation, reduced inventory, better delivery, and more effective value analysis that has brought lower prices.[14]

essentially a contract to purchase a specified quantity over a period of time at an agreed-upon price—were complemented by key bonding behaviors by each party. Zenith "desourced" its previous supplier of dampers for this application. Alta purchased special manufacturing equipment and made financial investment in prototypes beyond Zenith's reimbursement schedule. *Both parties made concrete behavioral pledges to the relationship, in addition to reaching a verbal agreement.* They were nearing the commitment phase.

Commitment

Commitment is a lasting desire to maintain or preserve a valuable, important relationship. Thus, this commitment phase is characterized by the parties exchanging significant resources. When the parties share a common belief in the effectiveness of future exchange in the commitment phase, they dedicate resources to maintain the relationship. Some buyers use a panel of suppliers to act as tribunals to arbitrate disputes. Buyer and seller may exchange employees in order to fully identify with the trading partner. Other means of cementing relations include the dedication of equipment and systems, and even anniversary celebrations to reinforce the critical social bonds between the two companies. Commitment enables relationships to survive either party's foul-ups and environmental disturbances—blizzards, fires, truckers' strikes—that are neither party's fault.

Exhibit 2–5
A Model of the
Process of
Channel
Relationship
Termination

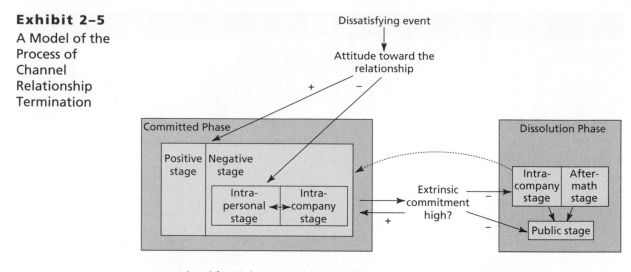

SOURCE: Adapted from Robert Ping and F. Robert Dwyer, "A Preliminary Model of Relationship Termination in Marketing Channels," in Gary Frazier, ed, *Advances in Distribution Channels Research* (1992). Used with permission from JAI Press, Inc., Greenwich, CT, and London.

Two months after reaching the "Release to Tool" agreement, Zenith hired a new purchasing director who was charged with instituting major cost reductions in parts purchasing. Alta renegotiated a new price schedule. Meanwhile, Alta's paint supplier caused several prototypes to fail corrosion tests. The relationship survived this breakdown because Alta secured a more capable paint supplier prior to the testing of production samples.

Dissolution

In the early phases of relationship development, either partner can walk away from the exchange without trouble. As mutual dependencies increase and the costs of switching to another exchange partner take on significance, ending a relationship can become a knotty problem. **Dissolution**—termination of an advanced relationship—can make assets dedicated to the relationship obsolete and require additional search, negotiation, and set-up costs for both parties. Indeed, it took more than a year for Alta and Zenith to forge a supply relationship. In some cases, costly litigation and emotional scars can add to the toll of termination.

What little research we have in this area suggests that dissolution is a multiphase counterpart to the process of relationship development.[15] Briefly, we know that parties remain in business relationships for two broad reasons: (1) they want to remain—the relationship is financially, strategically, or psychologically rewarding—or (2) they have to stay—exit is too costly, or no alternatives exist.

If a party wants to be in the relationship, it doesn't matter so much that it might have to be. Thus, Exhibit 2–5 indicates that the effects of a dissatisfying event depend on the overall attitude of the offended partner toward the relationship. If the attitude is favorable, as reflected in the arrow to the *positive stage,* episodes of dissatisfaction will be endured or redressed. When the partner has had to endure several letdowns and occupies the *negative stage,* lingering dissatisfaction darkens the view of the future held by the

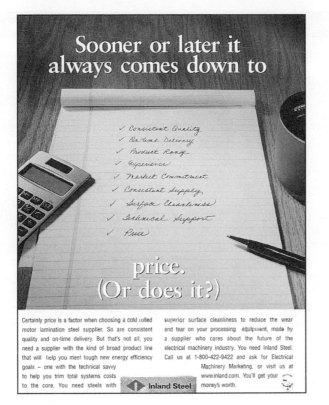

"custodian" of the relationship, perhaps a sales manager or purchasing director. This person with day-to-day responsibility for the relationship sorts through the options in an *intrapersonal stage,* then makes a case to the firm's top management in the *intracompany stage.* For example, the marketing manager at a medical insurance company may note the sustained weak performance of a particular agency, despite a variety of assistances and slack for extenuating circumstances, and make a presentation to the home office to terminate.

The *intercompany stage* features formal dialogue between the two firms to address the status of the relationship. Likely, the insurance company will give 30 days notice of termination of the agency. Cause may be given as substandard performance or policy breaches. Then in the *aftermath stage,* we can look for the dissemination of public accounts of a breakup and counterpart accounts for internal consumption only at the respective firms. Let's not expect company and agent always to tell the same story.

Model Assessment

The marriage metaphor seems to apply to business relationships in many contexts. For situations that allow gradual testing and expanding reliance on a trading partner, the metaphor seems particularly useful. It focuses on mutual problem solving, the development of efficient routines, and the reinforcement of trusting behaviors. The perspective also lends its insights particularly to exchange relations between firms that have a key individual doing deals and renewal.

Because it does not recognize (1) the dynamics of decision making by the cross-functional work teams, which are becoming common at large firms, and (2) different levels of authority of relationship custodians across organizations, the marriage metaphor

---

2–1

BUSINESS 2 BUSINESS

The Challenge of Cross-Cultural Partnerships

McDonald's is not the only western company trying to build business relationships in China. Although rigorous research has only just begun to study the process, we can identify a number of obstacles to the development of effective and lasting business partnerships. Perhaps due to the Confucian ethic stressing harmony in society and strong interpersonal bonds, business partnerships and joint ventures in China hinge on interpersonal relationships.

In initial interactions, managers from Chinese and western cultures must first develop a level of trust that allows greater interdependence. How do business professionals overcome language barriers and a history of hundreds of years as adversaries? The Chinese culture exhibits a reliance on an extended family or in-group called *zijiren*. Western culture is more individualistic and measures time in shorter increments. Does it surprise you that some western firms fracture relationships by prematurely pressing for written contracts? Would you expect some Chinese businesses to seek deals that in a demonstrable way "serve China"?[16]

---

represents a gross simplification of the process. The model also is nearly silent on the effects of the larger exchange network on the relationship, such as Alta's suppliers or even their suppliers. We will amplify these in a later section. Likewise, because the model neglects the business equivalent of marriage without courtship, the next section will discuss alternative means of securing relationships.

Safeguarding Relationships

A variety of mechanisms can be used to cement strategic relationships. These mechanisms take on particular significance when there is no real chance to test the relationship. Indeed, some exchanges involve large-scale and long-run commitments. It may take 15 years to complete an oil field installation or start up a chemical plant. The Department of Defense has planned for 20-year horizons in the development of certain new weapons systems. When Apple brought Sony in as a supplier of key components in its notebook computers, there may have been little opportunity for either partner to prove itself directly, in the specific relationship, prior to committing to substantial quantities at preset delivery schedules. Savvy business purchasers and marketers will set up terms and unique structures for the exchange to ensure its effectiveness over the long run.

Think back to the Hewlett–Packard laser printer that needed special fasteners. HP and prospective suppliers seem likely to be motivated to establish an effective working relationship. At the same time, each is uncertain about the other, not to mention facets of its own business.

House Calls

Perhaps HP could send a couple of its managers to visit prospective suppliers. Do they have smooth-running shop floors? Is a supplier's personnel competent and dedicated to quality? Does it have access to the technology to do the job in the future? Activities such as these were part of the development of the Zenith–Alta relationship and are called **supplier verification**. They are formal efforts to obtain evidence of supplier capabilities and commitment. From a marketing perspective, it is important to recognize that the expertise, dedication to quality, professionalism, teamwork, and all-around customer focus of the supplier organization—not merely the sales rep—speak volumes to the prospective customer.

Trading Places

Buyers and sellers may exchange personnel to provide assurances. Procter & Gamble engineers assist their suppliers with the setup and testing of new production processes, such as the cutting of material for use in disposable diapers. Intel invited its furniture supplier to bring its expertise to reside in Intel's growing 1,600-person office in New Mexico. The supplier met with the building planners, Intel customers, and construction contractors, thereby reducing planning time. The furniture supplier then placed all orders, assuring accuracy and tight coordination with its factory.[17] In this same way, HP could request its custom fastener supplier to come to its plant to become familiar with its workings and oversee the supply function.

Managing Dependence

Alternatively, HP might set up two suppliers or do some of the manufacturing itself to avoid vulnerability to failures or "hold up" by the sole supplier. This is one example of a generic safeguarding strategy called **dependence balancing**.[18] In this approach a buyer reduces its dependence on the supplier by cultivating relationships with other exchange partners. You can easily see how the number one supplier might be motivated to give exceptional service if HP has a very attractive backup supplier. Recognize that this strategy may confound work flow by (1) introducing variation in delivery and parts performance and (2) stretching the supplier coordination and management resources across two partners. That is, the buyer may need to host two or more supplier teams in its product design efforts.

Supplier Pledges

We saw this versatile strategy at work in the vibration dampers case when Zenith desourced its previous supplier. That bold move came after months of trust development with Alta at a time when it was important to signal its commitment. It also motivated Alta to reciprocate by investing in specialized machinery.[19]

Similar pledges could likewise be initiated by a supplier. Consider a supplier with a proprietary product. The supplier can empathize with a prospective buyer that is very reluctant to commit to any exclusive source, perhaps risking price gouging or restricted supply after production or marketing commitments that make switching impractical. As a pledge of good faith intentions to give good service and fair prices over the course of the relationship, the supplier could license its proprietary know-how to another company. This licensee would then be poised to serve the buyer in the event of performance breakdowns by the original source.

Contracts

The same effect, sustained commitment to the exchange, is sometimes achieved by inventive means of distributing the ownership of assets involved. For example, if HP wants a specially manufactured part that no other firm is known to need, prospective suppliers will require assurances that their investments in the ability to produce this product will

Baja Oriente joined AlliedSignal's roster of preferred suppliers by cutting costs more than 5 percent annually. In return, Baja sales to AlliedSignal are up 1100 percent.
Axel Koester/Sygma.

pay out. Perhaps the parties could hammer out a complex contract with terms for long-run purchases at preset prices, with contingency clauses for every foreseeable circumstance—good and bad. But chances are good that the negotiators cannot anticipate every possible circumstance. Writing a rule now for how the parties will behave in the new environment four years from now could take more meetings than either firm wants to attend.

This problem of indefinite haggling can be solved by HP's ownership of the machinery to produce the part. HP can buy the machines to install in the supplier's plant, acquire and set up the supplier, or start up its own facility from scratch. Ownership of just the machines still leaves some control issues unsettled—issues such as training, maintenance, repair, and exclusivity. But these issues are not beyond the limits of contracts. **Relational contracts** are contracts that don't try to bring every future contingency up for consideration in the present, but establish means of continuous planning, adjusting, and resolving conflicts. Relational contracts can specify decision-making authority by issue (material standards, shutdowns, training, and maintenance) and establish procedures or structures for planning to assure ongoing effective exchange.[20] Relational contracts are apt to play a key role in McDonald's' supply management in China.

Ownership

Vertical integration, bringing a function or technology within the boundary of the firm, assures continuity in the relationship because suppliers are now hierarchically connected employees. That is, employees work in an environment of formal rules, authority, reporting structures, and special responsibilities. Goals tend to be shared and, overall, control of activities is enhanced. Firms make a strategic choice to use distributors or their own sales force, outside research agencies or their own research department, third-party logistical services or their own traffic department, contract suppliers or in-house manufacturing, and much more.

Coordination of the selling, research, transportation, manufacturing, or other functions can be enhanced by a firm's own formal and informal communication systems, structured work roles, and decision-making processes. But there are real downsides to this solution to the safeguarding problem. Vertical integration swells fixed costs and may

---

2–2

BUSINESS 2 BUSINESS
Make-or-Buy Carburetors?

Rochester Products develops and produces carburetors and fuel injection systems. Product testing is quite extensive because fuel distribution systems play such a key role in a car or truck's operation and because systems must perform in a wide range of situations. Indeed, the systems need to operate in both Alaska and Tucson, in both Denver and Miami. They need to perform using gasolines that conform to different standards across the country. Are you surprised to learn that Rochester Products is a division of General Motors? Assess the benefits this gives to GM. What other means besides outright corporate ownership could GM use to be assured of good fuel systems?

---

not well duplicate the motivation of owners of independent businesses. Integration also broadens the activities a firm tries to perform well and can dilute managerial focus. In short, it can't solve very many problems without seriously complicating the question, What business are we in? We will expand on this issue in Chapter 6.

Relationships in Larger Networks

We began this chapter with a quick review of the magnificent ability of markets to coordinate work. Then we focused on the special challenges of developing and safeguarding relationships, which are necessary for the exchange of complex, specialty, and risky products. This focus on buyer–seller relationships can be myopic, however, because the parties are not the only entities in the marketplace. They are connected in a network, a much larger and strategically significant *web* of organizations. We provided a preview of the significance of the network in our brief discussion of dependence balancing. In two examples, a party attempted to manage a focal relationship by purposely structuring another relationship. Hakan Hakansson, a leading expert in business networks from Sweden, paints the picture quite vividly. He reminds us that Swedish film makers like to make movies about marriage. The intrigue in these movies, however, invariably comes from introducing a third person. Intrigue in business relationships comes from new buyers (rivals to the incumbent), from new vendors, or from customers of the buyer or suppliers to the supplier. In any case, we agree with Hakansson that a triangle makes for drama.

But relevant business networks can be much larger than triangles. Mr. Ma is so busy in China because McDonald's' successful relationships with its franchisees depend critically on the network of suppliers to those outlets. Similarly, Rob Bestwick runs a public relations company with just four employees. His sustained growth is a result of a network of independent copywriters, designers, photographers, and other technical specialists that enable him to compete as a fleet-footed "virtual company."[21] In the automotive field again, Chrysler has reorganized its entire product development process around the concept of simultaneous engineering. In practice this involved six Mexican firms in the engine design for a new generation vehicle.[22]

If we back away a bit from the intimidating complexity of networks, we should be able to focus on the essential linkages for resources and skills in the creation of value. Consider George Washington Carver, a scientist most often celebrated for his development of scores of products made from peanuts. But Carver was not simply a productive laboratory dabbler. His efforts with "goobers" followed his vital research and demonstration projects involving crop rotation. His work at Tuskegee Institute was aimed at increasing cotton yields among Alabama's struggling small farmers. Planting peanuts restored nitrogen to the soil, enabling rich cotton harvests in subsequent seasons. Carver and the farmers seemingly had a productive relationship. But the farmers' success with peanuts glutted the market. Their bountiful harvests had no value. Thus, not until consumer preferences for peanut butter cookies built demand for peanut butter processors, which bid up the price of peanuts, did cotton growers benefit significantly from crop rotation. George Washington Carver's endeavor to develop markets for peanuts reflects his insight into the connectivity of any enterprise to the larger network creating value.

You know from Chapter 1 that today's business marketing is not just peanuts. Multiple firms interacting with one another are using and discovering a host of mechanisms to coordinate their activities, of which price is but one. Consider Airborne Express, which has gained significant market share in the urgent-delivery business by knowing and handling its clients' shipping needs. In effect, becoming a firm's shipping department, Airborne and its client (say, Xerox or an industrial catalog company) together serve the shipper's customer base. Other firms enlisted by Airborne—independent consultants, software companies, local couriers, commercial airlines, and more—become part of the value-creating network as well.

The concept of networks is not new. Indeed, in the long history of trade the prevalence of family enterprises, cartels, guilds, and conglomerate trading companies is undeniable. The scarcity of truly autonomous enterprises with strictly defined boundaries belies their dominance in formal economic models of the marketplace.

Unfortunately, the complexity of business networks and the infancy of scholarship in the field limits us to largely descriptive insights. But Dave Wilson and Kristian Moller, top business scholars from the United States and Europe, respectively, contend, "Network thinking represents the most novel conceptualization about the nature of industrial markets and industries. . . . The emerging results suggest, however, that network concepts help to understand industrial markets in a more realistic fashion."[23]

Summary

Markets represent a powerful system for coordinating exchange. They allow work to be divided among specialists and allow value to be determined by customers. But there are technical limits to the effectiveness of markets. Incomplete information about product performance, buyer or seller integrity, and hidden costs not well reflected in price limit the utility of market exchange. For complex products and uncertain transaction environments, buyers and sellers must find additional means—complementary to the price system—for coordinating their behavior.

In some environments, buyers and sellers can forge high-performance relationships by a process akin to courtship. It includes gradual probing, reinforced risk taking (trust), language and norm customization, and overall deepening of dependence. The request for adjustment and accommodation are key signals of the value of the association and allow expansion into other exchange activities. We used the running example of the new product development efforts for automotive vibration dampers to illustrate the processes of relationship development.

But some contexts simply do not allow parties to taper into a relationship. These must be set up in advance to safeguard each party's investment and ensure long-run performance. Supplier verification, exchange of personnel, and dependence balancing provide some assurances of continuity and performance. On another plane, the parties can strategically manage dependence through third-party relations. Relational contracts and vertical integration complete our illustration of the vast array of options.

Finally, we must not neglect to consider the nesting of each relationship in a larger business network. Each firm's connections to other players in the web of exchange relations will determine their competitive position to provide value.

Key Terms

attraction	just-in-time (JIT)	reverse marketing
awareness stage	relationship	spot exchange
commitment	justice	strategic partnership
dependence balancing	norms	supplier verification
dissolution	outsource	trust
expansion stage	power	vertical integration
exploration stage	reciprocation	
	relational contract	

Discussion Questions

1. Evaluate the ability of spot markets to provide adequate resources for an organization seeking to purchase

O-rings	storage racks
data entry services	payroll software
custodial services	office furniture
applications engineering	small electric motors (components)

2. Would a company marketing these products be interested in developing long-run relationships with any customer? Why?

3. Write a series of events that might well typify a developing relationship between an office furniture dealer and a growing investment company.

4. Is it possible to develop a corresponding series of events reflecting a relationship between this investment company and its phone system vendor?

5. Imagine you are concluding a very productive meeting with your finance professor regarding the conduct of a feasibility analysis of a business venture you have dreamed about for a long time. You've never had such a supportive and caring professor before, yet there is a pained expression in Dr. Roberts' face when you ask to borrow one of his books. What safeguards can you provide Dr. Roberts that you'll return his book in good condition?

6. Marketing authors Robert Morgan and Shelby Hunt argue that trust and commitment are the central variables for understanding relationship marketing. Other scholars have suggested that power is the key variable. Explain which variable you believe is key.

7. A small group of parents in Kentucky formed a private, independent school. It opened recently in classrooms rented from an urban church with an oversized physical plant and a shrinking congregation. School officials forecast enrollment growing from about 40 in year one to about 120 over the next four years. Ample space for over 100 was available at the church, low-cost terms were agreed upon, and an option to renew for up to four years at the same terms was signed. The pastor answered to the church council and recently wrote the school board president that because the school opened with 80 students instead of 40, the consistory wanted to double the rent. How do you respond? Could this relationship have been set up better?

8. Describe a situation in which an important business relationship developed because of other loosely connected business relationships involving the parties.

9. Many franchisers require their franchisees to follow strict operating procedures or face termination and forfeiture of large sums of money. In some circles this state of affairs prompts discussions of the abusive power of franchisors over their franchisees. But the chapter suggests these termination provisions might be considered for their use as a safeguard. Explain.

10. Explain the student recruitment imperatives for a top business school using a network perspective on value added.

Internet Exercise

Franchising is a unique business marketing format. The franchisor selects franchisees from applicants who have the necessary financial resources and meet other qualifications. Then, each party to this partnership brings unique skills and resources to the enterprise. Usually, the franchisor lends a brand image, operational expertise, and siting assistance. The franchisee brings capital and initiative.

WWW
I N T E R N E T

Delve into McDonald's' web site to determine the financial resources a McDonald's franchisee would need. Examine the means by which the franchisor makes money. Evaluate this structure in the light of the chapter's discussion of safeguarding relationships.

Cases

Case 2.1   Mac OS Licensing

Apple Computer began its bold Mac OS licensing program in 1994, hoping to increase its market penetration in publishing, design, and database applications against competitive pressure from PC powerhouses Microsoft and Intel. A key ingredient to this program was a joint effort by Apple, IBM, and Motorola to create the Common Hardware Reference Platform (CHRP). This move freed Apple from the exclusive responsibility of hardware design and brought in broad industry participation. In the CHRP introduction, then Apple CEO Michael Spindler said, "We believe today's announcement is good news for anyone who believes in innovation, competition, and responding to customer needs."

Enter the Mac clones. Power Computing began shipping Mac systems in May 1995 and sales quickly soared. Clone maker Umax also racked up business. After touting its speed and then besting Apple systems in many computer magazine reviews, Power Computing reached annual volumes of nearly $400 million by Summer 1997.

As Apple struggled and prodigal founder Steve Jobs began to assert more influence in the company from his seat on the board, there were signs that licensing would end. In a filing at the Securities Exchange Commission, Apple said, "The benefits to the company from licensing the Mac OS to third parties may be more than offset by the disadvantages of competing with them." Indeed, sales data indicated that, rather than expanding the market, clone makers were carving up Apple's customer base. Apple's CFO said, "I would guess that somewhere around 99 percent of their sales went to the existing customer base."

On September 2, 1997, Apple announced that it would acquire Power Computing for $100 million in common stock and cease licensing new technology to other clone makers such as Umax and Motorola.

1. What did Apple hope to gain by licensing? Is this option open in the future?
2. What were licensees looking for? Where do they go without new Apple technology?
3. Could the license arrangements have been structured differently?
4. How did customers fare under licensing?

SOURCE: Stephen Beale, "Apple Eliminates the Top Clone Vendor," *MacWorld,* November 1997, pp. 30–31; Galen Gruman, "Why Apple Pulled the Plug," *MacWorld,* November 1997, pp. 31ff.; Kaitlin Ouistgaard, "Apple Kills Clone Market," *Wired,* September 2, 1997, *www.wired.com/news.*

Case 2.2   *Just-in-Time JIT*

You're the director of purchasing at a telecommunications company in Seattle and you've just gone to meet your sister-in-law for coffee at a little cafe off Rush Street. Earlier this week you arrived in Chicago to attend the National Association of Purchasing Managers Convention. As you waited in the cafe, you couldn't help but hear the conversation in the opposite booth. A group of three increasingly rowdy purchasing agents from different companies were clearly from the same convention.

One they called Xavier was from Tex Implements. He was warmed up and getting loud. "I just want to know how I'm supposed to get the best price from Prespec Spring, when I cannot even ask for a bid from anyone else."

"You think that's bad?" retorted a stocky guy called Hank, a street-wise purchasing manager at a Big Three auto company. "I got this dude from Magma in my department telling us how many hoses of which type we've got to get each month."

"We've got the same JIT II baloney. I call it 'JIP Too,' " said the woman in the teal suit.

You hoped you had done a better job getting the purchasing people at your firm committed to the concept of vendor consolidation, sole sourcing, and partnering, but the conversation prompted you to jot a few notes. At tomorrow's conference luncheon you were slated to accept an award for your company for purchasing excellence. You had been planning to make a few simple remarks off the cuff, but your napkin now had a short summary of the motivation and strategic payoff for this "new era in procurement."

Additional Readings

Claycomb, Vincentia ("Cindy"), and Gary L. Frankwick, "The Dynamics of Buyers' Perceived Costs during the Relationship Development Process," *Journal of Business-to-Business Marketing* 4, no. 1 (1997), pp. 1–37.

Dwyer, F. Robert, Paul H. Schurr, and Sejo Oh, "Developing Buyer–Seller Relationships," *Journal of Marketing* 52 (April 1987), pp. 11–27.

Fein, Adam J., and Erin Anderson, "Patterns of Credible Commitments: Territory and Brand Selectivity in Industrial Distribution Channels," *Journal of Marketing* 61 (April 1997), pp. 19–34.

Gundlach, Gregory T., Ravi S. Achrol, and John T. Mentzer, "The Structure of Commitment in Exchange," *Journal of Marketing* 59 (January 1995), pp. 78–92.

Gundlach, Gregory T., and Patrick Murphy, "Ethical and Legal Foundations of Relational Marketing Exchanges," *Journal of Marketing* 57 (October 1993), pp. 35–46.

Leenders, Michiel R., and David L. Blenkhorn, *Reverse Marketing: The New Buyer–Supplier Relationship.* New York: The Free Press, 1988.

Leuthesser, Lance, "Supplier Relational Behavior: An Empirical Assessment," *Industrial Marketing Management* 26 (1997), pp. 245–254.

Metcalf, Lynn E., and Carl R. Frear, "The Role of Perceived Product Importance in Organizational Buyer–Seller Relationships," *Journal of Business-to-Business Marketing* 1, no. 3 (1993), pp. 63–85.

Mohr, Jakki J., Robert J. Fisher, and John R. Nevin, "Collaborative Communication in Interfirm Relationships: Moderating Effects of Integration and Control," *Journal of Marketing* 60 (July 1996), pp. 103–115.

Moller, Kristian, and David Wilson, eds. *Business Marketing: An Interaction and Network Perspective.* Boston: Kluwer Academic Publishers, 1995.

Morgan, Robert, and Shelby Hunt, "The Commitment–Trust Theory of Relationship Marketing," *Journal of Marketing* 58 (July 1994), pp. 20–38.

Norris, Donald G., and Kevin M. McNeilly, "The Impact of Environmental Uncertainty and Asset Specificity on the Degree of Buyer–Supplier Commitment," *Journal of Business-to-Business Marketing* 2, no. 2 (1995), pp. 59–85.

Rubin, Paul H., *Managing Business Transactions.* New York: The Free Press, 1990.

Thompson, Grahame, Jennifer Frances, Rosalind Levačić, and Jeremy Mitchell, eds. *Markets, Hierarchies & Networks: The Coordination of Social Life.* London: Sage Publications, 1991.

Vlosky, Richard P., and Elizabeth J. Wilson, "Partnering and Traditional Relationships in Business Marketing: An Introduction to the Special Issue," *Journal of Business Research* 31 (May 1997), pp. 1–5.

Chapter 3

Purchasing and Materials Management

FLORIDA FURNITURE INDUSTRIES

Florida Furniture Industries (FFI) began life in 1930, producing cypress garden furniture. In the Great Depression, however, garden furniture was a luxury that few could afford, so the company switched to bedroom and dinette furniture. Since then, the company has grown from 10 to 650 employees, with annual sales over $50 million. ●

As with most furniture manufacturers, FFI management has to keep a close eye on costs to stay in business. Furniture sales are influenced by economic conditions. A few wrong purchasing decisions at the wrong time can spell disaster for a manufacturer. ●

Fortunately for FFI, it has made the right decisions at the right time—like the decision to build its newest plant. Because it could secure economic development loans below prime interest rates, it was able to expand at a time when other plants were closing. FFI was able to pick up much of its equipment for its new plant at liquidation auctions, at prices significantly below manufacturer's list price. ●

FFI also keeps operating costs low by building strong relationships with strategic vendors, such as the one that supplies the company with mirrors. While glass is a commodity available only from a few large manufacturers, there are quite a few companies that add the silver backing to turn the glass into mirrors. FFI, though, maintains a close relationship with one vendor that looks out for changes in the marketplace that can affect FFI. When necessary, the company can order ahead and take advantage of price changes. ●

Paying just a few dollars more per unit for raw materials can mean a loss on that particular product. With a keen eye to the raw materials market, however, FFI is able to thrive and grow in a tough and highly competitive market.

Since FFI does not yet have a web site, visit the National Home Furnishings Association's at: **www.homefurnish.com**

Learning Objectives

A key competitive advantage for Florida Furniture and for all other firms is an ability to control costs. One major input in their overall cost structure is their purchases. Therefore, attention to the purchasing function is important for firms trying to create or maintain a cost advantage or, at a minimum, a cost competitiveness. At the same time, marketers must understand the purchasing function in order to create effective marketing programs.

After completing this chapter, you should be able to

- Discuss how effective purchasing and materials management provide a competitive advantage.
- Illustrate strategies designed to provide the proper supply and tell why these strategies are used.
- Explain total cost of ownership, value analysis, and other forms of economic purchase evaluation.
- Describe the processes that purchasing uses to evaluate vendors and their offerings, as well as how the process varies depending on the organization's experience.
- Recognize the major ethical issues facing purchasing agents and how they respond to those issues.
- Understand differences in government purchasing and compare government needs in industrialized nations with those of developing countries.

The purchasing department has an important role to play in any organization. Controlling costs and managing cash flow are key issues that affect the ability of an organization to thrive. These issues are impacted by marketing programs, as you will see.

The Importance of Purchasing

Purchasing is a strategic weapon. Companies like FFI that can source effectively can create a competitive advantage by building better value into their own products.[1] As you've already learned, value can be increased by delivering more benefits or by lowering costs; strategic purchasing can make contributions in both areas.

Business marketers can also make contributions to the value delivered by their customers. Astute business marketers find ways to offer more benefits at the same cost or else lower costs to benefit their strategic purchasing partners. In the next section, we examine the contribution purchasing makes to the firm so that we can understand how we, as business marketers, can support their contribution.

Purchasing's Contribution to the Firm

As you've just read, a key contribution to the success of the firm is purchasing's ability to keep costs of supply down. That is not, however, the only contribution that purchasing makes. The three most important elements of the purchasing department's function are to

Provide appropriate levels of supply of the right product or service

At the correct level of quality

For the lowest total cost.[2]

Providing Supply

An important contribution of the purchasing department is to provide the right product or service in the correct amounts when needed. There are several important elements to recognize. First, purchasing has the responsibility to ensure that the right product or service is provided. For example, Florida Furniture Industries (FFI) manufactures bedroom furniture, making its frames from poplar. Pine may cost less, but it is not as hard as poplar and also does not provide as much flexibility with the final finish. Poplar can be made to look like cherry, maple, and even pine, but pine always looks like pine. The market demands a number of finishes; not everyone likes pine. If purchasing accepted pine instead of poplar, the price of the wood would be less, but the negative impact on other areas would be too great. Purchasing must ensure that the right product or service is provided.

The other important element is availability. The product or service must be available at the right time. FFI's lumber buyer keeps a watchful eye on the prices of lumber, ordering up to six months' production needs when the price is right. If the price isn't right, however, she sometimes has to buy anyway. Otherwise, all three plants would shut down, costing the company hundreds of thousands of dollars per week. If she buys too much, it costs more money due to higher carrying costs. Managing availability can be a delicate operation for the purchasing department.

One availability strategy is **just-in-time (JIT)**, the concept of shipping products such that they arrive at the customer's location exactly when needed. As sketched in Chapter 2, this strategy reduces inventory carrying costs to next to nothing because little or no inventories of supplies are needed. Too often, though, suppliers bear the costs of carrying the inventory if the buyer and supplier don't share information and coordinate plans.

In order for suppliers to reduce their costs (for if the costs are simply shifted from buyer to supplier, the costs would be reflected in a higher price), they are turning to **concurrent manufacturing**, which means the suppliers schedule their own manufacturing

Florida Furniture's lumber buyer makes sure that the company has enough wood of the right quality bought at a competitive cost so that the company can operate profitably.
Courtesy Florida Furniture Industries.

based on the shipment needs of their customers. The ideal situation is that the part rolls off the supplier's manufacturing line and into the truck, and then it's shipped to the buyer's plant and rolled off the truck right into the manufacturing line. Concurrent manufacturing means that the supplier can also keep inventory costs down, because the supplier can engage its own suppliers in JIT systems. If the entire supply chain produces and ships based on demand, then inventories for the entire chain are kept to a minimum, reducing costs for the entire chain.

JIT and concurrent manufacturing are not just for suppliers of component parts. JIT is used in shipping supplies to hospitals, in shipping paper to offices for use in copiers, and in many other instances where the buyer is not a manufacturer using the product in the manufacturing process. For example, some plumbing supply manufacturers schedule their manufacturing based on sales of their products. When a plumber purchases a bathtub or sink from the plumbing supplies distributor, the distributor orders another. The manufacturer makes a small run of tubs or sinks, depending on the orders received.

When JIT works well, there is a much higher exchange of communication than with regular (non-JIT) suppliers. Research concerning JIT buyer–seller relationships indicates that such communication concerns quality, cost, and performance issues, not just shipping issues.[3]

Still, the supplier must quickly know when the customer needs a shipment. An important technological development that enabled many firms to use JIT was **electronic data interchange (EDI)**, the use of electronic transmission of data between buyer and seller to order and maintain product inventory. Allegiance (formerly known as Baxter), a medical supply company, created a competitive advantage by pioneering EDI with the hospitals it serves. EDI significantly reduces the costs associated with buying and storing medical supplies, because purchase orders are generated automatically by computer when inventories approach the reorder level. Inventories can be reduced and shipments by Baxter to hospitals are just in time. Not only that, the buyer saves an average of $54 in processing costs for every transaction conducted via EDI.[4] When first introduced, EDI gave Baxter a significant competitive advantage because it ensured supply availability while lowering inventories. EDI is also necessary to support JIT and concurrent manufacturing.

Exhibit 3–1

Overall
Communication
Frequency with
JIT Supplier

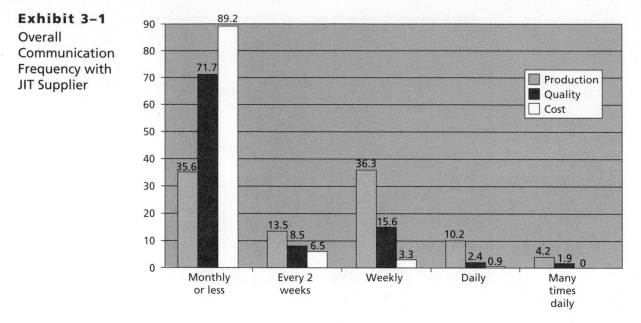

SOURCE: Adapted from Leslie Richeson, Charles W. Lackey, and John W. Starner, Jr. "The Effect of Communication on the Linkage between Manufacturers and Suppliers in a Just-In-Time Environment." *International Journal of Purchasing and Materials Management* (Winter 1995) pp. 21–29.

EDI is used most in the chemical industry and in health services.[5] Most companies that use EDI have only just started doing so and most companies have fewer than 10 percent of their suppliers hooked up to an EDI system. Perhaps what is more important for marketers, however, is that research indicates that buyers prefer doing business with vendors who have EDI capability. Buyers believe that EDI provides their organization with a strategic competitive advantage by ensuring a constant supply; business marketers may achieve a competitive advantage by offering EDI to their partners.

The use of information technology such as EDI and transportation technology has significantly reduced the costs of acquiring supplies. Inventories as a ratio of total sales, for example, have been cut to approximately 17 percent, the lowest in U.S. history. Freight costs have dropped from 6.5 percent of sales to 6.2 percent, in part because information technology such as EDI has made the entire purchasing and materials management process more efficient.[6] For these benefits to accrue, companies have to communicate more frequently, as you can see in Exhibit 3–1.

The Correct Quality

There are grades of lumber that denote quality, with quality in this case being how clear the wood is and whether it is free of knots, cracks, and other defects. If FFI accepted a low grade of poplar, then a lower yield is obtained from the lumber. Yield is typically around 52 percent, meaning that for every 1,000 board feet of rough lumber, only 520 feet are usable. A lower grade means not only fewer acceptable board feet, but problems later in manufacture. The entire manufacturing process may slow down because at each stage of manufacture, more effort would be needed to ensure that the quality of the final product was acceptable.

If the highest-grade lumber possible were used, it would cost more, resulting in a product too expensive for FFI's market. The consumer may not be willing to pay the extra cost for having perfect poplar in the frame, particularly when such perfection adds

3–1

FROM THE FIELD
ISO 9000—A Growth Industry

One of the fastest growing industries in business is a small set of consulting services designed to help companies achieve ISO 9000, the set of global quality standards. Established in 1987 by the International Organization for Standardification in Geneva, Switzerland, ISO 9000 is the first set of quality standards to achieve global acceptance.

For many companies, the decision to seek ISO 9000 (or ISO 14000 for advanced organizations) certification is often initially a marketing decision. They think it will look good on their company's resume to have the certification. After all, many customers are beginning to demand that their suppliers meet ISO 9000 standards. Certification requires registration and successful completion of an arduous certification process to prove that a firm meets the standards, but once it has achieved certification, access is gained to many markets around the globe, particularly in Europe. ISO 9000 standards have become so important that ISO 9000 consulting is listed as one of the top 25 growth industries in Hong Kong!

Donna Vyinski, quality assurance manager for Omni North America, was one of those who saw only the marketing potential at first. "We thought we'd be able to turn the heads of a Dow or a Dupont, that we'd really be able to increase market share." But as the company began to implement the discipline necessary to achieve ISO 9000 status, it quickly found huge gains in efficiency and productivity.

Marketing benefits have accrued, too. Vyinski reports that 20 to 30 percent of the company's clients stayed with it just because of the drive toward certification. And, as Omni North America's customers and potential customers begin their own certification process, they will need the help of vendors that already have ISO 9000 status, vendors like Omni North America.

Source: Barry Lynn, "Service Companies Go ISO," *Export Today* (March 1995), pp. 33–34; Bradley C. Mart, "Hong Kong Goes Shopping," *Export Today* (March 1995), pp. 36, 38, 40.

nothing to the strength or appearance of the final product. Choosing the right level of quality is an important element in the purchasing function, because quality impacts manufacturing and marketing in both cost and potential contribution.

Many companies recognize the importance of providing the right level of quality, and even work with suppliers of their suppliers to make sure that quality is high enough. Church & Dwight, makers of Arm & Hammer baking soda, buys little yellow boxes for the baking soda. Church & Dwight purchasing agents worked with cardboard makers that supply Church & Dwight's carton suppliers in order to know what quality of cardboard to specify so that bright yellow box would always look the same.[7] As you can see in From the Field 3–1, quality improvement is becoming an important industry of its own.

The Lowest Total Cost

As we said in Chapter 2, controlling the cost of supply can have a significant effect on a firm's profitability. As shown in Exhibit 3–2, suppose a firm's annual sales are $50 million, with a profit margin of 10 percent of sales, or $5 million. In general, companies spend about half of their sales on purchased parts, materials, and services,[8] so this company would spend about $25 million per year. If the company was able to save 10 percent on its purchases, it would add $2.5 million to its profit, an increase to profit of 50 percent! The company would have to sell another $25 million to have the same effect on profit. Each dollar saved through careful purchasing can have a direct impact on the bottom line.

Exhibit 3–2

Saving Money Affects the Bottom Line!

Annual sales	$50 million	$75 million
Profit margin (10%)	$5 million	$7.5 million ($2.5 million more)
Cut purchases by 10%, save	$2.5 million	Don't cut purchases
Total profit	$7.5 million	$7.5 million

Cutting costs has a more direct affect on profits than increasing sales, which is why so many companies watch their purchasing expenses so carefully.

Delivery and order size as well as quality influence the final cost of a purchase. If FFI buys the highest grade of poplar, then the cost of purchasing is higher than it has to be. Similarly, if FFI buys the lowest grade of poplar, then costs associated with manufacture are increased. Right now, the company buys up to six months' production requirements at a time, but what if the company could buy twice the usual amount (or a year's production needs) and save 10 percent? The cost of purchasing lumber would decrease, but the costs associated with carrying that extra inventory would rise through increased insurance costs, use of working capital (cost of money) to acquire the inventory, mortgage on the new property required to store the lumber, and so on.

The purchase price, therefore, is not the only cost that the purchasing department must contend with. Delivery, storage, service, and more can add costs. Several concepts are used by purchasing departments to examine and compare costs; these are the total cost of ownership, economic order quantity, and value analysis.

Total Cost of Ownership

Many factors can influence the **total cost of ownership**, the total amount expended in order to own a product or use a service. If we are talking about a piece of equipment, total cost of ownership includes delivery and installation costs, service costs to maintain and repair the equipment, power costs to run the equipment, supply costs, and other operating costs over the life of the equipment. All of these costs must be added to the actual purchasing and financing prices in order to determine the total cost of owning that equipment.

Similarly, services have a total cost of ownership. We have to take into account supplies, inventory (in the case of services, what we are paying to have a trained person available, whether that person is our employee or a service provider's), delivery, and other costs of ownership. For example, if we do our own marketing research, we have to pay the research personnel each month, whether they are currently engaged in a research project or not. Many companies are outsourcing services so that they can reduce the total cost of ownership. **Outsourcing**, discussed in detail later in this chapter, means buying from another firm.

For component parts and raw materials, like the poplar purchased by FFI, we have to account for delivery costs, inventory carrying costs, the impact of the product on manufacturing costs, and other costs. In all situations, we also have to include the costs associated with purchasing. In 1995, one company found that it was spending $250 for processing each purchase order for business forms. For every $1 it spent on forms, it was spending another $3 for ordering, storing, and distributing the forms![9]

Economic Order Quantity

A method of evaluating ordering and inventorying costs is to determine the economic order quantity. The **economic order quantity (EOQ)** is the quantity that minimizes both ordering and storing costs. As mentioned earlier, FFI buys up to six months of

Exhibit 3-3

Forward Buying
Forward buying in March and September causes spikes in sales, followed by low levels of sales as inventories smooth out.

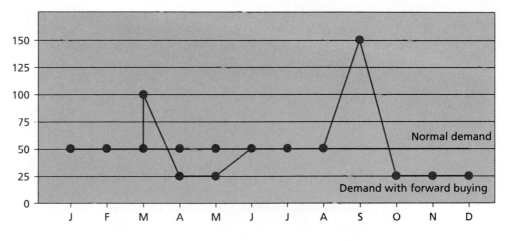

inventory. Any more than that would raise costs and not be economical. Those costs would include paying for additional space to store the lumber, additional insurance on the lumber, fire prevention costs, and the interest on the money that the firm would lose by having to pay for the extra lumber.

One strategic outcome of EOQ analysis that can occur is forward buying. **Forward buying** is buying in larger quantities than are currently needed because the discount is greater than the carrying costs. While a seller may appreciate forward buying if it helps clear out inventories, forward buying is usually an unintended negative consequence of a poor pricing decision. Forward buying creates a spike in sales (see Exhibit 3–3), which can lead to stock-outs and damage to relationships with accounts that can't get orders filled. Buyers will buy a lot more than they immediately need in order to get the cheaper price, which can then cause the manufacturer to run out. Later, when prices return to normal, demand is low so the company begins to produce less, which can increase manufacturing costs per unit, cause plants to sit idle, and create other problems.

An effective response to the problem of forward buying is to separate the order quantity from the shipping quantity through an annual contract. We'll talk more about this in Chapter 14 on pricing, but the idea is that it costs less for a company when it can plan ahead and stabilize its manufacturing over the year. These savings can be passed along to the customer, which will agree to purchase the year's needs from the manufacturer but accept delivery throughout the year. This schedule allows the seller to lower the price but maintain margin because costs will be lower. JIT can represent one form of such a contract, but a JIT system doesn't have to be in place for annual contracts to be effective.

Value Analysis

Value analysis is a thorough review of the costs and value associated with a component part. A component part is a part of the finished product—for example, a gas tank on a lawn mower or keypad used on a telephone. The value analysis can be used to redesign the part for more economical or efficient integration into the final product. The value analysis concept was developed in the 1940s by General Electric, and is often a part of the product design process. Value analysis, though, can be done afterward as well. For example, FFI has redesigned some products in order to standardize parts that it purchases, like drawer handles and other hardware. The standardization means a lower purchasing cost, more efficient inventorying, and other costs.

Value analysis must also consider the value-in-use. For example, FFI has switched to drawer guides (the tracks on which drawers slide in and out) that are easier to install. The installation time has been reduced, so even though the part costs more than other types of guides, the total value-in-use is less because of installation savings. Further, FFI has calculated an additional value to the consumer because these guides typically last longer and operate more smoothly.

When conducting value analysis, the firm considers what, if any, alternatives exist. The key question is whether the firm can achieve the same or greater value for less cost? Sometimes, the vendor's salesperson can conduct a value analysis and suggest savings. For example, Emerson Electric had up to three labels on the back of their products. Their vendor, Moore Business Forms, suggested combining the labels into one, saving Emerson Electric significant label costs but also saving Emerson manufacturing costs because only one label had to be applied. The value of the single label was greater than just the reduction in the cost of the labels themselves.

Purchasing Philosophy

In Chapter 2, you learned about the different types of relationships that are possible between buyer and seller. In this section, we will discuss a related topic, purchasing philosophies that buyers may use to guide their actions. This topic is related to the types of relationships because a company's philosophy toward purchasing will limit the types of relationships in which it can engage.

A traditional purchasing philosophy, the **adversarial purchasing philosophy**, is to have several vendors for each product. This philosophy was developed in order to increase competition for the buyer's business. Such competition is believed to lower prices while increasing the level of service and attention paid to the account. In one recent study, for example, having two sources reduced costs for some purchases.[10] At the same time, buying from a large number of suppliers can lower the quality of the relationship with suppliers, which can lead to availability problems during times of shortage as well as other problems. Still, many companies still engage in purchasing guided by the adversarial philosophy.

Buyers using an adversarial approach see the supplier as an enemy or at least as the opposition. The approach is based on caveat emptor (let the buyer beware) and assumes that the supplier will take the buyer for all there is, unless the buyer takes an adversarial position and fights for all it can get.

The Total Quality Management movement influenced purchasing philosophy by creating an alternative to the adversarial approach. This alternative, called **partnership purchasing** or **preferred supplier systems**,[11] seeks to maximize the benefits of collaboration between the buyer and a few suppliers. Buyers operating under this philosophy seek out the best suppliers they can find and then work to develop close relationships, particularly in areas of strategic importance to the firm.

In general, partnering relationships are more likely to be established with vendors who provide one or more of the following:

- High–purchase-volume materials, components, or products of strategic importance.

- Specialized products requiring information and training for effective use.

3–1

BUSINESS 2 BUSINESS
Is It Time to Say "Goodbye"?

In the past decade or so, many organizations have consolidated their purchases, reducing the number of suppliers, in order to (1) forge stronger ties and more collaborative relationships with a select few and (2) obtain significantly lower prices based on high-volume discounts. With changing management and competitive positions occurring at both buyer and seller firms, the aims of a sole sourcing arrangement may not be jointly understood. Consider this testimony about a key customer from a business marketer in the electric motors field. Can you think of similar dynamics that test a relationship?

"Our dealings with this account have been both fruitful and difficult. The business volume is significant but it is labor intensive, and problematic to service this account. . . . My personal complaint is their tendency to say 'fix this problem or we will go elsewhere.' There are not that many other places for them to go. Other people in the purchasing department there were not as quick to respond this way as the current staff. Also, this account is not as significant as it once was, due to lost market share for them. Their corporate culture is still like it was when they were larger and more powerful."

- Services that require specialized knowledge for cost reductions or performance.
- Materials that no other supplier can provide.[12]

These areas are usually those that contribute directly to the value provided by the buying firm in the supply chain, such as in the component parts of the finished product. Within the relationship, the two organizations work to increase value for both parties.

One frequent outcome is that significantly fewer suppliers are needed. Xerox, for example, dropped over 90 percent of its vendors, going from 5,000 to 400 suppliers when it adopted this philosophy. Whirlpool is currently reviewing suppliers, planning to eliminate half of its 2,500 suppliers and form partnerships with the remainder.[13] Each partner supplier provides Motorola with more products than do non-partners, gets first shot before non-partners at any new business, makes more profit than non-partners, and at the same time, provides Motorola with higher quality than Motorola can get from non-partners at a lower cost than non-partners can charge.

Single sourcing occurs when a company selects one supplier to satisfy all needs in a given area. Some students confuse single sourcing with partnering, but single sourcing can occur in an adversarial setting and need not imply a long-term collaborative relationship. For example, a company may decide to buy all of its maintenance supplies from one vendor but negotiate adversarially, trying to cut the best deal for itself without any thought of the consequences to the supplier. There is much more to partnering than single sourcing. Indeed, single sourcing without partnering can prove risky, for without the commitment of a partnership, the supplier will be free to operate adversarially too. Caveat emptor!

One difference between single sourcing and partnering is that buyers make investments related to the partner. These investments (which might mean the purchase of a computer compatible with the supplier's EDI system, for example) help bind the partners together.[14] In a single sourcing situation without partnering, there are no such investments, and the buyer is free to look elsewhere when demands are not met.

Single sourcing can lead to higher costs, as the Department of Defense has learned. It has long used single sourcing based on the theory that (1) high investments are needed to build weapon systems for which there is only one customer and (2) companies willing to make such investments should be rewarded with all of the business. What the Department of Defense has learned through experimentation, though, is that costs are lower when two vendors are used instead of just one. Organizations that engage in single sourcing should not assume that costs will be lower and should balance any higher costs with other benefits that can be obtained.[15]

Purchasing is an important contributor to the profit potential of any organization. Purchasing contributes to the profitability of the firm by controlling acquisition costs, assisting in the control of manufacturing costs, and ultimately influencing marketing costs. Purchasing also contributes by making sure that the right product or service is available when needed, in the right quantity and at the right quality, all for the lowest total cost. In the next section, we explore the processes that purchasers go through when examining products.

Supplier Evaluation

An important job of the purchasing agent is to evaluate potential suppliers and their offerings. The effects of purchasing on a firm's competitive ability are great, so companies pay close attention to how they evaluate suppliers. Marketers must also understand the process, for they are the ones being evaluated. Understanding the process is like understanding the rules of any game; if you don't know how to score, you are unlikely to win.

Buy-Grid Model

The **buy-grid model** is a version of a theory developed as a general model of rational organizational decision making, explaining how companies make decisions about, for example, where to locate a plant or make a purchase. The buy-grid model has two parts: the buy-phase model and the buy-class.

You've probably seen the buy-phase model in a management class as the rational or extensive problem solving model or in consumer behavior as a high-involvement model. This **buy-phase model** suggests that people go through a series of steps (or phases) when making a decision, beginning with problem recognition. They then search for alternatives, evaluate the alternatives, and select a solution, which is then implemented and evaluated. (See Exhibit 3–4.)

For example, when an organization needs new office space, crowded conditions help force recognition of the need. The next step is to define the type of product needed: Does the organization want to build a new office building, add on to an existing building, or simply find a larger place to rent or buy? As the organization continues to examine its needs, detailed specifications such as the size and number of offices are created. If the decision in the second step was to build, an architect would help create specifications by drawing plans. Then suppliers would be contacted, including those recommended by the architect. Step 5, acquisition and analysis of proposals, involves receiving and reviewing bids from each contractor. The architect and the executives would meet, evaluate the proposals, and select a contractor (step 6). Step 7 involves the creation of a contract specifying when the building will be completed, what it will look like, and when payments will be made. Evaluation begins as the project begins, but continues well after the organization moves in.

Exhibit 3–4

Steps in the
Buying Process
(Buy-Phase
Model)

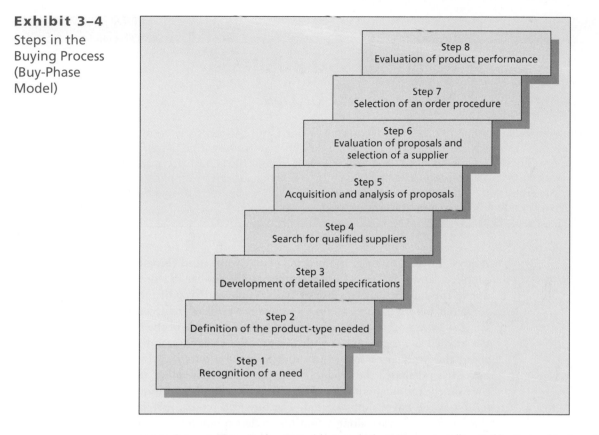

Step 8
Evaluation of product performance

Step 7
Selection of an order procedure

Step 6
Evaluation of proposals and
selection of a supplier

Step 5
Acquisition and analysis of proposals

Step 4
Search for qualified suppliers

Step 3
Development of detailed specifications

Step 2
Definition of the product-type needed

Step 1
Recognition of a need

SOURCE: Barton A. Weitz, Stephen B. Castleberry, and John F. Tanner, Jr. *Selling: Building Partnerships.* Second edition. Burr Ridge, IL: Irwin/McGraw-Hill, 1995.

Many firms have well-established purchasing policies and procedures that formalize the steps of the model.[16] In particular, government agencies establish and follow purchasing policies. For example, many state agencies are required to solicit bids from at least three vendors for any purchase over $10,000. *Set-asides* are programs designed to aid small and traditionally disadvantaged firms, such as women- and minority-owned businesses. These programs require federal government agencies to actively search and give preference to vendors that meet certain criteria. Set-asides are one example of formal purchasing policies that guide purchasing behavior.

As observers of buying behavior quickly realized, many organizational purchase decisions do not involve that much work, or include each and every step every time. A second element, the buy-class, was added, resulting in a grid. **Buy-class** refers to the type of buying decision, based on the experience of the buyer with a purchase of a particular product or service.

Organizational researchers realized that once a decision was made, products were bought automatically over and over; recognizing a problem might simply mean recognizing that the company is low in an item and needs to order more. The complete process was used only for **new buys**, products or services never purchased before. Automatic purchasing described what happened with **straight rebuys**, and only two steps were required. These steps are need recognition and placing an order.

At other times, however, a product or service would be bought again but not automatically. When a company was contemplating a rebuy but wanted to shop around, the process would include most or perhaps all of the steps—hence the term **modified**

3–2

BUSINESS 2 BUSINESS
Make or Buy?

In applying value analysis in order to cut costs, FFI has sought to find overseas sources for some components, including drawer fronts and tops of pieces like chests and dressers. At the time we write this, several suppliers appear to offer lower prices than FFI's own costs of manufacturing the parts, but the company hasn't made a decision. What are some of the hidden or potential costs of buying those parts from someone else? Since FFI is the current in-supplier, what might the challenges be in creating a partnership with a new supplier?

---

rebuys. In this instance, the process may involve need recognition, an evaluation of suppliers, and a decision—a process that can be similar to a new buy. The difference is not in the number of steps but in the amount and type of information that must be collected before a purchase can be made. Modified rebuys can also be similar to straight rebuys or new buys, depending on the specifics of the situation. In a new buy, the buyer has no experience with the product or service and must become educated about the product or service in order to make a purchase. In a modified rebuy, the buyer has purchased the product or service before. Therefore, the buyer will not spend time on education about the product itself, but about the various vendors and their offerings as the buyer shops around. The buy-grid model, therefore, describes how purchasing practices vary along a continuum depending on the buyer's experience in buying that particular product or service.

The personal computer industry is an example of how a market changes with experience. When the PCs were new, salespeople were needed to fully explain benefits and educate buyers. Buyers, particularly buyers in departments other than the data processing department, needed a lot of information in order to understand what PCs could do for them, how PCs work, and what was needed to be fully operational. Now PCs are sold in stores or through direct mail with little personal sales effort. Buyers are knowledgeable and can make their decisions without the marketer's help. In some organizations, computers are ordered through an 800 number on a straight rebuy basis. Note, though, that a PC purchase is still a new buy for some people. While the market may have moved more to a straight rebuy or modified rebuy, some salespeople will still meet new buy buyers and will find that these buyers will require more information and postsale service than buyers with more experience.

Some product decisions may never become true straight rebuys because of the importance of the decision. For example, fleet managers buy automobiles, trucks, and vans for their organizations each year. In some situations, they may simply pick up the phone and order a few more Ram vans or F150 pickup trucks, but in most cases, more work will be done. Offerings of several vendors will be considered and a contract will be negotiated because the size of the purchase is too great to do automatically. Modified rebuys are those situations where the same product or product type is being purchased that has been purchased before, but most of the decision steps are still taken.

Modified rebuys occur for several reasons, and we've already discussed the importance of the purchase. Other reasons include changing technology that improves product performance and requires re-evaluation of vendors and their offerings, dissatisfaction with the performance of a supplier and/or the product, changing prices, or even a change in the personnel involved. Some organizations periodically review all vendors and regularly conduct value analyses, even though there may be no obvious problems.

Value analysis is one situation that can turn a straight rebuy into a modified rebuy. When a company is closely evaluating a particular part, one question that is asked is if the part is available elsewhere for less. As the answer is sought to this question, **out-suppliers** (those suppliers whose products are not considered in a straight rebuy) are given the opportunity to earn the business. **In-suppliers** (those suppliers whose products are ordered automatically in a straight rebuy) must prove value or create new value by re-designing their offering. Thus, the purchase moves from being a straight rebuy to a modified rebuy.

Buy-Grid and Marketing Practice

The theory suggests that more information is needed by the buyer to make a new buy than when making a modified rebuy, and almost no information is needed for a straight rebuy. To use this model, a company would look at the degree to which a market is buying a product for the first time. If most of the market is buying the product for the first time, methods of communication such as personal selling may be used in order to provide the most information. Advertising would contain a lot of detailed copy that described the benefits and how the product worked. Over time, as the market grows more familiar with the product, less educational methods of communicating may be used, such as catalogs. Exhibit 3–5 illustrates some of the marketing differences depending on the amount of the market's experience in buying the product.

Another marketing implication is that an in-supplier would like purchases of its products to be straight rebuys. Annual contracts are one method of creating straight rebuys. For example, Xerox offers its customers an annual supply contract. Each time a department is low in copier supplies, the purchasing department orders automatically from Xerox, perhaps using EDI. Out-suppliers would be locked out until the next time the contract comes up for review.

When buyers don't have experience, marketing strategies can provide buyers with the information they need to make a decision. Marketers consider how buyers use that information to be very important. In the next section, we examine how buyers compare vendors and products.

Multi-Attribute Decision Making

In both new and modified rebuys, the vendor and product evaluation stages are important times for prospective vendors. One method used to explain the vendor and product evaluation stage of the buy-phase model is the multi-attribute model. The **multi-attribute model** is based on the idea that people view products as a collection of attributes or "bundle of benefits," and provides a picture of how alternatives are evaluated. Each benefit is how a particular feature satisfies a particular need. Where this model fits the buy-grid model is in the evaluation-of-alternatives stage for new or modified rebuys; in the straight rebuy, there is no evaluation of alternatives as the product or service is ordered automatically, perhaps using EDI.

For example, you may want high gas mileage, a comfortable interior, and a sporty exterior in a car (three needs). While an aerodynamic design may improve gas mileage and provide for a sporty exterior, it does nothing for the inside! Therefore, there must be some method of accounting for a particular product's ability to solve all three needs.

Exhibit 3–5

Marketing Implications of the Buy-Grid

Buy-Phases	Marketing Element	
New Task		
All steps of the buying process are taken, with emphasis on product definition and development of product specifications.	Advertising	Detailed, educational; must try to get users to try product, substitute for old method.
	Promotion	Use demonstrations at trade shows to show how it works.
		Offer free trials or demonstrations at the customer's site.
	Selling	Heavy emphasis on understanding customers' needs and showing how new product satisfies needs better than old methods.
Modified Rebuy		
Less emphasis is on product definition and more emphasis is on search and evaluation of suppliers.	Advertising	Use comparison advertising to show differences between your product and similar products.
	Promotion	Customer site demonstrations, hospitality events at trade shows.
	Selling	Protect relationship with current customers with plant tours, special trade-in pricing and other offers.
		Anticipate or respond quickly to changes in customer needs.
Straight Rebuy		
Need recognition and purchase are the only steps used.	Advertising	Use reminder advertising.
		Build image for company.
	Promotion	Hospitality events at trade shows.
	Selling	Any personal selling is designed to build relationships.
		Automate the purchasing process, perhaps through EDI.

Each need is more or less important than other needs, depending on the organization or individual making the purchase. For example, a company may be purchasing fleet vehicles that salespeople will use to transport customers. A comfortable interior and stylish exterior would be important. A company purchasing fleet vehicles for salespeople to use to get to remote areas may place the same emphasis on a comfortable interior but not care a great deal about the exterior's appearance. Each firm would place a different importance level on each attribute, as shown in Exhibit 3–6. On a scale of 1–10, with 10 being most important, one firm might rate exterior appearance an 8 while another rates it only a 3. On the other hand, the second firm rates interior comfort as very important or 9, while the first only gives it a 2. This rating system is important, but isn't enough to determine which vehicle to purchase.

Each firm must also then rate each car on how attractive and comfortable it is. For a Chrysler, you may rate it a 7 for appearance and a 4 for comfort, while another buyer gives it a 6 and a 9. The Honda, however, you give a 6 and a 9, while the other buyer gives it an 8 and a 7. (See Exhibit 3–7.)

The next step is to multiply the weight by the rating and then sum the scores, as shown in Exhibit 3–8. So you would multiply 8 by 7 and 2 by 4 to obtain scores for the Chrysler, and then sum the products (56 and 8) to arrive at the total (64). For the

Exhibit 3-6

Importance Level
of Car Features
for Fleet
Purchases

Car Feature	Buyer 1	Buyer 2
Exterior appearance	8	3
Interior comfort	2	9
Gas economy	4	5
Trunk size	7	7

Exhibit 3-7

Car Ratings

Car Feature	Buyer 1		Buyer 2	
	Honda	Chrysler	Honda	Chrysler
Exterior appearance	6	7	8	6
Interior comfort	9	4	7	9
Gas economy	8	6	9	6
Trunk size	6	9	5	8

Exhibit 3-8

Car Scores

Car Feature	Buyer 1			Buyer 2		
	Importance Level	Honda	Chrysler	Importance Level	Honda	Chrysler
Exterior appearance	8 ×	6 (48)	7 (56)	3 ×	8 (24)	6 (18)
Interior comfort	2 ×	9 (18)	4 (8)	9 ×	7 (63)	9 (81)
Gas economy	4 ×	8 (32)	6 (24)	5 ×	9 (45)	6 (30)
Trunk size	7 ×	7 (49)	8 (56)	7 ×	5 (35)	8 (56)
Total		147	144		167	185

Honda you would multiply 8 by 6 and 2 by 9, then add the products (48 and 18) to arrive at the total for the Honda (66). Based on these scores for just the two features, you would buy the Honda. Even though the Chrysler outperformed the Honda for your most important feature, the difference in comfort was so great that it outweighed the appearance.

We've asked our students if they actually calculate scores using ratings and weights. A few admit to this practice, but most believe that no one would be this formal. In organizations, however, you will find formal rating sheets used by purchasing departments to rate different suppliers and their offerings. Exhibit 3–9 is an example of a rating sheet used by Chrysler to evaluate potential suppliers.

A marketer would use this information by first determining what the most important attributes are, and then designing the product to rate the highest on those attributes. If you are a salesperson, however, and a particular buyer rated a competitor higher on an important attribute, you may work to change the importance of the attribute in the mind of the buyer if the product can't actually change.

Multi-attribute models are not just for evaluating potential suppliers. Companies use multi-attribute methods to analyze the performance of current vendors, too. Purchasing teams that include purchasing agents, engineers, manufacturing personnel, and other

Exhibit 3–9
Sample Vendor
Analysis Form

	5 Excellent	4 Good	3 Satisfactory	2 Fair	1 Poor	0 N/A

Supplier Name: _____   Type of Product: _____

Shipping Location: _____   Annual Sales Dollars: _____

	5 Excellent	4 Good	3 Satisfactory	2 Fair	1 Poor	0 N/A
Quality (45%)						
Defect rates	____	____	____	____	____	____
Quality of sample	____	____	____	____	____	____
Conformance with quality program	____	____	____	____	____	____
Responsiveness to quality problems	____	____	____	____	____	____
Overall quality	____	____	____	____	____	____
Delivery (25%)						
Avoidance of late shipments	____	____	____	____	____	____
Ability to expand production capacity	____	____	____	____	____	____
Performance in sample delivery	____	____	____	____	____	____
Response to changes in order size	____	____	____	____	____	____
Overall delivery	____	____	____	____	____	____
Price (20%)						
Price competitiveness	____	____	____	____	____	____
Payment terms	____	____	____	____	____	____
Absorption of costs	____	____	____	____	____	____
Submission of cost savings plans	____	____	____	____	____	____
Overall price	____	____	____	____	____	____
Technology (10%)						
State-of-the-art components	____	____	____	____	____	____
Sharing research & development capability	____	____	____	____	____	____
Ability and willingness to help with design	____	____	____	____	____	____
Responsiveness to engineering problems	____	____	____	____	____	____
Overall technology	____	____	____	____	____	____

Buyer: _____   Date: _____

Comments: _____

SOURCE: Chrysler Corporation.

managers are used to develop the rating systems. Rockwell International's Defense Electronics Group was one of the pioneers of formal supplier rating systems with the development of its Supplier Rating and Incentive Program (SRIP). This system first identifies events, or problems with supplier service that require Rockwell personnel to take action. Examples of events are overshipments, undershipments, and rejection of products upon receipt due to damage. Each event requires a Rockwell employee to take some action, such as seeing that overshipments are returned and a credit issued.

When the Rockwell employee has to take an action, a cost is involved for that employee's time. For example, Rockwell found that in 1990, it cost $275 to return something to a supplier and $120 to follow up on a late shipment. These costs can be summed for each supplier, which Rockwell does on an annual basis to develop a Supplier

Performance Index. The company can then analyze the quality of performance for each vendor. Rockwell's system has been adopted by such companies as Northrup, Motorola, and Honeywell.

Companies with high performance on SRIPs advertise their high ratings in order to attract more business. Buyers recognize that the quality of service is reflected in the total cost of ownership; poor quality does raise the cost of doing business. Companies that perform poorly will face difficulties no matter how well their products perform.

Buyers also evaluate suppliers for elevation to partner or preferred supplier status. The SRIP procedure is one method of evaluating suppliers, but it provides only supplier performance information. Other factors are important when deciding with whom the buyer wants to partner. When considering a candidate for preferred supplier status, Bethlehem Steel uses six sets of criteria: capability, which includes an SRIP analysis; organizational motivation and quality of employees; financial health; corporate culture; willingness to commit to a partnership; and ethics. Using a multi-attribute model, suppliers must pass minimum thresholds on each set of criteria and then reach an overall score before being offered preferred supplier status.[17]

The buy-grid model helps us understand how buyers make purchases that meet their organization's needs. In the next chapter, we'll learn how buyers operate as individuals in organizational purchases and how those individual factors can influence buying. In the next section, however, we'll discuss trends that are affecting purchasing departments and how they operate.

Trends in Purchasing

Purchasing departments are very important to the success of an organization, as we saw earlier in this chapter. As companies select and implement various strategies, purchasing is always involved as resources are gathered to support those strategies. As a result, one trend is to increase the professionalism of the purchasing agent. Purchasing departments are not immune, however, to the influences of the economy. Therefore, trends caused by the economy as well as trends in organizational strategy influence the purchasing department. One economic trend is downsizing of organizations, while outsourcing and cross-functional sourcing are strategic trends affecting the purchasing department.

Downsizing

Economic factors have caused many companies to **downsize**, or to lower the number of employees through early retirement and layoffs. In a recent study of purchasing agents, 55 percent said their departments had been moderately to radically downsized.[18] Layoffs mean that fewer purchasing agents are available to purchase the same amount of material for the organization. One agent said, "My department is now procuring twice the amount with one-third the staff."[19] Purchasing agents have to either work harder or find ways to be more productive—that is, to buy more in the same amount of time.

Purchasing agents are buying more in the same amount of time by buying more from the same vendors. Reducing the number of vendors is another strategy. Both of these strategies are designed to reduce shopping around, an activity that many purchasing agents do not have time for. In addition, reducing the number of vendors means fewer invoices to pay, fewer shipments to receive (because the vendor can send more in one shipment), and other productivity boosters.

These strategies also increase the importance of developing strategic relationships with customers because if your customers do not have time to shop around, neither do the customers of your competitors. Growing your business by taking sales away from competition may become more difficult.

Reducing the number of vendors also means that larger purchases are made. Increasing the size of business awarded to each vendor has, in turn, increased the importance of negotiation skills for both buyer and seller. For marketers, an increase in negotiated business will mean more pressure to lower prices as buyers negotiate harder.[20]

Some shopping around has to occur, however, because current vendors are not always totally satisfactory or may not have what is needed. One shopping activity that purchasing agents are turning to is visiting **trade shows**, which are like temporary business marketing shopping malls. In one day at a trade show, a purchasing agent can visit with 30 or more vendors and come away with a good idea of who can solve the organization's need.

Outsourcing

Outsourcing is the process of finding another organization to supply the buying organization with a product or service, usually one that was previously created in-house. Outsourcing is a strategic trend, caused in part by a trend in strategy where companies focus on their core businesses. As one buyer for Conoco said when discussing the outsourcing of employee training, "The bottom line is that we are in the business of producing oil and gas, not training our employees."[21] Therefore, a company in the oil and gas business would want to hire someone to do anything that didn't directly involve making oil and gas products. As an example, Conoco may hire an ad agency to do all of its advertising, an exhibit company to handle all of its trade shows, and a marketing research firm to conduct all of its research.

Global outsourcing is a strategy that takes advantage of lower costs or specialized labor. For example, New York Life, Cigna, and Metropolitan Life outsource underwriting and claims processing operations to Ireland, taking advantage of operating costs 30 percent lower than in the States and a well-educated staff.[22] Pacific Data Services has been contracting data entry services to China since 1961. In Japan, over 3,500 people work in office parks linked to their U.S. customers by satellite. They do data entry and other clerical duties for U.S. companies.[23]

Outsourcing affects the purchasing department because it changes the way purchases are made. For example, outsourcing a subassembly may mean that fewer purchases are made, but the final purchase may require more input from the design department or a tighter communication link with manufacturing. As you can see from the examples, outsourcing can also have a major impact on the organization because important responsibilities are being moved outside the business. Companies that outsource poorly can be significantly hampered in their ability to compete.

Outsourcing has also meant continued growth in the services sector. Much of what is outsourced is services, such as marketing research, advertising and promotion services, training services, and other services that were formerly done by organizational employees, although more companies are also outsourcing production.[24]

Stronger Relationships with Sellers

As just pointed out, outsourcing means that important responsibilities are now being moved outside the organization. In addition, companies are trying to reduce the number of vendors and increase the amount of business with each vendor. These factors combine

Exhibit 3–10

Cross-Functional
Purchasing Team
For a Bakery
Buying a Freezer

Team Member	Role
Plant manager	Evaluate impact on production process
Marketing manager	Provide estimates of sales
Sales rep for Steak and Ale	Provide primary customer's input
Comptroller	Evaluate financial aspects of purchase
Production supervisor	Offer input on training needs and other aspects that might affect line workers

to increase the importance of strong relationships with suppliers. We've talked about this trend in the previous two chapters, but, as you can see, other trends influence the importance of relationships too.

Communication channels have changed greatly as a result of this trend. With direct communication, buyers can talk directly to key personnel and know that their needs will be met.[25] Buyers like Peak Electronics, for example, believe so strongly in the need for direct communication that they gave manufacturing line employees authority to contact suppliers directly and handle problems as they occur.[26] Smart marketers are finding ways to increase direct communication between their company and their partners.

Cross-Functional Teams

Cross-functional sourcing teams are purchasing teams that include members of various functional areas within the firm, and sometimes include personnel from suppliers and customers too. These teams are formed to develop cost-reduction strategies, create sourcing strategies, and handle other purchasing functions.[27] Cross-functional teams are designed to take advantage of the different types of expertise that reside in the various departments across the organization. For example, a team may be composed of members of the marketing department, who can offer projections concerning customer reaction to changes, as illustrated in Exhibit 3–10. In this situation, a bakery whose primary customer is Steak and Ale created a cross-functional team to examine all purchases involving manufacturing processes.

Cross-functional teams work best when given the resources needed (particularly securing services and help from others and time), when suppliers participate, and when the team is given the authority to run itself. Combined with a need for authority is the need for good leadership, which is often the responsibility of the purchasing professional.

From a marketing perspective, it is apparent that potential suppliers should seek to actively participate in their customers' cross-functional sourcing teams. For this to occur, salespeople must understand what cross-functional teams are, how to recognize such teams in their clients' organizations, and how they can participate. In addition, salespeople have to be given resources that allow others in their own organization to participate. Buyers need the expertise of the selling organization's engineers, finance personnel, and so forth in order to fully benefit from the seller's participation.

Exhibit 3–11

Who Is the Professional Purchasing Agent?

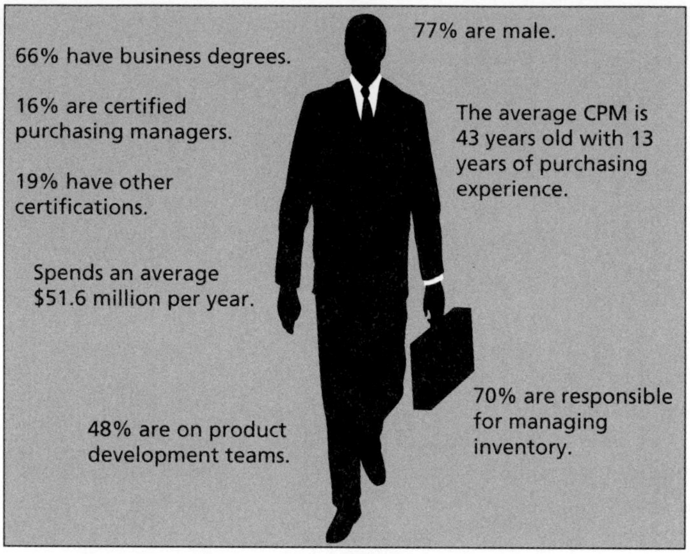

66% have business degrees.

16% are certified purchasing managers.

19% have other certifications.

Spends an average $51.6 million per year.

48% are on product development teams.

77% are male.

The average CPM is 43 years old with 13 years of purchasing experience.

70% are responsible for managing inventory.

SOURCE: A Ridour, "Profile of a Purchasing Professional," *Purchasing,* July 13, 1995, pp. 56–72.

Professionalism in Purchasing

Another trend is toward increasing the professionalism of the purchasing function. The National Association of Purchasing Managers has contributed much to the development of professionalism by encouraging and providing certification for purchasing managers. Those who are certified as professional purchasing managers must pass a battery of tests that indicate knowledge (and adherence) to the profession's code of ethics (which we will discuss later in this chapter) as well as procedures of purchasing. Because of the importance of purchasing to the bottom line, many companies are also encouraging their purchasing agents to seek certification. Exhibit 3–11 profiles the purchasing professional.

These trends, while discussed in the context of private industry, are also affecting the way the government buys. In the next section, we take a close look at government purchasing in order to successfully market to the world's largest buyer.

Purchasing in Government

The government is the largest single buyer, the largest single employer, and the largest landlord. For example, the federal government buys about $500 million in desktop PCs each year, while state local governments buy twice that![28] This kind of purchasing power makes selling to the government an important consideration for many businesses. The government, however, has a different agenda than private organizations, which influences the way the government makes purchases. For example, minority set-asides are programs designed to encourage the development and growth of minority-owned businesses. Reaching social and political goals, such as minority ownership of businesses, often influences government purchasing policies, which we will examine in this section.

Companies who provide infrastructure products and services, such as highway construction, are finding developing countries to be highly profitable and growing markets.

Courtesy Ingersoll-Rand Company.

Political and Social Goals

In developing countries, such as many of the countries in Asia, governments are very interested in developing their country's **infrastructure**, or the transportation, communication, and other utilities. These governments recognize that for their economies to develop, they must be able to provide businesses with clean water, electricity, natural gas, efficient transportation, and reliable communication. As a result, U.S. companies are snatching up infrastructure opportunities in many developing countries. Ellicot Machine Corp. (of Baltimore, Maryland) sells dredging equipment in virtually every Asian country, dredging equipment that is used to create ship channels and clear harbors.[29] While the U.S. government may be the single largest purchaser in the world, the market created by foreign governments is very large and desirous of finding suppliers from any country that can meet their needs.

The U.S. government encourages the development of minority-owned, women-owned, and small businesses through set-asides. The government also attempts to achieve social goals through compliance programs. **Compliance programs** are programs where purchasers must be in compliance with federal guidelines in order to be eligible to supply the government. The government has used compliance programs to advance affirmative action programs for women, minorities, and the handicapped.

Minority subcontracting programs are another way that the government encourages the development of minority-owned businesses. **Minority subcontracting** programs require general contractors and other major suppliers to allocate a certain percentage of the total contract to minority-owned subcontractors. For example, a company building a research park for the EPA may have minority subcontractors to install the plumbing, lay the carpet, and other such jobs that are part of the overall contract.

The Department of Defense

The Department of Defense is the largest single buying agency in the federal government, accounting for an estimated 80 percent of all government purchases.[30] Composed of the military branches (the Army, Air Force, and Navy), the Department of Defense also contains the Defense Logistics Agency (DLA). The DLA purchases all of the facilitating services and products as well as MRO items. The purpose of the DLA is to secure volume discounts by buying for all of the military such items as copiers, office supplies, and office furniture.

As mentioned earlier, the Department of Defense developed many single sourcing arrangements, in part because of the huge investment needed to develop weapon systems. Frequently, few vendors are even capable of bidding; for example, only Raytheon and General Dynamics entered the Sparrow air-to-air missile contract competition. The department, however, is now trying to develop additional vendors for many products, having found that multiple vendors can lower cost. In addition, due to its spreading purchases among suppliers, more suppliers learn how to do business with government, which further increases competition for government business. The increased competition should lead to lower prices and higher-quality products.[31]

Non-Defense Buying

The rest of the government uses the General Services Administration in a fashion similar to the DLA; in fact, the DLA makes most of its purchases through the GSA. The GSA supplies government agencies with office space, facilitating services and products, and MRO items. The GSA and the DLA are the two most important agencies because of the volume of buying for which they are responsible.

The GSA negotiates the price to be charged the government, but in many cases, the GSA does not actually make the final purchase. Each agency can then make its own purchase directly, receiving the GSA price and using a GSA-approved vendor. (Many companies have copied this model of approving vendors at headquarters and allowing each division or local office to make the final purchase decision.) For example, the GSA has negotiated copier prices with several different manufacturers. The Federal Highway Department office in Fort Worth, Texas, can choose the copier it wants from any of those approved vendors and make the purchase themselves.

The GSA does not get involved in all of the non-Defense buying, though. NASA, for example, buys space shuttles and space communication systems entirely on its own. The GSA does not have the expertise necessary to make those kind of purchases.

Marketing to the Government

The size of the federal government of the United States, combined with the various social, political, and economic goals that influence government purchasing, make selling to the government a complicated and arduous task, especially in comparison with selling to private industry. To assist potential vendors, the government has created booklets such as *How to Sell to the Air Force* and *Doing Business with the Federal Government.* Information on opportunities to sell to the government can also be found in the *Commerce Business Daily,* which is how Professional Restoration Inc. found the opportunity described in From the Field 3–2. In addition, government agencies have purchasing agents that seek

3–2

FROM THE FIELD

Restoring History Wins Government Contract

When President Clinton, South Korean President Kim Young Sam, and more than 100,000 people, including veterans and their families, attended the dedication ceremonies in late July for the Korean War Memorial in Washington, D.C., entrepreneurs Patricia Ghiglino and Reinaldo Lopez experienced tremendous pride. Their company, Professional Restoration, Inc. (PRI), under a subcontract, had built the monument's free-standing granite memorial wall and circular reflecting pool. "We took part in history in building the Korean War Memorial," says Ghiglino. "It is a hard feeling to describe, but it is an honor for us, especially being foreigners."

When Lopez began working in the U.S., he concentrated on sculpture, but he grew disillusioned with the business side of art when he was forced to take legal action against a gallery on grounds it had not paid him for work it had commissioned. Ghiglino encouraged him to look in other directions. In *Commerce Business Daily,* a publication that advertises available federal contracts, she found a call for bids to construct two entrances for the disabled at the Smithsonian Institution's Visitor Center, a landmark known as the Castle.

The job involved working with Seneca sandstone, a delicate, multilayered stone. Because of the Castle's historical significance, says Ghiglino, "it was critical that the stone be perfectly cut and carved to match the existing building stone."

Since PRI, their start-up firm, had no track record, Ghiglino offered a "free sample"—Lopez would actually do a small portion of the job—to convince the Smithsonian that PRI could do the whole project. By doing the demonstration and submitting the lowest bid, PRI clinched its first contract—a $200,000 job.

Among the company's most notable projects was the rehabilitation of the lobby of the Washington Monument. PRI is also restoring a 90-year-old Italian mosaic floor in Bancroft Hall at the U.S. Naval Academy, in Annapolis, Md. The job entails fabricating 15,000 small marble pieces custom-cut from individual molds.

In 1994, Ghiglino, president of PRI, was named National Businesswoman of the Year by the U.S. Hispanic Chamber of Commerce, and PRI was named a Blue Chip Enterprise for the District of Columbia in the Blue Chip Enterprise awards program, sponsored by Connecticut Mutual Life Insurance Co., the U.S. Chamber of Commerce, and *Nation's Business.* The program honors firms that have overcome adversity and become stronger.

With PRI now established as a regional company, Ghiglino and Lopez—both now American citizens—have larger ambitions. "Within the next five years," says Ghiglino, "our goal is to be known as the best restoration company nationwide."

Source: M. Courtauld McBryde, "Restoring History," *Nation's Business* (November, 1995), p. 15.

out qualified vendors and are specialists in set-aside, compliance, or subcontracting programs. These agents are valuable sources of information for the vendor with little experience in marketing to the government.

As mentioned earlier, the GSA negotiates a price and, when successful, places that vendor on the approved vendor list. Each agency can then do business with that vendor. If you aren't on the list, then an agency cannot purchase from you. The first step, for many vendors, is to become an approved vendor. Then each agency has to be sold and marketed to as if it were a separate customer.

Entertaining potential clients is a regular activity in many industries. Some companies, though, have policies forbidding their purchasing personnel to accept a meal from a salesperson so that there is never any question of unfair influence in a purchase.
Courtesy NCH Chemical.

In major purchases, particularly when products are being built to specifications, pricing can be negotiated one of two ways. For example, when NASA negotiates to buy a new space shuttle from Rockwell International, NASA can negotiate a fixed price. A **fixed-price agreement** means that if it costs Rockwell more to build an item than it thought, Rockwell has to cover the higher costs. Or NASA can agree to a **cost-plus contract**, which means that NASA will reimburse Rockwell for all of its costs plus a certain percentage for Rockwell's profit.

Both cost-plus and fixed-price agreements are negotiated when selling to foreign governments too. In addition to the issues we've already discussed about how governments buy, marketers to other governments must consider the type of government and political system. In China, for example, one must not only understand the purchasing process of the agency making the purchase, but also the hierarchy and decision-making process of the local Communist Party office.

Selling to any government can be a difficult process made complex by the number of regulations involved. Selling to governments can take much longer than selling to corporations, require significantly more paperwork, and result in lower prices and margins. Still, the size of purchases made by governments makes them an attractive market for many business marketers.

Ethics in Purchasing

Ethics in business are an important topic today. Issues such as price fixing, under-the-table kickbacks, and other shady practices continue to fill the media. Frequent cases, such as the CEO of a construction firm arrested for bribing government officials, create the perception that often sellers are unethical.

Ethics are of particular concern to purchasing management. The executive of the selling firm may offer a bribe, but it takes a recipient for the bribe to occur. Buyers are just as susceptible to the economic pressures facing salespeople that influence ethical behavior. In this section, we will examine the key ethical issues facing purchasing and what companies are doing to encourage ethical behavior.

What Are Ethics?

Ethics are moral codes of conduct, rules for how someone should operate that can be utilized as situations demand. Codes of ethics are rules developed either by an industry association or by a company or some organization, but individuals also develop their own codes. Individual ethics can be developed through experience and through education. When conduct fails to meet the ethical needs of society, laws are passed; for example, the Robinson–Patman Act was passed because business failed to price products in a fair and ethical manner.

For ethical behavior to occur, the person must first recognize the ethical implications of the situation and then be motivated to act ethically. Knowledge of right and wrong is not enough; the individual must want to do what is right. Situational factors, such as the probability of getting caught, may influence some people's behavior, while others will always do what they think is right (or what is wrong, depending on their moral state) no matter what the situation.

Ethical Issues Facing Purchasing

In purchasing, there are several key issues concerning ethics that revolve around the concept of fair competition. Fair competition means that any competitor has equal opportunity to sell to the buyer and equal access to information from the buyer. Actions such as bribery are unethical because they give one competitor an unfair advantage. Therefore, one issue facing purchasing is *equal access to the buying opportunity*.

Another basic issue is *responsibility to the buying organization,* the buyer's employer. For example, bribery may add to the cost of the product by raising the price, which is not the best thing for the buying organization. In addition, a buyer who has been bribed may not perform the buying duties completely, which means that the organization is not assured of getting the best solution for its needs.

These two dimensions of equal access and responsibility are the basic guidelines for evaluating ethical actions in purchasing. Let's now take a look at how these guidelines can be applied to purchasing situations.

Receiving Gifts

Gifts of some type are accepted by an estimated 97 percent of all buyers and gift giving has long been an accepted practice.[32] Most businesses believe that giving gifts is an effective activity that enhances their selling ability by strengthening relationships. Research, though, indicates that gift giving is not as effective as managers think and may cause problems for vendors.[33]

Xerox Corporation offered a joint promotion with an airline company where the buyer of a copier got a certificate good for one round-trip flight to anywhere in the United States. The value of the certificate could be as high as several hundred dollars. This type of promotion is called a gift with purchase. There were two problems with the specific program. First, buyers kept the coupon for themselves instead of surrendering the coupons to their organization. Second, the value of the gift was too high. While policies vary from company to company on whether a gift can be accepted, IRS regulations allow a seller to deduct only $25 when giving a gift. Any gift worth several hundred dollars is questionable ethically. Therefore, the Xerox promotion was halted because it was perceived by buying organizations' managements to be a bribe. The perception existed that buyers were buying Xerox copiers just to get the tickets; the ticket gave Xerox unfair access and Xerox may have been an irresponsible choice for the purchasing organization.

When gifts are given is another issue. The same gift sent out after the purchase, with no prior knowledge among the purchasers, might have been acceptable because the gift could not have swayed the decision. It was not offered to induce purchases, but to thank buyers. In situations involving repeat purchases, however, the choice is not so black and white.

Expensive lunches, entertainment such as golf games and sporting events, and trips are also considered gifts. Some companies, such as IBM, do not allow their employees to accept anything from a vendor. Mead Paper, for example, has an annual golf tournament for its customers, but the IBM buyer cannot participate. By company policy, that buyer cannot accept so much as a cup of coffee from the Mead representative. Yet in other industries and companies, entertaining clients and prospective clients is accepted.

Access to Information

Buyers have access to a lot of information. Having that information can be a competitive advantage. How that information is used can become an ethical issue. For example, suppose a purchasing agent is considering three vendors. If the agent tells one vendor the budget but doesn't tell the others, then the vendor with the budget information has an unfair advantage.

Buyers and sellers sometimes work closely together in developing products. Sellers also give some buyers sneak previews of products. In these situations, buyers are often asked to sign **nondisclosure agreements**, which means that they will not share any information about the new products with anyone who has not also signed such an agreement. If a buyer were to offer this information in a trade to wrangle concessions from another vendor, the buyer could be sued. More importantly, the buyer would be guilty of unethical conduct.

Encouraging Ethical Conduct

We've talked at length in this chapter about the importance of purchasing to the firm's success. Ethical conduct is a major contributor to effective purchasing; unethical purchasing can damage a firm because it will pay too much for lower-quality products. In addition, there is always the threat of legal action for unethical conduct.

Just as importantly, however, unethical conduct represents a breach of trust. Selling organizations have to trust their buyers on many levels, and trust is particularly important in building long-term partnerships. Without that trust, the buying organizations will not be privy to sneak previews of new products and will be unable to make fully informed decisions. Ethical sellers will look elsewhere to form strategic alliances, which will damage the competitive ability of the unethical firm.

The senior management of most companies wants their companies to operate ethically, but even if they did not care that much about ethics, it is good business practice. To encourage ethical behavior, many companies have developed specific and extensive policies concerning purchasing. These policies cover such things as when is it acceptable to receive a gift and how large a gift may be, issues concerning entertainment, and how a purchasing department will select products. For example, policies may dictate when sealed bids must be used, when the vendor with the lowest price has to be given the business, and other purchasing decisions.

Policies alone are not enough, however. Employees have to understand the policies and know how to apply them. For this reason, companies require their purchasing employees to undergo regular training about the policies.

Knowledge of the policies, however, is also not enough. Employees have to be motivated to follow the policies. Management can encourage employees to follow the policies by setting good examples and by punishing those who fail to follow the policies. When these two actions are viewed by purchasing employees, they know that the policies are real, and they will be motivated to act within the guidelines that management has set.

Summary

Effective purchasing can be a source of competitive advantage for a company. Purchasing's responsibility is to provide an adequate supply of the right product or service at the best possible price. Purchasing's ability to effectively achieve this responsibility is affected, however, by manufacturing and marketing considerations. Reducing purchasing costs can have a negative impact on manufacturing and/or marketing, so purchasing must consider the needs of manufacturing and marketing when making decisions.

Many organizations are turning to just-in-time (JIT) systems, which means that they receive products and materials just in time to use them. JIT can reduce inventory carrying costs significantly. Suppliers are incorporating concurrent manufacturing as a way to supply the JIT needs of the customers without increasing their own inventory costs. Electronic data interchange (EDI) is electronic data transmission between the buyer and seller that is used to order products and can facilitate the implementation of a JIT system.

Purchasing the right quality of product or service is an important responsibility of the purchasing department. Quality is ultimately defined by the consumer; purchasing has to work closely with marketing and manufacturing to ensure that the proper quality of products are purchased.

Purchasing also has the responsibility to provide products and services at the lowest total cost. Lowest total cost, however, includes many elements beyond the initial purchase price. Purchasing departments, therefore, examine the total cost of ownership over the life of the product. Many companies are turning to outsourcing services as a method of reducing the total cost of ownership because of the high costs associated with retaining service personnel on staff.

To arrive at the lowest total cost, companies have tried to determine the economic ordering quantity. Forward buying is one practice that can result, having negative consequences for the supplier. Another practice is value analysis, which is a method of examining the total cost of ownership.

Traditionally, purchasing agents have had an adversarial philosophy toward their suppliers, but this is changing to a more collaborative and partnering philosophy. Preferred supplier systems are means that companies use to develop stronger relationships with their vendors. One outcome of the shift toward partnering is the growth in single sourcing, although single sourcing by itself does not necessarily mean a partnership.

Several steps are required to select vendors. The buy-phase model describes each step that organizations go through when making purchases for the first time (new buys). Modified rebuys may require fewer steps, while straight rebuys are often simply automatic purchasing when inventories are low. Out-suppliers encourage value analysis in an effort to move straight rebuys into the modified rebuy category, so that they will have a shot at the business.

To evaluate suppliers, companies compare and weigh benefits using a multi-attribute process. This process requires purchasers to enumerate the desired benefits and rate the importance of each benefit. Then each vendor is evaluated and scored on each benefit. The rating of importance and the vendor's score are multiplied for each benefit, and then summed to arrive at a total score. The vendor with the highest score is the one whose product is selected. Companies such as Rockwell International use a formal process like this when evaluating current suppliers as well as potential suppliers.

Downsizing, outsourcing, and cross-functional purchasing teams are several trends that are influencing purchasing departments today. These trends are also affecting the way companies have to market their products and services.

Purchasing is an area where ethics are very important. Two basic dimensions guide ethical issues in purchasing: fair access and responsibility. Two activities are especially worrisome: gift giving plus information access and use.

Government purchasing represents a major economic influence in every country. Developing countries are especially concerned with making infrastructure purchases. Other countries may want to achieve social and economic goals through programs such as minority set-asides. For major purchases, a cost-plus or fixed pricing agreement may be negotiated.

Understanding how purchasing operates is very important. The purchasing department is involved in over 40 percent of all purchases made by organizations, and nearly all purchases involving MRO items and materials that go into the manufacturing process.

Key Terms

adversarial purchasing
  philosophy
buy-class
buy-grid model
buy-phase model
compliance program
concurrent
  manufacturing
cost-plus contract
cross-functional
  sourcing teams
downsize
economic order quantity
  (EOQ)

electronic data
  interchange (EDI)
ethics
fixed-price agreement
forward buying
infrastructure
in-supplier
just-in-time (JIT)
minority subcontracting
modified rebuy
multi-attribute model
new buy
nondisclosure
  agreements

outsourcing
out-supplier
partnership purchasing
preferred supplier
  systems
single sourcing
straight rebuy
total cost of ownership
trade shows
value analysis

Discussion Questions

1. When does gift giving become unethical? Are there any times when a salesperson accepting a gift from a purchasing agent could be construed as unethical?

2. Assume that graduation is here and you've been offered a job with the choice of two cities. Create a multi-attribute matrix listing all of the factors that would influence your decision and the appropriate weights for those factors. Please don't read ahead on this question; it is important that you create the chart before you find out what cities you are to rate. The rest of the question is at the end of this series of questions.

3. Assume you are the purchasing agent for Florida Furniture Industries. The company is anticipating the purchase of a new computer system that will integrate purchasing, production, and accounting activities. Your job is to create the specifications for the new system using a multi-attribute matrix. How would you go about it?

4. In this chapter, we discussed a number of trends and how they affect purchasing. Which trend do you think is most important? Why? Which is least important and why? What trends do you think we've overlooked?

5. Go back to the list of product types in Chapter 1. Which ones do you think are most likely to be purchased as straight rebuys and which are likely to be modified rebuys? Why?

6. Assume that you are the outsupplier for MRO items. How would you get that purchase changed from a straight rebuy to a modified rebuy? Would it make a difference to your ability to create a partnership if the purchase was made by the purchasing department or the maintenance department? Justify your answer.

7. What do you think are the challenges to getting a customer to accept your company's EDI system? What would the benefits be and how would you present them? How would it affect your presentation if the customer had not used EDI or JIT before? How would type of product influence their decision?

8. Discuss how buying in the U.S. government is different from buying in for-profit organizations. If you are a citizen of a country other than the United States, discuss how buying by your government is different from for-profit organizations' buying.

9. Discuss why three specific companies not mentioned in the chapter should be aggressively pursuing foreign government business. Based on what you know about these companies, which one do you think is doing best in selling to foreign governments? Why?

10. Assume you are negotiating with the Air Force about developing a new weapon system. Do you want a fixed-price or cost-plus agreement? Why? Now assume you are negotiating for the annual toilet paper contract with the Air Force. Which type of agreement do you want and why?

2 (Continued): Rate Atlanta and St. Louis and calculate the scores for each city. Is the final decision what you thought it would be? Did you feel like you fudged any numbers (ratings or weights) so that the model's outcome would match your original feeling about each city?

Internet Exercise

INTERNET

Hit the ISO home page (**www.iso.ch**), then select *Introduction to ISO*. Answer the following questions:

1. What is the ISO? Why was it created and how does it work?

2. Go back to the ISO home page and then select *ISO 9000 News*. What are ISO 9000 and 14000?

Cases

Case 3.1 Human Performance Systems

Joyce Davis leaned back in her chair and reflected on the sales call she made that morning. Her company, Human Performance Systems (HPS), provides safety training in order to bring manufacturers into compliance with OSHA regulations. She also had the data to prove that the training saved companies money by reducing the number of manufacturing accidents. What Joyce couldn't understand was why Bob Jackson, owner of Jackson Molding, was so adamant that he couldn't afford the training.

"Bob, you can't afford not to do this," she told him. "You have had three accidents this month, losing 23 workdays." (Three employees missed five days each, while another missed eight, for a total of 23.)

"I don't pay them for lost workdays. That makes them more careful." He stared at her defiantly. "Therefore, I don't need training."

1. What benefits could Human Performance Systems' training provide Jackson Molding? Think through the various ways HPS could save Jackson money, among other benefits.

2. What is important to Bob? Why?

3. How could Joyce use the multi-attribute matrix to change Bob's mind?

Case 3.2   Conroe Tire & Retread

Conroe Tire & Retread sells tires for heavy equipment, such as off-road mining and forestry vehicles and construction equipment. The company also retreads the tires and provides services in the field. Because customers' equipment is considered production equipment, a flat tire means a loss of production. Quality service is an important element in Conroe's business.

Art Kendall is the manager of Conroe's service business. His responsibilities include managing a fleet of 12 heavy-duty pickup trucks that are used to reach customers' equipment in the field for service. Art buys three trucks each January, retiring each truck after four years of service. For the previous two years, he purchased Dodge trucks from the Conroe Dodge dealer, dealing directly with owner Bill Bowfield.

Today, December 20, Bill stopped by Art's office. After saying hello and asking after the family, Bill said, "Come on, Art, I want to show you something I have outside in the truck." As they walked outside, Bill continued, "I know you like to hunt and I thought you might appreciate this little Christmas present. You've been a good customer the previous two years, and I'd like to say thank you with this." From the inside of his truck, Bill pulled out a new Browning Citori shotgun.

Art eyed the new gun with appreciation, knowing that it retailed for at least $1,200. The custom carving on the stock, with Art's initials, probably added another $500 to the cost of the gun. He held it, admiring the balance, and then sighted the gun as if about to shoot. He thought about how nice it would be to use this at the annual dove hunt that Conroe sponsored for its customers.

1. Is there any ethical problem with Art accepting the gift? Why or why not?

2. What factors could affect your decision?

Additional Readings

"Adopting Suppliers," *Purchasing Executive Bulletin* (May 25, 1994), pp. 1–3.

Drumwright, Minette E., "Socially Responsible Organizational Buying: Environmental Concern as a Noneconomic Buying Criterion," *Journal of Marketing* 58 (July 1994), pp. 1–18.

Freeman, Virginia T., and Joseph L. Cavinato, "Positioning Purchasing," *Marketplace: The ISBM Review* (Fall 1989).

Chapter 4

Organizational Buyer Behavior

CABLE & WIRELESS

Long-distance services vary little from one supplier to the next. Either the call gets through or it doesn't. So how does one supplier separate from the others? ●

For Cable & Wireless, a British company offering long-distance services in the United States, the answer is through personal sales support. Cable & Wireless does very little advertising, relying on sales representatives to get in the door by showing comparative pricing and then offering additional services such as customized billing in order to add value and win the account. With larger companies, the salesperson focuses on the telecommunications manager. But for smaller companies, the rep will call on the CEO first. ●

AT&T, on the other hand, aggressively advertises in a variety of media. An ad in *Sales & Marketing Management* might portray a hotel chain's reservations manager trying to figure out how reservations will be taken because the 800 reservation line is down. Another ad might illustrate what happens to a plant manager when the data line between the plant and a supplier isn't working and a crucial shipment isn't made. These fear appeals are designed to get others outside the telecommunications department involved in the purchase process. AT&T combines this advertising effort with telemarketing for smaller businesses and personal account service for larger companies. ●

Sprint has a sophisticated program aimed at large companies that audits telecommunication needs of every department of the organization. Similar programs are available, on a lesser scale, for smaller accounts. Price is important, but not the main element of their strategy. Sprint emphasizes its technology and reliability as well as price.●

Each of these companies has selected a different marketing strategy not just to be different. These long-distance suppliers believe their strategy will work because each strategy offers what they believe buyers need in order to make a decision. And each of these suppliers also believes that its strategy is the best one for the way its buyers make decisions. Which one is right? Only time, market share, and profitability will tell.●

Visit the web sites of ATT, Cable & Wireless, and Sprint: **www.att.com, www.cwi.net., www.sprint.com**●

www.att.com
www.cwi.net.
www.sprint.com

Learning Objectives

In order to develop profitable relationships with buyers, it helps to understand how they make decisions. This chapter describes the theories of how buyers in organizations buy products and services.

After reading this chapter, you will be able to

● Explain, using the most prominent theories of organizational buyer behavior, how individual needs may override or influence the rational decision-making process.
● Predict marketing action based on the choice of a particular buying theory.
● Describe the influence of risk on buyer behavior.
● Illustrate how these theories work in concert with partnering.

In the previous chapter, you learned about the influence of the purchasing department and the rational methods of making purchase decisions. You also learned about the importance to the buying organization of making sound economic decisions. In all organizations, however, it is people who make the final decisions—and they have their own agendas, quirks, likes, and dislikes. In this chapter, we explore the individual. You will find the theories presented here useful when making decisions about what products to market, how to set prices, what communication vehicles and sales approaches to employ, and other marketing decisions.

Theories in Use

Everybody has theories. We may not always express them, but we have our own explanations for why things work the way they do, why someone did something, or how to make something happen. Even when we don't consciously think about or express our theories, we hold beliefs such as if X happens, then Y will happen. Theories are our rules (like "don't bathe near a window during a thunderstorm or you might get struck by lightning"); they guide our behavior. Our theories may not always be correct, but they are what we use to understand our world and to make sure that we operate safely and profitably.

Decision makers in business have theories too. They decide to take action—to lower a price, for example—because they believe that X (a lower price) will lead to Y (greater sales). In this chapter, we will examine several theories about how buying works in organizations. It is important to understand the various buyer theories so you can make an informed model of your own that you can then use to guide your marketing decisions.

Understanding how things work, such as how people make buying decisions as part of their job, can help managers figure out what to do when situations change. For example, there were a number of real estate developers, such as Craig Hall and Trammell Crow in Dallas, who were very successful when inflation was 16 percent and interest rates were high. Their theory was that the price of real estate was increasing faster than interest rates. When inflation went under 10 percent, these developers went broke or suffered serious losses and setbacks because their loans were at interest rates well over 10 percent. One reason was that they understood how to make money under one set of conditions (high inflation and interest rates). When conditions changed (rates went down), their methods were no longer viable. Developers who succeeded (or simply survived) did so because they had a better understanding, or theory, of how the economy worked and were able to adapt their methods to the changing situation. Such adaptation can be a function of good theory.

You have already been exposed to one (set of) theory: the theory of relationships marketing. In this chapter, we will explore several individual buying theories—that is, a group of theories designed to explain individual buyer actions rather than organizational relationships. These theories are the buyer behavior choice theory, the buy-grid model, the reward-measurement theory, role theory, and the buying determinants theory.

People Make the Decisions

You may have gotten the feeling in Chapter 3 that, without bribery, the best solution for the organization is always purchased. Organizational buyers, however, do not always seek to maximize the benefits for the organization; sometimes they seek to maximize benefits for themselves, as you see in From the Field 4–1. In addition, relationships are between people, and buyers consider personal relationships skills as one important aspect of purchases.[1] After all, purchase decisions are not made by heartless, hyperrational machines. Purchase decisions are made by people. These buyers go home and become consumers, so as individuals operating in an organization they sometimes exhibit behavior that looks just like shoppers at a Wal-Mart.

For example, one buyer for BellSouth was also a veteran of the Pacific theater of World War II. As a result of his war experiences, this particular buyer would purchase nothing that was Japanese-made when alternatives, especially American-made alternatives, were available. When Bridgestone (a Japanese company) purchased Firestone, he slowly but surely replaced all of the Firestone tires on BellSouth vehicles with Cooper

---

4–1

FROM THE FIELD

Buy Me One, Too!

As a sales rep for Minolta Business Systems selling copiers in Fort Worth, Texas, Dan Gary has had his share of tough sales situations. "We have a great line of copiers, but not everyone's needs can be met by our products," notes Gary. "Still, I try to work with the buyer in determining what is needed so we have a stronger chance of winning the business."

Gary developed a strong relationship with the buyer at one account. "I always try to do a great job, and this was one of those times where everything went like it was supposed to." The buyer appreciated Gary's effort. The only problem with buying his product was that a certain type of original had to be copied daily, and Gary's had difficulty picking it up.

"The buyer, though, had two hot buttons," notes Gary. "He couldn't turn his back on those production needs with that original, so he bought a copier from someone else to handle that. But he also liked the personal attention and quality of service that we had given him and that he knew he could count on in the future," so the buyer also bought a system from Gary.

Gary believes that most buyers have two sets of needs, and that he wins most of his business by taking care of the personal needs of the buyer. "Almost all vendors can take care of the buyer's company's requirements, but few really take care of the buyer." Still, he usually doesn't see them buy a separate copier for each set of needs!

---

tires, Cooper being a U.S. company. The buyer's motivation in choosing a vendor may or may not have had an obvious impact on his company in terms of cost or product performance, but as long as the product would perform at a reasonably competitive price, his motive to do business with a U.S. company dominated the decision.

Reward–Measurement Theory

Reward–measurement (RM) theory represented a major advance in the way theorists thought about buying behavior because the theory recognized that there are benefits to be gained in addition to those delivered by the product. For example, a buyer may choose a product in order to win accolades from the boss. The essentials of this model are also the name of the model: If you can understand how performance is measured and rewarded, then you will understand how and why the buyer will make a purchase.

Reward–measurement theory is an expectancy theory of organizational buyer motivation, similar to expectancy theories you may have been introduced to in management. RM theory points out that buyers are motivated by both **intrinsic rewards**, or those rewards they give themselves (feelings of satisfaction, for example), and **extrinsic rewards**, or rewards given by the organization (e.g. salary, promotion). All rewards are not equal, however. **Valence**, or the degree of importance or value attached to a reward, varies from person to person in a fashion similar to the multi-attribute model discussed in the previous chapter.[2] For example, in Exhibit 4–1 the important reward is a raise, which is an extrinsic reward.

Valence alone does not tell us what the buyer will do. Another important element is **perceived probability** (usually just called probability), or the perception that effort on a particular set of tasks will lead to accomplishment of performance outcomes that will, in

Exhibit 4–1

Reward–
Measurement
Theory

Motivation	=	Valence	×	Probability
Office manager wants to buy the lowest-priced fax possible and is willing to shop around (spend a lot of effort)		because she can get an important raise		if she can negotiate a discount, which she estimates is likely.

turn, lead to the desired rewards. In other words, the buyer says, "If I do this, then I will get a reward." In our example, the buyer has estimated the probability of negotiating a discount. The RM model says that probability times valence determines the individual's level of **motivation**, or the amount of effort that the buyer is willing to expend to engage in that set of tasks, as you can see in Exhibit 4–1.

Perceptions of probability are dependent on the organization's measurement system, which is how the buyer's performance is graded, and the person's ability to successfully carry out the tasks, particularly for extrinsic rewards. If the measurement system can tell the difference between good and bad decisions, then perceptions concerning probability should be greater because good performance will be identified. If the measurement system doesn't tell the difference, then how well the buyer performs may not matter, at least in terms of receiving rewards from the organization. The organization will not be able to determine if the buyer did well.

For example, suppose an office manager needed to buy a new fax machine. Chances are that the manager's performance evaluation will not discuss how well she made that purchase; there is no system of formal purchasing measurement for that person. Or there may be a system of evaluating her cost control relative to her budget, but that is all. That system would not be able to tell if the fax was the best one suited for the needs of the office, if it arrived on time and worked well, or any other factors relating to the purchase. On the other hand, purchasing agents are evaluated on the basis of product performance, on-time delivery, and total cost, which should influence their probability perceptions.[3]

Each person also considers his or her own ability to carry out the tasks, a perception called **self-efficacy**.[4] For example, people who have never participated in the purchase of a telephone switching system may be concerned about their ability to tell the difference between good and bad products. They have low self-efficacy perceptions. Someone who says, "I can't do that," is not likely to volunteer to participate in a purchase; someone with high self-efficacy may be more motivated.[5]

Marketing and Reward–Measurement Theory

Xerox faces a problem when selling copiers, for example, because many buyers of copiers are not evaluated on their buying abilities. Buying a copier is something they do outside their normal job functions, unless they are purchasing agents or senior administrators who purchase office equipment regularly. In situations where measurement systems aren't designed to evaluate an employee's copier purchase performance, performance may become an either/or decision: Either the copier works or it doesn't, therefore, either the person made a good or a bad decision. In this type of all-or-nothing situation, it is important for vendors such as Xerox to provide high-quality service and products because they may not get a second chance if there are any problems.

Marketers can increase perceptions of self-efficacy by increasing the buyer's experience or knowledge. Demonstrations and free trials are ways that marketers increase self-efficacy. Also, advertising and other marketing communications that increase knowledge about products can increase a buyer's perception of self-efficacy.

Buyers choose to do certain tasks (such as see demonstrations) based on the probability associated with those tasks. How much and how well they do the tasks is a function of their motivation, which takes into account the valence for rewards associated with the purchase.

As marketers, if we understand the valence attached to the various rewards and how performance is measured, then we should be able to predict the amount of effort expended by the buyer on tasks involving information search, number of bids requested, and other purchase activities. We can also begin to understand what products might be purchased in which situations.

For example, in the long-distance industry, AT&T has been the dominant player in the United States for decades. Buying AT&T is a safe decision; with AT&T's track record of service, market share, and product quality, anyone who recommends AT&T is not going out on a limb. If the buyers in a particular market have a high valence for security, AT&T might be selected. For example, many L.L. Bean customers order over the phone. L.L. Bean management, who evaluate the performance of the telecommunications manager who buys long-distance services, probably place a high value on reliable service. But if buyers in a market are rewarded for cutting costs, Sprint, Cable & Wireless, and other vendors may have a better chance. Similarly, Cable & Wireless is viewed as a safe decision in Great Britain, while AT&T is perceived as more risky. You can see that this application is very similar to the multi-attribute model in that valences and attribute ratings can be viewed in a similar fashion.

Comparing Reward–Measurement and Multi-Attribute

How does the multi-attribute model (from Chapter 3) compare with reward–measurement theory? First, RM theory (1) recognizes intrinsic rewards such as feeling good about making the right decision or having pride in making a contribution to the success of the organization and (2) acknowledges that sometimes buyers operate to attain intrinsic rewards exclusively. For example, a telecommunications buyer who likes to get good deals would be more likely to do business with Cable & Wireless.

Second, RM theory recognizes that extrinsic rewards are a function of the reward–measurement systems of the organization, and not a function of the product. In organizational buying situations, few buyers actually benefit directly from a purchase. At L.L. Bean, for example, the telecommunications manager does use long-distance services. At Florida Furniture Industries, however, the buyer doesn't personally do anything with the poplar that she buys. Her rewards are based on the evaluation of her performance as a buyer, not as a user of wood.

Recognize, too, that buyers may still use a multi-attribute model when making a decision, even though they may be concerned with intrinsic rewards and the reward–measurement system of the organization. Intrinsic rewards may be influenced by attributes of the vendor's offering; for example, that telecommunications buyer who likes to get a good deal will weigh price more heavily than other buyers. Reward–measurement theory means that the buy-grid (new buy, modified rebuy, or straight rebuy) may not be as important as the reward structure, because effort is a function of probability and valence, not experience with the product.

Exhibit 4–2
Behavior Choice
Model

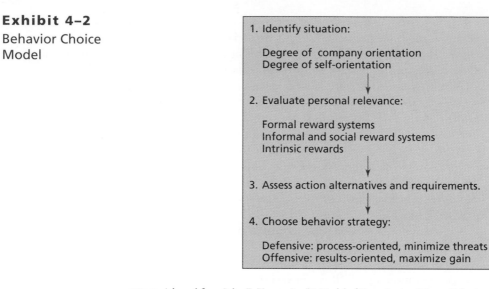

1. Identify situation:

    Degree of company orientation
    Degree of self-orientation

2. Evaluate personal relevance:

    Formal reward systems
    Informal and social reward systems
    Intrinsic rewards

3. Assess action alternatives and requirements.

4. Choose behavior strategy:

    Defensive: process-oriented, minimize threats
    Offensive: results-oriented, maximize gain

SOURCE: Adapted from John F. Tanner Jr., "A Model of Organizational Buyer Behavior Choice," *Proceedings,* Southern Marketing Association, 1987, pp. 355–58.

Behavior Choice Theory

What happens when reward systems for effective buying are nonexistent for many purchasing participants?[6] Behavior choice theory was developed in order to understand buying behavior when multiple and perhaps competing reward systems are present, or when no reward system is obvious to the buyer.

Behavior choice theory states that buyers go through a choice process to arrive at decisions of *how* they will buy, as opposed to the choice process of *what* will be bought modeled as part of the buy-grid.[7] Behavior choice theory is illustrated in Exhibit 4–2. The first decision is to decide what type of situation they are in. For example, a buyer may believe that the purchase is an opportunity to show decision making skills; as a management development opportunity, the purchase is more important than as an opportunity to obtain a particular product. The management development opportunity benefits the individual participating in the decision, whereas the product may benefit the company. This decision of the relative value of benefits and the type of situation leads to an orientation that influences the buyer's behavior throughout the rest of the purchase process.

The degree to which the individual works to achieve personal benefit is called **self-orientation**, while the degree to which the individual works to achieve benefit for the company is **company orientation**. Self-orientation and company orientation operate independently so one purchase situation could result in both high self-orientation and high company orientation. For example, a buyer may work hard to review several vendors because the purchase decision is an opportunity to exhibit promotable managerial skills, and the buyer's self-orientation would be classified as high. At the same time, the service being purchased may be crucial to the company's performance, which may also motivate the buyer to review several alternatives. This latter motivation is an example of a high company orientation. In this example, the buyer is both highly self- and company-oriented.

The second stage of the choice process is to evaluate personal relevance. In this stage, the buyer examines the reward structures, both formal and informal, associated with the situation as defined in stage one. Thus, a buyer who defines the situation as an opportunity to purchase a product is going to engage reward structures associated with the product, such as satisfaction with the product. A buyer who sees the situation as an opportunity to show off decision-making skills, however, will engage reward structures that might include promotions, management recognition, and the like.

In the third stage, the buyer assesses action alternatives and requirements. In this stage, the buyer looks at the amount of control over the task; does he have any choices in what he can and can't do. Company policies and procedures may limit the choice of buying activities; for example, company policy may require that he solicit at least three bids.

The final stage of the model is the selection of a strategy. There are two types of strategies: **offensive strategies** (strategies designed to maximize gain) and **defensive strategies** (strategies designed to minimize loss). (We'll talk more about reducing risk later in this chapter.) Using our telecommunications example, AT&T would be a defensive choice because it is safe—no one was ever fired for buying AT&T. Other defensive strategies would include asking the boss to make the decision, getting as many people involved as possible in order to share the blame if things go wrong, and paying attention to the process rather than to the outcome. The latter strategy is useful because if the product doesn't work out, the buyer can say, "Well, it is the vendor's fault. We did everything right in our selection process. We viewed 55 different models, evaluated 40 bids, and so forth."

Choosing an off-brand for service would be an offensive strategy, designed to maximize gain through saving the company the most money or making a name for oneself as an innovator. The selection of a strategy, either offensive or defensive, can relate to a single orientation. For example, a buyer may want to get the company the best deal possible (high company orientation, offensive strategy) but at the same time minimize personal risk (high self-orientation, defensive strategy).

The process of purchasing, then, can be decided by the strategy of the buyer, not experience with the product, as suggested by the buy-grid. Experience with the product should influence the choice of a strategy; for example, an inexperienced buyer may be more likely to select a defensive strategy. Other factors, such as reward–measurement systems, risk associated with the purchase, visibility of purchase participation, and management level of the individual, will also influence the selection of strategy.

Based on the strategy and action alternatives, the buyer selects a series of tasks. For example, when we mentioned viewing 55 models and evaluating 40 bids, we were discussing examples of tasks that may be selected to fit a defensive strategy. The actual purchase depends on the outcomes of those tasks.

Marketing and Buyer Behavior Choice

An example of this theory in use is Intel's "It Takes You There" campaign for the Pentium processor. Intel recognized that purchasers of computers in many situations have a high degree of self-orientation. PC purchases in organizations are initiated by individuals who believe that their old PC inhibits their productivity. Yes, the company gains when those individuals are more productive, but it is what the PC does for them individually that makes them initiate a purchase of a new unit. Intel played on the theme of personal advancement with the corporate version of "It Takes You There," getting 25,000 corporate buyers to visit its booth at the Comdex trade show, a show where Intel would normally expect only 8,000 visitors in its booth.[8] Intel took advantage of the high self-orientation of buyers and encouraged an offensive behavior strategy in order to get buyers to ask for new computers.

The buying center for an MRI scanner in a hospital may include the three types of people shown below: the technician operating the equipment (end user), radiologists (gatekeepers), and the hospital administrator (decision maker).

Pete Saloutps/The Stock Market; Mug Shots/The Stock Market; Jose L. Pelaez/The Stock Market.

Going back to our telecommunications example, think about why AT&T would advertise its long-distance services to marketing managers using fear appeals. By creating a fear of what will happen to those individuals if their long-distance service goes down and customers can't call in their orders or service requests, AT&T was attempting to promote a defensive strategy. Its hope was that the defensive strategy of choice would be to select the vendor with the reputation for service, AT&T.

So far, though, we've really only looked at the behaviors of individuals within organizations. What happens when several people are part of the decision process? Role theory is useful in understanding those situations, especially when used in concert with the theories we've already discussed.

Role Theory

Role theory has been applied to a number of social situations, such as families, friendships, and organizational buying. In general, **role theory** suggests that people behave within a set of norms or expectations of others due to the role in which they have been placed. For example, your instructor would act one way toward you because of the instructor role (and you would act in the student role). But if you also served on the city council with that instructor, your actions toward each other would be governed by another set of norms and expectations in your roles as council members.

When a person makes a purchase decision alone for an organization, the decision is said to be **autonomous**. When more than one person is involved, the group of participants in the company are called the **buying center** or **decision-making unit (DMU)**. Role theory helps us to understand how those participants interact because it defines the roles people take when involved in purchases.

Roles in the Buying Center

In organizational buying, several roles have been identified. The **initiator** starts the purchase process by recognizing the need, while at the other end of the process is the **decision maker**, the person who makes the final decision.[9] (There could be several decision makers who may vote on the final decision; this is covered in greater detail later in this chapter.) The **controller** controls or sets the budget for the purchase.

Exhibit 4–3

Who Participates in the Buying of CPA Services?

Buying Center Members	1	2	3	4	5	6
Chairman of the board		X				X
Audit committee				X		X
Chief executive officer	X	X	X	X	X	X
Chief financial officer	X	X	X	X	X	
Treasurer		X				
Internal auditor						
Controller	} All three participate in fewer than 10 percent of surveyed firms.					
Others						

1 = Initiate process (initiator role)
2 = Recommend alternative CPA firms (influencer role)
3 = Provide information on CPA firms (gatekeeper role)
4 = Evaluate firms (influencer role)
5 = Recommend firms (influencer role)
6 = Make final decision (decision maker role)
Audit Committee and other executives are also users.

SOURCE: Adapted from 12. Lynn, Susan A. (1987), "Identifying Buying Influences for a Professional Service: Implications for Marketing Efforts." *Industrial Marketing Management* 16, 119–130.

The **purchasing agent** is the person who actually makes the purchase. If the decision maker tells a subordinate to order another box of copier paper, then the subordinate is the purchasing agent for that purchase. Often the person with the official purchasing agent title does much more than just order the product, but many students confuse the role with the title. The purchasing agent role can be filled by anyone in the organization, while the person filling the purchasing agent job may play several roles in a purchase.

Influencers are those individuals who seek to affect the decision maker's final decision through recommendations of which vendors to include or which products are best suited to solve the organization's needs. Influencers can also affect the evaluation of the organization's needs.[10] Sometimes **users** are part of the buying center and try to influence the decision; sometimes, other influencers will represent the users' perspective. Even when users don't participate, they influence the decision when decision makers consider the users' needs or ability to implement the decision.

Gatekeepers control information into and out of the buying group or between members of the group. Sometimes gatekeepers can actively influence a decision by determining what information is made available to the decision maker. For example, in one study, an engineer was the primary contact with the vendors. The engineer controlled all of the information, deciding what to pass along to others in the decision. The result was that the engineer was able to slant perceptions of the vendors by choosing which information was passed along, and the final decision reflected his own personal preferences.[11] Secretaries can also be gatekeepers, as when they screen telephone calls for their boss.

For example, the CEO of an organization is likely to begin the search for a CPA firm to audit the company's books. The chief financial officer (CFO) is likely to serve as a gatekeeper by providing information about candidate CPA firms to other members of the buying center. The final decision, however, is most likely to be made by an audit committee and the CEO. As illustrated in Exhibit 4–3, other participants include the treasurer, the controller, and the internal auditor, all of whom are users of the financial information collected and examined by the CPA firm. The CEO, CFO, and controller are also most likely to set the budget to be spent on an audit by a CPA firm.[12]

Exhibit 4–4

An Example of Time Fragmentation in Buying Centers

Stage 1: *need recognition*
Bill and Dawanda recognize a need for a new lathe.

Stage 2: *definition of product type needed*
Joe, their supervisor, tells Purchasing to get a new metal lathe with a 5,000-RPM motor and computerized input.

Stage 3: *development of detailed specifications*
Joe, Bill, and Dawanda meet with Jackie in Purchasing to develop detailed specifications.

Stage 4: *search for suppliers*
Jackie and Frank in Finance visit a trade show and identify four potential suppliers.

Stage 5: *acquisition and analysis of proposals*
Frank receives all proposals and evaluates financial aspects. He sends a copy to Joe for technical evaluation.

Stage 6: *evaluation and selection of supplier*
Joe and Frank meet to select the supplier.

Stage 7: *selection of an order procedure*
Joe sends a purchase order to Jackie. Jackie issues the PO to the vendor.

Stage 8: *implementation and evaluation of performance*
Dawanda and Bill install the new lathe and try it out; they report to Joe that it works well.

Dimensions of Buying Centers

One misconception that students sometimes have is that a buying center means that a committee is formed, with individuals designated as a gatekeeper, influencer, or some other role. Cross-functional sourcing teams, discussed in Chapter 3, are formal examples of buying centers and are growing in use, but more often, the buying center is a changing, complex, and informal group.[13] Initiators, for example, may not be involved again once they've set the purchase in motion. Or initiators may also act as influencers and as gatekeepers. Influencers may seek to influence only which needs will be considered, only which vendors are considered, or only which product is selected, or all three elements of the decision.

Time Dimensions
One characteristic of buying centers, then, is that members come and go. This characteristic is called **time fragmentation**. The more people are involved for only short periods of time in the process, the more fragmented the buying center is over time. If the same people are involved through the entire process, the buying center is not fragmented. Exhibit 4–4 illustrates how the decision to select a metal lathe might be time-fragmented. As you can see, Bill and Dawanda only participated in three steps, Joe in five, Jackie in three, and Frank in three. Nobody participated in every step in this highly time-fragmented purchase.

Note, though, time fragmentation is not the same as the length of time for the decision to be made. The metal lathe purchase may have been accomplished in just a few days. Some decisions can take a long time without involving a high degree of time fragmentation if the same people stay involved.

Exhibit 4–5

Vertical and
Horizontal
Dimensions of a
Buying Center

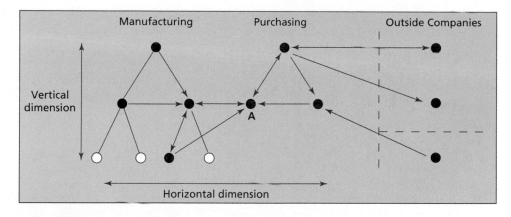

SOURCE: John F. Tanner Jr., "Buying Center Formation Process," unpublished dissertation, University of Georgia (1988).

Time fragmentation is important to understand for marketers. If a decision involves a number of people who move in and out over time, their influence is limited to only a few stages. The marketer must balance that influence with the cost of reaching those people. For example, if the marketing manager is involved only in determining what is needed, is it worth it to AT&T to spend the money advertising in marketing magazines? Perhaps, particularly if AT&T advertises why that marketing manager should request certain features.

Length of time is also an important consideration for the marketer. Shortening the decision cycle is always a goal for salespeople because a shorter decision cycle means that salespeople can move on to other prospects and increase their overall sales performance. Length of time to make a decision can seriously impact marketing efforts.

Decision making time is lengthened when buying centers are large and/or composed of many personnel who are inexperienced in making purchase decisions. Outsuppliers, those who are not established with the buyers, can actually benefit when decisions take longer and more information sources are utilized because they have the opportunity to plead their case. Shorter decision cycles tend to favor in suppliers.[14]

Vertical and Horizontal Dimensions

Two other dimensions of buying centers are **vertical dimensions**, or how many layers of management are involved, and **horizontal dimensions**, or how many departments are involved. Both of these dimensions relate to the number of people involved.[15] Decisions concerning component parts, for example, tend to be wide, involving members of the purchasing department, design engineers, manufacturing personnel, and upper management, as illustrated in Exhibit 4–5. Along the vertical dimension, that same decision may be considered tall if the vice president, many middle managers, and workers from the manufacturing line participate. A long-distance services decision, however, may be narrow, made entirely within the telecommunications department, and relatively short, involving only a director of telecommunications and a telecom manager.

Wide buying centers present difficult challenges for marketers. Many different people must be reached in order to accomplish a sale. Advertising has to be placed in a wider variety of trade publications than when buying centers are narrow. For example, if all long-distance buying centers for large buyers included marketing managers, manufacturing personnel, customer service and sales managers, and upper management, then Sprint

BUSINESS 2 BUSINESS
When Buyers Are Sellers

Office furniture is an interesting market that demands careful application of buyer behavior theory. Steelcase and Herman Miller are leading manufacturers, but rely on dealers–distributors to serve regional markets. These resellers serve organizational customers that may wish to (1) furnish a new office building, (2) equip an expanded training area, (3) appoint a refurbished storage room turned into a lobby, or (4) tastefully decorate the new VP's work space. Meanwhile, most markets are served by a few dealers in used office furniture. What organizational buying model seems most apt in two of these four situations?

would want to advertise in sales magazines, marketing magazines, manufacturing magazines, and financial magazines. Cable & Wireless, though, seeks smaller companies. If the purchase is autonomous (the most narrow buying center possible) and made by the CEO, then Cable & Wireless might advertise in *Nation's Business,* a magazine aimed at CEOs of small companies.

The vertical dimension alone is not as challenging. If all buying center participants are within the same department or functional area of the buying firm, they are likely to participate in the same media. These buyers would go to the same trade shows, read the same magazines, and so forth. The real challenge would be for the salesperson to uncover the true decision makers, for organizational position may not reflect who really will make this particular decision. For example, the salesperson would need to discover if the telecom manager makes the decision or simply rubber stamps the recommendation of a subordinate who investigated the various vendors' offerings.

Marketing to Buying Centers

Traditionally, it was thought that the best marketing strategy would be to determine who typically participated in the decision and then work to satisfy the needs of the participants.[16] In the purchase of component parts, for example, research has found that engineering, purchasing, and upper management each play roles. Engineers are concerned about products meeting performance specifications, while upper management worries about costs. A vendor would create marketing communication campaigns aimed at the engineers separate from those campaigns aimed at upper management. Features might be designed to the engineers' specifications but within the budget set by upper management.

Recently, however, marketers have begun to recognize that it is important to influence who might participate in the buying center and to what extent.[17] For example, Sprint may have a product that greatly outperforms the AT&T set of services. If users don't participate in the decision process, other members in the buying center may not be capable of judging just how much Sprint outperforms AT&T. Sprint should work to make **champions**, or **advocates**, of the users; that is, it should attempt to get users to influence the decision in their favor.[18] (Note that AT&T has attempted to preempt that strategy by advertising directly to marketing managers.)

When Buying Centers Occur

In some organizations, buying centers occur because of organizational policy. For example, in government agencies, purchases over a set dollar amount are often reviewed by a committee. In city governments, this committee may be the city council or a finance committee, depending on the size of the purchase. Hospitals and other institutions also have committees that review purchases of certain types.

In situations not governed by policy, buying centers are more likely to occur when risk associated with the decision is great. **Risk** is usually thought of in terms of the probability of an outcome and the importance or cost associated with the outcome. For example, the risk of lung cancer for a nonsmoker is low, not because a nonsmoker with lung cancer is any less likely to die than a smoker with lung cancer but because the probability of getting lung cancer is less for the nonsmoker. A low-risk decision, therefore, is either one with a high probability of a positive outcome or one where the outcome itself is relatively unimportant.

Sources of Perceived Risk

Risk can come from any number of sources. There is **financial risk**, also called economic risk, associated with the cost of the new product and with the potential for lost revenue if the product breaks down or doesn't perform as advertised. **Performance risk** is the risk that the product will not perform as intended. Performance risk and financial risk can occur at the same time if the performance of the product is crucial to the financial performance of the firm. For example, if a piece of manufacturing equipment breaks down and the production line must stop, then sales may be lost. Both financial and performance risk would be realized in that situation. If a piece of equipment breaks down while under warranty and the breakdown doesn't slow down production, only performance risk would be realized, because there would be no financial loss. Performance and financial risks are highly correlated, for it is rare that a loss of performance would not have some financial impact.

Another form of risk is **social risk**, also called ego risk, or risk that the purchase will not meet the approval of an important reference group.[19] The important reference group could be co-workers or it could be the buyer's immediate supervisor. As we discussed in terms of the buyer behavior choice model, purchase situations can be seen as opportunities to please others, such as one's boss, as well to purchase a product for what the product itself does.

Organizational buyers reduce their perceptions of risk in three ways.[20] To reduce risk, buyers gather more information, remain loyal to present suppliers, and/or spread the risk, either to other members of the firm or among suppliers.

Using Information to Reduce Risk

When collecting information, buyers seek help from a number of sources illustrated in Exhibit 4–6. Commercial sources are those sources controlled by the marketer, and include advertisements, brochures and other sales literature, personal selling efforts both at the customer's location and at trade shows, and product manuals. Noncommercial sources are sources outside the control of the marketer, and include word-of-mouth from colleagues within the organization, professional associates, and consultants as well as articles in trade publications.

The exhibit illustrates the overall relative usefulness of each source, as rated by buyers in a study conducted by the Simmons Research Bureau. Other research indicates that impersonal sources are more widely used early in the process, with personal

Exhibit 4–6
Sources of
Information

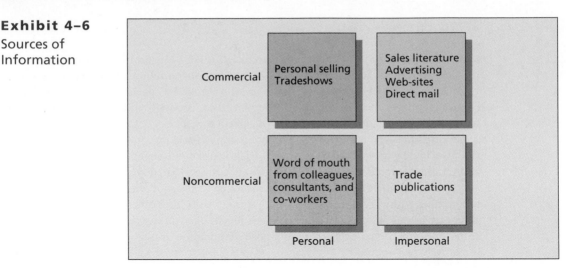

SOURCE: Barton A. Weitz, Stephen B. Castleberry, and John F. Tanner, Jr. *Selling: Building Partnerships.* Second edition. Burr Ridge, IL: Irwin/McGraw-Hill, 1995.

sources growing in importance over the course of the decision. That research also indicates that noncommercial sources are relied on more heavily than are commercial sources.[21]

Research indicates that salespeople can reduce risk through such efforts as demonstrations, samples, or free trials, and salespeople are often the most important source of information for buyers.[22] These efforts increase buyers' experience with the product, giving them the ability to more accurately evaluate product performance, which reduces their perceptions of risk. Demonstrations, samples, and trials are particularly useful when the issue is performance threshold because these marketing efforts prove performance.

Companies may also use advertising to educate buyers, providing information through details in advertising copy in order to reduce perceptions of risk. As you can see in the accompanying photo, AT&T presented detailed advertising to help buyers make decisions concerning the use of an on-line business service. Case studies can also be used to prove performance and provide buyers with important information concerning product or service performance that can enhance their ability to make the decision.

Guarantees, such as AT&T's long-distance services guarantee to pay for any lost business should the lines go down, are ways that marketers can reduce risk. Guarantees, though, are only as good as the reputation of the company that offers them. An unknown's guarantee may not mean much to a business buyer.

Using Loyalty to Reduce Risk

Risk can both help and hinder the development of relationships. One purchasing strategy to reduce risk is to remain loyal to a known supplier—for example, to always buy from AT&T. In essence, this strategy results in converting the decision into a straight rebuy, because other vendors are not considered. By converting decisions into straight rebuys, a poor decision is unlikely as long as the vendor continues to satisfy. With many firms downsizing, purchasing agents and other managers do not have the time they once had to evaluate all purchase decisions carefully. Therefore, they will only evaluate those decisions where the close examination of alternatives will result in benefits that outweigh the costs of looking. When a company routinizes a decision (makes it a straight rebuy), the opportunity is there for a vendor to build a relationship. Recognize, however, that

This AT&T ad has a lot of copy in order to educate readers. This information should help buyers make more informed decisions, thereby reducing their risk.

Courtesy AT&T; agency: McCann–Erickson, Inc.

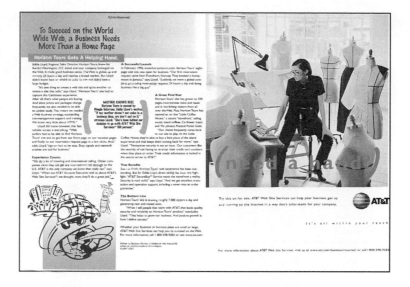

the decision was made routine because the product being purchased is relatively unimportant, a factor not likely to contribute positively to the development of a partnership. Habit or lazy purchasing behavior is not the same as a partnership.

Spreading the Risk

In contrast to the strategy of remaining loyal, buyers may consider many vendors when performance or economic risk is great and the benefits of looking around outweigh shopping costs. For example, the purchase of a telephone switching system can be a million-dollar decision. In a decision this big, most companies will shop around. Shopping around, though, is not just a risk reduction strategy—it can be used for other reasons. Shopping around is one way to spread risk when risk is large.

Similarly, buyers may elect to spread purchases among several vendors so that if one vendor does not live up to promises, others can take up the slack.[23] Spreading purchases among several vendors reduces performance risk. For example, a company that purchases gas tanks from Plastech may also purchase identical tanks from two other vendors. If Plastech was unable to deliver one order, the buyer would simply pass it along to the next vendor. In most cases, neither this strategy nor the shopping around strategy of risk reduction promotes partnerships; however, recognize that a partnership is unlikely anyway if the buyer cannot depend on a vendor.

Finally, one way to reduce risk, especially social risk, is to have others involved in the buying process. For a self-oriented buyer, one defensive strategy is to increase the size of the buying center. Having others involved can also add to the total expertise of the buying center, reducing the risk of a poor purchase decision. Many government agencies, particularly cities where a city council must make the purchase decision, hire consultants in order to take advantage of their expertise and minimize the risk of making a poor choice. Consultants are often used in high technology decisions and other infrequently made decisions when the organization perceives a need for expertise it does not have.

As you can see, many factors influence why individuals operate as they do. These factors can include experience with the product, the perceived risk in the decision, and the reward–measurement systems of the organization. There are also factors beyond the individual level that influence purchases and marketing decisions. These factors are best described by the buying determinants theory.

4–2

BUSINESS 2 BUSINESS
Buying Global Services

You own a large firm that sells worldwide. What roles do you think your marketing, technical support, manufacturing, and purchasing departments play in the decision to choose a long-distance supplier? How would

Sprint reps find out those roles if it has no other major accounts like you? What risks would be present for each individual in the buying center? How would Cable & Wireless's worldwide capabilities give it an advantage?

Exhibit 4–7
Buying
Determinants
Theory

Environmental factors

Market factors

Organizational
factors

Individual
factors

Buying Determinants Theory

Buying determinants theory—a rather general theory of why buyers buy—can help us integrate the previous theories. As you see in Exhibit 4–7, the theory describes behavior as due to the combined effects of four factors: environmental factors such as government regulations and technology; market factors, such as size and number of competitors; organizational factors, including company size, corporate culture, and policies; and individual factors, like age, experience, and education of any individual person involved in the decision.

In this and the two preceding chapters, we've already begun an examination of the buying determinants model, because we've looked at many of the individual and organizational factors that influence decision processes. One trap, though, that students may fall into is thinking that business marketing comes down to only personal selling, or the individual dealing with each individual decision process. The buying determinants model is useful because it offers a framework for combining buyers into groups and recognizing buying patterns, patterns that enable marketing managers to create marketing strategies.

Individual Factors

Individual factors are demographic and psychographic factors (psychological factors) that influence an individual's buying behavior. These factors can include age, education, and title or organizational level of the buyer, or they can be psychological factors such as

Exhibit 4–8
Expanded Buying
Determinants
Theory

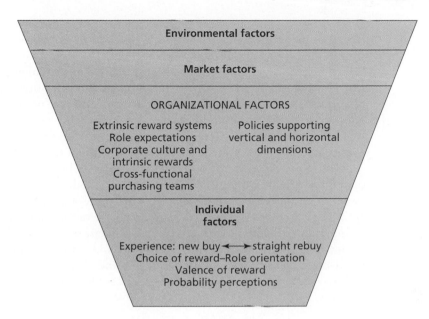

Environmental factors

Market factors

ORGANIZATIONAL FACTORS

Extrinsic reward systems   Policies supporting
Role expectations   vertical and horizontal
Corporate culture and   dimensions
intrinsic rewards
Cross-functional
purchasing teams

Individual
factors

Experience: new buy ←→ straight rebuy
Choice of reward–Role orientation
Valence of reward
Probability perceptions

the propensity to take risks. One of the individual factors that has been found to influence buyer behavior is experience, or years in purchasing. Experience reduces risk because uncertainty can be more accurately evaluated, and it increases the probability that the individual will buy alone, rather than creating a buying center.

At the individual level, we've already seen that a buyer's perception of risk and choice of reward system are two factors that influence behavior. A buyer's experience is another. An experienced buyer may not search for information as much as one with little experience. Therefore, as you can see in the expanded description of the buying determinants in Exhibit 4–8, individual factors include those such as the perceptions that drive motivation.

Organizational Factors

Organizational factors are characteristics of the organization that influence buying behavior. They include the size of the company, profitability, corporate culture, distribution of power, organizational policy, and other factors. For example, who participates in the selection of CPA services varies depending on large versus small buying companies. Small buying companies were less likely to have an audit committee, among other differences.

Reward–measurement systems are another set of organizational factors that influence buyer behavior, as we discussed earlier. We also recognized organizational factors when we discussed the relative risk associated with a purchase and when we examined the role that the type of organization (such as government agency) could have on the purchase process.

Market Factors

Market factors are the characteristics of the market that influence buyer behavior. Market factors are the number and relative size of competitors and the number and relative size of customers in a particular market. The number of competitors can be affected by the availability of substitutes. For example, Loctite Corporation makes glues and industrial adhesives. Screws, rivets, and other fasteners are competitive substitutes for Loctite's products in some markets. With so many substitutes in the market, competition can become quite heated. Buyers in such highly competitive markets may be wooed by so many suppliers that building relationships can be tough. On the other hand, vendors who can show creativity in solving problems over time can develop long-term relationships in such highly competitive markets.

The number of customers is also an important market factor. As discussed in Chapter 1, organizational markets are relatively small in terms of the number of customers.

Relative size of buyers can also make an impact on buying behavior. A buyer for GM can pull a lot more weight when purchasing auto body parts, for example, than can the owner of an independent body shop. Buying strategies, such as negotiating price, that are available to the GM buyer may not be available to the body shop owner.

In organizational markets, buyers may sometimes compete for sources of supply. Controlling supply costs or simply assuring continuity of supply can be major competitive advantages. The number of buyers and their relative sizes can influence individual buyer behavior depending on the competition for better products and better terms.

Environmental Factors

Environmental factors have had a great impact on how decisions are made.[24] **Environmental factors** are those characteristics of the world beyond the market level, and include the economy, technology, political factors, and social factors. As an economic example, many companies downsized due to economic pressures of global competition and slowing economies, as we discussed in Chapter 3. From the Field 4–2 illustrates how buying changes across transitional economies.

In some industries, technology is having a great impact. For example, computer technology is rapidly changing the publishing industry. In a few years, you may not buy text books for some classes but may purchase a CD instead. Look at this from your publisher's perspective: What could this mean in terms of the production equipment required? Similarly, this environmental factor will impact the market for printing presses.

The government's actions are also an important environmental factor. Trade treaties such as NAFTA and GATT may determine who your main competitors and customers are. Turkey processor Plantation Foods, for example, found new markets in Mexico soon after the passage of NAFTA. Then the peso was devalued (due to economic factors) and Plantation could no longer make a profit in Mexico. The company temporarily slowed its marketing efforts in that country.

These environmental factors, in combination with market, organizational, and individual factors, greatly influence buying behavior. Marketers examine these factors in order to find patterns, which they can then exploit by adapting their marketing strategy. Based on how these marketing managers view their world and how it works, they develop strategies to take advantage of the opportunities provided in their markets. In the next chapter, you will see how marketers examine market and environmental factors in order to assess marketing opportunities as part of the strategic marketing process. The foundation for this process is a solid understanding of how buyers buy.

4–2

FROM THE FIELD

Buying Equipment in Transitional Economies

In Eastern Europe, dramatic changes continue to occur. Countries used to a centrally planned economy have transitioned to a free economy and must now learn to compete on a free-market basis. In Africa, changes have been just as dramatic, although not always political. African countries must also face global competition, as they develop their industrial base.

Being a member of the global marketplace means buying equipment from global vendors. How have these transitions influenced buying practices in those two parts of the world?

In the Czech Republic, past formal relationships have been broken or disrupted. Users, who once had no say in the purchase, now have greater control, cutting the time involved and leaving a number of past key participants in an advisory role. What was once a highly bureaucratized process with many stages and lengthy deliberations is now straightforward and problem–solution focused. Still, many buyers are uncertain as to how to handle their new-found power in the marketplace.

Nigerian equipment purchasing is more developed. Nigerian companies are more likely to continuously search for new suppliers, keeping registers of potential suppliers. Nigerian buyers are also less likely to rely on references and more on their own judgment, wanting to see demonstrations, visit with sales engineers, and evaluate technical specs closely. Recognizing their global opportunities, these buyers constantly scan the environment for better sources of equipment.

Source: E. D. Bamgboye, "Equipment Buying in Nigeria," *Industrial Marketing Management* 21 (1992), pp. 181–85; Johan Roos, Ellen Veie, and Lawrence S. Welch, "A Case Study of Equipment Purchasing in Czechoslovakia," *Industrial Marketing Management* 21 (1992), pp. 257–63.

Summary

Theories are a picture of how the world works. This chapter presented several theories of how buying works in organizations. The first theory presented in this chapter was reward–measurement theory, which states that a buyer's motivation to engage in purchasing tasks is a function of the person's perceived probability and the valence of rewards associated with participation in the purchase. Perceived probability is the perception that effort will lead to outcomes that will result in the reward.

The second theory presented was buyer behavior choice theory. This theory states that buyers go through a series of steps in deciding what tasks they will perform. The steps are, first, determining the degree to which they should adopt a company orientation or a self-orientation and, second, determining whether to adopt a defensive or offensive strategy. Company orientation is the degree to which they attempt to satisfy company goals, while self-orientation reflects the degree to which they attempt to satisfy their own goals. An offensive strategy is one designed to maximize gain. A defensive strategy minimizes loss. Then they decide on which tasks to perform, which leads to the purchase of a product.

Role theory describes the roles that people can take on when more than one person is involved in the purchase. The group of people who participate is called the buying center, and they can be initiators of the purchase, influencers, the decision maker, the purchasing agent, a gatekeeper, controller, or any combination of these. Buying centers can be examined in terms of time fragmentation, of horizontal and vertical dimensions, and of governance, or how the centers make decisions.

Buying centers are often formed to minimize risk—either financial, performance, or social risk. Marketers can reduce perceptions of risk through guarantees, warranties, free trials, free samples, or demonstrations of the product. Marketers also attempt to reduce risk by educating buyers through advertising and other forms of promotion.

Buying determinants theory is a general theory of why buyers buy, and incorporates the effects of environmental, market, and organizational factors on the individual. Buying determinants theory enables us to examine markets for patterns in buying behavior, which will be helpful to remember when we discuss market segmentation and strategy in the next chapter.

Key Terms

advocate	financial risk	purchasing agent
autonomous	gatekeeper	reward–measurement
behavior choice theory	horizontal dimension	theory
buying center	individual factors	risk
champion	influencer	role theory
company orientation	initiator	self-efficacy
controller	intrinsic rewards	self-orientation
decision maker	market factors	social risk
decision-making unit	motivation	time fragmentation
(DMU)	offensive strategy	user
defensive strategy	organizational factors	valence
environmental factors	perceived probability	vertical dimension
extrinsic rewards	performance risk	

Discussion Questions

1. Everyone has theories about what it takes to be successful. What is your theory? What assumptions underlie your theory? You can usually pick out assumptions by listing your "causes" or "becauses." These are statements in your theory where you say "Because of . . . , then such and such is true." What follows "Because" is an assumption.

2. Compare and contrast the buy-grid model, reward–measurement model, and behavior choice model. Which model do you think is right? Why? Why are the other models wrong or merely less right?

3. Create your own buying behavior theory, based on what you have read in the first four chapters of this book and on your own experience.

4. A bank is looking to purchase a new PC-based computer system. Who do you think would play each of the roles in the buying center? What would be the roles of the president, office manager, average teller, manager of customer service, or any other manager? What characteristics or personal interests would influencers have?

5. Assume that the bank in question 4 is buying 25 PCs, one for each manager and loan officer. This bank has one location and $50 million in assets. Another bank has 125 locations across the northwest United States, with nearly 700 loan officers and 50 managers. It too is looking to buy 25 PCs. Is the risk the same for each

bank? Why or why not? If you were responsible for such a decision in each situation, what factors could influence your personal risk?

6. A wood products manufacturing plant must buy cyclone separators, equipment that collects sawdust out of the air in the plant in order to provide a healthier work environment. What differences in criteria for evaluating proposals might be used by (a) the purchasing department, (b) the company treasurer, (c) the CEO, (d) the plant manager, and (e) the head of the legal department? Illustrate your answer by using the multi-attribute matrix from Chapter 3.

7. Answer question 4 again, but this time, consider the roles that the different people would play in the decision process. Using the buy-phase model, when would each person in question 4 be involved? Create a chart like Exhibit 4–3 showing how each person participates in the purchase of CPA services in the chapter.

8. Do you think that people tend to buy offensively or defensively over time? Or do people vary from situation to situation? If people vary, what causes that variance? If people don't vary, why?

9. Assume the industry your company sells to is one that typically uses buying centers. What implications does this have for you as a marketer? What implications would it have if you were a salesperson? What would be different if the purchase was usually made by only one person in the firm?

10. How does a buying center differ from a cross-functional purchasing team (from Chapter 3)?

Internet Exercise

Open the AT&T home page (**www.att.com**) and click on the business services line. This should take you to a page that offers an option *success stories.* Click on this and then go to one of the success stories. Each story will tend to focus on one person. Discuss how this person made the decision to go with AT&T, using one of the theories from the chapter. Be specific with quotes to illustrate why you are using that theory.

Cases

Case 4.1   Wabash Waste Management

Wilson Puckett, president of Wabash Waste Management, had a stack of proposals on his desk from several truck companies. Two of the companies, Roper and Rollins, offered trucks on a lease basis, while three dealers wanted Wabash to buy their trucks. In the past, Puckett always purchased the trucks. Which proposal would be best, he wondered, as he picked up the proposals for the third or fourth time.

Wabash Waste Management is an industrial waste recycling company. It picks up grease and oil from several manufacturing facilities in a regional area, cleans the grease and oil, and then sells it to a company that packages the material for resale. Wabash also picks up frying grease from restaurants for recycling. The company was about to enter a new regional market, and needed four new trucks to pick up the used oil and grease.

The trucks were tank trucks with a pump that pumped the grease or oil from a holding tank at the restaurant or manufacturing plant. Darnell Gates, fleet manager, wanted Puckett to choose the Hauler2000, a tank truck with a McLaren pump capable of pumping 50 gallons in about five minutes. It has a capacity of 5,000 gallons. The truck is rated at 10 miles per gallon of gasoline and has one of the better maintenance records of all of the trucks. The Hauler2000 is one of the trucks for sale, but could be leased through Wabash's bank.

On the other hand, Betty Roberts, vice president of finance, has been pushing the Roper offering, a Fleetwood truck that pumps 50 gallons in 10 minutes. The Fleetwood tank holds 4,800 gallons of grease or oil, and the truck gets 12 miles per gallon of diesel. The lease option on the Fleetwood is the most attractive of all of the proposals, according to Roberts. In addition, by leasing through Roper, the company does not use any of the credit from the bank, keeping that free for some other needed purchases. The company has operated too close to the edge, and needs to fill some excess capacity in order to make enough profit.

Gates told Puckett that the Fleetwood is too slow and would lead to at least three fewer pickups a day by each truck. Three drivers have also told Puckett that the Fleetwood is a deathtrap, with a bad safety record. These drivers also told Puckett that the current fleet will need at least two trucks replaced in the next year. The maintenance manager, however, thinks the company could get by with replacing only one truck, and he also likes working on the Fleetwood better than the Hauler2000.

1. List the roles that each person is playing in this buying center. Then discuss the dimensions of the buying center. Who do you think is most important, other than Wilson Puckett, and why?

2. Discuss risk from the perspective of each member. Assume you are one of the dealers and discuss how you would reduce the risk for each member.

3. Assume that the buying center as described in the case is an accurate picture of the average buying center for tank trucks. How would this information influence your marketing activities? Be as specific as possible.

Case 4.2   Alcan Buys New Equipment

Fred Glasberg is calling on Alcan's Louisville plant. Alcan is one of the world's largest aluminum companies. Fred sells extrusion equipment used to manufacture aluminum pipes and wiring. Patti Schock, chief engineer for Alcan, is concerned about productivity. She wants a six-month lease on the equipment because if up-time isn't better than 97 percent, she wants to be able to replace it with competitive equipment. She had a team of her engineers observe a demonstration by Fred. She also asked accounting to prepare its own analysis of the financial information to see how it compared with Fred's.

Bill Cirrus, also with Alcan, is a rising junior executive. He is pushing for Alcan to consider a Chinese vendor because he believes that buying equipment from China will open the China market up for the Alcan aluminum products made in Louisville. Bill is the director, international markets, and reports directly to Vice President of Marketing Sharon Cron. Bill is trying to get approval for a trip to China for Patti, Jim Murray (VP of manufacturing) and Sharon to see the Chinese equipment.

1. Explain Patti's and Bill's motivations in terms of the reward–measurement model. You will need to make some assumptions about their jobs so be sure to state those.

2. Now explain each buyer in terms of the buyer behavior choice model. Again, be sure to state the assumptions you will need to make.

3. What should Fred Glasberg do? Which model of behavior would be most useful to Fred and why?

Additional Readings

Bristor, Julia, "Influence Strategies in Organizational Buying: The Importance of Connections to the Right People in the Right Places," *Journal of Business to Business Marketing* 1, no. 1 (1993), pp. 63–98.

Bunn, Michele D., "Key Aspects of Organizational Buying: Conceptualization and Measurement," *Journal of the Academy of Marketing Science* 22 (Spring 1994), pp. 160–169.

Jennings, Richard G., and Richard Plank, "When the Purchasing Agent Is a Committee," *Industrial Marketing Management* 24 (1995), pp. 411–419.

Settle, Robert B., and Pamela L. Alreck, "Risky Business," *Sales & Marketing Management* (January 1989), pp. 48–52.

Wilson, Elizabeth J., Gary Lilien, and David T. Wilson, "Don't Ignore Buying Committee Group Think," *ISBM Insights* 1, no. 2 (1991).

Wilson, Elizabeth J., and Arch G. Woodside, "The Relative Importance of Choice Criteria in Organizational Buying: Implications for Adaptive Selling," *Journal of Business to Business Marketing* 2, no. 1 (1995), pp. 33–58.

Part II

Foundations for Creating Value

Now you know that business markets are different from consumer markets in many regards: size and volatility, channels and sales complexity, and purchasing standards and processes. You also have a foundational understanding of how value-creating activities are coordinated not just by markets but also by different types of relationships. The chapters in Part II take us to the business marketer's engine room.

Chapter 5 looks at opportunity and access to the rewards of more and better customers. The best business marketers recognize their advantageous position to serve and their potential rewards from delivering more value to current customers. We describe the structure and content of a customer database and illustrate its utility for spotting opportunities and measuring the lifetime value of customers. With a lifetime value perspective, we can rightly regard the acquisition of new customers as a capital budgeting enterprise—an investment in a productive asset—rather than an expense. Of course, the development of new markets and the acquisition of new customers pivot on useful segmentation models. We review several approaches to segmentation in business markets and discuss the criteria for an effective segmentation scheme.

Chapter 6, an overview of strategic planning, is neither the first nor the last perspective you'll encounter that tackles the vexing problem of strategy formulation. Our emphasis in the chapter is on the definition of purpose and the match of distinctive competencies to opportunities. This matching process favors firms that act with a sophisticated understanding of the competitive forces in the product market. Furthermore, because the pace of technology and global nature of competition make almost any competitive advantage short-lived, the only real strategic edge comes from an organization's ability to learn to disrupt the status quo and adapt.

Any business that takes its eye off customer satisfaction, quality, and routine review of its mission and strategy will also fail to finish the race. This is the stuff of Chapter 7. We chart the roles that marketing plays in a learning organization and the partnerships marketing personnel must forge with all functional areas. The skills for partnering are outlined in a manner that should enable you to contribute positively to the teamwork needed to deliver value efficiently and thereby satisfy and retain customers at a profit.

Chapter 5

Market Opportunities
Current and Potential Customers

FEDEX

Frederick Smith began Federal Express with a clever idea and a network of financial backers. He saw countless businesses needing rapid delivery of small repair parts, blueprints, and other documents. His plan was to use a fleet of planes to fly by night, out of sleepy airports, to a central hub in Memphis. There all parcels would be sorted and bundled for their destination, and flown out again to the still quiet airports. Then before lunchtime, snappy fleets of trucks would deliver components, perishables, documents, and more to the addressee. The concept was supported with award-winning advertising and a customer focus. ●

What a stunning example of the impact of entrepreneurship! Although financial losses were substantial, it was critical to keep the system running while awaiting volume growth. But the growth did come. Many companies began using overnight air shipment in place of parts inventories warehoused in multiple locations throughout the country and beyond. But it was the document business that exploded. In 1983 the *Chicago Tribune* claimed, "The overnight letter and package delivery business—the procrastinator's dream—has been called the most important development for harried businessmen since the invention of the copier." ●

A few years later, however, there was more parity among the players in the overnight delivery business. While all carriers faced the adverse impact of the fax machine on their document volume, perhaps none faced it more than Federal Express, the leader by far in next-day letters. New businesses beyond documents were needed. ●

FedEx developed a new pricing schedule for heavy packages, hundred-weight rates, and it promoted the program especially to select customers known to ship heavy items. FedEx launched a similar program to its chemical and related customers to tout its ability to handle "dangerous goods." In a prize-winning program, FedEx used its own route personnel to deliver fresh-baked coffee cakes to high-volume shippers to announce Saturday delivery. People in the office that Saturday shared the news of this service as they shared the goodies. To develop new customers, FedEx made a special pitch to catalog merchants, or (as its program dubbed them) "you who serve the mail order shopper." Today Lands End, L.L. Bean, Spiegel, and more make FedEx delivery available to their customers for a small additional charge. A key benefit has been to enable last-minute shopping, effectively lengthening the Christmas season for catalogers.[1]

Visit the FedEx web site at **www.fedex.com**

Learning Objectives

In this chapter you will learn to think creatively and boldly—like FedEx — about finding new opportunities. We will underscore the favorable circumstances and possibilities for gaining increased business from current customers. We also develop options for gaining new customers. Both arenas require formal evaluations of market potential and can be well served by marketing research. We aim to sharpen your perspective on opportunities and acquaint you with some of the key managerial tools.

At the conclusion of the chapter you should be able to

- Seek to maximize the value of current customers.
- Outline the basic structure and capabilities of a customer database.
- Discuss the relative strengths and weaknesses of alternative means of customer research.
- Illustrate how suppliers and customers can collaborate to find opportunities.
- Segment business markets on the basis of industry codes, buying processes, benefits sought, media and memberships, and other criteria.
- Assess the utility of any market segmentation scheme.
- Apply basic models to evaluate the potential of market segments.

We don't promise to map every sector of market opportunities, nor do we review every known tool of market evaluation. But we give you what we hope is enough to jump start your perceptual vigilance and imagination in order that you may soon seize the day.

117

Finding Opportunities

The witch is melted, Scarecrow gets a diploma, Tin Man gets a heart, and the lion gets a medal for valor. But do you remember what Dorothy gets from the phoney Wizard of Oz? That's right: a reality check. She learns that what she thinks she wants—out there over the rainbow—is probably right there in her own backyard. Sadly, too many businesses have let their houses fall into ruin while they chased rainbows. That is, they neglected their current customers in order to chase opportunities elsewhere.

The word *opportunity* comes from the Latin *opportunitas,* meaning fitness or advantage. It represents a favorable circumstance, a propitious moment, or a promising course of events that bodes well for the attainment of a goal. Marketing opportunities derive from the "fitness" of a company to serve a specific market. They result from a seller's proximity, competencies, skills, and resources that can be brought to serve an identified customer or segment profitably. The seller's ability to provide value is its competitive advantage in that particular arena.

Markets among Current Customers

Business managers have often noted the tendency of about 20 percent of customers to account for 80 percent of sales. A closer look at some companies shows even greater skewness—perhaps more than 75 percent of sales from fewer than 10 percent of accounts. Firms that sell to automobile companies or the military, of course, might not experience the 80–20 rule or 75–10 situation simply because there are only a handful of potential accounts. Both phenomena—the 80–20 distributions and firms selling to small numbers of customers—dramatize the importance of managing important groups of accounts if not individual account relationships in business markets.

Best Customers

How much of its marketing budget should a firm allocate to efforts that serve its best customers? In the abstract, any firm should spend and spend until the payoffs from additional marketing efforts are no longer in excess of incremental expenditures. *Spending until marginal revenue equals marginal costs, and marginal costs are rising* is the basic profit maximization approach many of you learned in economics class. In practice, this approach can be followed for narrow promotions and some specific marketing expenditures. For example, Federal Express promotions are usually measured against a control group of customers that matches the target group in every way but participation in the promotion. Thus, in the "Dangerous Goods" program that promoted FedEx's capability to ship toxic, caustic, and flammable materials, the additional daily volume over three months was twice as high in the promotion group as in the control group. This translated into over $20 in revenue per dollar of marketing expenditure. With variable costs per shipment so low in the overnight shipping business, this program certainly increases profits from one group of current customers. From this point FedEx could expand the program to other accounts, intensify the program with this same group of customers, or both.

Unfortunately, the payoffs from many other marketing expenditures are not so easily determined. A computer company's commitment to staff a 24-hour service line is justified not so much on the hard data showing the profitability of the service as it is on a commitment to market leadership (or catching up to competition) and need to signal commitment to customers. A credit card company hosts an annual weekend of recreation and entertainment for its best business customers. This extravagant "thank you" builds goodwill and channels of communication. The credit company hopes this translates into increased business or **account retention**, the percentage of accounts that continue doing business with the seller each year. But, we can think of no practical way of gauging the effectiveness of the event on such criteria.

Customer Maximization

Many companies find that it is much easier to get current customers to do more business than it is to get business from prospective customers. Many of those who have never transacted with the company know the company and its products, *but are just not interested.*

To illustrate, note that most metropolitan newspapers derive a significant portion of their advertising revenue from auto dealers in their readership area. Nevertheless, a number of new superdealers in the midwest have elected to use *no newspaper advertising* in their promotion mix, relying instead on radio image advertising and highly targeted direct mail and telephone follow-up with referrals. How the local newspapers long to win over such accounts!

But that door seems effectively closed for now. Newspaper ad managers can use their time and talent more productively developing programs for the car dealers, real estate agencies, and department stores that are already buying ads. Indeed, Lee Enterprises in Davenport, Iowa, a media company publishing 19 newspapers, has expanded current client relationships by collaborating with its best advertisers on special events, preferred customer programs, and even the distribution of product samples.

New Products

The same logic for increasing the volume of light and medium accounts applies to their potential for purchasing new products. Current customers know the company, its service standards, its dedication to quality, its technical capabilities, and more. With them the seller enjoys a level of credibility and trust that has yet to be measured and tested among noncustomers, even bright prospects. Thus, a marketing research company with a new forecasting technique or model is apt to develop and find keenest interest among its current clients. Similarly, FedEx tested a service for next-afternoon delivery—priced lower than its next-morning–delivery service—paying particular attention to responses by its best customers in the test region.

Network Payoffs

Account retention and penetration motivate our attention to current customers in the preceding discussion. But current customers can be strategic assets in other ways too. Foremost, every business must seek to understand fully its role in the value chain. By enabling one's customer to better satisfy its downstream customers, achieve market share growth, or compete in new markets, one's company stands to grow too. For example, Johnson Controls worked very closely with Chrysler in the design of interiors for its cab forward cars. Chrysler's success from the Intrepid and its siblings play out in high volume for Johnson Controls.

Indeed, customers are a vital source of new product ideas. In 1995 students and a handful of recruiters at the University of Cincinnati requested the development and institutionalization of what is now a highly sought and successful course on marketing and the new information technology. Prospective students and potential recruiters would never have given such input. Similarly, BOSE speaker design teams frequently help suppliers to meet their tough specifications and quality standards for new plastic and metal parts. Those suppliers who measure up not only reap more purchases from BOSE, but they are more competitive at other accounts as a result. From the Field 5–1 recaps product development by a more complex network.

Certain customers may gain the company access to new accounts and markets. A consulting company that does an excellent job for one of the leading hospitals in St. Louis is apt to benefit greatly from the client's influence with hospital administrators in Kansas City, Chicago, Peoria, Evansville, and Louisville. Clearly, the value of a customer is more than its profit margin impact in the most recent accounting period.

Finding Opportunities with Customers

Opportunities to do additional business with current customers can be identified by informal and formal means. Feedback through the sales force and service and delivery personnel should be encouraged and rewarded. Their frequent contact with customers and empathic dialogue makes them attuned to developing customer needs. **Empathic dialogue** is active listening and identification with customer concerns, resulting in customer-centered communication and problem solving. The Loctite Corporation developed an inexpensive dispensing system for liquid adhesives primarily as a result of the insistence by its sales force that it should fill a dire need among heretofore neglected prospects, small manufacturers who could use a lot of adhesive if they could get their hands on a reasonable dispensing system.

Marketing research companies and consulting firms frequently spark—and sometimes frame—their client's next project. Because Cincinnati-based Hydrotech had helped engineer its principal's hydraulic systems into one of Cincinnati Milacron's machine tools, Hydrotech had the knowledge and track record to tackle other evident hydraulics needs at Milacron.

Leading companies periodically profile their top accounts and formally develop strategies for greater penetration. They seek to understand the sales forecasts and business strategies of key accounts. They formally model the purchase process and identify the roles of key members of the buying team, perhaps as influencer, user, gatekeeper, or decider.

Database
Some business marketers serve so many customers that account management is critically supported by computer database systems. United Parcel Service and Federal Express, for example, serve thousands and thousands of accounts. But even a small Denver medical lab must efficiently manage customer relationships with hundreds of area physicians.

Consider ScheduTrax, a small, fictitious software company that we will use to illustrate a number of typical database structures and applications. Selling desktop business software for scheduling and staffing, ScheduTrax has over 10,000 customers. An increasing number of companies are using part-time employees and trying to accommodate the flexible schedules their full-time people need to raise families, attend school, serve the community, or serve jail time. They use ScheduTrax programs to incorporate these complex constraints while scheduling staff, various operations, and service loads.

In the ScheduTrax database each customer comprises a record. Each record contains the following key elements:

User's name(s)

Company

Street address

City, state, and ZIP code

Phone and fax numbers

5–1

FROM THE FIELD

Opportunities in the Network

Sweden's logging industry faces a significant problem: cutting frozen timber at the mill. One saw equipment manufacturer worked with several of its suppliers to develop a small prototype band saw. The product was tested successfully at a small mill. This drew the attention of the large, opinion-leading mill in the region where a new, bigger adaptation of the test saw was installed. Unfortunately, serious breakdowns resulted; weakness in the steel and welded seams were deemed the problem.

Fortunately, the large mill forged a technical cooperation agreement with a blade manufacturer, and later brought in the steel supplier and welders. It took several years, but eventually the new processes were established, and the saw equipment manufacturer found success.

The map of the key linkages in this value-creating process shows the importance of even remote participants in the network.

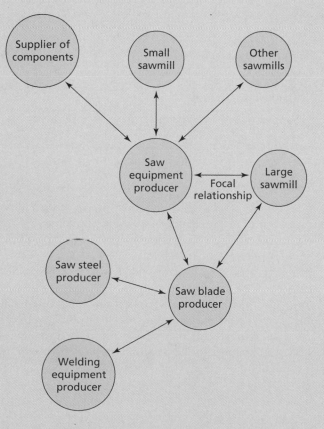

SOURCE: Adapted from James Anderson, Hakan Hakansson, and Jan Johanson, "Dyadic Business Relationships within a Business Network Context." Used with permission from the *Journal of Marketing,* published by the American Marketing Association, vol. 58 (October 1994), pp. 1–15.

Exhibit 5-1   ScheduTrax Decile Report

Decile	$ Spent	No. of Customers	Cum. No. of Customers	% of Customers	Cum. % of Customers	Average Purchases
1	632,771	162	162	2%	2%	$3,906
2	632,771	290	452	3	5	2,182
3	632,771	366	818	4	9	1,729
4	632,771	430	1,248	4	13	1,472
5	632,771	521	1,769	5	18	1,215
6	632,771	606	2,375	6	24	1,044
7	632,771	890	3,265	9	33	711
8	632,771	1,126	4,391	11	44	562
9	632,771	1,423	5,814	14	58	445
10	632,771	4,316	10,130	42	100	147
Total	6,327,710	10,130		100		625

Source code (origin of initial order)

Initial purchase date

Original purchase dollars

Purchase (upgrade) history

   Transaction dates

   Transaction amounts

   Source code of transaction

   Product type

Firm characteristics (industry, number of employees)

User demographics and lifestyles

Of course, the database requires both proper setup and ongoing maintenance to serve as a seed bed of market opportunities. Let's presume those challenges are addressed elsewhere in your business program and examine a couple of simple reports to illustrate opportunities among current customers.

Exhibit 5–1 is called a decile report. A **decile report** orders the firm's customers from best to worst, on the basis of purchase volume for the period, summarized by tenths. (Admittedly, we have heard executives give the same name—decile report—to tables summarizing purchase activity for fifths or twentieths of the revenue base.) At the bottom of the left-hand column, Exhibit 5–1 reports that ScheduTrax has achieved a little over $6.3 million in sales. The bottom of the next column to the right indicates that the sales came from a little over 10,000 customers. Thus, average spending per customer, in the bottom right, is $625.

Each row in the report, however, helps the marketing manager break free of the tendency to think about the "average" customer. The customers are far from equal in the significance of their purchases! For example, ScheduTrax's weakest customers—in row 10—don't even spend a quarter of the average and they represent 43 percent of the customer base! Now compare decile 10 against decile 1: A handful of best customers spend 26 times as much as the worst.

Exhibit 5–2

ScheduTrax
Account Profiles

ACCOUNT NO.	2207		
FIRM	Billy's Tavern	BUSINESS	Food Svc-Rtl
	2295 Riverside		
	Valdosta, GA 31602		
	9125551234		
CONTACTS	Bradford, Jimmy	DEMO CODE	2012
	Manager		

TRANSACTION SUMMARY

ORIG DATE	09/24/96	LAST PURCH	07/18/97
ORIG $	$159	CUM $	$3,882
ORIG SOURCE	M63	NO. TRANS	13
MODE	Phone		
PMT	AmEx		

ACCOUNT NO.	1761		
FIRM	Midwest Auto Parts	BUSINESS	Auto parts-Rtl
	27912 Telegraph Rd		
	Detroit, MI 48034		
	8105559999		
CONTACTS	Wolscheid, Emily	DEMO CODE	4302
	Office Manager		

TRANSACTION SUMMARY

ORIG DATE	03/04/92	LAST PURCH	08/26/96
ORIG $	$139	CUM $	$4,891
ORIG SOURCE	DM26	NO. TRANS	19
MODE	Phone		
PMT	PO, Amex		

The decile report is simple, but quite helpful to the business marketer. How well do we know our best accounts? Which accounts get invited to the trade show reception? Which ones get a card and which ones get the two-pound box of chocolates with a card that says, "Thanks for your business" at the end of the year? FedEx often tests promotions to its best customers in a particular service category and then expands the program to successively less important customers as long as returns are positive. Perhaps there are some accounts that have continued to get our marketing attention—mail and phone calls—that just don't seem worthwhile any more. We start to ask where else can we put such marketing effort to yield better payoffs.

Some of the preceding questions invite other questions. The very best accounts could be studied one by one. Exhibit 5–2 assembles the profiles of two specific customers to enable account strategies. Customer 2207 is relatively new and in the restaurant business. Customer 1761 is a retail auto parts chain and has been our customer since 1992. These data support telephone and direct mail efforts at ScheduTrax. Marketing communications with 2207—and with those accounts in like circumstances—might convey special appreciation for adapting the software and provide application tips for foodservice firms—perhaps scheduling wait staff with high absentee rates. Customers akin to

Exhibit 5–3   ScheduTrax Profile of Customers in Deciles 2–4

Type of Business	No. of Accts.	% of Deciles 2–4	Last Year's Purchases	Cumulative Purchases	% Adaptation of Companion Products			
					Graph1	Pay1	Pay2	Phonlink
Education	43	4%	$75,163	$159,458	44%	31%	18%	9%
Entertainment	27	2	47,196	159,458	34	20	14	17
Nursing care	217	20	379,313	1,009,902	40	22	28	18
Manufacturing	72	7	125,855	372,069	33	19	22	11
Professional serv.	128	12	223,742	797,291	29	40	15	12
Retail	380	35	664,235	1,754,041	15	22	13	16
Transportation	104	10	181,791	584,680	48	20	28	20
Other	115	11	201,018	531,528	47	27	25	22
Total	1086	100	1,898,313	5,315,276	31	25	20	16

1761 would receive affirmation of the long-running business relationship and might be sought as test sites for updates and new product prototypes. Indeed, the database can be mined for insights into user needs and motivations. Customers can be meaningfully grouped by size, industry, longevity, purchase volume, applications, and so on to enable a full range of marketing communications and customer service.

Individual customers in the second, third, and fourth deciles at ScheduTrax may not represent the sales volume to justify such close analytical attention, although firms with higher purchases per customer than ScheduTrax may, indeed, give close attention to key accounts in deciles 3 or 4 or elsewhere. Eventually, at some level of customer significance, we forsake individual account analysis to find significant patterns and groups of customers in these deciles.

Exhibit 5–3 profiles the groups of customers in deciles 2 through 4. Notice that 35 percent are in the retail business, including chains and specialty shops. Among these purchasers of our scheduling software, only 15 percent have adopted Graph1, the new companion software that gives (1) graphic display for departments or stores and (2) personal schedules addressable to each employee. The low adoption rate among retailers seems to be in sharp contrast to the nursing care segment, where 40 percent of the customers have bought Graph1. Maybe we should think about putting together a promotion to these 323 customers—the 85 percent of 380 retail customers that do not have the Graph1 software.

Customer Research

Astute readers should be asking a key question here: Before running the promotion, why not talk to several current customers to learn their priorities and circumstances? Indeed! The database supports two different research approaches: focus groups and sample surveys.

Focus Groups   **Focus groups** bring a small group of customers together to discuss a specific topic or issue. Our software company, ScheduTrax, might try to bring 6 to 12 customers together at a trade show or in three or four different cities where they conduct business. The meeting can be set up at a local hotel or conference facility or could be arranged to take place at the special facilities of a marketing research company. These might be quite elaborate. Most allow videotaping and direct observation through a one-way mirror. This allows ScheduTrax representatives who watch the focus group to give the moderator some additional directions for the interview.

A qualified focus group moderator can uncover buying motivations and new uses for products.
Courtesy Nordhaus, Inc.

The moderator is an experienced professional, often with advanced behavioral science training. After providing a brief icebreaker and general introduction to the topic, the moderator generally tries to let the group carry on the conversation. His or her concentration should be on the discussion, along a general outline of topics needed to be covered in the discussion. Because the interview is taped, the moderator can let the group talk, with ample opportunity later to analyze comments and extract stimulating quotations.

No two focus groups are identical. Each has different participants, perhaps from different positions in diverse organizations, from different industries, and/or from different parts of the country. Depending on the nature of the topic and the diversity of the user segments, most companies conduct several focus groups, although the incremental value of each additional group interview will taper off after three or four, or maybe not until a half dozen.

The focus group is best used to generate ideas, gain insights into customer needs and constraints, and develop hypotheses about market opportunities. ScheduTrax might learn that department managers, who used to schedule dozens of part-time employees every two weeks, have split into at least two distinct groups: (1) those who have handed off this task to a staff person and (2) those who have used the software themselves to begin or expand their array of desktop personal productivity aids and decision support tools. Managers in the second group appear to represent an opportunity for ScheduTrax.

It is important to note that the focus group is not a fitting procedure for measuring market share potential or forecasting adoption rates. The focus group reveals a spectrum of customer motivations, suggests differences in usage patterns, provides close contact with actual customers, and thus stimulates thinking about new products and services and how better to market existing products. Focus groups do not provide quantitative results like percentages or sales estimates.

The popularity of focus group research rests on three major factors. First, it is supported by the efficient and accurate access to customers afforded by the database. Just imagine the daunting task of finding 10 moderate users in the automotive repair business in Jacksonville without using a customer database. Second, focus groups can be conducted quickly and relatively cheaply. Depending on the scale of compensation for participants, the amenities of the facility, and the moderator's fee, focus groups can cost between $1,200 and $5,000 each. Finally, focus groups almost always yield a surprising customer insight and some new ideas.

Siemens Medical Systems, Inc. manages customer satisfaction using a survey that asks customers to rate its performance on several dimensions.

Courtesy Siemens Medical Systems

SIEMENS

Satisfaction Survey

Using a scale of 1-5, please check how you rate us:	
5=Extremely satisfied **4**=Very satisfied **3**=Generally satisfied (neutral, met the requirements)	**2**=Very dissatisfied **1**=Extremely dissatisfied **N/A**=Not applicable

The Sales Process

	5	4	3	2	1	N/A
1. The availability of your sales representative	O	O	O	O	O	O
2. The product knowledge of your sales representative	O	O	O	O	O	O
3. The quality of information and follow-up provided by your sales representative	O	O	O	O	O	O
4. Commitments by your sales representative were honored	O	O	O	O	O	O
5. The quality of information and advice provided on the changing health care environment by your sales representative	O	O	O	O	O	O
6. The ability of your sales representative to provide economic and financial justification	O	O	O	O	O	O
7. The creativity and attractiveness of financing programs provided by Siemens	O	O	O	O	O	O
8. Clear and concise proposals provided by your sales representative	O	O	O	O	O	O
9. How satisfied were you with the performance of the sales representative during the course of this transaction?	O	O	O	O	O	O

What specific suggestions do you have to improve the sales process? _____

The Purchasing Process (Order Processing, Delivery)

	5	4	3	2	1	N/A
1. Clarity and accuracy of invoices	O	O	O	O	O	O
2. Was the system delivered when expected?	O	O	O	O	O	O
3. Were changes in delivery dates communicated in a professional and timely manner?	O	O	O	O	O	O
4. Was the system correctly delivered as specified in your quotation?	O	O	O	O	O	O
5. How satisfied were you with delivery notification?	O	O	O	O	O	O
6. If your site was unprepared for delivery at the time of equipment arrival, did Siemens provide adequate assistance?	O	O	O	O	O	O

If NO, please explain: _____

	5	4	3	2	1	N/A
7. If some items were missing, were you notified of delivery dates of these items?	O	O	O	O	O	O
8. Were you satisfied with the purchasing process?	O	O	O	O	O	O

What specific suggestions do you have to improve the purchase process? _____

The Installation Process

	5	4	3	2	1	N/A
1. Quality of site planning. How satisfied were you with site and installation planning information and support prior to the start of installation? (e.g., preparing the site for installation with regard to room layout, electrical requirements, special cabling, networking requirements, etc.)	O	O	O	O	O	O
2. Were you satisfied with communication from Siemens personnel during installation of the equipment?	O	O	O	O	O	O
3. How satisfied were you with the overall installation process?	O	O	O	O	O	O
4. At the completion of installation, was the department left clean with professional appearances maintained?	O	O	O	O	O	O
5. Was the equipment turned over to you on a mutually agreed upon schedule?	O	O	O	O	O	O

If NO, please explain: _____

What specific suggestions do you have to improve the installation process? _____

The Training Process

How satisfied were you...

	5	4	3	2	1	N/A
1. With the training provided by the Siemens Applications Specialist?	O	O	O	O	O	O
2. With the training provided by the ICON course conducted in Hoffman Estates?	O	O	O	O	O	O
3. With the overall training process?	O	O	O	O	O	O
4. Was on-site training conducted at a time that met the department's requirements?	O	O	O	O	O	O
5. Was course training in Hoffman Estates conducted at a time that met the department's requirements?	O	O	O	O	O	O

What specific suggestions do you have to improve the training process? _____

Thank you for your participation in this study. Please place this completed questionnaire in the enclosed, self-addressed stamped envelope and mail it to:

Barbara Franciose, Group Vice President
Siemens Medical Systems, Inc.
Nuclear Medicine Group
2501 North Barrington Road
Hoffman Estates, Illinois 60195

Surveys Chico Marx stated the role of survey research quite clearly in the Marx Brothers' classic *Duck Soup:* "So how'm I gonna fin' ow what I gotta fin' ow if he no' tella me what I wanna fin' ow?" (Translation: So, how am I going to find out what I need to find out, if he won't tell me what I need to find out?)

He is saying that there are limits to what we can infer from behavioral information in the customer database. Likewise, focus group insights are typically exploratory. They seldom afford quantitative estimates of market size, for example. The **sample survey**—a questionnaire administered to a representative group of a particular population—is a versatile approach to problems that involve asking people questions. But it too has limits, which is why companies often use many types of research.

Surveys can be administered to customers in three primary ways: (1) personal interview, (2) mail, and (3) telephone. Personal interviews allow good depth of questioning and probing. Answers can be clarified and feedback from product demonstrations or physical stimuli (e.g., a fabric or warning siren) can be ascertained. But the expense of sending interviewers to the field to secure elusive appointments and visit geographically dispersed customers is often prohibitive. Thus, a compromise approach may be some focus groups or an attempt to see customers one-on-one at a trade show.

Questionnaires can be administered very efficiently by mail. But it is critical that the researcher design the survey with the nature of the current business relationship in mind. The recipient of the survey is a current customer, not a stranger. Thus, a number of imperatives govern the contact.

In most cases the researcher must acknowledge and affirm the relationship in the cover letter. Typically the survey aims to strengthen the relationship. Thus, affirmation of the relationship serves to motivate customers to reveal unmet needs and points of supplier weakness. Respondents should be given hope to realize greater satisfaction from within the current relationship, instead of seeking other sources. Even if the researcher's objective is to identify customers for disengagement, it is prudent to sever the exchange amicably, with minimal turmoil or stress.

Second, the survey must ask only questions that cannot be answered by information on the customer database. This is a matter of both credibility and courtesy. How believable is a cover letter affirming the importance of the relationship with Howard Supply when it is followed by a survey that asks for "volume of total purchases from us last year"? Out of respect for our customer's time and competing job demands, we should not ask survey participants to look up or compile information that we have in the database. In this same spirit, it must be clear to the survey respondent or informant whether the data are being compiled for statistical summaries or to augment the database.

No survey should be used to mask selling activities. **Sugging** is the unethical practice of using marketing research as a guise for selling. "Hi, this is Randy from Business Research Service. I'd like to ask you a few questions about office productivity. . . . Do you have a copy machine? . . . a fax? . . . laser printer? I'm going to switch you to Richard, who will tell you about the new three-in-one copy–printer–fax from Bosco." Sugging grossly misleads and "spoils" the marketplace for legitimate marketing research activities.

Finally, the questionnaire layout and length must reflect an overall appreciation for the respondent's time and effort. Ask the important matters first. Provide a post paid return envelope. A fax number makes it easy for respondents to give quick returns and to ask questions to the researcher.

Unfortunately, many mail surveys age in a customer's in-basket for several weeks. Some surveys will never return, despite the best procedures: telephone prenotification, a postcard reminder, premiums or cash inducements, and sending duplicate surveys to nonrespondents. Some recipients simply can't or won't give the time to the task; others don't want to answer the questions; many simply forget.

Telephone surveys represent a partial solution. Indeed, the ScheduTrax company could put two staff members—or a couple of students from this class—on the phone this afternoon and have summary tables from 400 or more interviews by tomorrow. This task is supported by inexpensive software that allows interviewers to follow a script on the computer screen, enter responses as they are given, conduct basic statistical analysis of the collected data, and display results in report format.

Telephone surveys have two key drawbacks. First, the telephone is a more intrusive medium than the mail. The interviewer may be interrupting a customer's schedule and may not receive enough of the customer's time to complete the survey. A key challenge will be to hold the respondent's interest through the entire set of questions that meet the information objectives of the researcher. It is wise to ask the most important questions up front.

Second, some businesspeople are very hard to reach by telephone. For example, pharmaceutical companies find it very difficult to survey physicians by telephone. When they are in the clinic, doctors are attending to patients, scribbling or dictating reports, and otherwise on the move. (Some drug companies have found that doctors are more responsive to mail surveys—that is, when they are printed on the back of $100 checks! Thus, the data come in as the checks are cashed.)

Joint Development and Testing   Many products in business markets require ongoing adjustments and developments after the purchase. Computers and other installations require frequent vendor–customer interactions and joint activities to hone operations,

---

5–2

FROM THE FIELD
Supply-Side Opportunity

While the chapter material emphasizes the garden of opportunities in the firm's customer base, buyer–seller relationships provide opportunities for both parties. Alcoa's project leader for material handling systems, Ken Main, paints a critical role for their vendors:

> We accomplished a lot of our efforts from the design of this material handling system through what I call vendor integration meetings. These are held on a monthly basis starting in December, as we were selecting vendors and getting them on board . . . We were depending upon our MAP (a material acquisition program at Alcoa) vendors to supply us with the utility that would allow us to send these defined message packets that we established. . . . All this was documented for our vendor use in what

I call a vendor integration document, which has become more or less the Bible by which we check and are doing our systems performance checking.[2]

Thus, formal interactions for material handling system development are important to purchasers as well as materials suppliers. Suppliers who participate in regular meetings with their customers the way Alcoa has invited its key vendors to do find themselves in a context to discover what strategic and operational issues keep their customers awake at night; what words, symbols, and communication channels are most reliable; what impediments prevent the full collaboration of a customer's personnel in the value creation process; and more.

---

adapt to new work requirements, and ensure the development of critical know-how at both organizations. For example, a vendor of pollution control devices called scrubbers will participate in the testing of its systems at an electric power company because both firms need the other's expertise and both recognize the emission control needs at multiple plants. This is discussed in greater detail in the product development coverage of Chapter 8.

Customer Visits If spending time at a customer's venue to test concepts and problem solve has value, it should come as no surprise that business marketers have been stepping up the frequency and complexity of customer visits. Hewlett–Packard is the oft-noted leader in design of and payoff from customers visits. Calling on a subset of key customers, using cross-functional teams, and following protocols that take the parties out of the conference rooms, a customer visitation program can be a powerful tool. Opportunities get spotted in operations, in the formal presentations of goals and plans, and—perhaps most uniquely—in the frank disclosures of customer's headaches and identification of problems.[3] From the Field 5–2 illustrates some of the parallel payoffs for customers.

The Acquisition of New Customers

Now that we have emphasized and illustrated the ocean of business opportunities with current customers, we can take up the matter of new customer acquisition. Notice our terminology. Some texts talk about *getting* new accounts or *winning* customers, but these terms suggest the essence of conquest. We want to underscore the process as one of securing a vital strategic asset. When the potential exists for a long-run relationship with customers, their acquisition should be regarded as an investment.

Most organizations make investment decisions on the basis of return on investment rates, net present value, or months (years) to reach break-even. When University Hospital buys a new magnetic resonance imaging (MRI) system, it estimates a multiyear stream of revenue from patients against the installation outlay and projected operating costs.

An increasing number of companies have begun to formalize a similar approach to customer valuation. **Customer lifetime value (LTV)** is an estimate of the net present value of the stream of benefits from a customer, less the burdens of servicing the account or managing the relationship. For a basic illustration, consider a public accounting firm, which will often serve a client for many years. The revenue from this relationship represents the chief benefit stream. The burdens include the direct costs of audits and reports, plus the costs of maintaining the account—training, entertainment, periodic meetings, even the annual Thanksgiving turkey gift baskets to the client's personnel. With this LTV perspective, a client billed $30,000 per year can take on six-figure significance. Likewise, a small environmental engineering firm doing $50 of overnight shipping per week can represent $10,000 in net present value to FedEx.

Let's develop a greater understanding of the mechanics of LTV by returning to the ScheduTrax example. Exhibit 5–4 shows the purchase history of a group of customers at our software firm. Although some customers are one-shot buyers, the majority tend to purchase ancillary software products and upgrades over their lifetimes. Thus, the benefit stream from a new ScheduTrax customer goes beyond the initial software purchase.

To calculate lifetime value ScheduTrax uses a four-year horizon—after acquisition—and a 20 percent estimate for average direct costs. With customer mailing and quarterly telephone contacts, annual account maintenance costs are expected to average about $20 to recent customers but are characteristically lower to "older" customer segments. That is, recent purchasers get more marketing attention from ScheduTrax.

Because most accounts are rather small and ScheduTrax wants to postpone decimals in the lifetime value calculations, it evaluates the LTV of 100 customers. The middle of Exhibit 5–4 maps the "migration" of 100 acquired accounts into different segments defined by the recency of their last purchase. Notice that over the first year some (60 percent) historically rebuy and remain "recent" buyers; the other 40 "age" into year-ago customers. Projecting the distribution of customers in the second year after acquisition involves calculating the expected purchasers from two segments: 60 recent buyers and 40 year-ago buyers. The former segment provides ScheduTrax 36 buyers (.6 × 60); the latter provides 16 buyers (.4 × 40). The 24 nonbuyers in the period from each of the two segments accordingly "age" into the next recency category. Accounting for buyers in the third year after acquisition involves estimates from three segments: recent buyers, year-ago buyers, and two-years-ago buyers. The process is repeated in the fourth year, when buyers come from four segments defined by years since last purchase.

The profit model in the bottom portion of Exhibit 5–4 reflects the historical pattern at ScheduTrax that customers who have not recently purchased show a lower probability of purchasing and a lower expected amount of purchase. The profit forecast reflects the gross profit from all groups of purchasers in each future period, less the service costs associated with the segment specific marketing program. At the bottom, cash flow is discounted at 10, 15, and 20 percent to highlight the sensitivity of the valuation to ScheduTrax's opportunity cost of money.

As you can see, LTV is a statistical estimate. It hinges on the relevance of historical data, the proximity of the horizon, the choice of a discount rate, and the accuracy of anticipated account maintenance charges. At no business is it a known constant, like the force of gravity on the earth's surface, 9.8 m/sec^2. Nevertheless, using the best available data in concert with one's explicit assumptions about buyer behaviors, LTV

Exhibit 5–4   ScheduTrax Lifetime Value Analysis

					Expected customer migrations following acquisition			
Yrs. since the last purchase	Purchase probability	Expected $ purchases	Account service costs	Acquisition period	1st yr. after acquisition	2nd yr. after acquisition	3rd yr. after acquisition	4th yr. after acquisition
0	0.60	$90	$20	100 → customers	60.0	36.0 16.0 52.0	31.2 9.6 4.8 45.6	27.4 8.3 2.9 1.9 40.5
					40.0	24.0 24.0	20.8 14.4 19.2	18.2 12.5 11.5 17.3
1	0.40	$60	$10					
2	0.20	$50	$ 4					
3	0.10	$50	$ 2					

Profit forecasts

Acq +1   [60 buyers ($90)] × .8 gross profit − [100 accts × $20 service/acct] = $2,320

Acq +2   [36 buyers ($90) + 16 buyers ($60)] .8 gr. profit − [60 accts × $20 + 40 accts × $10] = $1,760

Acq +3   [31.2 buyers ($90) + 9.6 buyers ($60) + 4.8 buyers ($50)] .8 gr. profit − [52 accts × $20 + 24 × $10 + 24 × $4] = $1,523

Acq +4   [27.4 buyers ($90) + 8.3 buyers ($60) + 2.9 buyers ($50) + 1.9 buyers ($50)] − [45.6 accts × $20 + 20.8 × $10 + 14.4 × $4 + 19.2 × $2] = $1,345

Discounting profits:	NPV @ 10%	NPV @ 15%	NPV @ 20%
Acq +1	$2,109	$2,017	$1,933
Acq +2	$1,455	$1,331	$1,222
Acq +3	$1,144	$1,002	$ 881
Acq +4	$ 919	$ 769	$ 649
LTV/100 customers	$5,627	$5,119	$4,686

5–1

BUSINESS 2 BUSINESS

LTV as a Motive to Relate

Chapters 2 and 3 introduced the nature of business markets and purchasing by spotlighting the shift in supply management away from countless small decisions. Auto companies, computer firms, and heavy equipment manufacturers once made thousands of decisions as they purchased from scores and even hundreds of suppliers. Since the mid-1980s purchasers have consolidated suppliers, moved toward global sourcing, and sought long-term supply partnerships. Consultant Adrian Slywotzky sums up the shift:

> The number of decisions has moved from thousands to hundreds, the number of suppliers from hundreds to dozens, the length of contracts for single-year to multiyear, the scope from regional to global. Fewer decisions, higher stakes, higher rewards, and much higher risks.[4]

The impact is vividly illustrated in Ford's supply strategy for the Mondeo, a world car. Winning suppliers were awarded purchase volume for not just 200,000 units—U.S. domestic volume—but 700,000 units anticipated across the globe. Furthermore, good performance gives suppliers a powerful advantage for converting their initial one-year contract into a long-running relationship via a three-year renewal. What was once a 200,000-unit decision has become a 2-million–unit decision.

Do you think the parties to trading relationships such as these dabble with lifetime value analysis?

should be estimated and applied as a key yardstick for planning customer service strategies, assessing customer acquisition programs, and more. In the next section we will use the LTV calculations from Exhibit 5–4 as we explore a few of the more common means of acquiring new customers.

The Search for Look-Alikes

The ScheduTrax customer mix we examined in Exhibit 5–3 showed a concentration of retail chains and nursing staffs. Maybe these two sectors represent our best growth opportunities. But let's not jump to this conclusion. Maybe this software has particular appeal in those sectors of the economy. Perhaps these are the markets in which ScheduTrax has concentrated its marketing effort. Perhaps the majority of businesses operate in these two sectors. Simply put, we need to augment information from the customer database with additional market data.

Exhibit 5–5 does just that. Market effort scores on the far right are the average of reports given by top management. Market size estimates come from a mailing list company that has compiled data from the Yellow Pages and other directories from across the country.

Now we can see that although ScheduTrax has a high number of retailers as customers, they represent just a small percentage of the market. ScheduTrax has attained only this modest level of penetration despite intense marketing effort. In contrast, hospital nursing directors are just 20 percent of the customers in deciles 2 to 4, but they have received just moderate marketing effort, and represent a 30 percent penetration rate. Seemingly, ScheduTrax has a strong appeal in this market. Opportunity knocks!

Exhibit 5–5   ScheduTrax Account Profiles with Penetration and Effort Scores

Type of Business	No. of Accts.	% of Customers	Last Yr's. Purchases	No. of Organizations in the Business	Market Penetration	Sought Mkt. Penetration	Effort Index
Education	355	0.035%	$164,520	18,271	2%	2%	4
Entertainment	263	0.026	189,831	38,864	1	3	3
Nursing care	2,046	0.202	1,252,887	6,820	30	35	3
Manufacturing	739	0.073	455,595	431,278	0	2	4
Professional serv.	1,195	0.118	746,670	678,957	0	5	5
Retail	3,525	0.348	2,202,043	980,241	0	3	5
Transportation	1,043	0.103	651,754	13,289	8	6	3
Other	962	0.095	664,410				
Total	10,130	1.000	6,327,710	2,167,720			

Note: Market penetration is ScheduTrax accounts/number of organizations. Sought mkt. penetration is ScheduTrax accounts/number of organizations in the business receiving marketing effort from ScheduTrax, reflecting other segmentation criteria (e.g., firm size) and nth name testing of certain segments.

Let's suppose the ScheduTrax marketing folks tell their advertising agency about their interest in developing the hospital market. Two weeks later the agency proposes a well-conceived program that integrates mail, telephone, and a demonstration disk for their top software product. Certainly, the proposed campaign is superior to anything ever done in this industry—it's creative, dramatic, and sensitive to market needs, the graphics are stunning, and it has a powerful close. ScheduTrax managers are now head scratching. Is it worth the agency's price tag, $45,000?

If we work the numbers a bit, we can see that ScheduTrax needs to get 375 orders of its introductory system to break even on this marketing program. That is, at a price of $150 and an 80 percent gross margin, the break-even volume is $45,000/$120 per order. In a target market of just 4,774 prospects (market size, less currently served ScheduTrax accounts), this represents a lofty response rate, 7.8 percent. No program at ScheduTrax has ever pulled more than a 5.4 percent order rate.

But isn't it shortsighted for ScheduTrax to require the acquisition program to produce what amounts to a one-year payback period. Indeed, the one-year break-even criterion smacks of conquest marketing. ScheduTrax is better advised to consider acquisition program costs against the expected LTV from new accounts. This new break-even number of customers is given by setting $45,000 = ($120 + LTV/acquired customer) × (no. of new accounts). Using the most conservative LTV estimate from Exhibit 5–4, we can solve for the break-even response rate.

> At lifetime break-even:
> $45,000/($120 gr. profit from initial purchase + $4,686 LTV/100 customers) = 267
> 267 customers to break even/4,774 = 5.6%

This break-even response rate is one-third smaller than the target for conquest marketing! Although still on the high end of the range of ScheduTrax experience, the strength of the agency proposal is apt to get it the go-ahead.

In summary, a firm's customers represent the intersection of its past marketing efforts and the competitive strengths of its offering to the target market. A business has an opportunity to acquire new customers that "look like" existing customers when the firm's

5–2

BUSINESS 2 BUSINESS

Stick with Me, Folks

The Loctite Corporation developed an inexpensive dispenser of industrial adhesives, hoping to penetrate small assemblers and achieve its corporate goal of being the world's number one adhesives company. Frankly, internal enthusiasm for the new dispenser, the Bond-a-matic 2000, was quite weak. The product was to sell at a low price, to be within the dollar range of purchasing authority at the manager level, and not be a capital item, so its margin was way below those of other Loctite dispensing equipment. The marketing program to launch it had a break-even market share of nearly 30 percent! Viewed as a singular product offering, the Bond-a-matic appeared to be a loser.

But from another perspective, the product had substantial promise. Might the availability of a low-cost dispensing system spur small assemblers to switch from metal fasteners to adhesives? And might the incremental adhesive sales generated by the Bond-a-matic more than recoup the heavy customer acquisition costs?

With gross profit from the Bond-a-matic only about twice that from a pound of adhesive (about $20), what LTV would you estimate from 100 Bond-a-matic adopters?[5]

What other firms will join the likes of Meritor Automotive of Troy, Michigan, to participate in the continuing industrialization of China?

Courtesy Meritor Automotive.

offering represents a good match to their needs and the firm hasn't fully penetrated the segment. If the firm's market share in the segment is already high, the segment may be practically saturated. The search for opportunity might be better directed elsewhere.

Finding and Developing New Markets

Our thirst for oil has brought us into some of the harshest environments on earth: the North Sea, the Arabian deserts, the Alaskan tundra, and the Andean jungles. In parallel, the quest for new business has brought companies to many vexing and precarious markets. What parts suppliers will serve the fledgling automotive industry in Vietnam? What broadcasting and telecommunications opportunities are unfolding in Russia? What consulting and analytical service companies will strive to serve the exploding credit card field in the Pacific rim?

Exhibit 5–6

Secondary
Information
Sources

Just a few years ago a business marketer would call the public library to make sure the number one business reference librarian was on staff that day, and then plan to camp there most of the afternoon. Today, most of those eye-taxing microfilms and dusty bound onion-skin documents are available on the World Wide Web. Here are some key starting points for your specific subject searches:

1. The University of Michigan Document Center is a compendium of statistical resources on the web. Data on agriculture, business and industry, economics, energy, education, foreign governments, transportation and more are neatly indexed and available at: **http://www. lib.umich.edu/libhome/Documents.center/index.html**

2. Thomas Register is a directory of businesses sorted primarily by industry and geography. The database can be searched to identify and access companies in a particular line of trade or region. For example, a search for companies that provide controls for oil field pumps reveals 19 companies, some of which have hyperlinks to on-line catalogs. Thomas Register maintains several specialty directories as well. Access this source at URL **http://www.thomasregister.com**

3. North American Industrial Classification System Manual details the entire classification system and is available at **http://www.census.gov/epcd/www/naics.html**

Use your search engine to find a bevy of specialty resources. For example,

1. To find architects in the southwest or contractors in New England, try Directory of Building Trades at **http://www.buildingtradesdir.com/**

2. To land conventions at your new conference center, try the Directory of Associations at Convention Central: **http://conventioncentral.com/**

Geographic expansion is the most frequently used means of business growth. Of course, not every new territory is a strange new land. An industrial laundry service in Dearborn, Michigan, can open new plants in Lexington, Kentucky, and Knoxville, Tennessee, without coping with (entirely) new languages or currencies. Nevertheless, it may find unique competitive pressures and special customer needs in each new market.

Sometimes a business can transfer its experience in one industry to another. Sealed Air Corporation manufactures a variety of packaging materials, from Jiffy bags and foam to plastic bubble wraps. With slight production modifications, the bubble wrap material can serve as solar blankets for swimming pools. F&W Publications is a business publisher that developed a strong position in one trade—writers—and then developed new magazines for other trades—professional artists and woodworking hobbyists.

Business marketers can use a host of research resources and tools to find new markets. Government agencies, trade groups and publications, and various compilers publish statistics on industry trends and market structure (number of competitors, their size, product prices, and buying criteria) that are highly accessible to the business marketer. Exhibit 5–6 highlights some of the often used public and commercial sources.

Of course, our key customer research tools, focus groups and questionnaires, can be administered to prospective customers. Compared to their use with current accounts, one should expect greater difficulty in securing focus group participation. Likewise, survey response rates will generally pale in comparison to customer surveys. This makes for sticky inference. Imagine a survey that nets a 15 percent return rate; two-thirds of the respondents express keen interest in the product concept. Does this mean the product appeals to two-thirds of the market . . . or only to two-thirds of 15 percent—in other words, a mere 10 percent of the market?

Market Segmentation

This is not your first marketing class. You know that market segmentation involves partitioning the general need for a solution to a class of problems into smaller clusters involving distinct markets. These clusters are comprised of buyers or potential buyers that share similar traits, buying patterns, information needs, benefits sought, psychographic profiles, product experiences, industry participation, and the like. But the purpose is not to simply slice and dice, nor to produce snappy bubble charts or tables. The segments are meaningful to the extent they are differentially responsive to different marketing programs. And a business opportunity rests in segments where our firm has an ability to serve customers better than the rest at a profit.

We like the way English author Simon Majaro emphasizes this notion of fit in his definition of segmentation: "a strategy that enables the firm to maximize the results of a given marketing effort by exploiting clearly identified strengths in relation to a submarket which is either inadequately satisfied by other [suppliers] or where the firm is particularly well placed to do an effective job."[6] This perspective provides plenty of room for creative segmentation schemes and different segmentation tools. It also recognizes that not every product is a breakthrough and that the competitive arena is rarely docile. Let's illustrate some typical segmentation approaches in business markets and highlight the opportunities of "fit" they reveal.

Industrial Classification Systems: SIC to NAICS

The **Standard Industrial Classification (SIC) codes** were developed by the U.S. government to collect and disseminate meaningful information on different sectors of the economy. Since the 1930s the SIC system has organized the nation's economy into 10 divisions. Within each division are two-digit designations of major groups of companies, categorized on the basis of their primary output. Each major group is comprised of three-digit designated industry groups, which are comprised of several specific industries designated by four-digit codes.

After decades of use by business marketers to classify customers and label target markets, SIC codes have now been replaced by a new systems called **NAICS** (pronounced "knacks"), the **North American Industrial Classification System**. Although trade lingo, promotional literature, and company planning documents are sure to include some SIC holdover classifications, NAICS establishes a common code between the United States, Canada, and Mexico. It is compatible with the United Nations' two-digit system of industry classification, ISIC, and has been designed to include industries in services and emerging technology fields.

NAICS is based on a six-digit hierarchical code, thus allowing for finer distinctions between industries than SIC does. This finer-grained approach begins at the first level. NAICS groups the economy into 20 major sectors. Newly created sectors including Education Services (61); Health Care and Social Assistance (62); Art, Entertainment, and Recreation (71); and Accommodation and Foodservices (72) were previously lumped into the SIC division called Service Industries. Exhibits 5–7 and 5–8 contrast and detail the new codes.

As a segmentation tool, NAICS and its predecessor SIC codes help the business marketer assess the size of a particular industry for which its product is thought to have particular relevance. For example, FedEx targeted companies in SIC 5961, "Nonstore retailers—catalog and mail-order houses," to generate leads where it might negotiate a contract for handling some or all of its package delivery. Similarly, if your company has

Exhibit 5–7

NAICS Sectors and Their Corresponding SIC Divisions

Code	NAICS Sectors	SIC Divisions Making the Largest Contributions
11	Agriculture, Forestry, Fishing, and Hunting	Agriculture, Forestry, and Fishing Manufacturing
21	Mining	Mineral Industries
22	Utilities	Transportation, Communication, and Utilities
23	Construction	Construction Industries
31–33	Manufacturing	Manufacturing
42	Wholesale Trade	Wholesale Trade
44–45	Retail Trade	Retail Trade Wholesale Trade
48–49	Transportation	Transportation, Communication, and Utilities
51	Information	Transportation, Communication, and Utilities Manufacturing Service Industries
52	Finance and Insurance	Finance, Insurance, and Real Estate
53	Real Estate and Rental and Leasing	Finance, Insurance, and Real Estate Service Industries
54	Professional, Scientific, and Technical Services	Service Industries
55	Management of Companies and Enterprises	Financial, Insurance, and Real Estate auxiliary establishments in all industries
56	Administrative and Support, Waste Management, and Remediation Services	Service Industries Transportation, Communication, and Utilities Manufacturing Construction Industries
61	Education Services	Service Industries
62	Health Care and Social Assistance	Service Industries
71	Arts, Entertainment, and Recreation	Service Industries Retail Trade Finance, Insurance, and Real Estate
72	Accommodation and Foodservices	Retail Trade Service Industries
81	Other Services (except Public Administration)	Service Industries Finance, Insurance, and Real Estate
92	Public Administration	Public Administration Service Industries

SOURCE: Paul Zeisset and Mark E. Wallace, "How NAICS Will Affect Data Users." U.S. Bureau of the Census, 1997.

developed an emergency safety bath for treating chemical accidents, it is useful to know how many chemical companies might need to be equipped with such a device. Alternatively, a producer of plastic diaphragm pumps may wish to craft different sales and advertising messages for different industries. It is likely that prospects in the chemical industry are seeking corrosion resistance while prospects in the pharmaceutical field will need information about purity and cleanliness.[7]

Understand that the NAICs codes are not perfect. Codes are assigned to each physical facility on the basis of the predominant output at the location. Although predominant output is supposed to be regarded in terms of value added, accounting difficulties often

Exhibit 5–8   Examples of NAICS Hierarchy

NAICS Level	Example 1		Example 2	
	NAICS Code	Description	NAICS Code	Description
Sector	31–33	Manufacturing	51	Information
Subsector	334	Computer and electronic product manufacturing	513	Broadcasting and telecommunications
Industry group	3346	Manufacturing and reproduction of magnetic and optical media	5133	Telecommunications
Industry group	33461	Manufacturing and reproduction of magnetic and optical media	51332	Wireless telecommunications carriers, except satellite
U.S. industry	334611	Reproduction of software	513321	Paging

SOURCE: Paul Zeisset and Mark E. Wallace, "How NAICS Will Affect Data Users," U.S Bureau of the Census, 1997.

lead to classification on the basis of sales. Large firms with multiple products emerging from a single site will still have only one code. Firms interested in marketing to specific six-digit SIC classifications may wish to look at its specialization and coverage ratios, available around March 1999 in the *Census of Manufacturers,* to keep an eye on their targeting efficiency. The **specialization ratio** indicates the percentage of total shipments by firms in a classification that is accounted for by the particular product of that specific code. A tightly focused industry has a high specialization ratio; most of the total business done by firms in this code is in the field coded. The **coverage ratio** reports the percentage of product shipments accounted for by firms actually assigned the classification of the product. Thus, a high coverage ratio means that firms producing the bulk of this product or service actually are accounted for in the category.

Company Characteristics

Company sales, number of employees, number of locations, degree of vertical integration, and other fairly observable traits can be powerful segmentation variables. Because of differences in service needs, buying criteria, and expertise, many business marketers classify customers on the basis of size. Often the breakdown features Fortune 500 firms, other named accounts, midsized firms (say, those with $10 million to 90 million in sales), and small businesses. It is difficult for a business marketer to dominate across the size spectrum. Although Xerox is the world's leading copier company, its sales are topped by both Canon and Sharp among low-volume users.

Buying Processes

Business marketers often find it productive to sort prospective customers on the basis of how they buy. Is it a new task or a rebuy? Personnel from different functional areas may participate in the decision at some firms, while at others participation is limited. Some prospective accounts use a bidding process, others do not.

Some buyers work with a strict "purchasing mentality," meaning that they simply seek the lowest price on tightly defined products, such as corrugated boxes, printing, or bulk chemicals. Other buyers may rely on a buying center that takes a broader view of supply in the value creation process. Perhaps packaging is not just an afterthought, but a means of ensuring quality through storage and transport, an avenue for distinguishing the brand, and part of a process that offers opportunities for efficiency gains in the use of labor and working capital (especially inventory). For a supplier with excellent sourcing capabilities and efficient operations, the first type of buyer is its bread and butter. For a supplier with a distinguished sales force of packaging expertise, the latter type of account is its mainstay.

Benefits Sought

Most business marketers find it difficult to be all things to all customers. When customers differ in the priorities they place on specific performance dimensions, marketers must be sure to properly match their offering to the segment seeking what their product does best. An electric motor company found its low-horsepower motors had special appeal for users in regions where electricity rates were high because they provided significant savings in operating costs. Users of motors in cheap-electricity settings put stock in other performance criteria, such as durability, torque, and ease of mounting, depending on their application.

A motor manufacturer that wants to serve several segments will need a carefully conceived positioning strategy. **Positioning** is a loosely used term that generally refers to marketing efforts to secure a valued categorization in the mind of a customer. Serving customers in a segment that values economy, the product perceived to have reliability and low operating costs will have a winning position. For the customer seeking performance in extreme heat situations, a seller must establish credibility as a provider of superior cooling or high stress tolerance. Because it strains credibility that a single product can be best across the diverse criteria of several segments, we typically see multiple product lines and distribution channels reflected in multiple positioning strategies.

A major manufacturer of large-scale electrical equipment (e.g., transformers) used a sample survey of potential customers—investor-owned electrical utilities, municipalities, rural electrification cooperatives, and industrial firms that generated or distributed electrical power—to identify customer characteristics, different levels of favorability toward the company ("switchability"), and preferences for product performance dimensions, as well as beliefs about the relative strength of the manufacturer on these dimensions. So electrical equipment buyers gave importance and performance ratings on criteria such as price, appearance of the product, availability of spare parts, ease of installation, energy loss, maintenance requirements, and so on. From statistical models based on the switchability and benefits-sought data, the manufacturer was able to segment the 7,000-customer market into 12 distinct segments. Targeting the "switchables" in each segment with unique direct mail messages—emphasizing the particular performance benefits and products the analysis identified as most important—the manufacturer achieved documented sales gains of 15 percent and more, compared to markets where the positioning strategy was not applied.[8]

Finally, as competing firms grow in their understanding of a market, each adapts what it regards as apt positioning strategies. Of course, what the customers perceive, believe, and retain become more important than the actual symbols, messages, and media used in the positioning campaigns. Now customer perceptions of the similarities in offerings start to take on special significance in the structure of the market. Perceptual maps represent a class of tools that help to reveal customers' mental picture of the marketplace. Typically beginning with customer survey data indicating the degree to which pairs of

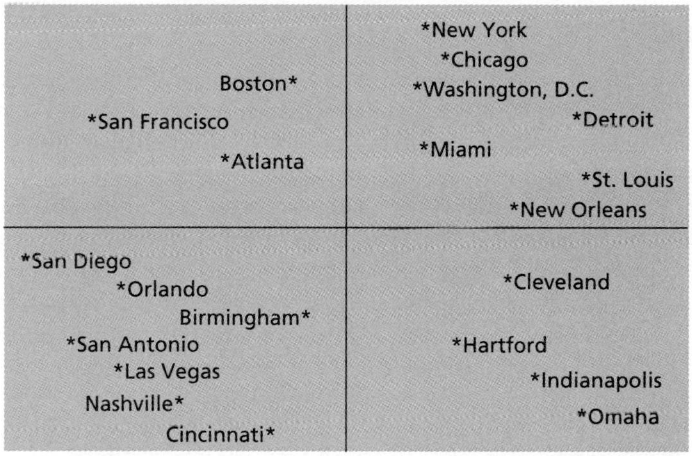

Exhibit 5–9

Perceptual Maps Reveal Opportunities into the Dimensions Customers Use to Discriminate among Products and in the Gaps and Clusters of Competing Products.

This map represents the similarities of potential convention cities as perceived by conference and convention planners at midsized associations, those with memberships between 5,000 and 10,000. What labels would you give the x and y axes? How would you recommend the city of Indianapolis promote itself?

products are regarded as similar, researchers apply a mathematical algorithm that puts the products in two- or three-dimensional space in a way that has similar products in close proximity (see the example in Exhibit 5–9). Marketing personnel often find value from perceptual maps because they can reveal (1) new dimensions on which customers seem to be discriminating among products, (2) clusters of competitors defined by customers, not by NAICS, and (3) opportunities for positioning products in new ways.

Memberships and Media

Creative marketers have successfully served business market segments defined by membership in professional societies, trade associations, and even readership of a particular publication. If members of an association or professional group represent a population likely to have a significant number of potential buyers, it makes good sense to give them marketing attention.

Why not capitalize on what you know about association members in the design of your marketing program? Use the language of the particular group (e.g., Chem show attendees, Business/Professional Advertising Association members, pharmaceutical manufacturers) to convey your firm's understanding of their needs and to tout the benefits of your product measured against the member's priorities. Ads for a particular publication, direct mail copy for a specific association, and trade show materials for a defined group of attendees all reflect tailored marketing activities derived from segmentation based on memberships.

By now you should have a good sense for the assortment of variables that can be used effectively to segment business markets. We have not exhausted the possibilities. Certainly, geography, language, conformity to industry or government standards, affinity groups, usage of other products, or qualifying behaviors can be used as well. Even the simple classification of a professional title can be a powerful segmentation variable. FedEx would not send a Secretaries Day card to Joe Bagadonuts on the shipping dock, even though Joe—like many secretaries—makes the call to use FedEx.

We are certain to illustrate many of these segmentation possibilities in later chapters that discuss marketing program development and control. But before we leave the discussion of segmentation, let's take stock of the essence of a useful segmentation approach.

Segment Criteria

One's objective in this process is to define good market segments. Good markets are identifiable, accessible, and substantial. These criteria work well to discipline the tasks of gauging opportunities and directing marketing effort. **Identifiable** members of market segments can be enumerated and evaluated. Imagine a cardiologist who developed a healthy heart program for overworked and overweight executives. Is there a practical way to identify such individuals? The cardiologist might advertise her service and/or invite prospects to a power breakfast seminar or a free risk screening. Prospects might not be so willing to identify themselves, however, if the service were for coping with chemical addictions.

Accessibility means that members of a market can be reached or impacted by some directed marketing activity. American Express knew that to get companies to adopt its corporate card, an American Express sales rep had to get some time with the prospect firm's chief financial officer. Years of advertising, direct mail, and attempted sales calls still left 400 attractive but inaccessible accounts.

The ability to approach or address known prospective customers is necessary but not sufficient to make an opportunity. That market must be **substantial**, promising sufficient business to justify the efforts to serve it. Customer lifetime value is a useful criterion in an assessment of a target market. Unfortunately, a firm's history with its current customers may provide very little basis for estimating the LTV of customers from entirely new markets.

Market Assessment Tools

Substantial markets can be revealed by a number of estimation techniques. One very powerful approach is the use of scenarios. **Scenarios** comprise a forecasting technique that requires managers to write explicit anticipated futures and articulate the chains of events that would need to occur to make the future happen. For example, Royal Dutch Shell tuned its supply strategy when its scenario process in 1973 found no compelling reasons for Arab states to increase their crude oil production.[9] Furthermore, one of this book's authors helped an environmental management company determine the market for certain types of training. The task involved getting accurate counts of employees in different industries who handled hazardous and toxic materials, plus an assessment of the likelihood of new government regulations that—by fiat or new economic sanctions—would impact the training demand.

A related approach involves hard thinking and analysis of how the product fits into the value-added process. This approach is sometimes called the **buildup approach** or **factoring**. Market estimates by this approach come from building up the materials or parts units needed in a specific application or from specific accounts. For example, potential demand for a surgical staple designed for closing Caesarian sections can be estimated from a count of the average number of staples needed to close a typical C-section, times the number of C-sections performed in different countries. Projections in each country are apt to show different trends, based on differences in hospital protocols, fertility patterns, and population distributions.

The same basic approach can be applied using survey responses from prospects (e.g., responses to "What volume of beer do you plan to brew in the coming years?" could help in estimating demand for water, yeast, and hops) or from members of the sales force (e.g., "What accounts are apt to replace their copiers in the next 12 months?")

Likewise, the volume of certain materials, logistical services, or MRO (maintenance, repair and operating) goods can be compared to finished products output in a statistical series. A **statistical series** is an estimation technique that uses the correlation between

Exhibit 5–10

Using a Statistical Series to Estimate the Drywall Market in S. Metro

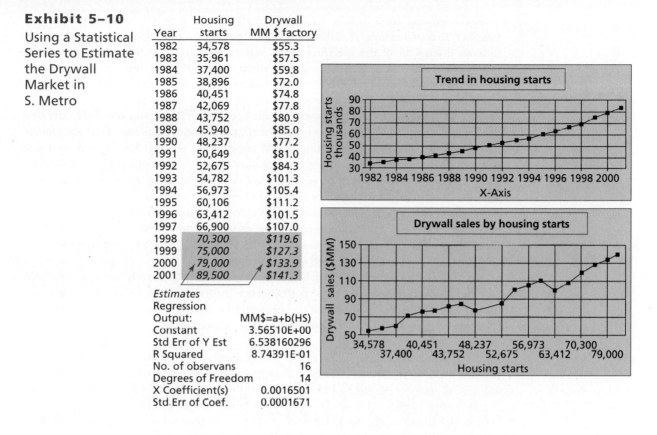

Year	Housing starts	Drywall MM $ factory
1982	34,578	$55.3
1983	35,961	$57.5
1984	37,400	$59.8
1985	38,896	$72.0
1986	40,451	$74.8
1987	42,069	$77.8
1988	43,752	$80.9
1989	45,940	$85.0
1990	48,237	$77.2
1991	50,649	$81.0
1992	52,675	$84.3
1993	54,782	$101.3
1994	56,973	$105.4
1995	60,106	$111.2
1996	63,412	$101.5
1997	66,900	$107.0
1998	*70,300*	*$119.6*
1999	*75,000*	*$127.3*
2000	*79,000*	*$133.9*
2001	*89,500*	*$141.3*

Estimates

Regression Output:	MM$=a+b(HS)
Constant	3.56510E+00
Std Err of Y Est	6.538160296
R Squared	8.74391E-01
No. of observans	16
Degrees of Freedom	14
X Coefficient(s)	0.0016501
Std. Err of Coef.	0.0001671

demand and some other set of economic activities to yield a forecast. For example, Exhibit 5–10 plots a hypothetical relationship between gypsum sales and housing starts in a metro market. The top graph shows a fairly consistent trend in housing starts. The bottom graph shows a good, but not perfect, association between housing starts and drywall sales; their correlation is .93. To forecast sales, the linear relationship between housing starts and drywall sales can be applied in the bottom of the exhibit using projected housing starts for the next four years as the x values.

Summary

This chapter has emphasized the value of current customers as a treasure trove of opportunity. Because not all customers are created equal, it makes sense to develop distinct programs for different accounts and groups of customers. Best customers deserve special attention and marketing effort to retain and expand their purchase volume. Their familiarity with and trust of the company often make current customers a rich market for new products. And high-quality working relationships with select accounts often provide strategic connections to other opportunities in the business environment.

We highlighted the customer database in a brief overview of tools for finding opportunities among current accounts. The database is structured to support account management activities with best customers as well as targeted communications and programs for specific customer clusters. It also supports customer research by identifying potential focus group and sample survey participants.

Focus groups are a loosely structured interview of 6 to 12 individuals brought together at one location. A skilled moderator guides the participants in a rather free-flowing discussion of the specified topics. Often repeated in different locations with new participants, focus groups are an excellent means of exploring customer motivations and product-related behaviors, generating ideas, and provoking new questions about opportunities.

Surveys also belong in the customer research toolbox. The one-on-one field interview can be a rich source of information, but travel and personnel expenses limit its application. Instead, companies try to bring several respondents together for a group interview (focus group) or use alternative communication channels—mail or telephone—to complete the interview. Both must be administered with proper appreciation of the customer relationship that circumscribes this particular interaction.

Mail surveys can be quite detailed and conducted at low cost. But even with all the tricks for garnering high response rates, responses may come slowly, or from the wrong informant, or never at all. The phone solves the turnaround problem, but often at a cost of frequent callbacks and shortened questionnaires.

The tools of customer research can be applied to the search for new markets, usually as complements to secondary market information from various trade and government sources. Unfortunately, prospective customers seldom participate to the same degree as current customers, making nonresponse a vexing issue for statistical estimation.

We affirmed the tendency of an increasing number of companies to treat customer acquisition as an investment. We have long given lip service to the notion that customers are a vital asset for the firm, but only recently have significant numbers of businesses begun to put a dollar value on the worth of the asset. Customer lifetime value (LTV) is a statistical estimate of the net present value of the cash flow from an account or group of accounts. LTV is not a hard number to be mechanically applied to the quest for new customers that look like current money-making accounts. LTV is better regarded as a perspective and tool involving significant judgment.

To evaluate opportunities to acquire new customers, it is critical to segment the market in a judicious manner that enables the matching of company strengths to unmet or underserved customer needs. Business markets can often be segmented meaningfully using industrial classification systems. SIC and the new NAICS codes are hierarchically structured classifications of businesses based on their principal output, with 20 two-digit sectors plus four-digit industry groups and six-digit U.S. industries.

The chapter demonstrated how business markets can be segmented on the basis of organizational buying processes, benefits sought, and memberships. We highlighted the role of segmentation for positioning strategies and previewed the means of segmenting according to the prospective customer's location, language, personal characteristics, business behaviors, usage of other products, and more.

As we consider potential market segments, we should recognize that opportunity is related to three criteria: Members of the segment must be identifiable, accessible, and substantial. Segments can be substantiated by a variety of analytical tools. We highlighted the utility of scenarios, the buildup or factoring approach, and statistical series for segment evaluation.

Key Terms

accessible (segment members)

account retention

buildup approach

customer lifetime value (LTV)

decile report

empathic dialogue

factoring

focus group

identifiable (segment members)

North American Industrial Classification System (NAICS)

positioning

sample surveys

scenarios

SIC/NAICS coverage ratio

SIC/NAICS specialization ratio

Standard Industrial Classification (SIC) codes

statistical series

substantial (segment potential)

sugging

Discussion Questions

1. Caller ID has become a popular option for consumer home telephones, especially among single women and busy professionals. In business, the feature has been in use for several years at some companies. They speak of its significance for improving customer service. Explore the potential of this feature in a modern information technology environment.

2. A small local graphics firm uses Quicksilver, a downtown courier service, to send art and proofs to clients, printers, and photographers in the conduct of its business. Sketch a framework for estimating the lifetime value of this account to Quicksilver.

3. Assess the utility of your university's information system to provide decile reports, decile profiles, and the like to support marketing efforts that maximize customer value and support the quest for look-alikes.

4. The university president has now indicated that all the student information management functions will be outsourced. How does a potential IT service firm differ from Quicksilver in its estimate of the LTV from its customer, the university?

5. The Holden brothers were experienced in travel and event promotions and explored the opportunity to sell promotional literature—especially maps—to chambers of commerce. They planned to sell advertisements in the literature to area businesses, including chamber members, returning a portion of the ad revenue to the chamber of commerce client organization. What would be some of the key impediments to testing this concept in two or three focus groups? What three objectives would motivate a telephone survey of chambers of commerce from the World Directory?

6. Write a scenario depicting the campus recruiting process by AT&T or Shell Oil company in the year 2010. Now, what enabling conditions must be met for this scenario to occur? What business opportunities become manifest to (a) campus career development and placement centers, (b) image makers, (c) resume consultants, and (d) multimedia conferencing?

7. Your company has just developed a polymer to extend the life of asphalt by 40 percent. The polymer is added in the manufacturing process and represents just .01 percent of the asphalt mass. Define the market opportunity for this product on the criteria of being identifiable, accessible, and substantial.

8. When a financial institution switches from one phone or computer system to another, the original supplier is rightly apt to regard the account as lost for good. Because the actual switch had to overcome significant costs—investments in equipment, habits, and the painful setup period for the new systems—the original supplier is out in the cold, with little chance of ever returning to favor. For these types of account, lifetime value gets a highly deserved focus from vendors. It is an effective motivation for quality, logistical efficiency, and responsiveness because it is highly sensitive to the retention rate. Plot the eight-year LTV for an account that nets your firm $40,000 per year as its annual retention probability moves from .5 to .9.

9. You have invented and contracted the manufacture of a light-weight parts container that can be reused hundreds of times. Your research into global experiences with returnable parts containers indicates that government and industry in many countries are paying close attention to Germany, where returnable containers have been mandated. Meanwhile, voluntary use has expanded in tightly integrated firms where economic efficiency gains have been experienced. Develop a segmentation framework for your product.

10. What cautions would you issue to the expansion-minded distributor from Chicago thinking about planting a drywall warehouse in the market described in Exhibit 5–10? He has used the exhibit's statistical model to predict sales (and make cash flow analysis) over the next 10 years.

Internet Exercise

From the FedEx web page (**www.fedex.com**) identify a new service being offered, perhaps a new international service or delivery option. Now, think of two industries for which such a service is apt to be particularly appealing.

1. What are the NAICS codes for those two industries?

2. Use the Thomas Register to find the addresses of two firms in each of these industries near your home or school.

3. Sketch an agenda for a FedEx customer visit to these accounts. You should find tips for planning such visits on the web as well.

WWW
I N T E R N E T

Cases

Case 5.1 Gleason Printing

Amy Morton is marketing manager at Gleason Printing. For nearly seven months she has been researching the printing needs at the Metro Alliance for Wellness, a consortium of hospitals and therapy centers in Uniopolis. Amy figures that, excluding forms and billing, Metro contracts for about $800,000 in commercial printing business each year. Granted, some of the jobs involve special imaging or sizing that doesn't match Gleason's printing capabilities. But there's about $600,000 in business that Gleason could do well. It's been rumored for some time that Metro is looking for a printing supplier to get involved in its internal operations, setting up a communications network for electronically transferring images and text—primarily for shared creative input and rough copy checking—that would enable even more rapid and efficient contact with its various stakeholders. Indeed, Metro's CEO often appears on the lecture circuit talking about harnessing technology, the efficacy of the "virtual organization," and the need for the modern enterprise to "negotiate favorable terms" with *all* its stakeholders.

Morton has also researched the systems and intranet parameters that Metro needs for this vision. Assuming Metro bought all the hardware, any printer in on the setup would have to invest approximately $400,000 in installation, training, and testing—and, frankly, the numbers could well be twice that estimate. Morton was grateful for Metro's enthusiastic response to her proposal for some "in-context research," which basically would be a chance to live with Metro systems and personnel to better understand the issues and activities at Metro. Still, she needs to review what might come from the research—she is just not sure if Gleason should seek the business.

Case 5.2   Market Segmentation at WCP

B. J. Wickett and Jennifer Modabe were looking at market and share data recently distributed by the analytical staff at WCP (formerly Watson Cooking Products), a midsized manufacturer of institutional foods and supplies. WCP used its own sales force and a system of regional distribution centers to service customers nationwide. Advertising in trade publications and a substantial commitment to industry trade shows supported the efforts of the professional sales force.

B. J., a recent hire from a consumer packaged goods firm, argued that WCP had neglected key industries. "Look at these numbers! WCP is on the verge of becoming a minor player unless we boost our marketing here, here, and here," he exclaimed, pointing to the following table.

Jennifer countered that really no firm had been able to dominate every segment. "Furthermore, we should leverage our current channels and within-industry reputation by further penetrating markets where we are strong."

The recent analysis of the market for cooking oils produced the following data:

Institutions Accounting for These Amounts of Total Spending on Oils (Est. WCP Share)	Highest 25%	Middle 50%	Smallest 25%	Total volume	Number of firms
Hospitals	400 (50%)	2,000 (30%)	3,000 (50%)	$200	5,400
Hotels	5,000 (20%)	28,000 (15%)	30,000 (40%)	700	63,000
Restaurants	24,000 (25%)	80,000 (45%)	180,000 (20%)	900	284,000
Universities	—	—	—	—	—

1. What opportunities for WCP are indicated by this analysis?

2. Suggest a more refined segmentation analysis for one of these opportunities that meets the criteria of being identifiable, accessible, and substantial.

Additional Readings

Anderson, James, Hakan Hakansson, and Jan Johanson, "Dyadic Business Relationships within a Business Network Context," *Journal of Marketing* 58 (October 1994), pp. 1–15.

Barclay, Donald W., and Michael J. Ryan, "Microsegmentation in Business Markets: Incorporating Buyer Characteristics and Decision-Oriented Determinants," *Journal of Business-to-Business Marketing* 2 (1996), pp. 3–35.

Boyd, Harper, Ralph Westfall, and Stanley Stasch, *Marketing Research.* Homewood, IL: Richard D. Irwin, 1993.

David Shepherd Associates, *The New Direct Marketing: How to Implement a Profit-Driven Database Marketing Strategy.* Homewood, IL: Business One Irwin, 1990.

Day, George S., Allan D. Shocker, and Rajendra K. Srivastava, "Customer-Oriented Approaches to Identifying Product Markets," *Journal of Marketing* 43 (Fall 1979), pp. 8–19.

Dwyer, F. Robert, "Customer Lifetime Valuation to Support Marketing Decision Making," *Journal of Direct Marketing* 11 (Autumn 1997), pp. 6–13.

Gensch, Dennis H., "Targeting the Switchable Industrial Customer," *Marketing Science* 3 (Winter 1984), pp. 41–54.

McQuarrie, Edward F., "Taking a Road Trip: Customer Visits Help Companies Recharge Relationships and Pass Competitors," *Marketing Management* 3 (April 1995), pp. 8–21.

Nash, Edward, *Database Marketing: The Ultimate Marketing Tool.* New York: McGraw–Hill, 1993.

Roberts, Mary Lou, "Expanding the Role of the Direct Marketing Database," *Journal of Direct Marketing* 11 (Autumn 1997), pp. 26–35.

Zeisset, Paul, and Mark E. Wallace, "How NAICS Will Affect Data Users," U.S. Bureau of the Census, 1997 **(www.census.gov/epcd/www/naicsusr.html).**

Chapter 6

Marketing Strategy

MORGAN STANLEY

In the Fort section of Mumbai (formerly Bombay), India, we enter an historic turn-of-the-century building. The elevator is not working, so we hike up the dilapidated stairs to the fourth floor. Ta-da! It's a state-of-the-art financial office—Indian professionals at their computer workstations, supported by full-service power lines and telecommunications equipment. We have arrived at Morgan Stanley, the largest U.S. investment bank in India.●

Morgan Stanley has undertaken bold initiatives around the world: Johannesburg, Jakarta, Beijing, Sao Paulo, Geneva, and Singapore. Led by its aggressive president, John J. Mack, Morgan Stanley aims to ride the world's dramatic turn to capitalism. It is betting that sprouting free markets will show double-digit economic growth rates that eventually yield profits and wealth.●

Established in 1935 to continue the investment banking business of J.P. Morgan & Co., Morgan Stanley & Co. came on the New York Stock Exchange in 1941, created the first computer model for financial analysis in 1964, and developed equity research, sales, and trading in the 1970s. The 1980s saw Morgan diversify into governments and money markets, tax-exempt and mortgage-backed securities, and other lines. The formation of Morgan Stanley Global Services in 1987 accelerated overseas expansion. In 1994 Morgan Stanley initiated the first domestic Indian mutual fund. In 1995 it invested $35 million in a joint venture with the People's Construction Bank in Beijing. In 1996 it started a fund management company with a local partner in Malaysia.●

In tune with Chapter 5's logic of opportunity, Morgan's strengths seem to match its pursued segments. Indeed, one industry observer calls Morgan Stanley the "premier emerging markets firm." Another says, "They are the broadest in scope and the most daring to move into new places and they have a very large commitment." The topic of customer commitment is taken up in detail in Chapter 7, but we can preview some key facets by noting that part of Morgan Stanley's commitment derives from its ownership structure—it's 40 percent employee-owned. Another part is a result of Mack's efforts to "break down fiefdoms" within the company and push hard in markets where competitors were cutting back.

Asked about the risks to the vaunted Morgan Stanley name, the uncertainty of developing markets, and the vigorous and diverse competition in the global arena, Chairman Richard Fisher says the risks require intelligence and cost-consciousness. "I think we have the most resources and the most conviction. I could be wrong. We won't know for five years whether we are right."[1]

You can visit Morgan Stanley at **http://www.ms.com**.

Learning Objectives

In this chapter, we want to examine how firms in business markets develop the vision and plans to make major initiatives with long-term impact. In the process, you will learn to think more strategically. In military jargon a **strategy** involves the science and art of conducting a campaign—achieving some end—on a broad scale. We distinguish strategy from tactics on the basis of scope, the magnitude of resources applied, and the duration of impact or consequences. **Tactical decisions** occupy the narrow, limited, and short-run poles of these dimensions.

In an important departure from the military metaphor, business strategy seldom concludes with a vanquished "enemy." Morgan Stanley's strategy to establish a leadership position in the financial markets of emerging capitalistic economies will not end with the "surrender" by Goldman, Sachs. There will still be Merrill Lynch, First Boston, and others. In product markets around the world, new demands from users and adaptive competitors will continue to bring new strategic challenges. A goal in this chapter will be to offer ideas for enabling the organization to learn and adapt.

At the conclusion of the chapter you should be able to

- Describe the key elements of a business strategy.
- Conduct a SWOT analysis of an organization with which you are familiar.
- Analyze the structure of competition, considering five forces.
- Give examples of the fleeting nature of competitive advantage.
- Outline firm characteristics that should enable learning and the creation of dynamic strategies.

Why a Strategy?

With just a small number of passengers and a worn-out cabin crew, the mischievous pilot came on the PA: "Ladies and gentlemen, this is your captain speaking. I have a bit of bad news for you tonight. Our navigation equipment and radio have cut out on us. We don't know where we are. On the brighter side, folks, we're making very good time."

It is easy for any organization to get so occupied with day-to-day operations that it buries its sense of identity and loses touch with where it is headed. Every member of the crew seems busy, but not even the pilot knows if the ship is on course. We suspect you have fallen into this trap more than once yourself. Perhaps your preoccupation with class assignments and midterms—not to mention your job or family pressures—have kept you from taking the school's career search workshop or charting your own plan to land a good entry-level position. Unless we give some time to reflecting on what we are about, what we want to achieve, and what matters on the way to those goals, we face a very good chance of sinking under the weight of urgent but increasingly unimportant activities.

Furthermore, once we have settled and formally stated what we want to achieve and become, we need a plan to reach the desired ends. We can compare the process to vacationing. First, we need to determine what we need and can reasonably attain. Do we need rest or excitement? Do we want to test our physical skills and stamina or refresh our family ties? Can we afford a week or two away? What's the budget? Once you determine that you need a break from the pace of the city and need to renew old friendships, you might negotiate a bit with your friends before settling on a week of backpacking with three friends from high school in Yosemite National Park. Notice the apparent key needs underpinning the "mission": personal refreshment and renewal, outdoor recreation, and friendship investments.

With the mission determined, the remaining components to the strategy center on the means of achieving it. Obviously, this foursome will need to make travel arrangements. Do they fly and find a rental car or do they look to you to tune and put new tires on your '89 Suburban? What camping gear do they need? Should needed items be purchased, borrowed, or rented? And how should the trip be provisioned? Should each hiker pack independently? Maybe the most experienced (or most idle) should purchase food and other supplies. With this metaphor in mind, let's take a closer look at business strategy.

Elements of Business Strategy

The word *strategy* has become commonplace. Straining the military metaphor reviewed in the opening of the chapter, you have probably heard the term used to describe plans to bring world peace, revitalize a downtown business district, halve the high school dropout rate, build a nest egg for retirement, plan a vacation, complete a major class assignments, or even get through Friday afternoon traffic. But we are talking about a *business strategy* in this chapter. We want to be sure we share the same understanding of what it actually is. A business strategy should develop or reiterate a formal mission statement—which we will discuss later in the chapter—and address four fundamental issues—which we take up now.[2]

Product Markets

What markets do we serve with what products? To replay some of the essentials from Chapter 5, no company has the luxury of being able to serve every segment of potential customers. We have to consider how well equipped we are to serve different groups, relative

to the strength of our competition in those segments. The breadth of our product line is motivated by the diversity of preferences in the market, but simultaneously constrained by production and operational economies, by managerial and marketing complexities, and by limited financial resources. In large part, the products we offer to particular markets define the focus and direction of our company.

The implications of market served are vivid in the airlines, where Southwest Air concentrates on low-price, no-frills flights between carefully selected pairs of cities. Meanwhile, US Air and others emphasizing larger coverage via hub-and-spoke strategies have to emphasize service and connections.

Perhaps even more dramatic is the strategic significance of market selection in the computer field. For example, Cray Research, Inc., has concentrated on building supercomputers for research-intensive applications; NCR Corporation emphasizes parallel processing machines that can be bundled and used to manage large marketing and financial databases. Digital opted to not offer machines to the growing personal computer market in the 1980s. Meanwhile, IBM has chosen to participate in several business markets with a range of large, mini-, and personal computers. Microsoft, on the other hand, has the highest market value of any player in the computer field, but it makes nary a disk drive or monitor.

Exhibit 6–1 reveals another important and more dynamic way to consider the products and markets served. This graphic highlights the basic means by which an organization can grow. There are only four. A firm can seek greater **market penetration**—that is,

Exhibit 6–1
Product Market
Growth
Opportunities

	Present products	New products
Present markets	Market penetration	Product development
New markets	Market development	Diversification

SOURCE: Reprinted from Igor Ansoff, *The New Corporate Strategy* (1988), p. 83, with the permission of the copyright © owner, John Wiley & Sons, Inc.

endeavor to gain a larger share of the market in which it currently competes with its existing products. Hertz freshens its advertising and keeps its service levels high in an effort to raise its share of business car rental. Alternatively, a firm may pursue **product development**, trying to serve customers in markets where it already has a presence with a new array of products. Microsoft would like users of MS Word, EXCEL, and PowerPoint to adopt its web browser, Internet Explorer. **Market development** is the counterpart: Current products are taken to new markets. Clearly, Morgan Stanley is bent on a strategy of market development, taking its know-how and financial services to new and emerging markets. Lastly, an enterprise may pursue **diversification**, an aim to serve new markets with new products, just as BBI added a management consulting service to its Burke Institute seminars and BASES new product testing repertoire in order to broaden its account base as well as deepen its relationship with each client.

Of course, strategic alliances and partnerships must be included as key facets of the product market selection component of strategy. We have already shown how new products can be developed effectively, with fast cycle times, in collaborations with customers and suppliers. Alliances for new product development enable the firm to access technology and other types of resources that would be quite difficult to acquire or grow entirely within a single firm. At the same time, large financial, physical, and personnel commitments—as well as the expected payoffs in market access or new products—heighten the significance of managing such relationships effectively.[3] We should note, too, the popular phenomenon of alliances with competitors. For example, Intel has entered an alliance with Hewlett–Packard to develop a single computer chip that runs PCs and large computers.[4] Certainly, competitors make promising partners because they know the stakes of new product development and share an understanding of the markets and the language of the industry. But a lack of trust and poor safeguards on proprietary knowledge often thwart the effectiveness of such alliances.

We know from our earlier chapters that partners can also play a strategic role in supply strategy, distribution functions, research and development, and more. Because firms must negotiate favorable terms of exchange with several varied partners, the portfolio of interfirm relationships takes on strategic importance.

Resources

Financial and other resource considerations lead up to the next key question: *what level of investment in the product market?* We may be trying to convert the business to cash by selling off assets or selling the whole operation. Indeed, a family business with no offspring willing to run it when Mom and Pop retire may follow this *divestment* strategy.

On the other hand, significant investment will be needed if the firm is seeking to enter and secure a footing in new markets or grow its share in a mature market. To make good on its promise to make "the fastest chips in the newest applications," Intel spent $2.3 billion on R&D and another $4.5 billion on capital expansion in 1997.

Between these poles a firm might make only the necessary investments to maintain the current position or investments—even forgoing maintenance—to bleed the life out of the firm. In your very neighborhood there is apt to be an aging urban school, a struggling printing business, or a small and dingy office supply store down the street from Staples. A "milking" strategy certainly has its place.

Objectives and Plans

A business strategy also has to develop *the detailed aims and action plans for the functional areas*. A host of questions must be addressed in this portion of a strategy. Will special emphasis be given logistics for customer service or will the firm decentralize manufacturing to provide short supply linkages to key customers? Will the firm need a strong advertising campaign or will it need to support distributor activities that play key roles in product differentiation? How important is supply management, relative to other facets of the value creation process? How can the sales, service, and operations people at the branches be encouraged to work as a team?

In many markets, careful analytical attention and planning are given to the product line—its scope, composition by functional feature and durability, horizontal and vertical connectivity, price, and so on. A computer company must consider the relationship of each model to the others it markets. What is the positioning strategy for each model and the array of accessories and peripherals? Engineering, purchasing, manufacturing, and logistics must collaborate in the formulation of supporting goals and activities.

The growing interconnectivity in today's information environment has posed new challenges for computer makers. For the small and midsized firms that want network services, manufacturers are relying more heavily on their value-added resellers (VARs). But at least two distinct action plans are evident. The approach used by Digital and Compaq favors Internet and/or intranet technology to provide technical and strategic support to a broad base of VARs. The other approach, exemplified in moves by IBM and Apple, provides increased service (e.g., lead generation, training) and incentives for an elite group of VARs.[5]

Of course, the remainder of the marketing mix must also be tightly formulated. Advertising and distribution strategies must be worked out to support the intended positioning and product line strategies. The roles of the sales force with respect to each product and customer group (e.g., end user category or type of reseller) need to be fit with the advertising and telephone marketing strategies. Also, pricing strategies need to be in harmony with the advertising, selling, distribution, and manufacturing strategies.

Additional Facets of Strategy for a Stable of Businesses

Organizations that are comprised of multiple businesses—GE, North American Rockwell, American Express, Magna, and many others—have at least two other significant components to their strategy. They need to resolve the problem of how to allocate resources strategically to the different business units. They must also manage the mix of businesses to achieve positive outcomes from the intersecting operations, resources, and markets among the businesses.

Resource Allocation

The assignments of key people, teams, and tasks to different facilities or plants need to be worked out. Financial resources—both internally generated funds and external capital—will seldom be sufficient to meet the requests of every line manager. "Projects" must be sorted and evaluated on different criteria in the firm: How risky is each of these endeavors? What return on investment will each yield? Is the venture consistent with the goals and aspirations of the company? Can the proposals develop new and relevant skill sets? Does the proposal access new and significant markets? Is the proposal so bold as to imagine we can change the rules of the game in our favor?[6]

Business managers make a strong pitch for their projects to their counterparts in other divisions as well as to corporate-level decision makers. In turn, the corporate-level executives decide to invest in the set of projects believed most likely to improve the financial, social, and market positions of the corporation.

Synergy

To guide the resource allocation process, the multibusiness organization should have an explicit understanding of the synergies sought from its mix of businesses. **Synergy** means that the whole is greater than the sum of its parts. International Paper Company is really much more than a paper company. Its distribution business is called ResourceNet, a $10 billion enterprise operating 275 warehouse and store locations plus a delivery fleet. As a result, International is well equipped to service retail customers, commercial printers and publishers, manufacturers, sanitary maintenance companies, quick printers, and more with dedicated stocking, just-in-time services, and technical support.

Synergy can also derive from systems and know-how. The Dunfey Hotels Corporation operates several hotels, few of which share the same name. It may seem puzzling that it could run successful business and convention hotels, some airport hotels, and a handful of luxury hotels in the major cities, all under different names and different marketing strategies. But its success does not stem from economies in advertising or from an otherwise developed common brand. Rather, the management knows how to position properties in unique markets and deliver satisfying lodging experiences. In this case, clearly we cannot find the source of synergy without looking deeply at the company's culture and planning systems.[7]

We offer a word of caution about synergy. It can be elusive, surprising, and overpromised. For example, several companies have tried to acquire technical expertise thought to be essential to their future operations by acquiring marketing research or engineering firms. On paper, the plans have looked sound: experts at making and selling will team up with experts at innovating, analyzing, or forecasting. The plan unravels, however, when the key scientists, analysts, or econometricians at the acquired firm get frustrated by the new ownership, reporting structure, or such. They then bolt to another firm or begin their own. Plans and incentives need to be well conceived and implementation must be sound in order to realize potential synergies.

Final Words on Business Strategy

A business **strategy** can exhibit different levels of detail and analysis, and can focus on horizons 2 to 20 years out. Critical elements in any strategic plan include (1) product markets served, (2) resource commitments, and (3) objectives and plans for each functional area. Firms with multiple business units must include two additional elements in their strategies: the resource allocations to the different businesses and the synergies expected from the mix. Clearly, these are similar to the second and third elements in any strategy, performed at a higher level of aggregation of the product markets served.

Developing Strategy

It may be several years before you make it to the top floor of corporate headquarters or take the helm of your family's business. In the meantime you should expect to contribute in several ways to your company's strategic planning process. In an entry-level sales position, you may find the firm using input from you and other field sales personnel for business forecasts. Your proposals for account and territory development might also be sought in the planning process. If your career progresses toward greater supervision of people and programs, perhaps including profit responsibility, your participation in the planning process will greatly expand. Until then, you will have a chance to hone comprehensive planning skills if you pursue entrepreneurial opportunities or take up community projects.

The Process for Strategies

Exhibit 6–2 depicts three strategic planning models. Although the presentations differ, all three contain common elements—a process for reflecting on the purpose of the enterprise, a situation analysis that attends to both environmental and organizational elements, some more careful consideration of the competitive forces in specific markets, and the detailed objectives, budgets, and plans for strategy execution.

It is noteworthy that activities are not sequenced identically in the three models. That is a clue that each model is a gross simplification. As such the summary diagram overstates the linearity of the process. Strategic planning is not a series of self-contained steps connected in a perfunctory way and guaranteed to yield action plans for profits. Indeed, many of the strategy process elements can be addressed simultaneously and iteratively between functions and levels in the organization.

This section of the chapter will discuss the key elements of the strategy process, but we don't pretend that there is a formula or rigid mechanism for the process. When a soccer team comes back together after the off-season, each player must regain her aerobic fitness, her touch on the ball, and her tactical senses for support and creating space. A good trainer will recognize those three components for effective preparation. Perhaps the coach will have the team run a series of sprints up a steep embankment, juggle, and work in a 3 v. 1 drill. Obviously, sprints could be run at the end of practice and small numbers games could hone all three components; those three outputs needn't be developed singularly and sequentially. Let's take a closer look at the key elements of the strategy development process.

Situation Analysis

Strategies are built on a solid foundational understanding of the organization's mission. The mission, in turn, derives from recognition of key capabilities, constraints, aspirations, resources, and constituencies in the task environment. This section will introduce some important perspectives for organizational and environmental analysis.

We have a number of tools available for situation analysis and goal setting. This section provides an overview of SWOT analysis, a powerful tool for internal and external strategic assessment. We spend a short time introducing the concept of organizational mission and its explicit sense of purpose. To bolster your own confidence and inspire creativity, we illustrate a number of devices for distilling details and conveying strategic insights. We then build up to a separate section that introduces a framework for evaluating the structure of competition.

Exhibit 6–2
The Strategy
Process
Model 1

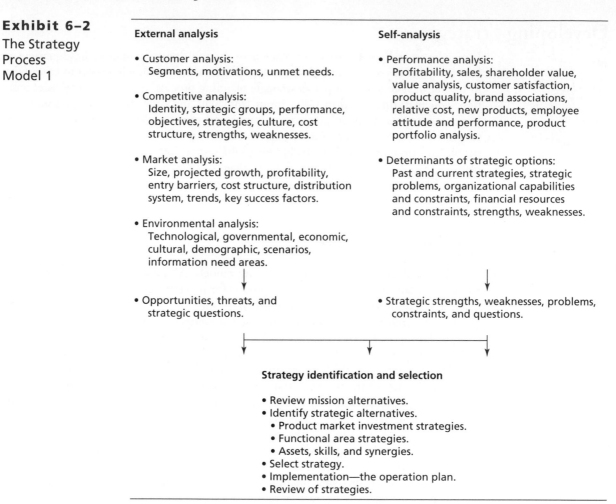

External analysis

- Customer analysis:
  Segments, motivations, unmet needs.

- Competitive analysis:
  Identity, strategic groups, performance,
  objectives, strategies, culture, cost
  structure, strengths, weaknesses.

- Market analysis:
  Size, projected growth, profitability,
  entry barriers, cost structure, distribution
  system, trends, key success factors.

- Environmental analysis:
  Technological, governmental, economic,
  cultural, demographic, scenarios,
  information need areas.

- Opportunities, threats, and
  strategic questions.

Self-analysis

- Performance analysis:
  Profitability, sales, shareholder value,
  value analysis, customer satisfaction,
  product quality, brand associations,
  relative cost, new products, employee
  attitude and performance, product
  portfolio analysis.

- Determinants of strategic options:
  Past and current strategies, strategic
  problems, organizational capabilities
  and constraints, financial resources
  and constraints, strengths, weaknesses.

- Strategic strengths, weaknesses, problems,
  constraints, and questions.

Strategy identification and selection

- Review mission alternatives.
- Identify strategic alternatives.
  - Product market investment strategies.
  - Functional area strategies.
  - Assets, skills, and synergies.
- Select strategy.
- Implementation—the operation plan.
- Review of strategies.

SOURCE: Model 1 reprinted from David Aaker, *Strategic Market Management* (1992), p. 23, with permission of the copyright © owner, John Wiley & Sons, Inc.

SWOT Analysis

One of the most productive and memorable planning tools is a **SWOT analysis**. This is a self-assessment framework for examining our **S**trengths and **W**eaknesses, our **O**pportunities and **T**hreats. Strengths include the pockets of excellence *in the firm,* perhaps a strong sales office in Birmingham, a good supply relationship with XYZ, a good inventory system, or a solid financial position. Weaknesses are also characteristics of the firm itself and may include products with poor market positions, a lame channel of distribution overseas, a disadvantageous cost structure, or yesterday's technology. Aging assets, a locational disadvantage, or thinning talent in a key area represent weaknesses.

In this level of analysis, opportunities are favorable conditions in the firm's task environment. They can be recognized in access to growing markets, a market of escalating distribution service standards—standards we can meet—and new laws or regulations that might foreclose competitors. Threats are potential adverse conditions in the firm's

Exhibit 6–2
Continued
Model 2

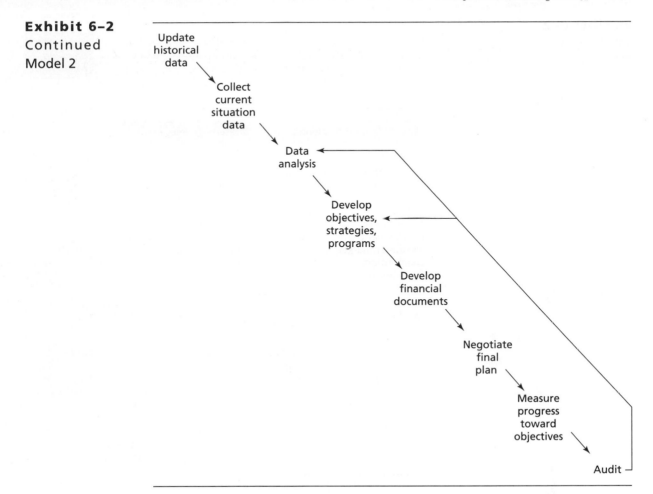

SOURCE: Model 2 reprinted with permission from Donald Lehmann and Russell Winer, *Analysis for Marketing Planning,* Plano, TX: Business Publications, Inc. (1988), p. 8.

environment. A margin squeeze from vigorous price competition and increasing input prices is a threat, as is a regulation that forecloses a particular input or distribution option. In the dean's office at your school, an analysis akin to the SWOT shown in Exhibit 6–3 (p. 159) may be one of the key working documents for goal setting and the revelation of distinctive competencies.

King of SWOT   A good SWOT analysis has several distinguishing characteristics. First, it is *honest.* Despite its receiving three professional awards for design excellence, it would be wrong to consider your firm's design team a strength if consumer acceptance is low or there have been departures of key personnel. An honest label on the strength would be a "strong reputation among product design professionals." Morgan Stanley enjoys a worldwide reputation for its expertise and professional integrity. Morgan must face up to the real threat in many new markets that a single foul-up in an emerging market can dash its reputational strength beyond recovery in the local setting.

Second, the analysis must be *broad* in focus. A distributor assessing trends for opportunities and threats should look at situations in markets outside its trade area. For example, T-Shirt City, a Midwestern wholesaler of shirts and sportswear to the screen printers

Exhibit 6–2
Continued
Model 3

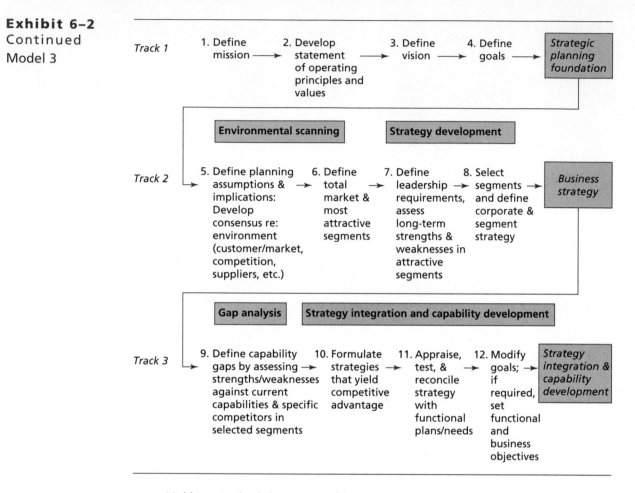

Track 1

1. Define mission →
2. Develop statement of operating principles and values →
3. Define vision →
4. Define goals →
Strategic planning foundation

Environmental scanning | **Strategy development**

Track 2

5. Define planning assumptions & implications: Develop consensus re: environment (customer/market, competition, suppliers, etc.) →
6. Define total market & most attractive segments →
7. Define leadership requirements, assess long-term strengths & weaknesses in attractive segments →
8. Select segments and define corporate & segment strategy →
Business strategy

Gap analysis | **Strategy integration and capability development**

Track 3

9. Define capability gaps by assessing strengths/weaknesses against current capabilities & specific competitors in selected segments →
10. Formulate strategies that yield competitive advantage →
11. Appraise, test, & reconcile strategy with functional plans/needs →
12. Modify goals; if required, set functional and business objectives →
Strategy integration & capability development

SOURCE: Model 3 reprinted with the permission of the Free Press, a Division of Simon & Schuster, from Christopher Meyer, *Fast Cycle Time: How to Align Purpose, Strategy, and Structure for Speed* (1993) p. 92; copyright © 1993 by Christopher Meyer.

and embroidery business, has observed margins shrinking across the country, has witnessed consolidation at the manufacturing and wholesaling level, and has seen its thinning customer base replicated in other markets.

The anticipation of customer needs requires a close look at the competitive pressures faced by each customer or customer group. Similarly, the business environment of direct and indirect suppliers must be considered. We also recommend that SWOT analysis be conducted at different levels: key products, lines of business, divisions, and countries.

Third, a SWOT analysis should consider *multiple time horizons* and label features of each dimension as such. For example, a drought in the Grain Belt is an immediate threat to flour and cereal processors; its impact on costs and eventual market prices must be considered. Firms in this industry such as Peavy and Cargill should also look ahead to new transport systems that may make inputs accessible that are currently remote. Evidence of new dietary habits, signs of breakthroughs in grain preservatives, and emerging package recycling imperatives ought to be considered. Even the durability of current strengths must be factored into the analysis.

Exhibit 6–3

Composite SWOT Analysis of the B School at Bliss State

I. Strengths
  A. A solid faculty base, particularly new faculty
    1. Improving research and professional activity and reputation
    2. High percentage of excellent teachers
    3. A number of research stars
  B. An undergrad program that offers
    1. The co-op program
    2. Opportunity to enter *College of Business Administration* (CBA) as freshmen
    3. Identifiable majors
    4. Some excellent undergrads
    5. Extensive student involvement
  C. A strong evening MBA program
  D. Several strong PhD programs
  E. Several centers with unique niches and solid support
  F. A large reservoir of potential goodwill, presently untapped
  G. Increased visibility from basketball success
  H. Decision-making autonomy within university
  I. Adequate facilities—good physical plant
  J. Urban location
II. Weaknesses
  A. A faculty characterized by
    1. Apathy
    2. Low expectations: tenure, aspirations, amount of work
    3. Many faculty not doing research or doing research with little impact
    4. Low levels of externally supported research
    5. Several departments in disarray
    6. Poor interdepartmental relations
    7. Inconsistent departmental workloads
    8. Distribution of faculty across departments that doesn't match our mission
  B. An undergraduate program characterized by
    1. An "average" undergrad student body, with a very wide range of abilities
    2. An aging curriculum that is inefficient and too specialized
    3. Lack of solid undergraduate recruiting
    4. Students distracted by work demands
    5. Lack of student identification with CBA
  C. An MBA program featuring
    1. Excess capacity in daytime MBA
    2. A part-time MBA longer than many prospective students would prefer
    3. A me-too curriculum
    4. Delivery in only one location
  D. Strong student–community ties, reducing the possibility of broader placement, visibility
  E. Weak management development programs that are not supported by faculty
  F. Low level of alumni and community support, including external funding
  G. Reputation that hasn't kept up with improvements in CBA
  H. Lack of support (financial or otherwise) from central administration for CBA's goals. CBA is expected to be a cash generator for the university
  I. Inadequate centralized administrative services: student recruiting and placement, public relations, information systems
  J. Inflexibility created by the unionized environment
  K. Lack of a galvanizing strategy
  L. Facility inadequacies: case classrooms, office space, technology
  M. Aesthetics of urban location
III. Opportunities
  A. Capitalizing on the strengths noted above, particularly by
    1. Expanding and promoting the co-op program
    2. Expanding the evening MBA program
    3. Encouraging high-impact faculty research

Exhibit 6–3
Continued.

B. "Fixing" certain weaknesses, particularly by
1. Upgrading management development programs
2. Making the MBA program more accessible (shorter, more locations, etc.)
3. Improving community and business relations, including fund raising
4. Revamping the BBA curriculum to teach more efficiently and effectively
5. Changing the organizational structure and choosing more appropriate administrators
6. Improving marketing efforts
7. Increasing the amount of externally funded (contract) research
C. Responding to new standards of accreditation
D. Use of our urban location and improved business ties for teaching innovations, expanded placement, and research possibilities
E. A large local market, particularly for evening MBA
F. An untapped market for joint MBA programs with engineering, law, medicine

IV. Threats
A. Declining interest in majoring in business (due to demographics and attitudes)
B. Actions by competitors to enhance their programs
C. Potential loss of strong faculty
D. Lack of faculty optimism and enthusiasm
E. Stable, if not declining state support for higher education
F. Dissatisfaction among businesses with the education business schools provide
G. Increasing accountability
H. Changed standards of accreditation
I. Negative attitudes by central administrators, particularly concerning the importance of sponsored research as a basis for BSU resource allocation
J. A tight job market

SOURCE: SWOT analysis used with the permission of the dean at "Bliss State."

Finally, because the SWOT analysis is built on *perceptions* of the firm and its environment, it is good to get the perceptions from several individuals or groups. Have purchasing, marketing, sales, human resources, and traffic departments each do SWOT analyses. This should broaden the scope of the analysis and capture strategic implications that stem from a variety of assumptions.

SWOT Recap It takes two mirrors to show how the back of your hair was cut. And most of us also run our fingers through it. A SWOT analysis works similarly. We're not saying that strategy begins with a good haircut. It begins with a good look at the enterprise—front, back, up close, down deep. And it takes stock of the firm's external environment. How has it changed in the last few periods? What do we anticipate in the time ahead? Is our firm poised for success in the current and anticipated environment? Are we ready to track the changing environment and maintain a leadership position therein? Or have we faced up to the reality of our problems? Perhaps the discomfort of the recent period can no longer be endured. Maybe top management is ready to lead the firm to make radical change. Whatever the case, an honest, broad, and timely examination from multiple perspectives is needed for reliable self-assessment via SWOT.

The Mission
In the strategic process of self-analysis, a company will often pause to reconsider its **mission statement**, a formal expression of why the organization exists. This sense of purpose works well to frame key strategies and day-to-day decisions. It also helps with the enculturation process needed when new employees join the firm or two firms merge.

Exhibit 6–4
Mission
Statements

We aim to be a leading and flexible world manufacturer of audio acoustic products, meeting the needs of our customer, employees, and shareholders.

Polish electronics manufacturer

We aim to be the friendliest Saudi bank which best anticipates and responds to the needs of our customers, employees, and shareholders.

leading Saudi Arabian bank

Fast, flawless, and simple delivery of value as perceived by our customers such that Digital becomes the benchmark toward which others can strive.

Digital South Pacific

To improve the health status of the people we serve. We pursue our mission by providing a full range of health-related services, including prevention, wellness, and education. Care is provided with compassion consistent with the values of our organization: respect for all people, stewardship, delighting customers through commitment to quality, response to community needs, respect for our spiritual heritage, valuing differences.

an alliance of hospitals in the Midwest

Become the premier custom sales research company offering the highest-quality product, the most responsive client service, the most flexibility, and the fastest service in the industry.

a national custom research corporation

SOURCE: The first three mission statements are reprinted from *Practical Business Re-Engineering*, 2d ed., p. 47, by Nick Obolensky. Copyright © 1994 by Nick Obolensky. Used with permission. All rights reserved.

Developing a mission from scratch or reassessing a prior mission statement can be a useful strategic exercise. Broad company participation in the visioning process necessary to develop a mission often yields new insights, a renewed sense of purpose, and broad-based commitment.

Even without broad participation in its development, a mission statement serves to clarify the goals and values of the enterprise to all constituencies or stakeholders in the firm. Most organizations can place the majority of their stakeholders into one of four key categories: customers, suppliers, employees, and owners. Are the stakeholders recognized in the sample mission statements in Exhibit 6–4?

Strategic Spectroscopy

A spectroscope is an optical instrument for forming and analyzing the spectrum emitted by an object or element. Physicists know that each element emits a different type of radiant energy. Each is distinguished by the different color bands on its spectrum. Although we know many managers who long for a marketing spectroscope, they accomplish the same objective by using a raft of tools that simplify and summarize the complex. We have already discussed some of the input data: customer surveys, industry studies, focus groups, and segmentation analyses. From here strategic planners need to grasp the big picture and trends. This need compels most managers to use graphics and charts in place of multiple, detailed tables. Managers and their analysts may move mountains of data, but now comes the time for visual tools that summarize the big picture.

Let's illustrate with a model that's been reinvented in many of our own student teams. Exhibit 6–5 derives from survey data asking customers (1) to rate the company's products on different functional attributes and (2) to indicate the degree to which each attribute is important. The graphic combines the data in a most illuminating way, reflecting an implicit management theory that the firm should do best what customers value most. In this

6–1

BUSINESS 2 BUSINESS
Your Mission

As a student in business marketing, you can benefit from having a mission statement. This is not a self-help seminar, but with just some rudimentary tools we can direct the effort and point to some key benefits. If you take some time over the next few days now to develop your personal mission statement, we think you will find a greater appreciation for the mission statement of a business organization. And we suspect you will produce a useful platform for finding personal success.

Management consultant Stephen Covey underscores our need to find balance and synergy in four principal spheres: physical, mental, spiritual, and social.[8] In each of these areas, list some of your strengths, shortcomings, and obstacles to overcoming the weaknesses. Where do you see your strengths in these areas overlapping? Identify some of the most important roles in your life (e.g., student, coach, employee, spouse, parent, son or daughter). What will be your accomplishments when you look back at your life from ages 30, 50, and 70?

With the insights from these exercises, write a private mission statement. Covey argues effectively that a good mission statement is true to one's inner self, reflects use of unique talents to serve others, integrates the four needs spheres, is anchored in truth, deals with the significant roles in your life, and inspires. But mix in a good measure of humility in order to cope with setbacks, be robust to disturbances and sidetracks, and admit the possibility that you may indeed have another mission. The payoff is a clarity of focus—doing what's important, attending to the right factors in the strategic environment, and running ahead of the pack.

Exhibit 6–5
Wants–Gets Grid

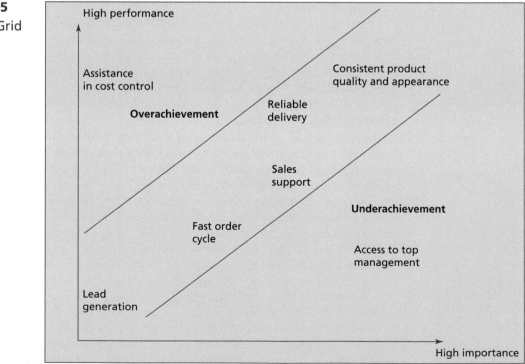

Exhibit 6–6
Conceptual Map

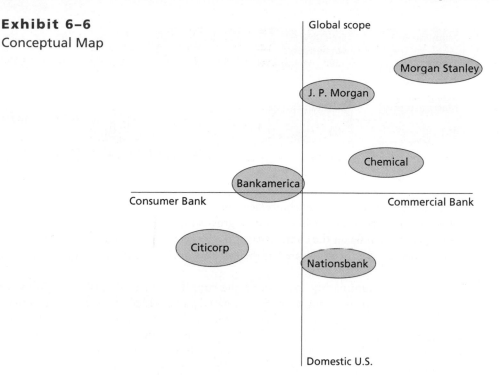

sense, attributes below the diagonal represent underachievement; those above the diagonal represent overachievement. Why put company resources to tasks that are not important? The result is a Wants–Gets Grid, simple but demonstrably illuminating.

The same sort of creativity can be applied to summarizing segment data and market share information. Exhibit 6–6 illustrates the oft-used strategic planning graphics called the conceptual map. A **conceptual map** is a picture of abstract ideas, options, persons, or companies on two or three key variables. The perceptual maps we discussed in Chapter 5, made from the subjective perceptions of customers, are one type of conceptual map. The vice president of marketing can make effective use of a conceptual map showing the evolution of shrink wrap applications in industrial markets. Alternatively, an export manager can effectively convey shipment volumes and products to various country clusters by a conceptual map.

Exhibit 6–6 represents a composite of perceptions of a commercial banking segment. It simplifies their perceptions about the lending postures of several large banks. Much better than the surveys or their summary in 50-column spread sheets, the graphic maps the consumer versus commercial lending emphasis of the banks against a scale of their global presence. The analysis can be repeated for different points in time and using different indicators of globalism.

The tool is an effective internal communication device. One banking expert's insightful view of the nature of competition in commercial banking was represented in a "radar screen" that included some unconventional and potential competitors to commercial banks. In this vein, one bank executive recently remarked, "I used to track six banks. Now I have to track over 100 different financial service firms who are competing for my customers' accounts. Measuring where the money is going is getting tougher. Parsing through the data is getting harder and harder. It gives me a headache."[9]

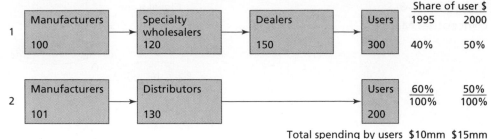

Exhibit 6–7
Value Chain Analysis
Numbers represent cost of goods sold at each level, indexed to inputs of manufacturers in channel 1.

					Share of user $	
					1995	2000
1	Manufacturers 100	Specialty wholesalers 120	Dealers 150	Users 300	40%	50%
2	Manufacturers 101	Distributors 130		Users 200	60% / 100%	50% / 100%

Total spending by users $10mm $15mm

The conceptual map is headache remedy of sorts. It's a communication instrument and tool for understanding. It is a model, a gross simplification of the real situation. It helps us to get a handle on the complexity of the real thing without all the messy details. But if the model were as complicated as the real situation, it would no longer work as an analogy.

It can also be illuminating to examine the supply chain to identify key points of value added. Exhibit 6–7 compares the estimated value added chain of two products from the same industry; share of market through channel 1 is climbing while share of market through channel 2 is waning. The numbers reflect use of average factory direct costs in channel 1 as the base. Although manufacturers in channel 2 are a bit less efficient, they nab higher prices from their distributors, and distributors enjoy 30 percent margins in their sales to end users. But the real action seems to be happening "downstream" in channel 1. In channel 1, dealers earn 50 percent gross margins on a sales level that has grown much faster than channel 2's. The market seems to be shifting toward a preference for dealer services! When this type of analysis is combined with other data on the environment (segment trends, technology, market share histories), we can get deep insights into the evolution of the product market, the emerging value priorities. In the computer field, this evolution manifests a diminished value from chips, and even sharper decline from hardware and peripherals. We note increasing value provided from operating systems, applications, and network functionality.

These three tools are merely representative of the grids, bubble charts, flow diagrams, and other graphics that can be used in the strategy process. We have underscored the need for broad and multilevel inputs for situation analysis. These tools and your own creativity can work effectively to synthesize and convey meaning.

Now, the value added chain and the dynamics of any industry can be more systematically studied within a comprehensive framework addressing the structure of competition. Although competitive analysis is technically a situation analysis tool, we take up the topic of competitive analysis in a separate section mainly for organizational purposes. As you will soon see, it contains a significant body of detailed material.

Understanding Competitive Pressures

Profits are the economic rewards to a business for providing value to customers better than the rest and running an efficient operation. If we briefly examine a few sources of profit, we can get a good preview to the upcoming discussion of the anatomy of competition. Competition is more than industrial rivals cutting prices in an effort to gain market share. It has a structure that can be described and analyzed.[10]

Exhibit 6–8
Five Forces of
Competition

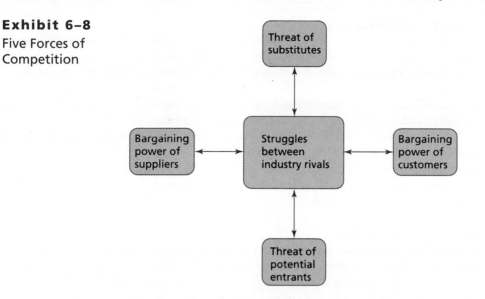

Let's begin with the profit impact from a gain in share of a growing market. The struggle for market share fits well with our commonsense notion of competition. But let us presume a gain of one share point brings a manufacturer a well-earned profit increase of $50,000. Is it likely we would regard some other means of earning an additional $50,000 as inferior? Would the dollars be less valuable if they came from, say, an ability to charge higher factory prices to dealers? Of course not. The dollars gained in net profits from share of market increases and from price increases are the same value.

In the same manner, as we showed in Chapter 2, profits can increase by using effective supply strategies, perhaps reducing spoilage, downtime, or ownership costs to achieve a $50,000 bump in profits. Finally, we might find $50,000 in new profits from regulations that foreclose a toxic substitute product from competing or beginning to compete for our accounts, thus relieving a degree of price pressure from our line.

Five Forces

The scenarios above suggest that firms have improved profit capabilities to the extent that they can withstand price pressures in the business environment. If we pause to reconsider each scenario, we see that price pressures come from five distinct sectors. Depicted in Exhibit 6–8, the **five forces of competition** are

1. Rivalry among firms in the industry.
2. Powerful customers.
3. Powerful suppliers.
4. Threat of substitutes.
5. Threat of potential entrants.

Rivalry in the Industry

Not all businesses face the same amount of price pressure from their competitors in the same business. In Atlanta during the 1996 Olympics, hotels enjoyed great pricing latitude because demand outpaced the supply of local rooms. Like the lodging business, other industries are partitioned by natural boundaries or customer purchasing constraints. Indeed, Morgan Stanley's selection of specific countries reflects both the promise of growth and a relative scarcity of competitors in the arena.

If industry rivals offer relatively undifferentiated products or if demand is significantly less than overall capacity, firms will tend to find intense rivalry. Price competition frequently intensifies in declining markets because firms try to grab market share to cover fixed expenses that can't be shrunk as rapidly as the market. T-shirt City is a wholesaler in such a situation of intense rivalry.

Powerful Customers

Their abilities to contract for large purchases make large customers attractive to many business markers. The seller's risk is that large buyers may press hard for price concessions, effectively squeezing out profit opportunities. Another possibility is delayed payments or returned products, both of which can sink an undercapitalized firm.

Powerful Suppliers

A manufacturer that relies heavily on a unique input for its product becomes vulnerable to price hikes or other means of "holdup" from the supplier. Of course, the unique input may provide a means of differentiation for the manufacturer. The "Intel inside" sticker on a desktop computer provides many buyers assurance of a top-quality Pentium processor, no matter what the brand name on the PC. The buying firm must carefully weigh the benefits from depending on a powerful source of supply. A key question may be what the future supply situation looks like. Perhaps there will be alternative suppliers when patent protection expires or when another source—maybe even one internal to the firm—has been brought up to speed.

Threat of Substitutes

Industries are typically defined by their channel position and their output. Are they manufacturers or distributors? Do they sell chemicals or rolled wire? Notice that user considerations get no mention. But clearly, if a buyer regards the products from two different industries as substitutes, the makers of those products must be considered competitors. The competitive pressure from products in a different industry can affect prices just as well as substitutes within the industry. A trucking firm will vie for business from some shippers that can also ship the commodity by rail or plane. Soft drink bottlers can use corn syrup or cane sugars as sweeteners.

Frankly, this competitive force has been the cornerstone of competitive analysis in marketing since the infancy of survey research. A hospital purchasing manager may not only compare prices and capabilities of different makers of diagnostic equipment, she may also examine the services of independent laboratories. But, while marketing research has long aimed to describe competition in terms of customer perceptions of substitutes, we may have underplayed the importance of some of these other structural dimensions of competition.

Threat of Potential Entrants

Rapidly growing or profitable markets tend to attract new sellers. And newcomers can change the competitive landscape in several ways. First, new participants in the market increase the productive capacity serving the market; therefore the existing demand from

Exhibit 6–9
Barriers to Entry

Product differentiation	If customers are loyal to brands because of effective advertising, customer service, or unique features, it will be expensive for a new firm to overcome that loyalty.
Economies of scale	Technical matters of production or distribution often demand that new players spend heavily to enter the industry on a large scale, or come in at a cost disadvantage.
Capital requirements	Consider the financial requirements to enter shipbuilding, mining, pharmaceuticals, or public accounting fields. One must cover the heavy equipment and fixed site requirements, plus finance inventories, R&D, start-up advertising, and sales.
Access to distribution channels	A new entrant to the business copier field will have to find and motivate dealers to add another model to their assortment or develop their own distribution and sales system. The former route is often confounded by exclusive dealing terms enjoyed by entrenched makes of copiers.
Cost disadvantages unrelated to size	This is a potpourri of possible advantages enjoyed by incumbents: a premium site, low occupancy costs (a paid-off mortgage), patent protection, lots of experience, access to inputs, etc.
Government policy	Licensing requirements, regulated distribution, and safety and pollution standards can limit or foreclose entry.

customers has to cover more fixed costs. Second, a new rival will fight to increase market share, perhaps displacing incumbents in the assortments of resellers or underbidding the established firms. Third, new rivals can bring new or substantial resources to the fray. Resources might be a reputable brand name brought to a new arena, (e.g., 3M in fertilizers, Digital in PCs) or could include technical expertise (Samsung in the Asian auto market) or financial muscle (Wal-Mart in food service).

Barriers to Entry

A keen analysis of competitive forces will seek (1) to gauge the barriers to entry in the particular industry and (2) given a sense of what it takes to enter, to identify the significant potential entrants into a field. If barriers are high, incumbent sellers enjoy a shelter from competitive pressures. **Barriers to entry** are the obstacles a potential entrant must overcome in order to compete in a market. Essentially, they are like the prerequisites you need to satisfy before you can take a particular course; they are the capabilities or resources necessary to succeed in a market.

Antitrust lawyers and economists have identified six types of barriers to entry. We need to turn their motivation inside out, because we are looking at barriers to entry from the firm's perspective. That is, Department of Justice and FTC lawyers are concerned when barriers create a monopoly and thereby restrict output and choice, impairing the customer satisfaction focus of the market mechanism. However, business executives, from a strategic business perspective, know that better profit opportunities exist in markets insulated from new entrants. Furthermore, even as a potential entrant to a market, we should carefully size up the skills and resources needed to compete. Thus, we briefly review the barriers to entry in Exhibit 6–9.

Barriers in Flux

In today's global business arena, dynamic and uncertain conditions describe most markets. For example, technology may radically affect the scale economies in an industry. In the marketing research field, powerful desktop computers and flexible software enable many small start-up companies to begin to offer marketing research *projects*. Meanwhile, capital requirements have escalated for firms participating in the new marketing research *systems* field. They need superpowered computers to clean and merge scanner data with information on geodemographics, promotions, and media activities as well as to develop, test, and apply new "products"—analytical models and report formats in tune with client needs. Analytical and customer service talent plus strong corporate reputations represent new barriers to entry.

Change can also affect other entry barriers. For several software companies the Internet has served as a distribution channel, enabling the description and delivery of demonstration and shareware products without the costly headaches of gaining access to and managing performance of a dealer network. Remember also that patents do expire and, prior to their expiration, many patented products have been displaced by innovations. Indeed, new circumstances and the transmission of knowledge enable new firms to leapfrog the reputation and experience edge held by incumbent firms. For decades, petroleum companies turned primarily to Red Adair to extinguish well head fires. When hundreds of well head fires were left by the Iraqis in Kuwait at the end of the Gulf War, scores of newcomers and novel methods were enlisted in the fire fight.

Spotting and Defending against Potential Entrants

We can better scan the horizon for potential new entrants with an informed sense of the barriers to entry to our market. What businesses have the ability to complete the "package" of skills and resources to compete in our market? Have they given any signals of their intention to enter? Some of the signals we should look for include a potential entrant's discussions with or purchases from suppliers. Note also the skills of the people they have recently hired from our field or a related field. Perhaps they paint their growth strategies broadly in their annual reports and are lining up dealers or sales reps at trade shows, field testing products and systems, or inviting presentations from advertising agencies. In short, we should be very attentive to potential competitors and the signs they provide about their marketing objectives and strategies. We should prepare defensive strategies or position the firm in a manner that deters the entrant. Vigorous defense of a position discourages other potential entrants who observe the high stakes of entry.

Strategic Implications of the Five Competitive Forces

If you know that your backpacking trip will take you through snowy mountain roads and swampy hiking trails, you would be wise to put on your snow tires and double up on insect repellant. Similarly, if you know the nature of competitive challenges in your market, you should be sure your firm is adequately prepared to meet them. Every firm has both strengths and weaknesses, but it is how they match up against the competitive structure of the market that determines success.

Solar Kids was a company launched in Ohio to provide computer training to children in schools and in after-school programs. The firm repositioned itself to serve business and government markets as Solar Comp in the face of a changing competitive structure. Specifically, the situation of slow-paying, price-sensitive, and difficult to aggregate customers was made even more difficult with the emergence of new rivals in the training field. Many of the new competitors were started by victims of corporate downsizing, a phenomenon that at the same time boosted the demand for outside training at the new "lean" enterprises.

Both brochures courtesy Solar Comp Computer Training Center.

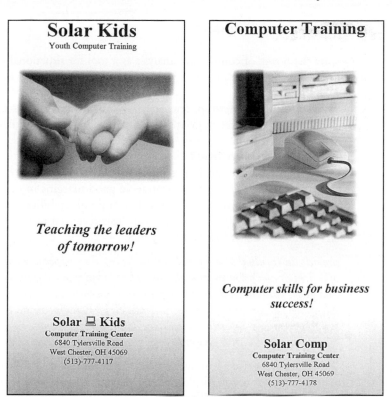

Solar Kids
Youth Computer Training

Teaching the leaders of tomorrow!

Solar ⌨ Kids
Computer Training Center
6840 Tylersville Road
West Chester, OH 45069
(513)-777-4117

Computer Training

Computer skills for business success!

Solar Comp
Computer Training Center
6840 Tylersville Road
West Chester, OH 45069
(513)-777-4178

Three broad types of action plans are implicated by competitive analysis. A firm will want to *choose its competitive battlegrounds judiciously.* If it is the low-cost producer, it might enjoy profitable business from a large, powerful buyer. A firm that is disadvantaged on the cost side should probably not pursue business from the powerful buyer, but compete in another customer sector where quick response and specialized technical service are critical. Solar Kids, a Cincinnati-based computer training company, faced up to the waning profit opportunities at elementary and high schools: lots of rivals, impoverished and slow-paying customers. It changed its name to Solar Comp and moved into corporate training, where competition pivots on expertise with the latest applications software and personal productivity tools.

Innovative organizations will sometimes pursue a strategy designed to *change the competitive structure of the industry.* Advertising and a sophisticated means of programmed merchandising for resellers may transform a market characterized by small regional manufacturers into one dominated by a few national marketers. In markets where this has occurred (e.g., construction adhesives and sealants), the new competitive structure creates barriers to entry through new distribution requirements and product differentiation by branding.

The third strategic approach is to *anticipate and exploit change* in the competitive structure of the industry. Our challenge is to look carefully at each competitive force, understand its root causes, and forecast its impact on the profitability of an industry. Then, with insight and mobility superior to our competition, we try to secure a position to capitalize on the evolution of the field. In the opening vignette to this chapter, we profiled the moves by Morgan Stanley to stake out a commercial presence in developing market economies. It is a reasonable bet that its growing experience and reputation will earn it superior profits and up the stakes for potential rivals in these emerging markets.

Cautions and Limitations

Despite the power of competitive analysis as a tool for situational insights and general options for broad strategic moves, it is not the do-it-all Swiss Army knife. Competitive analysis leaves plenty unsaid in terms of designing an organization structure and control system. Company culture, leadership, and learning are not in the lens of competitive analysis. These facets of business strategy are critical. We address them in the section below.

Sustainable Advantage?

If we use the five-forces analysis to position our company in markets where barriers to entry protect us and where we can preserve good margins in our negotiations with customers and suppliers, we risk complacency and vulnerability to innovative competitors. Commenting on the types of situation analysis reviewed in this chapter, Columbia University professor Richard D'Aveni says they

> *provide an invaluable set of tools for analyzing the competitive environment and position of a firm at any point in its evolution. They identify some of the key sources of advantage at a given point in time. As firms maneuver to create these advantages and erode the advantages of competitors, these static models provide important insights. However, they fail to recognize competitive advantage as a fluid and dynamic process. Advantages that worked in an industry's past only continue to work in a relatively static environment.[11]*

Indeed, competitive advantage is fleeting, as is evident in so many fields. For example, Cincinnati Milacron was displaced by Japanese firms as the number one machine tool company in the world. Milacron responded with new, low-priced products in the expanding plastic injection molding field. *Business Week's* annual ratings of top business schools have shown several different number ones in the past decade. What software company is secure from the actions of its rivals: innovation, nibbling at the fringes of its customer base, technology leapfrogging, new alliances, and so on?

The speed and intensity of competition in an ever-increasing number of business markets demand a strategic emphasis on a new set of organizational strengths.[12] Depicted in Exhibit 6–10, these strengths include

Superior stakeholder satisfaction	We focus on customers, employees and associates, shareholders, and top management, in that order of priority.
Strategic soothsaying	We are looking for advantages in the future, anticipating customer needs, and building the strengths we will need for future success.
Positioning for speed	We need flexibility and adaptability to compete in a changing environment, especially to preempt the moves of other players.
Positioning for surprise	Disruption derives from the ability to move covertly and creatively in ways competitors don't anticipate.
Shifting the rules of competition	A true innovation practically destroys the previous business format. New distribution channels (machine tools) or process technology (printing) have the potential to shape new rules.

Exhibit 6–10
The Ability to
Disrupt Markets

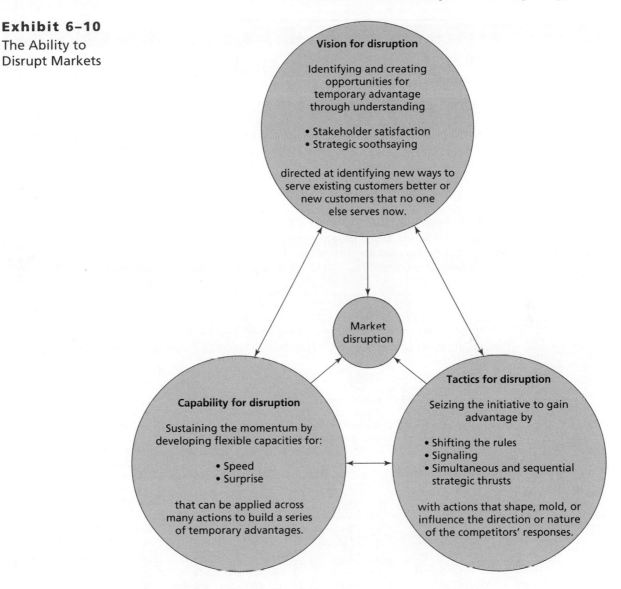

SOURCE: Reprinted with the permission of the Free Press, a division of Simon & Schuster, from *Hypercompetition: Managing the Dynamics of Strategic Maneuvering* by Richard A. D'Aveni. Copyright © 1994 by Richard A. D'Aveni.

Signaling strategic intent	We want competitors to highly regard our commitment to defend positions or penetrate markets. This enhances the credibility of our threats and diminishes the necessity that we will have to carry them out.
Simultaneous and sequential strategic thrusts	We must not get enamored with the competitive clout of a single strategic asset (e.g., deep pockets or product quality) because those can be easily predicted. Multiple assaults and the series of contingent moves ought to be formulated.

6–1

FROM THE FIELD
Komatsu v. Caterpillar

Between 1981 and 1984 Caterpillar's share of the world's earth-moving equipment slipped from 50 to 43%. Japanese manufacturer Komatsu surged over this same period from 16 to 25% of the world market. Before this skirmish, Caterpillar seemed unbeatable as it followed a "Perpetual Motion Machine" for sustainable advantage: It provided dependable machines, strong service and high world volume. The high volume yielded scale economies and enabled high R&D investments, which led to further quality enhancements, which commanded price premiums and high margins, thus a loyal dealer network. On it churned.

Intending to halt Cat's relentless machine, Komatsu devised a bevy of strategies to cripple each component. Under the company code name "Maru-C" (encircle Caterpillar), Komatsu moved aggressively in four key competitive arenas:

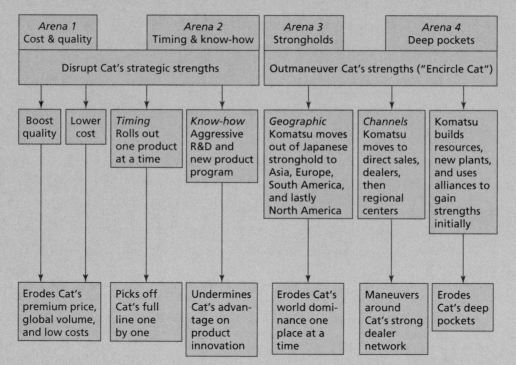

Komatsu: A Strategy of Disruption to Derail "The Perpetual Motion Machine"*

*Based on research by Chris Bartlett

In 1985 Komatsu took a hard hit from a 20% devaluation of the yen against the dollar. With most of its production in Japan, Komatsu had to bump prices and relinquish price leadership to Cat.

Source: Reprinted with the permission of the Free Press, a division of Simon & Schuster, from *Hypercompetiton: Managing the Dynamics of Strategic Maneuvering* by Richard A. D'Aveni. Copyright © 1994 by Richard A. D'Aveni.

Exhibit 6–11
Organizational
Types

Prospector
Likes being first mover
Detects early signals of opportunity and moves on them
Competes in new markets or with new marketing methods
Operates in a broad domain of products and markets

Defender
Aims to find and secure stable product market positions
Offers limited range of products
Is not at the forefront of technology
Ignores dynamic events on the outside of its core area of operation
Defends market position with low price plus quality and service

Analyzer
A combination prospector–defender—less aggressive with innovation and change than prospector, but not so attached to stability and efficiency as defender
Very selective in developing products and pursuing opportunities
Seldom a first mover, but often a strong second or third, offering high quality and service

Reactor
Lacks a well-defined strategy
Product mix is inconsistent
Not a risk taker, not aggressive
Takes action generally under environmental pressures

SOURCE: Adapted from R. E. Miles and C. C. Snow, *Organizational Strategy and Process,* p. 29, copyright © 1979 by McGraw–Hill. Used with permission of McGraw–Hill.

These New 7-S's enable firms to "disrupt" the status quo in markets to achieve temporary advantages. If the advantage is regarded as short-lived, the strategic aim will be to develop a follow-up disruption that yields another advantage. From the Field 6–1 profiles Komatsu's disruption strategy against Caterpillar.

The Organizational Context for Competing

Organizational and environmental analysis enable us to take stock of strengths, weaknesses, opportunities, and threats. A framework for competitive analysis helps us identify "fitting" positions for our business within the economic structure of a market. If we build from this static analysis to forecast cost and quality trends, the evolution of distinctive skills and know-how, the development of new barriers to entry, and the likely distribution of financial resources, we can begin to see what resources and skills we will need to protect our turf, minimize adverse impact, survive on carrion, or disrupt markets and achieve a series a temporary victories.

Indeed, organizations respond differently to their competitive environments according to their strategic personality or character.[13] Organization researchers have verified four archetypes: **Prospectors**, **Defenders**, **Analyzers**, and **Reactors**. Exhibit 6–11 profiles each, showing still another tool for evaluating competitors. Notice that only Prospectors and, to a lesser degree, the Analyzers are inclined to define and disrupt the competitive arena to their advantage. What is it that drives these two types? What is the power supply or organizational engine that drives industry leaders? We argue that the firm's pervasive and deep-rooted market orientation is that engine.

Market Orientation

Of course, industry competition motivates customer service, logistical efficiency, and the search for production economies. But as customer needs are changing, new market opportunities arise, and technology expands the realm of possibilities, success should favor the truly market-oriented enterprise. "A **market orientation** is (1) the systematic gathering of information on customers and competitors, both present and potential, (2) the systematic analysis of the information for the purpose of developing market knowledge, and (3) the systematic use of such knowledge to guide strategy recognition, understanding, creation, selection, implementation and modification."[14]

Unique Character

The unfortunate state of affairs is that a market orientation is rare. Yet quite clearly, as the orientation develops in the culture of an organization, it becomes a significant resource for sustaining a competitive advantage. Compared to its internally focused competitors, a market-oriented company selects its target markets more wisely and offers a product mix better matched to customer preferences. Although it may face the same risks as any other firm when it comes to neglecting market intelligence or acting sluggishly in an environment requiring adaptation, its knowledge of customers and competitors is apt to overcome occasional errors. Superior self-knowledge will reveal the source of its competitive advantage and it will then be protected.

Market Orientation Payoffs

Because many firms give lip service to being market-oriented, the truly market-oriented firm may not be easily recognized by its inwardly focused competitors. And market orientation is not something one puts on like a new T-shirt. It requires supportive administrative and social systems, formal and tacit routines, and employees who incorporate the orientation into their entire work lives.

At least three payoffs point to a sustainable competitive advantage from a market orientation. First, a market-oriented firm should benefit from better marketing programs, efforts that fit the needs of customers. In general, it realizes efficiencies from precision targeting and avoids trouble because it is adaptable. Second, the market-oriented firm is difficult for competitors to spot easily. Because talk is cheap, lots of organizations say they have a sophisticated customer focus. But the truly market-oriented will only be revealed over long time periods. Thus, the market orientation has a stealth character. Finally, a market orientation is apt to be unique. It is typically a very distinctive skill because it is complex, intangible, and inimitable. Two competing distributors could match each other in offering bar-coded parts, overnight delivery, and Internet ordering. But matching on market orientation—values and systems for market knowledge and strategy development—is not as easy as buying a scanner, hiring more drivers, or contracting for web site development.

Organizational Learning and Memory

So far in this chapter we have defined business strategy, identified key elements in a strategy (product market emphasis, objectives and plans, synergies, etc.), highlighted critical facets of the strategic planning process (SWOT, mission formulation, competitive analysis), and flagged the imperatives for sequential disruptions of market and a market orientation. Now we must emphasize the ability to learn and transfer knowledge as vital skills for both the development and execution of business strategies. Indeed, they represent the critical prerequisites for the judicious selection and development of other strategic resources and skill sets.

Eddie Robinson has coached the Grambling University football team to over 400 wins. If we analyze his world-record success, we find that he acquires superior resources—scores of his players have shown their athleticism in successful careers in the NFL. He also demands dedication in training, assignments, and practice. Stamina, strength, and good play execution result. Coach Robinson also carefully studies films of upcoming Grambling opponents. With his staff, he formulates a specific game plan, a strategy to neutralize the strengths of the opponent, exploit its weaknesses, and mask Grambling's own vulnerabilities. But the opposing coaches are doing homework too. On any given game day, weather, injuries, and "the breaks" can foil a game plan. Time and again, Coach Robinson has been able to diagnose breakdowns, spot new opportunities, and anticipate opponent reactions. He and his team constantly make adjustments on the sideline or in the short halftime break. Clearly, the ability to learn (1) in the formulation and rehearsal of the game plan and (2) in the heat of the struggle has proven itself to be a competitive advantage for Grambling.

What Is Learning?

You have been in college for some time now. One measure of its value so far might be to ask you to define learning. Students in our classes often give the following answers: "information," "facts and concepts you can use," "knowledge," "skill acquisition," "discovery," "to memorize." Although learning touches upon all of these, we like the very concrete definition from McGee: "**Learning** is when we connect new information to what we already know. We're learning when we can say, 'Hey, that's just like _____.' "[15] The ancient Egyptians made awesome and lasting architectural structures knowing only that a triangle with sides measuring 3, 4, and 5 units produced a perpendicular. Later, in the 6th century BC, the Greek mathematician Pythagoras gave his famous theorem. (The square of the hypotenuse is the sum of the squared adjacent sides, "just like the Egyptian's 5–4–3 triangle.") And sooner or later in statistics class you learn the concept of Euclidian distance, perhaps saying, "Oh, that's like the Pythagorean theorem!"

We can now define the **learning organization** as one that consistently creates and refines its capabilities by connecting new information and skills to known and remembered requisites for future success. Recognize implicit humility in this definition; it does not presume *all* success factors are known. It surely includes the endeavors by the organization to learn more about what are the requisites of future success.

Managing Organizational Learning

Management scholars have only just begun to investigate how one creates and maintains a learning enterprise. One useful way to represent the process is the multiplicative model shown in Exhibit 6–12. A key feature of this type of model is that if any variable is zero, the product of the remaining variables is zero, in which case we do not have a learning organization.

Visionary Leadership   Ronald Reagan was twice elected president in landslide proportions. Many pundits credit Reagan's success to his ability to communicate a clear vision for his administration: cut and simplify taxes, grow the economy, and rebuild the

Exhibit 6–12
Requisites for the Learning Organization

| Visionary leadership | × | Target & trajectory | × | Information systems | × | Creating & striving | × | Execution |

SOURCE: Adapted from Calhoun Wick and Lu Stanton Leon, "From Ideas to Action: Creating a Learning Organization," *Human Resource Management* 34, no. 2 (1995), pp. 299–311, with permission of the copyright © owner John Wiley & Sons, Inc.

U.S. military. Hernan Cortes conquered the Aztec empire—some 200,000 warriors—with 508 soldiers, 16 horses, 10 bronze cannon, four falconets, and 13 muskets. Cortes attacked when retreat seemed proper, he praised the valor of his defeated opponents, and made peace with the Aztec's enemies. His vision—in speech and action—to take the Gospel to the New World, find fame in this fantastic adventure, and claim wealth beyond compare motivated superb effort and loyalty in his men.[16]

POSCO, Korea's giant steel maker, is driven by the company motto of "3 Bests," meaning best quality, minimal pollution, and zero accidents. Boeing's vision directing effort on the new 777 was even simpler than POSCO's: "Working together to produce the preferred new airplane family."[17] Indeed, a vision should be simple and easily communicated throughout the business.

We are not out to replay our discussion of organizational mission in this section. The emphasis is on leadership. Organizational leaders determine whether the vision is concrete or wimpy. Cortes scuttled his ships after landing to end any doubt about commitment. GE's CEO, Jack Welch, has to follow through with rewards and divestitures when he calls for all GE products to be first or second in their markets.

High-profile CEOs are the subject of many articles and lore. But visionary leadership for the learning organization must extend throughout the organization: the executive committee, the senior partners, the regional heads, and department and branch managers. Especially in the nebulous assignment "to improve capabilities to attain success"

In Pohang, Korea, POSCO operates the world's third largest steelmaking facility. Dubbed the "factory in the garden," it aims for zero defects, zero accidents, and zero pollution.
Courtesy POSCO.

6–2

FROM THE FIELD
The Learning Organization of Coopers & Lybrand

Coopers & Lybrand L.L.P. (C&L), one of the world's leading professional services firms, provides services for enterprises in a wide range of industries. The firm offers its clients the expertise of more than 16,000 professionals and staff in offices located in 100 U.S. cities and (through its member firms) more than 66,000 people in over 125 countries worldwide. C&L offers financial advisory services, business assurance, consulting, and human resource advice to businesses around the world.

In the mid-1990s C&L identified learning as a strategic competency of the firm. "Improving our ability to learn continuously appeared to be central to dealing with the changes we saw in our markets—changes in clients, competitors, relationships, and services—fundamental shifts in our environment. Further, we saw learning as critical to enhancing and realizing the value creating potential of our organization," says Judith Rosenbloom, vice chairman of learning and education at C&L.

To create a learning culture in its corporate environment, C&L tried to formalize its definition: a culture in which every person in the company is dedicated to increasing the capacity for action. In support of this new credo the firm tries to provide opportunities to learn and be consistent with its reinforcing signals and actions. This first stage was coded into a three-point philosophy:

1. "I'm responsible for learning and for building my value through learning, and for actively sharing what I've learned."
2. "The firm is responsible for articulating the competencies required for success and for giving me the opportunities and the environment in which to learn."
3. "My boss is responsible for articulating to me my immediate learning priorities and for giving me the modeling, coaching, and feedback that will allow me to be successful."

C&L sees learning as much more than training. Although over 300 training courses are taught at C&L, learning is sought in countless interpersonal exchanges, role models, and practice opportunities—such as its Partner Camp. "I found this to be critically important because we're an organization that keeps score on everything," say Reed Keller, head of C&L's Human Resource Advisory. "In our competitive environment, it's hard to practice. You can't hit any fouls. You can't experiment with your client skills. It's hard to innovate safely. And so with Partner Camp, we tried to create an environment where we could have practice fields, to work on the future, rather than always debate the past."

Of course, C&L has found significant barriers. First, this initiative has brought a whole new vocabulary to the firm: *coaching, team building, reflection*. And achieving commonality in meanings has been a challenge. Second, C&L recognized it didn't have all its needed expertise in-house. It formed learning partnerships with other organizations and consulting firms. Its three-day, hands-on case experience for new partners at the University of Virginia's Darden School of Business was a smashing success. It yielded 120 "ambassadors for learning," bringing the culture to every corner of the enterprise.[18]

every supervisor is a role model in character—prudent, just, constant, and sober—as well as a potential champion of innovation, skill development, risk taking, and success sharing.

Target and Trajectory   It takes resources and plans to create a learning enterprise. When a firm's leadership has determined to build a learning culture, a program and administrative structure must be designed. A timetable should be developed to specify when each enabling phase or critical event ought to take place. It took Xerox six years to move from its first "Leadership through Quality" initiatives to winning the Malcolm Baldrige National Quality Award. Even a firm with a rich tradition of managing intellectual and moral capital must attend to the maintenance of these strategic assets. What programs, tracking measures, and new hiring criteria should be applied or reviewed? From the Field 6–2 profiles the learning initiatives at Coopers & Lybrand.

Information and Value Systems   We have already discussed situation analysis, SWOT, competitive analysis, customer satisfaction studies, and more. The learning organization develops *systems* to gauge internal matters: efficiency, employee morale, and cross-functional knowledge. Value systems encouraging honesty and information sharing and quashing the need to cover up errors with the need to fix problems are part of the equation.

Other systems must focus on the external environment. Competitive intelligence can be gained by talking to distributors, monitoring advertising and trade shows, reading corporate annual reports, tracking dialogue on the Internet, and more. Recognize good ideas from customers, competitors, foreign markets, and elsewhere. David Luther, senior vice president of quality at Corning Inc., says, "It's absolutely crazy to reinvent something that somebody else has done."

Creating and Striving   Vision, plans, and information are certain to be bland and feeble if not energized by creative effort. To create means to bring something into existence, to make something original. What does it take to be creative? Well, researchers in a variety of fields have told us that creative people tend to be or have:[19]

Curious	Persistent	Imaginative	Visual thinker
Sense of humor	Motivated and energetic	Energetic	Unique
Independent	Eclectic taste	Hard-working	Confident
Observant	Avid reader	Ambitious	Able to see the big picture

Thomas Edison claimed that creativity was 1 percent inspiration and 99 percent perspiration. That essence is reflected in the preceding traits and in our experience with effective managers. The creative professional works hard. Their efforts are efficient in the sense that they don't try to force fit a tired solution to a new challenge and they often recognize the payoffs that can come from finding new ways to frame problems. They recognize that a crisis in sales force performance may be a training problem, a motivation problem, or even a selection problem. By examining the data from different perspectives, the creative manager tends to see the limits of existing routines and the need for new solutions at any level of operations or position in the value-added chain.

Execution   Nike's slogan "Just Do It" captures the flavor of postindustrial culture. The learning organization has the same urgency to act, but it tackles a bigger agenda. Unlike the couch potato charged by Nike to get out there and play tennis, the learning organization must "Do the Right Thing" and "Do It Right." Coach Robinson can send the right play to be called in the huddle, but if blocks are missed, pass routes are sloppy, or the ball is fumbled, then the play called doesn't matter.

Learning organizations know the competitive advantage to be gained from execution. Lear Seating can deliver a car seat system ready for installation within two hours of the time it was ordered. Kuper Maintenance emphasizes fix-it-right the first time, knowing the nuisance and frustration that come from lingering problems at its customer's physical plants.

6–2

BUSINESS 2 BUSINESS
Listen Up!

Learning organizations listen to their customers. An airline customer told the aeronautical engineer at Boeing that he wanted a jet with a fuselage that could change size. Regarding the request as a technical impossibility, the Boeing engineer delved a little farther: "Why do you want such a plane?"

The customer explained, "We don't know 10 years from now what size plane we will need. If we had the flexibility to shrink or expand the size of the plane, it would help us meet future travel demands, even those we cannot anticipate."

Largely as a result of this exchange, Boeing reframed its notion of a plane's interior. It created a plane with quick-change seats and movable galleys—the flexible interior. The 777 can be outfitted for packing in vacation travelers or accommodating the need for room among business passengers traveling overnight.[20]

What business are you familiar with that really listens to its customers? Why do you say that? Who does the listening? How does listener input get translated into action?

Quality execution takes practice. So learning organizations make or find practice fields. They simulate market situations in training sessions. They use customer quotations and other feedback to tune systems. They hone routines in low-risk environments, perhaps in isolated test environments or in cooperation with a key supplier or customer with a shared stake in the excellence of operations. For example, Microsoft may pilot test a new operating system or software application at organizations that are apt to find and stretch the limits of functionality. Not only are kinks ironed out, but "new wrinkles" may be added to enhance system performance.

Summary

This chapter has pointed to the significant probability that you will give forecasting input to your company's strategic planning process. Although many planning models can be summarized in crisp flow charts and path diagrams, appreciate the iterative and multiple tasking character of planning in action.

You may also be asked to provide a SWOT analysis. Consider the various internal and external forces within your bailiwick and try to convey them to top management. Conceptual maps, value-added chains, and customer profiles will be helpful in this regard. These are just a small sample of singular situation analysis tools. Recognize that most students will plug into the planning process of their employer. For formulating a strategy for your own company or organization, we strongly recommend you use a variety of approaches. Of course, do not forget to spend time talking with and listening to members of your stakeholder groups—customers, suppliers, employees, owners—first hand.

We spent several pages on the analysis of competition. The heat of competitive pressures comes not only from intense rivalry among firms in the same industry chasing the same group of customers, but also from negotiations with powerful customers and suppliers. We must also regard the full range of existing and potential alternatives to our products as competitors. For example, potential customers of our information technology consultancy can consider other consulting firms, outsource their operations, or develop an internal strategic support staff.

Potential entrants to a market represent a fifth competitive force. The chapter underscored the importance of choosing one's competitive arena judiciously. By developing strong service organizations or channel relations, a business may thwart potential entrants who don't have the time, resources or know-how to serve customers that value these dimensions. Alternatively, a firm investing in high-efficiency, high-volume productive capacity needs to capitalize on this strength in securing large accounts, where few other players can hold their own in the slim-margin trade terms. In sum, stress the unique and inimitable.

Market-oriented firms recognize the fickleness of customers and the fleeting nature of any sort of competitive edge. Thus, getting and staying market-oriented is a competitive advantage in its own right. The foundation for the market orientation, in turn, is an organization that learns. The learning organization has visionary leadership, thorough plans, and good control systems. The learning organization manifests persistence, creativity, and an ability to execute.

Key Terms

analyzer	learning	prospector
barriers to entry	learning organization	reactor
conceptual map	market development	strategy
defender	market orientation	SWOT analysis
diversification	market penetration	synergy
five forces of competition	mission statement	tactical decision
	product development	

Discussion Questions

1. "Plans are nothing. Planning is everything." Can this be true?

2. The conduct of a SWOT analysis seems rather straightforward. But problems arise as both external and internal factors intersect. To illustrate, Sealed Air Corporation prided itself on its technical leadership and consultative sales force in the packaging field. Does this strength become a liability when effective, low-cost competitive offerings begin to flood the market? What would you say are the corporate strengths of, say, Microsoft, 3M, and United Parcel Service? Are there environments where these strengths become weaknesses?

3. "Analyzing a competitor's current strengths and weaknesses and playing strengths against weaknesses may work in the short term but is not an effective long-term strategy in a dynamic environment. . . . Consistently playing against the weaknesses of a competitor is both predictable and a strategy that ultimately builds its weaknesses into strengths. A tennis player who serves to his opponent's weak backhand will eventually force the opponent to develop a stronger backhand. Then the first player faces a rival with a strong forehand and a strong backhand."[21] Do you agree? Is there another strategy?

4. Analyze the structure of competition in the overnight delivery business using the five-forces model. Although Federal Express and UPS dominate, with respective market shares of about 45 and 20 percent, Airborne Express has been the fastest growing courier in the 1990s. Airborne has neglected small accounts and worked intimately with select companies to solve comprehensively their complex shipping needs. Is this advantage sustainable?

5. Chapter 6 sketched the role of conceptual maps and other models to cope with the complexity of markets and business planning. A lesson on this point is the Battle of Midway, required reading in the U.S. Naval Academy. In the aftermath of the sea battle that changed the direction of the war in the Pacific, it seems that the Japanese overplanned and overrehearsed. They followed static assumptions and enjoyed an abundance of resources. Japanese Admiral Isoroku Yamamoto "succumbed to the temptation of taking on a broad set of objectives (capture Midway, attack the Aleutians, destroy the U.S. fleet). As underdogs with limited resources, the Americans were constrained to pursue a simpler, more straightforward mission: defend Midway Island. As a result, their strategic responsibilities were much different: to be alert to whatever opportunities might arise within the context of their single mission and to be sufficiently flexible to act on them."[22] Use web and library sources to sketch a time line and simple set of maps to show the key events at Midway. (Try **http://www.geocities.com/ Colosseum/Arena/2951/english.html**) Contrast this to a corporate example (e.g., DeLorean Motor Cars, Beatrice, Osborne Computer).

6. Interview two business executives—the higher their rank the better. Ask them for their company's mission. Then invite them to tell you how it came about and how it affects the direction and activities of the company.

7. Our experience indicates that few student organizations on a college campus can show a history of sustained effectiveness. Analyze this phenomenon by considering the impediments to organizational learning in this context. Can you identify exceptional organizations on your campus? How have they overcome the impediments to learning?

8. What are the key strategic decisions facing managers at General Electric, Netscape, Apple, or Delta Airlines?

9. The senior partner at a rapidly growing marketing research company (from 30 to 80 employees in two years) described his company mission but indicated his reluctance to put it on paper because it might limit flexibility and adaptation to client needs. Is he missing something or is he onto something?

10. Is it possible for organizational learning and memory to be liabilities in a fast-changing market?

Internet Exercise

Mission statements provide direction for all individuals in an organization, framing decisions and guiding policy. If well connected to a firm's distinctive competencies, a mission statement is specific. It will make little sense if hung on the wall of another organization.

Visit the home pages of two or three firms in this chapter, and compare their mission statements with those of one of their competitors. For example, you might visit Coopers & Lybrand at **http://www.pwcglobal.com/us** (its new identity comes from its recent merger with Price Waterhouse). Then surf to a competing national accounting firm, such as Arthur Andersen at **http://www.arthurandersen.com** or KPMG (which merged in 1997 with Ernst and Young) at **http://www.kpmg.com.** You may be surprised to find that some firms do not publish a mission statement on their web site. Might there be valid reasons for keeping the mission proprietary?

Cases

Case 6.1 Intel Inside on the Outside

Compaq Computer is the world's largest supplier of personal computers. Its desktop PCs, servers, and portables are used in almost every type of business. Do its customers worry what microprocessor serves the machines? Do they care whether it's Texas Instruments, Hitachi, NEC, Toshiba, or Motorola? Yes, they do!

After nearly two years of reliance on other suppliers, in January 1995, Compaq returned to Intel as its primary chip supplier, again putting "Intel Inside" its computers.

Intel—the world's largest chip maker—is an industry leader in product development. It spends over $1 billion in R&D a year in a continuing cycle of innovation and obsolescence.

Compaq clearly values the technical product development savvy at Intel. The two companies entered a cross-licensing agreement under which they have agreed to a worldwide nonexclusive patent license. "Since both companies have strong patent portfolios, our agreement provides an open environment that allows us to continue to deliver innovative products to our respective customers," said Paul Otellini, senior vice president of Intel World Wide Sales.

"In addition, we are very happy that Compaq is returning to the Intel Inside® program. Intel has worked very hard to ensure that this ingredient marketing–promotional program is successful for our customers."

Thus, beyond the cross-licensing of patents, the two companies joined in marketing efforts. Compaq has reentered the Intel Inside® program and will use the Intel Inside logo in its products, packaging, and advertising.[23]

1. Do you think it wise that Compaq became so dependent on a supplier?

2. Can you identify other companies besides Intel that develop a brand for a component part? What entry barriers does this strategy pivot on?

Case 6.2 Petrex: Competition in Emerging Markets

The Petrex Corporation is an environmental services company that has been a leader in the field of chemical storage, disposal, and cleanup. Management at Petrex routinely monitors—and participates in—local, national, and international environmental policy forums. Recently there have been indications that the Environmental Protection Agency and Federal Emergency Management Agency will push to have regular filtration (every 24 to 36 months) of the diesel fuel that is stored in tanks for emergency power generation at nearly 12,000 hospitals and nursing care facilities.

The equipment to conduct these filtrations is widely available. Anyone with a small tanker truck can attach the filtration device and be in business within a few days. Thus, as demand for diesel fuel filtration may go from zero to nearly 5,000 jobs at $300 to $500 at the issuance of new regulations, start-up suppliers can appear just as quickly.

Petrex has tanker trucks it can retrofit and commit to this opportunity, but there have been heated debates in the company. Some argue that the potential sales numbers are too good to pass up and that Petrex is one of only two firms that could well participate as a nationwide supplier. Petrex already has waste disposal contracts with about 15 percent of the firms apt to be affected by new regulations. Others have cautioned that this is a new game—a mundane operation compared to the complexity and risk in most of its jobs. Also, the field is wide open to any local tanker jockey who wants to put down the $3,000 to outfit a truck.

Describe the competitive forces at play in this opportunity and justify a recommendation to Petrex.

Additional Readings

Abrahams, Jeffrey, *The Mission Statement Book: 301 Corporate Mission Statements from America's Top Companies.* Berkeley, CA: Ten Speed Press, 1995.

Best, Roger J., *Market Based Management.* Upper Saddle River, NJ: Prentice Hall, 1997.

Byrne, John A., "Strategic Planning," *Business Week* (August 26, 1996), pp. 46–52.

Covey, Stephen R., A. Roger Merrill, and Rebecca R. Merrill, *First Things First.* New York: Simon & Schuster, 1994.

D'Aveni, Richard, *Hypercompetition: Managing the Dynamics of Strategic Maneuvering* New York: The Free Press, 1994.

Day, George S., and David J. Reibstein, eds., *Wharton on Dynamic Competitive Strategy.* New York: John Wiley & Sons, 1997.

Fulmer, Robert M., "A Model for Changing the Way Organizations Learn," *Planning Review* (May–June 1994), pp. 20–24.

Geci, John, "Presenting the Winner of the 1997 Peter F. Drucker Strategic Leadership Award: FedEx's Frederick W. Smith," *Strategy and Leadership* 25 (September–October 1997), pp. 30–31.

Hamel, Gary, and C. K. Prahalad, *Competing for the Future.* Boston, MA: Harvard Business School Press, 1994.

Harley, Robert F., *Marketing Mistakes.* New York: John Wiley & Sons, 1995.

Hunt, Shelby, and Robert Morgan, "The Comparative Advantage Theory of Competition," *Journal of Marketing* 59 (April 1995), pp. 1–15.

Krinsky, Robert, and Anthony C. Jenkins, "When Worlds Collie: The Uneasy Fusion of Strategy and Innovation," *Strategy & Leadership* 25 (July–August 1997), pp. 36–41.

Slywotzky, Adrian J., *Value Migration.* Boston: Harvard Business School Press, 1996.

Slywotzky, Adrian J., and Fred Linthicum, "Capturing Value in Five Moves or Less: The New Game of Business," *Strategy & Leadership* 25 (January–February 1997), pp. 5–11

Spekman, Robert E., Theodore M. Forbes III, Lynn A. Isabella, and Thomas C. MacAvoy, "Alliance Management: A View from the Past and a Look to the Future." *Working paper.* Cambridge, MA: Marketing Science Institute, 1995.

Webster, Frederick, "The Changing Role of Marketing in the Corporation," *Journal of Marketing* 56 (October 1992), pp. 1–17.

Chapter 7

Weaving Marketing into the Fabric of the Firm

GENERAL ELECTRIC

General Electric is a name familiar to most people. What may not be familiar to most marketing students is the contribution GE has made to the management of marketing. GE, with industrial products making up 80 percent of its business, has been one of the leaders in the development of product management theories and practices, for example. Now GE is one of the leaders in developing theories and practices that weave marketing into every activity of the firm.●

The payoff has been great. Sales have increased 15 percent per year through 1997 and the return to shareholders was 45 percent in 1995. And unlike many companies that are breaking up into smaller companies in order to survive, GE is committed to growing even larger than the $90 billion in sales it enjoyed in 1997.●

As its top three executives wrote in the 1995 annual report, "Our dream, and our plan, well over a decade ago, was simple. We set out to shape a global enterprise that preserved the classic big-company advantages—while eliminating the classic big-company drawbacks. What we wanted to build was a hybrid, an enterprise with the reach and resources of a big company— the body of a big company—*but the thirst to learn, the compulsion to share, and the bias for action*—the soul—of a small company" (emphasis added).●

Learning, sharing knowledge, and a bias for action are important characteristics of the marketing-oriented firm. As GE continues to grow at a rapid pace, it also continues to develop better and more comprehensive marketing practices that permeate the organization.●

Visit the GE web site: **www.ge.com**●

Learning Objectives

In forward-thinking companies like GE, the marketing function has taken on increased significance in recent years. As companies recognize the importance of the customer, marketing's importance grows because of the responsibility for the customer. In this chapter, we examine the role of marketing in carrying the voice of the customer to the rest of the firm. In Chapter 6, we learned about strategic planning; in this chapter we learn how marketing builds internal partnerships in order to devise and implement the most effective strategic plan possible.

After reading this chapter, you should be able to

- Describe the role marketing plays in creating and maintaining a learning organization.
- Describe the internal partnerships that must be developed with marketing.
- Illustrate the partnering process for various internal partnerships.
- List the skills that are needed by marketing managers to build internal partnerships.

The concepts of marketing orientation and learning organization were first introduced in Chapter 6. In this chapter, we explore how those concepts must be carried into every activity of the firm so that the value delivered by the value chain is maximized.

The Fabric of the Firm

Visit friends on another campus, and you may find a very different college experience. What makes each university unique is the unique culture, the values that began as reasons for starting each university, and the forces that have shaped that university's past and will shape its future. Visit Texas A&M and you'll find a military tradition; more Aggies have won the Congressional Medal of Honor than graduates of any of the service academies. Just 60 miles up the Brazos River is Baylor University, with its very different culture shaped by close ties with the Southern Baptist church.

Organizational culture is the collectively held values, ideology, and social processes embedded in a firm.[1] When we entitled this chapter "Weaving Marketing into the Fabric of the Firm," we meant that marketing should be such an integral part of that culture that marketing activities are not identifiable with just one department but are part and parcel of the activities of virtually every employee. Implementing the marketing strategy becomes the responsibility of everyone, not just the marketing or sales departments.

When marketing values are embedded into the culture of a firm, then marketing managers have one important additional responsibility: to carry the customer's voice to the rest of the firm. The medium by which this is accomplished is organizational learning; the result of such learning should be a reinforcement of the market orientation of the firm.

Marketing Orientation and Organizational Learning

Organizational learning is an important element in the continued success of any organization, and a market orientation is the principal cultural foundation for successful learning. As you read in the opening vignette, GE is committed to creating a culture with a "thirst to learn," a commitment that is paying off with superior performance. As defined in Chapter 6, a learning organization is one that consistently creates and refines its capabilities by connecting new information and skills to known requisites for future success. Where do these "known requisites" come from? From the customer. **Known requisites** are requirements for success that have been identified by the firm; thus, the market-oriented firm is able to generate customer requirements that are then part of the learning process.

For example, Stork, a Dutch manufacturer of ships, machinery, and industrial coatings, suffered a sharp downfall in profits over a five-year period. The company had been dedicated to developing technology; a shift to dedication to clients was the first step in the turnaround. The company wasn't revitalized until it learned how to identify customer needs and to share those needs (known requisites) throughout the organization.[2]

Organizational Learning Further Defined

At the most basic level, organizational learning is the process of developing new knowledge that has the potential to influence behavior.[3] Presumably, learning facilitates behavior change that leads to better performance. For example, GE marketers learned that products could be managed using portfolios similar to financial portfolios. The outcomes included the development of a portfolio method of product management discussed in the next chapter, as well as overall performance improvement in GE's sales and earnings. In fact, GE's approach made such good sense that it has been incorporated into numerous textbooks, including this one.

Exhibit 7–1

Types of Learning
Generative learning
occurs when we
break through a
learning boundary
caused by a faulty
assumption or
conclusion.

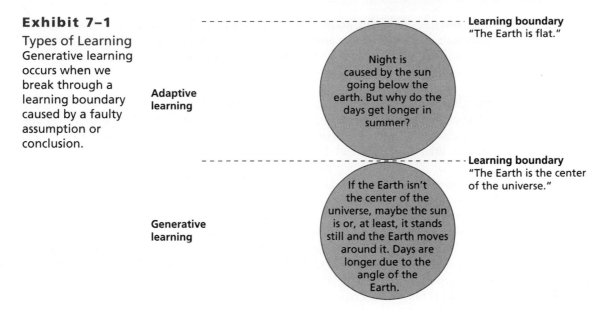

There are two types of learning: adaptive (single-loop) and generative (double-loop). In the next section, we'll define both types of learning and discuss why both are important to organizational success.

Learning Types

Adaptive (single-loop) learning is learning that occurs within a set of constraints, or learning boundaries. In a marketing process situation, adaptive learning is learning how to change within a system, but the system is defined by the individual's or organization's learning boundaries. **Learning boundaries** are assumptions and beliefs held by the organization that limit learning. For example, consider the theories held about what causes night and day when people assumed the world was flat. It would be impossible to think of the earth spinning on an axis and see night as a shadow if the world was assumed or believed to be flat. Any learning that took place within the assumption of a flat earth only enabled someone to adapt to changes within the boundaries of that assumption, and is illustrated in Exhibit 7–1.

Generative (double-loop) learning is the creation of knowledge that occurs when changing assumptions and beliefs. Recall that in Chapter 3, we discussed that everyone has theories of how the world operates. Theories are based on assumptions and beliefs, but also limit what new beliefs can be created. Generative learning requires that the firm build new theories of how things work; generative learning occurs when we change our theories as to *why* systems are effective. Generative learning is also a form of learning that occurs when learning boundaries are shattered by changes, rather than when changes occur within those boundaries. Going back to our earlier example concerning causes of night and day, if we just change our belief that the Earth is the center of the universe and consider that perhaps the sun is, then we cannot explain night and day. We must also reconsider whether the Earth is flat and stationary. Both boundaries, as illustrated in the exhibit, are called into question.

An example of learning boundaries was presented by Ted Leavitt in the classic article, "Marketing Myopia." In that article, he illustrated that railroads lost their competitiveness because they failed to see other modes of transportation as competition. Instead, they focused on being better railroads, rather than better forms of transportation. Seeing competition only as other railroads is a learning boundary; railroads have since broken through that boundary and are now intermodal carriers.

Generative learning is difficult; suspending one's assumptions is hard because assumptions are not always easy to identify and are also difficult to distinguish from fact. For example, mankind saw light and dark every 24 hours and believed the sun to move because that is what they saw. Tracing that conclusion back to the assumption that the Earth is flat requires several steps in logic that seem obvious to us now. More difficult is tracing back assumptions about how a market operates and distinguishing between what has been observed about that market and what was assumed.

Marketing often creates learning boundaries. For example, if AT&T defined its corporate long-distance market as companies needing long-distance services to *talk* to customers and far-flung employees, the Internet could not exist. This is an example of "tyranny of the served market" or being so focused on one traditional market that the organization is blind to unconventional business opportunities.[4] What usually happens in situations where a company is a captive of its market is that another company is formed and takes its place by capturing the unconventional opportunity. Thus, one important responsibility of the marketing manager is to encourage exploration of new markets, without undue focus on limited markets.

Organizational Learning and Competitive Advantage

Many executives have said that the only truly sustainable competitive advantage is to be able to learn faster than competition. A company that creates a truly innovative product can expect competition in 9 to 15 months, on average. The advantage gained from being first in the market can only be sustained if the company continues to learn and stays ahead of competition. For example, Lotus was once the dominant spreadsheet software company but did not maintain its early-market advantage because it could not learn how to integrate its software with other applications as quickly as Microsoft did. From the Field 7–1 reveals one facet of learning passion at Microsoft.

Note that this does not mean that all organizational learning is good. Organizations can learn the wrong things, such as concluding that the initial high sales of a new product were due to its features rather than to its low relative price and availability. As soon as even lower priced models become available, that new product will fail.[5]

Further, companies can get caught in competency traps, which are a form of learning boundary. A **competency trap** is any skill or technology that a company sticks with due to comfort with the familiar, in spite of evidence that better alternatives may exist. For example, Apple's reluctance to embrace the DOS environment has doomed Apple to being a niche player in the computer market. In this case, Apple's operating system may be superior, but the better alternative would be one that should lead to greater sales. (We could also make the case that the market has been caught in a competency trap represented by the DOS operating system, at least until the advent of Windows 95.)

Since learning is key to creating competitive advantage and since bad learning can have serious negative consequences, it behooves all managers to study learning processes and tools. Perhaps, though, it is more important for marketing managers to understand organizational learning methods since known requisites are derived from customer requirements.

7–1

FROM THE FIELD
Who's That behind Microsoft's Success?

Everyone has heard of Bill Gates, but Steve Ballmer is the unsung hero behind the success of Microsoft. Behind only Bill Gates and Paul Allen in terms of Microsoft stock ownership and worth $5 billion, Ballmer was responsible for developing Windows and destroying IBM's market share for OS/2. To stay current as the executive vice president for sales and support, Ballmer sometimes immerses himself in a region, living for a few months in Europe or acting as a sales manager in Phoenix in order to get a better feel for what is going on.

Searching for a better way to measure the market for network servers, Ballmer first tries to understand the market. For 15 minutes, he scribbles boxes and lines with different magic markers, creating a cognitive map of the market. Finally, he spots a connection between two parts of the market he hadn't noticed before. That small connection will be the basis of a marketing strategy for network servers into the next century.

In an industry where no company has been able to really maintain dominance from one computing era to the next, Microsoft wants to be the first to continue to dominate. Using data from public sources like investment reports and news accounts, Ballmer keeps picking at the data until he finds new ways to understand the market. "That will be a valuable asset for us, to understand this market in ways that others don't" (Ramstad, B4).

Source: Evan Ramstad, "Microsoft Ascribes Portion of Success to Marketing Guru," *Waco Tribune Herald* (Sunday, July 14, 1996) p. B4.; Jeffrey Young, "The George S. Patton of Software," *Forbes* (January 27, 1997), pp. 86–87.

How Marketing Learns

Organizational learning is comprised of three processes: information acquisition, information dissemination, and shared interpretation, as seen in Exhibit 7–2. Marketing's role in acquiring information, via marketing research, feedback from the sales force, and other methods, is an important element in the acquisition of vital information for the rest of the firm. That information is then disseminated through interpersonal communication and reports created as a function of internal partnerships. Together, as internal partners create a shared interpretation of the information (in other words, decide what the data mean for the organization), they can create an effective strategy to take advantage of what has been learned.

Further, marketing acquires and disseminates information for its own use through competitive intelligence, environmental scanning, accounting systems, information systems, case studies, experiments, and benchmarking. What we will discuss now are tools of learning, tools that are used to create new knowledge or understanding from the information acquired and disseminated in a market-oriented learning organization. The tools we will discuss are cognitive mapping, experiments, learning laboratories, and tools for learning from others.

Cognitive Mapping
Cognitive mapping is a learning tool that is used to explore mental structures of beliefs and assumptions. In one respect, cognitive mapping is used to draw one's theories; the map is a diagram of cause-and-effect streams.

Exhibit 7–2
How Marketing
Learns

Information Acquisition →	Information Dissemination →	Shared Interpretation
Marketing research	To	Through
Sales and service feedback	Marketing management	Brainstorming
Enivornmental scanning	Senior management	Planning
Competitive intelligence	Manufacturing	Other processes
Other learning tools	Engineering and R & D	
	Finance	

Cognitive maps are useful for identifying one's learning boundaries. Each link between a cause and its effects can be considered for what it really is—a tested conclusion or an untested assumption. For example, a cognitive map can be used to derive the potential causes of day and night, as discussed earlier. Once these learning boundaries are identified, generative learning can occur by altering assumptions.

For example, suppose one assumption is that as price goes down, sales go up. Yet more than one marketer has found that if price goes too low, quality is questioned and sales decrease. In some cases, marketers have actually seen sales increase when prices increased. Suspending the assumption that as price goes down, sales go up, marketers can create new strategies that increase sales with higher prices. Exhibit 7–3 illustrates two different cognitive maps for determining how many stores Kinko's should have in a city or area.

When a marketing team creates a cognitive map together, then a shared understanding is created. By stating beliefs and probing to uncover the assumptions that underlie those beliefs, each individual's cognitive map can be explored. Then the team's cognitive map can be created and tested.

Experiments

Experiments are tests of cognitive maps. For example, Kinko's could test both maps by conducting experiments on the incremental impact to individual and area sales when a new store is opened. Test markets are one form of experiment, as are rolling launches. Companies use a rolling launch when they introduce a new product to a limited market so that they can test the effectiveness of the marketing campaign and so that they can make sure that operational issues, such as the training of service personnel, are working appropriately. The product is then launched across the rest of the market in phases. Both test markets and rolling launches give the organization the opportunity to learn from market reaction to the product introduction.

Learning Laboratories

Learning laboratories are environments set aside for learning. For example, companies such as Motorola and Johnson Controls have created special campuses for training and other learning experiences. Even corporate museums, such as Johnson's Global Controls Center, are being used as learning laboratories. Exhibits of products in use, company history, and other informational exhibits make up the museum, and the area is used for training, simulation of customer experiences with products, and other forms of learning.

Exhibit 7–3

Two Cognitive Maps

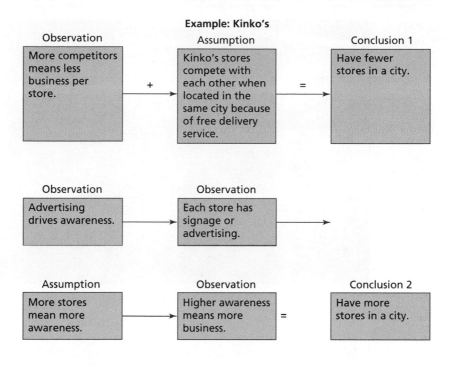

Activities in a learning laboratory might include experiments, but can also include computer simulations and other models of the real world that enable managers to practice, to learn how to learn, or to simulate decision outcomes. Role playing, such as that used in sales training and customer service training, is an example of a learning activity in a learning laboratory.

Scenarios   Scenarios are often used in learning laboratories to enable management to predict outcomes from decisions. A **scenario**, first used in Chapter 5 as a forecasting tool, can be defined as a focused description of different futures presented in a coherent manner.[6] Thus, for a single decision, all possible outcomes might be listed and probabilities estimated for the likelihood that each outcome might occur. Factors that affect the probability of each outcome are then identified; the recognition or identification of these factors is where the learning takes place.

One critical aspect of learning is that information is shared and managers across the organization share an understanding of opportunities and threats facing the organization. Scenarios can help create a shared understanding simply by forcing the sharing of knowledge. For example, creating a budget for promotion activities can be accomplished using scenarios. Each budget alternative would be examined by creating scenarios regarding potential outcomes for that level of expenditure. Royal Dutch Shell is one company that uses scenarios to develop marketing plans and to create a shared understanding of what is expected to occur. As plans are launched and results come back in, the shared understanding enables staff to go to plan B or some other appropriate plan for that particular scenario.

Case Studies   Case studies can also be used in learning laboratories to share learning throughout the company. The case study method can be used to search for causes when evaluating outcomes within a functional area. For example, when a company has a

Role playing, such as that done by Johnson Controls, is one form of learning in a learning laboratory, where people can practice and make mistakes without serious consequences.
© Chris Corsmeir

wildly successful new product, it should conduct a case study on how that new product was developed so that the process can be repeated. Similarly, if the product is a complete failure, examining how it was created can be used to avoid such problems. Product development areas in other divisions can use such cases to learn how to develop products more efficiently and with greater probability of success.

Xerox used the case study method after launch of the 3300 copier. This copier could have been a total disaster because it frequently jammed and set the copy on fire. But the company acted swiftly and pulled it from the market before any lasting damage was done. A case study indicated that the drive to turn the product out to market in a certain period of time meant that key quality tests were not conducted. These lessons were put to use in the development of the Ten Series, a product line of copiers that captured significant market share from global competitors.

Xerox has divisions that make other products too. Using the 3300 case and the Ten Series case, the company has taught important lessons to developers of such products as laser printers and facsimile machines. Case studies can be valuable tools for disseminating and creating a shared understanding in many areas of marketing, not just product development.

Strategic Planning   The strategic planning process itself can serve as a learning laboratory. A learning laboratory is an environment for learning; remember that strategic planning involves removing the planners from daily firefighting so that they can step back, consider the big picture, and make plans for the future. For generative learning to occur and to develop strategies that create systematic performance improvement, strategic planning must be done in an environment that allows for free thinking without fear of penalty. Activities such as brainstorming must be encouraged.

For example, Minit Corporation (a major service business) used the strategic planning process to bring managers together and explore corporate values. Over 300 managers in 27 countries ultimately participated and learned how what they do contributes to what the organization values.[7] From this experience, they were able to bring plans and activities into focus, which helped the company increase sales growth.

7–1

BUSINESS 2 BUSINESS
Organizational Learning and GE

In the 1995 General Electric annual report, the executives wrote that they wanted to preserve big-company advantages while eliminating big-company drawbacks. What big-company drawbacks make it difficult for learning to occur? How do big companies do a better job of performing as learning organizations? Do you believe it is possible to develop "the soul . . . of a small company" in a company as large as GE?

Learning from Others

Learners learn from others and do not seek to reinvent the wheel each time a wheel is needed. Benchmarking is one method of learning from others and includes examining the processes of others in order to copy what can be used at home.

Learning from others can also include learning from partners in joint ventures or strategic alliances, from consultants, at seminars, and via other external sources. Another form of learning from others is to be a learning customer. Virtually every large organization will purchase products from competitors in an effort to learn how to put its own product together in a more effective and economical fashion. Yet, learning from suppliers is also an important opportunity.

For example, John Paduch, vice president of sales for American Supply Co. of Gary, Indiana, saved one client over $1.5 million by showing how changing from stainless steel valves and pipes to cast iron would not reduce quality. That type of learning from value analysis (discussed in Chapter 3) is obvious. Less obvious opportunities for learning are also available from partners. For example, the Moore Business Forms accounting department presented a seminar on new accounting procedures to the accounting department of a customer.

A Commitment to Learning

When an organization is committed to learning, as GE is, it finds that learning can occur in many ways. For the marketing manager (you), commitment to learning must be personal and ongoing. Learning for an organization and the people that make up the organization is not simply about what needs to be done but also how to do it. This means that you must be committed to continuing to develop your marketing skills, industry knowledge, and other facets of professional development long after graduation.

Market-Oriented Companies

The management at GE is committed to creating a culture that supports learning. But it isn't just any learning or any knowledge. Rather, they seek specific knowledge that will enable their employees to do their jobs more effectively and more efficiently. The culture that will support the type of learning that GE management desires is one that is market-oriented.

A **market orientation**, first discussed in Chapter 6, has been defined as superior skills of understanding and satisfying customers.[8] When a firm has a market orientation, it is more likely to be financially successful and superior in many areas of performance, such as product development.[9]

A market orientation is the principle *cultural* foundation of the learning organization.[10] By cultural foundation, we mean that a market orientation must exist in the culture of the organization, and that such an orientation should be part of the values and norms of the organization. A company needs a market orientation in order to learn successfully. Recall our discussion of Stork, the Dutch company that had to develop an orientation toward customers and away from technology before it could learn the proper set of requisites.

At the same time, a market orientation is an outcome of successful organizational learning. The orientation is reinforced when the voice of the customer is carried to every part of the firm and becomes a driving force in daily operational decisions.

How Market Orientation Impacts Performance

Market-driven companies, or those with a strong market orientation, are superior in two important ways. First, market-driven companies do a better job of **market sensing**, or anticipating market requirements ahead of competition. Market sensing is the gathering of information from the market. Market research, such as that discussed in Chapter 5, is one form of market sensing, but market sensing can be achieved through listening to the sales force, observing competition at trade shows, and developing stronger ties with innovative customers and suppliers.

Similarly, the second important difference is that market-driven companies are able to develop stronger relationships with their customers and their channels of distribution. Stronger relationships include more direct lines of communication; instead of all communication going between a purchasing agent and a salesperson, interaction among engineers in all three firms (customer, manufacturer, and supplier) can occur. Stronger relationships can result in greater attention to the customer throughout the firm.

Neither important skill can develop, however, without the presence of adequate **spanning processes**, processes that link internal processes with the customer. New product development is one such spanning process, as it links market requirements with internal processes such as manufacturing. All companies have new product development processes; the difference is how the process incorporates the voice of the customer. Exhibit 7–4 illustrates the relationship of internal processes with spanning processes to link with customer requirements. In this exhibit, internal processes such as financial management are shown to link with spanning processes, such as order fulfillment, which then impact customer linking processes or other external processes. For internal processes to contribute to the value delivered by the value chain, there must be adequate spanning processes.

Internal Partnering to Create a Market Orientation

Yet internal and external processes are often in conflict, as different sets of objectives are sought. Internal partnering is one spanning process that, when done well, can result in managing such conflict so that it has a positive effect on the firm. **Internal partnering**, or creating partnering relationships with other functional areas (customers and suppliers within the firm), can also serve to carry market requirements to those managers in

Exhibit 7–4
Classifying
Capabilities

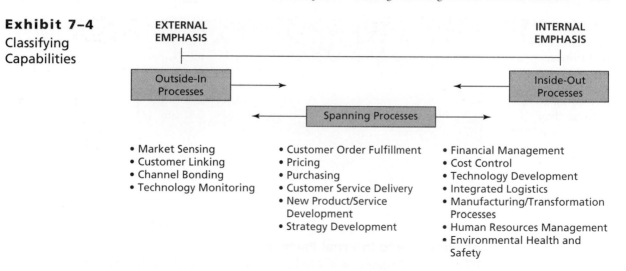

EXTERNAL
EMPHASIS

INTERNAL
EMPHASIS

Outside-In
Processes

Inside-Out
Processes

Spanning Processes

- Market Sensing
- Customer Linking
- Channel Bonding
- Technology Monitoring

- Customer Order Fulfillment
- Pricing
- Purchasing
- Customer Service Delivery
- New Product/Service Development
- Strategy Development

- Financial Management
- Cost Control
- Technology Development
- Integrated Logistics
- Manufacturing/Transformation Processes
- Human Resources Management
- Environmental Health and Safety

SOURCE: George S. Day, "Capabilities of Market-Driven Organizations," *Journal of Marketing* 58 (October, 1994), 37–52.

charge of internal processes. Internal partnering is a spanning process that creates a framework or environment for other spanning processes, such as postsale service, new product development, or market penetration and development processes. The result is a market orientation throughout the firm and not just in the marketing department.

Internal Partnering Carries the Voice of the Customer

Ron Williams, national accounts director for Champion Products, is a salesperson. Moreover, he has built many internal partnerships because he often sells for the *customer.* "I find myself selling the needs of the customer to senior management, manufacturing, customer service, or marketing every day," he says. One might think that members of those departments would just do what Ron says because it is in the best interest of the customer. Those managers, however, may have performance evaluation systems that conflict with what the customer needs. "For example, we may normally build a product a certain way. If the customer wants a slight modification, then I have to convince manufacturing and do that early enough that they can schedule the special production without driving their costs way up."[11] Ron works well with manufacturing and other areas of the firm because he has developed internal partnerships with the people in those areas.

In such situations, Ron is the voice of the customer. Other parts of the marketing department also take on the voice of the customer; for example, when new products are being developed (as discussed in the next chapter), it is the responsibility of marketing research to speak for the customer. If that voice isn't heard, then the product may be built to suit only the company's needs.

The customer's voice must be carried to many parts of the firm—internal partnering is one mechanism for carrying that voice. Recognize, though, that it is the marketing manager's responsibility to build these partnerships. Although a customer focus should pervade the firm, rarely have we seen information systems, employment selection systems, personnel evaluation systems, or other systems that encourage other departments to take the initiative. In fact, it is more likely that just the opposite is true, that there are incentives to not listen to the customer. For example, it costs manufacturing managers to change production from one product to another, yet a marketing manager may need to be able to offer different products in order to meet the customer's objectives.

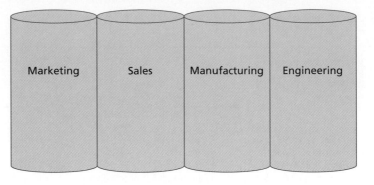

Exhibit 7–5

Silo Structure
No or little communication occurs between functional areas because they cannot leave their silos or cross through the walls.

Alternatives to Internal Partnering

What is the alternative to internal partnering? The Total Quality Management (TQM) movement of the late 1980s decried the silo organizational structure that typified many organizations at that time (and still does). A silo is a large cylinder several stories high in which grain is stored; some companies consist of a number of silo departments, with high walls built around them and no ability or desire to go between the departments. Each department does its own thing without regard for other functions in the firm, with communication between departments kept to a minimum, as illustrated in Exhibit 7–5. TQM proponents fought silo management because they recognized the importance of communicating customer requirements across all parts of the firm in order to develop a market orientation.

Internal versus External Partnering

In Chapter 2, we discussed the importance of building a partnership with customers and in several chapters, we've learned how to do that. We also learned in Chapter 3 that purchasing departments build partnerships with key suppliers because of the importance of managing costs and the contribution to innovation that such partnerships can bring. External partnerships, however, are just part of the story. One benefit of the TQM movement is that it forced companies to recognize that there are internal customers and suppliers, because each work process has inputs and outputs. Therefore, once marketing managers identify who supplies inputs for their work process and who uses their work outputs, they've recognized who the internal suppliers and customers are.

For example, when a salesperson takes an order from a customer, there is a piece of paper or an electronic record that spells out the terms of the agreement. The order contains vital information used by other departments; that information is input into their work processes, processes such as shipping the product, invoicing the customer, and recording the sale on an accounting ledger. The order is a product of the salesperson's work process (an output) and an input into other work processes, as illustrated in Exhibit 7–6. The salesperson, according to TQM, should view those other departments as customers.

Partnerships are characterized by open communication, trust, and commitment to the partner. Whether internal or external, partners are able to align their goals with the goals of the other. Internal partnering also requires open communication, trust, and commitment, but the alignment of goals is a little different. What happens when internal partnering is developed is that customer satisfaction becomes the **supragoal**, a goal against which other goals are aligned.

Exhibit 7–6
Order Fulfillment
Process: An
Example of a
Critical Spanning
Capability

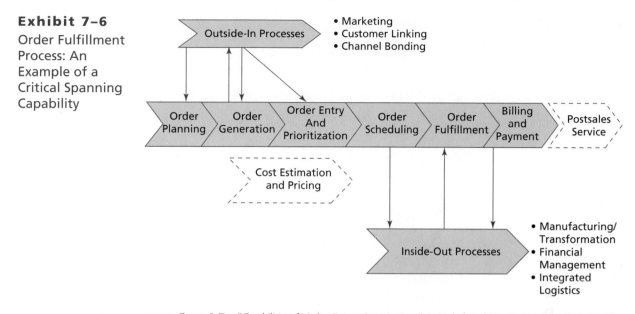

SOURCE: George S. Day "Capabilities of Market-Driven Organizations," *Journal of Marketing* 58 (October, 1994), 37–52.

Further, internal partnering is like external partnering in that the same stages of awareness, exploration, expansion, and commitment characterize the creation of a partnership.[12] Many internal relationships never progress to the partnership level because in non–marketing-oriented companies, lip service to the same supragoal does not support such relationships. As we've said earlier, there can be conflicts between functional areas in an organization. What should also be recognized is that if profitability is the supragoal, customer satisfaction may, at times, become of little importance. In such situations, each functional area may be able to contribute to profitability in ways that can damage customer satisfaction or make internal partnerships possible.

For example, Ross Controls is a company that makes pneumatic valves. Not too many years ago, it was slowly and painfully going out of business as profit margins fell and market share shrank. The company tried to cut costs so that prices could be lowered without hurting margins; the manufacturing department worked to cut costs by standardizing products and parts as much as possible, and by making longer runs of each product. As a result, the company had large inventories of products that were not always in demand, while it was unable to deliver some products because they were not scheduled for production for several months. When the company decided to make customer satisfaction the supragoal and offer custom products with faster turnaround than competition, prices were raised but so were profits and sales. Now financially healthy, the company is receiving worldwide acclaim as a leader because of internal partnerships based on delivering customer satisfaction.[13]

In the next section, we'll examine those areas of the company with whom the marketing manager works, their internal processes, and their needs and motivations. Then we'll discuss how they partner with marketing to create a market orientation.

Internal Partners

The business marketing manager interacts with many parts of the firm. Before we describe those areas, let's first define what we mean by a marketing manager. For the purposes of this discussion, a marketing manager is anyone on the marketing and sales management

Exhibit 7–7
Marketing
Interfaces

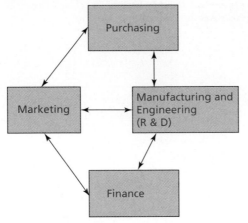

team, so we include marcomm (marketing communications) managers, sales managers, product managers, and others who serve as managers in the marketing function. Few of these managers will have all of the internal partnering responsibilities described here, but all of these responsibilities are part of one or more of those managers' duties.

Because partnering requires open communication, it promotes spanning processes and organizational learning. Marketing managers work with many areas of the firm, including manufacturing, shipping, finance, information systems, engineering, and (as you've probably guessed) just about every other area of the firm. In many cases, these areas work in the dark as far as customer requirements are concerned, particularly in silo organizations. They rely on the marketing manager to provide those customer requirements. The areas that marketing must partner with are illustrated in Exhibit 7–7.

Manufacturing

The Ron Williams example earlier in this chapter illustrates how marketing can work with manufacturing to provide customers what they need. There are three types of marketing–manufacturing situations that represent the range of customization: make to stock, make to order, and engineer to order.[14] In a **make-to-stock** situation, marketing supplies forecasts of demand and manufacturing makes enough to handle that demand. The company then draws on inventory to fill orders as they come in. There is no customization at all.

Make to order means that manufacturing or production begins making the product after receiving an order. Gateway Computers, for example, builds each computer by assembling the appropriate parts as called for on the customer's order. Customization, in this case, is handled by assembling stock parts into a custom-completed product, a process called mass customization. **Engineer to order** is complete customization, with the product designed from scratch to meet the customer's needs. In these situations, engineering is a key partner with manufacturing. (In Chapter 8, we'll talk about the engineering and research and development functions in more detail.)

In general, manufacturing is concerned with producing product at the lowest possible cost, so make to stock is the most desirable situation from manufacturing's situation. In most cases, this means that it wants long production runs, little customization, and low inventories of raw materials. Customers, however, want their order shipped immediately

This manufacturing facility operates in a make-to-stock situation, manufacturing products and storing finished inventory until sales are made.

© Ed Kashi; George Kavanagh/Tony Stone Images.

and custom made to their exact specifications—if not engineered to order, then at least made to order. Salespeople have to negotiate compromises between what customers want and manufacturing can deliver. Further, marketing managers must recognize manufacturing's responsibilities when making promotion plans, creating product line extensions, and making other marketing decisions.

Kaypro Inc., a manufacturer of portable computers, was unable to handle the conflict between marketing and manufacturing and went bankrupt as a result.[15] The problem was that what the salespeople were promoting was not what manufacturing was making. With inventories out of whack and cash flow drying up, creditors forced Kaypro into insolvency.

Marketers who have developed partnerships with manufacturing can coordinate promotion schedules to fit manufacturing schedules and vice versa. Further, the stronger the partnership, the greater the communication between marketing and manufacturing, which should result in greater success in a stronger market orientation in manufacturing.

Finance

As we will discuss in Chapter 14, pricing is a marketing function and several models are presented to aid in making pricing decisions. Yet, determining prices is not done entirely by the marketing department; as Exhibit 7–4 showed earlier, pricing is a spanning process. It is the finance department's responsibility to manage the company's cash flow, which includes setting prices at a level that contributes to profit, while it is marketing's responsibility to reflect the value a product delivers in its price.

Finance may also have responsibility for determining credit terms. Such terms would include when a customer has to pay as well as finance charges for overdue payments. Credit policies such as who gets credit are also part of the responsibility of the finance department. Strong credit policies may narrow the list of potential customers greatly, whereas loose credit policies may risk too much of the company's capital.

In the 1930s, a new trucking company called Central Freight needed trucks. A Ford dealer in a nearby town offered to sell the company the trucks and provide credit, something no other dealer would consider in those Depression years. Over 60 years later, that trucking company has several hundred trucks on the road from the same Ford dealer. Terms of the sale may be the province of the finance department, but (as that Ford dealer realized), there can be major marketing implications.

In the early 1980s, the telephone industry was heavily regulated and controlled by AT&T. An upstart company began providing long-distance services and needed some telephone switching equipment, which it wanted to purchase from Rockwell's Collins Commercial Switching. The only problem was that the sale was for $30 million, an amount equal to the customer's losses for the previous year. Should Collins extend credit? One of your authors (who worked in the marketing department) was asked to prepare a forecast for the customer's future sales to assist the finance department in working out appropriate credit terms. The company extended credit to that young firm, MCI, and they are still in partnership today.

Purchasing

Purchasing plays an important role in the product development process. The function of purchasing is to watch the company's purchasing dollars by developing policies and procedures that carefully husband those dollars. Product development, however, needs purchasing's estimates of component costs and performance (or quality) ranges, as these ripple through the value chain. It is easier to evaluate a supplier on the basis of cost than quality; after all, quality is determined by the customer and is not always as easily quantified. Purchasing, therefore, relies on the marketing manager to present the customer's definition of quality in a way that enhances the purchasing process, while the product development part of marketing relies on purchasing to meet the customer's cost needs.

From this discussion of some of the departments with whom marketing managers work, you should have some idea of the needs of other departments. At the same time, recognize that those needs may be in conflict with the needs of the customer. Making the largest profit possible, for example, conflicts with the customer's need to save money. The marketing manager's responsibility is to see that the customer's needs are met in a way that enables the company to meet its overall goals. At the same time, however, the marketing manager has to recognize that unless a firm is market-oriented, there may not be motivation for other managers to follow the marketing manager's recommendations.

Partnerships in Marketing

Partnerships must also be formed within the marketing department. In a recent session with a large industrial company, Tom Leigh (marketing professor and consultant) asked salespeople to draw pictures that illustrated their conceptions of the marketing department. One salesperson drew a large black circle and explained it by saying that marketing was a big black hole in which went the budget, ideas from the field, and so forth, but nothing ever came out. The marketing personnel, however, depicted their own salespeople as thieves, swindlers, and other despicable people.[16] So even within the marketing function, there can be breakdowns in relationships.

When a firm selects a particular marketing strategy, there should be decisions made at every level of the organization to support that strategy. One outcome of poor relationships in the marketing department is that marketing strategies are not implemented consistently across all elements of the marketing mix. A recent study found that over 25 percent of implemented sales strategies conflict with the overall marketing strategy,[17] which indicates the serious extent of poor relationships between sales and marketing. Reasons for the strategy–implementation mismatch were poor communication, misleading information promulgated by one or more departments, distrust and resentment between departments, and other factors that represent the opposite of partnerships. Cultural differences can also impair strategy, as Seagate Technology found. (See From the Field 7–2.)

7–2

FROM THE FIELD

One Company, One World

The challenge of creating a market-oriented company with a shared set of values is tough enough when all employees are from the same basic culture. When a company goes global, however, creating a corporate culture includes having to integrate world cultures. Seagate Technology may be based in California, but 6 percent of the company's $8.5 billion in sales are made in Germany. Sales offices and plants can be found in Australia, Korea, and, most recently, Malaysia.

Part of the job of creating one culture falls on the shoulders of the company's trainers, especially sales trainers. Disk drives are component parts, and salespeople can easily default to lowering prices and trying to sell the drives as commodities. Seagate's premium price is justifiable on the basis of the value the company delivers. But Roger Liston, sales trainer for Seagate, found sales reps in Australia were making friends but not making sales. In Asia, he discovered reps were uncomfortable with what they perceived to be inappropriate American selling methods. In both cases, Liston had to first learn the country's culture before he could adapt the corporate culture. After he learned the local culture, he was able to adapt Seagate's selling strategy, changing the sales method to fit local requirements.

Seagate's culture challenges extend to all parts of the corporation, as plants are being added in Asia and other continents. Making the challenge even greater is the company's acquisition binge. Recently, the company purchased several other companies in related businesses, companies that already had global operations. While the future looks bright for the industry, whether Seagate can successfully integrate all of these cultures into one corporate culture remains to be seen.

Source: Andy Cohen, "Small World, Big Challenge," *Sales & Marketing Management,* June 1996, pp. 69–73; Seagate home page, August 1996; Ramthan Hussain, "Seagate Sees Computer Sector Rebounding," Reuters News Service, August 11, 1996.

What happens when there is conflict in the marketing activities? There are few companies that will admit that they've had difficulties. One anonymous sales manager described a situation where a direct mail campaign was targeted to a small segment of the market not being called on by field salespeople. The campaign was so successful, however, that the marketing department sent direct mail offers to a much larger group and included 10 percent off the list price, a lower price than the field salespeople could offer. That larger group included many prospects of the field sales force, who lost sales to the direct mail offer, missing commissions and bonuses as well. To make matters worse, the field salespeople were expected to train the buyers on how to operate the equipment without any additional compensation.

A distributor for several electrical parts manufacturers reports that one manufacturer introduced a new product and shipped her an initial order. But she couldn't get brochures or any other written material for the product, nor was there any dealer training because those "weren't ready yet." Her sales rep had explained what it did and why she should carry it, but this was not enough information to really sell the product. Advertising in trade journals was focused on getting new dealers, not new customers. After two months of waiting, she sent it all back, and eventually canceled all of her business with that company. So as you can see, all elements of the marketing and sales plan must work together for a market opportunity to be fully captured.

Integrating Marketing Efforts

As we've discussed, marketing strategy must reflect a coordinated effort of product performance and two-way communication. Within the communication process must be integration of marketing efforts and messages, as discussed in Chapters 9 through 12. Further, what is communicated about the product must be accurate, or the position won't be supported. How can a company make certain that such integration occurs?

Several factors can encourage the appropriate level of integration within the marketing program. Clear strategic decisions, personnel stability, compensation systems that support the marketing strategy, and formal communication and organizational structures that encourage cross-functional interaction are among the more important.[18]

Clear Strategic Decisions

In one study that examined mismatches between marketing and sales strategies, an issue that surfaced was a lack of decisiveness on the part of senior marketing executives. For example, two sales managers said that, while formal strategy indicated that a product would be on the market for the next few years, informal signals from marketing management indicated that the product might be withdrawn. As a result, the sales force was not putting any effort into those products. Sales and marketing strategies are neither immediate nor irreversible; if management waffles on strategic decisions, then marketing and sales investments could be wasted and relationships (both internal and external) damaged.

Personnel Stability

Relationships take time to build. As mentioned earlier, internal relationships go through the same stages as external relationships. Moving people rapidly through the organization can mean that relationships between areas of the marketing department are never built. One manager in one study reported three marketing executives in five years; one salesperson told us he had three different sales managers in one year! While each successive manager had to try to quickly build rapport with each subordinate and superior, the whole sales team suffered because new relationships had to be built between each new manager and all of the other functional areas. When rapid personnel turnover occurs, the relationship cannot get past the exploration stage.

Compensation

A key issue that creates ill will is the fact that different groups within marketing compete for the same budget. Fights over budgets can create bad feelings and damage relationships. Budgets, though, are not the only "money" issue that can damage or enhance relationships.

Many companies are evaluating and testing compensation plans that encourage teamwork. For example, marketing managers may find that their pay contains incentives based on sales or contribution margins. When that is the case, they are incented to work more closely with the sales force. Morehead Supply is one company that pays quarterly bonuses to all marketing personnel if sales targets are achieved. Unlike profit sharing plans that the company also uses, these bonuses are specifically designed to encourage teamwork within the marketing–sales interface.

Compensation can also help turn budgeting into teamwork. By using a joint compensation system, all of those competing for budget end up being paid based on the same performance. As a result, they are more determined than ever to see that the budget results in

Exhibit 7–8
Functional
Organization

effective marketing. The issue, though, also affects how areas such as manufacturing, engineering, and other functional area bonuses are paid. When those areas are also compensated for customer satisfaction and teamwork, then those outcomes are more likely.

Organizational Structure

Compensation plans, though, should be supported by the appropriate organizational structure. The structure of the organization can enhance or inhibit the ability to create internal partnerships. In the next section, we discuss different types of organizational structures, as well as the different groups within marketing between whom partnerships are created.

Organizational Structure—Marketing Partners

Marketing is usually organized into four functional groups: sales, product development and management, marcomm, and marketing research. Sales may report to a marketing VP, along with the other areas of marketing, or may be entirely separate, as in the case of the organization that Tom Leigh was working with. Organizing by marketing function is called a **functional structure**. Exhibit 7–8 presents an example.

When many markets are served, remaining in a functional structure can actually become dysfunctional. Allocating appropriate resources to each functional group and to each market becomes too challenging, and a market structure is created. The primary difference is that each market gets its own marketing department, which may be further organized using a functional structure.

Customer-focused teams are a sales-led example of organizing around the customer in a hybrid format. The functional groups still remain, but are also organized around specific customers or customer groups. Each group is represented on the team and each representative is charged with ensuring that his or her area supports the customer-focused marketing strategy.

Structure and Formal Communication

The customer-focused team (CFT) formalizes communication between parts of the organization that should be communicating anyway. As a result, some level of communication is assured. It is still up to the marketing manager to ensure that the communication is timely and accurate.

Organizational structure is important to understand because it defines much of communication. In a functionally structured organization, for example, communication usually flows up and down reporting lines, as illustrated in Exhibit 7–9. Cross-functional communication only occurs at points when the managers of functions report to the same person. Customer-focused teams and other types of cross-functional organization structures remove formal communication barriers and require communication at the point of need.

Exhibit 7–9
Customer-
Focused Team
Structure

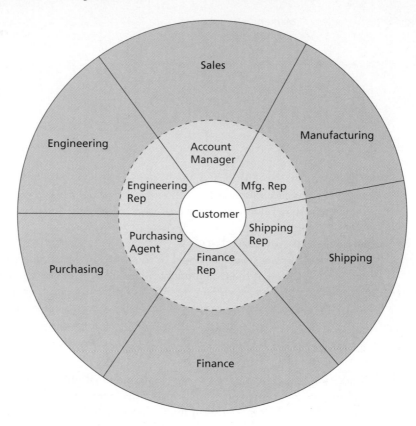

For example, under a formal communication structure, if a salesperson had a problem with shipping, then the problem would be reported to the sales manager, who might be able to call shipping or might have to report it to a regional level, depending on where a peer relationship existed. In the illustration in Exhibit 7–10, there is no equivalent of a district sales manager in the shipping department, so the information has to be passed along to the regional level. As you can imagine, the message gets garbled and delayed, which reduces customer satisfaction and also the job satisfaction of the salesperson who needs to get the problem resolved. In a CFT, the information goes straight from the customer to the responsible person in shipping or, at worst, through the account manager to the team member in shipping. The result is that the customer's needs can be assessed and satisfied.

The Learning Market-Oriented Individual

Important Internal Partnering Skills

Building partnerships has been a major theme of this book. In many respects, building partnerships with internal partners is no different than building relationships with customers. Several skills are useful in building internal partnerships, skills such as questioning and listening, negotiation, and financial and accounting skills. We'll discuss finance and accounting skills first, because they represent the language of business.

Exhibit 7–10

Communication Example
In a functional organization structure, communications have to wind their way through the chain of command, increasing the likelihood of miscommunication and lengthening the time to get a response.

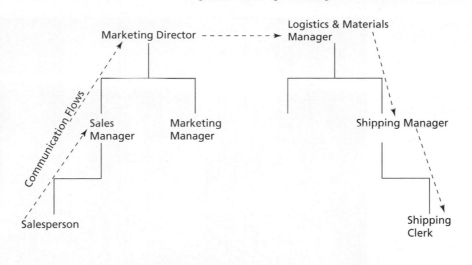

Finance and Accounting Skills

When we consider the mindset of those in the company who are not part of the marketing department, it is important to remember that almost everyone wants to do their job well. No one likes to fail. Engineers want to use their creativity to design successful products, finance managers want to beat the market by managing the company's investments well, and manufacturing managers want to operate a profitable, safe plant. In almost every situation, success is measured, at least partly, in terms of profit. The common denominator is the bottom line on the income statement.

Marketing managers who fail to understand finance and accounting fail to communicate well with other managers. They just don't understand the language. Understanding finance and accounting, though, is needed for more than just the sake of good communications; good business managers must understand these areas in order to make good decisions. Marketing managers at Federal Express, for example, are using profitability analysis in order to allocate marketing dollars to various accounts and market segments.[19] Dollars are then allocated to grow profitable accounts, not equally to all accounts. Those marketing managers have to understand accounting procedures in order to make wise investment decisions. We can't teach those procedures here, though. Our purpose is to sensitize aspiring business marketing managers to the importance of what they will learn in their finance and accounting classes.

Questioning and Listening

Understanding needs of others is the first step to building a partnership. Understanding the profit needs and cost structures of the internal partner is an important part of understanding their needs, but more is also required. The marketing manager must understand the individual's wants and aspirations as well. This level of understanding requires questioning and listening skills, the same types of skills needed among salespeople.

Negotiation

Understanding the needs of an internal partner, though, is not enough. That partner's needs must be aligned with the marketing department's needs, in terms of both the final outcome and the timing of the decision. **Negotiation** is a method of decision making

Marketers who can communicate with the language of accounting and finance will be understood by senior executives and are more likely to be successful.

Howard Grey/Tony Stone Images.

that is used to resolve conflicts; it is important for the marketing manager to develop skills that enhance the use of this method.

Negotiation is a mutual problem-solving process rather than an argument. When managers use negotiation to build consensus through tactics such as brainstorming rather than bullying, internal partnerships can be developed.

Create a Sense of Urgency One reality that marketing managers face is that their sense of urgency, or need to get something done now because the customer is waiting for it, is not always shared by the internal partner. Without a shared sense of urgency, the other party may not participate fully in the negotiation, so good negotiators are adept at creating a sense of urgency. Appealing to supragoals is one method of creating a sense of urgency. If the customer's needs are of paramount interest (and not the needs of the marketer), then that can help to create that sense of urgency to get the job done.

What Is Negotiated Intra-organizational conflict, or conflict between two departments or functional areas, is well suited to negotiation. Other methods of handling internal conflict can be used, too, but negotiation is the most often used method. Since negotiation can be used as a decision-making process in any conflict, it is important to recognize that, while it is advisable to hold to one's goals, you should be open to multiple means of achieving those goals. With this recognition, nearly anything is negotiable and the marketing manager creates a level of flexibility that opens new vistas for decisions—the opportunity is there for double-loop learning.

Be Prepared The first step in being prepared for negotiation is to have negotiation skills. There are many excellent books that can help you continue your learning of negotiation and conflict resolution. If your school's management department has a change management or conflict–negotiation course, you may want to take it. The second step is to recognize negotiation opportunities and plan accordingly. Since anything is negotiable, negotiation can occur at any time. If the manager has not prepared to negotiate, a competitive negotiator can win at the manager's expense before the manager even recognizes that negotiation is occurring.

7–2

BUSINESS 2 BUSINESS
From the Ground Up

The president of one of the top 25 research firms in the world told attendees at a career workshop, "I don't really care if you're a hotshot MBA itching to bring in business or a whiz-bang analyst with a yen to build statistical models. When you come to work for this research company, you're going to start with about 200 hours of telephone interviewing, and you'll probably assist the project managers in about 20 jobs before you get slotted for your specialty."

What do you think are the objectives of this type of training? Do you think this is a characteristic of a market-oriented, learning organization?

Summary

Marketing is an important element in the learning organization, and should be an integral element in the culture of all business marketing organizations. Learning organizations use marketing to determine known requisites (the requirements for success). Two types of learning occur in organizations: single-loop (adaptive learning) and double-loop (generative learning). Both types of learning can provide companies with competitive advantages when companies learn faster than their competitors.

Marketers can learn a number of ways, including through experimentation, cognitive mapping, and learning laboratories. Even the process of strategic planning discussed in Chapter 6 provides an opportunity for organizational learning. But not just any learning is useful; companies also seek to create a market-oriented culture in order to learn what can provide competitive advantage.

Market-oriented companies do a better job of market sensing, or anticipating requirements (known requisites). They also build stronger spanning processes so that information from customers can get to the areas within the firm where it will do the most good. Internal partnering can strengthen spanning processes and communication, and is a strategy effected by salespeople and marketing managers. Marketing staff and salespeople want to partner with their peers in finance, manufacturing, and new product development.

Market-oriented companies also integrate their marketing activities better than do companies that are not market-oriented. In the chapters ahead, we will discuss each of the marketing activities in greater detail, but it is important that you now understand how marketing efforts are integrated.

Marketing efforts are integrated when strategic decisions are clear and carry throughout all marketing activities. Further, internal relationships take time to build. For partnerships to develop, personnel stability is needed. Compensation plans should also take internal partnerships into account. Teams should be supported with team compensation and team organizational structures.

Professionals are also learning individuals. Business marketers must develop their finance and accounting skills in order to be successful businesspeople. Communication skills, such as questioning, listening, and negotiation, are also useful skills to learning professionals.

In the next set of chapters, we discuss various marketing activities such as product development and marketing communication. As you've learned in this chapter, though, these activities are not isolated accidents, but are part of an integrated marketing and corporate strategy.

Key Terms

adaptive (single-loop)
  learning
cognitive mapping
competency trap
engineer to order
functional structure
generative (double-loop)
  learning

internal partner
known requisites
learning boundaries
learning laboratories
make to order
make to stock
market orientation
market sensing

negotiation
organizational culture
scenario
spanning processes
supragoal

Discussion Questions

1. In 1965, the top three computer companies were IBM, DEC, and Honeywell. Computers were big and expensive, and controlled by the data processing department. Who are the top three computer makers now? Are hardware manufacturers the major powers in the industry? What learning boundaries inhibited IBM, Honeywell, and DEC from fully capitalizing on changes in computing?

2. Create a cognitive map that illustrates the relationships of organizational learning, market sensing, marketing functions, strategy development and corporate planning, strategy implementation, and evaluation. You may need to bring in other concepts from this and earlier chapters.

3. Consider your relationships with others in an organization that is important to you, preferably one in which you hold an office or position of leadership. Select three people in three different relationship stages. How do you know those relationships are in different stages? Specifically identify differences between the relationships.

4. The chapter lists some of the skills necessary to develop internal partnerships. How strong are your partnering skills? What could you specifically do to improve those skills over the next 90 days?

5. Consider student group projects. Do people want to work with you? How was your reputation created? What specific events contributed to that reputation? What can you learn from those experiences that could help you become a better internal partner?

6. Identify five negative consequences caused by poor relationships between (a) marketing and manufacturing, (b) marketing and finance, and (c) marcomm and sales.

7. Some companies experimented with separating sales and marketing completely. Sales sells products for several product-based marketing divisions, operating almost like manufacturer's representatives. Do you think these could be successful experiments? If so, under what conditions? (Be as specific as possible; don't say something like "if they had a good partnership." Be able to describe how that partnership would be built.) If not, why? (Again, be specific.)

8. How does industry experience become a learning boundary? What other types of learning boundaries can you think of?

9. Jack Welch, CEO of GE, says it is important for companies to have enemies so that you can be at war. Explain how this statement relates to the concept of a supragoal.

10. How does a professional marketing manager choose what she should learn? Relate your answer to the methods and types of learning presented in the chapter.

Internet Exercise

Check out the GE home page (**www.ge.com**). GE has a link to its business products and services (separate from its consumer products and services). Access this link. Then hit <u>visit</u> for a GE business site. Choose from any of the divisions, and then hit its recruiting or employment site. Select any job and read the job description. What can you learn about the GE culture from this job description? Go back to the home page and hit <u>employment opportunities.</u> There you should find a <u>first job opportunities</u> link. Go to that page and explore <u>internships</u> and <u>professional positions.</u> Again, read job descriptions and find evidence to support a conclusion of your assessment of their corporate culture. (Keep in mind that home pages change and these links may not be as direct as they were when we wrote this.)

WWW
I N T E R N E T

1. What is GE's culture like? Is GE a market-oriented company?

2. Quote the job descriptions to support your analysis.

Cases

Case 7.1   Turk Creative Medical

William T. (Bill) Turk, president and founder of Turk Creative Medical, was justifiably proud of his firm's growth to annual sales of nearly $50 million in only 20 years of operation. But a sense of uneasiness was growing as the company got larger. Except for a few old-timers, employees didn't stay very long. Worse yet, profits were going to be negligible for the coming year. That uneasiness, though, grew into definite crisis proportions the day Bill got the call from Maria Gutierrez, VP of Purchasing at Hillcrest Medical Corporation, a company that runs over 30 major hospitals.

"Mr. Turk, I've been a customer nearly as long as you've had a company. In fact, I was the one that got you to consider blanket purchasing agreements that made us a half-million–dollar customer. But I want to tell you personally that I'll not renew our agreement at the end of this month."

Bill almost dropped the phone, but he managed to blurt out, "Why?" Then Maria described defective products that resulted in nearly a 20 percent return, invoices that double-billed for the returned products and their replacements, and other problems. Try as he could, he could not get Maria to agree to even give him a shot at keeping her business. Her last words were, "Bill, you've got problems, big problems. And I'm disappointed that I have to even point these out to you—this shouldn't be a surprise."

After hanging up the phone, Bill began hunting and got the following information: Average days to receive payment came to 65; returns equaled 18 percent of sales for the past 90 days, equally divided among incorrect shipments and defective products; inventories grew to 20 days worth of sales, except for four top sellers that were backlogged one to two weeks; and average contribution margin was 16 percent, less than the target of 25 percent. Cost of goods sold had increased almost 10 percent in the previous six months, without any increases in the prices Turk charged. On the bright side, however, overall sales were 10% over projections.

1. What are the key problems and what are their possible causes? How could he find out if those causes were in fact the actual causes?

2. If the problems involve working relationships between departments, how can Bill improve those relationships? How can he create a culture based on a market orientation?

3. Turk has two other customers equal to Hillcrest in annual revenue; all other customers spend about $50,000 to $100,000 per year with Turk. Devise an organizational structure suited to this situation that can also handle the interdepartmental issues. Be specific as to who should report to whom and create one-sentence job descriptions for each person.

Exhibit 7–11
SSI Organization Chart

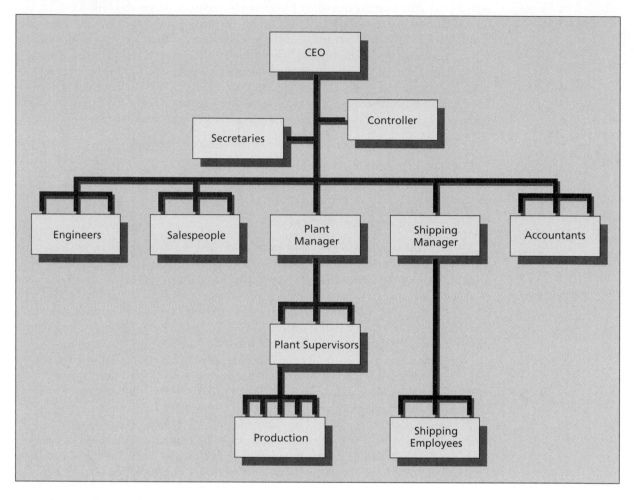

SOURCE: Barton A. Weitz, Stephen B. Castleberry, and John F. Tanner, Jr. *Selling: Building Partnerships.* Second edition. Burr Ridge, IL: Irwin/McGraw-Hill, 1995.

Case 7.2   Structural Steel Industries

It was nearly 5:00 on Friday afternoon when Charlie got the call from Laredo Construction. "Charlie, you gotta get someone out here now!" hollered its owner, Jack Belmont. "You guys tried to slip some foreign steel into our job, and now we gotta rip it all out. But we aren't going to do it. You are, and it better be done by Monday!"

Charlie could tell that Jack was furious, and he had every right to be. Jack's company was building a major complex at the naval base in San Diego. Because it was a job for the federal government, the specs called for all U.S. steel. Somehow, steel from Structural Steel's Mexican supplier had been mixed with the domestic steel and sent to Laredo. If a Navy inspector had seen it, Jack might even have had to forfeit a performance bond.

Structural Steel Industries (SSI) is a division of a larger steel fabricator. Steel fabricators take stock steel and make it into products. Miscellaneous steel fabricators, such as SSI, make custom steel components. SSI takes I-beams and other stock steel products and prepares them for assembly at a construction site. It cuts the steel to size, drills the holes for the rivets, and makes special beams and other steel products customized for specific buildings.

Exhibit 7–12
Process for Filling
an Order

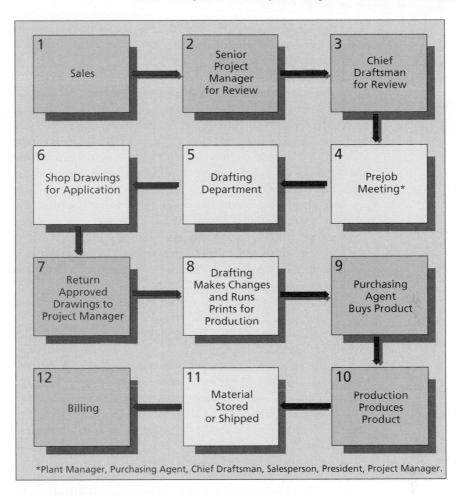

*Plant Manager, Purchasing Agent, Chief Draftsman, Salesperson, President, Project Manager.

SOURCE: Barton A. Weitz, Stephen B. Castleberry, and John F. Tanner, Jr. *Selling: Building Partnerships.* Second edition. Burr Ridge, IL: Irwin/McGraw-Hill, 1995.

The company, a small division, employs 45 welders and production workers (including a plant manager and four supervisors), 10 employees in shipping (including the shipping manager), two engineers, three salespeople, three project managers who work with salespeople and engineers to prepare bids, a controller, two secretaries, and Charlie (the chief executive officer).

Everyone from the plant supervisors on up (see Exhibit 7–11) talks with customers directly. Because the jobs are custom, a lot of communication takes place between the contractor, the architect, and SSI to make sure that everything is done just right.

In addition to a high degree of customer contact, each job requires a great deal of communication within SSI. As the flowchart in Exhibit 7–12 shows, all areas of the organization must interact throughout the project to ensure that SSI meets customer specifications.

After dealing with Jack, Charlie hung up the phone and buzzed Mary Longren, the project manager for Laredo's project. "Mary, who worked on the Laredo project?" Charlie queried.

"I did. Why?" she replied.

"I know you did. I meant, who was the engineer and who inspected the goods before shipping? I just heard from Jack Belmont. Seems as though some of the steel was from a Mexican mill."

"Oh great, just what we need. When is he building the structure?" she asked.

"He's already started. He wanted us to go to San Diego and rip the material out ourselves, but I've got him calmed down somewhat," Charlie replied.

"Was it all Mexican steel?"

Charlie sighed. "No, only about 40 percent. The good news is that only about half of that was installed before they realized the problem. But they can't do anything until we ship the right steel."

Mary muttered something that Charlie didn't quite catch. Then she said, "OK, I'll go get Manuel and Mark and get manufacturing going." Mary hung up the phone and then slapped her desk in disgust. To her ceiling, she said, "Why can't we get this right? Is it that difficult?" She left her office to find Manuel, the production manager, and Mark, the shipping manager.

She quickly located the two among a crowd at the break lounge. She glanced at her watch; it was a few minutes after 5:00. Mark and several others were laughing loudly as Manuel described his weekend plans.

"You can forget those plans," interrupted Mary. "Laredo called. It seems that 40 percent of the steel we shipped was from a Mexican mill. That's a federal job, so it all has to be domestic steel."

"Well, we can get to it next week," Manuel replied, with his hands on his hips.

" 'Fraid not, Manuel. Charlie wants it out this weekend."

"No way, Mary! We can't get all of that done this weekend. That was a full-week job." Manuel was almost shouting.

"Then we'll just have to get out what we can," she stated, noticing that Mark was smirking. "You can forget your weekend plans too, pal. You've got to get us domestic steel and get this shipped to San Diego as soon as a truckload is ready."

"Well, we'll just see about that," said Mark, slamming a Coke can into a trash container. "C'mon Manuel, let's go see Charlie." The two walked off, talking animatedly to each other. A few production workers got up and started to walk out.

"Hey, you guys can just wait right there!" yelled Mary. "You are going to get plenty of overtime today. And if you don't want it, Charlie will help you find another place to work." One worker acted as if he didn't hear and kept right on going. Two turned around and returned to the break area.

On Monday, Angela Davis, the salesperson who handled the Laredo account, called Charlie. "I got your message, boss. What's up?" she asked.

"Laredo got Mexican steel. We've managed to ship a little more than half of the stuff he had already installed, but it will be Wednesday before the final shipment goes out."

"That's just terrific. What's the matter with those people in manufacturing? Can't they read specs?" Angela asked. Laredo wasn't her largest customer, but it was one of her biggest, a class-A account.

"Well, Angela," Charlie replied, pausing for effect, "it wasn't on the specs. Nothing manufacturing got said domestic only."

"But they should have known. It was a federal job!" she protested.

"Why should they have known? Anyway, you better call Jack Belmont and let him know what's happening. I'll let you talk to Mark next so you can get the full shipment schedule." Charlie transferred Angela to Mark. As Charlie hung up, he wondered where he was going to make up for the loss he was taking on the Laredo project.

Angela was in no mood for polite conversation when she finally reached Jack at the construction site. "Jack, this is Angela. Have you received the first emergency shipment yet?"

"No, we haven't. But it better get here soon. My guys are just sitting around." Jack sounded grim.

"You should get it any time now. I talked to Mark, and it went out about 5:00 this morning, so it should be there by 9:00."

"Look, sister. If it's not here by 9:00, you might as well keep it. I can't afford to do business with you guys any longer." The line went dead as Jack hung up. Angela slumped against the wall of the pay phone booth, wondering what could go wrong next.

Source: Barton A. Weitz, Stephen B. Castleberry, and John F. Tanner Jr., *Selling: Building Partnerships,* 3d ed., (Burr Ridge, IL: McGraw–Hill Irwin, 1997).

1. Who was primarily responsible for the Laredo project mistake? Who else was responsible? Why?

2. Identify the managers who would be involved in a project and discuss what their priorities would be (e.g., the engineer would be most interested in the design itself). How should this company organize in order to create stronger internal relationships? In your answer, consider which relationships should be stronger.

3. What can be done to prevent these problems in the future, and who should make those corrections?

Additional Readings

Bennett, Joan Kramer, and Michael J. O'Brien, "The Building Blocks of the Learning Organization," *Training* (June 1994), pp. 41–49.

Hauser, John, Duncan Simester, and Birger Wernerfelt, "Internal Customers and Internal Suppliers," *Journal of Marketing Research* 23 (August 1996), pp. 268–80.

Kashani, Kamran, "Marketing Futures: Priorities for a Turbulent Environment," *Long Range Planning* 28, no. 4 (1995), pp. 87–98.

Kofman, Fred, and Peter M. Senge, "Communities of Commitment: The Heart of Learning Organizations," *Organizational Dynamics* 22, no. 2 (1993), pp. 5–19.

Konijnendijk, Paul A., "Dependence and Conflict between Production and Sales," *Industrial Marketing Management* 22 (1993), pp. 161–67.

Luthans, Fred, Michael J. Rubach, and Paul Marsnik, "Going beyond Total Quality: The Characteristics, Techniques, and Measures of Learning Organizations," *International Journal of Organizational Analysis* 3 (January 1995), pp. 24–44.

McGill, Michael E., John Slocum Jr., and David Lei, "Management Practices in Learning Organizations," *Organizational Dynamics* 21, no. 1 (1992), pp. 4–14.

Nevis, Edwin C., Anthony J. DiBella, and Janet M. Gould, "Understanding Organizations as Learning Systems," *Sloan Management Review* (Winter 1995), pp. 73–85.

Parker, Glenn, "Cross-Functional Collaboration," *Training & Development* (October 1994), pp. 49–52.

Pasa, Mehmet, and Steven Shugan, "The Value of Marketing Expertise," *Management Science* 42 (March 1996), pp. 370–88.

St. John, Caron H., and Earnest H. Hall Jr., "The Interdependency between Marketing and Manufacturing," *Industrial Marketing Management* 20 (1991), pp. 223–29.

St. John, Caron, and Scott Young, "Functional Coordination within the Global Firm," *International Business Review* 4, no. 3 (1995), pp. 341–54.

Smith, Suzanne Konzelmann, "Internal Cooperation and Competitive Success: The Case of the US Steel Minimill Sector," *Cambridge Journal of Economics* 19 (1995), pp. 277–304.

Strutton, David, Lou E. Pelton, and James R. Lumpkin, "Psychological Climate in Franchising System Channels and Franchisor–Franchisee Solidarity," *Journal of Business Research* 34 (1995), pp. 81–91.

Troff, Kristen, "Ally or Adversary? Working Effectively with the Sales Department," *The Exhibitor* (April 1995), pp. 26–29.

Part III

Business Marketing Programming

Part III prepares us to develop marketing programs that serve the customer and attain organizational objectives. Fittingly, Part III has seven chapters: four on marketing communications elements and one each on the management of product, channels, and price.

We start with what are generally the most strategic of the marketing variables. Chapter 8 looks at product development, including the role of suppliers and customers in the process. With large investments, long-run implications, and interactions with other marketing activities, product management across the life cycle is a critical strategic competency.

Chapter 9 deals with the management of interfirm relationships for the proper execution of channel functions—key tasks for providing apt service to target customers. Again, significant financial resources, a durable character of relations with channel partners, and connections to price, promotion, and other marketing variables make channels difficult to alter in the short run. Careful forecasting of customer needs, planning, and relationships open to adjustment are key.

Chapter 10 previews an integrative approach to marketing communications strategy. It pivots on the premise that individuals involved in the buying process—and members of other key constituencies—have different information needs. The communication vehicles covered in Chapter 11 (public relations, advertising, and trade shows), Chapter 12 (direct mail, telephone, and Internet), and Chapter 13 (personal selling) differ in their impact and cost efficiency for delivering the needed information to the targets. Thus, a marketing communications manager will play no favorites, but will blend the media synergistically to fit the message requirements of the product with the various needs of the target.

Finally, we take up pricing and negotiation in Chapter 14. We offer a comprehensive framework for pricing decisions that accounts for many factors—costs, demand, competitors, channel coordination, and regulations—and we speak to tactical issues in pricing. Brief coverage of price negotiation recognizes different strategies of bargaining and uses several principles of conflict management from Chapter 9 as a frame of reference.

Chapter 8

Developing and Managing Products

What Do Customers Want?

PRODUCT DEVELOPMENT AND MANAGEMENT ASSOCIATION

Who develops new products? Is it some guy tinkering in his garage? Or is it a highly paid laboratory scientist or engineer? ●

Just as often, the developer of an innovative product, at least a product to be used by other businesses, is neither an independent developer nor a manufacturer's employee. Just as often, the real new product developer is the user, the customer. ●

For example, in the PC and semiconductor businesses, all major innovations involving the process of producing semiconductors and assembling them on boards for use in PCs were developed by users, not by the manufacturers of the semiconductor production equipment or by manufacturers of components of PC boards. In fact, the first to make a printed circuit board was the U.S. Signal Corps (a part of the Army), a user of electronics. ●

These users did not want to become manufacturers of printed circuit boards or semiconductors. Rather, they couldn't buy what they needed so they made it themselves. When someone came along who was willing to make it, these users willingly began to purchase the commercial product. In addition, in the semiconductor and PC industries, some users worked closely with their suppliers in order to develop major improvements to the original product. Other users took the commercial product and modified it, making significant improvements that were later copied by the suppliers and added to the product offering. In all, 70 percent of the major or minor improvements in the printed circuitry industry were developed by customers, either independently or jointly with manufacturers. ●

Yes, many innovations come from garage laboratories and from corporate labs. But many also come from customers, which is another reason for developing partnerships with the right accounts. ●

Visit the web site of the Product Development and Management Association, **www.pdma.org** ●

Learning Objectives

Is having the right product the most important factor in marketing strategy? Some would argue so, saying that without the right product, no one will buy twice. All of the rest of the marketing mix might get someone to buy once, but if the product is no good, no one will buy again. For companies who wish to compete effectively over the long term, developing products that deliver value is essential. Developing products that deliver value by serving organizational buyers' needs is best accomplished when strong relationships exist between manufacturer and buyer. Then those relationships serve to ensure that value really is delivered.

After completing this chapter, you should be able to

● Apply portfolio and product life cycle approaches to managing existing products.
● Identify the process of developing products internally.
● Discuss the importance of lead users to the product development process.
● Indicate what partnering, with both suppliers and customers, means to the product development process.

Satisfying customer needs is an important objective in product management. As you will see, however, successful product management depends on the successful integration of many areas. Pricing, promotion, selling, and manufacturing are just a few of the organization's strategic areas that must operate in concert with product management in order for the firm to enjoy success.

What Is a Product?

What is a product? To some, a product is a collection of **features**, or physical characteristics of the tangible item or service. For example, a computer may have a hard drive capable of storing 5 gigabytes of information. Storing 5 gigabytes is a physical characteristic, or feature, of the computer. Getting a haircut completed in less than 30 minutes is a feature of a service.

Other people might think of a product as a collection of **advantages**, or reasons for having those features. For example, a 5-gig hard drive may mean that users can store a lot of software on their computer and not have to switch disks all of the time. Getting a haircut in under 30 minutes means it can be done during a lunch hour, saving time.

If you have one computer program that requires more memory, then you wouldn't buy that 5-gig computer or, if you did, you'd upgrade the hard drive or use a CD-ROM drive. At the same time, computer makers are finding that many people don't want to spend several thousand dollars for a high-speed, multitasking computer if all they want to do is surf the Net. What is important to a buyer is the **benefit**, or how the product or service satisfies a need. It is more useful for you to think of a **product** (we include services when we use the term product) as a bundle of benefits, a collection of solutions to needs and wants.

At the same time, it is important to recognize that simply having the benefits that a buyer wants is not always enough. Our product has to do something better than the competition or there is no **competitive advantage**. The buyer would be just as likely to choose the competitor's product.

In an earlier marketing class, you probably also learned that there is a core product and an augmented product. The **core product** is the tangible item and/or the customary services offered. For example, your company may purchase computers from a company that offers all new customers two hours of free training. That free training is part of the customary service that is part of the core product. If, however, the company also offers to provide you with free networking consulting to make sure that the new computers will work well with your current network, then the product has been augmented. The **augmented product** is that part of the offering that is somewhat customized for each particular customer.

Augmenting to Exceed Expectations   It is important to recognize the role that augmenting a product plays in creating customer satisfaction, particularly when discussing product development. Customer satisfaction is created when a customer's expectations for a product are met. Those expectations are created by the marketing and selling efforts and reflect the needs that the customer hopes to have satisfied. When the product fails to meet expectations, then we have a dissatisfied customer. When the product exceeds expectations, though, the customer feels like more was gained than was paid. Then we have an enthusiastic customer, one who will share this positive experience with others. An important method of enthusing customers is by carefully augmenting a product. How the product is augmented should vary from customer to customer, because not all customers' needs are the same and if the extra benefit was given to every customer, it would no longer be extra but expected.

Augmenting the product is important to understand when we consider building partnerships with our customers. Augmenting product offerings properly is a major contributor to building solid partnerships. Sometimes, augmenting products can lead to the development of new products as well. We will talk more about this throughout the rest of the book, because the idea of augmenting products to create enthusiastic customers is an important part of a sound marketing strategy. Decisions concerning new products, though, require an understanding of how product lines are managed, which is the topic of the next section.

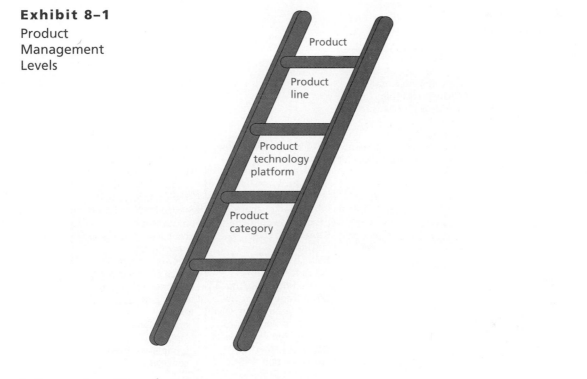

Exhibit 8–1
Product
Management
Levels

Product

Product
line

Product
technology
platform

Product
category

Managing Products

Few companies exist on just one product. Most have several lines of products designed to work together to satisfy a broad range of needs and desires, and (as you read in Chapter 6) companies organize these into strategic business units. An important element of business marketing is deciding which products to introduce or keep, which products to promote heavily, and which products to cut or market less vigorously. There are several different tools that managers use to manage their company's products, including the product development and life cycle, and product portfolio tools.

Before we can discuss these tools, however, it is important to recognize that product management tools can be applied at different levels. There are four such levels: the product itself (e.g., the Minolta EP300 copier), the technology platform (e.g., the microtoning system that Minolta used in several copiers), the product line (Minolta's EP line of copiers), and the product category (for example, plain paper copiers), as illustrated in Exhibit 8–1. A **technology platform** is the core technology that is often the basis for a **product line**, or group of products. A product line does not have to share the same platform, but sharing a platform is usually the case. Another example is the IBM line of Pro-Printers. The basic technology platform is the same (dot matrix PC printers), but each printer has a different speed and other feature differences. Keep these definitions of platform, product line, product category, and product in mind as we discuss product management tools such as the product life cycle (PLC).

Product Life Cycle

Products have been likened to living organisms. They are introduced to the market or have a birth. Then they grow (in sales), mature, and at some point, die out. This cycle of development, introduction, growth, maturity, and decline in sales is called the **product**

Exhibit 8–2

The Product Life Cycle

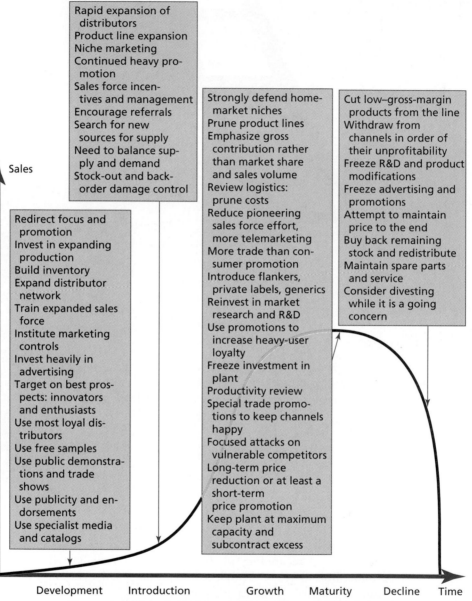

Development **Introduction** **Growth** **Maturity** **Decline** **Time**

The product life cycle has been used to guide marketing strategy.
Here are some common recommendations for each stage.

life cycle (PLC), and is illustrated in Exhibit 8–2. The cycle can be applied to individual products or to product platforms or categories, with differing implications as we will discuss. For example, daisywheel printing was a technology that used a wheel with a number of petals, like a daisy. Each petal contained a character and the petal was struck against a ribbon in order to print the character. Quality of print was high but speed was slow. This technology was introduced by a number of vendors, grew, matured, and then declined as it was replaced by newer technologies, such as ink jet and laser printing.

Within the life cycle of the daisywheel technology, however, companies introduced new products at different times; some grew and matured, while others died fairly rapidly.

Products can have multiple lives. While a product may fall out of favor in one market, it may find new life in another. When this occurs, the product begins a new life, with all of the same strategy issues that any new product faces.

Products may also die young. There is no guarantee that a product will live to maturity or even make it to the introduction stage. And unlike living organisms that have similar life cycles (for example, adolescence hits all of us at about the same period), products can go through the stages at very different rates. Depending on the barriers to adoption—high prices, complicated learning requirements, or entrenched competition—one product may have a growth stage of years while another may have a growth stage of only a few months. The PLC, though, does offer a useful tool for understanding product strategy.

PLC and Product Strategy

In most discussions of the PLC, you will find that the development stage is left out. In these discussions, products become products when they are launched. While we are not going to talk about the development stage in great detail until later in this chapter, it is important to recognize that products have a **development stage**, that stage in the product's life when it is designed and readied for market. Some products are never brought to market simply because someone else gets there first or leapfrogs. A product is **leapfrogged** when a competitor brings out a product that is at least one step better technologically. For example, Xerox introduced the 8-bit PC one week before IBM introduced its first PC, a 16-bit machine. IBM leapfrogged Xerox with a superior machine.

Leapfrogging can have serious consequences when it occurs so early in the life of a product, but leapfrogging can also occur in the development phase. Xerox had a word-processing software product that never made it to market because other products were coming out that were already better. Thus you can see that a key stage in the life cycle is the development stage. If it takes too long to bring a product to market, the product may die before it has a chance. One major trend in product management is to shorten the product development stage in order to lengthen the overall life. We'll talk about how companies are doing that when we discuss product development strategies later in this chapter.

When the product is first introduced to the market and potential customers are learning what the product is and does, it is in the **introduction stage**. Sales are relatively low and profits are unlikely as sales revenue is invested in creating awareness. If distributors or other middlemen are needed, getting their agreement to carry the product can be difficult because there is not yet a well-defined market for the product.

For truly innovative products, this stage requires marketers to educate buyers (and channel members) as to the function of the product. **Primary demand**, or demand for that type of product, must be created. Creating primary demand and educating the market can require a tremendous communication investment in advertising, trade shows, free samples or trials, and other marketing elements. Copy-cat products also have an introduction stage, as do new products that are improvements over existing products. Copy-cats do not have to educate the market, but do have to announce their presence. Improvements require some education but not as much as innovations do.

The second stage of the PLC is the **growth stage**, when sales and profits grow at a fast rate. Competition against an innovative product is most likely to enter the market in this stage, and vendors begin to differentiate their product in order to create **secondary demand**, or demand for a particular vendor's offering. Significant marketing investment may still be required in order to create a position for the product separate from others in the market.

The third stage is the **maturity stage**, when sales level off. Note that sales can level off for a product category, in which case that market is said to be mature. Profits are relatively high and marketing expenses should begin to decline. A new product or vendor, however, can enter the market and take away sales at the expense of competitors. For example, the plain paper copier market is a mature market, but new products are introduced regularly. Each product represents a slight improvement and, while none are truly innovative, each new copier product may go through all stages of the PLC.

In the maturity stage, product differentiation is even more important. With little or no product differentiation, price becomes more important and companies try to reduce costs. Companies that want to differentiate rather than lower prices try to augment mature business products with more services, or create images of differentiation through effective advertising and trade show promotion. Research indicates that successful companies don't always reduce their marketing investment in mature products; rather, they change the nature of their marketing communication to emphasize their competitive advantages.[1]

The final stage is the **decline stage**, or that stage when sales decline and products are removed from the market. Marketing investment may be cut and managers look for ways to milk the last few dollars of profit before withdrawing the product. In some cases, marketers look for new markets or new applications and the life cycle starts all over again. We'll talk more about the decline stage later in this chapter.

One caveat is appropriate here and in other areas as well. Business is like any other human endeavor; it suffers from fads and fashions. The product life cycle is a useful tool, but at one point, it was greatly overused and misused, just as TQM and reengineering have been more recently. All three of these basically sound concepts can significantly help businesses, but all three have been implemented incorrectly by managers who wanted to blindly follow what they thought to be a universal solution to all problems. With the PLC, managers misinterpreted life cycle signals, cutting investment off for products that were not ready to die (but that died anyway because of inadequate support), or pumping dollars into a product that was dying a slow and painful death. The PLC is just a tool, one of several tools for managing products. The PLC can aid in planning marketing investments and setting profit expectations, and it can provide a rationale for eliminating products, but the decisions should be made by managers with care, not with blind following of the PLC.

Product Portfolios

The same cautions apply to using a product portfolio. There are several types of portfolios. Perhaps the most famous is the one developed by the Boston Consulting Group and called the BCG grid or matrix. **Product portfolio management** suggests managing all products simultaneously as you would a financial portfolio, balancing risk and return among all product investments. Most models involve a grid, and suggest that product decisions should be based on where each individual product, product line, technology platform, or product category is along the combination of two dimensions.

The BCG grid is the simplest of the grid models, with dimensions of market share and market growth. This model has been criticized for being too simple and too similar to the product life cycle (which is also based on market growth).

A more advanced model developed by General Electric is called the GE grid (as illustrated in Exhibit 8–3). It has **market attractiveness**, or a composite measure of the potential for sales and profits in a particular market segment, and **business strength**, or the strength of our offering relative to other companies' products, as its dimensions. Attrac-

Exhibit 8-3
Product Portfolio Matrices

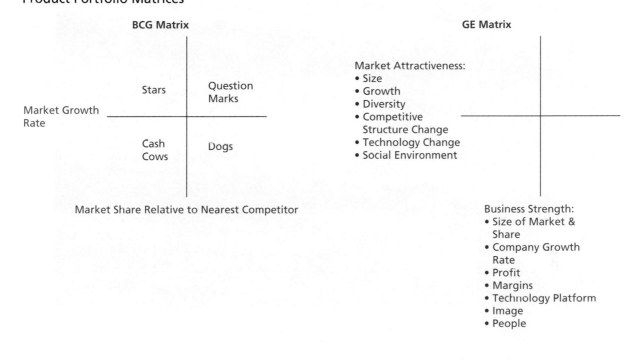

BCG Matrix

Market Growth Rate

| Stars | Question Marks |
| Cash Cows | Dogs |

Market Share Relative to Nearest Competitor

GE Matrix

Market Attractiveness:
• Size
• Growth
• Diversity
• Competitive Structure Change
• Technology Change
• Social Environment

Business Strength:
• Size of Market & Share
• Company Growth Rate
• Profit
• Margins
• Technology Platform
• Image
• People

tiveness determinants include market size, growth rate, competitive structure, industry profitability, and environmental (legal, social, etc.) factors. Determinants of strength can include our market share, our growth rate, the company's image, people resources, and other similar factors.

In the upper left corner of the BCG matrix, products are considered **stars** because market growth is high in a market where we control a large amount of the total market. Stars create cash through high sales but require high levels of investment in order to maintain or increase market share in that growing market. The investment made is in the form of marketing and distribution, as stars require more advertising, more personal selling, and the development of appropriate distribution in order to gain market share.

The hope is to turn stars into **cash cows**, which have high market share and strength in a steady market and are those products that should contribute the most to the company's profit. This contribution is possible because it should not take as much investment to maintain market share in a stable market as it does in a growth market; economies of scale and return on the investment of marketing dollars made when the market was growing should pay off. The assumption of low investment holds true if competition does not invest heavily to erode your share, or if technology also stays stable so that cost structures and sales remain stable. For example, if TI develops a method of manufacturing computer chips that reduces the cost of those chips by 25 percent, while the chips themselves have not changed, the market share figures will change because TI will undercut all other competitors' prices. Companies have to keep an eye on many factors in order to protect their cash cows.

Question marks are those products in high-growth markets that currently have low market share and may not be too strong. If the product's position can be strengthened, then the potential is for the product to become a star and perhaps a

Raytheon's line of aircraft can be managed like a portfolio of financial investments.
Courtesy Raytheon Company.

cash cow when the market stabilizes. Question marks require a great deal of investment, using cash generated from cash cows, in order to be successful. Investment alone, though, is no guarantee of success. Success still requires wise investment into sound marketing strategy.

Products with low share in a poor market are called **dogs**. These products are usually thought to be in the decline stage of their life. Some products become dogs after beginning as question marks while others become dogs after a long life as cash cows. In most cases, dogs are not worth much investment and most companies want to withdraw dogs quickly from the market.

Note that the PLC also involves two dimensions: time and sales. One property of time, however, is that you cannot go back. With product portfolios, products can move along both dimensions in either direction—if overmilked, a cash cow can become a dog, while with the right opportunity and investment, a dog can become a cash cow, for example. One problem with the use of portfolio matrices is that decision makers assume that products follow a PLC beginning as question marks, moving to stars, then cash cows, then dogs. The reality is that movement can occur between any two quadrants. While it is unlikely that a dog can become a cash cow, it can happen.

Even the more advanced portfolio models, however, have been criticized. Criticisms such as an overdependence on internal investment sources and ignoring capital markets as a source of funds for investment in new products, problems with defining market share, and the overemphasis on current products without much regard for future markets have caused some businesses to turn away from portfolio approaches. These tools, though, can be used effectively when the executive recognizes these limitations and makes an accommodation. For example, potential technology platforms that may replace current technology platforms have to be considered when planning how much to invest in any current product.

Of course, the use of the PLC and portfolios requires products to be managed. In the remainder of this chapter, we will discuss product development, both internal and customer-led.

New Product Development

New products are launched and old products withdrawn from the market at an increasingly rapid rate. Estimates are that more than one-third of new products ultimately fail.[2] Many companies such as 3M set corporate objectives that include sales or profits from products that don't exist yet. At the same time, new product development and the costs associated with launching a product are so great that a single product launch can mean the difference between profit and loss for many companies. As a result of the intense risk associated with new products, many marketing strategists believe that the key to success lies in solid planning.

Risk and New Product Decisions

The most basic decision in product management is the go–no go decision. Do we launch (or continue developing) the product, or do we kill it now? There are two types of risk associated with this decision: investment risk and opportunity risk. **Investment risk** is the risk that we decide to go ahead with the product, it fails, and we lose some or all of our investment. **Opportunity risk** is the risk that we decide to kill a product and thereby lose all of the revenue we would have gained if it had been a success. In marketing research class, you probably learned about these types of risk as Type I and Type II errors involved in making decisions based on what we observe relative to our hypotheses. Keep this in mind, because for new products not yet launched, the go–no go decision is often based on marketing research. As a marketing manager, you need to recognize when you've set up the decision process in order to minimize either investment risk or opportunity risk.

Several factors will impact your decision. For example, the size of the investment relative to the fiscal health of the firm can determine your willingness to assume investment risk. A company with $2 million in annual revenue may not want to risk $1 million in new product development, whereas the potential loss of $1 million to Du Pont may be minimal.

Another factor that impacts risk is the newness of the product. A product new to the company but similar to others available in the market is less risky in terms of market acceptance of features (which should reduce investment risk) than a product that is completely new to the world. The sales potential for a me-too product is less than for a completely new product too, so the opportunity risk is lower.

Based on consideration of the risks involved, decision rules are set that minimize either investment or opportunity risk. For example, suppose you believed that 5 percent market share was essential to the success of the product, so market research is conducted to estimate market share. If the answer was 4.8 percent, is that close enough to go ahead and launch? It depends. If investment risk is more important, you may decide that the risk of not reaching 5 percent is too great, and the answer is no. If opportunity risk is more important, then you may decide to continue with the product launch.

8–1

BUSINESS 2 BUSINESS
Intel's Market Risks

Consider Intel, the manufacturer of the Pentium and other computer chips. A constant flow of new products is needed but at the right speed. If Intel moves too quickly, software designers won't keep up and there won't be demand for the new chip. If Intel is too slow, then competitors that can move more quickly will capture market share. What are Intel's risks when developing the next new PC chip? What risks face the company should the market move toward less sophisticated computers designed more for Internet browsing than heavy-duty computing? How can Intel minimize those risks?

The process used to develop new products can reduce the risk. In the next section, we'll discuss product development processes that companies use to keep a constant flow of new products.

Internally Developed Products

Large business marketing organizations have a staff of product developers, while small businesses may simply pull someone off the manufacturing line. Research indicates that success, though, may require hiring someone primarily for product development.[3] In either case, there are those business experts who believe that the key to success is to develop a solid process for creating new products internally (within the company).[4]

Seven Steps in the Internal Product Development Process

The essential steps of an internal product development process are presented in Exhibit 8–4.

Generating Ideas   As mentioned earlier, a key to the entire process is a constant flow of new ideas. New product ideas can come from many sources: suppliers, customers, salespeople, marketing research, and competitors, as well as others. The challenge is to get the ideas submitted; if employees don't know what to do with ideas (whether they got the idea from their own inspiration or it was given to them by someone like a supplier or customer), then the idea will never be considered.

Promoting a central location for submitting new product ideas is especially critical if there is no New Product Development Department or otherwise obvious location. Employees must also believe that their ideas will be taken seriously, so following up with a phone call or letter to acknowledge receipt of the idea is important, as is letting the originator know of the final decision.[5] Another element that can spur new product ideas is to recognize those individuals who contribute ideas that turn into successful products. Such recognition can include awards or cash bonuses.

Screening and Preliminary Investigation   Screening involves examining new product ideas to see if they are worth investing any time at all. Screening is a first look at the following factors, in order of importance:

- Consistency with corporate objectives.
- Ability to serve customers' needs.

Exhibit 8–4

The Internal
Product
Development
Process

Idea generation. In this step, the basic idea is created. The key here is to have a steady flow of new ideas.

Screening and preliminary investigation. In this stage, ideas are examined for fit with corporate objectives, current product offerings, and other factors to see if it is worthwhile to continue developing the ideas into products. Information is gathered to determine development costs and time, potential sales, and other factors that influence whether the process should continue.

Specifying features. Detailed specifications for the product are developed. These specifications should be centered around features that lead to desired benefits, as expressed by customers and channel members.

Product development. The purpose of this step is to develop and test a prototype of the product in the lab (called alpha testing), based on the specifications developed in the previous step.

Beta testing. Beta testing is field testing, or testing the product at the customer's location, to see if the product will work under real world conditions.

Launch. Finally, the product is brought to market.

Evaluation. The product is evaluated and elements of the marketing program are adapted to fit changing market conditions.

- Market potential.
- Competitive advantage gained with the product.
- Ability to manufacture and service the product.

Many companies with formal planning systems will weight each criterion and any sub-criterion. For example, Du Pont may consider the fit with corporate objectives to be 35 percent of the decision while competitive advantage may be 20 percent. Ability to manufacture may be only 5 percent if Du Pont can protect the competitive advantage with a patent and contract the manufacturing to someone else. Some companies are using expert systems, or computer modeling programs, to screen new products.[6] In any event, the purpose is to determine if the idea is worth spending money to develop further.

If the answer is yes, the product concept is worth pursuing, then a more detailed examination of the factors that will contribute to the product's success is undertaken. When screening, we examined the product concept for potential success. Now we consider such questions as which market segments will be interested, why will they be interested, and how will competition react. The data that we obtain are then fed into the next stage, when the product is designed in terms of what it will do. Keep in mind that the product can still be killed at any time.

In marketing research classes, you will discuss the decision to conduct marketing research as a balance between the costs of research versus the benefits delivered by the new information. It is often in the preliminary investigation that the marketing research process begins (unless the new product was suggested by research). You must balance the cost of doing research against the potential for being leapfrogged. Cost of research includes not only the dollars spent on gathering the information, but the time it takes. The market life of the product may depend on the speed with which you can bring it to market; if you spend too much time on research, the product will have a shorter life because you gave competition time to develop a competitive product, too. Spend too little time on research and you may end up with a product that few buyers want.

Keep in mind, too, the investment and opportunity risks and sources of those risks. The newer the product to the market, the more you may want to spend in time and resources on research. For an innovation, it is often important to spend more on planning, in order to get the product developed right, than on later stages in the process. If you introduce the product and it isn't exactly right, a competitor will copy and improve on your idea, stealing your market.

Specifying Features   Based on your research in the preliminary investigation, it is now time to begin specifying features. This stage is when you begin to decide just what the physical characteristics, or features, of the product or service will be. At this time, you should also begin working with suppliers. Companies can shave a great deal of time off of the product development cycle if they will follow the example of the Japanese and solicit assistance from suppliers as early as possible. When suppliers are involved early, product planning can benefit from their insight. They are also more aware of the cost parameters associated with the product that will influence the product. If suppliers are brought into the loop later, then the product design may not meet cost requirements, causing the need for redesign and an addition of months to the development cycle.

Product Development   Once the features are specified, the actual product is designed and prototypes are developed for lab testing. One strategy to speed up the development process is to divide the product into component modules, which can then be designed concurrently. More designers may be needed, but the additional cost is made up in the speed in which the product is brought to market.

Manufacturing should be involved in this process because how the product is designed will impact how it is manufactured; sometimes, simple changes in product design can have a major impact on product cost. Many companies are also bringing in suppliers at this stage in order to take advantage of their expertise. For example, Plastech, a small plastics manufacturer in Gainesville, Texas, was supplying gas tanks to a lawn mower manufacturer. By changing the position of the fill spout, Plastech was able to manufacture the tank using existing molds, lowering their costs and their price to the manufacturer. More importantly, the new position also made it easier for the mower manufacturer to place the tank on the mower for assembly. A potential bottleneck in the assembly process was avoided because both the supplier and the company's own manufacturing department were involved in the product development process.

Using supplier expertise can also reduce the cost of designing. Instead of needing, say, 30 in-house designers, five teams of four in-house designers plus two supplier's designers per team are used. The speed of design is much quicker, while at the same time, the suppliers can participate intelligently to keep later production costs low.

For example, suppose a module has a target cost for parts of $25 per unit. By having the supplier participate in the design, not only does the company save money on the design costs, but the supplier can ensure that its prices are kept within that $25 limit. Otherwise, a design may be created that cannot meet the production cost targets.

The design process involves creating prototypes, or versions of the product that are then tested to make sure that they meet performance specifications. For example, a software company would test a word processing program to make sure that it works with IBM ProPrinters or HP Laserjets.

Beta Testing   But will the software work the way customers want it to in real world conditions? That is the objective of beta testing. **Beta testing**, or **field testing**, is testing the product by letting customers use it in real world conditions. Not all companies beta test, because competitors can get an early peek at the product, the test can delay the launch of the product, and a weak product can significantly damage relationships with customers who use it. Beta testing does make sense when the product represents a new platform, rather than a product extension, because the likelihood of unforeseen problems is greater.

The rush to get products out can cause companies to skip the beta testing stage. Among the countless examples of companies that rushed products out too quickly include Intel with its Pentium processor (although Intel recovered very well) and Xerox with its 3300 copier (which jammed and caught fire often).

When companies do decide to beta test, key questions to answer include how long the test should last. In most cases, the beta test is really designed to see if the product delivers the benefits in the minds of customers for whom it was designed. The beta test is not usually a test of how well the product works—finding out that the copier catches on fire is not the kind of result you would usually expect from a beta test, as that kind of result is usually caught in a lab test. What you are really trying to answer is questions like whether customers like the speed of the copier and how the document feeder works.

Xerox did an interesting version of the beta test when it designed the Memorywriter line of electronic typewriters. It hired 2,000 temporary secretaries to work with prototypes in all stages of the design. When the product was ready for market, instead of beta testing at a customer site, Xerox brought in more temporaries to type away and make sure that the product met the needs of secretaries. One reason Xerox chose this route was to keep competitors from learning about the product. An IBM repair technician, for example, might have seen one in an office at Chrysler if Xerox beta tested it there.

Launch   Finally, the product is launched in the market. Companies must develop a launch strategy based on the innovativeness of the product, service needs related to the product, and other factors.

The innovativeness of the product, or the degree to which the product represents a new technology or new way of solving buyer needs, influences how the product is launched. Potential customers must be educated about the innovation and shown how it will solve their needs. Products that are not innovative, that represent add-ons or extensions of an existing technology or copies of competitive products, do not require the same education-focused launch.

Service needs related to the product also influence how the product is launched. The greater the need for accompanying service, the more training of support personnel is required before the product can be launched. IBM, for example, cannot launch a line of printers until there are enough trained service technicians to support the product. For this reason, some technology-based companies will conduct a **rolling launch**, or launch the product in certain areas, rolling to new areas as support personnel are trained and ready. Of course, launching globally is an option, too, as you can see in From the Field 8–1.

We will discuss promotion and service issues, and other details of marketing products at the appropriate points in the book. For now, recognize that launching with a big splash isn't always the best strategy, and that the launch strategy is influenced by a number of factors such as the innovativeness of the product and service–support issues.

Evaluation   Once the product is launched, the launch itself must be evaluated. We will devote an entire chapter to the evaluation of the marketing strategy, as well as discuss how each element is evaluated. Here we will focus on the evaluation of the new product development process and market launch.

Three factors guide the evaluation of the product development process. First, what was the time to market, from conceptualization to launch? Many companies set time targets for bringing new products to market so we must first examine if we met those targets. These targets reflect the competitive nature of new product development. There is a significant advantage to be gained by being the first in the market, called the **first-mover advantage**.[7] Companies can also gain just by looking like they were first or by

8–1

FROM THE FIELD

The First Global Launch

Microsoft's Windows95 launch was touted as the first global product launch ever. Getting Microsoft ready for the launch meant making sure not only that the software was fully developed, but also that the channels of distribution had enough copies of the software to handle sales, that customer service could handle customer calls about problems during installation, and that salespeople were trained to sell the product. All told, Microsoft spent $700 million just getting ready for the launch.

One reason the launch cost so much was the extensive beta testing that Microsoft put Windows95 through. The beta period lasted eight months longer than most, in part due to the tremendous programming complexity of the product but also in part due to a strategy of using the beta test to build excitement for the product. As beta users discovered the value of the new software, they told their friends. This positive word-of-mouth created a demand for the product that helped make the launch possible.

Other companies that want to launch globally may not have $700 million, or even the $200 million that Microsoft spent just on advertising. Industry experts suggest that direct mailing to current Windows users (which requires, of course, that a database be in place), in-ad coupons, and other forms of direct response marketing (none of which were used by Microsoft) could be employed to successfully launch a business product without significant cost.

Even without direct response marketing, the launch was extremely successful. Analysts forecast sales of Windows95 to exceed 175 million copies by the end of 1998.

Source: Ian Katz and Azeem Azhar, "Start Me Up . . . It's Windows Time," *The Guardian* (August 19, 1995), p. 36; Jake Kirchner, "Windows 95 Launch: The Day After," *PC Magazine* (October 10, 1995), p. 30; Alan Maites, "Windows 95 Ad Blast Missed a Major Step," *Advertising Age* (October 9, 1995), p. 14; Jim McConville, "$200 Million Windows Ad Push," *Broadcasting & Cable* (August 28, 1995), p. 16.

introducing a product soon after the original product was introduced by a competitor, but introducing it with a bigger and more effective launch. Time in the development process is an important element in being able to capture a first-mover advantage.

The second factor evaluated is the cost of development. Development costs can be significant, and once money has been invested in a product, it is considered a **sunk**, or irretrievable, **cost**. The company hopes, of course, to recoup that cost by selling the product. The point here is not whether the product is profitable, but whether the process brought a finished product to the market within the budget. The company will also evaluate the success of the product, but what we are focusing on now is the evaluation of the new product development process, so the focus is on whether the process stayed within the budget.

Another important consideration is the financial return. Companies set return-on-investment targets that reflect their profit relative to the investment it took to make that profit. Similarly, they want to know how long it will take to break even (for profit to cover the development costs), also known as the **payback** period. So when Intel spends $5 million to create a new processor that generates $10 million in profits in the first year, it only takes six months to cover development costs, a short payback.

Finally, were we able to create the desired competitive advantage? In other words, did the new product development process result in a product that has a sustainable competitive advantage relative to other products that are available? If so, the opportunity for rewards

Exhibit 8–5
Average Importance of Computer Printer Benefits

Benefits	Average Importance
Cost under $500	10
Quality of print	9
Speed	8
Noise	6
Printer size	5
Number of fonts	4
Type sizes	4
Cartridge life	4

are great, which can offset long, costly development cycles. If not, then the company will have difficulty covering those costs. One method of increasing the likelihood of creating a competitive advantage incorporates the value chain concept first introduced in Chapter 2.

Quality Function Deployment

The value chain can represent how suppliers and customers can work together to create value through new products. At the heart of the product development process involving the supplier and customer is the quality function deployment method. The **quality function deployment (QFD)** method is a process of linking customer needs to product attributes.[8] QFD requires that a company be close to its customer and involve the customer in the product development process so that customer needs are understood. Marketing research, the sales force, and other parts of the organization can provide input from the customer, as we've discussed. From the customer, though, comes a list of requirements or desired benefits that the product must offer. As you can see in Exhibit 8–5, these are listed in a column for a new computer printer. By also incorporating the multi-attribute model of buyer decision making, we can recognize the importance, or weights, attached to each desired benefit, which is in the second column.

In addition to the needs of the customer, the company has needs that must be met and design considerations that must also be taken into account. For example, the profit margin must be acceptable, which places an upward limit on costs. Also, competitive offerings must be considered, for the new product must be superior in some manner or customers won't buy it. There are also design considerations such as the technology platform that will be used and how different benefits can be accomplished by using different features.

For example, in our computer printer situation, we've listed several design considerations across the top of the chart in Exhibit 8–6. These include what toning system (the type of ink) is used, how the paper will move through the system, and the on-board software. If we select the best toning system available, we increase the quality of print (noted by the plus sign) but at greater expense (identified by a minus sign). In addition, it may take a larger printer. If we want to keep the printer small and use that toning system, then the toner cartridge may not have as long a life.

With the addition of competitive information in the far right column (Exhibit 8–7), designers can recognize the competitive requirements of the new product as well. As you can see, the Capson is strong in quality of print, while the Hewlett–Bell is stronger in noise and paper-handling systems. Thus, a product that can be both high-quality and quiet has a chance to capture market share from both Capson and Hewlett–Bell.

Exhibit 8–6
Design
Considerations in
Computer Printer

Benefits	Average Importance	Toning System	Paper Feeder	On-Board Software
Cost under $500	10	–		
Quality of print	9	+		
Speed	8		+	
Noise	6		–	
Printer size	5	–		
Number of fonts	4			+
Type sizes	4			+
Cartridge life	4	–		

Exhibit 8–7
Competitive
Analysis

Benefits	Average Importance	Toning System	Paper Feeder	On-Board Software	Poor 1	2	3	4	Excellent 5
Cost under $500	10	–							
Quality of print	9	+							
Speed	8		+						
Noise	6		–						
Printer size	5	–							
Number of fonts	4			+					
Type sizes	4			+					
Cartridge life	4	–							

= denotes the Capson, *denotes the Hewlett–Bell.

The resulting matrix can aid designers in recognizing important trade-offs. For example, the designer can increase the speed but at the same time costs and noise may increase. The advantage to the designing firm is that the document is the framework for superior communication between the engineers designing the product, manufacturing, and marketing. QFD is a mechanism that allows the product to be developed in smaller modules simultaneously, speeding up the development process without a loss of important communication. With QFD, all of the modules should fit together when designed. The QFD process also provides a framework for involving suppliers.

Channel Involvement in New Product Development

As was discussed in Chapter 3, companies sometimes use value analysis (the examination of a particular part or module for its contribution, or value, relative to its cost). As we said, suppliers are involved in the value analysis because they may be able to offer ways to reduce cost without lowering value or else to raise value without increasing cost. Early supplier involvement is more likely to occur when strategic partnerships have been established; preferred suppliers are invited to participate and therefore get first crack at new business. QFD is a form of value analysis because each module is developed in terms of the value it provides.

When suppliers are involved, new solutions can be offered to solve trade-off difficulties. For example, if a supplier can offer a motor at the same speed but a cheaper price, the new printer may meet the cost and speed requirements. Having suppliers involved in the QFD process gives them the creative opportunity to add value to the final product.

Other channel members, such as distributors, can also play an important role in the new product development. Often, distributors and other channel members are close to the end users and are able to provide information about likely customer response and desires. Having channel members involved also helps to ensure distribution, for if channel members won't accept and carry the product, it won't reach the customer. As we read in the opening vignette, however, customers also play an important role in the development of new products.

Customer-Led Product Development

The purpose of marketing is to serve the needs of the buyer at a profit. The customer must play a role in the development of the product in order to ensure that the product meets the needs of the customer. The actual role of any specific customer, however, can vary greatly. Earlier, we discussed the role of customers in developing new product ideas through marketing research. We also discussed the role that partners play when beta testing products. In these situations, the development process is still led by the manufacturer. For other situations, such as those described in the opening of this chapter, customers lead the development of the product, sometimes from start to finish. In this section, we'll examine the issue of product design from the customer's perspective. Then we'll talk about customer-led product development.

Make or Buy?

Suppose the customer determines a need for which there are no obvious solutions (in terms of products or services available) or for which the available solutions seem expensive. The organization must consider whether they can make or create their own solution. Similarly, when the organization is considering the assembly of a product, each component may be purchased in parts and assembled by the company or else bought in modules already partly assembled, or raw materials can be purchased and the organization may consider making the components internally.

When products are already commercially available, economies of scale usually mean that the company can buy the products for less than what it would cost to make them. A company that makes casings for computer monitors, TV screens, and other similar products assembled by many companies can probably make casings for Sony screens cheaper than Sony can. When companies make these components to Sony's specifications for inclusion in Sony products, they are called **contract manufacturers**. Contract manufacturers are often able to provide components cheaper because they are able to spread the investment for machinery over more products, are able to use the machinery more efficiently, and have a higher volume. As From the Field 8–2 reports, a recent trend has been to farm out more business to contract manufacturers.

Lead Users

Sometimes, though, the products aren't readily available, affecting the manufacture of the company's product. When this occurs, some organizations innovate in commercially useful ways. For example, as described in the opening scenario, the original designer of the printed circuit board was the U.S. Army's Signal Corps. The Army needed a way to miniaturize communications equipment and seized upon the idea of the printed circuit

8–2

FROM THE FIELD
Outsourcing Is a Growth Industry

Outsourcing is one of the hottest trends in manufacturing. As companies examine their manufacturing cost structures, they are realizing that specialists can often make parts at a much lower cost. As Ken Cihlar of Ci-Dell Plastics can illustrate, contract manufacturers can also make parts better. As he describes, "we were able to remove a step from the process by molding a hole into the part, which our customer had been drilling out instead. And everything we did made the part stronger, too."

Another contract manufacturer, Guico Machine Works, just doubled the size of its machine shop in order to handle its business. As a global provider of metal parts to the heavy equipment industry, Guico has enjoyed constant growth.

Guico and Ci-Dell Plastics, like many other contract manufacturers, can make parts for many customers while spreading the capital investment over all customers. This gives contract manufacturers a much lower overhead to absorb, lowering their prices. At the same time, their specialization into one area (like plastics for Ci-Dell or metal machining like Guico) means that they bring expertise that their customers don't have but need. Better products at lower prices—no wonder that outsourcing is a growth industry.

Source: Michael Barrier, "Precision Tooled Ambition," *Nation's Business* (December 1995), pp. 14, 16; Dale D. Buss, "Small Firms, Big Clients," *Nation's Business* (December 1995), p. 22.

board, designed it, and produced the first. It looked for potential suppliers; after all, the Army is not in the business of printing circuit boards. In this instance, the Army served as a lead user, or a user that develops its own solutions to problems using available technology in a new or innovative way. **Lead users** face needs that will be general in the marketplace, but they recognize these needs months or years before the market is aware, and/or they are able to generate solutions to needs independently of manufacturers.[9]

Companies that seek a product innovation position in the marketplace should look for lead users among their customers. Strategically, lead users are accounts for which partnering relationships should be developed. They possess important insight into the evolution of their needs and the needs of customers similar to them, as well as knowledge of how those needs can be met. Such knowledge can be invaluable when developing new products.

Lead users can be identified in a number of ways. Lead users can be found participating at the conferences of trade associations. These conferences often include seminars concerning the most pressing problems facing a particular industry. Since lead users are those users that have found solutions to problems before others in their industry, you may find them presenting their solutions at conferences.

Lead users can simply be the source of new product ideas, or they can work with product designers. For example, Diamond Shamrock had a vice president of future systems, whose department was charged with planning for technology five years and further into the future. Software engineers from several vendors met regularly with this person and his department at Diamond Shamrock, co-developing computing and communication platforms. Diamond Shamrock benefited because it could more wisely plan computer purchases. The vendors gained valuable expertise that resulted in more marketable products.

Lead users can be identified among the speakers at trade conferences and seminars.
Richard Pasley/Stock Boston.

Keep in mind that the channel of distribution may separate the user from the manufacturer. Product development processes should also include distributors, either as suppliers or as customers, when they are part of the marketing channel. Often, a distributor can represent many suppliers or many customers, bringing additional valuable expertise to the process. The objective, of course, is to increase the probability of success, which is the topic of the next section.

Success or Failure?

The ability to develop successful new products is necessary for a company to thrive over the long term. Yet, nearly one in three new products will fail. While this failure rate is significantly lower than that for consumer products, the company with an expensive failure on its hands is just as unhappy. In this section, we discuss some of the factors that have been found to be related to a particular product's success or failure.

Components of Success

In general, there are five key components for success. (See Exhibit 8–8.) First, the company has close ties to a well-defined market, so it is able to anticipate customer needs. Product advantage is the dominant factor in success, according to research.[10] Second, the company can be characterized as being highly integrated and market-oriented, which means that the sales force is not the only part of the company close to the customer.[11] There is close coordination between all who participate in the new product development process. Third, the company has competitive advantages in technology and production capability, with which the new product is a good fit. These first three factors should result in a product or service that is unique and delivers superior benefits.

The fourth element is that the company has a strong marketing proficiency. The final element is that the new product launch is adequately financed and takes advantage of the marketing proficiency. These factors were identified in studies involving tangible products and services. In addition, it helps to choose a market with a high growth rate. These factors aid success because even a superior mousetrap must be marketed well.

Exhibit 8–8

Factors
Influencing New
Product Success

- Close ties to a well-defined market that lead to a product advantage
- Highly integrated and market-oriented company
- Competitive advantages in technology and production
- Strong marketing proficiency
- Strong financial support

What all the studies on new product success boil down to is that companies that focus on their **core competencies** (what they do best that gives them competitive advantage) and provide the greatest value to the customer are most likely to win the new product contest. The astute student will also note the importance of sound marketing practice, for it is marketing's responsibility to build those relationships with customers, to coordinate the new product development process, and to launch the new products. Further, timing is an important factor affecting new product success. In the next section, we'll discuss how to shorten the development process.

Accelerating the Development Process

Several case studies indicate that one important element in successful new product development is finding ways to bring products to the market more quickly. In one study, it was found that German companies are much faster in developing new products than U.S. companies.[12] The result for U.S. companies may be an overall decline in competitiveness if development cycles aren't accelerated, for (as we mentioned earlier in this chapter) product life cycles are growing shorter. Accelerating the development process can significantly improve an organization's chances to achieve a first-mover advantage, an advantage that can be retained for many years. Four strategies have been found to significantly shorten the process: Streamline each stage of development; develop products in parallel; launch products simultaneously in world markets; and use upgrades strategically.[13]

Streamline Each Stage

Streamlining each stage means being as efficient as possible in each stage of the design process. Streamlining can mean, for example, screening each new product idea within 24 hours of receipt at the central location designated for new ideas, rather than at a quarterly idea review meeting. Streamlining can also include simplifying the process, sometimes as easily as by reducing the number of people who have to approve designs before work can proceed.[14] Design can also be streamlined by taking advantage of computer design technology, such as that used in the pharmaceutical industry that enables chemists to analyze chemical compounds in a fraction of the time spent doing it manually.

Involving customers in the design process has many benefits, one of which can be faster development. Involving customers streamlines the design process when companies get feedback early in the process, avoiding blind alleys and design mistakes.

Develop Products In Parallel

Breaking a product into modules and developing it in parallel means that more designers can work on the product simultaneously, accelerating the design process substantially.[15] The high level of communication between each team of designers required by QFD

8–2

BUSINESS 2 BUSINESS

Building Relationships with Lead Users

In the opening part of this chapter, you read about the Army's role in the development of semiconductors. Suppose you are a salesperson for TI, a semiconductor manufacturer, and your customer is the Signal Corps, a lead user. Who would you want in your company to begin building relationships with people in the customer's organization in order to take advantage of their innovative abilities? How would you begin? What would you hope to offer those people in the Signal Corps so they would want to work with your personnel, and how would you convince your company's engineers that they should work with the Signal Corps?

improves the likelihood that the modules can be assembled without fear of a lack of fit. Without that communication, new product development might be like building a railroad by starting from both ends and working toward the middle, only to have both lines miss by a couple of miles.

Xerox developed its Ten Series copier products by combining the best of each of its global partners: Fuji Xerox in Japan and Rank Xerox in Europe. Japanese optics were combined with European paper handling systems to create a higher-quality line of copiers, reducing development time by more than 25 percent. The result enabled Xerox to leapfrog several Japanese competitors and regain market share in the midvolume market.

Recognize, too, that it takes a lot of time to create the processes that support a new product. Companies have to devise marketing communications plans, develop brochures and advertising, create training packages, and the like. Often, these ancillary processes and products are designed concurrently with the design of the new product in order to minimize total development time.

Launch Products Worldwide

Earlier we noted that some companies engage in a rolling launch in order to train service personnel and minimize the impact of the investment required to support a launch. On the other hand, rolling launches give competitors the opportunity to capture markets with copycat products. When possible, a global launch means faster sales acceleration, which leads to a faster return on the new product investment. This return can then be used to support further product development.

Use Upgrades Strategically

Windows95 was launched with significant fanfare. But since the product was originally designed to be a Macintosh look-alike, why didn't Windows offer more functionality the first time it was launched? Because Microsoft was using upgrades strategically. Rather than take the long time necessary to get a product that was (1) fully compatible with DOS-based software already available and (2) capable of Maclike functionality, the company launched a product it felt met the big concern, ease of use. Many companies can launch a product that meets the most important need much more quickly than if they try to fine-tune the product to meet every need. By launching a product

Exhibit 8–9

How Mitsubishi
Got a 10-Year
Head Start
through Strategic
Use of Upgrades

Year 0: Mitsubishi launches new product.	Competitors notice, begin process of new product development to copy Mitsubishi—projected time to market is five years.
Year 1: Mitsubishi launches upgrade.	Competitors still try to develop their version of product—four years to product.
Year 2: Mitsubishi launches another upgrade.	Competitors still try to develop their version of product—three years to product.
Year 3: Mitsubishi launches another upgrade.	Competitors still try to develop their version of product—two years to product.
Year 4: Mitsubishi launches another upgrade.	Competitors still try to develop their version of product—one year to product.
Year 5: Mitsubishi launches another upgrade.	Competitors now ready for market, but their products are equivalent of Mitsubishi's product of five years ago—add the five needed to design the upgrades and they're 10 years behind!

meeting the most important need quickly, they gain the first-mover advantage. By then upgrading regularly, they can maintain that advantage. The key is to incorporate planned upgrades in the product strategy from the beginning; otherwise, you may get leapfrogged.

The best example is likely to be unfamiliar to most students. Mitsubishi took this approach, launching a new air conditioner, then launching upgrades every year to improve performance, reliability, and ease of installation. As illustrated in Exhibit 8–9, the new product took competitors by surprise. With their four-to-five–year development cycles, they were about 10 years behind Mitsubishi when they finally got a product out, assuming the same development cycle for each upgrade. While 10 years may seem like an exaggeration, the U.S. company that used to lead the market now trails Mitsubishi miserably and buys its products from Japanese competitors.

Keys to Innovation

Innovation can mean many things, such as innovative marketing strategy, innovative corporate structure, or innovative manufacturing processes. In this chapter, our context is new product development, which is dependent on creativity leading to innovation. Some companies are better at innovating than others.

In a study focusing on flexible manufacturing equipment, innovative companies were found to have a corporate culture that supported innovation. This culture is dominated by a desire for the firm to grow, to improve, and to take advantage of all possible opportunities. Innovative firms tend to focus on opportunity risk while non-innovative firms focus on investment risk.[16]

A business marketer that wants to encourage innovation must first create the right culture. Understanding the culture of innovation can also aid salespeople and other business marketers in identifying innovative customers for they are likely to be lead users. Understanding the culture of innovation should also influence the selection of suppliers to the organization, for innovative suppliers can aid the business marketer in gaining competitive advantages. The wrong culture can be a major barrier to success.

Exhibit 8–10
Special
Challenges of
Services

- *Perishability.* Services can't be stored, like physical products can, which makes anticipating demand much more critical.
- *Intangibility.* Services can't be touched or seen, so marketers have to (1) ensure that customers understand the value that services provide and make (2) the benefits seem more tangible.
- *Reliability.* Services can vary a great deal in terms of quality, depending on who is performing the service. Someone can have a great experience one time but a horrible experience the next time. Managing quality carefully is a challenge for services companies.

Challenges to New Product Success

A number of research studies have examined new product or service successes versus failures. Most of the failures can be attributed to the inability to meet one of the criteria for success. Thus, most products that fail do so because the firm does not have a market orientation throughout, or there is poor coordination, or the firm does not have or does not use a technological advantage. These factors contribute to a product that does not provide value.

Another key factor in product failure is poor marketing, either through failing to launch the product with adequate or appropriate support, or by pricing the product inappropriately.[17] Again, the marketing department plays a key role in determining the success of a new product or service and, ultimately, the success of the firm.

Services face additional challenges. Pure services must overcome all of the same barriers as products, in addition to those factors related to such characteristics as perishability, tangibility, and reliability. Services cannot be produced and stored until needed in the way that products can. For example, if Hilton builds a hotel and rooms go empty, those unpaid nights are lost forever. If Hilton misanticipates demand or if demand varies widely for a particular location, the hotel may fail. Exhibit 8–10 reviews the special challenges of business services, such as architectural services, financial and banking services, accounting and auditing services, and other services that businesses use.

One difficulty with new services is getting potential users to understand what the services do, what benefits they provide. Employee Resource Management (ERM), a South Carolina company that transfers client company employees to its own payroll and then leases the employees back to the company, relieves its clients of many of the problems associated with human resource management. The problem is that ERM solves so many of the clients' problems and makes human resource management look easy that once the problems are fixed, clients think ERM isn't needed anymore. ERM management has to constantly educate the customer, so that the client continues to recognize the value ERM provides.[18] This education can be difficult because potential users can't touch or see the product because it is intangible.

Harvesting a Product

At some point, all good things must come to an end. So it is with a product's life. When the product no longer contributes to the firm's success, then it is time to stop production and turn resources to more profitable ventures.

When to Harvest a Product

Products are not harvested or terminated just because they are unprofitable or because they are classified as dogs. Several considerations must be reviewed, of which cash use and contribution to profit are two. For example, a product may be profitable and selling at a reasonable rate, but if investment (or cash) can be diverted to an even more profitable product, the company may decide to harvest the first product. Or a product may not be profitable after overhead is allocated, but have a positive contribution margin otherwise. If the company were to stop selling that product, overhead would have to be reallocated elsewhere, perhaps making another product look unprofitable.

Customer demand should also be considered. Some products are useful because they mean that customers do not need multiple vendors. For example, Wallace Computer Services sells ribbons and ink cartridges for computer printers, including ribbons for the now unpopular daisywheel printer. If Wallace did not offer daisywheel printer ribbons, customers would have to buy those ribbons from someone else. Customers who have some daisywheel printers, as well as laser and ink jet printers, might decide to buy all of their printer supplies from a Wallace competitor if they couldn't also get their daisywheel supplies from Wallace.

Challenges to Harvesting

Products are managed by people, and sometimes people overinvest their egos in a particular product. This may make it difficult to halt producing a product, particularly if the product was designed by the owner, for example.

Similarly, a product may not be eliminated because of the jobs that might be lost. Every day we see fights in Congress over what plane the Air Force will build; many times, these fights may be about saving jobs (and votes) rather than what is best for the Air Force. Similar situations can occur in companies unwilling to lose good personnel. Political difficulties can make harvesting products a challenge.

Summary

The first step in product management is to understand that a product is viewed by the customer in terms of what the product does, not what it is. A product, therefore, is a bundle of benefits, or a bundle of need satisfiers. Companies that can exceed expectations by adding desired services or augmenting the core product can achieve a significant competitive advantage.

Products have a life cycle consisting of five steps: development, introduction, growth, maturity, and decline. The technology platform's life cycle can be separate from the life cycle of the product itself. A technology platform's life should be longer, but leapfrogging can quickly end a platform's usefulness.

As products go through the life cycle, marketing emphases will change. For example, early in the life of a technology, the issue is simply creating primary demand. During maturity, however, a company wants to maintain the product's position or increase it relative to competitors.

Product portfolio management is a set of management tools that recognizes that companies manage many products in the same manner as they do financial investments. Products can be classified as dogs, stars, question marks, and cash cows. Marketing efforts, or investments, will change, depending on the product's classification.

New product development processes are more important than ever due to shorter average life cycles. At each step of the process, management must make the decision to continue or kill the product. Influencing the decision are the risks, both investment and opportunity risk.

Internally developed products begin as an idea that must be screened to determine if it is worth further development. Features are specified and then a prototype is created. A small run of the product is manufactured and beta, or field, tested. Then the product is launched and evaluated.

An important element to successful business marketing is to develop products with customers. Through understanding the value chain and using quality function deployment, an internal development process can include customers and suppliers. The resulting product should have greater value (and greater likelihood for success) than one generated entirely internally.

Lead users can lead product development. Lead users recognize needs months or years before the rest of the market recognizes those needs, and they generate their own solutions. Smart business marketers identify lead users and build them into the new product development process.

In general, five factors are key to success. The first three relate to the company's ability to identify needs and satisfy them: close ties to the market, highly integrated and market-oriented organization, and competitive technology and production advantages. The second two relate to the company's ability to market products: strong marketing proficiency and the resources necessary to launch the product.

Shorter average life cycles, though, mean that successful companies must also develop new products more quickly than before. Therefore, companies are trying to streamline each stage of the process, developing products in parallel, and launching globally in order to preempt launches by competitors. Innovative companies are finding ways to create new products quickly, and an important element in their success is their corporate culture of innovation. Barriers to new product success usually relate to a failure to secure one of the five keys to success.

Products must also be withdrawn from the market at the appropriate time. Companies have to consider not only each product's profit and loss statement, but also the impact that the product has on the sales of other company products. Sometimes, a money loser has to be kept in order to round out a product line, maintain a foothold in a market, or for other strategic reasons.

New products are the essence of growth for most companies. Managing products well and creating processes for continuous product development are important aspects of business marketing, particularly in today's market of short product life cycles.

Key Terms

advantage	contract manufacturer	field testing
augmented product	core competencies	first-mover advantage
benefit	core product	growth stage
beta testing	decline stage	introduction stage
business strength	development stage	investment risk
cash cow	dog	lead user
competitive advantage	feature	leapfrogged

.. market attractiveness   product life cycle (PLC)   question mark

maturity stage   product line   rolling launch

opportunity risk   product portfolio   secondary demand

payback   management   star

primary demand   quality function   sunk cost

product   deployment (QFD)   technology platform

Discussion Questions

1. Consider the personal computer for a moment. In one column, make a list of all of the benefits that you derive from a personal computer. In a second column, list the features that provide these benefits. Is this product augmented in any way and how might that differ if you were a business user? What is the core product?

2. A big issue for salespeople who work on straight commission is this: On what products will they place their emphasis during a sales call? For these salespeople, time with the customer is their most important resource, so they have to choose how to use that time. Draw a blank product portfolio matrix and decide how much time should be spent on products within each square, assuming equal numbers of products in each of the quadrants. What are your reasons for each decision?

3. Can a product enjoy multiple life cycles? If so, how? If you were a salesperson with a product in each stage of the product life cycle, what percentage of your selling time would you allocate to each product?

4. Some authors have combined the life cycle and portfolio matrices into one model. How would you do that? What are some limitations of the model?

5. The chief engineer for Portland Purifiers, a maker of industrial water filters with annual sales of $5 million, has an idea for a new product that would represent a major (and patentable) improvement over current market offerings. She estimates that the development of the product will cost half a million dollars, including tooling the manufacturing line. The last product launch cost about $200,000 in marketing and promotion costs. She thinks the product would sell for about $50,000 and should sell 75 units in year 1, 140 in year 2, and then level out at 200 per year. Contribution margin is 40 percent. Should the company continue with this project? What do you need to know about the company in order to understand its decision to go or not go ahead? What is the payback period?

6. What criteria would you use to determine which customers would make good beta test sites? Would you want to choose lead users? Why or why not?

7. Several ways of developing new products were discussed in the chapter. Make a list of all of the ways, and then discuss which methods would lead to greater innovations and which would be more likely to lead to incremental additions or better versions of the same thing.

8. Shred-All is a security company that takes company documents (on paper, disk, or any other media) and destroys them. Shred-All had a difficult time when the service was launched because companies failed to recognize a need for the service. Describe the investments Shred-All needed to make to prepare to launch the company so that you can understand the "inventory" that it had to manage. Then discuss how you would overcome barriers to success if you were Shred-All's management. Finally, how would you educate potential customers so they understood the need for your service?

9. One component of success is to have a highly integrated and market-oriented company. You are the marketing manager. How will you contribute to the integration and market orientation of your company?

10. Is a competitive advantage always a benefit? Why or why not?

11. What are the potential ethical issues in obtaining innovations from customers? For example, if a salesperson sees a customer using the product in a new way or with some modification, are there any ethical issues in copying the new application or modification?

Internet Exercise

Open the Product Development Management Association's home page (**www.pdma.org**) and select the <u>Outstanding Innovator Award</u> option. Answer the following questions:

1. What process was used to select these innovators? Who are the most current winners?

2. Go to the home page of one of the current winners. (You may have to search for it.) Identify a new product and evaluate how innovative that product is. What seem to be its competitive advantages? What would be the buyer's motivation for buying it?

WWW
I N T E R N E T

Cases

Case 8.1   Washington Waterproof

Sue Guidry, president of Washington Waterproof, hung up and stared at the phone. She had just finished talking with George Hernandez at NorWest Technologies, one of Washington Waterproof's largest OEM customers. Or at least it had been one of the largest customers. She had called George to learn why NorWest was no longer buying Temolentum, a chemical that made fabrics less likely to tear, thus improving the ease of cutting and sewing fabrics. George had told her that another company had introduced a product that was cheaper and easier to apply, making Temolentum obsolete. Sue had seen the product at a trade show and had been worried about how it would affect her sales. Now she knew.

Washington Waterproof began in 1933 with one product, a chemical that waterproofed fabric. Since then, the company has expanded into other industrial chemicals such as a product applied to exterior walls after they have been painted. The chemical prevents spray paint from adhering to the wall's paint, which means that graffiti can be washed off quite easily. Washington sells its products directly to users and OEMs through a manufacturer's rep network, meaning that none of the salespeople are employees of Washington. They represent Washington and other chemical companies, and are independent contractors.

Sue Guidry took over Washington Waterproof when her father, Bill Washington, retired six years ago. Bill was a chemical engineer, and under his leadership, the company developed most of its current products. Sue's expertise, however, is marketing, and in the six years that she has run the company, no new products have been introduced. Patent protection is running out on some of the company's products and Sue is beginning to panic. If Washington is to continue to thrive, or even survive, it must develop new products.

1. Set up a system that would encourage new product ideas and development for Washington. What resources or personnel would you want to have?

   2. Washington's salespeople are not company employees but independent contractors. How, then, can Sue identify and build relationships with lead users? Would you consider NorWest Technologies to be a lead user? Why or why not?

Case 8.2   NorTex Distributors

Cedric McElroy examined sales results for the year that just ended. His company, NorTex Distributors, had just completed the best year ever in terms of total sales, but profits as a percentage of sales had actually decreased. NorTex Distributors represents several electronics manufacturers, selling switches, transistors, semiconductors, and other electronic parts made by six companies in the Pacific Rim to telecommunications and computer companies in the Dallas–Fort Worth area. McElroy employs six salespeople who work on straight commission based on total sales.

As he reviewed sales by manufacturer, he realized that the biggest drain on profits was sales of Doosun products. Doosun is a Korean company that makes transistors. Intense competition for that business, combined with a lack of new products from Doosun, drove prices and margins down during the year. As McElroy looked at his figures, he thought back to one of his own sales, a $700,000 order that included about $100,000 of Doosun products. He really had to discount the Doosun products in order to compete with the new Hibachi transistor. But without a transistor, he probably would have lost the sale entirely.

At the same time, however, McElroy realized that the new Kinetec line of electronic switches was a potential bright spot. Introduced only three months ago, already the line accounted for 60 percent of NorTex's switch sales, which were just over 10 percent of NorTex's total sales. Profits were not great on the line, however, because McElroy had to discount it to get people to try it.

   1. What factors should McElroy take into account when considering whether to drop the Doosun line of transistors?

   2. In what stage of the PLC is the Kinetec line? What can McElroy do to speed acceptance of the product without discounting the price? What will signal to McElroy sufficient acceptance that discounting is no longer needed to get the sale?

Additional Readings

Andrews, Jonlee, and Daniel C. Smith, "In Search of Marketing Imagination: Factors Affecting the Creativity of Marketing Programs for Mature Products," *Journal of Marketing Research* 23 (May 1996), pp. 174–87.

Athaide, Gerard A., Patricia W. Meyers, and David L. Wilemon, "Seller–Buyer Interactions during the Commercialization of Technological Process Innovations," *Journal of Product Innovation Management* 13 (1996), pp. 406–21.

Besemer, Susan, and Karen O'Quin, "Analyzing Creative Products: Refinement and Test of Judging Instrument," *Journal of Creative Behavior* 20, no. 2 (1995), pp. 115–26.

Ettlie, John E., "Product–Process Development Integration in Manufacturing," *Management Science* 41, no. 7 (1995), pp. 1224–37.

Germain, Richard, "The Role of Context and Structure in Radical and Incremental Logistics Innovation Adoption," *Journal of Business Research* 35, (1996), pp. 117–27.

Griffin, Abbie, and John R. Hauser, "Integrating R&D and Marketing: A Review and Analysis of the Literature," *Journal of Product Innovation Management* 13 (1996), pp. 191–215.

LaBahn, Douglas W., Abdul Ali, and Robert Krapfel, "New Product Development Cycle Time: Influences of Project and Process Factors in Small Manufacturing Companies," *Journal of Business Research* 36 (1996), pp. 179–88.

Langerak, Fred, Ed Peelen, and Harry Commandeur, "Organizing for Effective New Product Development," *Industrial Marketing Management* 26 (1997), pp. 281–89.

Large, David, and Donald Barclay, "Technology Transfer to the Private Sector: A Field Study of Manufacturer Buyer Behavior," *Journal of Product Innovation Management* 9 (1992), pp. 26–43.

Menon, Ajay, Bernard Jaworski, and Ajay Kohli, "Product Quality: Impact of Interdepartmental Interactions," *Journal of the Academy of Marketing Science* 25 (Summer 1997), pp. 187–200.

Moorman, Christine, "Organizational Market Information Process: Cultural Antecedents and New Product Outcomes," *Journal of Marketing Research* 22 (August 1995), pp. 318–35.

Rochford, Linda, and William Rudelius, "How Involving More Functional Areas within a Firm Affects the New Product Process," *Journal of Product Innovation Management* 9 (1992), pp. 287–99.

Chapter 9

Business Marketing Channels: Partnerships for Customer Service

CINCINNATI MILACRON

Cincinnati Milacron is one of the nation's largest makers of machine tools and plastics processing machines. It also makes computer controls and software for factory automation, and it produces precision grinding wheels, metalworking fluids, and metal-cutting tools.●

For many years Milacron's sales people were its crown jewels. With strong engineering backgrounds and high salaries, by industry standards, Milacron's reps used a consultative selling approach. Customer needs were carefully defined and machines were often produced to order. Delivery occurred a few months after order.●

But then Japanese tool makers entered the fray. They offered solid and versatile machines, built up inventories at regional distribution centers, and sold through distributors and agents at radically competitive prices. Of course, deliveries occurred within a few days of orders and Milacron's market share plummeted. Reacting to competitive pressures, Milacron souped up its advertising and sales literature, started building speculative inventories using overseas manufacturing, and squeezed its sales force for increased productivity.●

Because the competitive pressure in tools was simultaneously occurring in its robotics division, a Milacron task force aimed to make revolutionary products for plastics molding. In 1991 the team succeeded in making small injection molding machines that could sell for a fraction of traditional models' price. There was one little snag, however: Their margin would not afford company selling expenses. *They would be sold through industrial distributors.* Throughout the 1990s Milacron products such as Elektra, Ferromatik, and Vista brand injection molding machines have led the market. They are sold by capable distributors working in partnership with Milacron. Perhaps it was inevitable that in 1995, Milacron switched from an internal sales force to a partnership approach with a distributor sales component for its quarter-billion-dollar machine tool business too. ●

Visit the Milacron web site at **http://www.milacron.com** ●

Learning Objectives

Marketing channels are systems organized to deliver products and related services. They save buyers the costs of searching and waiting. Because of the breadth of tasks needed to be done, most channels are comprised of multiple businesses. To be effective, these firms typically work as partners to coordinate their activities to serve ultimate customers and to remain competitive as a "team."

We begin the chapter with an orientation to the reasons for channels and an introduction to some of the types of businesses involved. We then provide a model for channel design and take up the key issues of channel management.

At the conclusion of the chapter you should be able to

- Describe the functions of a marketing channel.
- Classify the various intermediaries used in business marketing.
- Analyze customer needs for channel service outputs.
- Design a channel system that can (1) provide customers with the services they want and (2) attain a competitive advantage.
- Discuss the challenges of managing channel relationships and coordinating activities across organizational boundaries.
- Frame a basic make–buy analysis involving different distribution system functions.

What is the Marketing Channel?

Business marketing channels are systems designed to close numerous gaps between the manufacture and use of products. Some of the gaps are between places. For example, coal is efficiently mined in enormous quantities in China and the Dakotas. But it must first be graded and transported before it can be used at the university or metropolitan power plant. Coal is hardly a commodity one might ship by overnight air. Thus—to close another type of gap, a time gap—the power plant's supply depends on accurate information about coal in transit by rail and barge, plus probably occasional truck deliveries from a local depot. The marketing channel functions to sort the output, break bulk, and deliver.

These physical distribution tasks are not the only ones performed by a channel system. A builder who picks up attic fans at a Contractors' Warehouse (CW) not only enjoys the convenience of a local supply source, but might get a tip or two on installation from the floor personnel at CW, have to pay for the goods only in the next 30 days, and grab some shingles and flashing in the same trip. In this instance, the dealer—a channel partner of the fan manufacturer—provides sales help, financing, and an assortment of other products. We are apt to find several builders using CW to the same ends.

So notice in the top portion of Exhibit 9–1 that five builders transact directly with six material suppliers. Each channel is very short. No **channel intermediaries**—organizations that facilitate the transfer of title between the producer and user of a product—are involved in the supplier-to-builder channel. But the whole system requires 30 (5 × 6) transactions. The bottom of Exhibit 9–1 shows a longer channel. Between supplier and builder we find a distributor carrying the lines from all six material suppliers, and serving all five builders. Notice that in this longer channel only 11 (5 + 6) transactions are needed to serve the builders—and the suppliers.

So let's forget—for the time being—the superior services the Contractors' Warehouse might provide over direct from factory orders (e.g., sales help and an assortment of materials). We've shown that adding an intermediary can reduce the number of transactions in a system. Channels can affect the efficiency of buying and selling.

Channel Value

This simple example of the trading efficiency provided by a channel intermediary preempts frequent criticism that marketing channels are to blame for excessive prices. You may have leveled such a claim yourself at one time or another. Perhaps when you found out the body shop was going to charge you $130 for the new side view mirror on your Toyota, you blamed the long channel between manufacturer, jobber, local distributor, and dealer for the difference between what you and Toyota pay.

But a dealer's price for one mirror installed by tomorrow afternoon is not really the same as the unit price paid by a car manufacturer buying tens of thousands of mirrors, with several months' lead time. A better comparison point is the $130 versus your directory assistance calls to find the manufacturer, plus the long distance calls and faxes to get your order placed—using your credit card number—and the express delivery charges. And all this presumes the item is in stock, you have correctly identified the needed mirror, and the manufacturer is even set up to handle small orders and credit cards.

Channel Outputs and Costs   When we consider channel costs, we must really look deeper into what is getting done by the channel and what other means we might have of achieving the same end. Any marketing channel exists to provide specific service

Exhibit 9–1
Trading Efficiency
from an
Intermediary

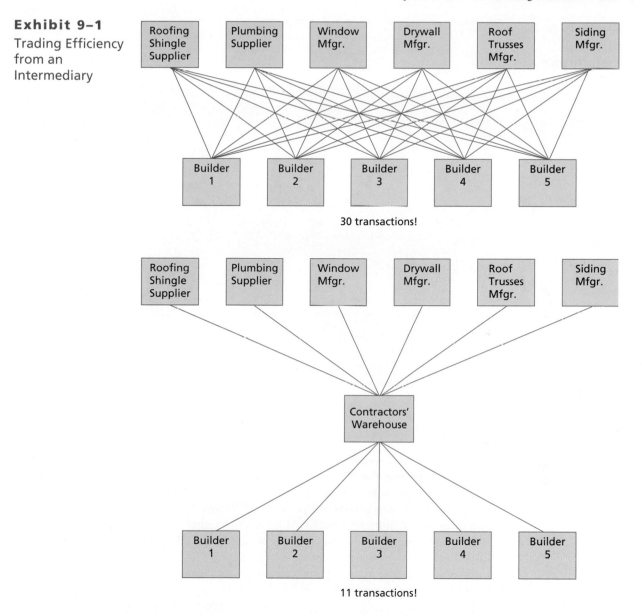

outcomes that are valued by the supplier and the buyer. Exhibit 9–2 formalizes the chapter's opening discussion. The horizontal axis is an abstraction representing a combination of channel service outputs: fitting quantities are available, convenient selection and order are the rule, and we see rapid delivery, wide assortment, installation or application assistance, and so on.[1]

None of these services can be provided without cost. You know that oil by the tanker costs less than oil by the drum or liter; 20 distribution centers cost more to operate than 10; overnight delivery costs more than second-day; it takes a huge showroom or catalog to display office supplies or building products, but only a kiosk or trifold brochure to peddle mousepads or insulation batts; and distributor service and support require higher prices (margins) than self-serve alternatives. Thus, Exhibit 9–2 shows channel costs rising with the provision of increased levels of service.

Exhibit 9–2
Channel
Performance and
Costs

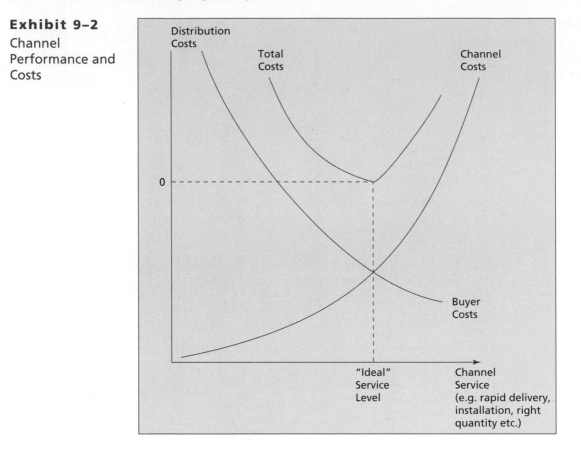

Buyer Effort and Costs   But as these channel service outputs increase, the work required by a buyer—and the associated cost of this work—decrease. For example, a law office that can purchase letterhead in lots of 2,000 instead of 10 reams has less office clutter and saves on inventory investment. More of these saving accrue if the printer can replenish the stationery in just 72 hours instead of three weeks. An environmental engineer who can take the hazardous waste seminar locally saves the cost of airfare to the national training center. A purchasing agent who can get all the factory's lubricating oils from a single supplier saves on the costs of searching for and haggling with numerous vendors of specialty lubricants. Finally, a sales office that gets dealer installation assistance and training on the new copier saves on its own start-up efforts and avoids downtime resulting from misuse of the machine. In sum, many functions in the conduct of business—and their associated costs—can be shifted between buyers and members of the channel.

A Best Channel Structure?   Economic pressures on the exchange network tend to move the channel to the structure that yields minimum total costs, point zero in Exhibit 9–2's curve representing the sum of buyer's costs and the costs of the commercial channel. Inefficient intermediaries will find their business going elsewhere, perhaps to more competitive intermediaries, but also perhaps to their suppliers, or their customers, who decide they can do certain functions for themselves.

Of course, habits, vested interests, and social and political ties can impede the evolution to this minimum-cost "ideal." For example, a company trying to use catalogs to sell routine supplies and its sales force to sell more complex products may nevertheless have to "buy peace" with its reps by providing them a small commission on the catalog orders in the territory.

Allegiance Corporation distributes medical supplies and instruments directly to the hospital floors at Seton Medical Center. In close partnerships, Allegiance and Seton share information and coordinate activities for cost control and quality health care.

John Storey

Noncompetitive markets can likewise thwart more efficient systems for a time. For example, many municipalities have found that they can save money by outsourcing water and wastewater management to independent companies in the chemical process industry.[2] In essence, a water management company is an intermediary in a new, more efficient channel system. But more than economics determines the channel structure for any municipality. Outsourcing is dubbed "privatization" in government. Regardless of its true economic merits or, in other cases, demerits, use of such an intermediary often serves as a political lever for elected officials, strikes fear in the hearts of municipal employees, and mobilizes union opposition.

Part of the evolutionary equation must be the cooperative spirit between channel participants. As we have discussed in prior chapters, when buyers and seller collaborate, they often find ways to coordinate activities to eliminate waste or gain impact. For example, Skyway is a transportation company that uses electronic communications and the Internet to allow its customers to track the location of orders 24 hours a day. Certainly this innovation affects needed inventories at both customer and shipper locations.

In this vein, let's not presume there is a single and permanent "best channel." Because of technology, experience, innovation, regulation, and the variability of costs of different system inputs (e.g., jet fuel or telecommunications), the minimum-cost channel and the ideal service level are moving targets.

Channel Member Profits   In a competitive environment channel, members receive compensation that corresponds to the value they add to the product. For example, a small manufacturer of computer peripherals needs a dealer network not only to inventory and display its line, but to demonstrate its products and ensure proper use with different operating systems. Dealer compensation in the form of margins may be more than 50 percent for such a role in differentiating the product in the value-added chain. In contrast, dealers simply taking orders for stock office or medical supplies play a much smaller role in the value-added chain; their margins will be quite thin.

Similarly, we see the market rewarding unique excellence. The hydraulics distributor, Hydrotech, with the distinct capability to provide applications engineering assistance to its

OEM account, Cincinnati Milacron, is highly sought and valued as a channel partner—by both suppliers and customers. Such uniquely skilled intermediaries are apt to preserve their margins and enjoy market leadership without resorting to the deep discounts offered by distributors who lack the expertise or credibility.

Types of Channel Intermediaries

To this point we have provided a justification for channels of distribution in general. We have referred to different types of channel members, but have not provided formal introductions. This section briefly reviews a number of the major types of organizations in business-to-business marketing. Actually, there are more types than we can afford to cover here. Simply keep in mind that several industries feature unique channel institutions that combine attributes of the forms we review next.

The Ownership Distinction

We distinguish two major classes of business marketing intermediaries on the basis of whether or not they own the goods they sell. **Merchant wholesalers** are intermediaries who take title to the merchandise. Sometimes called **industrial distributors**, merchant wholesalers include a number of subtypes, which differ in the functions they perform. **Agents** and brokers represent the other class of intermediaries, they do not buy or own the goods they sell.

Why is product ownership such a key distinction? Product ownership brings with it a substantial business commitment. It involves cash or financing to purchase, requires proper storage and handling, and always includes risk of spoilage, theft, or obsolescence. Consider a small distributor doing $10 million in sales with 20 percent gross profit. Stocking an inventory sufficient to turn over four times per year requires an inventory investment alone of $2 million. Add to that the racks and bins, forklifts, systems, security, and more to see that the *ownership* commitment is substantial.

A third class of intermediaries consists of **manufacturers' sales branches and offices**. These are wholesaling operations that a manufacturer owns and operates. For example, General Electric Supply Corporation is an electrical supplies distribution subsidiary of the General Electric Corporation. Similarly, in the plumbing field Arnstan–American Standard has a distribution subsidiary, Crane Supply Company.[3]

Any such subsidiary may have a measure of autonomy within the corporation, but its ownership by the manufacturing organization distinguishes sales branches and offices from the independent merchant wholesalers and agencies introduced above. Later in the chapter we will revisit some of the concepts from Chapter 2 and elsewhere in the text regarding the strategic costs and benefits of vertical integration, particularly the distribution functions.

Other Distinguishing Functions: Merchant Wholesalers

Full Service

Some merchant wholesalers, called **full-function wholesalers**, provide a broad array of services for their suppliers and customers. Exhibit 9–3 highlights the range of functions a full-service distributor is apt to provide. In essence, with a little foresight and candor from the buyer, the distributor can serve as an extension of its purchasing department. Similarly, good product training and marketing support from the manufacturer can enable the distributor to be an effective partner in the execution of sales and service functions. A good distributor partner enjoys a strong reputation in the regional industry or product area. Inventory levels should be sufficient to provide ready supply to users. Its

Exhibit 9–3
Functions
Performed by
Distributors

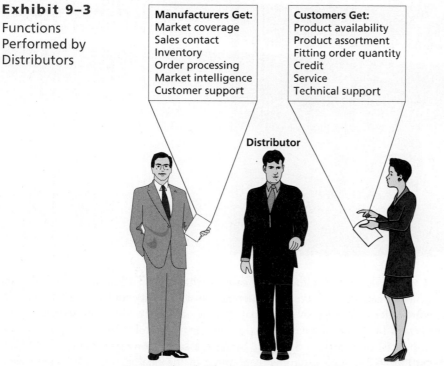

Manufacturers Get:
Market coverage
Sales contact
Inventory
Order processing
Market intelligence
Customer support

Customers Get:
Product availability
Product assortment
Fitting order quantity
Credit
Service
Technical support

Distributor

SOURCE: Adapted with permission from Bert Rosenbloom, *Marketing Functions and the Wholesaler-Distributor: Achieving Excellence in Distribution.* (Washington, DC: Distribution Research and Education Foundation, 1987).

sales force is knowledgeable and gives adequate attention to current customers and the tasks of developing new accounts. The distributor also provides market intelligence and new product ideas to both its suppliers and customers.[4]

In several product categories the distinction between wholesaler and retailer is blurred. Computer dealers, office supplies resellers such as Office Max and Staples, and warehouse clubs such as Sams sell to households. But they sell substantial volume to what some call the soho segment—the small office and home office—as well as to schools, restaurants, event marketers, and other organizations.

Selective Service

Many channels consist of **limited-function wholesalers**. These firms don't provide the full spectrum of services listed in Exhibit 9–3. For example, **single-line wholesalers** don't carry an assortment of items, perhaps just seed corn or certain chemicals. This concept can be carried further to **specialty wholesalers**, firms carrying a very narrow line and supporting that with technical expertise and consultative selling. An example is High Ocean Products Co., a Redmond, Washington, distributor of sea-frozen, sashimi-grade fish.

Merchant wholesalers also include **cash-and-carry distributors**, firms that provide no buyer financing or delivery. Many cities have downtown produce markets with several cash-and-carry wholesalers serving restaurants or other institutions. A **drop shipper** or **desk jobber** buys products from a supplier but never takes physical possession; instead they are delivered directly to the user. Bulky products such as coal and gypsum board are often drop shipped.

If one can job (wholesale) from a desk, one ought to be able to job from a truck. A **truck jobber** carries all its inventory on a truck and services customers on a frequent basis or route. The Snap-on-Tools distributor calling on service stations and garages is a truck jobber. This can be an effective means of reaching a market of small customers constrained by high search costs.

Snap-on dealer Jesse Renfrow (right) and technical representative Alan Joffray (background) help Mario Rodriguez (left) offer Snap-on tools—and new ways to grow his business.

Courtesy Snap-On Inc.; photo by James Schnepf.

Finally, we should recognize the role of catalog wholesalers. While almost any distributor will have a catalog to serve as a reference and ordering tool for customers, the **catalog wholesaler** relies exclusively on mail, phone, and fax orders from its catalog and does not have a field sales force. Selling through catalog wholesalers such as Quill (for business products) or American Scientific Surplus, a supplier wants a high level of market penetration, its products prominently featured in the catalog, and wholesaler inventories sufficient to fill orders promptly.

Management Issues with Using Merchant Wholesalers

Key management challenges for manufacturers using distributors—full service or otherwise—include sustaining distributor sales support for the line. A distributor with 200 reps calling on 10,000 hospitals and medical labs can't possibly satisfy every supplier's wish for a high percentage of its overall selling effort. When distributors carry strong competing makes or private-label merchandise, the problem becomes even tougher. High margins on top-quality products, fitting trade promotions, advertising, and the manufacturer's own selling activities will be required to motivate distributor efforts.

Manufacturers also complain about distributor shortcomings in market development. They point to a short-run orientation and a tendency merely to take orders on stock items instead of calling on *new* accounts and demonstrating *new* products. This difficulty can be a manifestation of a deeper problem, lack of manufacturer–distributor trust in the relationship. Perhaps distributors have seen the manufacturer terminate other wholesalers when markets grew big enough to support its internal sales force. Sometimes selling effort is discouraged by too much competition from other distributors in the region selling the same line. Maybe the technical specialists or other missionary sales work evidenced by the manufacturer are thought to be a prelude to designating large customers its "house accounts" no longer serviced by the distributor.[5] In these cases the manufacturer should work primarily to restore trust with channel partners before tinkering with incentives or channel system redesign.

Many wholesale businesses are small, family-run operations. Frequently, the success of the enterprise is attributable to one person. What is the state of this person's health? Is he or she ready to retire or step out of day-to-day operations? Can the manufacturer see or assist the distributor in planning management succession? If we do not see a certain depth of leadership and continuity, suppliers and customers alike should hedge against breakdown of the current arrangement by cultivating other channel options.

The David J. Joseph Company is one of the world's first and largest scrap metals brokers. The $1.5 billion company headquartered in Cincinnati, Ohio, trades in ferrous metals around the world. The company builds, refurbishes, leases, and sells railroad box cars; and it has eight automobile shredders capable of processing up to one million cars a year. These activities are highly synergistic with its brokerage business. Joseph Company's professional brokers use sophisticated electronic communications and a network of supply and demand contacts to spot and act on opportunities around the world.

As summarized on the company web page (http://www.djj.com):

The Joseph Company offers overseas buyers and sellers an insider's view and expert's perspective of the U.S. market. At the same time, we offer domestic customers access to an in-depth knowledge of overseas markets that can enhance their own operations.

Our goal is to benefit both metals producers and metals buyers alike, creating long-term partners.

Agent Intermediaries

Among the channel institutions not taking title, **manufacturers' agents** sell the lines of noncompeting principals for a commission. A **principal** is the manufacturer or other person or firm who contracts for the services of the agent in its own behalf. Their job is to promote the line, develop new accounts, and take orders. When a manufacturer of radio receivers uses manufacturers' agents to sell its products, it avoids the overhead associated with its own sales force. Also, the commission compensation of an agent makes selling a variable cost. Agents typically bring knowledge of the regional market, established client relationships, and a modest assortment and affiliation advantage from the other *noncompeting* lines. They are a rich source of information on innovations in the industry for customers and often can be counted upon to go the extra mile to solve problems such as scarce supply situations or adaptations to new uses.

Agent commissions vary by industry. Agents representing automotive OEMs earn about 5 percent commissions. Electronic products agents can earn between 7 and 12 percent. They often work under contracts requiring only 30 or 60 days termination notice. This means that the contracts themselves provide little assurance of longevity. More important are performance and *strong working relationships*—with principals and agency customers. When these characteristics bond the parties, both principal and agent may be motivated to invest in training, materials, and other productive assets of the relationship.[6]

Brokers

Brokers bring buyers and sellers together, typically in environments where buyers and sellers lack the information needed to connect with one another. For example, scrap metal and used machinery can originate from any of thousands of businesses. But who are the likely buyers and where are they? Brokers succeed by maintaining information on demand and supply situations. They can be engaged by either buyer or seller and receive

Exhibit 9–4

The Functions of Different Types of Channel Intermediaries

	Holds Inventory	Holds Title	Promotes	Negotiates	Provides Credit
Merchant wholesalers					
Full-function or service wholesalers;	●	●	●	●	●
Limited-function wholesalers					
Drop shipper (desk jobber)	○	●	◑	●	●
Cash and carry wholesalers	●	●	◑	●	○
Wagon (truck) jobbing	◑	◑	◑	●	◑
Rack jobbers (service merchandise)	●	●	●	●	●
Wholesaler-sponsored (voluntary) chains	●	●	●	●	●
Retailer cooperative	●	●	●	●	●
Agents and brokers					
Brokers	○	○	●	◑	○
Manufacturers' agents	○	○	●	○	○
Selling agents	○	○	●	●	○
Commission merchants	●	○	●	●	●

● = High levels of involvement in this function.
◑ = Only some modest involvement in this function.
○ = Does not perform this function.

a commission from the engaging party. Brokers often attend to an array of details associated with the execution of the exchange, perhaps negotiating the purchase, setting up delivery, and tracking. From the Field 9–1 profiles the Joseph Company, one of the top brokers in the world in ferrous metals.

Exhibit 9–4 summarizes the functions performed by the channel institutions we have just introduced. We have also included types of intermediaries that we have not discussed in the chapter. For purposes of this chapter, their role is sufficiently outlined in the table. Use it for reference when analyzing cases or considering channel design problems beyond those taken up in the next section.

Marketing Channel Design

Marketing channel design is certainly a fitting topic to take up after a discussion of marketing strategy. Remember that strategy involves a commitment of *significant resources* in a *coordinated* manner for outcomes over a *long period*. By this measure most channel

Exhibit 9–5
A Model for
Channel Design

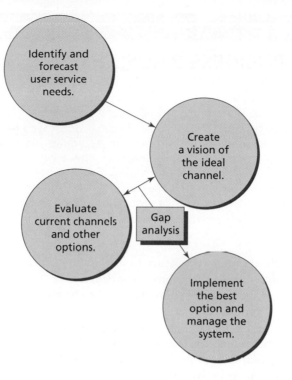

SOURCE: Adapted with permission from the MAC Group, now known as Gemeni Consulting, Inc., *The Planning Forum: Differentiation through Channel Strategy: Concepts and Practice* (May 1, 1990).

decisions are essentially strategic: inventories, sales forces, distributor support programs and other channel activities involve large financial outlays. Hundreds and perhaps thousands of people—very likely housed in two or more distinct organizations—need to coordinate their activities. Furthermore, the whole structure is difficult to reconfigure or dismantle because implicit and explicit coordination processes, customized work habits, and special equipment *get dedicated* to making the system work.

The channel design process consists of four primary steps: (1) Identify and anticipate end user needs for an array of channel services, (2) Create a vision of an ideal channel that could provide customers with those services, (3) Evaluate current channels and all practicable options against this ideal system, (4) Implement the best practicable option and set up for ongoing channel management. Exhibit 9–5 shows these steps. Let's take up each in detail.[7]

Identify and Anticipate User Needs

You have a good sense of the menu of channel services from this chapter's opening discussion of the purposes of channels. In the planning process, we need to go beyond the abstract notion that customers want convenience and quick delivery. We need to attend to different needs that exist across different segments. Air conditioning systems for schools and government offices don't require the same emergency service and component replacement standards as systems for hospitals, theaters, or large computer installations. Small bakeries have different delivery and assortment needs than a microbrewery, and both differ from their large-scale counterparts.

BUSINESS 2 BUSINESS

Service Needs by Segment

Think about the demand for two types of replacement automotive parts: (1) tires, batteries, and accessories (TBA) that generally wear out and (2) crash parts: fenders, tail lights, trim, and so on. Now, make a small two-column table listing (1) the services sought by an end user of each product type (e.g., locational convenience, product information) and (2) the channel activities that are apt to be involved in providing these services. Which channel will have higher costs—the TBA or crash parts channel—as a proportion of end user price?

Within each segment, we must try to identify the entire array of services sought. To say that customers are seeking "convenient delivery" or "setup assistance" does not lend enough detail to the planning effort. We need to be more explicit: Convenience comes from delivery before business hours, within a two-hour window, using returnable cartons. We need to dig deep to learn that "setup assistance" for one segment means delivery of tubing in machine-feeding bins to the work stations on the factory floor; for another it means resetting the tube bender–beader to the new product.

In short, the channel service outputs we described in just a half-dozen dimensions at the start of the chapter get sliced into perhaps a score or more benefits.

Create a Vision of the Ideal Channel

The channel system that yields the service outputs identified in the first phase may very well not exist. Recall that when Cincinnati Milacron developed low-cost plastic injection molding machines, it knew that the product's low-price position and scattered target market precluded use of its own sales force. It needed an outside sales force. But which one? No distributors had ever carried such a product and there was doubt that an agency could be adequately supported logistically from factory inventory to provide the needed delivery time and availability.

Thus, the ideal channel featured a low-cost sales force, equipped with product knowledge and motivated to assist with machine setup, installation, and some training. The machine itself supported easy entry into the plastics business and its low cost made it affordable to small firms, even startup companies. Thus, potential customers were numerous, and actual prospects difficult to identify. The ideal channel would need to generate and qualify leads efficiently to allow the sales force to follow up efficiently. Many customers would want financing and rapid delivery once they made the purchase decision. Parts and supplies would need to be readily available. Postsale service could be a little slower than instantaneous.

Assess Options

We have profiled a number of types of channel intermediaries, firms that specialize in several channel functions. In this stage of the planning process we want to consider the adequacy of these different business types. Examine the viability of a system using

Exhibit 9–6

The Economics of Direct and Indirect Distribution

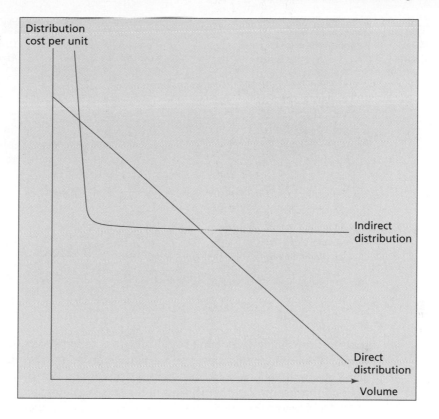

full-service wholesalers. Compare that to a hybrid system using limited-function whole-salers and manufacturer-performed functions. Frequently, a manufacturer will increase its participation in different channel functions—lead generations, presale service, expedited shipments, after-sale service, and training—and wonder if its "full-function" wholesalers are rightly labeled.

Can we use combinations of intermediaries to achieve the majority of the sought outputs? Consider an electronics components manufacturer that uses its own sales force for market development activities such as trade shows, seminars, and low-key visits to purchasing managers. Agents are relied upon to sell and get orders. Most shipments are made from the factory. Federal Express and a single inventory in Memphis are used for urgent small orders.

Sometimes different structures are required in different parts of the country. That is, in medical and electrical products we find two or three national distribution organizations available. Still, other distributor firms compete quite effectively with the nationals within geographic regions or within certain customer groups. In this situation, the alternative channel structures involve not merely different business types but different specific companies.

Face it, some options we might consider are simply beyond company capabilities. Examine the graph in Exhibit 9–6. It shows that sales and distribution costs per unit are consistent over a large range of volumes. But at very low volumes, the curve elbows upward as the manufacturer faces stiff resistance from distributors.

Distributor interest in a new product from a small company may be negligible until the start-up firm has done some channel activities itself to "buy" channel support or demonstrate demand for the product. Even if intensive personal selling is involved, the

Exhibit 9–7

Gap Analysis: Channel Options versus Ideal Channel

Channel Service Outputs	Company Sales and Distribution Centers	Distributors and Small Company Service Staff
Product knowledge of sales force	2	6
Customer relationship of sales force	5	3
Assortment match	6	3
Inventory investment	7	2
Inventory controls	2	5
Delivery cost	5	3
Delivery reliability	3	3
Product setup	1	5
Customer training	1	4
Emergency service response	2	5
Total gap score	34	39

KEY: 0 = match to ideal; 10 = gross mismatch to ideal.

start-up firm simply lacks resources to initiate a national sales force. Instead, the firm might sell on consignment, focus on a regional market, or use direct response advertising and a strong telephone marketing staff to demonstrate demand, (i.e., push out to the right on the graph). Early participants in the personal computer field, such as Apple and Hyundai, followed this approach prior to generating dealer interest.

In the channel design process, each alternative can be evaluated against the ideal structure. It is rare that any alternative matches up to the ideal because each option is bounded by constraints in resources and know-how as well as coordination difficulties and incompleteness in performance evaluation.

Many managers have found that overall assessments of channel options are enabled by a feature-by-feature comparison. **Gap analysis** is a set of tools for comparing performance outcomes or expectations on specific criteria. Exhibit 9–7 shows a gap analysis for two channel options against the ideal. It relies on a mix of objective measures as well as scaled subjective inputs from managers. The decision maker can follow a weighted or unweighted point system to tally an overall gap score. Coca-Cola Foods used this approach to change its channel from a hybid of brokers and its own sales organization, to one that used brokers exclusively and compensated them on a detailed performance-based commission structure.

Exercise caution here, however. Many decision makers imagine that tools such as gap analysis deliver a greater level of precision than they can possibly provide. In hospital emergency rooms patients are immediately given a preliminary exam and triaged, or classified into one of three treatment groups: (1) give urgent care or more thorough exam *now,* (2) wait for available care and observe, and (3) treat as if there is no emergency. Scoring alternatives in a gap analysis should serve the same basic purpose. It lets management look closely at what appears to be the best of several options and it disqualifies the worst options.

In contrast, the analysis in Exhibit 9–7 favors the company sales force over the use of distributors. Although this means significant inventory investment and a lot of relationship building, the payoffs appear in distinctive customer service on such dimensions as

Dell Computer's web site might be the world's most productive computer sales showroom. Sales in 1998 averaged over $5 million per day.

product setup, customer training, and emergency service. Thus, this analysis can sometimes lead to a channel structure that is shorter than the existing channel, eliminating an intermediary. Especially when margins are high and intermediary performance is suspect, any manufacturing organization is apt to consider eliminating the distributor or agent. Other computer manufacturers have noted Dell's ability to do over $5 million a day by its web page. Should all others now strive to sell direct? It might well cost them their dealer support.

Heed our warning: Eliminating an intermediary does not eliminate the need for performing the channel functions. Firms that try to vertically integrate the functions of an intermediary often underestimate the full scope of functions or neglect a number of costs of doing business.

Implement and Manage

Channel structure or strategy selection must include consideration of how to set it in place and how to make it work. Although the complexity and scope of channel structure change urge one to move carefully and methodically, competitive realities and vulnerability to opportunism in any adjustment period call for swift execution. We take up these two challenges next. From the Field 9–2 previews the challenges of changing channels.

Tough Competitors   What can a competitor do to disrupt the channel implementation process of its rival? If the strategy calls for enlisting distributors, competitors may try to "load up" distributors with inventory so they see no need to carry a new line. Many distributors pledge not to carry competing lines in exchange for a manufacturer's pledge to restrict product distribution through other distributorships.[8] In the face of a potential entrant in the channel, they can use some heavy-handedness with distributors, making broad interpretations of their exclusivity contracts, and contending the new product is competitive with their lines.

Sometimes the competing incumbent supplier will challenge the adequacy of a distributor or agent's selling effort, requesting more people in the field or the promotion of fewer products to the target market. In the face of pressure from an important supplier, a reseller or agent will show some reluctance to carry the new items.

Saboteurs   The channel intermediaries themselves can thwart even the best channel strategy. How much selling effort would you give if you got word that your principal was terminating your agency in favor of a company sales force in three months? Would a terminated distributor work hard to get equipment repaired or defects replaced? Will payment for final shipments be made promptly and completely? In the local market, performance breakdowns will tend to be attributed to the manufacturer. As the battle for accounts now rages between the distributor and the brand, situations can get ugly.

Speed and Redundancy   Of course, channel redesign can feature disintegration, where internally performed functions are spun off to intermediaries. Then the opportunity to reassign personnel may soften the shock on individuals from the change, but in harsh competitive environments, there may be no place to move personnel internally. Like the bitter intermediaries above, disgruntled employees can jeopardize account relationships and operations.

Thus, channel structural change must be communicated carefully and executed swiftly. Because contractual obligations may require 30 to 60 days notice for termination, it may be wise to operate parallel channels—redundant operations—during the wind-down period. This affords a measure of slack for learning new routines and serves as a buffer against some types of opportunism. Redundant systems also provide a backup for current accounts that should not suffer through the transition.

Channel Management: The Politics of Distribution

The justification and planning sections of this chapter have emphasized the economic function of marketing channels. This matches the text's perspective on value creation and provides a very useful normative framework. But let's not pretend that market share, efficiency, and return on investment are the only goals motivating functional arrangements and activities in channels. The interfirm relationships we find in marketing channels exhibit political as well economic phenomena.

Your understanding of the value-added chain makes our discussion of interfirm partnerships for achieving channel services quite plain. This section delves deeper into some of the *behavioral* factors that interact with margins, performance standards, purchase terms, multipage sales contracts, and other *economic* factors. Because trading between firms inescapably involves human beings who have limited mental capacity, incomplete data, different goals, and feelings, it is critical to address some of the key behavioral dimensions of channel management.

Relational Exchanges

Organizations exchange because it is beneficial to do so. These are voluntary associations, at least at the beginning. Each firm expects to be better off by trading some of its resources for the resources of another. A distributor carries a line of products it thinks

9–2

FROM THE FIELD

Managing Channel Change at Milacron

It is seldom easy to change distribution channels. In the case of Cincinnati Milacron, an internal sales force was replaced with independent distributors. Read how Penton Media, Inc., one of the country's leading business information and marketing service companies, assisted Milacron's changeover.

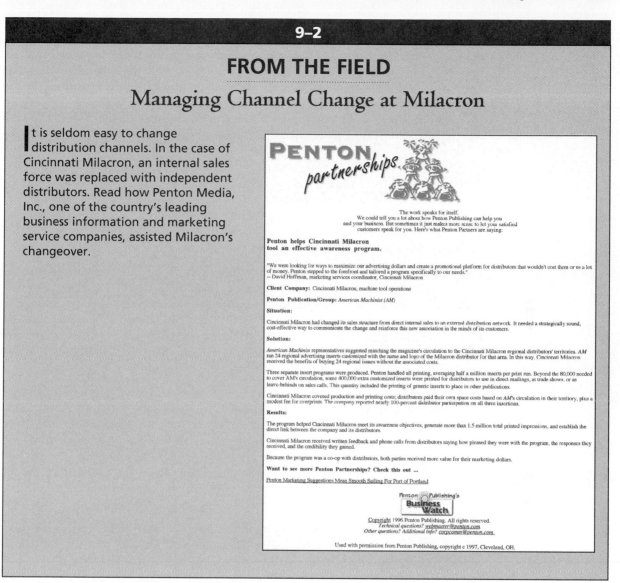

will sell in the industries it serves in its market area; the supplier concedes the distributor's margin as payment for the distribution functions performed. Mutual gain is expected from the exchange.

But exchange between channel members has a little different character than, say, a contractor hired to paint a couple of offices or other *transactional* exchanges we illustrated in Chapter 2. It will take both distributor and supplier several months or longer to ascertain accurately the benefits of their exchange. And what looks okay after six months may sour in the next for any number of reasons. With the investments each party makes in the exchange—inventories, delivery systems, product knowledge, selling approaches, brand image—not to mention sticky termination provisions in sales contracts, channel associations are seldom transactional. Channel members are generally relational exchange partners.

Channel members will need to make adjustments to their relationship because they depend on each other in dynamic environments over time. New demands may arise at the distributor level, perhaps affecting inventory costs or selling efficiency. New competition may motivate discounting, which shrinks the margins that were allotted to compensate for the long selling cycle. At the supplier end, new profit requirements from the division may demand a cut in print advertising, an activity regarded as an important source of leads by distributors. Perhaps the supplier is broadening its product line and sees strategic payoffs from more in-house selling activities.

Conflict and Its Types

Conflict is felt or enacted tension between parties—in this situation, channel members. The source of this tension can reside in the different goals of the members, preferences for different roles or activities, and sometimes in different perceptions of the task environment.

Goal Conflict   Most agency relationships have a degree of inherent goal conflict in that manufacturers push for higher and higher sales, while agents must be concerned with profit—that is, sales (commissions) less expenses. Even on this goal, agents are not apt to seek some hypothetical maximum profit, but some satisfactory level that affords their sought lifestyle. In manufacturer–distributor relationships we often see different growth aims. Manufacturers generally are more aggressive, caring particularly more about their product category than the distributor's overall growth.

Means Conflict   Conflict over how things get done arises when channel members dispute how the EDI system will be implemented, who will solve a customer complaint, who will prospect and cultivate accounts and who will close, who will service mail order customers, what accounts will be house accounts, and how much inventory is appropriate. This is a big arena for conflict. Often the activities have different costs for the parties, but simply compensating the more efficient member to do the task is difficult when performance is costly to measure. How does the other party know when the tasks are done and whether they're done well?[9]

Conflicting Views   The problem of monitoring performance leads well into the third source of conflict: different perceptions and theories. For example, sometimes distributors won't follow up on leads generated by manufacturer advertising because they believe the leads are lousy. And as leads sit too long or receive half-hearted follow-up, sure enough, the leads play out as poorly as the distributor expected. Different views of reality also clash over how much inventory is appropriate, how many sales calls a certain customer type should receive, how many items in the line will be carried, and whether sales are down because of market softening or flagging effort in manufacturer advertising. Or is it poor intermediary selling effort?

Conflict Consequences

First, we should recognize that the elimination of conflict chokes a relationship. Any partnership with vitality has conflict. But will conflict prove destructive, or will conflict have some valued function? The managerial challenge for channel members is to enable conflict to be addressed positively and to harvest constructive outcomes. If disparate goals are not reconciled, at least one party will go unsatisfied and perhaps the relationship will fail. If parties work at cross purposes or redundantly, the system will get trounced by a competitive channel. If the parties do their work according to different views of the world, coordination will be impossible, and critical functions may go undone. Again, the relentless tide of competition will swamp such a poorly coordinated channel.

Responses to Conflict

Social scientists have cataloged a handful of primary reactions to conflict: exit, voice, loyalty, aggression, and neglect.[10]

"I'm Out of Here!"   **Exit** means leaving a relationship. This is a bold move and is perhaps difficult to see as a positive approach to conflict. But recognize that exit ends what may have been a prolonged period of squabbling. It also signals important limits: "You can't push us any farther" and "We have an option." Although the focal relationship terminates, the abandoned party sometimes processes the signal and makes adjustments in its relationships with other channel partners.

"What I Really Need Is . . ."   **Voice** involves some means of articulating dissatisfaction. A leader in a negotiation seminar once described a conflict between two roommates. They were cooking late one night and each used a recipe that called for an orange. With only one orange in the house and the nearby stores closed, the cooks argued over who needed it more and who had eaten the second to last piece of fruit. Alas, they halved the orange and each halved the recipe. One roommate then squeezed the juice of half an orange into the bowl; the other grated the peel.

Sadly, the parties had argued over means and never clearly voiced their respective goals. Had they done so, it would not have taken much problem solving at all to find a solution satisfactory to both parties.

Not every conflict problem has such an obvious win–win solution, but many do when they are accurately and fully framed and creativity is applied. We advise conflicting parties to hold fast to their goals. Be clear about what they want from the relationship. Compromising on one's objectives takes no creativity. Put imagination to the task of finding a means that meets goals of both parties. Usually, the pie is bigger than first thought.

Voice is a critical process for uncovering the origin of the conflict. Consider the conflict situation described earlier involving a distributor's low regard for manufacturer-generated leads. It seems highly unlikely that the manufacturer aims to generate weak leads, although there may be a misplaced emphasis on getting large numbers of leads. The distributor, meanwhile, has no interest in doing all lead generation itself. It makes good sense for the manufacturer to do the national print advertising needed. The conflict resides not in goals, nor significantly in preferred activities. This seems to be a conflict resulting from both parties working with tainted or incomplete information.

Remember from Chapter 2 that an exchange partner requesting adjustment—an act of voice—implicitly signals that there is potential benefit from staying in this relationship. There is a measure of confidence that the request will be entertained by the other party. Thus, there is hope that the other sees longer-term payoffs from the relationship too.

"Aye, Captain."   **Loyalty** is steadfast perseverance in the face of conflict's felt tension or abuse. Suppose you exhibit loyalty in a conflict situation. You see conflict of interests, inappropriate roles, or wrong-headed perceptions, but you hold onto hope that the other will (1) eventually come around or (2) prove you wrong. More typical of alumni patience with a new football coach or a spouse's steadfastness in a rocky marriage, loyalty in business marketing channels characterizes struggling new-channel relationships, non-profit partnerships, and channel members tied by family bonds.

9–2

BUSINESS 2 BUSINESS
Voice Supports Problem-Solving

The conflict of lead quality is common in business marketing channels. One tact taken by some manufacturers is to make joint calls on a sample of leads. Another is to give distributors five business days to follow up before passing the lead to an internal sales force. A more integrative approach is to enlist a third organization, a telephone service bureau, to receive the inbound calls generated by advertising, qualify leads on the spot, and electronically distribute them to regional distribution sales offices within 24 hours, at a price to distributors of $4 each. Ads that generate an abundance of nonqualifiers tend to be rooted out by the expense of fielding all the 800-number calls. Distributors generally are less inclined to let purchased leads languish, and the $4 fee partially offsets the service bureau costs. See how accurate representation of the problem

and creativity are so critical to the conflict management process.

Dr. John Graham is a marketing professor who has conducted conflict resolution workshops around the world. He has frequently used the following game to see if exchange partners can solve problems together.[11] One person or team is asked to play the role of buyer, another plays seller. The parties have only their own profit table and make offers and counteroffers for three different products as they try to discover what is important to the other party and then come to terms of agreement that are profitable for the whole transaction. Each is out to make the most it can, regardless of what the other earns. Payoffs from each price for the two players are shown in the accompanying table. Can you see a win-win solution to this particular exchange?

PAYOFF MATRICES FOR NEGOTIATION GAME						
	Buyer Profits			Seller Profits		
Prices	Product 1	Product 2	Product 3	Product 1	Product 2	Product 3
A	40	24	16	0	0	0
B	35	21	14	2	3	5
C	30	18	12	4	6	10
D	25	15	10	6	9	15
E	20	12	8	8	12	20
F	15	9	6	10	15	25
G	10	6	4	12	18	30
H	5	3	2	14	21	35
I	0	0	0	16	24	40

Hint: Buyer and seller have complementary priorities on which to make concessions. Buyer wants the A-level prices on Product 1; Seller wants I-level prices on Product 3. E seems fair for Product 2. Profits work out to 52 for each at these terms.

"You Dirty #@!"   **Aggression** includes open or covert actions intended to injure the conflict party. Yes, this includes hurtful words and shoving on the golf course or in the office. More common are retaliatory business practices that accelerate a downward trust spiral. Regis Blahut, a manufacturer's agent in Wexford, Pennsylvania, notes that one of his "principals had some internal problems which resulted in new management and a total misunderstanding of what a sales rep does for a living. As a result, a significant commission due is in jeopardy."[12] Delayed shipments or payments are just an example. Other aggressive behaviors include tardiness in communications, empty promises, bait-and-switch, violating assigned territories, or simply going through the motions in assorted channel roles.

Sadly, aggression tends to add fuel to the sparks of conflict. As trust deteriorates and negative sentiments harden, it becomes quite difficult to restore the relationship to gain some value from the conflict situation. Acrimonious terminations, tarnished reputations, and costly litigation that often drags on for years are the sorry fruits of this strategy when played to the hilt.

"Ho-Hum."   **Neglect** means to leave the conflict untreated, perhaps allowing the relationship to atrophy or fade in significance. A distributor often does 70 percent of its business with less than 15 percent of its suppliers. If one of its suppliers of the remaining 30 percent is unreliable in delivery or order fill rates, how much effort should the distributor give to straightening out the situation? No redress in this situation is not really loyalty or perseverance; it's a case of minimal interest in the conflict. Akin to the early stages of the relationship development process reviewed in Chapter 2, the parties in this situation are not deeply dependent on each other—at least the distributor has little stake in this supplier. If performance slides further, the distributor can cut back on selling effort or inventory, or even replace with another supplier. If things improve, perhaps the supplier's share of the distributor's business will climb too. In neither case have we seen proactive effort by the distributor.

Structures for High Performance and Conflict Management

Rather than relying on ad hoc activities to address conflict—and other operational or strategic matters—participants in some channels establish formal mechanisms.

Private Referee   A manufacturer may enlist managers from a subset of its distributors to serve on a distributor council or planning panel. The distributor council then is a forum for all distributors to air complaints, underscore competitive threats, identify opportunities for better coordination, and give input on channel strategy for better customer service or serving new markets. Dayco Corporation in Dayton, Ohio uses its distributor advisory council to provide suggestions for new channel policies and programs.[13] Large distributors set up similar panels of suppliers.

Third-Party Solutions   So channel members in dispute can avoid the costly and highly uncertain route of litigation, some channel relationships and trade associations have established third-party systems for conflict resolution. Akin to a corporation's internal grievance procedure for employees, distribution channel members can agree to seek a mediated resolution before an industry referee. For example, the retired founder of Businessland computer stores, once the largest company-owned chain of PC dealers, was enlisted to mediate a dispute between the chain and one of its key suppliers, Compaq.[14] Other arrangements can provide for arbitration.

Empathic Mechanisms   Three other approaches deserve mention here. Some organizations assign the task of managing channel member relations to a particular manager. This person's title could be dealer advocate, ombudsman, or director of trade (supplier) relations. In essence, they are diplomats, contacts for channel members with problems, firefighters, and initiators of policy changes.

Channel members can attain better understanding of each others' managerial challenges and find forums for constructive dialogue by joining each other's trade association. Chemical manufacturers, for example, will attend meetings of the National Association of Chemical Distributors (NACD). Many distributors will participate in the manufacturers' meetings.

Finally, consider the utility of exchanging personnel. By bringing reps to the factory for several days, or sending production people into the field with sales reps, better empathy results and shared perceptions of the value-added process result. If longer periods of exchange are feasible (say, a distribution executive in residence at the supplier for six months or more), the implicit reasons for supplier's routines become verified or tuned, and new understandings of the other's operating environment enable joint problem solving for distribution channel competitiveness.

Some Final Words on Conflict

We view the marketing channel as a set of interdependent institutions performing functions necessary to provide customers with valued services and time and space utility. Because the goals, skills, expectations, and perceptions of the firms in a channel are different, the potential for conflict is ever present. But this stress over what to aim for, who does what, and in what vision of reality is a double-edged sword. If properly managed, it can lead to more efficient operations, identify opportunities for growth, enable marketing innovations, and prompt the whole channel system to improve its competitiveness. Accordingly, we discussed several means for gleaning the positive outcomes from conflict.

Not all system improvements benefit every member of the channel. And even if a particular change might actually bring mutual gains, it is often the case that at least one participant doesn't see it that way. In addition, some conflicts hinge on the distribution of system payoffs (or losses). This reality prompts us to attend to another critical facet of the politics of distribution, power.

Power in the Channel

In Chapter 2 we briefly introduced the concept of power between organizational buyers and sellers. Again, **power** is a property of a relationship deriving from one member's dependence on another for valued resources—resources that are not readily available elsewhere. It is a potential to get another to do something that he would not otherwise do. Because each party is somewhat unique in skills, resources, and connectivity to other candidates for exchange, seldom is power distributed equally in a relationship.

Some inevitable power inequalities in channels are quite subtle or shifting, especially in light of changing technology and markets. For all practical purposes, such relationships can be regarded as balanced. Nevertheless, many channel relationships reflect unbalanced dependence or asymmetrical power distributions. Consider a billion-dollar distribution company and its hundreds of small suppliers, a large manufacturer and its agents doing $150,000 in commission, and finally, a large OEM and its MRO supplies provider.

You should not be surprised: Power too cuts both ways. Lord Acton cautions that "absolute power corrupts absolutely," and we have the historical evidence of the abuses of mercantilist monopolies, Nazi genocide, and Tiananman Square to support him. In marketing channels we want to examine how a powerful firm might judiciously use its resources—not to exploit—but to *lead* the interfirm system, effectively coordinating the behaviors required to deliver value to customers.

Sources of Power

In an exchange relationship one party can depend on the other for a variety of resources: discounts, selling assistance, promotional ideas, affiliation, access to new markets. We want to take a portion of this section to identify some of the key resources and those too often neglected.

Carrots and Sticks   Probably the most common means of coordinating channel behavior involves the use of rewards and punishments. **Reward power** is the ability to provide payoffs to a party for specified behaviors or outcomes. A principal may promise an expense-paid trip to Hawaii to any agent selling $.5 million in a quarter. A distributor might be given 12 cases for the price of 10 for ordering during a particular period or participating in a supplier promotion.

Coercive power is the ability of one channel member to mediate punishments to get another to do what it otherwise would not do. A supplier may threaten to set up another sales or distribution relationship or terminate a distributor if the quality of selling effort is not up to standards. Likewise, a distributor can punish a supplier by delayed payments, withholding sales efforts, trimming inventories, and terminating also.

Rewards and punishments are a very direct means of changing another's behavior. They work by altering the outcomes of the particular action. Neither approach affects the other's motivation for the behavior itself. That is, rewards and coercion don't compel others to comply for the rightness of the act. But sometimes if a channel member can witness other positive outcomes of compliance, it will begin to internalize the behavior.

Punishments tend to move the channel members apart, fracturing their sense of solidarity and possibly alienating the punished party. We can expect a member to mask noncompliance in the face of punishments. Therefore, a coercive channel member must also implement a monitoring system. But policing and other detection systems, similarly risk alienation. Intentions to maintain a working relationship should bridle a member's application of coercive power.

People generally seek rewards and enjoy "prizes" significantly more than avoiding punishments. Auditing behavior too is a little easier with rewards because channel members staking claim to rewards will tend to document their own compliance. Nevertheless, even the use of reward power can be overdone. Relationships can get muddled when members do every little thing in order to claim the goodies. A sense of pressure mounts as one works without a grasp of the real reasons for performing the channel functions. Think about it: We want our agents making monthly calls on "A" accounts because they agree with us on the service level needed with these particular customers—not simply because they earn more chances to golf at the Greenbrier!

Persuasion   The ability to get a channel partner to change behavior by bringing it to the point where it sees the merit in the activity is a type of power too. This ability stems from three key power bases: information power, expert power, and referent power. **Information power** resides in a channel member's reliance on facts and figures, models, and insights from its partner. A manufacturer that invests in a market-tracking system that can provide product category forecasts for different regional wholesalers will possess information power over the buying and inventory activities of its wholesalers. Agents have information power over their principals in areas of customer buying cycles and the competitive products they are considering.

Image   Information power can be well complemented by expert power. A source's **expert power** is the ability to gain a target firm's compliance based on that target's regard for the source as knowledgeable. The target doesn't need to read the source's analysis or follow the logic. It's the source's *reputation* as an expert in the eyes of the target that brings behavioral change. Because a key requirement for the use of information power is gaining the target firm's attention to the information, expert power seems to work well in concert with data and models.

Another power base that rests in the perception of the target firm is **referent power**, the potential to influence another based on the other's desire to identify with or be like the source firm. The firm with referent power in some relationships will be able to change its partner's behaviors by modeling those behaviors or making simple requests. A manufacturer's reception for its agents at a trade show builds rapport and identification. When training sessions occur and new planning systems are introduced, any agents' tendency to emulate the manufacturer enables channel coordination.

Authority   The last dimension of channel power we need to discuss is called legitimate power. This is not to imply any illegitimacy in previous dimensions. This basis of power stems from one of two roots: tradition or contract. In **traditional legitimate power**, the source is able to direct the behavior of the target because cultural norms support the source. A supplier can rightly ask that distributors properly handle paints or adhesives that would not perform properly if frozen or overheated. The culture maintains the value that customers deserve a product that performs up to promises. Other examples of the power of tradition are resellers' final say on prices to customers and a host of operating issues (business hours, employee qualifications). **Legal legitimate power** is explicit authority over certain behaviors granted to the source in a sales agreement or contract. For example, a distributor may agree to not carry competing lines and to recognize the penalty of termination for a breach. Similarly, a manufacturer may promise service within a specified period of time when distributors call for it.

Unlike traditional legitimate power, legal legitimate power is often obtained in a trade for some other resource. Holiday Inn franchisees agree to change the sheets and clean rooms according to franchisor-established standards because it pays to be a Holiday Inn. They would never agree to follow the 200-page book of standards for the Tanner and Dwyer Lodge. They want the green and orange sign in front, they need the national reservation system. Simply put, the Holiday Inn franchisees trade some of their freedom—meaning they grant the franchisor legitimate authority over some matters—in order to gain anticipated rewards.

Final Words on Power

Channel systems are often comprised of multiple organizations holding different stakes in the success of the system. Without leadership, the organizations may work at cross purposes and operate in a manner devoid of customer focus and efficiency. Channel leadership is the judicious use of power to coordinate channel member behaviors. A member's power stems from another's dependence on the member for scarce resources. We have described and weighed the merits of using different power resources: rewards and punishments, information, expertise, identification, and legitimacy. These resources can be applied to affect specific behaviors by channel partners. Power can also be used to affect more permanent properties of the channel relationship such as contractual provisions and even ownership.

Relationship Forms in Channels

This section elaborates on the idea that channel members can apply their power not only to specific behaviors, but to the establishment of enduring *structures* for exchange. As a result, channel members interact to coordinate their work in four classes of exchange systems. Here we rely on some of the notions from Chapter 2 to detail alternative contractual and ownership structures of marketing channels. We discuss four classes of channel systems: transactional, administered, contractual, and corporate.

Transactional Channels

In **transactional channels** the members trade at arms length. Each firm operates on its own, with no significant coordination with its channel partners. An insurance company planning its company picnic may buy 500 #10 duro bags from a cash-and-carry wholesaler. A church group staging a community Thanksgiving dinner might buy 300 pounds of potatoes from the riverside produce market. As you can see, finding channels that exemplify no relationship characteristics is quite difficult. This form is rare. We use the description largely as an end point in the classification scheme.

Administered Channels

Members of **administered channels** recognize their participation in a larger system, but they interact without a formal chain of command or a set of rules. Coordination results from an ad hoc division of labor and informal leadership. The leader has no legal legitimate base of power, but mobilizes social and economic resources to coordinate behaviors for competitiveness. The use of promotional allowances and discounts to load resellers or blitz a market area are quite common but don't represent the systematic approach to lead or administer the entire channel. In contrast, Allegiance Corporation administers hospital supplies channels by analyzing hospital needs, trimming the variety of items ordered, and planning just-in-time deliveries. With its Sabre system, American Airlines was first to provide a computer reservation system to agents. Many credit this program for American's leadership in U.S. air travel. Sealed Air coordinates its distributor efforts in stocking and selling various packaging materials using programmed sales aids and stocking guidelines.

Contractual Channels

Contractual channels are tightly coordinated by formal procedures and pledges of ongoing exchange. Nonrefundable fees and 5- to 10-year agreements are common devices to ensure longevity. We mentioned the Holiday Inn franchise system earlier in the chapter. Other franchising operations in business markets include ServiceMaster in the field of building maintenance and custodial services, Insty-prints in printing services, Manpower in employment services, and Avis in rental cars.

More narrow in scope than these franchisor–franchisee systems are *authorized* wholesalers and dealers. Under these systems, resellers are allowed to promote that they are authorized by the manufacturer to carry a particular line. In return, the resellers agree to

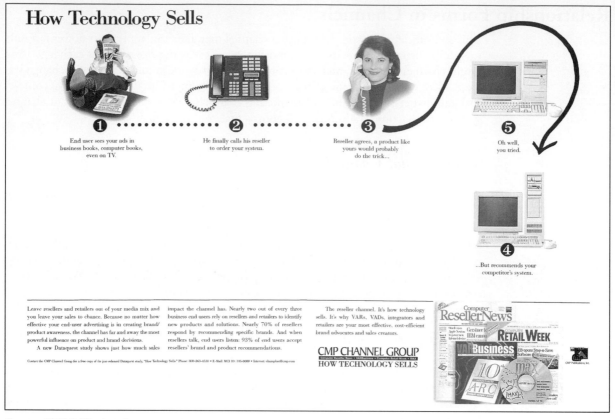

Courtesy CMP Publications, Inc.

meet specified service standards.[15] An authorized Apple dealer must stock a range of Apple products and software, attend training programs, use promotional material from Apple, and provide information about market conditions.

Corporate Channels

It is difficult to imagine total integration of all channel functions: delivery, selling, promoting, customer feedback, inventory, ordering, service, and so on. In **corporate channels**, what we tend to see are high degrees of vertical integration in the sales and distribution functions. A firm that uses its own sales force, its own fleet of trucks, from its owned distribution centers is highly integrated, even though it may use UPS for next-day shipping of orders taken at night at the telephone service bureau it uses in off-hours.

Ownership provides a significant measure of control over channel functions because one's own employees are generally more inclined to take direction than are associates of an independent organization. It can safeguard investments that have no use outside of the relationship. For example, if we spend heavily to develop a brand image, but buyers of the product rely on personal sales reps for information about the product, we will want to be sure we can control the selling process. Corporate ownership provides a number of coordination advantages that arise from employees working in close proximity, using common communication standards, and following explicit procedures.[16]

Of course, "owning" a channel function does not guarantee that you can perform it well or economically because of scale. Intermediaries specialize in certain functions. Therefore, intermediaries can often perform activities cheaper and better than a vertically integrated firm.

Thus, to close the chapter on a note similar to its launch, if we are a manufacturing firm unhappy with the support we are getting from our distributors, we must look very carefully at the costs and likely effectiveness of performing distributor functions ourselves. Based on the dispersal of accounts and the selling tasks, how many calls per day can our own reps make? How many calls per year are demanded by the market? How many reps will it take? Can we deliver products by UPS from a central inventory? Does the "recaptured" distributor margin allow us to internalize? Do we have the investment capital and do we really want to be in this business?

Exhibit 9–8 details this type of analysis for a manufacturer currently using distributors. With distributor margins averaging 35 percent, we know that the factory sales of $26 million must be 65 percent of distributor sales. Thus, total distributor sales volume is about $40 million, and margin is about $14 million. Looking at the estimated costs of performing the distributor functions—selling, sales management, inventory, and accounts receivable—we sort start-up from annual costs. Then we can evaluate the magnitude of savings, if any, against the investment needed.

Of course, the analysis is just as informative for the evaluation of a corporate sales and distribution system. Like Cincinnati Milacron in the opening vignette, the make–buy analysis can point the way to dis-integration and a focus on a narrower set of competencies as well.

Summary

Marketing channels are multifirm systems at work in the flow of products from producer to user. Their purpose is to deliver needed services, spatial convenience, and time utility to customers. They represent a highly strategic decision arena in that they are expensive to establish, costly to coordinate, and difficult to adapt to new environments.

Practically no firm can perform all the complex functions of sorting, assorting, transacting, risking, delivering, promoting, and servicing involved in providing sought channel outputs. Firms specialize in these functions and realize profits by performing them better and more efficiently than manufacturers, buyers, or others in the channel.

Many different kinds of intermediaries operate in business markets. We make a major distinction between merchants—who take ownership of products—and agents—who do not. Ownership brings substantial investment and risk. Other subclasses of intermediaries can be distinguished on the basis of their performance of several channel functions.

The emphasis on channel functions and institutional structure should not lead us to neglect their social and political dimensions. Because channel members have different goals, different preferences for routines, and different views of the world, but still must depend on each other, the potential for conflict is ever present. Conflict can tear a system apart or prompt members to reassess motives, innovate, buttress, and survive.

The major responses to conflict by individual channel members include exit, voice, loyalty, aggression, and neglect. At the industry, trade group, and relationship levels, conflict resolution mechanisms can be established to improve system competitiveness and to resolve disputes fairly and efficiently, while avoiding the uncertainty, acrimony, and glacial pace of court action.

Exhibit 9–8 Analysis for Integrating the Distributor Functions

The Setting: A manufacturer doing factory sales of $26 million sells exclusively through distributors who earn an average margin of 35%, unless they discount radically from manufacturer's list price. Distributors call on 5,000 customers an average of six times per year and finance receivables for 30 days. Inventories turn abour four times per year, and overall are four times the current factory inventories of about $1 million. Customers pay no explicit delivery charges now, but the manufacturer's accounting people estimate that UPS and other delivery modes can be achieved from central stores at about 10% of prices to users.

Estimating Revenues	The manufacturer selling direct—all other things equal—stands to realize total distributor revenue. Thus, its current sales of $26 million represent just 65% of distributor revenue. The distributors' 35% margin is missing here. Thus, total sales to end users is $26 million/.65 = $40 million, and incremental gross margin for the manufacturer is the $40 – $26 = $14 million currently earned by distributors.

Can the manufacturer perform the channel functions for less than what it "pays" distributors, $14 million?

Converting Functions to Costs

Selling costs:	5,000 customers × 6 calls/yr. = 30,000 calls per year
	A company salesperson working 250 days per year, making four calls per day can make 1,000 calls per year. → Thirty salespeople are needed in the field. Add four sales managers. Plan (est.) to pay $58,000 per year plus another 50% for expenses each.
	Managers will cost $100,000 plus 100% in office and clerical.
	Total selling cost: $3.41 million. Cash needed for payroll and expenses → (say) $.5 million
Inventory:	Inventory investment increases from $1 million to $4 million = $3 million
	Estimate inventory carrying costs (interest, spoilage, etc.) @ 20% = $.6 million
Financing sales:	Estimate 1/12 of sales at 10%. With manufacturer selling to end users, sales—all things equal— are $40 million at distributor prices. Thus, the balance sheet will require $40/12 = $3.33 million in accounts receivables. There is an interest or opportunity cost of carrying these receivables of $3.33 × .1 = $.333 million.

Start-up costs:		Annual expenses	
Cash for selling expenses	$ .50 million	Selling	$3.41 million
Inventory	3.00	Inventory	.60
Receivables	3.33	Receivables	.33
Total investment needed	$6.83 milllion	Total yearly costs	$4.34 million

Compare current distributor margin	$14.00 million	
To new expenses	$ 4.34 million	
Savings	$9.66 million/yr.	on an investment of $6.8 million is a very nice return. It would be so even if distributor discounts cut their margin in half!

The interdependence of channel members means that power is a character of their relationships. Power can be used to exploit or coordinate. We defined and illustrated how six bases of power can be used to coordinate channel behaviors, or structure the exchange for the potential to coordinate behaviors.

Finally, the chapter reviewed four basic structures by which channel members exchange. In rare cases exchange is characterized by arms-length, transactional dealings. Even between independent organizations there is a measure of informal administration and coordination. Contractual arrangements provide for legitimate power to coordinate channel activities and are exemplified in licensing and franchising relationships.

Corporate systems benefit from employee commitment, communication efficiency, and tighter administrative control, but require significant financial resources, technical know-how, and motivational mechanisms. We provided a framework for examining the economics of making or buying channel functions.

Key Terms

administered channels

agent

aggression

broker

cash-and-carry
  distributor

catalog wholesaler

channel intermediary

coercive power

conflict

contractual channels

corporate channels

desk jobber

drop shipper

exit

expert power

full-function wholesaler

gap analysis

industrial distributor

information power

legal legitimate power

limited-function
  wholesaler

loyalty

manufacturer's agent

manufacturer's sales
  branch or office

marketing channel

merchant wholesaler

neglect

power

principal

referent power

reward power

single-line wholesaler

specialty wholesaler

traditional legitimate
  power

transactional channels

truck jobber

voice

Discussion Questions

1. As of 1999, South Korea has opened its doors to foreign colleges and universities to establish programs for its peoples. Go through the steps of channel design to a channel of distribution for your school to serve the Korean business education market.

2. Most steel is ordered and shipped directly from the steel mill. Still, a significant percentage of steel is sold through steel service centers, wholesalers that carry a wide assortment of specialty steels, bars, I-beams, wire, sheet steel, and so on. Identify the likely channel service outputs sought by two or three of the following businesses: small steel fabricators, rail car manufacturing, commercial construction, tool manufacturing, saw blade manufacturers, and environmental engineering. What channel structure do you expect for each?

3. With the great diversity of market segments, many manufacturers actually use multiple channels: direct sales, distributors, dealer networks, catalogs, and perhaps some private brands for other manufacturers or resellers. What is the potential for conflict in such a system? Can it be managed in the way territories are configured or margins structured?

4. The World Wide Web has enabled electronic markets. The new marketplace has been especially important for recyclable materials. Surf the cyberwaves for brokers or cooperative exchanges (such as the Chicago Board of Trade at **http://cbot-recycle.com**) in the area of wood by-products, crumb rubber, plastics, or scrap metal. Prepare a short summary of the operation.

5. In many markets across the United States, certain cement contractors have enjoyed a rapid growth and profitability using new minisized cement trucks. The trucks don't come into play for street paving or parking garages, but they compete quite effectively for smaller jobs. Speculate about the types of work (segments) that would be served well by the smaller trucks. Give a list of four to eight benefits sought by these segments that are probably well delivered by this new form.

6. A great deal of social science research in the area of conflict resolution was motivated by geopolitical and racial tensions. One model from the foreign relations sphere is called GRIT (for Graduated and Reciprocated Initiatives in Tension-reduction). When conflicts approach a flash point, GRIT begins when one party makes a unilateral concession or withdrawal—without becoming vulnerable—and invites the other to reciprocate. When the other does, another concession is made and so on.

   In 1996 the state of Ohio terminated all vehicle emissions testing when it canceled its contract with the test provider. The State said E-check lines were too long, tests were poorly done, and prices were too high.

   How do you think the GRIT approach could be applied to channel conflict such as this?

7. At the XYZ computer company, dealers' calls have lit up the phones for the past two weeks. Dealers are complaining that XYZ's venture into TV advertising has brought thousands of business customers to the store, but after an hour or more of hand-holding, the prospects leave the store looking for a better price. And it seems that many are finding the better prices at about a dozen authorized dealers that placed huge orders when told of the TV campaign and that now offer deep discounts.

   Is this the kind of "trouble" every manufacturer longs for, or is this a serious problem?

8. Beer and wine distributors average about 18 percent gross profit, but less than 3 percent net profit. What marketing activities account for the expenses that eat up this gross profit margin? List as many items as you can.

9. Imagine that Caterpillar would like its heavy equipment dealers to change their operations. Selling is to be done from a large, regional showroom supported by new information technology and professional salespeople. Service will be done at a greater number of locations, giving convenient and rapid attention to service needs. For most of its current dealers, the investment requirement for this change is about $1 million.

   Illustrate Caterpillar's use of at least four different power bases (reward, information, etc.) to gain dealer participation in this strategy.

10. What type of channel relationship structure will enable the most and richest communication between members? Why?

Internet Exercise

Allegiance Corporation sells surgical instruments, oxygen masks, test tubes, intravenous solutions, patient care supplies, instruments, and thousands of products and services needed by hospitals, laboratories, and other health care. It boasts nearly $5 billion in sales in 1997.

Allegiance is a 1996 spinoff from Baxter International, with roots tracing to American Hospital Supply, a Chicago-area company founded in 1922. The company's leadership position in the field of hospital products distribution derives, in part, from its comprehensive product assortment and its delivery reliability. But Allegiance does more. It manufactures many of its products and has expertise in hospital supply management.

Visit the Allegiance web site at **http://www.allegiance.net** to learn about a program it established in which it partners with customers to achieve specific cost savings. Moreover, find out what it takes to set up a relationship that promises to split documented payoffs between the partners.

WWW
I N T E R N E T

Cases

Case 9.1 Steel Service Center

Years ago, metals were distributed mostly by small companies. They typically processed and shipped small quantities to small metalworking shops. Today metal service centers play a key role in the supply chain. They stamp, cut, and otherwise transform plate steel, coiled metals, bars, and other semifinished metal products into other forms that metalworking companies can use in further processing or assembly.

"These days, few so-called metal distributors simply warehouse metal. As manufacturers continue to curtail in-house production and administrative functions, the service centers are evolving from simple distributors to complex providers of processing and information technologies. In many ways, this evolution reflects the trend toward outsourcing: As producers concentrate on making metal and steel customers concentrate on making their own products, each side is willing to outsource more tasks to the metal service providers."

As we note the changing service standards in the field—metals with greater strength, more complex shapes, and other attributes, JIT deliveries, and materials management services—it's important for manufacturers, top service centers (such as Reyerson Tull, Thyssen, and Russel Metal), and customers in construction, automotive, machinery, and other fields to anticipate the needs for the future.[17]

Based on globalization trends, technological advances, and economic policy, what are some of the key avenues for growth we might see in metal distribution in the next five years?

Case 9.2 Marshall Industries

In 1992 Robert Rodin became president and CEO of Marshall Industries, one of the largest electronics distributors in the United States. Sales have doubled since then, hitting $1.16 billion in 1996. Observers attribute Marshall's amazing growth to a number of innovative moves: a versatile web site including NetSeminars and Live Help, full warehouse automation, a no-commission sales force, and round-the-clock service.

Marshall serves 40,000 customers. Rodin says that if you ask his customers what they want it comes down to three things: "they want everything *free, perfect, and instantly.*" Talk about your ideal channel!

Well, Marshall has built the customer focus and invested nearly $50 million to strive toward those goals. Here's a clear demonstration of both. On midnight the Saturday before Christmas, managers at Cabletron Systems in Rochester, New York realized they had insufficient parts to run Sunday's three shifts. Cabletron started calling distributors in a panic, thinking the best that could be done was a Monday order. But Cabletron's call to

Marshall's Boston office was rerouted to a live operator at Marshall's California headquarters. Key Marshall representatives were paged at a Christmas party and zipped to the 260,000–square-foot warehouse, where they pulled the needed parts and got them on a Boston-bound flight that night. They arrived at Cabletron in time to avoid a shutdown.

Recently, White Mountain DSP (digital signal processors) announced that its development tools for Texas Instruments DSPs would be distributed by Marshall. Its fit into the White Mountain channel strategy was summarized succinctly by its president, Peter Siy: "Marshall's virtual distribution strategy, 24 hours, seven days a week manned technical service center, combined with White Mountain's comprehensive tool solutions for TI DSP developers, offers engineers unprecedented support throughout the entire DSP development cycle."[18]

Should Marshall's approach be emulated by other distributors in this industry? How about in other business sectors? Are there ways to compete against Marshall?

Additional Readings

Anderson, Erin and Barton Weitz, "Determinants of Continuity in Conventional Industrial Channel Dyads," *Marketing Science* 8 (Fall 1989), pp. 310–23.

Anderson, James, and James Narus, "Turn Your Distributors into Partners," *Harvard Business Review* 64 (March-April 1986), pp. 66–71.

Bello, Daniel C., Li Zhang, and Harash J. Sachdev, "The Quasi-Integrated Export Marketing Channel," *Journal of Marketing Channels* 5, no. 1 (1996) pp. 59–90.

Boyle, Brett, F. Robert Dwyer, Robert Bobicheaux, and James Simpson, "Influence Strategies in Marketing Channels: Measures and Use in Different Relationship Structures," *Journal of Marketing Research* 29 (November 1992), pp. 462–71.

Dahlstrom, Robert, and F. Robert Dwyer, "The Political Economy of Distribution Systems: A Review and Prospectus," *Journal of Marketing Channels* 2, no. 1 (1992), pp. 47–86.

Dant, Rajiv, and Patrick Schull, "Conflict Resolution Processes in Contractual Channels of Distribution," *Journal of Marketing* 56 (January 1992), pp. 38–54.

El-Ansary, Adel I., "Strategies for Improving Sales Force Effectiveness in Wholesale Distribution," *Journal of Marketing Channels* 3, no. 1 (1993), pp. 5–21.

Fein, Adam J., and Erin Anderson, "Patterns of Credible Commitments: Territory and Brand Selectivity in Industrial Distribution Channels," *Journal of Marketing* 61 (April 1997), pp. 19–35.

Frazier, Gary L., and Walfried M. Lassar, "Determinants of Distribution Intensity," *Journal of Marketing* 60 (October 1996), pp. 39–51.

Hlavacek, James, and Tommy McCuistion, "Industrial Distributors: When, Who, and How?" *Harvard Business Review* 61 (March-April 1983), pp. 96–101.

Johnson, Jean L., and Gregory S. Black, "The Effects of Relationalism and Supplier Replaceability on Industrial Distribution Channel Outcomes," *Journal of Marketing Channels* 5, no. 2 (1996), pp. 25–44.

Lusch, Robert F., and James R. Brown, "Interdependency, Contracting, and Relational Behavior in Marketing Channels," *Journal of Marketing* 60 (October 1996), pp. 19–38.

O'Callaghan, Ramon, Patrick J. Kaufmann, and Benn R. Konsynski, "Adoption Correlates and Share Effects of Electronic Data Interchange Systems in Marketing Channels," *Journal of Marketing* 56 (April 1992), pp. 45–56.

Osland, Gregory E., and Lloyd M. Rinehart, "Negotiation in Channels of Distribution: Conditions, Behavior, and Outcomes," *Journal of Marketing Channels* 3, no. 2 (1993), pp. 111–28.

Pelton, Lou E., Davit Strutton, and James R. Lumpkin, *Marketing Channels: A Relationship Management Approach.* Burr Ridge, IL: Irwin, 1997.

Rangan, V. Kasturi, Melvyn A. J. Menezes, and E. P. Meyer, "Channel Selection for New Industrial Products: A Framework, Method and Application," *Journal of Marketing* 56 (July 1992), pp. 68–81.

Reuer, Jeffrey J., and Terrence J. Kearney, "Information Advantage and the Development of Direct Selling Strategies in the Airline Industry," *Journal of Marketing Channels* 3, no. 4 (1994), pp. 1–18.

Simpson, James T., and Brent W. Wren, Buyer-Seller Relationships in the Wood Products Industry," *Journal of Business Research* 39 (May 1997), pp. 45–52.

Stern, Louis, Adel El-Ansary, and Anne Caughlin, *Marketing Channels.* Upper Saddle River, NJ: Prentice-Hall, 1996.

Zemanek, James E., Jr., and James W. Harden, "How the Industrial Salesperson's Use of Power Can Affect Distributor Satisfaction: An Empirical Examination," *Journal of Marketing Channels* 3, no. 1 (1993), pp. 23–45.

Chapter 10

Integrating Marketing Communications

INTEL

Imagine 25,000 corporate buyers visiting you in a three-day period. Each buyer watches an eight-minute video presentation about your product and then visits with four or more of your partners to see your product in use. When the buyers go home, they see commercials on television, reinforcing what they've already learned about your product. Then a letter arrives in the mail with a special offer and a salesperson visits those buyers who are about to make a decision. ●

This scenario was actually just a part of Intel's communication strategy to promote the Pentium. At the Consumer Electronics Show, 25,000 buyers for computer retailers, distributors, and organizational users crammed into the Intel booth to learn more about the Pentium processor when it was first introduced. Buyers also picked up a "passport" listing all of Intel's software partners. As they visited each of at least four booths, they had the passport stamped. When the buyers returned the passport to the Intel booth, they were given free software to take home, software provided by one of the Intel partners. And as mentioned earlier, Intel's follow-up strategy included direct mail and television advertising along with personal sales calls. ●

Intel's dominance of the PC processor chip market is due in large part to the successful branding of its products and its Intel Inside campaign. When the Pentium was introduced, that dominance was supported by the integrated communication plan that launched the product. ●

Visit the Intel web site: **www.intel.com** ●

Learning Objectives

To many people, marketing is all about communication. Certainly, communication by marketers is the most obvious marketing activity. There is also no doubt that communication by marketers is an important activity. In this chapter, we explore marketing communications, setting the framework for closer examination of such activities as advertising and trade shows in later chapters.

Your objectives for this chapter should be to

- Understand the nature of communication and dialogue in the marketplace.
- Relate various marketing activities to an overall communication strategy.
- Understand how strategy would vary depending on the application of buying theory and market position.

It has been said, "Build a better mousetrap and the world will beat a path to your door," but that simply isn't true. The world won't know where the door is if no one tells them, nor will you know it is a better mousetrap if you don't get buyer reaction. Successful marketing communications are an essential element in any marketing strategy.

The Power of Marketing Communications

Received in the mail was a postcard, offering $5,000 for each time you signed your name. All you had to do was send $19.95 for the kit to get started in your own business as an official document signer! Does this sound too good to be true? You bet. While this offer was clearly a scam (yes, someone actually sends that out so there must be buyers somewhere), we've all been disappointed by products that don't live up to their billing.

Even a casual observer should see that marketing communications play an important role in selling products. What the preceding example should illustrate, however, is that marketing communications are also the basis for customer satisfaction. A good product will not be satisfactory if expectations are set too high.

On the other hand, profit will be lost if expectations are not set high enough. Think for a moment about how you judge a price. When faced with two apparently equal products, which do you choose? The one with the lower price. But if you're convinced that there is an additional value greater than the price difference, you'll select the higher-priced product. That additional value is your profit in the transaction, and buyers are often made aware of that profit through effective marketing communication. The result for the seller is a higher price and a higher profit than could have been gained if the greater value was not proven.

So as you can see, marketing communications do three things:

- Marketing communications create buyers.

- Marketing communications set expectations.

- Marketing communications improve profits.

Underlying the ability of marketing communications to accomplish these objectives is the ability of the communicator to prove value. A basic premise of this book is that marketers must create value in order to create profit—the product has to deliver value for the buyer. Marketing communications can help buyers to recognize the value offered, and prove that the marketer can deliver that value.

Integrated Marketing Communication Strategy

Developing an integrated communications strategy is really a part of the strategic planning process discussed in Chapter 6. Here we are focusing on a portion of the overall strategy: How will we communicate with our (prospective) customers? This communication should be two-way, so that we can incorporate customer feedback into our implementation and make necessary adjustments. Rather than being a strategy that we launch and then sit back, watch, and hope it works, communication strategy involves making adjustments as we go. As measures are taken and feedback is received, changes are made and communication improved.

Integrated Marketing Communications

The basic premise for integrating marketing communications has probably been around since the beginning of marketing. Consider the traditional circus that would send someone ahead to each town to put up posters announcing the circus's arrival, which would be heralded by a parade and the excitement of watching a big tent being raised by a team of elephants. If the town had a newspaper, each event would be covered in articles coveted by the circus as free publicity.

Integrated marketing communications (IMC) is strategic, two-way communication targeted to specific customers and their needs, all coordinated through a variety of media.[1] Business marketers are more likely to capitalize on the power of integrated marketing communications than consumer marketers.[2] Coordination is a powerful element of an integrated communications strategy. Still, many companies find integration difficult due to turf battles and a reluctance to invest in the needed databases.[3] When different departments are responsible for different elements in the communications strategy (say, an advertising department, a direct response or direct mail department, and a trade show and events department), each is reluctant to give up control over its respective area and fight each other for a piece of the marketing budget. A result is that the communication strategy is fragmented, rather than integrated. Let's look at each important element of the definition of integrated marketing communications.

Integrated Marketing Communication Is Strategic

Integrated marketing communication is *strategic* in that the content and delivery of all messages are the result of an overall plan. The result is that messages across all communication channels work together to create the appropriate position and result in the right action. Delivery of messages is synchronized so that synergy can be reached. For example, remember how Intel timed television ads to reinforce the Pentium introduction after the Consumer Electronics Show.

Integrated Marketing Communication Is Two-Way

IMC is a two-way dialogue. Without feedback, marketers may never really know if anyone is listening. Feedback is shared within the organization for learning purposes, so that the strategy can be adapted to fit customer needs and provide value. While a single point of communication may be one-way (for example, an advertisement in a magazine), the point here is that any communication such as an advertisement should be part of and reflect a dialogue with customers.

Integrated Marketing Communication Meets Customer Needs

With laserlike precision, integrated marketing communication *meets the information needs* of the buyer, results in the desired position, and secures the appropriate action at the right time. If IMC does not provide value to the buyer, then the buyer will not participate in the dialogue. IMC seeks the answer to the question "What does the buyer want or need to know in order to make the next decision?" That decision may be to visit the booth at a trade show or to place an order or to elevate the vendor to preferred account status. In any event, if IMC does not meet the information needs of the buyer, there is no reason for that buyer to interact with the marketing communication.

The IMC Strategic Planning Process

The integrated marketing communications strategy process, illustrated in Exhibit 10–1, begins with setting goals, creating the overall message, and then determining how the various modes of communication will be used. The next step is selecting specific channels of communication, creating the specific messages for those channels, and implementation. Based on results, messages are altered and adapted to more accurately reflect the original intended message, in order to achieve the strategic goals. In this chapter, we will focus on the first three steps, as the other steps will vary greatly depending on the media used. Those issues—placement, measurement, and adjustment—will be handled in greater detail in Chapters 11 through 13, where we will also discuss message creation in greater detail.

Exhibit 10–1
IMC Strategic
Planning Process

1. Set communication goals.
   Who is the audience?

   What do you want them to do with the information?

2. Determine roles for each medium.

3. Create messages.

4. Place messages in appropriate media.

5. Measure results.

6. Make adjustments in messages and/or media.

Setting Goals

The first step in the strategic communication planning process is to set goals based on the strategic marketing goals. For example, assume we are going to introduce a new product and we set a goal of 20 percent market share for this product. Our communication goals would be derived from the market share goals. Market share is just one marketing goal that would influence communication goals. Total sales goals, market penetration goals, and others should influence the selection of communication goals.

Understanding marketing goals helps communications planners determine the audience for marketing communications. Therefore, the goal-setting process for communications planning includes determining the audience and deciding what the marketer wants the audience to get out of the communication.

Who Is the Audience?

Understanding who the audience is depends a great deal on how the market has been defined, as well as how the buying center operates. Assume for the moment that your company sells plastic components made to custom specifications. The market is any manufacturer that uses plastic components. From Chapter 4, though, we know that members of several different functional areas may be involved in the purchase of component parts. Engineering, purchasing, manufacturing, and upper management may all play a role in the purchase. We really have four audiences, not one.

Further, marketing objectives may involve multiple market segments. For example, the plastics components manufacturer may sell plastic components to computer manufacturers, stereo and consumer electronics manufacturers, and aircraft manufacturers. Each of these market segments represents a different audience.

What Should the Communication Say and Do?

When the marketer asks the question "What should the communication say and do?" the answer lies in what the audience is intended to do with the information. To understand this better, the hierarchy-of-effects model was created to understand the process that the audience goes through when interacting with marketing communications.

10–1

BUSINESS 2 BUSINESS
Killing Bugs

Intel suffered tremendous negative publicity when it was learned that the Pentium chip had a serious bug. Some have argued that Intel's response to the negative word-of-mouth (primarily over the Net) and other PR problems could have been handled by a more proactive communications strategy regarding bugs in the chip. Others have even called for legislation requiring software and chip makers to publish a list of known bugs or defects in their products. What should Intel have done to avoid the problem, assuming they knew about the flaw and couldn't fix it any sooner than they did (which was after they launched the product)? Should there be a legal requirement for software companies to publish known bugs and, if so, how would you work that into a marketing communications plan? How should a list of bugs be made available?

Hierarchy of Effects

The **hierarchy-of-effects model** is used by many companies when planning communication campaigns because it describes the stages through which the audience progresses when interacting with marketing communications. These stages are awareness, interest, desire, and action, as illustrated in Exhibit 10–2; the pyramid shape is chosen in order to reflect the reality that not everyone who is aware becomes interested, nor does every interested person desire the product and then take action.

Awareness is created when potential buyers become acquainted with the product or brand. **Interest** is the next step, and reflects the buyers' desire to learn more about what (e.g. product, brand, company) is being discussed. **Desire** is the recognition by the buyer that when the needs occur, that is the brand or product to buy (or the company to visit at the trade show, or the home page to visit, etc.). **Action** is the desired behavior that we want the audience to do.

Thus, the model helps marketing communications planners recognize different types of communication goals that must be set. Communication goals are usually set on two levels: strategic goals and tactical goals. Strategic goals are goals set for a communication strategy; tactical goals are desired outcomes for specific communications. There are also two types of goals set: positioning and action goals.

Strategic Goals   **Strategic goals** are what you want the overall strategy (in this case, the communications strategy) to accomplish. For example, a communication strategy may emphasize a new product introduction. Strategic goals would be set to drive the planning of messages and media selection.

Exhibit 10–2
Hierarchy of
Effects

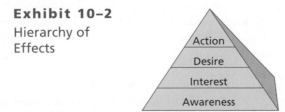

Exhibit 10–3
Goal Grid

	Positioning	Action
Strategic	Intel takes you where you want to go with your computing	Market share Total sales New account sales
Tactical	Remember Intel theme after leaving trade show	Number of visitors to booth who attend video presentation

Tactical Goals   As mentioned earlier, **tactical goals** are desired outcomes for specific communications. For example, a tactical goal may include the number of qualified leads who respond to an ad in a magazine, or the number of prospects generated at a trade show. As you may recall from the previous chapter, leads are potential buyers; the more a lead is *qualified,* the higher the probability of purchasing, but in general, less is known about leads than about prospects. A **prospect** is someone for whom we know needs, budget, and timeframe for purchase. Tactical goals may include both lead generation and prospect generation or other goals. Note that these goals require a dialogue, or two-way communication, for without a dialogue, we would not know if the person was a prospect.

In addition to two levels of goals, there are two types of communication goals: positioning goals and action goals. As you can see in Exhibit 10–3, positioning and action goals can also be set at the strategic and tactical levels.

Positioning   As discussed in Chapter 6, a product's **position**, or place in the mind of the buyer, is determined by the buyer's evaluation of the product along every dimension relative to all other offerings. Then, depending on the application and other situational issues, the buyer selects a product. For example, if a buyer wants to build a simple, inexpensive computer to operate a printer on a network, a 286 processor may be sufficient. If a computer to search the Internet is needed, a Pentium may be selected. Or the buyer may decide to buy a chip by Motorola or Cyrix (Intel competitors) if cost is important.

From a communication perspective, the goal is to create the proper position so that the product will be selected given the right set of buyer needs, which is a strategic objective. The position is the intended message of the overall communications plan. A product is created on the basis that enough buyers would face the right set of circumstances, including their needs, budget, and availability of potential substitutes. When a company communicates that the product belongs in a certain place in the sphere and the buyer agrees, then the firm has positioned the product appropriately. It occupies the appropriate spot within the buyer's head and that buyer would be predisposed to act favorably toward the product, if given the right set of needs and budget. Going back to our marketing goal of achieving 20 percent market share, we would then be successful if the right set of circumstances (buyer needs and budget) occurred at least 20 percent of the time.

Keep in mind that positioning goals can be set for individual products and for companies. For example, you've probably seen computer commercials for many brands on TV that end with the Intel Inside symbol and jingle. Those commercials support the importance of the Intel brand processor as the right choice, whether it is the Pentium processor or an Intel MMX chip. These commercials create a brand image for the Intel company.

A key goal for our communication strategy is the position we desire to achieve. A position is not just a communication goal, however; we must also design a product that has the attributes we say it has, offer it at the appropriate price, and so forth. If

Exhibit 10–4

The Buying
Process for
Pentium
Processors

Awareness: Buyers become aware through articles in trade publications that Intel is introducing the Pentium processor.

Interest: Buyers become interested in seeing the Pentium processor when they receive an invitation to visit the Intel booth at the Consumer Electronics Show.

Desire: Buyers desire the Pentium processor after they visit the Intel booth and see the video, and then visit software vendors' booths and see how the Pentium makes the software faster. Desire is further enhanced by television commericals.

Action: Buyers who indicated that a decision is approaching receive a letter with a special offer. Action is taken when the salesperson calls to visit the buyer.

we want to communicate that our processor is faster, we must first build a faster processor. There would never be any repeat business if we created a position for which we could not deliver.

We noted earlier that the position is the intended message. It is unlikely that one message will completely communicate a position, or that the position will be permanently retained by the audience. For that reason, communication often has tactical goals. For example, in order to occupy a position in the mind of a buyer, the buyer has to associate certain characteristics with the product. If speed is one characteristic, then Intel might measure buyers' perceptions of speed after they've received a communication. Or Intel might ask buyers if they recall the Intel slogan (it was "Intel Takes You There" at the Consumer Electronics Show) or logo. Tactical positioning goals are desired outcomes relating to specific communications messages that contribute to the achievement of the strategic positioning goal.

Action Goals   Another objective for communication is to cause the receiver to take an action, the ultimate step in the hierarchy of effects. It may be that the desired action is to give blood to the Red Cross, to vote for a particular candidate, or (in the case of Intel's preshow communication strategy) to visit its booth at the show. **Action goals** are set for those communications that are intended to cause the receiver to do something.

Examples of action goals in business marketing are

- The number of visitors to a trade show booth who bring coupons from a direct mail campaign.
- The number of inquiries received from an ad in a trade publication.
- The number of appointments set for field salespeople by a telemarketing program.
- The number of orders received from a catalog mailing.
- The number of surveys completed and returned.

All of these goals reflect desired actions to be taken by the receivers. Note that sales are one action goal and that other actions may also be appropriate—including giving feedback. The choice of an action goal depends on what you want the communication to do.

Choosing an action goal should also reflect the buying process. For example, Intel's Consumer Electronics Show strategy was based on buyers following a specific decision process, as you can see in Exhibit 10–4. A buyer makes a number of decisions, as we discussed in Chapter 4, before actually making the purchase. Choosing which vendors to consider, deciding if and when to see demonstrations, and making other decisions are a part of the overall purchase process. Action goals should reflect an understanding of the decision process and the potential impact of marketing communications on that process.

Challenges in Goal Setting

Setting goals for communication strategies has special challenges. Creating a desired position and getting someone to do something can seem like two separate objectives. In addition, a position is really held in the mind of the buyer; unlike an action, you can't directly observe a position. Integrating communication goals and developing appropriate measures of performance are two challenges in setting communication goals.

Integrating Marketing Communication Goals Suppose a company's advertising discussed its service quality, its employees' commitment to excellence, and the investments management has made in upgrading every area of the firm. What would a buyer's reaction be if the talk at the trade show booth centered on how cheap the company's products were? Two conflicting messages would be sent, creating confusion or disbelief in the mind of the buyer.

While such extreme conflict is rare, much more common is the creation of separate messages for each medium without regard for what is expressed through other channels. For example, an advertising campaign could focus on a particular product, but that product may not be given prominent space in the trade show. Or, in the same scenario, salespeople could be pushing another product at the expense of selling the advertised product. Integrated communications is just the opposite; each communication is designed to support the same overall objectives. From the Field 10–1 provides an example of how Alcatel, a global telecommunications company headquartered in France, successfully integrated its marketing communications.

Integrating goals requires understanding the impact of positioning on action. As we said earlier, a position is created so that when the need arises, the buyer is predisposed to doing business with you. Successfully positioning a product or company in the buyer's mind can also predispose that buyer to react appropriately to communication designed to create action. For example, advertising can create an image for a company that opens doors for its salespeople; a direct mail and advertising campaign can lead buyers to stop at a booth they see at a trade show. Integrating communication creates synergy, a synergy that begins by integrating the communication goals across media.

Setting Measurable Goals As you probably know from other marketing classes, effective marketing goals are measurable. The process of setting measurable communication goals can actually cause problems because the tendency is to set goals that can be easily measured, rather than devising measures to fit the goals. When you first read it, 8,000 visitors to Intel's booth probably seems like a reasonable goal; however, simply walking into the Intel booth did not contribute to the creation of their desired position. They rightly believed that unless a prospective buyer participated in the intended communication, then no contribution to the desired position occurred. But instead of setting a goal based on the available measure, they created their own measure.

A visitor wasn't a visitor at Intel's booth at the Consumer Electronics Show unless the person had seen Intel's video, been qualified as a potential buyer, received a passport, and then used it to visit Intel's partners. Visitors were counted on the basis of returned passports, which meant that the buyer had participated in the complete set of communications. Set the objective on the basis of what you want to do, then develop an appropriate measure; don't do something just because it is measurable.

At a trade show for contract manufacturers, one marketing manager was overheard bragging about the number of visitors to her booth. This same marketing manager had stationed two lovely models barely dressed in the booth to pass out literature. Another marketing manager at the same show also had a booth jammed with visitors because he had a golf game that was fun to play. In neither booth did they have any idea of which visitors were prospects, nor were visitors really given the company's message. Was the

10-1

FROM THE FIELD
Alcatel's Global Lightwave Traveler Flies to the Rescue

According to the Center for Exhibition Industry Research, the average person decides whether to read a direct mail piece in 11 seconds or less. Just reading the piece, however, is not enough for most marketing managers. For example, Andrea Wharton (exhibit manager for Alcatel, a French telecommunications company) needed to get people in the booth at the SuperComm trade show.

"Alcatel has many divisions, and five were to be represented at the show," notes Wharton. Each division shares buyers with other divisions and the overall objective was to leverage positive attitudes across all of Alcatel's divisions. An integrated marketing campaign was created that focused on Captain Alcatel, the Global Lightwave Traveler.

To launch the campaign, Wharton had a three-dimensional comic book (complete with the funny glasses) created that featured Captain Alcatel solving global telecommunication problems with products and services from the various divisions. This comic book was mailed to all preregistrants for the SuperComm show and a list of people generated from Alcatel's own database. The comic contained a ticket for an excursion on the Global Lightwave Shuttle, a self-contained ride that showed examples of all of the products represented in the booth. In addition to the preshow mailer, Alcatel's trade magazine advertising featured Captain Alcatel saving the world with Alcatel products.

"One important objective for us was, Would they remember the message even if they didn't visit the booth?" says Wharton. Although a primary objective of the campaign was booth traffic, Wharton believes Alcatel set a higher standard. "We also wanted to preselect visitors to the booth so we would have high-quality traffic."

Did it work? In addition to a 5.5 percent response rate of shuttle tickets, a survey of buyers by *Telephony* magazine found that Alcatel was recalled four times more frequently than in any period prior to the campaign. The survey asked for unaided recall, which is the strongest measure of advertising effectiveness other than actual sales. As Wharton says, "Captain Alcatel really came to our rescue—as far as I'm concerned, he's a real superhero."

show a success? They thought so. They devised a strategy to meet their objective: Fill the booth with visitors. Unfortunately, neither strategy contributed to building their position or convincing prospects to take meaningful action.

Roles for Each Medium

Setting integrated goals appropriately requires understanding the role for each medium. Marketers, though, must also recognize that media selection is also a function of the overall communication strategy. The important factor to remember is that communication goals, both strategic and tactical, determine media selection.

To understand the role of a particular medium, however, we must also understand the strengths and weaknesses of each medium. Let's take a brief look at each form of communication. (We'll examine these in greater detail over the next few chapters.)

Advertising
Advertising is the most obvious form of communication to most students. Advertising is one-way communication; while a buyer can respond to advertising by calling or faxing a response card, the message is not altered as a result of feedback. Business advertising is

Trade publications, such as these aimed at professionals in specific industries, are used by business marketers to reach their buyers.

Courtesy Crain Communications, Inc.

The vision of Crain Communications was boldly stated on page one of the premiere issue of *CLASS*, the company's first publication. As the organization grew from a one-man shop to one of the world's leading trade publishing houses with 27 publications in 15 offices worldwide, that philosophy still holds true today.

To get dollars-and-cents results in your advertising program, contact your sales representative at:

Crain Communications Inc

DETROIT	CHICAGO	NEW YORK
313-446-6000	312-648-5200	212-210-0100

PROUD PUBLISHERS OF:

Advertising Age	Crain's Chicago Business	Modern Physician
American Clean Car	Crain's Cleveland Business	Pensions & Investments
American Coin-Op	Crain's Detroit Business	Plastics News
American Drycleaner	Crain's New York Business	RCR Radio
Amercian Laundry News	Electronic Media	Communications Report
Automotive News	European Rubber Journal	Rubber & Plastics News
Automotive News Europe	Franchise Times	TIRE BUSINESS
AutoWeek	InvestmentNews	Urethanes Technology
Business Insurance	Modern Healthcare	Waste News
Business Marketing		

found in **trade publications**, or magazines written for a specific profession, industry, or trade. *Marketing Educator* is a trade publication that your professor probably receives. Other examples are pictured elsewhere in this chapter.

Business advertising is also found on television (remember the BASF ads!), radio, billboards, and other media. Strengths of advertising include the low cost per contact, an ability to reach inaccessible or unknown buying influences, and the ability to reach large numbers of potential buyers.

Advertising is used for many reasons, but because of the strengths listed above, advertising is often used for one of several related purposes. As illustrated in Exhibit 10–5, the roles of advertising are related and begin with a base of creating awareness and strengthening a company's position or image. Prospects are more likely to let salespeople into their offices when the salespeople represent known companies—and it is advertising that makes the companies known. The second role, then, is to create a favorable climate for salespeople. Even better is to have a prospect call and ask for a salesperson to visit. This is the third role of advertising, generating leads for salespeople. In some instances, customers will order directly from the advertising, so the final purpose of advertising is to generate sales. Note, though, that the form of the model is a pyramid to remind you that the primary purpose of advertising is to create awareness; advertising is used less often to generate sales.

Direct Response

Direct response communication is communication delivered directly to the prospect to obtain an action outcome. If you were to turn the pyramid in Exhibit 10–5 upside down, then you would have the roles of direct response. The most common is to

Exhibit 10–5
Roles of
Advertising

generate sales, followed by generating leads (or some other action, such as visiting a trade show booth), and so forth. Direct response communication can be delivered by mail, fax, or Internet, and includes catalogs. By selecting a particular trade publication or other medium, business marketers hope their advertising reaches prospects. With direct response, however, marketers should know more about the people with whom they are communicating than when advertising. At the very least, the marketer should know the receiver's name, for example. As you read in Chapter 5, companies can learn a lot about their customers by building a database and using that database to locate opportunities. A primary method of exploiting those opportunities is through direct response communication.

Direct response is also used for obtaining feedback from potential and current customers. We discussed surveys in Chapter 5, but it is important that you remember the need for two-way communication and feedback from potential and current customers. Direct response communication is an opportunity to receive feedback. We aren't suggesting that **sugging**, or selling under the guise of doing research, is appropriate; it isn't. Sugging is considered unethical because the basic premise ("talk to us, customer, all we want is information") is a lie. What we are saying is that market surveys are one form of direct response communication.

Public Relations

Public relations (PR) is the management function that focuses on the relationships and communications with individual and groups in order to create mutual goodwill.[4] PR is not just crisis management, like Intel had to do with the Pentium processor when it was discovered that it had a bug. PR is also creating good relationships with the media so that it is easier to get good news presented, as well as creating good relationships with other important constituencies.

PR plays a supportive role in most cases, and is used to inform audiences about the company and its products. PR, in the form of news stories, can have a lot of impact because the stories are actually written or appear to be written by someone other than a company employee or agent. Thus, the audience tends to give the stories greater credence. But compared to advertising, PR doesn't offer marketers the same degree of control over what is said, where it is said, and to whom, which can negatively impact the power of PR.

Trade Shows

Trade shows are temporary exhibitions of products and services. The first trade shows were open-air markets set up at fairs and festivals. Trade shows can contribute to both positioning and action goals. For example, recent studies indicate that 20 percent of all show attendees actually buy something at the show and 76 percent will ultimately purchase something they saw at the show. At the Consumer Electronics Show, Intel was not there to take orders but to create the position that wherever a buyer wants to go with personal computing, "Intel Takes You There" with the Pentium processor.

Trade shows offer the advantage of personal interaction, which gives the seller the opportunity to observe nonverbal communication as well as listen to verbal communication. Products can be demonstrated, particularly products that would be impossible to take to a customer or expensive to demonstrate otherwise. Trade shows can be very cost effective, bringing many buyers together with a sales staff, buyers who often have not had any prior contact with the selling firm.[5]

Telemarketing

Telemarketing is the systematic and continuous program of personally communicating with (potential) customers via telephone and/or other electronic media. Telemarketing can include e-mail communication, but the important element is that telemarketing is person-to-person. Telemarketing over e-mail is not sending a message to a million e-mail addresses, but it is responding to a prospect's query via e-mail. **Inbound telemarketing** is electronic communication initiated by the customer; **outbound telemarketing** is initiated by the marketer. Inbound can be used to take orders and for customer service. Outbound can be used to set appointments for field salespeople, invite prospects to visit the trade show booth, and other actions.

Telemarketing does include feedback, and messages can be immediately altered due to feedback. Depending on the channel of communication, little or no nonverbal communication occurs, which can be a drawback. Over the telephone, nonverbal communication would include pacing and the tone of voice, but over e-mail, no nonverbal communication would be possible. The opportunity for immediate feedback, however, is one advantage to telemarketing over blanket forms of communication such as advertising and direct response.

Most telemarketing campaigns have primarily action goals. For example, Vulcan Binder & Cover created a telemarketing program designed to reactivate dormant accounts (those that had not purchased anything within a period of time) and gain an appointment for the field rep. The action may be to provide feedback, as in the case of a customer service telemarketing call, or the action may be to purchase, set an appointment for a salesperson's visit (as with Vulcan), or agree to visit a trade show booth. Telemarketing is an action-oriented medium.

Personal Selling

At the most basic level, **personal selling** is interpersonal communication in which one person attempts to secure a purchase from another person. Personal selling can be accomplished using different methods, which we will discuss in Chapter 13. The advantages of personal selling are that communication can be adapted to fit the needs and personality of the buyer, the offer can be changed to fit the buyer's requirements, and the sale can be completed. Disadvantages revolve around the cost of personal selling; maintaining a sales force is expensive, requiring investments in management structures, training, and other items. On a cost-per-contact basis, selling is very expensive compared with other forms of communication. On the other hand, the quality of a sales contact should be substantially higher than advertising, for example.

Typically, goals for personal selling should reflect buyer actions. A successful sales call is one that advances the buyer to the next stage of the buying process. Salespeople can make other types of calls, such as training calls, service calls, and calls that strengthen the relationship. Different communication objectives would be set for each type of call, reflecting the nature of the desired communication.

Marketing Research

Marketing research is not usually included in the same conversation as selling or advertising, but marketing research is part of the overall communications mix. Marketing research can communicate to the customer that the organization is committed to the customer. Feedback is an important element in successful communication, and research is one avenue for feedback.

Create Messages

The idea of an integrated marketing communications plan is that each message delivered through each medium will achieve tactical positioning and action goals that support strategic positioning and action goals. Now that you have an understanding of the advantages and disadvantages of each medium, as well as the types of goals typically set for each medium, the next step in developing a communication strategy is to orchestrate the contribution of each medium.

In order to create specific messages, it is important to recall what the communications plan is trying to say. At the same time, however, the marketer must also understand what buyers already think and do, what information buyers need, and what competitive actions are currently (or could be) undertaken.

What Do Buyers Currently Think and Do?   Marketers need to recognize that buyers enter the market with preconceived ideas based on experience, education, competitors' communication, and other factors. Marketing communication never starts with a completely blank slate. Recognizing what buyers already think and how they purchase should significantly influence the design of any communication strategy.

For example, using the Buyer Behavior Choice model might enable the marketer to recognize that buyers see the purchase of plastic components as a minor task with little self-relevance. If so, there is little reason for buyers to shop around. Communication strategies might center on creating a position that it is easier to purchase from the marketer's company.

A marketer who subscribes to the reward–measurement theory would examine the reward–measurement systems for members of the buying center in an effort to predict buyer behavior. If purchasing agents were rewarded for reducing costs, then resulting communication strategies may focus on the firm's low-cost components.

What Information Do They Need?   Communication, particularly marketing communication, must serve the buyer. If marketing communication only serves the need of the marketer, the buyer will ignore it. When developing marketing communication strategy, it is important to consider the information needs of the buyer. If the product is a new buy, for example, the buyer needs information that will help in understanding what the product does. Conversely, if the decision is a straight rebuy, a buyer may only need to know where or how to buy it. Research has determined that buyers attend trade shows, for example, with three sets of information needs:

- They need to find vendors for a particular product.
- They need to explore different possible solutions to a problem they are facing.
- They need to stay abreast of the latest technology in their field.[6]

Successful trade show marketers attempt to deal with each set of needs for their visitors. A visitor whose information needs are satisfied is more likely to continue a relationship with the vendor who filled those needs.

What Are the Competitors' Actions? At the same time that a marketer is trying to create a position in the mind of the buyer, so are all of the marketers' competitors. Sometimes the desired positions are very similar, creating the likelihood of confusion for the buyer.

Additionally, competitors are unlikely to allow a company to achieve a desirous position without challenge. Marketers must consider what competitors are doing as well as how they are likely to respond. For example, each time Intel introduces a chip and creates a communication strategy, Motorola and Cyrix are also changing their communications strategy to counterattack.

Types of Communication Strategies

Strategies can be classified on the basis of what the company is attempting to achieve. While there are classification schemes for overall marketing strategies that you read in Chapter 5, to some degree, all communication strategies can be divided into either customer acquisition or customer retention strategies. For example, when Gateway Computers includes a special software offer with every computer invoice, the company is trying to retain that customer. On the other hand, when Gateway purchases a list of Compaq users and sends them a coupon to entice them to trade in their Compaqs for Gateways, Gateway is pursuing a customer acquisition strategy.

Customer Retention Communication

As you know, a key theme of this book is that customer retention and growth through current customers is an important, if not the most important, element in a business marketing strategy. As we discussed in Chapter 3, one impact of downsizing is that fewer people are available to make purchase decisions. One result of that fact and the drive to improve quality is that stronger relationships are needed with vendors. In addition, for some products of little strategic value, companies may buy repeatedly from the same vendor simply because the costs of shopping around (particularly in terms of time) do not outweigh expected benefits. Customer retention communication will be important to vendors in both situations.

Several communication mechanisms are used to achieve customer retention and growth objectives. These mechanisms take advantage of the customer's need to minimize costs associated with purchasing, in terms of both shopping behaviors and actual costs of processing purchases. Lowering costs raises the value. Several principles are at work in designing communication elements to achieve customer retention and growth (that is, growth within current accounts) objectives. These principles include communicating proactively, making it easy for customers to communicate, and making it easy for the company to respond.

Communicate Proactively Far too many business marketers assume that satisfied customers will buy again. These same marketers focus their attention on acquiring new customers, not realizing that competitors are stealing customers away just as fast as new ones are found. For this reason, successful business marketers communicate regularly and proactively with their customer base.

If a strategic partnership exists, communication will be a necessary element to maintaining the partnership. Direct lines of communication between functional areas in both firms (for example, between the seller's shipping department and the buyer's receiving department) will be created.

When the relationship is not strategic, however, proactive communication is just as important. Proactive communication strategies first identify every communication opportunity, such as when invoices are sent, when a technician performs service, or when a delivery is made. Then these opportunities are incorporated into the overall communication strategy. For example, a new catalog is included with the invoice, the technician leaves a customer satisfaction survey for the customer to complete and mail in, or the delivery person notices a competitive product and asks when the company began ordering that product. In each instance, a communication opportunity is seized and information is exchanged that can lead to additional selling opportunities.

Make Communication Easy   With so many hungry wolves in the marketplace ready to steal away your customers, it is important that business marketers make it easy for their customers to communicate. You know that your competitors' salespeople are always in your customers' offices, ready to sympathize with the least complaint. If you don't receive the complaint, you can't respond to it, but your competitors can. Similarly, if a customer is ready to order and you aren't there to take the order, it may go to competition.

Inbound telemarketing is one method of making communication easy. Providing customers with an 800 number to call, and then empowering the customer service representative so that complaints can be resolved immediately makes it easy for customers to offer their concerns. But the issue is not just making it easy for customers to complain.

Customers must also find it easy to reorder. Many business marketers are responding to this need by making EDI (electronic data interchange) available. As we've discussed in earlier chapters, customers can purchase automatically via computer exchange. When the customer's computer recognizes a low inventory, an order is automatically generated and sent to the vendor's computer. Baxter Healthcare is a company that has created a competitive advantage by making EDI readily available to its hospital customers.

Catalogs are used by business marketers to make it easy for customers to order. Premier Industrial, for example, sells more than 5,000 products. A salesperson only has time to explain five or six products on each sales call, so the catalog is an important method of generating additional sales.

Make It Easy to Respond   Everyone has had the experience of getting the runaround; calling and being transferred from person to person, none of whom seem capable of resolving the issue, is a customer's nightmare. Successful communication requires a receiver. Many companies, such as Vulcan Binder & Cover, are empowering every employee to be a receiver of information from customers. When a customer calls, the employee is given the responsibility for handling the customer's issue, even if the issue is outside that employee's usual area of responsibility.

Another important element in making it easy to respond is the creation of internal communication channels, as discussed in Chapter 7. For example, it is important to recognize that when the delivery person identifies a competitive inroad into a customer, that vital information has to reach someone who can respond. The most obvious person to respond is the sales rep for the account, but the delivery person won't know who that is. Open and regularly used channels of communication between internal areas of the firm must exist in order for the company to learn and to make use of that knowledge.

Customer Acquisition Communication

Customer acquisition communication must follow the same principles of proactive communication, making communications easy, and making it simple to respond. Customer acquisition communication, however, must also convince the buyer to receive the communication. In a customer retention situation, there is a natural communication link already established; that is not always the case with customer acquisition.

10–2

FROM THE FIELD

IBM Integrates Marketing Communication by Consolidating

IBM has had to learn the hard way that resting on one's laurels is a sure-fire way to lose those laurels. Competition has eaten away at so much of IBM market share that the company has had to refocus its strategy, particularly in the area of marketing communications.

With a company that spends $15 million on promotion (not counting advertising, sales, and trade shows) for just one of 13 divisions, and participates in over 1,000 trade shows per year, it is easy to see how marketing communications could be the spoon that ran away with the dish. In order to rein in its communications, the company has begun creating strategic partnerships with marketing communications suppliers, consolidating its communication efforts.

Furthermore, the company expects its remaining agencies to create their own alliances in order to integrate the company's marketing communications. Ogilvy and Mather (O&M), for example, is now the company's only advertising agency, but the company's trade show services provider is expected to work closely with O&M in

order to develop show communications that integrate with advertising. Similarly, Einson Freeman, the company's sole promotions agency, works closely with O&M and the show provider in order to tie promotions (such as free software with purchase) into advertising and show efforts.

IBM's strategy of consolidating marketing communications into a handful of supporting agencies is closely watched by other companies that want greater synergy in their own marketing communications. A recent presentation by the IBM trade shows director at the International Exhibitors Association conference was packed with exhibit managers who wanted to learn how IBM did it. As IBM's consolidation of advertising led to a shakeout in the advertising industry, many expect similar shakeouts caused by such consolidation among trade show service providers, promotions agencies, and other marcomm suppliers.

Source: Sally Goll Beatty, "Advertising: IBM Combines In-Store Promos Seemingly out of the Big Blue," *Wall Street Journal* (February 23, 1996), p. B 12; Kerry Smith, "Big Blue Makes Big Move," *Promo* (March 1996), p. 10.

Budgeting for Communications

Traditionally, the advertising budget was also the marketing communications budget. Salespeople did not require a budget because they were paid straight commission and they paid their own expenses or, if they were paid a salary, the sales budget was calculated separately. Other elements of communication were treated as afterthoughts and given only a small percentage of the total budget. When business marketers discussed their marketing communications budget, they meant their advertising budget.

With the advent of integrated marketing communications and recognition of the power of all of the forms of communication, new organization structures (like IBM's in From the Field 10–2) and strategic budgeting processes have been developed. Many methods exist to determine the communications budget and allocation among media; the choice may depend more on the sophistication of the marketer than any other factor. Before we examine how companies budget, though, it is important to recognize why companies budget.

10–2

BUSINESS 2 BUSINESS
Turf Battles

Earlier in the chapter, we mentioned turf battles as an obstacle to integrating communications. How can the budgeting process cause or reduce turf battles? Among whom would those battles occur? Review the opening vignette about Intel and From the Field 10–2 about IBM as you think about who would be involved in a turf battle. As you read the following section, think about how these methods can contribute to increasing or lessening turf tension.

Benefits of Budgeting

As anyone who has watched the federal government try to determine its budget knows, budgeting can result in disharmony, fighting, and even long-term feuds. Yet without budgets, spending can spiral out of control. For organizations, including the government, such a lack of control can be devastating. Yes, there will always be someone who uses the budgeting process to feather a nest, but budgets and the budgeting process have several benefits, including planning, coordination, and control.

Planning
Budgets should be part of the planning process. When decision makers recognize their budget constraints, they can evaluate alternatives in a realistic fashion. Far too often, budgets are set and then planning takes place. When planning occurs after the budgeting process, some tasks may be underfunded, while other areas may enjoy a surplus. So that each task can be properly funded, budgeting should be part of the planning process.

Coordination
Budgets should be part of the integration of communication. When resources are allocated among various forms of communication, the integrated marketing communications concept demands that all communication methods work together to create synergy. If coordination is attempted after budgets are determined, then integration may not occur because funds may not be available. For example, suppose Intel's trade show manager wanted the sales force to supply 12 salespeople to work the Comdex trade show. Sales would have to fly 12 salespeople to Las Vegas for a week. Whose budget will pay for the travel? If the trade show budget can't cover it and the sales manager had already allocated travel funds for other events, Intel's booth at Comdex may go understaffed. Good budgeting processes cause stronger coordination and support IMC; postbudgeting integration, or trying to integrate after the budget is set, is difficult.

Control
The importance of budgeting and how budgets are set is that budgets set boundaries on what can and cannot be done. These boundaries act as controls, providing decision aid to marcomm managers.

Exhibit 10–6

Breakdown Methods of Budgeting for Communications

Method	How It Works	Why It Is Less Desirable
All you can afford	The decision maker examines cash flow and sets the budget based on cost targets.	Budget is based on cash flow, which is based on sales. But if more sales could occur, then more could be "afforded."
Percentage of sales	Sales are forecasted and then a percentage of that forecasted sales is allocated to marcomm.	Same problem as with all-you-can afford method. Also, in many cases, the percentage is equal to the industry average or historical amounts, neither of which are related to the company's goals.
Competitive parity	Dollars are allocated to match one or more competitors' spending.	This type of budgeting assumes that competitors' sales are due to their communications, and that they are using dollars efficiently. It also assumes that our company wants to sell similar amounts and does not consider our competitive position.
Share of market–share of voice	Budget is 1.5 times desired market share for new products, or some percentage of the total industry's marcomm expenditures.	Similar problems as with competitive parity, particularly if budget is set as a percentage of last year's industry expenditures. It assumes that industry figures are accurate and that the desired share of voice will result in the desired level of sales.

Setting budgets is an important part of the planning process. The planning value of budgets, though, is influenced by the method used, as you will see.

Methods of Budgeting

As we mentioned earlier, budgeting is an important element in the planning of integrated marketing communications. Some methods of budgeting lend themselves to better planning and stronger integration. **Breakdown budgeting** methods, though, are those that begin with the manager setting a total communications budget, then allocating (breaking down) the budget to the various forms of communication. Attempting to integrate communications after budgets are set means that the planning and coordination benefits of budgeting are lost. While these methods are in common use, we don't recommend them.

Breakdown Budgeting Methods

The biggest reason that breakdown methods of budgeting are not recommended is that these methods depend on sales to determine the amount to be spent. Sales are supposed to result from our communications, but when the budget is set based on sales, then the logic is that communications result from sales! These methods are examined in greater detail in Exhibit 10–6.

For example, the all-you-can-afford method is a cash-based method of budgeting. The marketer examines the projected cash flow (generated from sales) and allocates as much as possible to communications. While this may seem like a very naive method of allocating funds, keep in mind that the method is an implicit element of every method. No manager is going to allocate more than the company can afford! The problem arises

Without proper budgeting for marketing activities, companies may find themselves without key elements of their marketing strategy, like this company that didn't fund enough money to adequately staff the booth.

when the all-you-can-afford method is the only method used. There is no strategy to determine how much you should communicate and the potential effects of communication are not fully considered. For example, the decision maker doesn't consider that more communication might mean greater sales, which means that the company could afford more communication.

Setting Budgets to Reach Strategic Objectives

The best method for budgeting in order to reach strategic objectives is the objective-and-task method. The **objective-and-task method**, also known as the **budget buildup method**, requires the decision maker to set the budget after determining the communication strategy. The method has three steps: defining objectives, determining strategy, and estimating cost. Of course, the decision maker will balance what can be afforded with what is desired. As the communications strategy is implemented and results become available, changes can be made to enhance efficiency and effectiveness.

One distinction that sets the objective-and-task method apart is that strategy precedes budgeting. With all other methods, communications strategy cannot be determined until the budget is known. The advantages for the marketer using the objective-and-task method are several: First, the budgeting process is less of a hindrance than in other situations. Effectiveness of a particular strategy can be examined—not just efficiency or cost. Second, the method is strategy-driven and learning-based. If tasks are based on objectives, and budgets are based on tasks, then the decision maker had better know with a reasonable degree of certainty that the tasks, or strategy, will achieve the objectives. The marketing communications manager justifies a budget based on performance, which requires learning which tasks work when and why. The objective-and-task method may require more sophistication on the part of the marketing decision maker, but should be the most effective when learning takes place.

Allocating among Media Choices

For most budget-setting methods, once a total communication budget is set, each form of communication will require a budget. If the objective-and-task method is used, however, each form of communication already has a budget, which is why that method is

Exhibit 10–7   Budget Buildup versus Breakdown

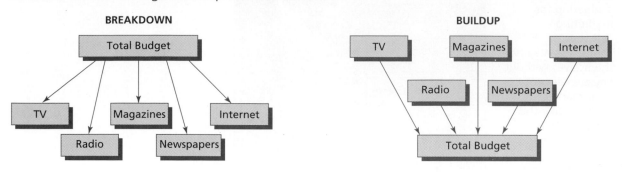

also called the budget buildup method. As objectives are set, tactics involving various media are created, along with a budget for each tactic and media. These are then added together to create the final budget. Thus, objective and task should lead to highly integrated communications. Exhibit 10–7 illustrates the difference between budget buildup and other methods.

How the budget is allocated among the various media is a measure of the degree of integration in the firm's communications. We can illustrate this idea with the all-you-can-afford method. If that method is used to determine the total budget, then the marcomm (marketing communications) director says, "We can afford only this amount on advertising, this amount on trade shows, and this amount on direct mail." Then the manager of each takes that budget amount and tries to develop a strategy. Any integration in communication is likely to be a function of sharing budget dollars to cut costs; for example, the trade show manager asks the advertising manager to mention in upcoming ads that the company will exhibit at the Widget Show. Yet, allocation of budget can be accomplished using the objective-and-task method within limits established by an all-you-can-afford total.

On the other hand, customer-acquisition communication may be fully integrated yet customer-retention communication may be separated. For example, should marketing research be part of the communication budget? What about customer service and customer satisfaction measurement systems—these involve communication with the customer. Billing and shipping are part of communication with customers, but it is unlikely that these elements of communication will be part of a marketing communications budget. The marcomm director should have input into the creation of communication via the channels of invoicing, shipping, and others so that corporate graphics will be used, and that the appearance of the communication will match that found in other media. These modes of communication, however, are unlikely to be found in the marcomm budget.

Summary

Marketing communications can create buyers when they become aware and desirous of the company's offerings, but marketing communications must also set the proper expectations. If expectations are set too high, then dissatisfaction will result. If expectations are set too low, then profits are lost because prices have to be lower to offset the lower perceived value.

Business marketing communications are much more likely to be integrated than are consumer marketing communications. IMC is strategic in that content and delivery are part of an overall marketing plan. IMC is also two-way communications, incorporating learning from customers into the design and execution of marketing communications. Customer needs can be met, which increases customer participation in the marketing communications dialogue.

The hierarchy-of-effects model profiles the stages that buyers progress through when interacting with marketing communications. Using this model, marketers set two levels of goals for their marketing communications: strategic and tactical. Strategic goals are the goals for the entire marketing communications plan, while tactical goals are those outcomes desired of specific communications. In addition, marketers set two types of goals: action and positioning goals. Action goals are those desired actions we want buyers to take, while positioning goals involve the attitudes and beliefs we want the buyers to have about us and our products. Positioning goals reflect the ratings we want our products to have in the customer's multi-attribute evaluation of the product.

There are many challenges when setting goals. Such challenges include integrating goals across the various forms of marketing communications and setting goals for performance that can be measured. The challenge with setting measurable goals is to make sure that what is measured will lead to desired outcomes such as increases in sales. Often, what is easiest to measure is the least important.

Several forms of media can be used to communicate with the market, including advertising, direct response, trade shows, telemarketing, public relations, personal selling, and marketing research. Choosing a medium for a particular message depends on a number of factors. Marketers should also consider such questions as who is the audience, what do they currently think and do, and what do they need to know when selecting a medium. Current customers, for example, already like our product, while acquiring new customers may require first creating a liking for the product.

Budgeting (another important decision set) can be accomplished by breakdown or buildup methods. Buildup methods are recommended because the dollar amounts allocated to various media are based on strategic objectives and are therefore more likely to result in achieving those objectives.

In future chapters, we will examine each type of marketing communication in greater detail. First, though, it is important to recognize that integrating marketing communications is important in order to achieve the highest level of response possible.

Key Terms

action

action goals

awareness

breakdown budgeting

budget buildup method

desire

direct response

hierarchy-of-effects
  model

inbound telemarketing

integrated marketing
  communications
  (IMC)

interest

objective-and-task
  method

outbound telemarketing

personal selling

position

prospect

public relations (PR)

share of market–share of
  voice

strategic goals

sugging

tactical goals

telemarketing

trade publications

trade shows

Discussion Questions

1. Misrepresentation is when, as a result of deceptive marketing communications, a customer believes a product will do something that it doesn't. Assuming no intent on the part of the seller to deceive, what could cause a buyer to hold incorrect expectations as a result of marketing communications?

2. What is AT&T's desired position among long-distance carriers? What is Sprint's? What, specifically, about their advertising led you to those conclusions?

3. Should all marketing research be part of an integrated marketing communications plan? Why or why not? If only some marketing research should be part of the plan, which part? Why?

4. Assume your company sells first-aid–CPR training and supply products to companies. They are required by OSHA to have someone trained and to have the proper supplies on hand. Assuming that most buyers are defensive (to minimize the threat of an OSHA fine), what would your strategic communication goals be? What would your primary message be? Relate your strategic goals and message to positioning goals.

5. Why has American business historically focused on customer acquisition strategies? How has that influenced marketing communication and the public's perception of marketing communication?

6. The field sales force is still the largest part of the marketing communications budget, but other areas are growing. Why?

7. How the budget is allocated may be the most telling sign of the degree of integration for a company's marketing communication. Why is that?

8. In a previous chapter, we discussed investment risk (the possibility of losing one's investment) and opportunity risk (the possibility of missing out on an opportunity). Discuss how these types of risk may influence the choice of a budgeting procedure.

9. Go the library and find a trade magazine. (It would help if the particular issue previews a trade show.) As you thumb through the magazine, identify five companies that seem to have a highly integrated communication strategy and five that do not. Be prepared to justify your choices.

10. Does changing to integrated marketing communications require organizational structure changes?

Internet Exercise

INTERNET

Go the Intel home page (**www.intel.com**) and select one of the pages aimed at business buyers. (When we looked last, there was one on TCO, or total cost of ownership.) First, state what you believe Intel's strategic and tactical goals are for that site. Then evaluate the site in terms of how well it achieves those objectives.

Cases

Case 10.1   McReynolds Manufacturing

After six years of stagnation, McReynolds Manufacturing finally made a change. The family-run business had done well in its first 20 years of operation, but Frank McReynolds' strength lay in his engineering ability, not in selling. And sales was the area that seemed to need the most help.

Elise McReynolds reviewed the sales data with a growing sense of despair. Her father had been after her to take over the marketing and sales departments ever since she graduated from college five years ago, but she wanted to learn what the field could teach her about sales and marketing. So her first job out of school had been with Xerox. But nothing she had faced as a Xerox salesperson had readied her for the numbers she saw now.

The first thing she did was divide the company's customers into four groups, each comprised of 25 percent of the total customers. The top group ranged in sales from $15,000 to $33,000, averaging $20,000 in sales per year. The second group averaged $12,000 in sales per year and ranged from $10,000 to $15,000. The next group ranged from $5,000 to $10,000 and averaged $7,000 per year in sales. The worst group averaged $3,000 in sales.

The company paid a straight 20 percent in commission, out of which salespeople had to pay all of their expenses. The company employed 20 salespeople and totaled almost $1 million in sales. The only other marketing that the company did was to appear in a couple of regional trade shows aimed at the oil service industry, McReynolds' primary target market.

McReynolds makes custom products. Because of setup costs and shipping charges, most orders under $6,000 actually lose the company 5 percent once they pay the 20 percent commission. The company breaks even when the sale reaches $10,000. Profit eventually reaches 10 percent at $20,000 and then flattens out.

Elise's first suggestion was to no longer accept any order under $5,000. "But Elise, we can't turn down business!" argued her father. "Some of those customers have been with us since we started the company. Others started out small, but grew. If we give them up now, we'll lose out in the long run!"

"But, Dad, we're losing money on those small orders," she replied. "And worse yet, those customers are none too satisfied with the level of attention they're getting. Did you listen to any of them at the Oil Supply show in Houston last month? Even our big customers were complaining."

"That's why I hired you—to increase sales from current accounts while increasing profits and improving customer satisfaction!"

What should Elise do?

Case 10.2   Budget Time

The conference room was filled with the friendly buzz of chatter between colleagues when Marisa Hernandez entered. As she sat, she noticed that she was the last of the marketing staff to arrive for the budget meeting.

"OK, now that Marisa is here, we can get started," smiled Tom Davis, director of marketing. "The purpose of this meeting is to review the budgets you have all submitted and then chop off 15 percent." This remark was met with nervous laughter, as Tom smiled ruefully. "Sorry, gang, but it's true. If we can't improve our profitability by another 5 percent, it seems that our parent company will sell us off after this year. So top management has asked everyone to reduce their costs by 15 percent without losing sight of their sales goals."

Marisa groaned. She was relatively new and was responsible for managing trade shows and other special events, but she had been there long enough to know that the company had been wasting its trade show money in the past. With a little re-arranging of the show schedule and the increase in budget she had asked for to build a new booth, she felt sure that she could increase the number and quality of leads enough to handle the 12 percent increase in sales that management had already asked for. Cutting 15 percent of the budget, though, eliminated the new booth.

Tom passed out copies of the summary budgets of each department. "Whoa, here's the culprit right here," exclaimed Shelly Tap, national sales manager. She slammed the copies to the table, saying, "Our trade show budget request is 30 percent higher than last year." Turning to Marisa, she said, "I can't cut our budget 15 percent and expect to reach the sales target, but if you cut yours to 5 percent less than last year's, that'll equal 5 percent of my budget."

"But if I can upgrade the quality of leads you get, as well as the quantity, you can still achieve your sales targets," replied Marisa, trying to hide her irritation. For some reason, she didn't hit it off with Shelly.

"Oh, sure. Everyone knows that trade shows are just a wild party. We haven't closed a lead from one in years." Shelly, along with all of the other staff, laughed. "Look, Tom, let's put our money where the results are, and that's in sales."

"Yeah, Tom, and you know how important advertising is to our image," added Brian Black, director of advertising. "We can't possibly cut 15 percent."

At this point, Marisa began to worry about keeping her job.

1. What type of information does Marisa need to justify her proposed budget? Where would she go to get that information?

2. Similarly, how would any other marketing managers justify their budget requests?

3. What type of budgeting does it seem the company does now? What should the company do? What challenges will Tom face in implementing a different budgeting process? How should Tom go about that implementation?

Additional Readings

Andrews, Jonlee, and Daniel C. Smith, "In Search of the Marketing Imagination: Factors Affecting the Creativity of Marketing Programs for Mature Products," *Journal of Marketing Research* 33 (May 1996), pp. 174–87.

Englis, Basil G., and Michael R. Solomon, "Using Consumption Constellations to Develop Integrated Communications Strategies," *Journal of Business Research* 37 (November 1996), pp. 183–92.

Hutton, James G., "Integrated Marketing Communications and the Evolution of Marketing Thought," *Journal of Business Research* 37 (November 1996), pp. 155–62.

Phelps, Joseph E., Thomas Harris, and Edward Johnson, "Exploring Decision-Making Approaches and Responsibility for Developing Marketing Communications Strategy," *Journal of Business Research* 37 (November 1996), pp. 217–24.

Rapp, Stan, and Tom Collins, "MaxiMarketing: The Concept and Its Implications," *Journal of Direct Marketing* I (Winter 1987), pp. 65–75.

Rust, Roland T., and Sajeev Varki, "Rising from the Ashes of Advertising," *Journal of Business Research* 37 (November 1996), pp. 173–82.

Schultz, Don E., "The Inevitability of Integrated Communications," *Journal of Business Research* 37 (November 1996), pp. 139–46.

Stevenson, Thomas, and Linda Swayne, "The Use of Comparative Advertising in Business-to-Business Direct Mail," *Industrial Marketing Management* 24, (1995), pp. 53–59.

Stewart, David W., "Market-Back Approach to the Design of Integrated Communications Programs: A Change in Paradigm and a Focus on Determinants of Success," *Journal of Business Research* 37 (November 1996), pp. 147–54.

Zinkhan, George M., and Richard T. Watson, "Advertising Trends: Innovation and the Process of Creative Destruction," *Journal of Business Research* 37 (November 1996), pp. 163–72.

Chapter 11

Communicating with the Market:

Advertising, Public Relations, and Trade Shows

COLORSPAN

When a better mousetrap is built, the world may beat a path to the inventor's door, but then, the purpose of a mousetrap is obvious. When ColorSpan of Eden Prairie, Minnesota, introduced the DisplayMaker oversized graphics printer, potential buyers looked at the DisplayMaker's output and said "Wow, great pictures. What do we do with them?" Until prospects knew how to take advantage of the DisplayMaker's features, nobody would buy.●

In order to educate the market, ColorSpan developed its "The Options Are Endless" campaign, an integrated marketing campaign that took advantage of the communication power of advertising and trade shows. In this campaign, advertising illustrated the various uses of the DisplayMaker, while trade shows were used to demonstrate productivity gains as well as the quality of the images created by the DisplayMaker.●

To add to the challenge, the DisplayMaker had potential in several different market segments. The simplest answer was to create separate messages for each market. But as Sandra Crowley, marketing communications vice president, notes, "The general need was the same across all markets—we had to show how the DisplayMaker would make the buyer more profitable." Using the same copy across all media, ads illustrated the DisplayMaker in use for that particular segment. Similarly, trade show graphics remained the same, but the demonstration was customized to fit the needs of the prospect. ●

The DisplayMaker opened up new markets for buyers, who were able to build a business around the DisplayMaker's output. The first step along the path of success, though, was educating those buyers on how to use the DisplayMaker. More than a mousetrap, the DisplayMaker needed creative advertising and personal demonstrations at trade shows in order to capture its market potential. ●

Visit the ColorSpan web site: **www.colorspan.com** ●

Learning Objectives

As you learned in the previous chapter, communication involves dialogue. It is not just one-way communication. In this chapter, we will examine specific communication tools and venues, some of which look like one-way communication. As you will see, however, astute business marketers are finding ways to make these methods part of an overall dialogue.

After completing the chapter, you should be able to

- ● Set goals for advertising.
- ● Develop advertising strategies to achieve those goals.
- ● Compare and contrast the types of advertising commonly used.
- ● Illustrate how subscription to a particular buying theory influences advertising strategy.
- ● Describe principles of sound public relations.
- ● Set goals for trade shows, and develop a trade show strategy.
- ● Illustrate the complete marketing mix of the trade show experience.

As you learned in the previous chapter, effective marketing communications not only sell the product, they also help the buyer set expectations for product performance. These expectations are then the basis for determining product satisfaction. In this chapter, we will learn how to communicate and build desire for the product, while also setting the proper expectations, through methods of communication to the larger market.

Exhibit 11–1
From Unaware to
Action

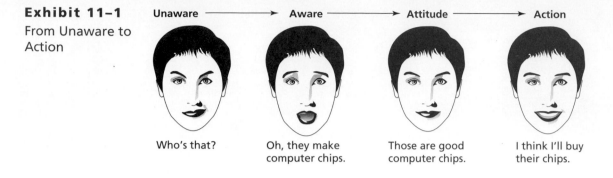

Unaware ——————→ Aware ——————→ Attitude ——————→ Action

Who's that?

Oh, they make
computer chips.

Those are good
computer chips.

I think I'll buy
their chips.

Advertising to Business

The biggest part of the marketing communication budget (not counting the cost of a sales force), is devoted to advertising. Advertising by businesses can serve many objectives but the primary objective is to talk to large groups. Those groups can be potential investors in the company, influencers of government regulation, and even buyers. Yet we discussed, in earlier chapters, how business markets are smaller than consumer markets in terms of the number of buyers, how important the personal relationship between buyer and seller is, and other factors that might lead students to believe that advertising is relatively unimportant. Why, then, is advertising so much a part of the budget?

Why Advertise?

John Wannamaker, a British executive, once said, "I know half of my advertising works; I just don't know which half." That somewhat facetious comment reflects the fact that we can't always see when advertising works. The action a buyer takes may have been influenced by advertising seen long before the action. Advertising, though, is important in business marketing because it does work—advertising does influence action.

As we discussed in Chapter 10, advertising influences action by creating awareness and strengthening attitudes, and advertising can also lead directly to action. As we discuss these benefits of advertising in greater detail, keep in mind that business marketers use advertising to communicate to any large group, not just potential customers. Advertising can be used to create favorable attitudes in financial markets, among potential suppliers, with government officials, and with other important groups.

Advertising Creates Awareness

Before a product is positioned in the mind of a buyer, the buyer must be aware of the product. Products for which the buyer is aware are part of the **evoked set**. As you can see in Exhibit 11–1, the process is one of the buyer becoming aware of the product, developing an attitude about the product (the attitude represents the position), and then acting. Advertising, because of its ability to reach so many prospective buyers, can create awareness.

For example, ColorSpan was an unknown company to most of the potential buyers for DisplayMaker. ColorSpan had to first make the market aware of both ColorSpan and DisplayMaker. Not only did neither the company nor the product hold a place in the mind of the buyer, the product platform (in this case, computer-driven printers) was unknown to the market. ColorSpan had to build awareness for several things, not just the product name.

11–1

FROM THE FIELD

Hewlett-Packard's Advertising Builds LaserJet Brand

Branding a product is usually a practice associated with consumer marketing. But Hewlett–Packard has built strong brand identification for its LaserJet printers. Using award-winning television and print advertising, HP has created brands of printers that are winning the battle for mind-share.

"When people shop for a printer, they generally go in with two brands on their mind, and walk out of the store with one of those two brands 90 percent of the time," says Arlene King, HP marketing communications manager. One of those two brands is HP's LaserJet.

The brand was introduced in 1993, with an integrated marketing campaign that involved television, radio, print advertising, and direct mail. That campaign won the Sawyer Award as

the best business advertising campaign. The current campaign, again winner of the Sawyer Award, was created after an analysis of focus group research and one-on-one interviews indicated that users and corporate buyers wanted reliability more than any other feature. The result was the "You do your job. We'll do ours." campaign, another integrated marketing campaign featuring television, print, radio, and direct mail. Perhaps even more important than winning another Sawyer Award are the outstanding sales results.

Source: Kate Bertrand, "HP Thrives on Powerhouse Brands," *Business Marketing* (February 1995), p. A5; Edmund O. Lawler, "HP Wins Second Sawyer in 3 Years," *Business Marketing* (January 1995), p. 13, and Edmund O. Lawler, "Fear Mongering It Ain't," *Business Marketing* (January 1995), p. 13–14.

Advertising Strengthens Attitudes

Once awareness is obtained, advertising can influence the creation of attitudes. A company's position is similar to the buyer's attitude toward the product, with one exception. A position is the summation of beliefs held about the product, but the attitude also includes how strongly the beliefs are held. A weak attitude can be easily influenced by information from either advertising or other sources. Advertising can strengthen beliefs about a product (thereby strengthening the position) or weaken beliefs held about a competitive product. Strong attitudes and brand preference were Hewlett–Packard's objectives, and as you can see in From the Field 11-1, its advertising was able to deliver in the form of increased market share.

Advertising Leads to Action

As described in Chapter 3, buying is the result of a series of decisions. While it is rare that an industrial buyer will purchase as a result of only seeing an advertisement, a number of actions can be taken as a result of seeing an ad. Prospects may send in cards asking for more literature, may visit the trade show booth, or may call an 800 number. For example, Voice FX includes an 800 number for prospects. Advertising can move prospects more quickly through the decision process when it leads to action.

Advertising Strategy

Advertising strategy consists of two elements: the creative plan and the media plan. Essentially, the creative plan is determining what the content of the message will be (encoding), while the media plan is choosing the channel of communication. Both plans should result from objectives set for the advertising communication.

Note how these ads show a number of ways for an interested buyer to follow up: an 800 number, a trade show booth, or the reader service card.

Courtesy FX Corporation.

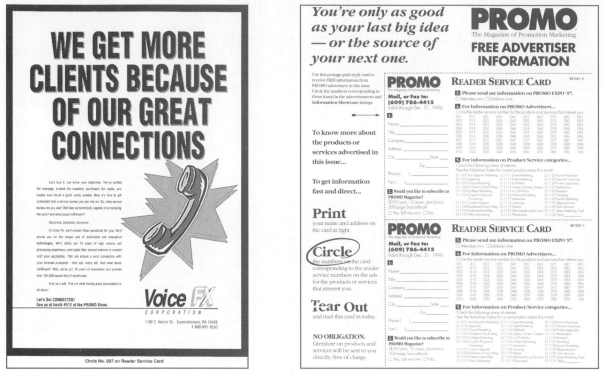

Determining Advertising Objectives

Advertising objectives include performance objectives, (what the advertising should do) and the audience, (with whom the firm wishes to communicate). Setting objectives is important in order to evaluate the success of the advertising and to learn what works and what doesn't, particularly since one can't always observe an immediate change in sales due to an advertising campaign.

As we discussed in the previous chapter, marketing communications objectives include both position and action goals. In Exhibit 11–2, we list a number of such objectives (and measures of performance) that are commonly used for advertising.

At the same time, objectives should state the intended audience. For ColorSpan's "The Options Are Endless" campaign, the objectives were to educate the market as to the profit potential for the new applications possible with the DisplayMaker. The audience included the three members of the typical buying center for DisplayMakers: a chief executive, the user, and the financial analyst. The advertising campaign had to address the needs of all three. Further, there were several different market segments, including professional photographers, trade show booth designers, and retail store designers. ColorSpan had to develop a single campaign that could still attract the interest and build desire among all of its market segments.

Determining the Creative Plan

The creative plan is based upon the objectives. The plan begins with the creative strategy statement, which is a summary of the objectives. If the desired position for DisplayMaker is based on total value due to highest quality and lowest total cost of

Exhibit 11–2

Examples of
Advertising
Objectives

Positioning Objectives
- Create a favorable climate for personal sales calls. (Examine sales call reports regarding the ability to see new accounts or other hard-to-reach accounts.)
- Support other communication channels. (Observe results of other channels.)
- Stimulate derived demand. (Observe sales of product later in the value chain.)
- Project a financially healthy image. (Examine reports by financial analysts.)
- Support distributors or other resellers. (Count the number of distributors who feature our product in their advertising or promotion.)
- Create favorable image among difficult-to-reach influencers. (Conduct surveys of attitudes among those individuals.)

Action Objectives
- Generate leads for field or telemarketing salespeople. (Count leads.)
- Increase attendance at a trade show. (Compare the number of visitors at the booth this year and last year.)
- Increase distribution of catalogs. (Sum the number of telephone calls asking for the catalog.)
- Secure investment in company through sale of stock or other methods. (Observe stock sales.)
- Generate sales. (Observe sales.)

ownership, then our creative strategy statement may be "To create a position of creating new and profitable markets for users who exploit the technology of the DisplayMaker."

From the creative strategy statement, an appeal would be developed. The appeal can be based on rational motives (such as showing increased profit) or emotional motives (how the decision maker might spend the extra profit). Exhibit 11–3 illustrates rational and emotional appeals. Then marketing managers would decide copy, theme, colors, headlines, and other creative elements. Every element of the advertisement would then contribute to achieving the creative objectives.

For example, ColorSpan illustrated DisplayMaker applications in each ad, with copy describing the new market that each application offered. One application was for graphics design firms, which could create and produce high-quality oversize graphics as large as 8 feet high and 10 feet wide. The capability of producing graphics that large opened up markets such as trade show booth graphics, backdrops for in-store displays, and other graphics markets that were not economically feasible without the DisplayMaker technology. Headlines emphasized the profits in new markets, with copy describing the application. Each element supported the creative objectives.

Media Selection

BASF, featured in an earlier chapter, uses a lot of television advertising compared to the average business marketing firm. Other forms of media include radio, outdoor advertising (billboards, signs on buses, etc.), as well as magazines and the Internet. Choosing the particular form of media is a function of cost and access. In other words, what does it cost to access the market? Another consideration is the quality of the message possible. Print ads are not the same as television ads, for example, and each medium has its communication advantages and disadvantages.

Magazines   Most business marketers rely on **trade publications**, or magazines written for a particular trade, profession, or industry. Popular business press, such as *Business Week* and the *Wall Street Journal,* are also important. One particular form of popular

Exhibit 11-3
Rational Ad Example

Courtesy United Van Lines; courtesy Group 1 Software.

Example of an Emotional Appeal (Fear Appeal Based on Fear of Not Knowing and Making Poor Decisions)

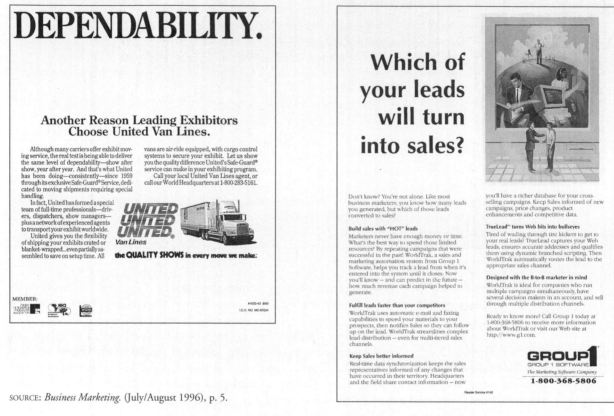

SOURCE: *Business Marketing.* (July/August 1996), p. 5.

press with business advertisers is in-flight magazines, such as American Airlines' *American Way* magazine. Busines advertisers favor these magazines because the readership includes a high percentage of business travelers.

As with most forms of marketing communication, marketers want to know that their advertising dollars are being spent on communicating with their desired market. For that reason, magazines with **controlled circulation**, (distribution only to qualified readers) have been developed. The magazines are distributed free to qualified readers, and *qualified* usually means that the readers play at least an influential role in the buying process. Since the magazine does not allow subscriptions to anyone who does not meet the purchasing criteria and because the magazine focuses on a particular profession or industry, advertising can be efficient because few readers will be nonbuyers for advertised products. Still, because these are nonpaid subscriptions, some advertisers wonder if these magazines are read. The readership of trade magazines, whether circulation is controlled or open, is verified by an independent company; the verification is called a **circulation audit**. Circulation audits tell marketers who gets the magazine, therefore, the marketers can determine if their ads are reaching the right buyers.

Interested buyers can respond to magazine advertising with **reader service cards**, or cards that are sent to the magazine publisher where the lead information is distributed to the appropriate companies. The cards are also called bingo cards because they are covered in numbers, like bingo cards. The reader circles the numbers corresponding to the various advertisers. Bingo cards make it easy for readers to respond because the card

11–1

BUSINESS 2 BUSINESS
DisplayMaster Budgets and Goals

When ColorSpan introduced the DisplayMaster, the product represented a major breakthrough in the way photography could be reproduced. Because it was so new, many potential buyers didn't really understand how to use it. To make advertising the product more challenging, the product has uses in many different applications for many different markets. ColorSpan executives wanted to have as great a reach as possible with its launch campaign, yet keep production costs low by creating only one ad. Budgets weren't high enough to support high reach. How would these budget-based decisions influence what goals could be set for the advertising? What creative limitations might their decisions have?

is ready to mail, only one item has to be mailed no matter how many companies the reader is interested in, and the reader only has to circle numbers. Look back at the Voice FX ad; it has "Circle No. 097 on Reader Service Card."

Faxback is another way to respond to trade publication advertising. It's similar to bingo cards. The only difference is that the reader faxes the information to the publisher instead of mailing it, and the advertiser faxes information to the reader to fulfill the request.

Bingo cards and faxbacks give the publisher information about the readers (what products they are interested in, for example) and about the ads to which they respond. Publishers can then use this information to sell advertising, select articles that are of interest to readers, and make other decisions. Including a few questions about title and purchasing responsibility further qualifies the magazine's audience, too.

Audience quality is the most important variable to consider when selecting a publication. Audience quality is high when the readership of the magazine is composed of important decision makers and key influencers for the advertised product. Some trade magazines, however, are more like new product brochures with very little editorial content or articles. Buyers are likely to only scan these types of magazines whereas magazines with strong editorial content are likely to be read more carefully. Ads in magazines with well-written articles relevant to your audience can have greater impact because the buyer spends more time with the magazine.

Overlap between trade publications should be considered when selecting magazines. For example, the trade show industry is served by *Trade Show and Exhibit Manager, Exhibitor Times, The Exhibitor* and *Trade Show Week*. One study by Cahners Publishing Company found that, in general, advertising in three magazines reaches only 2 percent more of the audience than advertising in two magazines, because most professionals read more than one magazine. **Reach** is the total number of buyers that see an ad. If Freeman Exhibit Company, for example, advertises in those magazines plus general marketing magazines like *Potentials in Marketing*, then overlap may waste advertising dollars by duplicating reach.

At the same time, however, overlap can help companies achieve the frequency of readership. **Frequency** is the number of times a potential buyer is exposed to an ad. Again, the choice of media should reflect overlap but be based on goals for frequency as well as reach.

Cost per thousand (CPM) readers is a critical variable in selecting trade publications, and can be calculated by dividing the cost of an ad's space by the number of readers (in thousands). For example, it may cost $600 to place an ad in *Potentials in Marketing*. If the readership includes a potential 2,000 buyers for the product advertised, then the CPM is $300 (or $600/2). While the publisher will quickly give CPM for the overall readership, it is important to recognize that not all readers are in the target audience. An astute mar-comm manager will calculate CPM on the basis of the total number of prospects in the total audience.

Broadcast Media   Television and radio are forms of broadcast media, and the audience is audited. In most cases, though, the audits do not determine the position or industry of a listener or viewer so many members of the audience may not be part of the desired market. Therefore, there is more waste, or advertising that reaches unintended audiences, be-cause only a small portion of the audience represents potential prospects. Sometimes, however, products have an appeal wide enough to warrant television and radio. Office products, for example, are not limited to a particular industry or profession. Southwest Airlines' "The Low Fare Airline" campaign is designed to attract business travelers who must travel frequently and within a budget. In cases such as office products and airline travel, broadcast advertising (both TV and radio) can be useful in building sales.

Companies also use broadcast media to build company images or to position a company. The BASF ads mentioned in Chapter 1 are a good example of corporate advertising that positions the company.

Television provides an advantage that the previously discussed advertising media cannot match. Television combines both sound and visuals, including full motion. Ads on TV can have more impact or involve the prospect more fully than ads in other media. On the other hand, the audience watching a particular TV show may not have enough prospects in it to justify the expense, and some argue that TV watchers are less involved than magazine readers.

Radio can also deliver the frequency and reach of TV and at a much more affordable rate. By advertising during commute time, radio advertisers believe that they are reaching their audience of business decision makers. The medium also allows for a high degree of creativity. With short production times, ads can be easily and inexpensively altered should the need arise. One difficulty with radio, however, is that it is difficult to purchase national coverage. Radio is used most often to encourage action within a local market and can also be used to support TV advertising. For example, Southwest Airlines also has a radio version of "The Low Fare Airline" campaign.

Electronic Media   Electronic media includes the Internet and World Wide Web. Home pages serve as a form of advertising that the audience seeks. The effectiveness of home pages is often measured in "hits" (the number of times someone looked at the page), yet many service providers, which provide advertisers with space for home pages, also audit the readership of those home pages so that advertisers know who hit the page. Creative home pages are often hit by other people who have to make their own home pages, by competitors, by the curious, and by accident, which means that some hits aren't worth counting. Additionally, while someone may hit a site repeatedly, it is difficult to determine new hits from repeats without an audit service.

Another limitation is that anyone can put just about anything on the Web. (Heaven's Gate, the mass suicide cult with a home page, is an example of what can be placed on the Web.) Credibility of messages is somewhat suspect to many potential buyers.

Many advantages exist, however, for Web advertising. First, it can be *interactive*. The person has to choose to enter a company's home page so there is more active participation than when reading a magazine, and the ad is next to the text of an article. Readers then select the additional information they want, continuing to participate in the communication.

Web pages like this one are becoming an increasingly important method of communicating with potential and current customers.

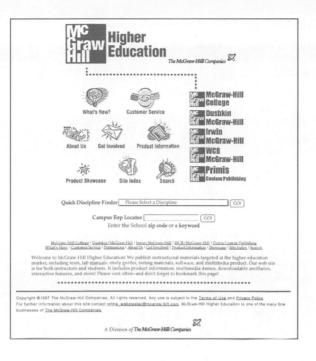

In addition, Web advertising is *responsive*. Because readers can choose from a wide array of information, they can get more information targeted to their needs immediately. Bingo cards are slow, and faxback, while quicker than bingo cards, is not as fast as Internet communication.

Finally, since Web advertising can offer readers the opportunity to provide feedback in a more conversational mode through e-mail, it can result in *two-way communication*. If a reader wants to comment on anything that was seen, she can do so by sending a message to the advertising company. This two-way advantage is why many companies turn to home pages to support their customer service efforts. While the company hopes for messages like "Send me 10 dozen!" the feedback could be questions about the product, requests for salesperson visits, and others.

Such was the case for the Faucet Outlet, a discount plumbing supply house. Initially, the company relied on catalogs mailed to plumbers, builders, and other plumbing supplies buyers. In just a year, however, sales taken from browsers of the company's on-line catalog represent 5 percent of the company's total business, and that amount is growing rapidly.

One problem with the Net is that searching for vendors can be difficult. IBEX, the International Business Exchange launched by the U.S. Chamber of Commerce, is one virtual marketplace designed to overcome that limitation. Companies that have IBEX software can enter offers to buy or sell, which are then matched. Through secure electronic mail, negotiation can take place between matches, anonymously if preferred. Once an agreement is reached, IBEX also offers both parties the ability to review each other's profiles, an important consideration when extending credit or depending on a vendor to supply a crucial product. Because IBEX is not an Internet service but a private network, users expect IBEX to provide greater security for transactions—still a major concern for transactions conducted over the Net.[1]

Banner advertising on the Net can also attract attention. Banners are those small advertisements that you see when you use a search engine like Yahoo or Lycos. These ads are proving to be successful business builders.

Exhibit 11–4   Advertising Measures

Measure	How It Is Calculated	How It Is Used
Recall	Surveys of magazine readers (or television viewers) asking which ads they remember seeing	Did the ad attract attention? Was it remembered? Assumption is that if the ad is remembered, it was effective.
Inquiries	Sum of bingo cards, faxbacks, or calls to the 800 number in an ad	Did the ad cause readers to take action? Were the people who responded really interested in buying the product?
Position	Pre-advertisement and postadvertisement surveys of attitudes toward a product	Did the ad change the market's attitudes toward our product? Is the attitude now what we want it to be, relative to attitudes about our competitors' products?
Reach	Using circulation or readership audits, the number of readers among the target market is calculated	Does this magazine reach our desired audience? Used to assess media choices, rather than the effectiveness of a particular advertisement.
CPM (cost per thousand)	Divide cost by readership, expressed in thousands	How does the reach of this magazine compare to the reach of a similar magazine, relative to how much each charges? Again, used to assess media choices.

Directories   Industrial buyers sometimes use directories to locate potential suppliers. Unlike consumers who can just open a phone book, organizational buyers can not always find suppliers in the Yellow Pages. Specialized directories, though, can serve the same purpose. Many trade publications include an annual directory of companies for a particular industry. There are also directories in which companies buy space. Like in the phone book, companies are listed but can also purchase ads. An example from the Center for Exhibition Industry Research can be used by show managers to book convention facilities or by marketing managers to find trade show exhibit makers.

Measuring Advertising Performance

Advertising performance is like all other forms of marketing performance; to evaluate whether advertising worked, the advertising manager must compare results with objectives. The real challenge, though, is to create measures that can enable that type of analysis. For example, if the objective was to change a position, then postadvertising surveys determining the relative position of the advertised product should be developed. (Refer back to Exhibit 11–2 for a list of objectives and measures.) All too often, though, objectives are set around what can be measured, such as the number of inquiries or CPM, which may not reflect the original objectives.

Another factor of concern to marcomm managers is the need to determine the efficiency of advertising. Efficiency is usually determined by comparing inputs with outputs or, in this case, advertising dollars are compared with results. Efficiency is relative, not absolute, meaning that we must compare a new advertising campaign against an old one or compare two new campaigns in test markets to learn which campaign is more efficient. Exhibit 11–4 lists different measures commonly used to measure advertising results.

EXAMPLE OF AN INDUSTRIAL DIRECTORY

Greater Pittsburgh Convention & Visitors Bureau
Joseph R. McGrath
President & CEO
Tel: (412) 218-7711, Fax: (412) 644-5512
Toll-free (800) 359-0758

Kansas City Convention & Visitors Bureau of Greater Kansas City
Wayne Chappell
President
Tel: (816) 691-3815, Fax: (816) 691-3855

Las Vegas Convention & Visitors Authority
Manuel J. Cortez
President
Tel: (702) 892-0711, Fax: (702) 892-7515

Las Vegas Convention & Visitors Authority
Terry Jicinsky
Marketing Research Administrator
Tel: (702) 892-2805, Fax: (702) 892-7685

Little Rock Convention & Visitors Bureau
Barry Travis
Executive Director
Tel: (501) 376-4781, Fax: (501) 374-2255

Los Angeles Convention & Visitors Bureau
Bob Moore
Executive Vice President
Tel: (213) 624-7300, Fax (213) 624-9746

Metro Toronto Convention & Visitors Association
Gino Giancola
Vice President, Sales
Tel: (415) 203-2600, Fax: (416) 203-6753

Metropolitan Tucson Convention and Visitors Bureau
Jana Rae Oliver
National Sales Manager
Tel: (520) 624-1817, Fax: (520) 884-7804

Nashville Convention & Visitors Bureau
Butch Spyridon
Executive Vice President
Tel: (615) 259-4730, Fax: (615) 244-6278

New Orleans Metropolitan Convention & Visitors Bureau, Inc.
Ed J. McNeill
Executive Vice President
Tel (504) 556-5050, Fax: (504) 556-5046

New York Convention & Visitors Bureau
Ruth Nadler
Director, Information Services & Research
Tel: (212) 484-1221, Fax: (212) 245-5943
Email: nyres@nycvisit.com

Orlando/Orange County Convention & Visitors Bureau
William C. Peeper
Executive Director/CEO
Tel: (407) 363-5800, Fax: (407) 370-5022
Email: Bill.Peeper@OrlandoCVB.com

Philadelphia Convention & Visitors Bureau
Michael J. Gamble
Vice President/Convention Sales
Tel: (215) 636-330, Fas: (215) 636-3327

Phoenix & Valley of the Sun Convention & Visitors Bureau
David S. Radcliffe
President & CEO
Tel: (602) 254-6500, Fax: (602) 253-4415

Saint Louis Convention & Visitors Commission
Greg Deininger
V.P. of Sales & Marketing
Tel: (314) 992-0620, Fax: (314) 621-7729

Salt Lake Convention & Visitors Bureau
Richard E. Davis
President/CEO
Tel: (801) 521-2822, Fax: (801) 534-4927

San Antonio Convention & Visitors Bureau
Steve Moore
Executive Director
Tel: (210) 270-8700, Fax: (210) 270-8782

San Diego Convention & Visitors Bureau
Christine Shimasaki
Vice President of Sales & Marketing
Tel: (619) 525-5201, Fax: (619) 525-5005

San Francisco Convention & Visitors Bureau
John A. Marks
President
Tel: (415) 227 2605, Fax: (415) 227-2602

San Francisco Convention & Visitors Bureau
Doug Neilson
Vice President, Convention Division
Tel: (415) 974-6900, Fax: (415) 227-2602

San Jose Convention & Visitors Bureau
Marian L. Holt
President & CEO
Tel: (408) 295-9600, Fax: (408) 295-3937
Toll-free: (800) SAN-JOSE
Email: sjcvb@sanjose.org

Seattle King County Convention & Visitors Bureau
Steven Morris
President/CEO
Tel: (206) 461-5800, Fax: (206) 461-5855

Singapore Trade Development Board
P.C. Tham
Director
Tel: (212) 421-2207, Fax (212) 888-2897

Tampa Hillsborough Convention and Visitors Association
Suzanne Cavanaugh
National Sales Manager
Tel: (202) 833-4943
Email: scavanaugh@thcva.com

Washington DC Convention & Visitors Association
Daniel E. Mobley, CAE
President and CEO
Tel: (202) 789-7000, Fax: (202) 789-7037

Exhibit Brokerage, Design, Production

Abex Display Systems, Inc.
Nick Drance
Vice President, Sales
Tel: (818) 764-5126, Fax: (818) 503-9955
Toll-free: (800) 537-0231

ABF Display Company
Jerol F. Fleck
President
Tel: (612) 647-0598, Fax: (612) 647-1008
Toll-free: (800) 647-0598

Adler Display Studio, Inc.
Ron Adler
Vice President-operations
Tel: (410) 366-6200, Fax: (410) 366-5876

Admore, Inc.
John Floros
CEO
Tel: (508) 793-2020, Fax: (508) 752-4076

Admore, Inc.
Robert J. Francisco
President
Tel: (508) 793-2020, Fax:(508) 752-4076
Toll-free: (800) 937-1341

Admore, Inc.
C.J. Floros
Comptroller
Tel: (508) 793-2020, Fax: (508) 752-4076
Toll-free: (800) 937-341
Email: mg2ma@aol.com

Admore, Inc.
Robert Nolette
National Production Manager
Tel: (508) 266-2700, Fax: (508) 266-2711

SOURCE: Center for Exhibition Industry Research *Directory*, Washington, D.C.

Public Relations

Public relations is the management function that focuses on the relationships and communications with individuals and groups in order to create mutual goodwill.[2] Some people define public relations (PR) as the quality of relationships with the various groups or individuals that comprise the public (including government, stockholders, and others), but we define PR as a management function in order to emphasize the importance of managing these relationships. PR is more than crisis management—effective marketing communicators do not wait for an oil spill to begin developing communicating with the various publics. Rather, effective marketing communicators seek to have strong, positive relationships before and in spite of any crises.

There are two forms of PR: publicity and public affairs. These forms of PR may overlap, but it is helpful to recognize the different categories separately first so that all PR requirements are identified.

Publicity

Publicity is often confused with PR, but publicity is only one type of PR. **Publicity** is the generation of news about a person, product, or organization that appears in broadcast or electronic media. For example, when ColorSpan launched Display Maker, it sent information to various magazines in hopes that the magazines would do stories on the new product.

Marketers try to get positive publicity, but several issues must be remembered. First, the information must be newsworthy and, unfortunately, negative information seems to be more newsworthy. That is why we see more stories about ethics violations, for example, than we do about successful turnarounds of failing companies. Second, there is no charge for publicity by the media, but no obligation to use it. Nor can the marketer control how such information is used. A major publicity campaign can require an investment of 1 to 2 percent of sales, as opposed to 5 to 20 percent for advertising, so publicity can be very cost effective when successful.

News releases are an important form of publicity. A **news release** (or **press release**) is a brief memo or report containing news information, such as the announcement of a new product, award, or change in management. Exhibit 11–5 presents tips for effective news releases.

Press Agentry   One form of publicity is **press agentry**, or the planning and staging of an event in order to generate publicity. For example, hosting a press party at a trade show and demonstrating a new product would be considered press agentry. There are other methods of achieving publicity, particularly negative publicity; press agentry encompasses much of what is done to create favorable publicity. Again, one key to success is to make the event newsworthy.

Press kits (or **media kits**) support staged events, and contain information about the event and key information for publication in news stories. These kits may include samples of the product, background information and product brochures, and any other information that will aid a journalist in writing an article about the event or the organization.

Another form of press agentry is the creation of speaker's bureaus, or lists of company officials who will speak at civic and industry events. For example, the Freeman Companies, a Dallas-based group of companies serving the trade show industry, has several executives who have prepared speeches. Based on a group's needs, the PR department matches the executive and speech to the occasion.

Exhibit 11-5
Checklist for
Writing News
Releases

- **Identify yourself.** Include the name and address of the company (preferably on a letterhead) and the name and number to contact for further information.
- **Provide a release date**—even if the item is marked "for immediate release."
- **Use wide margins.** Copy should be double-spaced for print media and triple-spaced for broadcast media.
- **Keep it short.** One page is preferred. If the release is longer, don't break in the middle of a paragraph.
- **Proof the copy.** Typos, grammatical errors, and other mistakes detract from the message.
- **Update your mailing list.** Editors change, offices move.
- **Don't call to see whether the editor received your release.** Editors don't like to be pressured.
- **Don't ask for tearsheets.** Don't expect the editor to send you a copy.
- **Don't promise you'll advertise if the item is published.** You'll offend the editor.
- If an article runs, **send a thank you** to the editor.

SOURCE: William F. Arens and Courtland Bovée. *Contemporary Advertising.* Fifth edition. Burr Ridge, IL: Richard D. Irwin, 1994.

Public Affairs

Many people contact companies for many different reasons. School children may write to learn more about business, a local government official may ask about a company policy, a local journalist calls with questions about employment figures, or a charity calls asking for a donation. All of these inquiries must be handled, and it is usually through a public affairs office. **Public affairs** is the part of PR that deals with community groups. In addition to the inbound examples just mentioned, there are two types of public affairs: lobbying and community involvement.

Lobbying   **Lobbying** is any attempt to persuade a government official or governing body to adopt policies, procedures, or legislation in favor of the lobbying group or organization. Lobbying is an important activity and can affect the outcomes of planned mergers and acquisitions, product introductions and recalls, marketing communication activities, and other activities of the firm. While we were writing this chapter, the government announced that set-aside programs (government purchasing programs setting aside contracts for minority- or women-owned businesses) would be ended. You can imagine that many minority and women's groups actively lobbied against the end of set-asides.

Community Involvement   A form of public relations is a company's community involvement. Such involvement can range from sponsoring a children's soccer team to underwriting the costs of charity events to loaning an executive to run a charitable organization. Many companies use their PR department to create relationships with organizations that can benefit from the companies' participation. The PR departments then secure participation from employees.

Trade Show Marketing

The trade show, or exhibition, industry is an exciting one because of the complexity of trade show plans, the excitement of traveling to exotic locales, and the pressure of managing the details necessary to pull a show together. In this section, we will examine trade shows primarily from the perspective of the exhibit manager. We'll also introduce the various service providers in this industry and discuss how trade show strategy is developed.

The Importance of Trade Shows

Trade shows rank second only to advertising in terms of the marketing communication budget (taking out personal selling). For that reason only, trade shows are important. The biggest reasons that shows are growing in importance are that buyers depend more on trade shows, trade shows can provide an opportunity for dialogue, and trade shows reach buyers that salespeople have not. Lest you think, though, that shows are only about meeting potential new customers, shows are growing in importance because of the opportunity to strengthen customer relationships. Relationships with the trade press can also be developed at shows. The bottom line is that trade shows create sales.

Buyers Depend on Trade Shows

One issue is that companies have downsized everything, including their purchasing departments. With fewer people to participate in purchasing decisions, buyers are finding it difficult to stay informed. They no longer have time to see salespeople unless a purchase is imminent. Therefore, buyers are depending on trade shows to provide information that they used to get in other ways. At a trade show, they can talk to 20 or more potential vendors in one day.

These buyers include your current customers as well as potential customers. Since buyers depend on shows to see new products and keep abreast of the latest information, trade shows should be important to business marketers.

Trade Shows Create Dialogue

The trade show experience can consist of dialogue with the prospect. To be sure, some attendees may only see the formal presentation and not enter into dialogue. Attendees interested in the company's offerings, however, will engage in dialogue, sharing their reactions to the offerings as well as information about their needs, decision process, and budget. This useful information can be passed along to the right salesperson. And, because attendees have also seen a demonstration, the sales cycle is reduced from an average of four sales calls to one.[3] Shows provide an opportunity for high-quality dialogue.

Trade Shows Reach New Prospects

With downsizing and reduced budgets, the only people who can afford to attend a trade show are decision makers and key influencers.[4] Many of these people were unavailable to salespeople in the field. (Either they wouldn't see salespeople or salespeople did not find their company.) Research indicates that many customers first identified as a prospect at a trade show were never called on by a salesperson prior to the show. Trade shows are an important opportunity to find new customers.

Trade shows are also useful for entering new markets. Many business marketers use trade shows to test a new market's reaction to their product, to find distributors in new markets, and to enter foreign markets. Such was the case with Link Technologies, which went to CeBIT, a European trade fair profiled in From the Field 11–2.

Trade Shows Strengthen Customer Relationships

Current customers also attend shows. Trade shows are an excellent opportunity for current customers to meet upper-level executives and offer input regarding company policies, strategies, and other decisions that affect customers. Personal relationships can also begin between top executives and key customers through meetings at trade shows.

11–2

FROM THE FIELD

Entering Foreign Markets through Trade Shows

IBM, Microsoft, General Motors, Alcoa—these large companies probably market their products in every free country in the world. Most companies, however, don't have the marketing muscle that IBM or GM have and may be afraid of the investment needed to sell their wares in another country, particularly a country on another continent.

But many small companies are finding that trade shows provide a venue for testing foreign markets without massive investment. With help from the U.S. Department of Commerce and from show management, small companies can encounter eye-opening results overseas. For example, at CeBIT in Hanover, Germany, some 450,000 visitors in eight days have the opportunity to pass by the eight U.S. pavilions, booths featuring over 350 smaller U.S. manufacturers. Even states, such as Florida, sponsor pavilions to showcase the wares of their home companies.

Link Technologies, of Atlanta, Georgia, wanted to find distributors for its products. "A lot of companies over here [in Germany] want to get out of manufacturing because of price pressure, so actually, we're looking for each other," says Jim Bourgeois, Link Technologies' director of sales.

Companies still unsure of exhibiting can participate in the U.S. Department of Commerce CEO program. The program provides the company with an office and an assistant who makes appointments with prospects during the show. Then the company can follow up later at the prospect's office. Almost every company that participates is convinced of the project's worth and exhibits the following year.

The key, though, is the bottom line. As MDS Distributors discovered, exhibiting overseas can seriously impact the bottom line. International sales grew from 20 percent to 75 percent of the firm's total sales in just five years of exhibiting at overseas shows.

Source: Jenny Tesar, "Many US CeBIT Exhibitors Were Small, First-Time Firms," *Computer Trade Show World* (April-May 1995), pp. 8, 15, "New from Around the Exhibit Industry," *ideas* (June 1996), pp. 12–14.

Customers also want to see new product demonstrations. New products often make their debut at trade shows. Customers who were not part of the product development process or haven't seen the final product will want to view these at shows.

Many companies also host customer appreciation events, such as Allied Van Lines' annual dinner and party at one of its key shows. When the show was in Chicago, Allied hosted its party at the Improv comedy club; when it was in Louisville, Kentucky, the party was hosted at the Derby Museum at Churchill Downs. These memorable occasions are wonderful opportunities to strengthen customer relationships.

Building Relationships with Trade Press

With new product introductions and other key announcements headlining every trade show, the trade press is there in full force. In addition to hosting press conferences for new product announcements, exhibit managers try to create opportunities for key executives and marketing personnel to meet and build relationships with members of the trade press. Trade press representatives are often included in special events such as Allied's annual parties. They may also seek interviews with executives concerning hot topics and current issues in the field, interviews they can get easily because top executives participate in the show. Trade shows provide an important venue for building and strengthening relationships with the media.

Setting Trade Show Goals

Seeing current customers, creating new customers, and strengthening relationships with the press—all are important functions of trade shows. Goals can and should be set for each function, yet most companies focus only on the acquisition of new customers. New customer goals include the number of leads, the number of sales, and the number of visitors to the booth; 3M Medical Imaging Systems, a company that manufactures X-ray and other medical imaging equipment, uses all three. It also sets goals for current customers, including the number of current customers who attend a function or visit the booth. 3M Medical Imaging salespeople are encouraged to set goals for each of their accounts who may attend. An example of such a goal might be to introduce a decision maker to a key executive in order to strengthen the relationship.

Companies should also consider press goals, or goals for meeting members of the media. 3M Medical Systems sets goals including the number of interviews given, number of people who attend press conferences, and number of media packets distributed. It also sets goals for the amount of press actually generated at a show, and evaluates its ability to actually get its story in print after the show is over.

Setting goals depends on the overall marketing strategy. For example, when 3M Medical Imaging Systems introduced a new product, press goals included the number of mentions of the product in the trade media. The highest-priority lead goal was the number of leads for that product. Then, based on these goals, the strategy for the show is determined.

Once goals are set, the next step is to select shows. Show selection is like media selection in advertising; many of the same issues such as reach have to be considered.

Show Selection

One of the primary responsibilities of an exhibit manager is selecting shows in which to exhibit. Factors that affect the decision include the expected audience at the show, the type of show, and cost of exhibiting. Selecting a show is basically a process of comparing the number of potential prospects at the show with the cost of exhibiting. Like advertising, choice may be made on the basis of cost per exposure.

Two measurements can be useful in predicting the number of prospects at a show: net buying influences and total buying plans. **Net buying influences** is the percentage of show audience that has influence in the buying process for the specific product exhibited. A trade show audience may include students, job seekers, competitors, members of the press, and other nonbuyers, as you can see in Exhibit 11–6. Additionally, not every buyer in the audience buys for every exhibited product category.

Total buying plans is the percentage of the audience planning to buy exhibited products within the next 12 months. Both figures, total buying plans and net buying influences, are often available from show management for the most recent show, and can be used to predict audience quality for the next show.

Other reasons for choosing a show may include the amount of press that participate and whether competition is there. Sometimes, not exhibiting may send negative signals to a market so companies can get locked into exhibiting at some shows just to show that their business is healthy. For example, when IBM decided not to exhibit at the National Office Administrators' Conference, attendees wondered if this meant that IBM was getting out of office equipment markets (i.e. typewriters and word processors). In addition,

Exhibit 11-6

Percentage of Attendees by Role in Buying Twenty-nine percent of first-time trade show attendees and 40 percent of repeat attendees have final say in the purchase of products exhibited, while 22 percent and 15 percent, respectively, have no role in purchase.

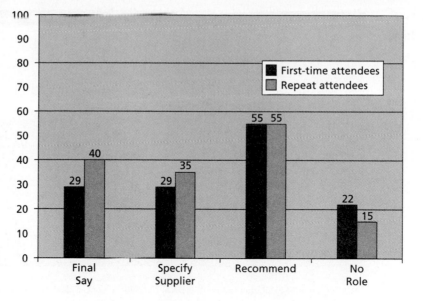

SOURCE: Center for Exhibition Industry Research, "Power of Trade Shows."

buyers go to shows because of the opportunity to examine a large number of vendors' offerings in one convenient place. The more competitors present, the more buyers who will attend.[5] Going where competitors go can be wise.

Choice may also be made on the basis of show type. There are several types of shows in which to exhibit: trade association conventions versus for-profit shows; regional versus national and global shows; and horizontal versus vertical shows.

Association-Sponsored versus For-Profit Association-sponsored shows are exhibitions that occur as a sideline to a convention and conference of a trade or professional association. For example, the California Dental Association has an annual convention that includes seminars on the latest dental practices plus an exhibition of dental equipment. Sometimes, companies exhibit at association shows in order to support the organization.

Some shows are created and run by for-profit companies. For example, the American Contract Manufacturers' Shows (Amcon) is a company that produces exhibitions for contract manufacturers. Seminars occur in conjunction with the show, but the primary focus is on the exhibition.

The exhibition portion of an association conference can be a big money-maker for the association. Attendance at the conference may be higher than at a for-profit show, but actual attendance through the exhibits can be low if attendees come only for the seminars. On the other hand, many marketers also seek to present at the seminars, thus increasing their visibility.

Regional versus National or Global Amcon shows are regional, which means that several versions of the show are held in various locations around the country. The California Dental Association is another regional show. Regional shows attract both regional exhibitors and regional attendees. Regional shows are usually the least expensive to participate in because they are smaller shows. Many exhibitors may not have a booth but simply use a table to display their offerings.

Exhibit 11–7
Leading Trade
Shows in the
United States by
Industry
Classification

	Number of Shows	Number of Attendees
Gifts and merchandising	29	725,300
Manufacturing and engineering	29	633,720
Computer and electronics	20	828,540
Jewelry and apparel	18	270,700
Sports and recreation	17	347,980
Hospitality and service	14	254,410
Food and beverage	13	252,690
Medical and related fields	11	139,950
Housewares–home and office	8	135,175
Broadcast and communications	7	120,900
Print–publishing and paper	7	88,630
Automotive and trucking	6	122,450

SOURCE: Center for Exhibition Industry Research, "A Guide to the U.S. Exposition Industry."

An interesting trend is that *regional* does not mean *domestic;* with NAFTA, some regional shows are international, drawing visitors from either Canada or Mexico, depending on the show's location. Shows that move from location to location each year and serve regions near a border are including Mexican or Canadian cities in their site selection. CeBIT Hanover Fair is the world's largest telecommunications show and brings visitors and exhibitors from all over the world to Hanover, Germany. Choosing a regional, national, or global show depends on one's market and marketing strategy.

Vertical versus Horizontal A **vertical show** is one that focuses on one industry or profession. Certainly, both Amcon and the California Dental Association meetings are vertical. Business expos sponsored by chambers of commerce or by the U.S. Department of Commerce to spur local and interregional business are examples of **horizontal shows**, or shows that include many industries and professions. For example, CinterMex, the convention center in Monterrey, Mexico, hosts an annual horizontal show designed to increase trade between Monterrey and Texas. The trend, though, is to vertical shows that narrowly define their target market. The narrower the audience, the more efficient trade show dollars can be because, with proper show selection, a larger percentage of the audience is more likely to be prospects. As you can see in Exhibit 11–7, the top 10 types of shows are vertical shows.

Show Marketing Strategy

Once a show is selected, marketing for the show involves three sets of activities:[6]

- Preshow promotion.
- Show management.
- Postshow follow-up.

The challenge facing the exhibit manager is that a complete marketing plan is required just for the trade show! Considering the attendee's show experience as the product, the exhibit manager is responsible for designing a product, promoting that product, and then following up with the customer.

Exhibit 11-8

An Example of an Advertisement Promoting Booth Attendance

Courtesy F. O. Phoenix Conocraft and Rack-N-Pack, Inc.

Preshow Promotion

Preshow promotion activities include direct mail and advertising as well as invitations from salespeople. Telemarketing is also done but to a lesser degree. Preshow advertising promoting booth attendance, if done at all, usually consists of a sunburst saying "Visit Us at Booth #215 at *(name of show)*" added to current advertising. (See Exhibit 11–8.)

There are two schools of thought concerning direct mail, which is the most popular form of preshow promotion. (We'll talk more about direct mail later in this chapter.) One school of thought is to mail to all preregistered attendees (or to all preregistered attendees who meet certain criteria). The objective here is to increase share of attendance or to increase the percentage of attendees visiting the booth.

Another school of thought says to mail to all potential attendees from the company's own database. Obviously, this school of thought requires that the company has a database. Alcatel mails only to preregistered attendees. Most of their shows attract a predominantly regional audience (usually 60 to 70 percent), even though the shows are global. Alcatel's belief is that a national or global mailing would not increase attendance sufficiently for a show.

On the other hand, research indicates that invitations from exhibiting companies is a primary reason that buyers attend.[7] Alcatel combines blanket direct mail with special invitations by salespeople. Salespeople call or hand-deliver invitations to prospects to encourage them to attend. The risk is that a prospect may visit a competitor's booth; on the other hand, if a competitor invites the prospect, the prospect may never visit the Alcatel booth. Alcatel uses invitations to increase the motivation to attend and to help build stronger relationships.

These Harlem Globetrotters are signing little basketballs in order to attract visitors to the Allied Van Lines booth at a trade show. Because almost all attendees at this show are involved in shipping decisions, Allied can effectively use a general attention-getter like meeting the Harlem Globetrotters.

The Show Experience

Strategy for the show experience usually involves three elements: the attention getter, the message, and the close. Careful consideration of all three elements can not only increase the likelihood of success for the show, but also increase the synergy of the show with other messages in other media.

The Attention Getter   The attention getter influences attendees to enter the booth. Invitations and offers for free gifts may encourage some attendees to stop by, but others either won't receive the invitation or will throw it away. As people wander the aisles of the trade show floor, booth design should include attention-getting elements that will entice visitors off the aisle and into the booth.

At the same time, however, some attention-getters can bring everybody into the booth, whether you want them or not. Magic acts, free pictures with a movie star, comedy routines—all have been used as attention-getters. If the audience contains a high proportion of prospects, then these types of attention-getters can be worthwhile. At times, however, such attention-getters can work too well, resulting in wasted time for booth staff who have to deal with unwanted visitors. The challenge, then, is to attract attention but only the attention of the desired audience.

One strategy is to hook attendee's attention and then move the desired attendee into another area of the booth for the appropriate interaction. Visitors who do not qualify as prospects are then free to leave as soon as the show is over. For example, Freeman Exhibit Co. recently used a mind reader as the attention-getter. His show focused on Freeman capabilities. When the show was finished, sales staff met with interested visitors and then invited them to other areas of the booth for one-on-one conversations.

The Message   Constructing the message is an important element in trade show strategy. Two considerations influence the construction of the show message. First, what are the positioning objectives for the products and services being offered; and, second, what are the action objectives? Any message must be consistent and integrated with messages sent via other channels.

Most of the message is delivered by the booth staff. Selecting staff appropriately is a delicate decision. Because the show experience is in-person and results in sales leads,

11–2

BUSINESS 2 BUSINESS
Using Trade Shows

A recent research report indicated that some smaller companies depend heavily on trade shows to close sales. Yet exhibit managers in large companies complain that management doesn't take the show program seriously—in part because 20 years ago, trade shows and conventions were just one big party. But the environment at trade shows has changed, with most attendees going to shows expecting to find new products and suppliers. How would you convince upper management that trade shows are a worthwhile part of the marketing communications plan? As a new graduate, how can you use trade shows to learn your new industry more quickly?

salespeople should want to participate. Salespeople, though, often dislike being away from their sales territory and may resist fulfilling their trade show responsibility. Technical staff, such as product development engineers, can provide visitors with the technical information they desire. Technical staff, though, may need supplemental training to prepare for the selling environment of a show. Top management is also needed.

The Close   Because the show experience is face-to-face, it should end with some indication of an agreement concerning what should happen next. Asking for this agreement is the close. The close may be a request to have a salesperson call, to send information, or whatever else is appropriate for the situation. If the visitor is ready to move to the next step in the purchase process, then the staff member in the booth should note that information so that the appropriate follow-up can occur. The staff member, however, will never realize what follow-up is appropriate unless the visitor is asked. Exhibit managers should always specify how to close to staff members and how to record the information for postshow follow-up.

Postshow Follow-up

Postshow follow-up is a critical element in the trade show marketing mix. In industries such as fashion, toys, and hardware, retailers place orders at the show. At most business marketing shows, however, few sales are made at the show, at least in the United States. (In Europe, more companies are likely to purchase at the show.) Getting the sales force to follow up on leads generated at the show is an important function.

Lead Follow-up   Based on the conversation at the show, leads are categorized, usually into three levels. Zenith Data Systems (ZDS) is one company that uses the three-level method. The A level is reserved for those leads who will make a purchase soon. These leads are faxed to the appropriate salesperson, so that the salesperson calls as soon as the prospect gets home. ZDS believes that *faxing* the lead to the sales rep shows the rep that the lead is important and deserving of immediate attention, thus increasing the likelihood of quick follow-up.

B-level leads are prospects who are interested but will make a purchase later. The amount of time separating A leads from B leads depends on the industry and the normal sales cycle, but in most cases, the time frame is 90 days. If B leads are passed along to the sales force, their sense of urgency for all leads decreases. Reps learn that most leads are a waste of time, which was the case with ZDS. It may not be worth their time to call immediately, either. Therefore, ZDS, like many trade show marketers, turns to telemarketing or direct response mail to follow up with B leads, allowing the sales force to focus on hot leads.

C leads are people interested in the product but with no immediate buying plans. Any follow-up with C leads will be minimal, probably via direct mail. ZDS sends a thank-you-for-stopping-by letter along with a brochure.

Communication   Shows are a venue in which a great deal of useful market information is available. Getting that information shared is an important element in a learning organization if learning is to result from the show. Information about new competitive products and programs (such as discount programs or joint marketing efforts like the Intel software partnerships) can be learned at shows. While at Rockwell, one of your authors had the job of going to competitors' booths and collecting brochures, as well as taking notes during competitors' presentations. This information was later used by the sales force in order to learn and understand competitors' strategies, as well as by the marketing staff.

In addition to competitive information, customer information is available. The seminar agenda can provide insight into key issues that your customers are facing. For example, if several seminars are presented on the subject of government regulation, then you can be sure that government regulation is an important issue for your customers. Companies who can respond, perhaps by helping customers comply with those regulations, will increase their market share.

Visitors to the booth respond to new products and programs. Learning organizations can take this feedback and use it to adjust marketing programs or new product introductions. For example, prospects may suggest minor changes to the product. If there is a mechanism for capturing that information and passing it along to the appropriate product developers, then important changes can occur. Otherwise, the information is lost and the company has missed a useful learning opportunity.

Postshow follow-up is an important activity but can often get lost in the rush to get ready for the next show. Yet it is really in the follow-up that the potential of trade shows is realized. Effective trade show marketers are effective because they don't allow their success at the show to wither and die for lack of follow-up.

Using Specialty Advertising

Specialty advertising is the use of products to advertise another product or company—for example, putting a company's name on pens and pencils, and then giving those away. Specialty advertising, also called premiums, freebies, and giveaways, is an important part of the trade show marketing mix, which is why we are discussing this now, but can be used with field sales or given through direct mail.

Split premiums are becoming popular, where half of the freebie is mailed to the prospect; the other half is given to the prospect after listening to the sales pitch at the booth. For example, a company might send one cufflink or earring in the mail, with the second available at the booth. Other popular forms of specialty advertising include premiums involving sports stars and other celebrities. For example, at shows Hank Aaron, career home run record holder, signs baseballs that are given to attendees.

Another popular form of premium is something that will be used regularly, like the software that Intel's partners gave away, described in Chapter 10. A sign company cleverly combined its product and marketing message into a NO SMOKING sign giveaway. Any

Exhibit 11–9   Measures of Trade Show Performance

Measure	How It Is Calculated	How It Is Used
Traffic counts	At various times of the day, the number of visitors in the booth is counted, then multiplied by a factor of time available to determine total visitors. Simpler methods are to estimate the number of visitors based on the total number of brochures given out, business cards collected, etc.	Did our exhibit program bring people into our booth? Some companies will also count the number of people in the aisles in order to see how well the booth pulled people in. (What percentage of aisle traffic actually entered the booth?)
Direct mail redemption	The booth staff counts the number of direct mail pieces redeemed (turned in) at the booth.	If preshow invitations or split premiums were mailed to attract visitors, the redemption rates tell us how effective the preshow promotion went.
Attraction efficiency	Divide the number of qualified prospects by the total attendees who meet the same profile. (That number is available from show management.)	This number tells us how well our exhibit program did in attracting the right audience.
Total press coverage	Number of interviews given, number of attendees at press conferences, press visitors to the booth.	While we can't measure PR effects until the press writes articles on our company, this can tell us if we attracted their attention at the show.
Anecdotes	The exhibit manager collects stories regarding which buyers came to the booth and what happened during their visit.	In some markets, a single sale can offset the cost of the exhibit program. Anecdotes provide exhibit managers with tangible evidence of exhibit success, examples that can flesh out what can be learned through other measures.
Recall	Postshow surveys by independent auditors ask attendees which booths they remember visiting.	Like recall measures in advertising, recall measures examine how memorable the booth experience was.

premium used regularly by the recipient has greater value to both the recipient and marketing company. The recipient appreciates the gift more, creating greater goodwill. The recipient also sees the marketing message more, increasing the value to the marketer.

Keep in mind that specialty advertising can be used in a number of ways, not just at trade shows. Specialty advertising can include logo-embossed merchandise given by salespeople to prospects, included in direct response mailings, or distributed through other methods. Specialty advertising is, however, very popular in trade show marketing because of the ability of specialty advertising to lure potential buyers to the booth.

Measuring Exhibit Performance

As we said earlier about advertising performance, the marcomm manager must develop measures that enable comparisons between objectives and results. (Exhibit 11–9 lists trade show measures.) While most companies want to generate qualified sales leads at a show, just counting the number of people who stop by, for example, doesn't result in a useful measure of performance. Companies should measure such things as the number of A leads as a percentage of the total audience. This measure is called **attraction efficiency** and tells us how well we did in getting people to the booth.

Another method of determining the return on a show is to estimate sales made as a result of show activities. Peterson Manufacturing, for example, estimates the number of sales that will be made by keeping track of prior shows' performance. The firm has learned that, for it, about 30 percent of qualified leads from a show will result in a certain level of sales over the next two years, which it can use immediately after a show to determine if the show was profitable.

Summary

In this chapter, we've presented three methods of communicating with large audiences: advertising, public relations and trade shows. Advertising is used to create awareness of the company and the product, to strengthen attitudes toward the company or product, and to lead buyers to act. Advertising strategy begins with setting specific communication objectives. Objectives can be related to the desired position or an action by the buyer.

At the same time, the objectives should include a description of the intended audience. Such a description makes media selection easier, and also helps the creator of the advertising to craft a relevant appeal. This appeal is further based on the creative strategy statement. Business marketers tend to rely more heavily on rational appeals, but emotional appeals are also used.

Media selection is the next step. Choices include trade publications, (some of which have controlled circulation), electronic media such as the Internet, and broadcast media. Bingo cards, faxback, and e-mail provide the audience with an opportunity to communicate with the advertiser.

Public relations is also an important element in the total communications plan. Publicity and press agentry are two forms of public relations. Public affairs, including lobbying, is another important form of public relations.

Trade shows are an important element of the communications mix, combining the mass audience of advertising with personal communication. Shows are important to buyers, too, because buyers use shows to shop for suppliers. Like other forms of marketing communications, it is important to set specific and measurable goals for a show program. Show selection is based on the number of buying center participants among the audience, based on information collected by the show manager. There are many choices of shows, such as those reaching a national or global audience or an audience within one industry.

Trade show programs consist of preshow activities designed to build traffic to the booth, activities in the booth, and postshow follow-up. Specialty advertising is a common part of the trade show program and can be used to build traffic to the booth, as well as increase memorability of the company.

Business marketers are growing more sophisticated in their advertising, PR, and trade shows efforts. Further, these are areas of marketing with increasing opportunities for college marketing graduates, perhaps more so than with consumer marketers. As with direct marketing, the subject of the next chapter, the future looks especially bright for students interested in mass communication areas of business marketing.

Key Terms

attraction efficiency	**CPM (Cost per thousand)**	**faxback**
circulation audit		**frequency**
controlled circulation	**evoked set**	**horizontal shows**

lobbying	press release	specialty advertising
media kit	public affairs	split premiums
net buying influences	public relations	total buying plans
news release	publicity	trade publications
press agentry	reach	vertical shows
press kit	reader service cards	

Discussion Questions

1. There is a quote in the chapter, "I know half of my advertising works; I just don't know which half." What makes it so difficult to know whether advertising is working?

2. "Sales are the lifeblood of this company. Any marketing communication that doesn't directly contribute to creating sales is wasted money." If you were the marketing communications manager, how would you justify advertising, PR, and trade shows to the VP of sales who made this comment?

3. What is the relationship of positioning statements and corporate strategy? Write out a separate positioning statement for Fed Ex, UPS, and the U.S. Postal Service with respect to corporate rapid delivery services. Base each statement on what you believe to be competitive advantages for each. Why is each one different from the others? How are these differences communicated in their advertising?

4. Schuster Electronics must sell to a buying center composed of design engineers, finance managers, purchasing agents, and others. How is it that an ad aimed at design engineers may upset finance managers and yet be ignored by purchasing agents?

5. A marcomm director has to choose three magazines in which to advertise. Assume they have equivalent editorial content. Given the following information about the magazines, which three should be chosen and why? Calculate CPM as part of your answer.

	% of Readership				Total Readers	Cost
	Users	Influencers	Decision Makers	Controllers		
Magazine A	15%	18%	8%	5%	30,000	$780
Magazine B	22	32	12	0	17,500	550
Magazine C	16	12	12	3	19,000	550
Magazine D	8	5	23	14	11,000	400
Magazine E	18	21	9	4	33,000	800

6. Can a personal interaction at a trade show take the place of a field sales call? If so, when?

7. Are some forms of communication more effective early in a product's life cycle than later? If so, when and why would which forms be more effective? If not, why not?

8. "We can grow our revenue and our profit more by taking care of the customers we already have," says the president of one firm. "For that reason, we will no longer

advertise." Is this a wise decision? Why or why not? Are some forms of media better suited to customer retention or customer acquisition? If so, which ones?

9. How can trade shows contribute to organizational learning?

10. How are the elements of advertising, public relations, and trade shows similar? How are they different?

Internet Exercise

WWW

INTERNET

Open ColorSpan's home page (**www.colorspan.com**) and print out a press release. What marketing objective(s) do you think it is trying to accomplish? Go back to the beginning page and hit its trade show schedule. What different markets do you see it addressing with its shows? Offer specific shows as evidence of what these markets are.

Cases

Case 11.1 DynaProducts

Jill Vivaldi picked up the last of three proposals, scanned it quickly, and then dejectedly tossed it back on her desk. Not one new idea in the bunch, she thought dejectedly.

Jill's company, DynaProducts, was searching for a new advertising agency. The company was the result of a merger between Dynamic Distributors Inc. and Robotic Products. Dynamic had earned a reputation as the materials handling company to turn to when faced with challenging materials handling requirements. The company specialized in creating customized materials handling systems for efficient warehousing of raw materials or finished products. Primary members of buying centers were warehouse managers, shipping and receiving managers, and the purchasing department.

Robotic Products, on the other hand, was known for combining materials handling systems with manufacturing systems in order to make the manufacturing operations more efficient. Plant engineers and plant managers were important members of the buying center, as were purchasing agents and finance executives.

Neither Robotic nor Dynamic actually manufactured anything; rather, their engineers assembled the best systems from components purchased from a number of manufacturers. Together, these companies will offer the best in complete materials handling systems, from the time raw materials are taken off a truck or railroad car to the time finished products are loaded into a truck or railroad car. The primary needs that they will meet are

- Materials handling systems to enable the use of JIT, and all of the benefits of JIT.

- Better space utilization, allowing for manufacturing capacity growth without acquiring new facilities (just new equipment).

- Reduced inventories, with more efficient manufacturing.

- Lower operating costs due to more efficient materials handling.

The challenge for Jill is to create an image for DynaProducts that capitalizes on the reputations of both firms. One proposal was from Dynamic's ad agency and another was from the agency handling Robotic's advertising—neither proposal seemed to capture the synergy of the new company. Jill had also asked another agency to bid on the contract, but this agency simply merged the two former companies' advertising together. She wants something bolder, more creative—something with immediate impact. Furthermore, she is unsure as to how to best reach a broader buying center.

1. Create a one-sentence positioning statement for DynaProducts. Feel free to rename the company in order to support the position. Then create a print ad based on that positioning statement. How would you alter that ad for publication in magazines aimed at the different members of the buying center?

2. Jill is focusing on advertising. Choose another medium of marketing communication to announce the formation of the new company and its position (instead of advertising). Then defend your decision. If you could only use one medium, which would it be and why?

3. How would you measure your results for advertising and for the second medium you chose? Be as specific and as complete as possible.

4. Should Jill go back to the three advertising agencies and ask for second proposals or should she find someone else? Why?

Case 11.2   Southeast Laser Technology

Trey Jackson and Alice Hernandez were working overtime again. Their start-up company, Southeast Laser Technology, had reached the point where a larger and steadier flow of sales was necessary in order to stay in business. As a contract manufacturer, Southeast Laser Technology manufactured small metal parts on contract for large OEMs. Using lasers, the company could make precision cuts in metal for parts used in computers, watches, manufacturing equipment, materials handling equipment, and anything needing small metal parts.

So far, the company sold primarily to high tech companies that understood the need for laser precision. Both Alice and Trey had sales backgrounds; their combined sales efforts were enough to get the company off the ground, but continued growth required more salespeople. There were plenty of low tech companies in the area that could benefit from Southeast's precision cutting.

Or at least, that's what Trey argued. "What we should do is a hire another salesperson," he said, as he drained the last of the coffee.

"That may be," said Alice, "but we need to expand to the rest of the region, too. If we hire someone and have her hit the market cold, like we did, think how long it will be before we see results."

"Hmm," responded Trey. Alice had a point. After all, it had taken the two of them six months to get enough sales to justify hiring one salesperson. Would it take one salesperson a year to do it alone?

"Look, the Southeast Business Expo is coming up, and the week after that is an American Contract Manufacturers' trade show. What we should do is exhibit at these shows to generate leads," Alice offered excitedly.

"Not a bad idea. Then when we hire someone, we'll have hot leads for them to handle right away," Trey replied. "Why, we might even find someone at the show to hire!"

The Southeast Business Expo is a show designed to introduce businesses to each other in the Southeast so that local suppliers can be found. The show is put on by the regional association of Chambers of Commerce. Everyone, from insurance companies to contract manufacturers like Southeast Laser to transportation firms to mining companies, will be there. The Contract Manufacturers' show has contract manufacturers exhibiting to design engineers. Run by Amcon, a company that sponsors six regional shows each year, the show will have about one-tenth the number of exhibitors as the Business Expo.

1. What should Trey and Alice expect from each show? Should their goals be the same for both shows? Why or why not? What should their goals be? Be specific and state how you would measure performance for those goals.

2. The company doesn't have the money for both preshow and postshow mailings. Which should the company do and why? Should it do the same thing for both shows?

3. By choosing trade shows, Trey and Alice have decided against several other methods of getting their company known to the marketplace. Evaluate their decision, comparing other promotion alternatives.

Additional Readings

Donath, Bob, Richard A. Crocker, Carolyn K. Dixon, and James W. Obermayer, *Managing Sales Leads: How to Turn Every Prospect into a Customer.* Lincolnwood IL: NTC Business Books, 1995.

Gilliland, David, and Wesley J. Johnston, "Toward a Model of Business-to-Business Marketing Communications Effects," *Industrial Marketing Management* 26 (1997), pp. 15–29.

Gopalakrishna, Srinath, Gary L. Lilien, Jerome D. Williams, and Ian K. Sequeira, "Do Trade Shows Pay Off?" *Journal of Marketing* 59 (1995), pp. 75–83.

Haley, Eric, "Exploring the Construct of Organization as Source: Consumers' Understanding of Organizational Sponsorship of Advocacy Advertising," *Journal of Advertising* 25 (Summer 1996), pp. 19–35.

Lohtia, Ritu, Wesley J. Johnston, and Linda Aab, "Business-to-Business Advertising: What Are the Dimensions of an Effective Print Ad?" *Industrial Marketing Management* 24 (1995), pp. 369–78.

Mudambi, Susan McDowell, Peter Doyle, and Veronica Wong, "An Exploration of Branding in Industrial Markets," *Industrial Marketing Management* 26 (1997), pp. 433–46.

Sharland, Alex, and Peter Balogh, "The Value of Nonselling Activities at International Trade Shows," *Industrial Marketing Management* 25 (1996), pp. 59–66.

Chapter 12

IMC

The One-to-One Media

SCOTT PAPER

A three-ton modern sculpture sits in the lobby, marble floors run to the elevator, a classy bistro pipes music through the open dining area. Problem: What towels will grace the men's room? Solution: Scottfold™, a soft, luxurious-feeling paper towel, dispensed one at a time, providing improved restroom appearance, high tenant satisfaction, and cost-effectiveness. Challenge: How to market "the solution" to property managers of Class-A office buildings. ●

Scott Paper Co., acquired by consumer products giant Kimberly-Clark Corp. in 1996, brings a strong business-to-business division to the merged $12 billion enterprise. To develop a program to secure trial of Scottfold™, Scott used Fried-Cassorla Communications, Inc. (Melrose Park, Pennsylvania) for its multimedia expertise. ●

Scott introduced the brand to prospects by mailing a free $50 starter kit, a rebate incentive for quick reply inviting a Scott representative to call. The package contained oversized personalized headlines: "Scottfold™ deals XYZ Company a winning hand!" Many aspects of the letter were personalized. A four-color brochure continued the playing card, "winning hand" theme with a lift-off action device. Prospects were urged to respond by one of three modes: fax, mail, or telephone. START, Scott's in-house telephone marketing staff, handled both outbound and inbound calls. They made appointments for Scott's field sales force. ●

Scott credits a 28 percent response rate to the mail package, backed by telephone follow-up. A sales gain of 80 percent is attributed to the joint impact of the mail campaign and the increased attention given the product by the sales staff. Looking back at the program, marketing development manager Randy Kates said, "We believe that this success is attributed to a well-rounded program consisting of the classic aspects of direct marketing. That includes clear definition of your target audience and database development, follow-up telephone work from our Scott START unit, paired with high-impact, highly personalized direct mailers."[1] ●

Visit the Kimberly-Clark web site at **http://www.kimberly-clark.com** ●

Learning Objectives

This chapter is a bridge between advertising and personal selling. The media we will emphasize—mail, phone, and other electronic forms—don't provide face-to-face contact. But they were developed to enable one person to communicate with another. We dub the chapter one-to-one media because it will greatly aid your understanding and, eventually, your effectiveness in the field, if you regard these marketing communication forms as dialogue. In essence they are closer to personal selling than mass communication in the communication mix.

Upon completion of this chapter you should be able to

● Map the range of utility for direct mail, telephone, and web sites in modern business marketing.

● Describe the essence of their appeal to business marketers.

● Plan and evaluate a direct mail program, recognizing the interplay of the mail package, list, and the "offer" itself.

● Outline key elements of a telephone marketing program, giving due attention to target's identity, target's motives, message scripting, and assessment.

● Frame the decision of whether to use a telemarketing service bureau or develop an inside telemarketing operation.

● Classify the major marketing objectives of web sites.

● Discuss a number of the synergies from combining mail with telephone—and other media efforts—in marketing communication programs.

● Select an evaluation process befitting the communication objectives of the program.

Direct Marketing

Direct mail, telephone marketing, web sites, fax programs, e-mail list serves, and the like often fall under "direct marketing" in meeting topics and budget headings. The Direct Marketing Association has tried to tackle the task of defining **direct marketing**:

> *An interactive form of marketing using one or more advertising media to effect a measurable response and/or transaction at any location, with this activity stored on database.*[2]

Four Essentials in the Definition

The definition is not perfect. For purposes of this chapter's discussion, four key elements can be teased out of the definition.[3] First, *it is marketing,* not something else. (Don't laugh. One company's sales force denigrated a niche rival for years for exclusively selling by catalog and a dedicated telephone sales staff. They ate a little crow when they started their own catalog program and inside telemarketing unit to serve small and remote accounts.) We will firmly establish the need for direct marketing activities in the modern business marketer's tool kit.

Second, *it precludes face-to-face interaction.* Personal selling and trade show education and hospitality are out, although they could well be supported by direct marketing activities. In practice we always include the telephone and the new electronic channels as "advertising media."

Third, *the definition implies uniqueness in seeking a "measurable response."* From Chapter 11 you already know that advertising, personal selling, and trade shows can generate responses. But remember that personal selling and trade shows were disqualified on the basis of their face-to-face character. That leaves advertising still up for discussion. The responses sought by direct marketing are *readily observable actions* that can happen almost anywhere in the marketplace. That means that only some of the responses sought in advertising count as measurable. Leads generated from a chemical company's ad in a trade magazine are readily observable actions, easily measured responses. The same company might tout its prowess for innovation and quality in other ads. Its sought response is awareness, excitement, or attitude formation—and these are not readily observable actions. We can only gauge knowledge, attitudes, and emotional responses with paper-and-pencil instruments, physiological measures (e.g., pupil dilation or galvanic skin response), and telephone surveys.

Database represents the fourth essential component of the definition. We know of no business that dials or mails randomly to potential customers. Whether aiming to acquire new customers or deepen the relationship with current customers, mail and telephone programs are built upon a database. At a minimum, the database is a list containing company names, addresses, and phone numbers. Often the database contains industry codes, personnel at key positions (VP purchasing, president), firm size, and purchase history as discussed in Chapter 5. On its own files any firm should record each type of customer contact, while external databases (e.g., mail or phone lists) purchased or rented for particular campaigns should be evaluated for their performance. Of course, respondents are added to the company database.

Definitional Gaps

Direct marketing is ever changing and its trade association definition is usually trying to catch up with these changes. As the emphasis on buyer–seller relationships has crystallized over the years, professionals who regard themselves as direct marketers began to forsake the request for a response occasionally. Indeed, chatty newsletters, specialty magazines, birthday greetings, and invented occasions to say "thanks for your business" have become part of the direct marketing repertoire. The practice is less common via telephone, but many organizations find it another useful way for personnel other than salespeople to stay in touch with customers.

Thus, it seems difficult to identify a use of the phone or mail that is not regarded as direct marketing. Personal selling is always excluded from the picture. But a broadcast and print advertisement can be regarded as direct marketing if it enables an easily observable behavioral response, such as a request for information or a direct order.

The next section of the chapter provides a brief overview of lists. The two following sections treat the unique facets of direct mail and telephone marketing and their frequent use in concert. We examine the range of communication goals pursued in the advent of the World Wide Web and conclude with a discussion of procedures for measuring the effectiveness of programs in the one-to-one media.

Lists

Outbound telemarketing and direct mail require a list. Lists can be generated from internal databases, such as the company's customer files, also called the *house list*. Lists can also be rented or purchased from external sources. For example, show management can provide exhibitors a list of preregistered attendees for a trade show. An insurance company trying to line up additional agents to carry its line may rent names of independent agents in the markets it wished to develop. In addition, trade publications are popular sources of lists.

Not all external lists are created equal. We can distinguish two broad classes of lists on the basis of their origins: compiled lists and response lists, basically the house files (customers and inquirers) of other companies.

Compiled Lists

Some business lists, called **compiled lists**, are assembled by companies that comb directories and public records, and even make physical observations. For example, American Business Information, Inc., collects data from Yellow Pages, Business White Pages, annual reports, and SEC information in concert with government data, business magazines, professional directories, and more. Over 14 million phone calls are made to update and verify the accuracy of records on 10 million businesses, 160,000 firms with 100 or more employees, hundreds of thousands of physicians and 1.5 million professionals (accountants, architects, dentists, attorneys, etc.).

The names from compiled lists generally can be rented for one-time-only use for $70 to $120 per thousand, with perhaps a $350 or 5,000-name minimum order. Reuse of the names constitutes theft and can be detected by a list provider from a few bogus names seeded into the list for such control purposes.

Sometimes multiple mailings are needed. For example, some direct marketing programs are intended to gather customer feedback, preferences, and more by questionnaires. In this setting, response rates to a mail survey can be increased when the direct marketing researcher (1) makes a telephone prenotification, (2) mails a personalized cover letter with the questionnaire, and then (3) follows up with a postcard reminder. For a higher price than a list for one-time use, the research company may purchase a compiled list in machine-readable format and use it repeatedly. Alternatively, data can sometimes be obtained on a subscription basis on CD-ROM or other computer medium—or even downloaded for a fee from the compiler's web site.

Response Lists

Who would you guess is the best prospect to enroll in a correspondence course in how to teach computer graphics: Margaret Smith, drawn from a compiled list of fine arts teachers in secondary schools, or Leonard Brown, a paid subscriber to *PC Graphics* magazine, or Julio Guerra, a six-months–ago buyer of educational software from the MacZone catalog? Direct mail professionals would bet on Julio, the recent catalog buyer, because he is *mail-responsive.* If we are asking potential customers to order by mail or phone, we will generally find that those with prior buying experience with the medium are most responsive. Lists of another company's previous mail or telephone purchasers or inquirers are called **response lists**.

Of course, the *PC Graphics* subscribers probably started or renewed their subscriptions by mail and, technically, could be dubbed a response list too. But magazine subscribers better reflect an affinity for the editorial thrust of the magazine than a propensity for mail order purchasing. Because almost anyone with a subscription to a magazine has signed on or renewed by mail, subscriber lists don't well identify the mail- or phone-responsive buyer.

Renting and Using Lists

Marketers typically obtain lists from compilers or brokers. List brokers are professionals serving both list owner and marketer. List owners pay brokers a commission (usually 20 percent of the basic rental price) for "merchandising" the list—fitting it with an assortment of other lists, matching it to marketer needs, and executing the exchange. Marketers rely on broker knowledge of their business and their insight into the character of different lists. Any broker can provide at least 95 percent of all the lists available, but usually a marketer relies upon and enjoys a close working relationship with just one or two.[4]

Compilers invest heavily in the collection and verification of data in the public or commercial domain, and then generate revenue in the rental and resale of those data. Compiled lists offer an opportunity to saturate a niche or larger market segment. But don't assume complete accuracy or coverage! In times of corporate restructuring, relocating, and so on, a portion of almost every database is obsolete within weeks of its entry. List users should ask compilers about deliverability guarantees and measures to verify and update data. Some trade publishers, such as Virgo Publishers, **telequalify** their subscription list, which means that they call each subscriber to verify that person's title, level of purchasing influence, and type of products purchased. Telequalified lists cost more, but there is less wastage due to mail going to people who never buy the offered product or to people who have moved or changed jobs. Some lists grow stale at a rate of up to 2 percent per month, so a year-old list can yield less than 80 percent coverage.

Business marketers sometimes complain that they get minimal service from their compiler or list broker. In part this stems from their relatively small impact on broker or compiler revenue. Your firm's interest in renting a list of 10,000 electrical supply wholesalers may be dwarfed by the broker's consumer goods clients renting names by the millions. Many business marketers enlist a direct mail or telemarketing consultant in this environment.

One-to-One Marketing Programs

The mail and telephone account for the vast majority of spending in the world of one-to-one marketing. One study pegs business-to-business spending on direct mail and telephone marketing at $4.5 billion.[5] In the exploding field of electronic commerce, the

List compilers gather data from public records and their own research to produce lists that mailers will rent or purchase.
Courtesy Acton.

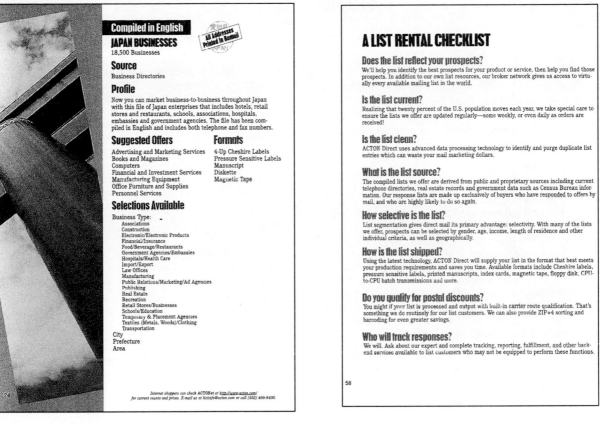

numbers are not so well established, but most agree that business marketers are making significant investments to discover and harness the potential of the Internet. The next sections discuss the management of mail, telephone, and Internet marketing efforts.

Direct Mail

Direct mail can provide business marketers with a number of advantages. Direct mail excels at delivering a personalized message at a precise point in time to a well-defined audience. The cost per contact is greater than print advertising but typically less than the telephone. Direct mail is almost always much lower than the $250 personal sales call. Indeed, from a comparative cost of one or more personal sales calls, some boldly creative and extravagant direct mail programs are executed.

Direct mail probably leads all other media options in terms of versatility. Your mailbox at home may be stuffed with promotions to apply for the American Express card, order your class ring at the campus bookstore, and renew you membership in the Sony CD club. While these examples hint at the range of communication objectives supported by direct mail, the staggering array of business-to-business direct mail is largely hidden. Use the "spectrum" in Exhibit 12–1 and a few examples to appreciate the multi-purpose utility of direct mail.

12–1

FROM THE FIELD

A 7-Page Invitation to the Pole

One of the most famous sales letters in business marketing raised $600,000 for the Admiral Richard E. Byrd Polar Center. And it was all done on a $5,000 budget! Without money for a slick four-color brochure, the letter had to paint the picture:

Dear Mr. _____

As Chairman of the Admiral Richard E. Byrd Polar Center, it is my privilege to invite you to become a member of an expedition which is destined to make both news and history.

It will cost you $10,000 and about 26 days of your time. Frankly, you will endure some discomfort and may even face some danger.

On the other hand, you will have the rare privilege of taking part in a mission of great importance of the United States and the entire world. A mission, incidentally, which has never before been attempted by man.

The letter went on to describe the purpose of the expedition, the itinerary, and the rarity of this opportunity, closing on page 7,

To reserve your place in the expedition, just drop me a note on your letterhead or personal stationery, with your deposit check for $2,500, made out to the United States Trust Company. Incidentally, if anything prevents your leaving as planned, you can send another in your place; otherwise cancellation cannot be accepted later than 30 days before departure. . . .

I hope we may hear from you soon—and that we will welcome you to the expedition.

Sincerely yours

Edward C. Bursk

Ed Bursk was then editor of the *Harvard Business Review*. All 60 seats on this North Pole expedition were booked. Direct mail consultant Dick Hodgson points to this classic to emphasize that "there is no such thing as a letter too long, just too boring."[6]

Communication Goals

Create Goodwill At the "please like us" end of the spectrum, direct mail is used to send gifts, greetings, thanks, and even apologies. The goal is *goodwill*. A Midwestern builder got into hot water with area real estate agencies when one of its now dismissed marketing employees sold a few homes directly, enabling the buyer to avoid the agent's commission, but really free riding on some of the agents' marketing effort. To repair damaged credibility and reenlist agent support, the builder used private couriers to deliver two-pound boxes of fresh-made, premium chocolates, a letter of apology, and a humble plea for "another chance." Of course, the message and the candy were shared throughout the offices. The builder enjoyed record showings that spring.

Develop Familiarity and Interest The theory motivating a mailer's interest in response lists can similarly anchor the communication objective to *establish mail responsiveness* and perhaps build or identify *interest in the general product category*. We have already noted that compiled lists often contain names of individuals with an aversion to mail. It may prove useful to execute a low-cost mail program that weeds out such nonprospects and that allows costlier programs to be applied to a better prospect pool. For example, the 3M Corporation sells overhead projectors through the mail. To establish mail responsiveness it first offered prospective buyers a Wharton School white paper on

Exhibit 12–1   Martiny & Company Direct Marketing Sales Spectrum

Please Like Us Because We're Nice (and the $$ will come) ——————————————— Please Give Us The $$ Now!

Public Relations/Good Will Mailings	Establish Direct Marketing Relationship	Establish Indirect Interest	Establish Direct Interest	Product/Service Demonstration	Traffic Builder	Selling to "Retailers" or Opinion Leaders	Mail Order
Get your prospects and customers to *like* you more than they like your competitors; ideal when perceived parity exits among competing products and services.	Cost effective way to identify prospects, especially when universe is very large; enhances profitability of future mail programs because you eliminate waste.	Offer or send sales information; *arena information*; can generate significant response rates by appealing to professional or personal motivation rather than specific services; inquiries are generally of a lower quality but greater quantity.	Offer or send information specifically about your products or services; best results are attained when audience is pre-qualified; excellent for customer retention.	Surrogate sales call; can "set up" prospect for actual sales call, offer a "rep-to-call," or send trial opportunity incentive.	"Drive" guest or prospect to a specific location	Persuade third parties to sell, refer or recommend your products or services; important mail marketing tactic when expert advice is sought.	Programs that seek to generate profit by selling a product or service that can be purchased via the mail; examples include financial solicitations such as credit cards, home equity loans, and investment services; books, newsletters, and other mail order items.

SOURCE: "Direct Marketing Sales Spectrum," reprinted with permission of Martiny & Company, Cincinnati, OH.

the effectiveness of overhead projectors in professional presentations. Those who ordered this free publication were then targets of mail promotions selling projection equipment.[7]

The use of the mail in a complex multistep selling process also involves the *generation of inquiries and leads.* This approach is common when we need to better qualify our target before mailing an expensive literature packet, a costly catalog, or a demonstration system.

There are two types of lead strategies: loose and tight. **Loose lead strategies** attempt to generate as many leads as possible, relying on a qualifying process to sort out good leads from bad. Markets with high turnover among buyers or many members in the buying center, new products, and forays into new markets are situations that call for casting the widest net possible.

Tight lead strategies seek to generate response from individuals who are already highly qualified. Obviously, the response generated from a tight lead strategy should be closer to the actual sale, if not the sale itself, than a loose lead strategy. Loose lead strategies look for anyone remotely interested; tight lead strategies look for buyers. Stable markets, limited selling capacity, and high-cost-per-sales-call situations require tight lead strategies.

A lead strategy will affect list choice and may also affect the choice of direct response medium. A tight lead strategy may combine direct mail with telemarketing aimed at a focused list, whereas a loose lead strategy may combine advertising with direct mail. Additionally, the type of lead strategy will also influence the message content, for more should be known about the members of a list used for a tight lead strategy. Thus, the message can be aligned more closely to the prospects' needs.

Provide Demonstrations   Under the right conditions the mail can, indeed, *provide a product demonstration.* Software demonstrations are widely distributed by mail. Video demonstrations can be provided for less than $5. We know of a hospital garment manufacturer that sent hospital buyers a small box containing water, a jar, two small squares of fabric, and instructions for a test comparing the migrations or "wicking" tendencies of the two fabrics. (Spreading fluids can transmit germs.) Interestingly, the program was designed to look not too slick—two colors, plain box, crooked label—like a resourceful salesperson put the simple program together.

Build Traffic   We have illustrated the use of direct mail to *generate traffic* to a trade show exhibit. Similarly, the mail can be used to spark calls to wholesalers or bring prospects to a dealer's showroom. Mita works in partnership with its select office system dealers to get potential customers to view its new models of copiers and faxes.

In a remarkably clever program IAMS works closely with kennel operators and dealers to keep puppies on the IAMS diet after they go home with new owners. Kennels receive $5 from IAMS for every new owner name. Within 24 hours of getting a name, IAMS mails a "puppy pak" of its specialty dog food and a letter identifying the location of IAMS dealers in the area.

Influence the Channel   Naturally, the mail can be used to *sell to retailers or other influencers.* Pharmaceutical companies are major users of mail to this end. If doctors, dentists, or veterinarians will accept and distribute drug samples, they are highly likely to write prescriptions for the same. (We've never visited a doctor who gave us a four-day supply of a drug sample and then wrote a script for a different drug to take us to the end of the treatment regimen.) In a dramatically successful dealer recruitment program, a former corporate sales rep sent personalized video presentations to 100 of his successful friends in the field, inviting them to join his new financial services company as agents.

Hewlett-Packard builds a compelling sales offer on a strong letter in an envelope that seizes attention. An informative brochure, a second letter attempting to close, and a rebate certificate/order card complete a model mail program.
Courtesy Hewlett-Packard; photo by Michael J. Hruby.

Direct Order Finally, direct mail efforts can seek purchases. Catalogs represent a significant source of revenue for computer accessories, office furniture and supplies, books, and MRO items. In 1996, catalog sales to business accounted for $28.6 billion.[8]

Other communications through the mail may solicit registrations at a professional conference, new subscriptions to a market scanning service, or the latest desktop project management software. From the Field 12–1 shows the power of direct mail in a most unusual invitation. Within an established business relationship, the mail allows efficient and pinpoint targeting of communications for renewals, product upgrades, and changes in operations. When these communications have primarily a goodwill objective, we cycle right back to the left-hand side of the spectrum to consider the "please like us" capability of the mail.

The Elements of Direct Mail

Direct mail has up to four elements: the envelope, the offer, the enclosure, and the reply. Not all direct mail will contain all four elements. Self-mailers, such as postcards and catalogs, don't have envelopes. Their mailing label is affixed to the actual direct mail piece and self-mailers usually don't have enclosures. The principles, though can be applied to all direct mail.

The Envelope The outer wrapping of the direct mail piece is the first element that can get the attention of the intended reader. The average business decision maker spends less than five minutes going through the mail—much may be thrown away without being opened, let alone read. According to the Direct Mail Institute, the reader will spend 11 seconds to determine whether to read a piece or throw it away. The envelope, then, carries most of the weight in the decision to read or discard the entire piece.

The first thing a person usually checks is the name and address, asking, Is this for me and did they get my name right? The second element is the return address. Mail is more likely to be opened when the reader recognizes the sender. First-class postage indicates that the mail is more important than cheaper rates show.

Odd-sized envelopes are more likely to be opened, but also cost more to send. Many companies are printing a benefit statement or some other attention-getter on the envelope to encourage prospects to open the package and read the contents. Exhibit 12–2

Exhibit 12–2

Getting Your
Envelope Opened

Create urgency	Use deadlines ("order by July 1!"), scarcity, (while supplies last!"), and simulated overnight mail.
Teaser headlines	Tantalize the target reader. Don't tell the whole story.
Envelopes with no return address	Sometimes they arouse curiosity. Don't send to customers.
Pointed versus rounded flaps	Rounded flaps look commercial. Pointed flaps are common in greeting cards, invitations, and other personal communication.
Address on the flap side	This saves the seamless side for a promotional message.

SOURCE: Adapted from Rene Gnam, "How to Make Your Envelopes Work Harder," *Direct Marketing to Business Report* (October, 1995), p. 15.

lists a number of ideas for increasing the attention-getting power of envelopes. Without neglecting attention to the functional necessities of the envelope—protecting the contents—recognize the importance of the envelope in getting the potential reader's attention.

The Offer   The offer is the description of the product or service offered, so the offer can include the interior of a catalog or a letter. It helps to think of the offer being conveyed in a letter because (1) it usually is in business and (2) even when the offer is conveyed by other means (e.g., sales call, catalog) the letter as a metaphor is quite fitting and powerful. Remember, the mail system was developed to enable one person to write a letter to another. We greatly underutilize the channel of communication if we simply stick a piece of advertising into an envelope. A brochure alone will not suffice.

An offer includes a description of the product or service, the benefits it provides, and the terms of purchase. But how these facets are communicated determines the success of the offer.

Begin with a benefit. The reader wants to know quickly, "What's in it for me?" Then enlarge on the benefit. Be as specific as possible so that the reader knows exactly what will be received. Some successful direct mail copywriters have used the position of the inside address on a letter as a benefit summary or teaser. Thus, they preserve the appearance of a letter, but use the format creatively to pursue the (action) objectives of the communication.

Proving benefits is important in any marketing communication, but particularly important in direct mail because even in multimedia programs it carries the majority of the burden of establishing credibility and must rightly anticipate objections. For example, it is not enough to say that the buyer will save money in the long run—offer proof. Proof can come in the form of case studies showing what other companies saved; endorsements are a similar form of proof. Additional sources include third-party research and articles reprinted or quoted from trade publications. Free trials or demonstrations also offer proof and should be used when completely proving value cannot be done in the mail package by itself.

The Enclosure   The enclosure plays a supporting role to the offer. Proof statements, such as case studies, can be part of the enclosure if separate from the offer. Free samples, computer disks or videotapes with video demos, or specialty advertising premiums can serve as enclosures. A **dimensional** is the term mailers use for an enclosure that is something other than flat pieces of paper.

Fed Ex uses a powerful headline in a letter's usual location for the inside address.

Courtesy Federal Express.

> *Federal Express will carry an unlimited number of your 2 day boxes.*
>
> *And each box can weigh up to 150 pounds.*
>
> Please return the enclosed card
> for a STANDARD AIR™ Coupon
> worth up to $11.50.
>
> We were going over our records recently and were pleased to
> see that you're a regular user of our Priority 1® overnight
> service. I'd like to say thanks very much for your confidence
> and we look forward to more of your time-sensitive shipments
> in the months ahead.
>
> At the same time, I thought I'd write and remind you of
> another opportunity you have to count on Federal Express.
>
> Those records we were going over also show that you do not
> currently use our economical, 1 to 2 day STANDARD AIR service.
> Now, I don't know why this is ... but if it's because you're
> giving your less urgent boxes to UPS or the Post Office*,
> I hope you'll give our STANDARD AIR a try.
>
> Just return the enclosed postage-paid card and you'll receive
> a Coupon worth up to $11.50. It's our way of letting you see
> exactly how our 1 to 2 day service compares to the competition.
>
> For example, just ask yourself these questions about UPS and
> the Post Office:
>
>   Do you get on-call pick-ups?
>   Do you get pick-up on Saturday?
>   Do you get discounts?
>
> *U.S. Postal Service

Although enclosures can serve attention-getting functions or as proof sources, enclosures should support and not overwhelm the offer. The offer is more important than the enclosure; no matter how much the buyer likes the enclosure, if there is no reading of the offer, nothing is sold.

The Reply Device   The reply closes the sale. To close a sale, the reply should do four things:

1. Tell the reader what to do: Respond. Leave no doubt in the prospect's mind as to what he or she is supposed to do: Order now. Call to set up an appointment.

2. Make the action easy and obvious. If you are asking for the sale, remember to ask for payment, too. If you are building a database of mail-responsive or otherwise qualified prospects, be sure to ask for the information needed. One direct mail piece sent out by a company included a plastic lobster; the recipient was told to fill out the card and bring it by the company's booth at a trade show in order to register for a free lobster dinner for four. Unfortunately, the mailer didn't include any place on the card to fill out the recipient's name and address! Readers won't spend much time looking for a way to respond. What you want them to do has to be obvious and easy or they won't respond.

3. Include a reason for acting now. When a supply is limited or the product is seasonal, there are genuine reasons for a buyer to act promptly. Other reasons can include a premium or discount for acting quickly. Otherwise, remind readers that the faster they act, the sooner they begin to receive the benefits of the product.

12–1

BUSINESS 2 BUSINESS
Impact from a New Dimension

Each year awards are given to the best art directors, copywriters, and electronic directors for their creative solutions to direct marketing problems. The Caples Awards are named in honor of direct marketing pioneer John Caples. One 1996 Caples winner in the business-to-business category was the creative staff at Catalyst Direct, Inc., not for a program they did for one of their clients, but for a self-promotion intended to bring in new clients.

The promotion mailed Soufflé à l'Orange to direct marketing managers at Fortune 1000 firms with the goal of getting past corporate gatekeepers and generating immediate interest in the Rochester, New York, agency. The supporting copy and foldout poster delivered the message: While everyone has the same recipe, not everyone gets the same results. By calling an 800 number, prospects were put in touch with the "master chefs" at Catalyst.[9]

When one needs to reach identifiable prospects with a high-impact message, the mail is a powerful tool. Dimensionals help to survive corporate mailroom filters on promotional mail and creatively support the message.

Think of a dramatic mail package that your dean might send to 50 CEOs in your college community to entice them to come to next year's case competition, a professionally executed showcase of undergraduate business talent.

---

4. End with a positive picture for the buyer. The last sentence should never be a selfish request for money; rather, reflect on the benefits the buyer will receive.[10]

The reply can be part of the offer. For example, a catalog should have ordering instructions and an 800 number in several places, such as the back cover and perhaps on an insert in the middle of the catalog. A sales letter should end with the reply, a paragraph devoted to how the prospect can take action now. The reply can also be echoed in separate elements, such as a business reply card that can be used as a faxback or mailed in, with an 800 number if the buyer wants to call now. Just adding an 800 number throughout a mailing can more than double a response rate.

Limitations of Direct Mail

Direct mail can work very well when all of the elements work together to secure the sale. While response rates may vary from less than 1 percent to 10 percent or greater, the value of each response can outweigh the cost and make direct mail very profitable. Still, it can take several weeks to design and execute a mail campaign. Nondelivery may shrink coverage by 10 to 20 percent. The recipient's crowded mailbox or overflowing in-basket may interfere with prompt attention and void any urgency in the copy.

Telemarketing

Telemarketing was defined in Chapter 10 as the systematic and continuous program of personally communicating with (potential) customers via telephone or other electronic media. An important point to note in that definition is that telemarketing is both systematic and continuous. *Systematic* means that the campaign is designed to cover a market segment thoroughly and completely. *Continuous* suggests that telemarketing is not a

Customer service representatives respond to inbound calls generated by advertising and hotline calls.
Earl Kogler/International Stock.

random event, but part of a specific strategy of communicating with customers. Telephone programs can be designed, tested, and implemented in as little as a few days. Thus, a learning organization may use the telephone both in its ongoing operations plus in rapid deployment fashion in times of opportunity.

Telemarketing generally triggers recollection of the credit card protection service pitch that came at supper time. But the world of business telemarketing is much different and much larger than that. There are two types of telemarketing: outbound and inbound. **Outbound telemarketing** means that the contact is generated by the marketer; **inbound telemarketing** is just the opposite, with contact initiated by the potential customer or customer. Outbound telemarketing resulted in $130 billion in sales for business marketers in 1995, so you can see that outbound telemarketing is an important marketing communications activity. Inbound telemarketing accounted for over $86 billion, including response to television advertising and catalogs.[11]

Telephone Versatility

By now you should be aware of other objectives the telephone might pursue besides sales. Indeed, there are several purposes or strategies to telemarketing. These include account management, field support, prospector, and customer service strategies.

Account Management   Many companies use telemarketing to serve accounts in a more efficient manner than could be accomplished with a field salesperson. For example, Shell Oil assigned its smaller dealers to a telemarketing sales force. These dealers were not buying enough to cover the cost of field sales calls. After one year of telemarketing account management, the dealers reported higher satisfaction levels because they felt they were getting more attention from their telemarketing rep than they used to get from a field salesperson. Average sales per dealer were also increased substantially.

A firm in the Midwest uses telephone marketing almost exclusively to sell computer software—some costing as much as $100,000. It employs this approach to serve accounts across the world. A central databank of product information and account records can be readily accessed by its technically skilled salespeople. With more efficiency than a rep in the field could offer, accounts receive technical support via phone, fax, and e-mail and get products by overnight courier. When used properly, telemarketing account management improves customer satisfaction and increases sales.

Field Support   In some cases, covering accounts with just a single salesperson is too difficult, yet the account requires personal visits in the field. For example, Schuster Electronics, an industrial electronics distributor in Cincinnati, found that its field salespeople were having difficulty maintaining contact with all of the members of the buying centers. Field visits were necessary, however, in order to work with engineers who design products using Schuster components. The company teamed each field salesperson with a telemarketing rep. Now, when the field rep visits an account, she doesn't have to try to see everyone or drop everything to handle a problem. The telemarketing rep can take care of many problems quicker and more effectively, while also handling follow-up calls on any new members of the buying center. One result has been that, while the company used to lose about 12 percent of its customers each year, now the company retains 98 percent of its customers.

Field support means that the telemarketing rep supports the efforts of an account manager who makes personal visits to the account's location. As in the case of Schuster, most successful firms in this type of selling team their field reps with individual telemarketers, so the result is similar to account management, but responsibility for the account is shared. In most cases, the final decision for account strategy rests with the field rep, not the telemarketer, but compensation for both is derived from combined performance.

Prospector   Similar to support activities, **prospector** telemarketing combines telemarketing with field efforts. The primary difference is that once a prospect is identified, the account is turned over to the field force. The telemarketer does not make any further calls on the account. In some cases, a telemarketer may work with an individual rep, but more likely, the telemarketer supports the efforts of several reps.

One company that found this method useful is Infisy, a manufacturing software company in Houston. After trade shows, the company had so many leads that had to be called that the field reps were swamped. Telemarketers called the leads, qualifying prospects over the phone and setting appointments for the field rep with those prospects who were going to make a decision soon. The company further expanded its telemarketing efforts by purchasing lists of decision makers for manufacturing software. Results were so positive that the company doubled its field sales force in order to handle the increased opportunity.

Another use of prospectors is to call **dormant accounts**, or those accounts that have stopped buying. Goodall Rubber, for example, uses telemarketing to reactivate accounts. Reactivated accounts are then turned over to field reps. Additionally, the company can gather useful information about why companies stopped buying from Goodall.

Customer Service and Orders   Most students think of customer service telemarketing as strictly inbound, such as the 800 numbers that you call if you need help with your presentation software. In business marketing, customer service can include both outbound and inbound calls. For example, customer service telemarketing can include follow-up telephone calls to ensure that field service was satisfactory. Burlington Northern/Santa Fe Railroad uses customer reps in its inbound call center to track any caller's order and tell where the shipment is and when it should arrive at the destination.

Customers also expect to find order-taking services on the telephone. Indeed, $34 billion in sales was achieved in 1995 by telemarketers from buyers ordering from catalogs.[12] In most cases, customer service reps take calls in the order in which they are received, rather than handling specific accounts.

Outside Service or In-House Telemarketing

Everyone has used the telephone for some commercial purposes or to coordinate activities. We've scheduled meetings, landed jobs, sold raffle tickets, and confirmed reservations. Indeed, we use this business tool everyday. So why should we bring in outside professionals to assist with telemarketing? When this line of thinking is combined with the prevalence of underutilized staff and phone lines at an organization, in-house telemarketing operations often spring up in a makeshift workspace. This is an accidental commitment to in-house telemarketing.

We would like you to consider the make-or-buy decision more strategically, certainly within your integrated marketing communications strategy, but also as part of your firm's mission and distinctive skill sets. Nearly 1,500 businesses provide telephone marketing services. Some have capabilities limited to lead generation and messaging. Others bring broad experience and capabilities to the tasks of strategic planning, program design, and implementation in coordination with other marketing efforts. What factors should one consider in choosing in-house or outside-vendor telemarketing services?

In-House Advantages   Four factors tend to favor in-house operations. The major strength of a good in-house telemarketing operation is *control*. Representatives can be intensively trained and more knowledgeable about company products and programs than an outside agency. Proximity allows closer performance evaluation, even though most telemarketing activities at outside service bureaus are highly auditable—clients can observe operations, listen to calls, and review computer-generated reports of connect rates, duration, and more.

A second and related strength is *access to the company database*. Although electronic data interchange (EDI) has become increasingly used between marketing companies, resellers, and fulfillment agencies, organizational boundaries still make for distortions and delays in the transfer and dissemination of information. A central database is usually more accessible and current for employees than outside vendors.

Third, special motivation programs and the sustained company culture may be able to *secure a high level of commitment* to a well-integrated operation that is unmatchable by an outside agency. But several professionals caution that this benefit may be an illusion. Jim McAllister at Matrixx Marketing observes, "Often, the telemarketing program has a champion who starts the in-house program with fanfare and company support and commitment. Once the champion leaves, the program is usually inherited by a subordinate without sufficient rank or it's attached to another department head's function. . . At this point the program stops evolving and it becomes static. It can't find a voice, can't command the resources in terms of personnel or systems. This lack of stature and status within the corporation prevents it from playing its proper role."[13]

Companies that attempt in-house telemarketing stand to attain one more key benefit: *they learn*. The individuals involved develop a unique set of skills and build experience in an area of growing importance to the company. As efficiency and effective performance improve, these skills increase in value and may be applied elsewhere in the firm.

Vendor Advantages   Outside specialists can be enlisted by any enterprise. Competition among telemarketing service bureaus and the relatively measurable tasks we give to telemarketing make outside vendors attractive candidates as partners in integrated marketing programs. Let's highlight a few of the potential advantages of outsourcing most telemarketing services.

The telephone is a powerful customer service medium, but can't always stand in place of a personal visit from the supplier.
Courtesy Mantek.

First, an outside company *skirts the investments* needed to do telemarketing. It avoids the need to purchase switching equipment, computers that distribute calls and generate productivity reports, ergonomic furniture, screens and script servers, headsets, trained heads, and more. An outside vendor has already made these capital investments and spreads the overhead costs across a broad base of clients.

Careful vendor evaluations should reveal *a high level of expertise* at a growing number of telemarketing agencies. Look at the experience base of an established agency and at its team of experts. They are apt to be experienced, trained, motivated to serve clients, and ready to go now. Is it reasonable to expect to be able to staff quickly an in-house operation with the same professionalism and expertise? Many firms find the talent pool quite shallow and the time needed to "grow" talent too scarce.

Let's elaborate on the timing issue to recognize the *nimbleness* provided by an outside vendor. Compared to starting an in-house operation, a telemarketing agency can put its people and systems to work on a program much faster. Quick start-up is often a competitive imperative for rapidly changing markets and technologies. Global markets and escalating customer service standards require 24-hour telephone access. A service bureau has staff and systems in place to provide such access. At the same time, when change dictates program termination, it is easier to shut down an agency operation than an in-house unit.

As you can see, strong arguments can be made for both telemarketing options: in-house and outside agency. In general, a firm's initial ventures into telemarketing seem best supported by outside vendors. Experience and broader programs can bring more operations in-house, but this evolution may flow out of a strong working relationship between the marketer and the telemarketing service firm. Jim McAllister at Matrixx paints this picture: "In cases where telemarketing can be truly large-scale, establishing a partnership relationship with a vendor is essential. Over time, the applications change and expand. These dynamics are difficult to deal with in-house. . . . However, a vendor can help the client through the evolution of using telemarketing—if a mutually beneficial partnership is forged. Over time the vendor may execute certain aspects of telemarketing; may help the client execute some in-house, may set up a separate facility for them or even operate an on-premise department—whatever is called for and makes sense over a long-term commitment."[14]

Limitations of Telemarketing

The telephone's strength is also—in a sense—its weakness. It may be great to get a call from your cousin in Germany on your birthday. It's helpful when the bookstore calls to say your order is in. But when you're studying for a critical exam, you don't want to receive a phone solicitation for a new marketing magazine. The telephone is intrusive. Give consideration to the time and duration of business calls. Respect your customer's requests not to be called.

While telemarketing is used to sell everything from 25-cent supplies to $10 million airplanes, telemarketing does have its limitations. For example, the products that Schuster Electronics sells require face-to-face visits so that design engineers and salespeople can work together. Some products are too complex for selling over the phone, for buyers cannot visualize the benefits without seeing demonstrations. Similarly, the buyers' needs may be so complex as to require personal visits in order to define and understand them. Although telemarketing can't be used to demonstrate products or get orders in such cases, we shouldn't neglect the clout of telephone marketing to take requests for additional information, identify decision makers and purchase cycles, qualify leads, schedule personal sales calls, issue appointment reminders, follow up on recent installations, and more.

Both sets of limitations identified in this section—intrusiveness and incompleteness—suggest the inadequacy of the telephone as a stand-alone medium. Indeed, a theme of these communication chapters is that there probably is no such thing as a stand-alone medium. Each medium has certain strengths and undeniable weaknesses. The challenge is to use the different media in concert. The weaknesses of one medium are compensated for by the strengths of the others. The next section briefly surveys the complementarity of these two one-to-one media: mail and telephone.

The Synergy of Mail and Telephone Marketing

Direct mail is probably peerless when measured on the criteria of personalization, amplification of benefits, and forcefulness of the call to action. Dimensionals can be used to get past office personnel who filter obvious promotional mail from their supervisor's inbasket. Moreover, a dimensional can effectively support the printed copy, and will sometimes be retained as a reminder of the sender and the message—a personalized coffee mug or a Tonka truck with seller's logo. Relevant, urgent, and creative as these may be, they still fall short in their capacity to allow dialogue.

In contrast, dialogue is the telephone's unique advantage in the mix. Of course, the telephone might match the mail in terms of urgency and call-to-action effectiveness, and it can be highly personalized too, but it can come in "cold" and fall short of vividness and detail—a key strength of the mail.

Lifting Response Rates

With careful planning, training, timing, and execution, the mail and telephone can be integrated into a highly effective program. A direct mail piece might net us a 2 percent response rate. By introducing the availability of a toll-free call in the mail copy and adding 800 telephone service, potential customers can ask their questions at their convenience with no cost to them. They find value in the ability to initiate this contact and put the seller in a reactive or adaptive mode. It is not uncommon to see overall response rate increases of 50 to 100 percent, to 3 or 4 percent overall.

12–2

FROM THE FIELD

Apes by Mail and Sales Force Support

To secure appointments with chief financial officers at prospective users of its Corporate cards, American Express mailed each at a highly targeted group of companies a series of dimensionals. Direct mail professionals use the term **dimensional** to refer to a three-dimensional package containing a gift or object supporting its message. The first package contained a 14-inch stuffed gorilla and a message about wrestling with travel and entertainment expenses, but no phone number or response card. Successive communications featured an 8-ball and padlock with fitting puns, each with an easier means of responding. Although the program secured a cumulative response rate of over 40 percent, responses came in at a rate that did not tax the follow-up capacity of the American Express sales force.

If we add carefully timed outbound calls to the program, we may well find another 100 to 700 percent lift in response, compared to the base case of mail only. The outbound call has been previewed by the mail package, it reminds the recipient of the prior communication, and it allows for interaction.

A Test for Synergy

The effectiveness of this approach is illustrated in a controlled test of two marketing programs directed at 25,000 small- to medium-sized businesses.[15] Test A featured heavy advertising in national publications and selected local radio. The mail part of the program included a prenotification postcard followed two weeks later by the direct mail package. The program in Test B focused advertising on business decision makers. One week following the initial ad, the direct mail phase began. Then, within 24 to 72 hours of receipt of the letter, outbound telemarketing was applied. Exhibit 12–3 summarizes the media mixes and outcomes.

Although Test B lacked the program visibility of A in the national publications, especially before the company sales force, it clearly bettered A in lead generations. On a cost per lead basis, the score was $200 to $67. But let's not forget the internal efforts to support sales force follow-up and belief in the quality of the leads from Test A. We will examine the quality of sales leads and follow-up in the next chapter.

About the Timing

Many students and professionals are surprised that telemarketing should follow so soon after the mail effort. They contend that calling prospects a day or two after they have received the direct mail hardly gives them a chance to respond; many recipients of the calls would have responded by mail. Hence, this is pushy and wasteful, they conclude.

But think about this for a few moments. We'll take up the waste issue first. Imagine a mailing to 1,000 potential customers can reap a 3 percent response rate if we allow three weeks of measurement. If we call two days after the mail is delivered, only 1 or 2 percent would have placed their order. Let's say 1 percent have ordered. That means 2 percent of the calls are "wasted" on eventual mail customers. But the cost of 20 calls in a program to reach 990 is barely significant.

Exhibit 12–3
Synergy between
Mail and
Telemarketing

	A: Traditional Budget Application		B: Synergistic Budget Application	
	Budget	No. of Leads	Budget	No. of Leads
Advertising	$175K	438	$25K	375
Direct mail	75K	812	63K	750
Telemarketing	—	—	162K	2,625
Total	$250K	1,250	$250K	3,750

SOURCE: Experimental results presented in Ernan Roman, *Integrated Direct Marketing* (Lincolnwood, IL: NTC Business Books, 1995).

Let's regard the cost of 20 "wasted" calls as a surcharge we pay to call potential customers when the impact of the direct mail package is fresh. Call recipients remember the questions that were left unanswered in the mail, or are reminded of the need to act now, or are directed to additional benefits. The combined impact of the two media more than pays for the "wasted" calls.

Similar synergies can be realized when the promotion mix includes other media and communication channels. For example, as Chapter 11 describes, many trade show managers use direct mail to build traffic to their booth. Likewise, inbound telemarketing may rely on the print ads in trade magazines to generate telephone calls. Xerox's laser printing division combines direct mail with field sales efforts, leading to a three-month (or 25 percent) reduction in average sales cycles![16] From the Field 12–2 shows a well-managed mail program that worked strategically within the capacity of the sales force.

Marketing on the World Wide Web

In its 1997 celebration of the best 200 business-to-business web sites, *Business Marketing* magazine opined that "the Web has the potential to be the most powerful customer-relationship–building tool ever invented. In three short years the internet has been transformed from an obscure communications network into a global marketing weapon."[17] In this rapidly changing medium, we can highlight a number of the key strategic applications for the business marketer.

Web Site Goals
Remember some of the web sites to which we have directed you in the prior chapters. You might be able to discern a spectrum of objectives for these different firms. On the one hand, some seem to be offering principally a public relations guide—a history of the company and a well-crafted mission statement. Others clearly aim at generating orders—if not by e-mail, perhaps through one of the regional sales offices or distributors in the directory page. The Direct Marketing Association has examined "best practices" in this new electronic medium and identified three categories of web site goals: strategic channel management, operational support, and traffic generation.[18]

Strategic Channel Management   Many companies have recognized that the Internet is a sales channel, a distribution channel, and a communication channel uniquely accessed by customers and prospects. Indeed, unlike with print or broadcast advertising, direct mail, or outbound telemarketing, the *customer initiates* the contact or site visit. And an increasing number of customers are showing a preference for this channel.

12–2

BUSINESS 2 BUSINESS
Rate a Web Site

In the mid-1990s many organizations felt pressure to develop company web sites. Their goals were not very clear. One marketing executive summed up his company's stance by saying, "We are very sure that we do not want to not be on the web."

Agencies with developing technical and marketing skills were hired to develop company web sites. They were often slow and pointless. Mission statements and company histories dominated the site. Sometimes graphics undermined the very character of the organization. And users visited because the support advertising for the site overpromised the timeliness and depth of information on the site.

Make or recall your last visit to your school's web site. It's an organization you know well now. How does it measure up in truth, user-friendliness, depth of relevant information, and scope of utility?

Therefore, the web site can be designed with the explicit aim of *targeting new customers.* For example, PhotoDisc is a company that supplies photographs to graphic artists to be used in books, magazines, and promotional literature. Like other vendors of "informational" products (e.g., software, research reports, and educational materials), PhotoDisc uses the web as distribution channel by making its pictures available for download. Instead of waiting four days for photo delivery, now customers have instant access—and can pin the blame on copywriting or somebody else in the publication process for a missed deadline.

If business opportunity lies with new customers who prefer to transact electronically, a business should not be surprised that many of its *current customers prefer to use the Internet* as well. In the face of slipping market share, Fidelity Investments went on the Internet to better serve its most active personal and institutional traders. This not only made trading more efficient and informed for Fidelity customers, it meant lower costs to Fidelity.

This potential for the Internet to be applied to *strengthen customer relationships* is well illustrated by FedEx. As you may recall, the FedEx web site provides details on all its services, allows customers to track their packages, takes orders for package pickup, and provides a question-and-answer forum. Moreover, FedEx offer a software package called VirtuaLink, which enables FedEx customers to develop and maintain their own Internet site featuring electronic catalogs, payment and order systems, and—of course—distribution support.

Finally, within this category of web site objectives we must underscore the versatility of the medium in *reseller support.* Fruit of the Loom, the giant T-shirt making subsidiary of Sara Lee, has increased the effectiveness of its distributor network via an on-line system that enables distributors to serve tens of thousands of T-shirt screen printers and other garment decorators. The system allows distributors to design electronic catalogs, integrate inventory with order processing, and manage supplies from all vendors.

Operational Support   Technical integration has enabled many firms to increase the level of service they offer to customers. At the same time service can be provided at lower costs. Instead of staffing or contracting for a 24-hour call center, the web site is always open. Orders can be taken and shipped with great efficiency. And with timely and accurate shipping and inventory data, an added benefit is more economical purchasing and manufacturing. Cisco Systems is a supplier of LAN systems and software, servers, and more. With 1996 sales of $4.1 billion, Cisco boasted the number three position in *Business Marketing's* 1997 top 200 business-to-business web sites largely because it allows customers—many of whom are quite sophisticated in the field of information technology—to design their own system, price it out, and order it on-line. Cisco takes approximately 30 percent of its orders this way and handles approximately 75 percent of its customer inquires on-line. As a result, Cisco reports shortened product lead time, higher accuracy, and a lot fewer product manuals than before it went on-line.[19]

Traffic Generation   None of the objectives discussed in the previous paragraphs will result if customers do not visit the web site. So, it is not at all frivolous to aim for a creative web site. Creativity should strive to apply technology for a competitive advantage and improved customer service. Stunning graphics for art's sake is the wrong path—especially if they take a long time to load on the user's screen or print on the user's equipment.

Use the web site to gather customer information and preferences that can lead to refinement of the site and personalization of the products and services presented. Tools are also available for tracking and analyzing site usage. These can provide directions for site changes. And a changing site seems best able to capitalize on the interactivity the web provides.

Web Site Synergy in Integrated Marketing Communications

The leverage of web sites on the effectiveness in other media—and vice versa—is only beginning to be explored. In contrast, the positive interactions between mail and telephone, and even between the other media in business marketing, have been widely studied in hundreds of marketing programs. We note that most business advertisers put a tag with their web address on their ads, but no integration is evident; we usually cannot discern any "team work" between the media. Remarkably, many web sites have no phone number and no address! This neglects the diversity of communication channel preferences in the market—address and phone are just as easy to include on a web page as the URL on the ad.

Clearly, the opportunities for integrated media abound. Dell computer ads, Marshall Industries ads, and others direct the reader to visit the company web site. In these examples, the web site serves as a problem-solving and selling center. As prospects visit a site and become known customers, they may be contacted and served by other one-to-one media. For example, customers who have not visited a firm's web site for some time can be called or e-mailed an invitation to visit again. Technically complex products can be profiled in direct mail and highly targeted trade magazines—but the details can await the reader's visit to the web site and perhaps an eventual sales call.

Marshall Industries has pioneered the use of seminars on the web. Thus, with no immediate selling objective, the site strengthens relationships with customers when used to train and educate customers in the capabilities of new products or the implications of new regulations. For selling and order placement, other media or other pages on the web site may well lead to a trade show or dealer network. In short, for maximum marketing impact, the web site should benefit from top management support and integration with other elements of the communications program.

Final Words on the Internet

Six years elapsed between the invention of the personal computer and its adoption by 10 million users. In contrast, the first 10 million users of Netscape's Internet browser came in just 10 months! Like an 800 number, the Internet allows boundless customer-initiated access that is free. The inbound telephone metaphor is limited, however, in that the information content of Internet-based interactions far surpasses that of the typical phone call.[20]

The successful pioneers on the web have used the system to achieve three broad types of objectives. The first we called effective channel management. It includes employing web sites to target new users, satisfy the communication channel preferences of existing customers, develop deeper relationships, and effectively deliver information-based products. Second, the web has been used to hike customer service levels and bring needed operational efficiency. Innovative companies have designed web sites to support customer problem solving, order placement, and delivery. Payoffs in inventory management, billing accuracy, and production planning have been realized. Finally, many firms have pushed the frontiers of creativity to attract and engage visitors to the site.

Despite its power and unfolding potential, the Internet is not a stand-alone medium. User preferences for different communication channels will persist and some communication objectives—such as drawing new customers or negotiating a custom service—will require other media and personal selling. Astute business marketers will orchestrate the role of the web site among roles of other media to fittingly attend to different segments, with varying degrees of product understanding and buying readiness as well as different information requirements.

Evaluating Communications Effectiveness

When telemarketing and direct mail seek immediate action—inquiries, orders, survey responses—the business marketer can use experiments to compare the effectiveness of different programs. **Experiments** involve the systematic manipulation of variables to allow the detection of cause-and-effect relationships.

In experimentation terminology, we use the term **independent variables** to designate the factors we manipulate (price, headlines, telephone script, copy strategy, etc.) or control by selection in our marketing program (size of firms targeted, list source, time since last purchase, etc.). The **dependent variables** are the effects or outcomes of the experiment. If we carefully apply experimental design principles, the differences on the dependent variables can be causally attributed to the independent variables.

Experiments enable marketing managers to develop an understanding of the effectiveness of communications. Tests comparing the effects of different alternatives on key objectives—dependent variables—make marketing activities accountable and enable managers to learn and adapt. Learning involves generating options, trial and error, making adjustments, and further trial. With learning, managers can improve the quality of their communication programs. Such learning is the primary objective of all evaluation processes.

Summary

The mail and the telephone were invented to allow one person to communicate with a specific other person. Both media can be engaged to achieve particular communication objectives across a spectrum ranging from awareness and liking to "give us the money now." As the primary media of direct marketing, mail and telephone marketing often are regarded as synonymous with direct marketing.

Precision targeting is enabled by in-house databases or outside lists. External lists represent the house lists of other companies or data compiled by firms from public records and directories. Usually, lists are rented for one-time-only use, but many compiled lists can be purchased or obtained on a subscription basis for multiple use.

Direct mail communications generally comprise four key elements: the envelope, offer, enclosure, and reply. Each has a role to play. While the envelope must protect the contents economically, the envelope also delivers the first impression of the mailing. The offer conveys credible descriptions of the benefits provided by the product and services and outlines the terms of payment and delivery. An enclosure—typically a brochure or video—supports the offer with graphics and drama. The reply device closes the sale or encourages the sought response, and must be simple to understand and execute. A breakdown on any one of these four essentials can cripple an otherwise sound mail program.

Telephone marketing consists of both inbound and outbound calling and can be performed by an external agency or a company unit. The in-house unit maximizes control and has full access of the internal database. It also enables the company to develop experience and skills in a growing business activity. But an outside vendor brings trained people and all the systems to the task, eliminating most of the needed capital investment. The outside vendor can set up and shut down quickly. We recommend that a business marketer forge a close working relationship with an outside vendor to develop telemarketing experience. Then see if it makes sense to invest in the training, hardware, and systems for an internal telemarketing unit.

Telephone marketing can also be used for a wide array of communication objectives, spanning prospecting, lead development and qualification, sales support, order taking, customer service, and even consultative selling.

Many firms are realizing synergies from integrated marketing programs that combine the personal intimacy and detail of the mail with the interactivity and urgency of the telephone. Generally it is highly effective—and not at all wasteful—to closely sequence mail and telephone contacts because overlap is small and the repetition of messages by a different medium reinforces those messages.

We used inbound telemarketing as a metaphor for the customer-initiated interactions on the World Wide Web. But web sites far outrun the telephone in their capacity to deliver information. Companies have used their web sites to bolster company image and develop brands, but increasingly we see web sites designed to manage channels of communication with new and current customers, open new channels, solidify existing channels of distribution, and develop stronger relationships with customers. We also see web commerce providing significant economies in customer service and logistical functions via more accuracy and speed in ordering, delivery, and inventory management. Many companies are striving to harness creativity and technology to make their web sites attractive and engaging without losing focus on customer needs and the tasks to be done. Effective web sites are part of an integrated marketing communication program.

Sound, accurate evaluation processes enable organizations to learn and adapt their communications programs. Because they typically pursue immediate and easily observed behavioral outcomes, mail and telephone communications can be evaluated with experiments. Experiments allow the detection of cause-and-effect relationships.

Key Terms

compiled list	experiment	prospector
dependent variable	inbound telemarketing	response list
dimensionals	independent variable	telequalify
direct marketing	loose lead strategy	tight lead strategy
dormant account	outbound telemarketing	

Discussion Questions

1. A number of marketing professionals have flatly stated that the telephone is not a stand-alone medium. Do you agree or disagree? Why?

2. Typically, is there a communication channel or media preference for parties in an established relationship? That is, do the parties settle into preferred means of communicating one-to-one? Please illustrate.

3. Compare direct mail, telephone, and print advertising on speed of communication to the market, beginning with resolution of the communication objectives and the creative strategy. How long does it take to create, produce, and deliver the message by each medium?

4. It's probably a bit far-fetched to sell grinders to the ceramic industry by mail. Nevertheless, we might identify several key communication objectives for mail in the selling process. Discuss.

5. Advertisers often use a cost per thousand (CPM) measure as a standard for first-cut comparisons across different media. CPM numbers might run $45 for a jazzy color ad in a trade magazine, $450 for a direct mail program, and $4,500 for a telephone effort. Briefly outline why mail and phone costs are often justified, despite the apparent advantage of the print medium.

6. In this same vein, we know that the average personal sales call in business marketing runs about $300. Identify three communication tasks each for mail and telephone marketing that stand to improve the productivity of a company's sales calls.

7. Much of our understanding of experimental design comes from agriculture, where different seeds, fertilizers, pesticides, and the like were tested in different soils or elevations for their effects on yield (bu./acre), harvest quality, and—when possible—profit per acre. Sketch the essentials of a marketing experiment to test two different copy strategies, two different price terms, and the order of the planned mail and telephone contacts for offering a training program targeted to 28,000 real estate appraisers in the United States. Identify and make the case for at least two useful dependent variables.

8. "Response rate tests are a trap. Sure, they allow you to hone your current program—always trying to beat the 'control' letter or top the proven script. But if you're not careful, all your efforts are tactical and no effort is expended on strategic market development or programs with longer-run payout." Comment.

9. Convince an industrial distributor why it should enclose a business letter to its accounts with the trifold brochure introducing its new lines. (The cost of the brochure is subsidized by the new suppliers.)

10. A pet food company designed a promotion to introduce a new doggie dental product to the market through veterinarians. The program called for both mail and telephone communications, but there were two competing theories at the company

involving which should come first: the phone call or the mail package. An experiment was set up by the firm's ad agency with close collaboration with an outside telemarketing service bureau. Which do you think did better in terms of generating requests for sample products? Why?

Internet Exercise

The following companies have received high marks from industry observers and trade publications for the quality of their web sites. Visit two or three to make your own assessment. Compare them on speed, match to intuitive structure, and overall effectiveness on the goals you believe the web site pursues.

In an imagined integrated marketing communication strategy, sketch the message, target, and relationship of at least three other media to these sites:

http://www.ibm.com
http://www.deere.com
http://www.pitneybowes.com
http://www.cisco.com
http://www.firstdatacorp.com
http://www.amp.com
http://www.goodyear.com.
http://www.hilton.com

WWWW
I N T E R N E T

Cases

Case 12.1 Direct Marketing the NanoV

NanoViz is a new company started by Billie Jean Hudak and Martin Wilkomen, two former tech heads, to develop and market small projection equipment for computer-driven presentations. For example, the current product line features four models ranging in price from $1,399 to $1,899. The firm's leading seller, the NanoV, sells for $1,599 and allows a presenter (a salesperson, professor, seminar leader, etc.) to connect the sandwich-sized projector to the video out port on almost any VCR or notebook computer. Clear images are then projected on an ordinary screen or—in a pinch—even a wall. One leading computer magazine recently reviewed the NanoV in its new products feature, calling it "the next best thing to buying a cinema."

Hudak and Wilkomen don't want to sell through intermediaries, having been burned in their earlier days by a large department store that reneged on a large order of another home entertainment product. The partners have asked you to pick up the pieces of the marketing plan begun by Billie's father, just before he had a near-fatal heart attack.

NanoViz is working with little cash right now. Over 90 percent of its $500,000 in assets are tied up in parts (30 percent) and finished goods inventory (70 percent). Product costs run about $330 at the bottom end of the line to about $710 at the top end. Direct costs on the NanoV are $759. About $40,000 is on hand now for marketing, but crisp and early sales could fund substantially more marketing activities.

The following costs illustrate a number of the media options available (M = 1,000; MM=1 million):

Four-color ad in *PC Tec* magazine (circ. = 1.1 MM)	$14,000
Black-and-white ad	8,000
Four-color ad in *Sales & Marketing Tips* mag. (circ. = 2.6 MM)	18,000
Black-and-white ad in *Wall Street Today* (circ. 21 MM per column inch)	600

Mailing lists:	"Big Business" (n=125,407)	$80/M
	University Info Technology directors (n= 27 M)	$70/M
	Razor Image catalog six-mo. hot list (n=49, 379)	$90/M
	Trade show exhibit and receptions/demo	$5K to 15,000

Web site development: $5M-$25M; $10,000/mo. for upkeep.

Postal charges as low as $.20

Telephone service bureau: outbound calls @ $1.50 ea.; inbound calls @ $4.50 ea.

Outline communication objectives against targets, appeals, media, and expenditures over the coming year.

Case 12.2 Direct Mail Testing at Precision Valve

Precision Valve Corp. was about to initiate a new program directed to municipal water utilities. With 12,000 utilities in its target market, some debate among the managers developed over whether the safety or economy should be stressed in the program. Using 400 labels printed in Zip code order, Precision Valve sent letters emphasizing safety to the first half and emphasizing economy to the second 200 utilities.

Is this a good experiment? Does it allow Precision Valve to attribute differences in response rate to the appeal in the letter?

It's not unusual for companies to test program A against B by mailing program A in March and program B in April. Is this a good experiment? To what else can we attribute differences between the two programs? Would it be better to mail A and B at the same time to a sample of prospects (randomly assigned) one half to each of the two programs?

Additional Readings

Alba, Joseph, John Lynch, Barton Weitz, Chris Janiszewski, Richard Lutz, Alan Sawyer, and Stacy Wood, "Interactive Home Shopping: Consumer, Retailer, and Manufacturer Incentives to Participate in Electronic Marketplaces," *Journal of Marketing* 61 (July 1997), pp. 21–37.

Best Practices in Interactive Marketing: A DMA Management Guide, prepared by Price Waterhouse. New York: Direct Marketing Association, 1997.

David Shepard Associates, *The New Direct Marketing.* Homewood, IL: Business One Irwin, 1990.

Dwyer, F. Robert, "Direct Marketing in the Quest for Competitive Advantage," *Journal of Direct Marketing* 1 (Winter 1987), pp. 15–22.

Forrest, Edward, and Richard Mizerski, eds., *Interactive Marketing: The Future Present.* Chicago: NTC Business Books, in conjunction with the American Marketing Association, 1996.

Frank, Malcom, "The Realities of Web-Based Electronic Commerce," *Strategy and Leadership* 25 (May-June 1997), pp. 30–37.

Harper, Rose, *Mailing List Strategies: A Guide to Mail Success.* New York: McGraw-Hill, 1986.

Hodgson, Richard, *The Greatest Direct Mail Letters of All Time,* Chicago: Dartnell Corp, 1987.

Hoffman, Donna L., and Thomas P. Novak, "Marketing in Hypermedia Computer-Mediated Environments: Conceptual Foundations," *Journal of Marketing* 60 (July 1996), pp. 50–68.

McDonald, William, *Direct Marketing: An Integrated Approach.* New York: McGraw-Hill, 1998.

Miller, Richard N., *Multinational Direct Marketing: The Methods and the Markets.* New York: McGraw-Hill, 1995.

"NETmarketing 200 Best B-to-B Web Sites," *Business Marketing* (November 1997), pp. 1ff.

Roman, Ernan, *Integrated Direct Marketing.* Lincolnwood, IL: NTC Business Books, 1995.

Stone, Bob, and John Wyman, *Successful Telemarketing.* Lincolnwood, IL: NTC Business Books, 1992.

"The Business-to-Business Census: A Benchmark Study of Marketing Spending and Practices," *Business Marketing* (June 1996) Supplement.

The WEFA Group, "Executive Summary," *Economic Impact: US Direct Marketing Today.* New York: Direct Marketing Educational Foundation, 1996.

Appendix

DMA's Guidelines for Marketing by Telephone

The structured use of the telephone to purchase or sell products or services, to obtain or give information to businesses and residences, or to collect funds or support for charities, political parties, and other non-profit organizations is known as telemarketing. "Inbound" telemarketing programs enable consumers to call companies to place orders or receive products, services, or charitable information. "Outbound" telemarketing programs are those in which companies call customers and potential customers to inform them of offers that may be of interest, to provide service information, or to raise funds. For the purposes of these Guidelines, all telephone calls made for marketing purposes will be referred to as "contacts." Those persons who call or who are called by telephone marketers will be referred to as "consumers."

More and more businesses today are using telephone marketing to meet the needs of their customers. Telephone marketing is a person-to-person marketing medium that enables companies to target their products and services to consumers who would be most interested in them.

The Direct Marketing Association's Guidelines for Marketing by Telephone is intended to provide individuals and organizations involved in direct telephone marketing with accepted principles of conduct that are consistent with the ethical guidelines recommended for other marketing media, and with all federal and state laws and regulations. These specific Guidelines reflect the responsibility of the DMA and telephone marketers to consumers, the community, and the industry.

Telephone marketers should be aware of the *DMA's Guidelines for Ethical Business Practice,* the more comprehensive guidelines for all direct marketing. The guidelines are self-regulatory in nature. Telephone marketers are urged to honor them in spirit and in letter. In addition, all telephone marketers should be familiar with the business compliance guides involving telephone marketing practices, for instance, *Complying with the Telemarketing Sales Rule* and *A Business Guide to the FTC's Mail or Telephone Order Merchandise Rule.*

These Guidelines do not cover all of the regulatory requirements that apply to marketing by telephone. Persons who engage in marketing by telephone should take appropriate steps to ensure that their practices comply with all relevant federal, state, and local laws and regulations, including the Telephone Consumer Protection Act (TCPA), the Telephone Disclosure and Dispute Resolution Act (TDDRA), and the Telemarketing

Sales Rule. For a listing of relevant laws and regulations and other DMA resources, see the Appendix to these Guidelines.

These Guidelines are part of the DMA's general philosophy that self-regulatory measures are preferable to government mandates whenever possible. Self-regulatory actions are more readily adaptable to changing technologies and economic and social conditions. Further, self-regulation encourages widespread use of sound business practices.

Prompt Disclosure: Identity of Seller/Purpose of Call Article #1

When calling a consumer, telephone marketers should promptly disclose the name of the seller, the name of the individual caller, and the primary purpose of the contact. Additional information to allow contact with the seller should also be provided.

All documents relating to the telephone marketing offer and shipment should sufficiently identify the full name, street address, or telephone number of the seller so that the consumer may contact the seller by mail or by telephone.

If a telephone marketer is placing or receiving calls on behalf of a seller, and the consumer inquires about the telephone marketer's identity or affiliation to the seller, the telephone marketer should disclose its own name, address, and telephone number as well.

Honesty Article #2

All offers should be clear, honest, and complete so that the consumer may know the exact nature of what is being offered and the commitment involved in the placing of an order or donating to a charity. Before making an offer, telephone marketers should be prepared to substantiate any claims or offers made. Advertisements or specific claims which are untrue, misleading, deceptive, fraudulent, or unjustly disparaging of competitors should not be used.

No one should make offers or solicitations in the guise of research or a survey when the real intent is to sell products or services or to raise funds.

Disclosure of Terms of the Offer/Tactics Article #3

Prior to asking consumers for payment authorization, telephone marketers should disclose the cost of the merchandise or service and all terms and conditions, including payment plans, the availability of refund and cancellation policies, limitations on use, and the amount or existence of any extra charges such as shipping and handling and insurance. At no time should high pressure tactics be utilized.

Reasonable Hours Article #4

Telephone contacts must be made during reasonable hours, as specified by federal and state laws and regulations.

Use of Automated Dialing Equipment Article #5

When using automated dialing equipment for any reason, telephone marketers should only use equipment which allows the telephone to immediately release the line when the called party terminates the connection.

ADRMPS (Automatic Dialers and Recorded Message Players) and pre-recorded messages should be used only in accordance with tariffs, federal, state, and local laws, FCC regulations, and these Guidelines. Telephone marketers should use a live operator to obtain a consumer's permission before delivering a recorded solicitation message.

When using any automated dialing equipment to reach a multi-line location, the equipment should release each line used before connecting to another.

Taping of Conversations Article #6

Taping of telephone conversations made by telephone marketers should only be conducted with notice or consent of all parties, or the use of a beeping device, as required by applicable federal and state laws and regulations.

Monitoring Article #7

Monitoring of telephone marketing and customer relations conversations should be conducted for purposes of training, quality assurance, and to ensure compliance with consumer protection laws and regulations. All employees should be informed of call monitoring, should be made fully aware of why and how call monitoring is done, and should be informed of the results of any monitoring.

Name Removal/Restricted Contacts Article #8

Marketers should remove consumers' names from telephone marketing lists upon consumer request and at no charge. Marketers should maintain and suppress names of consumers who do not want to be called as part of their in-house suppression practices and in accordance with applicable federal and state laws and regulations. Prior to the use of any outbound calling list of consumers, marketers should use The DMA Telephone Preference Service and, when applicable, The DMA Mail Preference Service name-removal lists. Names found on such suppression lists should not be rented, sold, or exchanged.

A telephone marketer should not knowingly call anyone who has an unlisted or unpublished telephone number, or a telephone number for which the called party must pay the charges, except in instances where the number was provided by the consumer to that marketer.

Random dialing techniques, whether manual or automated, in which identification of those parties to be called is left to chance, should not be used in sales and marketing solicitations.

Sequential dialing techniques, whether a manual or automated process, in which selection of those parties to be called is based on the location of their telephone numbers in a sequence of telephone numbers, should not be used.

Collection and Transfer of Data Article #9

Consumers who provide data that may be rented, sold, or exchanged for marketing purposes should be informed promptly and periodically thereafter of the potential for the rental, sale, or exchange of such data and of the opportunity to opt out of the marketing process.

Consumer requests regarding restrictions of the collection, rental, sale, or exchange of data relating to them should be honored.

Telephone marketers using Automatic Number Identification (ANI) should not reuse or sell, without customer consent, telephone numbers gained from ANI except where a prior business relationship exists for the sale of directly related goods or services.

Promotions for Response by 800-, 888-, and 900- Numbers Article #10

Promotions for response by 800- and 888- numbers should be used only when there is no charge to the consumer for the call itself and when there is no transfer from a toll-free number to a pay call.

Promotions for response by 900- numbers or any other type of pay-per-call program should clearly and conspicuously disclose all charges for the call. A preamble at the beginning of a 900- or other pay-per-call number should include the nature of the service or program, charge per minute and the estimated total charge for the call, as well as the name, address, and telephone number of the sponsor. The caller should also be given the option to disconnect the call at any time during the preamble without incurring any charge.

The 900- number or other pay-per-call should only use equipment that ceases accumulating time and charges immediately upon disconnection by the caller.

Children Article #11

Because children are generally less experienced in their rights as consumers, telephone marketers should be especially sensitive to the obligations and responsibilities involved when dealing with them. Offers suitable only for adults should not be made to children.

Pay-per-call services should not be directed to children under 12, unless the service is a "bona fide educational service." For promotions directed to consumers between the ages of 12 and 18, the advertising and the call should clearly disclose that parental or guardian permission should be obtained.

Prompt Delivery Article #12

Telephone marketers should abide by the FTC regulation regarding the prompt shipment of prepaid merchandise, the Mail or Telephone Order Merchandise (30-Day) Rule. As a normal business procedure, telephone marketers are urged to ship all orders as soon as practical.

Laws, Codes, and Regulations Article #13

Telephone marketers should operate in accordance with the laws and regulations of the United States Postal Service, the Federal Communications Commission, the Federal Trade Commission, the Federal Reserve Board, and other applicable federal, state, and local laws governing advertising, marketing practices, and the transaction of business by mail, telephone, print and broadcast media, or any other media.

SOURCE: Reprinted with permission. Copyright © 1997, Direct Marketing Association, Washington, DC.

Chapter 13

Sales and Sales Management

HEWLETT-PACKARD

What computer company is growing at eight times the industry rate? No, it isn't some start-up or lesser known company about to take over the PC business. It's Hewlett-Packard, and it is also the leading UNIX systems vendor in the world.●

Hewlett-Packard has achieved growth rates of 25 percent (from $20 billion in 1993 to $40 billion in 1997) because of two factors: product strategy and sales strategy. The sales strategy was based on two key principles: Free the salesperson to focus on selling and focus that selling effort on specific accounts. For example, Nancy Ewart, HP rep on the East Coast, sells only to banks. This focus on banks has enabled her to develop solutions to computing problems, rather than just push hardware.●

Salespeople were freed from spending time configuring systems. A salesperson in the past might spend 30 to 50 percent of work time in the office, drawing up plans for computer systems. Now, specialists do that, meaning up to twice as many sales calls can be made.●

If an overall 25 percent increase in sales is not enough, one division has grown sales 40 percent in an industry that is only growing overall at a rate of 5 percent! Customer satisfaction has grown, too. As one former IBM customer put it, "When you are dealing with HP they make you feel like you are their only customer . . . I call IBM, I get lost in phone mail."●

Visit its home page: **www.hp.com**●

SOURCE: Daniel S. Levine, "Justice Served," *Sales & Marketing Management* (May 1995), pp. 52–66; "HP Earnings Rise 25 Percent in Fourth Quarter; Revenue Increases 16 Percent; Orders Up 14 Percent," press release, **HP.com/pressrel/nov97.**

Learning Objectives

Most companies spend more on selling than any other element in their marketing budget. They spend so much because personal selling is an effective way to transact business.

In this chapter, we focus on the strategic nature of managing sales. As business marketers, it is important to recognize the many different options from which to choose within the sales function.

After reading this chapter, you should be able to

- Identify sales' strategic communication role.
- Select the types of selling used for different types of relationships.
- Outline the sales strategy associated with each type of selling.
- Compare and contrast organizational structures used to manage sales.
- Illustrate when to use different control and compensation programs.
- Discuss how sales force performance is evaluated.

Professional salespeople are an important element in business. When managed properly, they can contribute to the firm's success, as well as the value produced by the entire value chain.

369

Sales involves professionals satisfying their buyers' needs, such as a plant manager who wants to cut maintenance supply costs, an office manager looking for new computer software, or a doctor who needs to learn about new uses for an old medication.

David J. Sams/Tony Stone Images.

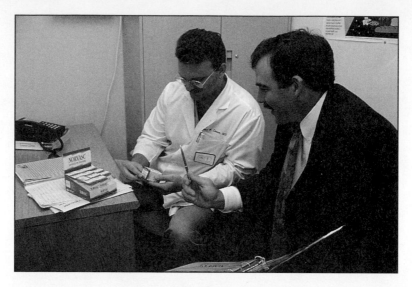

The Nature of Professional Selling

A major premise of this book is that sound business marketing creates value. Yet the public perception of selling is that salespeople deliver value only by accident. The perception is that salespeople are out to get the sale, no matter what—and if the product is really a good one, salespeople and selling really aren't needed.

This perception that salespeople are unethical is unfortunate, for a primary role of professional salespeople is to create value. Most salespeople believe strongly in the efficacy of their product. When this belief is combined with genuine concern for the customer, salespeople are free to create value.

Salespeople Create Value

A doctor with a patient who doesn't respond to traditional treatment is frustrated and unable to come up with a solution. The pharmaceutical salesperson describes a new therapy involving an old drug—the doctor tries it and the patient recovers.

A furniture manufacturer wants to expand but doesn't have the money. Salespeople (called loan officers) from two banks compete for the loan—the local bank wins because the salesperson identifies a free-enterprise zone where the company can expand and save money on taxes. The company builds a new plant and employs 200 more people.

A small manufacturer of trusses (components used in construction) has an old computer that seems to break down two or three times a month—always during payroll. Payroll checks are late and employees are grumbling. They wonder if the company has the money to pay them so they look for new jobs. A salesperson shows how replacing two peripherals can keep the old computer operational for at least a year, until the company has the money to buy a new one. Payroll checks are cut on time and key personnel stay with the company.

While these stories may seem melodramatic, they illustrate the way that salespeople deliver value. Salespeople add value by identifying customer needs and devising or delivering a solution for those needs. Salespeople are able to adapt (change) how a product is presented or even able to adapt the product itself so that it meets the needs of the buyer. Adaptation is something that other forms of marketing communication can't do. Such adaptation powers professional selling, because customers often don't know what they need or how to configure a solution for their needs. For example, how many new plants has the furniture manufacturer's management financed? The current management had never built a new plant before. The loan officers, though, had financed several. Similarly, the truss manufacturer's management were experts in building trusses, not computers. Professional salespeople create value by adapting to fit the needs of the buyer.

Professional Salespeople Are Ethical

As stated earlier, many students believe salespeople will do whatever it takes to get a sale. For example, in a study comparing the perceptions of sales managers and students, students believed salespeople to be less ethical than did sales managers. So those with more direct experience with business salespeople were more likely to report that salespeople have high ethics.[1]

What these findings probably mean is that students expect business to have its dirty dealing, manipulating, and so forth. Salespeople, however, have found that they can be successful and be ethical; in fact, to succeed it is necessary to be ethical. The nature of professional selling in the business-to-business environment supports and encourages ethical behavior. Taking a sales job in the business marketing environment does not mean that a compromise of personal values will be necessary to be successful. Perhaps to understand this more clearly, it is necessary to understand the role of the sales force in the organization.

Sales' Role in the Organization

Sales may be an expensive part of the marketing mix, but the sales function is important for many other reasons than just cost. The field sales force is responsible for managing the personal relationship between the company and the customers. From an integrated marketing communication perspective, salespeople bring the dialogue to life. How they go about their job of selling the product must be consistent with the positioning strategy of the firm and with messages sent through other channels.

Salespeople have further responsibilities, such as coordinating the firm's actions in order to satisfy customer requirements and gaining customer information (from their dialogue) and sharing that information so that appropriate product, marketing, and investment decisions can be made. In other words, the sales force plays a key role in the market-oriented organization.

Managing Relationships

In many cases, salespeople have the field responsibility of deciding which accounts to work with and which accounts to bypass. Other elements in the marketing communication mix do not have the same level of individual dialogue that enables the selling organization to adapt in the same manner as salespeople. Further, the sales force has the responsibility for determining specific account strategy, particularly with respect to how the relationship will be managed. Sales is also responsible for implementing the account strategy and ensuring customer satisfaction.

13–1

FROM THE FIELD
Building Long-Term Partnerships

Pat Lynch Eaton is national account manager for The Freeman Companies, one of the largest service organizations in the trade show industry. Her responsibility is to sell all of Freeman's services, including preparing and decorating convention halls for trade shows, building exhibits and trade show booths, and shipping and storing booths between shows. Pat says that "Working in the trade show industry is, to me, the ultimate challenge. I go to a city where I know no one and in three days, produce a product." That product is a trade show.

Pat believes her attitude of doing the job right leads to mutual admiration for her customer and her company. "I have a personal concern for my customer's results, as well as respect for what they do. And they have the same for me and for Freeman."

Sometimes that means doing things that other salespeople probably wouldn't consider—like staying up until 2 AM, typing attendees' names into the computer because her customers' computer went down and all of the registration information was lost the day before a show was to open.

Or like the time the fire sprinkler system broke at the close of the first day of a music show. "The system dumped several *hundred thousand* gallons of water on grand pianos, carpet and drapes, furniture—on everything." Pat got a work crew right in and they toiled all night. When the show opened the next day, it looked as if nothing had happened.

With this kind of customer service, Pat's customers know they can count on her and Freeman when they are in a pinch. And that kind of trust builds long-term partnerships.

Source: Barton A. Weitz, Stephen B. Castleberry, and John F. Tanner Jr., *Selling: Building Partnerships* (Burr Ridge, IL: Richard D. Irwin, Inc., 1995) p. 383.

Creating Customers for Life

Customer relationships should be managed such that the sales force achieves sales targets. Business is not about making friends, but making customers, preferably for life. For example, an office equipment and supply company can reasonably expect a small law firm to buy $83,800 in office equipment and supplies (not counting computers) over a 20-year period. If that office supply salesperson looks only for a copier sale and doesn't recognize the long-term value of the account, the additional revenue could be lost.[2]

Customer Service

Serving the needs of customers can include training on how to use the product or service effectively, handling customer complaints, and taking care of customer needs. A good example of taking care of customer needs, even though these needs may not be resolved by our product or service, is the story of Pat Eaton in From the Field 13–1.

Serving the customer well is important to all companies. One study found that 65 percent of the average company's business comes from current customers. Another study found the cost of acquiring a new customer to be five times that of keeping an old customer.[3] These figures point out the importance of taking care of the customer in any reasonable manner.

Coordinating Corporate Resources

Salespeople have the responsibility for making sure that the customer is satisfied, but often that satisfaction depends on someone else in the organization doing what should be done (as we discussed in Chapter 7). Salespeople depend on and interact with personnel from manufacturing, shipping, sales administration, credit, and billing, among others. For example, a salesperson may take an order and promise delivery in three months. Achieving that three-month target may mean that manufacturing has to schedule production of the order, shipping has to make sure a truck is available, and the credit department has to approve the customer's credit. If there's a breakdown in any one of those areas, the customer may not get the product when needed. It is the salesperson who coordinates with each of these departments to see that the product is delivered to the customer on time.

Gathering Information

Successful learning organizations gather, share, and act on information. Boundary spanning positions (those that cross beyond the organization's boundaries) are important information gathering and sharing positions. Sales and purchasing can be the two most important boundary spanning positions because of the type of information they gather. (We discussed the information gathered by purchasing in Chapter 3.) Sales' responsibility is to engage the customer in dialogue, or two-way communication to achieve mutual interests. Salespeople also gather information concerning competitors and market factors. Salespeople who only *tell* miss a great opportunity: the opportunity to listen.

Customer Dialogue

The salesperson is only one communication channel with the customer. Companies also communicate with their customers via newsletters, advertising, trade show exhibits, direct mail, marketing show exhibits, and other forms of communication such as marketing research. But because salespeople interact face-to-face with customers, salespeople are able to gather information and then act on that information in a way that brings additional value to customers.

The information gathered by sales concerns customer requirements—important information for the long-term success for any organization. If that information remains only in the mind of the salesperson, however, the organization cannot act to the fullest extent possible. Products will be developed that may or may not fit customers' requirements, for example, or pricing could be too high or too low, or any number of other suboptimal decisions could be made. Just as important as gathering the information is the sharing of customer information with decision makers across the organization.

Competitive Information

In addition to gathering information from the customer, the salesperson is gathering information about competitors and market forces such as the economy. While there are other channels of getting this type of information, salespeople can provide decision makers with timely and necessary information about a number of market factors.

For example, the first time management may hear of a new product is when a customer tells a salesperson about the competitor's proposal. It's more likely that pricing information, competitors' sales strategies, and similar information will be encountered first by salespeople than by any other source.

To summarize, the sales force is an important element in a firm's marketing mix because salespeople manage customer relationships to build sales, manage customer satisfaction by coordinating corporate resources, and gather key customer and market information. Other elements of the marketing mix may also perform some of these activities, but none do all of these activities all of the time and with the efficacy of the sales force.

Exhibit 13–1
Selling Strategies

Script-Based Selling
Customers' needs are similar.   Use same presentation from customer to customer.

Needs Satisfaction Selling
Customer needs vary among   Use questioning techniques to identify needs.
a set of common needs.   Present specifics about product to satisfy important needs.

Consultative Selling
Customer needs vary, with   Use questioning techniques to identify needs.
unique needs from buyer to buyer.   Create or assemble a custom solution to fit needs.

Strategic Partner Selling
Buyer and seller co-create needs and jointly develop solutions.

Sales Strategies and Customer Relationships

The sales force, including sales management, has the responsibility for developing and implementing account sales and relationships strategies. Yet, as we know from Chapter 2, not all accounts want, or are entitled to, the same level of relationship or service. In this section, we will review the types of customer relationships and then discuss the types of selling strategies appropriate for each one.

Types of Customer Relationships and Selling Strategies

In Chapter 2, you discovered a model that indicated two dimensions were important in determining the type of relationship. Each dimension represented the degree of commitment and motivational investment to the relationship, one dimension for the seller and the other for the buyer. In Chapter 3, you learned that buyers are more likely to want a strategic partnership when the product or service supplied is a key element in their ability to create value. Sellers, on the other hand, want strategic partnerships with buyers who are lead users (Chapter 8), represent a large amount of (potential) revenue, and/or provide status. (For example, consultants often list the names of their largest clients in order to gain credibility with the rest of the market.)

When there is little product and service differentiation, there is little need to partner from the buyer's perspective. Similarly, when needs are the same across all customers, buying processes are virtually identical, and all customers are relatively the same size, there is little need to partner from the seller's perspective.

In each case, there is a different type of strategy that can be implemented. There are four basic sales strategies that illustrate the potential range of possible strategies: script-based selling, needs satisfaction selling, consultative selling, and strategic partnering, as illustrated in Exhibit 13–1.

Script-Based Selling

In situations where customer needs do not vary much from one customer to another, script-based selling can be very effective. The product should be relatively simple and easy to understand. Also called canned-selling, **script-based selling** involves using scripts or memorized sales pitches from which the salesperson does not deviate. The method is used by Premier Industrial, a company that manufactures and markets over 5,000 maintenance, repair, and operations (MRO) items. For example, it markets a solder that is much stronger than the solder sold in a hardware store. (Solder is used to weld two pieces together that have to carry electric current, such as welding a wire to a contact on an electric motor.) The strength is evident in a simple demonstration during which the salesperson solders two ends of a paper clip together and asks the buyer to pull the two ends apart. The conversation may go something like this:

Premier salesperson: Do you ever solder anything on the equipment you maintain?

Maintenance manager: Of course.

Premier salesperson: Most guys I talk to resent having to solder the same thing over and over because the solder won't hold. [Buyer nods head to indicate yes.] If I can borrow a paper clip from you, I'll show you that won't ever be a problem for you again.

[Salesperson bends wire into a circle and solders it together.] Now pull that apart. [Buyer tries and fails.] Isn't that the kind of solder you need?

Maintenance manager: Yeah! That stuff's great!

Premier salesperson: How many spools will you need?

While many people may believe scripted selling to be outdated and obsolete, Premier is enjoying an enviable growth rate well in excess of 15 percent per year. Scripted selling is popular in telemarketing and in selling MRO items and other supplies.

Needs Satisfaction Selling

A more advanced method of selling is **needs satisfaction selling**, or a process of selling that involves identifying the buyer's needs and tailoring the sales pitch to fit those needs. Thus, needs satisfaction selling involves two components: identifying the needs and making the presentation.

Needs satisfaction selling works best when there is variance in needs across buyers and choices have to be made among products, as opposed to custom-made solutions. For example, the method is very popular with copier sales companies because the reasons for buying a new copier vary from company to company. In one case, the customer may make 50 copies each time whereas in another case, the customer may only make five copies at a time. In the first case, multiple-copying speed is important; in the second case, how fast the copier makes the first copy is important. In both cases, the total time spent at the copier can vary greatly depending on the model. The salesperson has to find out what the customer needs in order to recommend the right copier.

Consultative Selling

Consultative selling is very similar to needs satisfaction selling, but differs to a matter of degree. When a seller uses consultative selling, the solution choices are not simply a matter of choosing from an array of finished products. When truly using **consultative selling**, the seller is bringing specialized expertise into a complex problem in order to create a somewhat customized solution.

For example, the materials handling industry manufactures and installs customized equipment for moving products through manufacturing processes. Using belts, rails, wheels, hooks, motors, and so forth, products in the process of being manufactured are moved from one machine to the next. The assembly of standard materials handling parts into a customized system is an outcome of consultative selling.

In consultative selling, the salesperson is a consultant. More of the knowledge lies with the salesperson than with the customer in comparison to needs satisfaction selling. Still, there is not the commitment by the customer that exists when a partnership is created.

Exhibit 13–2
Stages in
Relationship
Building

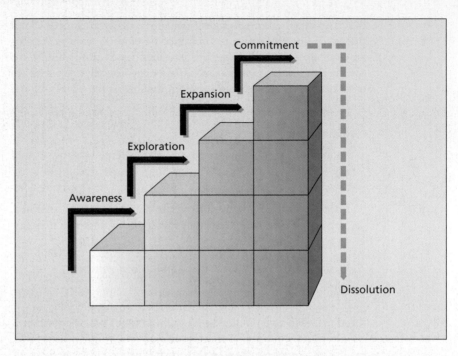

SOURCE: Barton A. Weitz, Stephen B. Castleberry, and John F. Tanner, Jr. *Selling: Building Partnerships.* Second edition. Burr Ridge, IL: Irwin/McGraw-Hill, 1995.

Strategic Partner Selling

Partnering as a sales strategy goes beyond consultative selling. In **strategic partner selling**, both parties share expertise and resources to create customized solutions and there is a commitment to joint planning for mutual benefit. As a sales strategy, partnership selling requires a commitment of resources well beyond that of just the salesperson and customer support staff. A company must also commit resources in all other areas of the firm in order to support the most effective creation of value possible. Further, the result should be a maximization of revenue for all areas of the company.

Partnering is more than just selling strategies aimed at increasing revenue within the account. In the next section, we will discuss selling strategies across the partnering cycle that are designed to lead to long-term commitment.

Selling across the Stages of the Partnership

In Chapter 2, you learned the stages of a strategic partnership, from awareness to dissolution. Here, we focus on the three middle stages—exploration, expansion, and commitment—because these stages separate discrete transactions and functional relationships (which stop at exploration) from strategic partnerships, as illustrated in Exhibit 13–2. Recall, too, the crucial role that trust plays in building a strategic partnership. In this section, we will discuss the selling strategies used in each stage that are designed to create trust.

Exploration

In the exploration stage, the relationship is defined through the development of expectations for each party. Each party, both buyer and seller, explores what the other party has to offer. The buyer tests the seller's product, how the seller responds to special requests, and other similar actions after the initial sale. At the same time, trust and personal relationships are developed.

Salespeople can improve customer satisfaction by making sure customers use the product correctly, as this salesperson is doing.
Courtesy NCH Chemical.

Beginning the relationship properly is important for the relationship to flourish over time. Keep in mind that the customer is excited about receiving the benefits of the product as promised by the salesperson. If the customer's initial experience is poor, it may be extremely difficult to overcome. Beginning the relationship properly requires the salesperson to set the proper expectations, monitor order processing and delivery, ensure proper use of the product, and assist in servicing the customer.

Set Proper Expectations   As discussed in previous chapters, customer satisfaction begins with setting the proper expectations. No marketing communications should inflate the buyer's hopes unreasonably. Long-term relationships are begun by making honest presentations of the product's capabilities and eliminating any misconceptions before the order is placed.

Monitor Order Processing and Delivery   Many people may work on an order before it reaches the customer, but it is the salesperson who is ultimately responsible for making sure that the product reaches the customer at the appropriate time. Business marketing is not like retailing where the customer chooses a product in stock and takes it to the checkout counter; rather, the order is placed and the product shipped at the appropriate time. Because products may not be immediately available from another vendor should delivery fall through, customers rely on companies to meet their delivery promises. Imagine what would happen, for example, if Florida Furniture couldn't get any raw lumber? The plant would shut down. Direct response and EDI have taken the salesperson out of the order–delivery loop in many cases, but in most instances, the salesperson is still responsible for making sure the company lives up to the delivery commitment.

Ensure Proper Use   Some buyers may not know how to operate the basic features of a product. If the product is not operating at maximum efficiency, the customer is losing value. Many firms have staffed a customer service department or tasked their technical support group with training customers, but it is still the salesperson's responsibility to make sure that the customer is getting full value. In England, for example, Thermofrost representatives train users in proper maintenance of their display and storage coolers. Proper maintenance not only increases the life of the coolers but also lowers electricity and repair costs associated with running the coolers.

Assist in Servicing   Although complaints signal customer dissatisfaction, their absence doesn't always mean that the customer is happy. They may speak out only when grossly dissatisfied or the purchasing agent may not be aware of any problems until users become furious. When salespeople assist technical support and customer service personnel in servicing the accounts, salespeople can learn why problems arise. Then they can address similar situations in other accounts before the problems grow into complaints.

Complaints can arise at any stage of the partnership, but when complaints arise during the exploration stage, the salesperson has the opportunity to prove commitment to the account. When customers sense that commitment, either through the handling of a complaint or through other forms of special attention, they may be ready to move into the expansion stage.

Expansion

When a salesperson does a good job of establishing the relationship by ensuring a successful initial experience, the opportunity is there for additional sales. Trust is developing, allowing the salesperson to focus on identifying additional needs and recommending solutions. Note that the following strategies for increasing sales are sometimes used in direct response situations, particularly telemarketing.

Generating Repeat Sales   In some situations, the most appropriate strategy is to generate repeat orders, particularly for supply items and other operating expenditures. For example, Morton provides salt and other cooking ingredients to food manufacturers like General Mills. The best strategy for a Morton's salesperson may be to ensure that General Mills continues to buy from Morton.

Generating repeat sales requires recognizing buying cycles and being present at buying time. For example, Kelly McCourt of Wallace Computer Services, a supplier of business forms and specialized computer papers, has Mrs. Baird's Bakery as one of her largest accounts. By understanding its usage volume, budgeting process, and ordering cycle, Kelly has been able to time her sales calls effectively. She's there when Mrs. Baird's wants her there, with the result that she's grown her share of its business from 20 percent to 70 percent and still climbing.

Salespeople should also continue offering special assistance through value analysis. For example, John Paduch, now vice president of sales for American Supply Co. of Gary, Indiana, saved one customer $1.4 million over a five-year period through various ideas, including one that reduced inventory by 47 percent. Not only did this earn Paduch significant reorders, he was nominated by that customer for *Purchasing* magazine's Top-Ten Sales Rep award.[4]

Upgrading   **Upgrading**, or **upselling**, is similar to generating reorders in that the same general needs are met, only upgrading involves convincing the buyer to use a higher-quality or newer product. The buyer selects the upgrade because it meets needs better than did the old product.

Upgrading is crucial to high tech companies. For example, when Digital Equipment Corp. launched the Alpha AXP, computer industry experts agreed that for the new product to succeed, the sales force had to secure upgrades from Digital's old VAD products. Otherwise, customers would turn to IBM or other vendors and Digital could lose their business forever.[5]

Full-Line Selling   Parker Hannifin (or simply Parker) manufactures and sells a line of industrial valves. These valves come in different sizes and are designed to turn off and turn on the pipelines for different types of materials—some toxic and others harmless.

Exhibit 13–3
Preferred
Supplier Criteria
for Suppliers to
Bethlehem Steel

- *Capability:* The purchasing team examines manufacturing, shipping, and administrative capabilities. Because Bethlehem requires significant monitoring by suppliers, even paperwork is scrutinized.
- *Organization:* Are employees dedicated? Is the company flexible or bureaucratic? Can it change as we change?
- *Financial health:* Bethlehem reviews audited financial statements to determine if the supplier is managed well.
- *Culture.* Does the corporate culture fit with ours? Do we want the same things and do we work in similar ways? Can we get along?
- *Willingness to commit:* Suppliers must be willing to commit the resources necessary to serve the account. For many suppliers, this means a full-time representative on Bethlehem's site.
- *Ethics:* Is the supplier trustworthy?

SOURCE: Adopted from Jean Graham, "A Simple Idea Saves $8 Million a Year," *Purchasing* (May 21, 1992), pp. 47–49.

Depending on the materials that go through the valves, different materials are needed to make the valves. Suppose a buyer manufactures a line of oil storage tanks for use in oil fields, refineries, gas stations, and other situations. If the company bought one type of valve from Parker and other valves from other manufacturers, the Parker rep may try to convince the buyer to buy all of its valves from Parker. Selling the entire line of associated products is called **full-line selling**. Many companies try to get their foot in the door with any sale, hoping to then blossom into full-line selling once the initial product has proven its value.

Full-line selling is not the same as full-line forcing, a practice used when a company has one top-selling product that it sells through distributors. Full-line forcing occurs when the company forces distributors to carry the full line in order to be able to sell the top seller. Full-line selling is a sales strategy that involves leveraging the relationship in order to sell the entire line of products.

Cross-Selling   Similar to full-line selling, **cross-selling** is selling additional products but these products may not be related. For example, the Parker salesperson may also try to sell meters and gauges along with the valves. Cross-selling works best when the salesperson can leverage the relationship with the buyer. Trust in the salesperson and the selling organization already exists; therefore, the sale should not be as difficult if the proper needs exist.

If the buying center changes greatly, cross-selling becomes more like the initial sale. For example, if Parker also has materials handling equipment, that equipment may be purchased by an entirely different set of people. For them, Parker has no reputation or relationship.

Commitment

When the buyer–seller relationship has reached the commitment stage, there is a stated or implied pledge to continue the relationship. Formally, this pledge may begin with the seller being designated a preferred supplier. While **preferred supplier status** may mean different things in different companies, in general it means that the supplier is assured a large percentage of the buyer's business and will get the first opportunity to earn any new business.[6] For example, at Motorola, only preferred suppliers are eligible to bid on new programs. Thus, *preferred supplier* is a buyer's term for partner.

To become a preferred supplier for Bethlehem Steel, a supplier must pass several criteria (including a willingness to commit to the relationship) listed in Exhibit 13–3. Research finds that many buyers examine the suppliers on criteria similar to those used by

13–1

BUSINESS 2 BUSINESS
Customer Power

Some customers try to take advantage of salespeople with special requests such as asking the rep to perform routine maintenance for free, or for free trials or samples. A customer may ask for free service in order to keep the account, or for a free trial with a big purchase as bait. How do you recognize which requests represent legitimate needs and are made in the context of good faith partnering and which requests represent an unfair use of the customer's power? What should a salesperson do to curb unfair and unnecessary requests?

Bethlehem Steel. While the salesperson may not be able to manage corporate culture, the salesperson can utilize appropriate selling strategies to lead the customer to the commitment stage.

Securing Commitment   Commitment in a partnership should permeate both organizations. The salesperson must secure commitment not only from the customer, but also from the rest of his own company. Senior management must be convinced of the benefits of partnering with the account so that the appropriate investments will be made. Additionally, the salesperson has to see that others in the organization are empowered to serve the needs of this customer. For example, if a customer has a problem with the billing process, the billing department should work directly with the customer to resolve the issue and design a more appropriate process. For other accounts, the billing department would probably be unwilling to make changes to the process.

Building Communication   For the billing department to handle a request for a new billing procedure, direct communication must occur between the department and the customer. Once in the commitment phase, the salesperson must take on a much stronger coordinative role and build direct lines of communication between the two organizations. In the previous stages, communication between the two organizations was really just between the purchasing agent or decision maker and the salesperson. Now, as illustrated in Exhibit 13–4, communication lines should be direct so that problems and opportunities can be identified and resolved as quickly and efficiently as possible. These direct communication lines are part of the commitment necessary to building partnerships.

As you have seen, the sales force plays an important role in the business marketing organization. How the sales force accomplishes that role is dependent on a number of factors, and one result is the choice of the most appropriate selling strategy. Selling strategy also affects the structure and practice of sales force management, which is the focus of the rest of this chapter.

Organizing the Sales Force

The sales function may be organized in many ways, depending somewhat on the choice of sales strategy as discussed earlier in this chapter. No matter how the sales force is organized, though, there is usually a sales executive in charge.

Exhibit 13–4
Communication
in the Partnership

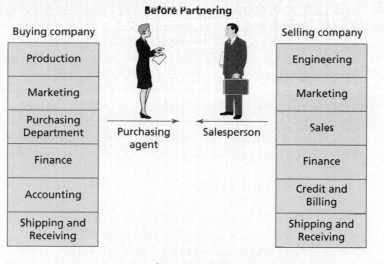

Before Partnering

Buying company

| Production |
| Marketing |
| Purchasing Department |
| Finance |
| Accounting |
| Shipping and Receiving |

Purchasing agent

Salesperson

Selling company

| Engineering |
| Marketing |
| Sales |
| Finance |
| Credit and Billing |
| Shipping and Receiving |

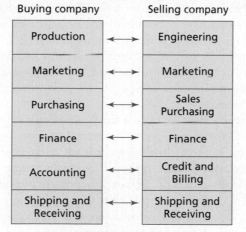

After Partnering

Buying company		Selling company
Production	⟷	Engineering
Marketing	⟷	Marketing
Purchasing	⟷	Sales Purchasing
Finance	⟷	Finance
Accounting	⟷	Credit and Billing
Shipping and Receiving	⟷	Shipping and Receiving

SOURCE: Barton A. Weitz, Stephen B. Castleberry, and John F. Tanner, Jr. *Selling: Building Partnerships.* Second edition. Burr Ridge, IL: Irwin/McGraw-Hill, 1995.

The Sales Executive

Depending on the size of the organization, the chief executive officer may fulfill the responsibilities and duties of the sales executive, or the marketing executive and sales executive duties may be combined into one position, or the sales executive position may be a stand-alone function. Irrespective of whether the person handles only sales duties or has other responsibilities as well, the sales executive is responsible for decisions such as the choice of sales strategy, the number and location of salespeople, the setting of sales quotas and designing of compensation plans, and sales forecasting. We've already discussed the choice of a sales strategy so we will focus now on the other responsibilities.

Size and Organization of the Sales Force

The sales executive determines how many salespeople are needed to achieve the company's sales and customer satisfaction targets. In addition, the executive must determine the type of salespeople needed. For example, the sales executive is the person who decides if a global account management team is needed or if local salespeople can handle all accounts. This decision, as well as other decisions concerning such factors as location and field management structure, are based on the executive's determination of the customer satisfaction level necessary to achieve sales targets.

There are many types of salespeople, including telemarketing representatives, field salespeople, product specialists, and account specialists. Sometimes there is overlap in responsibilities, such as when a telemarketer supports a field salesperson—both have responsibility for the same account. Usually, however, there are different responsibilities assigned to different types of salespeople, and companies often have more than one type.

Geographic Salespeople

Most sales departments are organized geographically at some level. The most basic sales force structure is to give each salesperson all accounts within a specified geographic area—here we have the **geographic salesperson**. Companies often combine geographic territories into branch or zone offices, which are further combined to create regions. Minolta Business Systems, for example, operates a geographic sales force. One rep may have responsibility for all businesses within three ZIP codes whereas a rep working in a downtown area may have responsibility for all businesses within three square blocks, depending on the number of businesses within each geographic area. The company attempts to balance the sales potential of each territory by determining how many businesses should be in a territory, and then dividing a city into areas that fall near the desired number of businesses. Geographic salespeople are used when all products serve the same general types of buyers.

Geographic reps are usually **field salespeople** (also called **outside salespeople**); that is, they call on accounts at the accounts' locations. **Inside salespeople** can also be found in business markets; these salespeople sell at the company's location. A telemarketer account manager is such a person. Inside salespeople also handle any walk-up business. Square-D, a supplier of electrical components, has inside salespeople who help electricians select the right parts and close the sale.

When only a geographic structure is used, the organizational structure is likely to be line-and-staff. A **line-and-staff organization** is one where those who conduct the primary tasks of the department (in this case, sales) are part of the line—their managers are called line managers—and all support personnel are staff. Authority and responsibility move up and down the organizational line, not across. A salesperson's responsibility for an account comes from the branch sales manager, who received that responsibility from the regional manager, who got it from the sales executive.

Companies may also organize their salespeople by account, and there are several ways to do this. In each method, the **account salesperson** has responsibility for specified accounts, rather than a geographic area. One method is to specify new account responsibility to one group of salespeople and current account responsibility to another group. For example, an RCA radio communications division uses field salespeople to develop new accounts and a telemarketing sales force to maintain accounts. Each telemarketer has a list of specified accounts and only that telemarketer works with those customers.

Similar customers often have similar needs, while different types of customers may have very different needs for the same product. In such cases, salespeople may specialize on one type of account. For example, Lanier has salespeople who only call on medical accounts. Similarly, Xerox has account salespeople who specialize in serving the education market, the legal market, or government accounts. These situations require special customer or market knowledge to be successful.

Companies also divide their accounts on the basis of size. Large customers, sometimes called **key accounts**, may have a salesperson assigned only to their account. If the account buys centrally for implementation or delivery nationwide, the salesperson is called a **national account manager** (**NAM**); similarly, global accounts are managed by **global account managers** (**GAMs**). These salespeople work with geographic salespeople to handle local needs, but all account planning, pricing, and even product development is managed by the NAM or GAM. Moore Business Forms has been a leader in using GAMs. Previously, for example, a local (French) Moore salesperson would sell to the American Express office in Paris, the Tokyo rep would call on the Asian office, and so forth. Each rep may have used a different strategy, different pricing, and so forth. Now American Express has a centralized purchasing office but needs global implementation; the Moore GAM calls on the central office but works with the Tokyo and Paris reps (and others) to make sure that local services are implemented properly.

Sometimes, a company may determine that a key account is a house account. A **house account** is handled by a sales executive and the company does not pay anyone commission on sales from the account. General Dynamics asked its suppliers to engage in this strategy and cut prices by an amount equivalent to the commission, but abandoned the strategy when it realized that service was also reduced. House accounts are generally not a good idea and should be served by an account manager.

Product Specialists

When companies have diverse products using different technology platforms, their salespeople will specialize by product category. The need for technology expertise is too great for any one salesperson to understand, so the sales force is organized by product. Hewlett-Packard, for example, has separate sales forces selling computers, electronic test equipment, components, medical test equipment, and analytical test equipment. Each sales force is geographically organized, and some may have account managers as well.

Product specialists must sometimes coordinate their activities with salespeople from other divisions. For example, a Hewlett-Packard test instrument salesperson may have an account that also purchases electronic components. Sharing that information with the representative from the component division can help build a relationship that pays off with leads for test instruments.

Sales Teams

In some industries, companies used product specialists to call on the same accounts, even the same buyers within each account. The buyers, however, grew tired of being called on by five, six, or even more salespeople from the same company, especially when it was obvious that there was no coordination within the organization. In response, companies began developing sales teams, headed by an account manager. In **team selling**, a group of salespeople handle a single account. Each salesperson brings a different area of expertise or handles different responsibilities.

One type of team is the field salesperson and telemarketing support rep whom we've already discussed. Another type of team is used in **multilevel selling**, where members of a selling organization at various levels call on their counterparts in the buying organization. The vice president of sales, for example, may visit the vice president of purchasing, as illustrated in Exhibit 13–5.

The most common form of team, though, may be one comprised of product specialists and coordinated by account managers and organized using a matrix. As you can see in Exhibit 13–6, the **matrix sales team** may have each product specialist working with three or more account managers. The account managers have total account responsibility

Exhibit 13–5

Sales Teams May Be Formed for Multilevel Selling

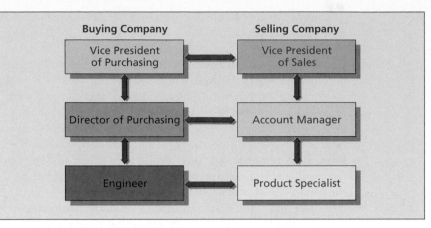

SOURCE: Barton A. Weitz, Stephen B. Castleberry, and John F. Tanner, Jr. *Selling: Building Partnerships.* Second edition. Burr Ridge, IL: Irwin/McGraw-Hill, 1995.

Exhibit 13–6

Matrix Team Selling Organization

In team selling, product specialists work with account managers. Account managers have total account responsibility, but product specialists are responsible for sales and service of only a limited portion of the product line, and may work with several account managers.

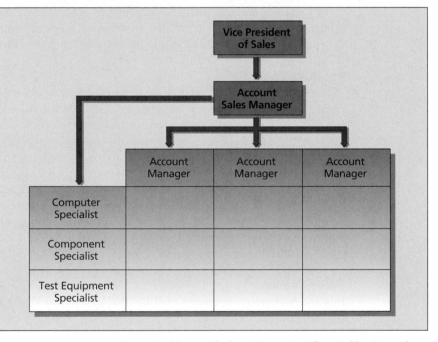

SOURCE: Barton A. Weitz, Stephen B. Castleberry, and John F. Tanner, Jr. *Selling: Building Partnerships.* Second edition. Burr Ridge, IL: Irwin/McGraw-Hill, 1995.

and bring in the proper product specialist only when needed. Consultative and needs satisfaction strategies work well under this type of organization, especially when specialized expertise is needed to satisfy customer requirements but there is too much expertise required to reside in any one person.

A recent innovation in organizing the sales force is the customer-focused team. The customer-focused team (CFT) is a structure that assigns customer responsibility to individuals across the organization, in sales and in other areas. Pioneered by NCR and Allegiance (a health care industry supplier), the structure resembles a wheel, with the customer as the hub. (See Exhibit 13–7.) In addition to product specialists, the account manager can draw on the expertise of a specific credit manager, a specific billing person, someone in manufacturing, and so forth. Each of these individuals has responsibility for

Exhibit 13-7
Customer-
Focused Team
Structure.

SOURCE: Barton A. Weitz, Stephen B. Castleberry, and John F. Tanner, Jr. *Selling: Building Partnerships.* Second edition. Burr Ridge, IL: Irwin/McGraw-Hill, 1995.

coordinating the efforts of her individual functional areas in order to achieve the account strategy. Further, they are part of the account strategy development process and are headed up by the account manager.

Note that these individuals will also have line managers. There is still someone in charge of all manufacturing. The innovation lies in the fact that there is someone in manufacturing (and each other area) responsible for developing account goals and strategies and seeing that those strategies are implemented and account goals are met. All of the company's resources can be more effectively directed toward the needs of the account, so when relationships are important, customer-focused teams are an excellent method of organizing.

Sales Force Size

The sales executive may select one or more of the preceding types of salespeople and structures, based on the relationship quality, the complexity or variety of products, market size, and other factors. The sales executive is also responsible for determining how many of each type should be employed. The objective is to achieve the sales potential by providing each company that wants to buy the opportunity to buy.

One approach to determining the optimum number of salespeople involves an analysis of the salesperson's **work load**, or all of the activities that a salesperson must do to cover a territory. For example, a salesperson may be able to make six sales calls each day, but when training, sales meetings, and customer service responsibilities are thrown in, only four days per week are available for making sales calls. In the average month, the salesperson could make only 96 sales calls (6 calls × 4 days × 4 weeks). Keep in mind, too, that the more successful a salesperson is, the more time will be needed for customer service.

		Sales Potential	
		Low	High
Market Position	Strong	Relatively fewer resources should be allocated here	Maintain sufficient resources to continue to reap the sales potential and strong position
	Weak	Assign to alternative method of communicating, such as telemarketing	Direct more sales resources here

SOURCE: Adapted from Raymond LaForge and David Cravens, "Steps in Selling Efforts Deployment," *Industrial Marketing Management* 11 (1982), pp. 187–88.

The next step is to allocate accounts such that all accounts will be called on with the desired frequency. For example, using the previous figures and assuming that there are 96,000 customers that you want called on at least once per month, then you need 1,000 salespeople. The desired number of calls per account will depend on a number of factors, including

- The sales strategy selected.
- The type of salesperson (geographic, account specialist, etc.).
- The nature of sales job.
- The nature of the product. More complex products require more calls.
- Stage of market development. A company entering a market has few customer service requirements and can use large territories.
- Competitive intensity. As intensity grows, so may the number of sales calls.

One method to determine work load focuses on sales potential and market position through use of the **sales resource allocation grid**. **Market position** means the strength of the company relative to competitors. It can be measured by market share, but should also reflect forecasts of future share. If a competitor has just introduced a new product that will capture a significant share of the market, it is foolish to consider only your current share. **Sales potential** is the total forecasted sales for the product category.

The sales resource allocation grid provides insight not only into the amount of activity needed in a particular segment, but also into the strategy that should be used. For example, when the position is weak but potential is high, more activity should be directed to strengthening the position. Conversely, when potential is low but position is strong, either activity should be designed to increase sales potential or a minimum of activity should be engaged in order to maintain the position, as illustrated in Exhibit 13–8. Then, based on the activity determined by position and potential, the number of salespeople are calculated.

Outsourcing the Sales Force

Not every business marketer that uses field or telemarketing salespeople uses its own employees. Manufacturers' reps, distributors, and telemarketing service bureaus can fill the requirement for salespeople without the fixed costs of hiring your own. Some companies even hire temporary sales forces for special needs, such as new product launches.[7]

Manufacturer's reps, distributors, and sales agents have to know the product and how it works in order to sell it for the right applications. Here, NCH is training salespeople in the use of an industrial cleaning product.
Courtesy NCH Chemical.

Advantages

There are advantages to outsourcing sales beyond just the costs issue. For example, manufacturers' reps and distributors are already in the field and already have relationships established with customers. When selected appropriately, they already have relationships with the customers you seek. Companies that are looking to enter a new market, particularly a foreign market, will use local distributors or manufacturers' reps in order to quickly penetrate the market through those established relationships.

Costs, as mentioned earlier, are variable, meaning that there are no selling costs to the manufacturer until the product is sold. There is no draw, only commission (or a profit margin earned by the distributor), and all selling expenses, such as travel or entertainment, are paid for by the distributor or rep. Therefore, less up-front investment is needed.

Disadvantages

There is one major drawback to using distributors and reps—a loss of control. In most cases, the manufacturer's product is just one of many being sold. There is no guarantee that the product will even be discussed in sales calls. Nor is there any guarantee that the product will be sold in the manner desired by the manufacturer. Some manufacturers that sell through distributors or reps invest in training and merchandising materials in order to increase the likelihood that the reps will focus on their product. A common complaint, however, among distributors and reps is that the manufacturers do a poor job in supporting them with selling materials and training. It seems that most companies that use reps and distributors simply give them the product and a commission or a suggested profit margin.

Often, it is up to the salesperson to decide how much resources will be put into specific accounts. These decisions, though, are usually guided by strategies developed by the sales executive. In the next section, we'll examine how sales executives direct the activities of the sales force through several different methods.

Directing the Sales Force

Once the sales force is in place, there remains the question of directing their activities. Part of the sales executive's responsibility is to ensure that the salespeople are working to achieve the company's sales and customer service objectives. Field salespeople are scattered over a wide area and operate without benefit of direct supervision. The sales executive faces the unique challenge of designing control systems that encourage each field sales manager and salesperson to maximize individual results through effective self-control. These control strategies often include quotas and compensation plans.

Quotas

Quotas are a useful control mechanism, as they represent a quantitative minimum level of acceptable performance for a specific time period. Two types of quotas are used: activity quotas and performance quotas. **Activity quotas** specify the number and type of activities that salespeople should do; for example, a new business call quota would specify the number of noncustomers representing potential new business that should be visited in a period of time. Activity quotas are especially useful in situations where the sales cycle is long and sales are few, because activities can be monitored more frequently than sales. For example, some medical equipment sales cycles are longer than a year, and a rep may only sell one or two units per quarter. Having a monthly sales target would be inappropriate, but requiring a minimum number of sales calls is reasonable. Here management assumes that if the salesperson makes the calls, the sale will occur. Activity quotas can be specified for many types of sales activities, such as number of current customer calls, demonstrations, proposal presentations, and other activities.

Performance, or **outcome**, **quotas** specify levels of performance, such as revenue, gross margin, or unit sales in a period of time. Often, sales quotas are simply a breakdown of the company's sales forecast. Other types of quotas, such as gross margin quotas, can be used to encourage salespeople to sell profitable products, not just the products that may be the easiest to sell. Companies may convert gross margin to points and then allow salespeople to achieve their quota by whatever mix of products they choose. For example, suppose an office equipment company enjoys a 30 percent profit margin on copiers but only 20 percent on faxes. Copiers may be worth three points each while faxes are worth two. If the salesperson's quota is 12 points, quota can be achieved by selling four copiers, six faxes, or some combination.

Good quota systems are fair, recognizing the potential in a sales territory as well as the constraints. For example, someone who has to call on accounts scattered across Montana, Idaho, and Wyoming can't make the same number of calls each day that a rep in Chicago can. Good systems are also attainable, yet challenging. Quotas should set standards that encourage salespeople to stretch and improve their performance, yet represent reasonable performance standards. Quotas that are perceived to be unreasonable may be ignored or, worse yet, may demoralize the sales force.

A quota plan should also be complete, yet easy to understand. A complete quota system is one that covers all important criteria on which salespeople are judged. Yet, the quota system has to be understandable, or salespeople will ignore it. The flexibility to handle unforeseen events (such as labor and transportation strikes, fire, and floods) is another characteristic of a sound quota plan. Sound quota plans motivate salespeople by providing goals and feedback on their performance relative to management expectations.

Compensation

The salesperson's compensation is usually tied to how well she achieves quota. When designed well, the compensation plan satisfies the needs of both the company and the salesperson. The salesperson needs an equitable, stable compensation system, but the company needs a system that encourages profitable sales and customer satisfaction.

Sound compensation programs

- Base rewards on results and efforts.
- Provide equal rewards for equal performance.
- Provide competitive rewards.
- Are easy to understand and implement.

Salespeople who perceive the reward structure to be unfair will be demotivated. Similarly, if they can't understand the system, then the system will have no impact on their activities or performance. And, if they can get more money elsewhere for the same work, management can wave goodbye, for they will go where the money is.

Types of Sales Compensation

Sales executives can choose to pay salespeople a straight salary, a straight commission plan, a combination of the two, and perhaps a bonus. Most firms pay a salary and a commission (a combination plan), with fewer than 4 percent paying only commission and about 5 percent paying only salary. Combination plans are used because most companies want a balance between "nonselling" activities such as taking care of customers (compensated for with salary) and sales activities (compensated by commission). Some salary provides salespeople with the security of knowing that they will receive a certain amount each month, which is another reason why some companies use salary as part of the compensation plan. Xerox, for example, uses combination plans, varying the percentage of total compensation allotted to salary based on how much customer care is involved. Jobs with little customer care and mostly customer acquisition pay about 60 percent salary and the balance is commission, while major account managers with lots of customer retention and customer care activities are paid about 80 percent salary.

Straight Salary   Under the **straight salary** plan, a salesperson is paid a fixed amount of money for work during a specified time. A quota system may be used to determine annual salary raises, but otherwise pay does not vary. Straight salary is best used when sales cycles are long, when a team of people is involved and individual results are difficult to measure, or when other aspects of the marketing mix (such as advertising) are important to closing the sale (such as may be the case for inside salespeople). Salary is also useful when the position requires more customer service activities than selling activities.

Straight Commission   A **straight commission** plan pays a certain amount for each sale, but there is no salary. The **commission base**, or the item from which the commission is determined, is usually unit sales, dollar sales, or gross margin. The **commission rate** is the amount paid per base item sold, and is usually a percentage (such as 10 percent of sales revenue or gross margin) or a fixed amount (such as $50 per sale). Using the preceding copier example, Exhibit 13–9 compares straight salary with two commission plans: one paying 10 percent of sales revenue and a point plan paying $100 per point.

Exhibit 13–9

How Different Types of Compensation Plans Pay

			Amount Paid to Salesperson			
Month	**Sales Revenue**	**Straight Salary**	**Straight Commission***	**Combination†**		**Point Plan**
January	$50,000 6 copiers 10 faxes	$3,500	$5,000	$2,500 (salary) 3,000 (commission) 4,500 (total)		$3,800
February	$60,000 6 copiers 15 faxes	3,500	6,000	2,500 (salary) 3,600 (commission) 5,100 (total)		4,800
March	$20,000 2 copiers 5 faxes	3,500	2,000	2,500 (salary) 1,200 (commission) 2,700 (total)		1,600

*Commission plan pays 10% of sales revenue.
†Commision portion pays 6% of sales revenue.
Note: Copiers are worth three points, faxes worth two, each point is worth $100 in commission. Also, the commission rates are used for example purposes only, to illustrate how compensation schemes work. Point plans, for example, do not necessarily always yield the lowest compensation.
SOURCE: Weitz, Barton A., Stephen B. Castleberry, and John F. Tanner, Jr. (1995), *Selling: Building Partnerships* 2e, Burr Ridge, IL, Richard D. Irwin Inc.

Exhibit 13–10

An Example of a Draw Compensation Plan

Month	**Draw**	**Commission Earned**	**Payment to Salesperson**	**Balance Owed to Company**
January	$2,500	$0	$2,500	$2,500
February	2,500	1,500	2,500	3,500
March	2,500	6,000	2,500	0

A draw is usually paid as part of a straight commission plan; a **draw** is a loan paid to the salesperson to provide stable cash flow; it's then repaid from commission. For example, the company could agree to pay the salesperson $2,500 per month. If the salesperson earns less than $2,500, the balance is carried over to the next month. An example of how this works is presented in Exhibit 13–10.

Straight commission ties pay directly to performance, but does little to engender company loyalty. Salespeople on straight commission are far less likely to do activities that they don't see tied directly to making a sale, activities such as paperwork, sales forecasts, and even customer service. Xerox experimented with a straight commission plan but found that customer service suffered, as did company loyalty among salespeople.

Companies engaged in transactional sales strategies and markets find straight commission to work very well. Premier Industrial, for example, pays a straight commission.

Bonus Bonuses resemble commissions, but a **bonus** is a lump sum payment for meeting a minimum standard of performance within a given period of time. The amount depends on total performance, not an individual sale. Bonuses motivate salespeople to overachieve quotas, and can be used in conjunction with either commission or salary or a combination plan. A salesperson who has made quota with three months left in the year can be motivated to

---

13–2

FROM THE FIELD

Is Your Compensation on Autopilot?

It was one thing when top management at Cargo Heavy Duty Inc. told the sales force they'd be switching from straight commission to an entirely redesigned pay plan. But then the specifics were unveiled: Each salesperson's prior-year earnings would be chopped in half and offered up as his new salary, which would be accompanied by a completely restructured commission program.

While this move didn't rouse whoops of joy from the sales force, it did accomplish a larger goal. By restructuring its compensation program, the Kalamazoo, Michigan-based trucking parts and service company was more precisely aligning its sales incentives with specific company objectives.

Cargo Heavy Duty centered the change around four key objectives. Increases in monthly volume, new customers, gross profit, and sales within higher profit product lines now determine commissioned earnings. Dale Fraaza,

company president, says the reasons behind the change were twofold: It wanted more control over the products sold and flat sales over the past two years had been partially attributed to a lack of sales aggressiveness. Until restructuring, there hadn't been any incentive for salespeople to move into uncharted waters with new product lines or accounts.

Fraaza says salespeople initially hesitated to accept Cargo's program, but that was expected in the wake of such a change. Salespeople met one-on-one with top management, company objectives were explained, both positive and negative scenarios were worked out, and ultimately each salesperson was shown how he could succeed with the new system. Will they succeed? Fraaza believes so, but only time will tell.

Source: Sue Kasten, "Smart Sales Compensation Programs Fuel Success: Is Yours on Auto Pilot?" *Sales and Marketing Strategies & News* (March 1996), pp. 1, 7, 9.

---

sell even more if a bonus is worthwhile. Xerox uses bonuses to motivate balanced performance. Salespeople can earn bonuses based on customer satisfaction ratings, total sales revenue, and revenue growth over the previous year. Thus, Xerox uses bonuses to encourage salespeople to take care of customers while also growing the business.

Combination Plans   As stated earlier, most companies pay some combination of commission and/or bonus and a salary under a **combination plan**. Such plans are also called salary plus plans, because they pay salary plus a commission or plus a bonus. The salary portion can engender loyalty to the company and represent pay for activities that benefit the company more than the salesperson, while the commission or bonus portion can motivate the salesperson. Research by the Dartnell Corporation indicates that while the number of combination plans is holding steady, the percentage of total compensation that is derived from commission or bonus has doubled over the past years, from almost 20 percent to almost 40 percent. From the Field 13–2 describes why one company has gone in the other direction, moving from straight commission to a combination plan.

The primary disadvantage of combination plans is that they can become very complex. Confused salespeople may unknowingly engage in inappropriate activity; sales management may even design the program such that salespeople emphasize the wrong products.

Note, though, that we are not talking about selling something to someone who has no need. While commission and bonus plans can encourage that type of behavior, let's first assume that our salespeople are ethical. If a salesperson is paid the same for faxes and copiers, then most likely, the rep would sell more of the easier one to sell. The company, however, would benefit if more copiers were sold because the gross margin is higher. Compensation plans affect the choice of where salespeople place their effort; good compensation plans encourage effort in the right activities.

Salary plus bonus plans are used when management wants long-term customer relationships and when teams are used. Long sales cycles also make bonuses effective. Salary plus commission encourages salespeople to increase revenue in order to get the commission, but also encourages nonselling activities that are paid for with the salary.

Companies sometimes cap earnings for their salespeople. A **cap** is a limit to how much a salesperson can make, no matter what the amount of sales. Caps can be unethical if salespeople are unaware of them. For example, one company paid a 10 percent commission. A salesperson who closed an $11 million sale, though, was only paid $100,000 because of the company's hidden cap. Caps are not particularly smart—if they're hidden, morale for the entire sales force is damaged when the cap comes to light. When not hidden, caps limit sales productivity.

Evaluating Performance

Sales executives aren't the only executives constantly evaluating the performance of their sales force. Every executive in the firm is interested in sales performance. Sales executives, however, are interested in more than total sales revenue; sales executives have to be concerned with sales productivity as well. In this section, we will discuss the various methods of evaluating sales performance following a five-step method.

Five Steps to Evaluating Sales Force Performance

As illustrated in Exhibit 13–11, the first step in any evaluation is to review the objectives for the activity being evaluated. While setting objectives is part of every planning process, results should be compared with what was desired so that overall objectives can be realized. For example, if the company set a target of a 20 percent increase in revenue and a market share target of 10 percent, management would be less thrilled with a 25 percent revenue increase if market share was only 8 percent. Management would realize that the market grew faster than 25 percent and the company must have missed out on some sales.

The second step is to gather the appropriate performance data. In a sales setting, this means observing both performance and activity (both outcomes and effort). The third step is to evaluate the influence of any uncontrollable factors. The sales force can

Exhibit 13–11

Five Steps to
Evaluate Sales
Force
Performance

- Review objectives.
- Gather appropriate performance data.
- Evaluate influence of uncontrollable factors.
- Identify problems or opportunities.
- Develop and implement strategy to resolve problems and take advantage of opportunities.

hardly be blamed for poor performance if the company was late in introducing new products; similarly, the sales force should not rejoice overly in any sales increases if they're due to the sudden bankruptcy of a key competitor. The economy, the weather, and other uncontrollable factors can influence sales performance. Identifying the impact of those factors enables sales executives to focus on how well the sales strategy is being implemented.

Based on these three steps, the company can then identify any problems or opportunities, which is the fourth step. These problems and opportunities are then fed into the strategic planning process and/or tactical actions are taken to minimize problems and take advantage of activities for the final step of the process.

Measures of Performance

Sales performance is measured in two ways. Outcome measures record performance concerning important results such as sales volume, total revenue, total profit contribution, number of new customers, and increase in sales from old customers. These numbers can be compared to performance or outcome quotas to determine if goals were met. These numbers alone, however, can be misleading. External factors, new products, and other issues can make performance look stellar or terrible in spite of anything the salesperson does.

That is why sales executives also measure activity, or a salesperson's effort. Again, activities such as new business calls, demonstrations, and proposal presentations can be observed and compared with quotas.

Measuring Productivity

When the measures of effort and output are combined, the sales executive can examine the efficiency of the salesperson or sales force. Combinations of activity and performance measures are productivity measures. We discussed these **conversion ratios** in Chapter 12 as they related to other marketing activities. For example, at Freeman Exhibit Company (one of the Freeman companies that Pat Eaton represents in From the Field 13–1), the sales executive examines the ratio of sales to proposals. The question is how many proposals were actually closed. Other conversion ratios might be the number of new business calls that turn into appointments, the number of appointments that are converted to demonstrations, and then the number of demonstrations that became sales.

If a sales executive has a map of the sales process, then a conversion ratio can be calculated for each step of that process. An example is found in Exhibit 13–12, which illustrates the typical sales cycle for Minolta Business Systems copier salespeople. Measuring conversions at each step can enable the sales manager to pinpoint problems that salespeople may encounter. These problems can then be rectified with training, changes in strategy, or marketing support.

Exhibit 13–12

Minolta Business System's Sales Cycle

Gain Appointment
100 calls—10% conversion

Qualify Prospect
10 appointments—50% conversion

Demonstrate Equipment
5 demonstrations—
40% conversion

Present Proposal
2 proposals—
50% conversion

Close the Sale
1 sale

SOURCE: Adapted from John F. Tanner Jr., *Trade Shows in the Marketing Mix* (Washington DC: Center for Exhibition Industry Research 1996).

Balanced Performance

In addition to examining the productivity or output of individual reps, the sales executive must also examine the productivity of the overall sales force in order to make such decisions as quantity discounts and deleting products from the product line. Therefore, examining average order size, order mix (which products are purchased with other products), and sales by product are important factors to consider. Low sales of a particular product may signal low demand for the product, a need to train the sales force in how to sell that product, or a need to change compensation.

Customer Satisfaction

With Total Quality Management movement came the drive for customer satisfaction. Now many companies measure customer satisfaction regularly and set satisfaction objectives for their sales force. IBM measures customer satisfaction at both the executive and salesperson level. These satisfaction ratings are part of the salesperson's performance evaluation—40 percent of salesperson compensation is tied directly to the ratings.[8] We will discuss customer satisfaction measures in greater detail in Chapters 15 and 16, but for now, recognize that customer satisfaction is an important part of many companies' sales force performance evaluation and compensation programs.

Other Measures

Salespeople have many nonselling activities to perform and also have to know a great deal about competitors, customers, and the industry. Sales managers often evaluate salespeople on their knowledge of the market, how well they work with others in the company, and other measures that are similar to those employed in the evaluation of any member of the organization. These measures are usually used only to evaluate individuals, but sometimes recognition of knowledge gaps or internal workplace problems across the sales force can trigger training or policy change.

Salespeople also have the responsibility for managing financial resources. If they travel, then travel expenses must be managed. Resources such as free samples, loaner equipment or products, trial units, and other costly resources are managed as well. Salespeople are evaluated on their ability to manage these resources within the budgets established by the sales executive.

Summary

Sales differs from other forms of marketing communication because sales is person-to-person. Salespeople create value by adapting their products to fit customer needs. Salespeople have further responsibilities that involve managing the relationship between buyers and their organization. Salespeople not only have to close sales, they also provide customer service and coordinate company resources so that the customer is satisfied.

Business marketers can choose from a number of sales strategies; we discussed four as being representative of the wide array of possible strategies. The first is script-based selling, which is used when there is little variation among customers. A more sophisticated approach is needs satisfaction selling, which works best when there is variance in needs across buyers and an array of finished products from which to choose.

Consultative selling may appear similar to needs satisfaction selling, but in this case, the buyer has less information about what is needed and relies on the consultant's knowledge to custom tailor a solution. Partnering, the fourth strategy, goes beyond consultative selling because of the long-term nature of partnerships. There are many sales strategies that can be used when partnering; these include cross-selling and full-line selling.

The sales function can be organized in many ways, depending on the sales strategy. At the top of the structure is the sales executive, who has responsibility for deciding the size and type of sales force. Most sales organizations are organized geographically at some level. The most basic level is to assign each salesperson a geographic territory.

Other sales organizations assign salespeople to accounts, including key accounts, national accounts, or global accounts. Still other firms organize by product. In some situations, companies need both account and product representatives, so they create sales teams to meet the needs of their customer. The account manager coordinates activities and determines sales strategies while product representatives and representatives from other areas of the organization carry out more specific objectives. Customer-focused teams are one type of team structure that includes representatives from manufacturing, billing, shipping, and other areas that serve the customer.

Sales force size is determined by the sales executive. One method of determining the appropriate number of salespeople is the work load approach, based on the expected number of sales calls that a salesperson can make. Of course, companies can, and do, outsource the selling effort. Some companies choose to use manufacturers' reps, or firms that represent a number of manufacturers. Telemarketing service firms are also available. Some companies even outsource selling temporarily, hiring temporary salespeople for special sales campaigns.

Once the sales force is in place, its activities must be directed. Quotas, or minimum levels of acceptable performance, are one control method. Quotas can be set for activities as well as outcomes. Compensation plans also direct sales activities. The sales executive can choose from salary, commission, and bonus, and may create a plan involving a combination of two plans or all three.

Sales performance is measured two ways: in outcomes and by activities. By combining outcomes and activities, conversion ratios can be calculated to measure salesperson efficiency. These three figures (outcomes, activities, and conversions) enable sales executives to compare salesperson performance. Salesperson performance measures also include data such as average order size and order mix so that decisions concerning pricing and product can be made.

Sales is the last element of the marketing communication mix that we examine. In the next chapter, we examine pricing strategies. Yet like the product itself, pricing must be consistent with the positioning strategy that we intend to communicate through advertising, trade shows, direct marketing, and our selling efforts. Position cannot be created through communication but must also be delivered.

Key Terms

account salesperson	geographic salesperson	performance quota
activity quota	global account manager	(outcome quota)
bonus	(GAM)	preferred supplier status
cap	house account	quota
combination plan	inside salesperson	sales potential
commission base	key account	sales resource allocation
commission rate	line-and-staff	grid
consultative selling	organization	script-based selling
conversion ratio	market position	straight commission
cross-selling	matrix sales team	straight salary
draw	multilevel selling	strategic partner selling
field salesperson	national account	team selling
(outside salesperson)	manager (NAM)	upgrading (upselling)
full-line selling	needs satisfaction selling	work load

Discussion Questions

1. Create a matrix that lists types of salespeople across the top and sales strategies down one side. Then for each strategy, determine when each type of salesperson is appropriate and why.

2. Should the salesperson handle all customer complaints or should the customer be told to call the appropriate department? Why or why not? Would your answer change if the account were in the exploration stage versus the commitment stage?

3. The sales executive notes that there is a 2-to-1 ratio of proposals, so an edict is published that requires all salespeople to double the number of proposals. What are the possible outcomes of such a command? (There are at least four.) In general, is such a requirement a good idea? How firm should the executive be on enforcing this policy?

4. Assume you are a NAM who must rely on geographic salespeople to service far-flung locations of your customer. They are paid 40 percent of their normal commission on every sale made to your account. (You get the rest.) The account, though, is complaining that service is really bad in certain parts of the country. What would you do and how would you do it? Why?

5. An experienced salesperson argues against salaries: "I don't like subsidizing poor performers. If you paid us straight commission, we'd know who could make it and who couldn't. Sure, it may take a while to get rid of the deadwood; but after that, sales would skyrocket!" Explain why you agree or disagree with this statement.

6. Describe how decile analysis could influence sales strategy. Organize a sales force using different types of salespeople for different accounts for the top decile, the two middle deciles, and the bottom decile.

7. Your company is planning to begin exporting to Mexico and wants to use local sales agents. What should you look for in a sales agent?

8. The soundest philosophy for building partnerships may be summed up as "It's the little things that count." List eight little things a salesperson can do that cost little or nothing but may be extremely valuable in building partnership.

9. Some companies have salespeople who work with distributors. Wicor, for example, makes pumps, and its salespeople help distributors display and promote the products. How would partnering with distributors differ from partnering with end users?

10. Your regional company sells hardware for cabinets and furniture to companies that manufacture those types of products. (Your company does not sell to retail stores.) Your 22 salespeople only sell in five states. What type of sales force structure would be best and why? If you don't feel that you have enough information to answer the question fully, what other information would you like to know?

Internet Exercise

Go to the Hewlett-Packard home page (**www.hp.com**), select HP Search, and enter Industry Solutions. This page lists a number of different industries; choose one. What you should see at this point is a list of case study titles, or articles about how HP helped a specific customer. (For example, when we looked at the industry Process Manufacturing, we found case studies on Starkist, Ore-Ida, and Sara Lee.) As you read the case study, list the actions the HP salesperson took to win the sale. Estimate the type or stage of relationship and provide specific evidence, such as quotes, to support your estimation.

Cases

Case 13.1   Fletcher Electric, Inc.

Molly Stevens, account manager for Fletcher, was pondering her next move with Tymco, her largest account. Fletcher manufactures a line of pumps, electric motors, and controls that are sold to companies that use Fletcher's parts in manufacturing all kinds of equipment. Tymco, a maker of street sweepers and other specialized industrial products, had purchased Fletcher controls for the past five years, but also purchased controls from several small distributors for specific applications when Fletcher's products couldn't meet the specifications. Molly originally sold the controls by proving to the engineering department that Fletcher's quality could meet its specifications and by demonstrating the controls' accuracy and long life. Then she convinced the purchasing agent that the pricing would be more stable with one major vendor than with multiple distributors. Since then, Molly has heard no complaints about Fletcher's products. Tymco even allowed a trade magazine to write an article about Tymco's experience with Fletcher controls.

Early last year, Molly was able to persuade the purchasing agent for Tymco to switch to Fletcher electric motors for several applications. Although engineering was not involved in this decision, Molly had to prove to the purchasing agent that the products were as good as the ones they were currently purchasing. Molly estimated that Fletcher had about 30 percent of the Tymco motor business, 30 percent went to Visa SA from Mexico, and the remainder of the business belonged to Smart & Co., which actually distributed several lines of electric motors imported from the Pacific Rim.

Last month, Molly received a call from the director of engineering asking for a meeting to discuss some issues with Fletcher motors. She was delighted, because one of the Fletcher engineers had suggested combining Fletcher motors and controls and shipping the units as one assembly. Molly felt that such a meeting would be a perfect opportunity to present the new idea. Molly created and presented a proposal to the engineering department that, if accepted, would mean doubling Fletcher's share of the electric motor business. The proposal would require some redesign by Tymco, but the savings over two years would be more than the redesign costs. After that, Tymco could increase profits by about 3 percent on those products. But several engineers pointed out that Fletcher was unwilling to manufacture controls for all of Tymco's needs and they were reluctant to make such a change with a company that was not willing to work closer with them. In addition, one engineer seemed very unhappy that the purchasing department had switched to Fletcher motors. She felt that the reject rate of 2 percent was too high; all of Tymco's other vendors were achieving lower than 1 percent rejects. At the conclusion of the meeting, the director of engineering said, "Molly, we've enjoyed a long and good relationship with Fletcher. And your idea is a good one. Right now, though, I don't think Fletcher is the company we should do that with. But we'll consider it and let you know."

1. In what stage of partnering is the relationship between Fletcher and Tymco?

2. Is there anything Molly could have done to set the stage for better acceptance of her proposal?

3. What should she do right now? If her visionary objective is to develop a strategic partnership with Tymco, is it still realistic? What should she do to achieve that visionary objective?

Case 13.2 Jackson Timers & Controls

Jackson Timers & Controls has the following compensation program: Reps are paid a $1,500 draw per month, with straight commission paid on a point system, and a bonus depending on quota performance. Here is the point system:

Product	Points/Sale	Quota
Digital wamometer	50	4 units/month
Lambadameter	40	5
Origameter	35	6
Cyclometer	25	8
Universal tricometer	5	45

Reps are paid $5 per point, or $5,175 plus a bonus of $500, if they sell quota for each product, for a total of $5,675. The total number of points to reach each month is 1,035, but they have to reach quota for each product to get the bonus. Here is the performance of the district:

Product	District Quota	Number sold
Digital wamometer	40	22
Lambadameter	50	78
Origameter	60	63
Cyclometer	80	82
Universal tricometer	450	479

Salesperson	Dig. Wam.	Lambada.	Origameter	Cyclometer	U. Tricometer	Total Points
Chonko	5	6	7	9	53	1,225
Dunn	1	7	5	8	45	930
Easley	0	6	5	8	44	835
Cooper	1	8	6	8	48	1,020
Madden	1	7	7	8	47	1,010
Moore	3	11	7	9	52	1,320
Roberts	2	9	7	11	46	1,210
Weeks	2	8	6	7	48	1,045
Johnson	3	8	7	6	48	1,105
Davis	4	8	6	8	48	1,170

	Dig. Wam.	Lambada.	Origameter	Cyclometer	U. Tricometer	Total Sales Calls
Sales Call Quota	20	20	10	10	10	70
Roberts	28	17	11	9	10	75
Weeks	24	24	8	8	7	71
District	27.2	18.6	9.5	10.4	9.7	75.4

1. Evaluate the district's sales performance. Draw conclusions on just where it is doing well and doing poorly. (Don't fix anything yet.) Justify your conclusions.

2. Compare Roberts' and Weeks' performances. What are some possible explanations for the poor digital wamometer sales?

3. The VP of sales says the problem is a compensation plan problem. How would you fix it?

Additional Readings

Anderson, Roph, Rajiv Mehta, and James Strong (1997), "Sales Training and Education: An Empirical Investigation of Sales Management Training Programs for Sales Managers." *Journal of Personal Selling & Sales Management* 17 (Summer), pp. 53–64.

Darmon, Rene Y. (1998), "The Effects of Some Situational Variables on Sales Force Governance System Characteristics." *Journal of Personal Selling & Sales Management* 18 (Winter), pp. 17–30.

Darmon, Rene Y. (1997), "Selecting Appropriate Sales Quota Plan Structures and Quota Setting Procedures." *Journal of Personal Selling & Sales Management* 17 (Winter), pp. 1–16.

Moon, Mark and Susan Forquer Gupta (1997), "Examination of the Formation of Selling Centers: A Conceptual Framework." *Journal of Personal Selling & Sales Management* 17 (Spring), pp. 31–43.

Sharma, Arun (1997), "Who Prefers Key Account Management Programs? An Investigation of Buying Behavior and Buying Firm Characteristics." *Journal of Personal Selling & Sales Management* 17 (Fall), pp. 27–40.

Chapter 14

Pricing and Negotiating for Value

DU PONT

From an antitrust trial involving du Pont de Nemours and Company we have extensive data on prices, costs, and sales of cellophane, the plastic wrap that continues to be used extensively today. This bit of time travel reveals much about prices through innovation, market adoption, line extensions, and competitive challenges.●

In 1923 the du Pont Cellophane Company was founded and cellophane was introduced at an average price that year of $2.51 per pound. Price reductions enabled and were enabled by production efficiencies over the next three years. At a price of $1.43 in 1927, volume increased substantially. The next year du Pont patented a process for moisture-proofing cellophane and the market potential jumped even more dramatically. In 1930 sales were 11.1 million pounds. Although about one-third more expensive than plain cellophane, prices on the moisture-proof product had dropped to $.38 by 1940, while the profit rate remained about the same.●

Mirroring the textbook product life cycle, in the 1940s cellophane was produced in many different forms: transparent plain and colored, moisture-proof heat-sealable transparent, heat-sealable colored, adhesive transparent, and so on. In 1945 prices ranged from $.33 to $.62 per pound. Volume was 95 million pounds.●

From its introduction, cellophane was never priced to match its substitutes: wax paper and glassine. It was always more expensive. But the steady decrease in prices "was intended to open up new uses for cellophane and to attract new customers." A bonus effect from expanding markets was a steady decrease in cost due to learned efficiency and scale economies.●

After World War II, du Pont and its competitor, American Viscose, faced rising material and labor costs. The accompanying table shows that in close harmony with Viscose, du Pont's prices rose across the product line in the postwar decade. In 1955 du Pont cellophane sales totaled 125 million pounds. The case is a fascinating preview of the determinants of price in business marketing: the benefits to customers and their price sensitivity, costs and experience, competitive pressures, the legal environment, and more.[1]

Visit du Pont today at **http://www.dupont.com/index.html**

Year	300 PT		300 MT		300 MSAT		450 MSAT	
	dP	AV	dP	AV	dP	AV	dP	AV
1945	.33	.33	.41	.41	.57	.57	.46	.46
1947	.42	.43	.44	.44	.54	.54	.55	.55
1950	.49	.53	.51	.55	.59	.64	.59	.64
1955	.62	.64	.59	.59	.66	.66	.66	.66

Key: dP = du Pont; AV = American Viscose; numbers 300 and 450 are thicknesses; PT = plain transparent; MSAT = moisture-proof, sealed, adhesive, and transparent.

Learning Objectives

The cellophane story hints at the connections between price and market penetration and experience, the interrelationships between products in a line, and the considerations of competitive behaviors. Indeed, it exemplifies the need to think about price comprehensively.

At the conclusion of the chapter you should be able to

- Describe a comprehensive framework for pricing decisions.
- Identify some of today's pricing pitfalls in business-to-business marketing.
- List the key interest groups in the pricing decision.
- Appreciate price as a strategic variable at the intersection of many factors: costs, demand, competitors, channel coordination, and regulations.
- Recognize the tactical value of price for cash and production flow, inventory control, promotion, and more.
- Demonstrate facility with the financial rudiments of pricing: break-even analysis, channel margins, simple pro forma income statements, and margin analysis.
- Manage prices of related products in the line, evaluate bid pricing opportunities, and apply principles of conflict management to price negotiation.

Exhibit 14–1

Pricing Principles in Practice

> You've got to have *X* percent margins; every product, every division has to have *X* percent margins. There's no way you can live without that margin.
>
> industrial marketing manager

> Prices decline 10 percent per year, so your costs must decline 15 percent per year.
>
> financial manager at high technology firm

> If we don't get this deal they're gonna walk. We're going to lose their business. We potentially may jeopardize this business.
>
> sales managers at information service company

> Whatever you do, do not underprice and leave money on the table!
>
> pricing manager, computer systems business

Adapted from Gerald Smith "Managerial Pricing Orientation: The Process of Making Pricing Decisions," *Pricing Strategy & Practice* 3, no. 3 (1995), pp. 28–39.

The Principles and Principals of Price

Prices are a source of frustration for many business professionals. Customers complain of rising prices, complicated discounts, and more. Within selling organizations, there is often a power struggle among people (the principals) over who sets price. This struggle often reflects an underlying conflict over the theories (principles) of price.

At an executive seminar some years ago, participants were asked to write the decision rules or "truisms" about price at their companies. Exhibit 14–1 summarizes some of the pricing principles that emerged from the exercise.[2] The exhibit illustrates the emphasis some companies place on margin maintenance, competitive pricing, and cost cutting, the importance of particular customers, and avoiding a price that is below the value of the product package. Although each principle has merit, we will want to find a proper balance of emphasis and fit within the marketing strategy of the firm.

"Too many cooks spoil the broth." When it comes to pricing business products, this saying points to a real risk. Cost accountants scrutinize buying, manufacturing, selling, and shipping. The financial managers know the target return rates for each arm of the enterprise. Marketing departments stay abreast of competitor prices and count the bids won and lost. The sales force knows the pressure on distributor margins. Every day they get asked for new discounts. And a growing number of end users compete in intense markets where cost containment has become a motto that is played out in supplier relationships. Meanwhile, the Environmental Protection Agency may demand new handling or disposal procedures, increasing costs of product inputs. Some ingredients may be specially taxed or have their availability and prices affected by import and export restrictions.

Each interest group has a tendency to emphasize a particular pricing principle in accordance with the criterion measures of its "turf." Thus, if we revisit Exhibit 14–1, note the origin of the different pricing principles. The marketing manager is evaluated each period on her operating margin. The financial manager frets about trimming costs ahead of prices. The sales manager considers price concessions in order to retain key accounts. Naturally, the pricing manager doesn't want tinkering with the "system" of prices resulting from careful value analysis.

Exhibit 14–2
A Model for
Managing Price

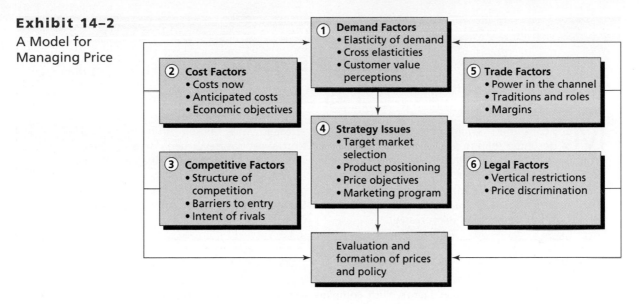

What Is Price?

Let's make it clear what we mean by price before we go any further. **Price** is the amount of money paid by a buyer to a seller for a particular product or service. Of course, the payment terms are a part of the price. Is payment due at delivery or at the end of the month? In what country's currency? Is freight included? How about service over the first 90 days? Buyers and sellers also know that price can be changed by adjustments in the financial terms or the product characteristics and its bundle of ancillary services. For example, adhesive prices can go from $60 a gallon to $66, or the price per can might remain at $60 while the can shrinks to 116.34 ounces.

Thus, a product can provide value in business markets not only when its invoice price is lower than the competitor's, but when its performance is superior. Performance includes quality, durability, and safety as well as energy efficiency, ease of operation, portability, and more. The fundamental job of the business marketing program is to establish and extend the sphere of benefits or value provided for a "price."

Second, we need to review the fact that no item is priced in isolation. Prices for countless items are connected in an exchange economy. With $20 in your pocket, you can take a friend to a movie and enjoy popcorn and a drink. But, if your car won't start and you have to take a cab to the cinema, you may have to forgo the popcorn or your friend. The same is true in business markets. As the price of freon has increased, the price of installed refrigeration equipment has climbed, and the demand for substitutes has pushed their prices higher. As buyers pay more for these inputs, there is less money to distribute to stockholders or spend on other inputs.

A Model for Price

Exhibit 14–2 maps the complex array of price determinants.[3] The model shows that prices are rightly determined by *demand factors*—price sensitivity, connectedness to other products, and customer perceptions—interacting with *cost factors* and *competitive factors* in the economic environment. At the same time, we must acknowledge the intersection

---

14–1

FROM THE FIELD
Fish Tales

Many consumers have read or heard reports of declining salmon populations in the world's rivers. As a result they have cut back on purchases when dining out or in. Yet fish farming is booming in Maine, Chile, Canada, Norway, and elsewhere. Farm-raised fish account for about half the world's salmon sales.

Meanwhile, salmon fishing in the Pacific Northwest has never been greater. Over 200 million came from Alaskan waters alone.

The irony is the declining demand in the face of surging supply. Prices have dropped from $.80 to $.05 per pound for Alaskan fishing crews.[4]

---

of market factors with company *strategy issues*—targeting, positioning, programming, and goals—within a marketing environment that is circumscribed by *trade factors* and *legal factors.*

In the remainder of this chapter, we will examine the pricing impact of six major factors in two major sections. The first deals especially with boxes 1, 2, and 3 from Exhibit 14–2, in a brief refresher of microeconomics. A short review of financial rudiments at the end of this section serves as a bridge from the clarity and internal consistency of economic models to the financial objectives of price management. The second major section treats an array of managerial issues arising primarily from boxes 4 through 6. Major subsections will address channel pricing, product line pricing, bidding, and negotiation. Specific legal matters arise within the subsections.

Cutting to the Quick: The Scissors Factors of Price

As a basic framework for pricing, recall the analysis you applied in your microeconomics class. Exhibit 14–3 shows the "scissors" of intersecting supply and demand functions in a market. The demand function is a downward-sloping line that represents the tendency of firms to purchase increasing amounts of our product—or additional firms to make purchases—as price declines. Supply and demand play out vividly in From the Field 14–1.

The steepness of this slope is determined by the availability of substitutes for the product. A product providing unique benefits exhibits a steep slope; its demand is **inelastic** or not very price sensitive. Products with lots of substitutes tend to be price **elastic**, meaning the quantity demanded is highly sensitive to changes in their price. An elastic demand function is flatter.

The product market demand picture can translate into firm-level demand curves in a number of ways. For example, the restaurant demand for salmon is downward-sloping—more chefs will feature salmon when they can buy the fish at low prices. Still, a specific Seattle fishing company or wholesaler has minimal pricing latitude. They sell at the market price because restaurants will go elsewhere if they try to price above the market. On the other hand, below-market prices are not apt to bring the supplier any more revenue than the market price. Essentially, any producer of a me-too product faces a flat demand function and has little pricing flexibility.

Exhibit 14–3
Supply and
Demand

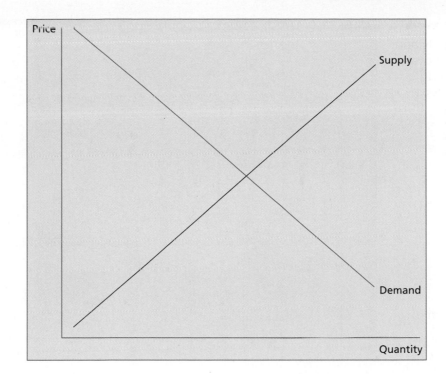

Only a firm providing unique value to customers enjoys a downward-sloping demand for its product and finds some pricing latitude. The amount of pricing discretion is rooted in the strategic advantages the firm uses to provide distinct benefits to customers. If a special lubricant can save a user $100 per machine in maintenance, it would be reasonable for a user to pay up to this level—whether the supplier's costs are $50 or $.50.

One company developed a new method of cleaning pipes in industrial furnaces. Using small propellants in a carrier gas to knock loose scale and coke deposits, this new process was called shotblasting. Compared to the traditional methods of cleaning, steam air decoking, or "turbining" (cutting or reaming out deposits), shotblasting was quicker, provided more energy efficiency for the system, and did minimal damage to pipes. The company used marketing research with prospective customers to find the priority and approximate dollar value of these advantages. It could then predict market share at different price and service configurations.[5]

Of course, the gently sloping downward demand curve we see in Exhibit 14–3 is an abstraction. In reality, the line may be more jagged or stair-stepped as substantial gains in purchases come at different price thresholds. Cellophane penetrated several successive applications as its price declined. Similarly, electronic controls for autos have seen expanded use as prices decline. We find that at certain prices new industries—lawn mowers or kitchen appliances—begin to use electronic controls at accelerating rates.

Meanwhile, back in Exhibit 14–3, the supply function is sloped upward. This represents suppliers' motivations to increase supply as prices increase. Higher prices prompt suppliers to hire additional shifts, use overtime, adjust capacity by subcontracting or retooling, and employ other measures to boost supply. This curve could actually be rather jagged too. For example, adding a second shift may provide just a small increase in our output because it replaces a good deal of first-shift overtime. But when we open a large

Exhibit 14–4

Often Supply and Demand Show Dramatic and Discontinuous Reactions to Price

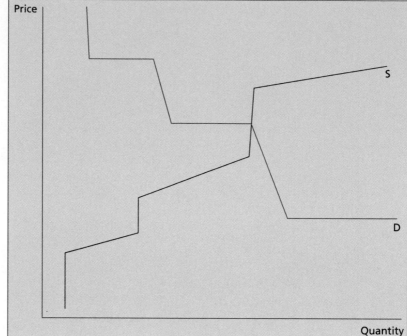

automated factory, supply surges at the current price; a rather flat sector of the supply function results. Furthermore, when *experience* can be expected to reduce costs—as in our cellophane vignette—we have suppliers driven to build cumulative volume and thereby secure a cost advantage. From the Field 14–2 profiles experience effects in both a labor-intensive and highly automated production setting.

The intersection of the two jagged functions, as shown in Exhibit 14–4, represents an abstract equilibrium price for our product. Practically, the "equilibrium" may be in a constant state of flux as needs change, technology advances, the costs of substitutes rise or fall, and supplies vary with weather, war, and whim. The simple model can nevertheless provide significant insights into the direction of future price pressures if we can develop tracking systems for the variables that affect supply and demand. Indeed, a classic study of a large petroleum company's pricing of gasoline in local markets, daily checking of market prices, internal product costs, and forecasts of overall market supply were key strategic variables.[6]

The Nature of Competitive Markets

As you know, economists have developed models of prices in several different market structures. Recapped in Exhibit 14–5, two of these—monopoly and pure competition—are rarely observed in practice. Most products have substitutes so it is not particularly useful to discuss monopolistic pricing in a business marketing text. Likewise, except for some minerals, metals, and agricultural products—and perhaps even in these areas—it is difficult to identify products that are undifferentiated across suppliers. Relationships supported by joint planning, delivery coordination, and an array of services can differentiate practically anything.[7] Thus, we won't discuss the price-taking situation of products in pure competition.

14–2

FROM THE FIELD
The Learning Curve

Kathleen Haefner stumbled into commercial upholstery when a friend asked her to renew the seats on a raft of cafe chairs for a new restaurant. She began with careful attention to original design and construction. Measures were double-checked. Assembly was tested and retested in process. The first chair took an entire day.

Chair 2 was knocked out the next morning. Chairs 3 and 4 were completed that afternoon. Ms. Haefner's output continued to improve until about halfway through the job, when things leveled off at about an hour per chair.

This example of the **learning curve**, the tendency of costs to decline with repetition, has been observed in countless studies. It is a component of a more encompassing concept called the experience curve. The experience curve reflects declining cost as a function of accumulated experience or output. Efficiency comes not only from repetition, but also from production and distribution innovations as well as product design simplification.

The accompanying table shows the forecast of experience-based economies in CD ROM manufacture. When such cumulative volume effects are anticipated, pricing strategy should aim to penetrate successive markets.

$0.15 =$ Learning curve constant
$\$2.00 =$ Average variable cost during first period
$2,000,000 =$ Average production per period

Period	Cumulative Production	Variable Cost/Unit	Percent Reduction	% Reduct. as Prod. Doubles
1	2,000,000	$2.00	0.00%	
2	4,000,000	$1.80	9.87%	9.87%
3	6,000,000	$1.70	5.90%	
4	8,000,000	$1.62	4.22%	10.12%
5	10,000,000	$1.57	3.29%	
6	12,000,000	$1.53	2.70%	
7	14,000,000	$1.49	2.29%	
8	16,000,000	$1.46	1.98%	10.26%
9	18,000,000	$1.44	1.75%	
10	20,000,000	$1.42	1.57%	
11	22,000,000	$1.40	1.42%	
12	24,000,000	$1.38	1.30%	
13	26,000,000	$1.36	1.19%	
14	28,000,000	$1.35	1.11%	
15	30,000,000	$1.33	1.03%	
16	32,000,000	$1.32	0.96%	10.33%

SOURCE: CD-ROM data courtesy of Michael V. Laric, Merrick School of Business, University of Baltimore (1997).

Exhibit 14–5

Economic Models of Market Structure

Most of the action in business marketing is in oligopoly and monopolistic competition.

Important dimensions / Types of situations	Pure competition	Oligopoly	Monopolistic competition	Monopoly
Uniqueness of each firm's product	None	None	Some	Unique
Number of competitors	Many	Few	Few to many	None
Size of competitors (compared to size of market)	Small	Large	Large to small	None
Elasticity of demand facing firm	Completely elastic	Kinked demand curve (elastic and inelastic)	Either	Either
Elasticity of industry demand	Either	Inelastic	Either	Either
Control of price by firm	None	Some (with care)	Some	Complete

SOURCE: Reprinted from E. Jerome McCarthy and William D. Perreault, *Basic Marketing* (Homewood, IL: Richard D. Irwin, 1987), p. 102. Used with permission of the McGraw-Hill Companies.

Oligopolies

Many business markets are **oligopolies**, characterized by just a few sellers. Each offers a product that is quite similar to the others. Consider Hertz, Avis, and National car rental firms or Owens Corning and Johns Manville in fiberglass insulation. Each firm may strive for a differential advantage in customer service, brand image, logistical excellence, or such. But any advantage tends to net only a narrow latitude for a price premium, and that advantage tends to be short-lived. Like the classic story of cellophane, imitation is the rule and pricing decisions of competitors are highly constrained and made with due consideration of the reaction by others.

As a result, firms see themselves competing in a market with a *kinked* demand, as shown in Exhibit 14–6. That is, at prices above the kink, demand is very elastic. Therefore, any attempt to raise prices above the current equilibrium zone will lead to sharp drops in volume. Going the other way, it is not likely that competitors will allow another's price cut to siphon their market share. Even not so radical price cuts stand to trigger a price war—a situation that certainly benefits customers in the short run, but which typically produces no winner on the supply side.

Monopolistic Competition

Another realistic case in business markets is **monopolistic competition**, a large number of differentiated sellers—such as corporate training companies, custom marketing research firms, and industrial distributors. In these fields, the actions of one firm have a smaller effect on others. Each seller brings some unique competency to the market and offers distinctively valued services and products, but, in the eyes of buyers, some other makes are tolerable substitutes. As a result, each firm faces a downward-sloping demand curve.

Exhibit 14–6

An Oligopoly's Kinked Demand Curve Has Elastic and Inelastic Segments

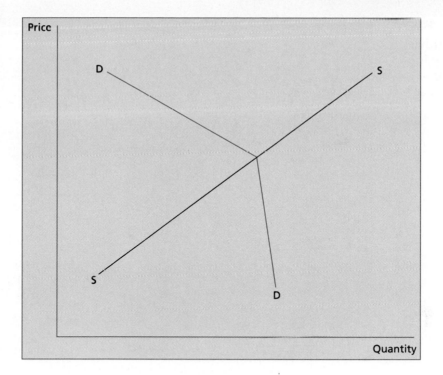

This is a useful case for illustrating the profit maximization model. Exhibit 14–7 shows the product's demand curve. Because each point on the line represents the quantity sold at a given price, it also represents the average revenue (AR) or price per unit. The line labeled MR is the very important function showing marginal revenue. Thus, if we can sell 200 units per month at $4 and 300 units at $3, the marginal revenue or additional sales is $100 [i.e., ($3 × 300) − ($4 × 200)].

The curve labeled ATC is the product's average total cost. This includes fixed costs that must be paid regardless of volume (managers' salaries, occupancy costs, advertising). Naturally, these produce high average costs at low volumes. But the ATC also includes the direct costs of producing and delivering the products (e.g., raw materials, direct labor, packaging). These costs start to swell the ATC at high volumes when crowded factory floors, overtime, stress, poor supervision, and the like begin to impair efficiency.

If managers at this firm could clearly measure costs and collect perfectly accurate market research, they would produce the quantity E per period. At this level of output, sold at price A per unit, the firm finds that marginal revenue equals marginal costs. Think about what this means. If the additional selling expenses are just a tiny bit less than the additional sales minus direct costs, profits increase. On the other hand, it would be folly to incur $101 in costs to gain another $100 in sales. Alas, profits are maximized at this price and quantity level—where marginal revenue equals marginal costs.

Graphically, the area of the rectangle ABEO depicts dollar sales, total revenue. The area of DCEO represents total costs. Their difference, shown by rectangle ABCD, is profit.

In monopolistic competition, firms have distinct skills, brands, and distribution advantages. They have no perfect substitutes. But firms making substantial profits tend to be emulated and draw competitive activity from rivals. This has the effect of reducing

Exhibit 14–7

A Competitive Advantage in Monopolistic Competition

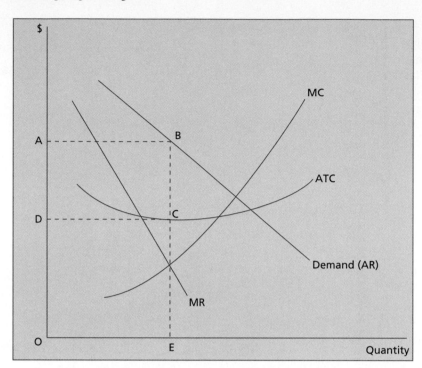

Exhibit 14–8

Unsustained Advantage in the Long Run in Monopolistic Competition: Average Total Costs Equal Average Revenue

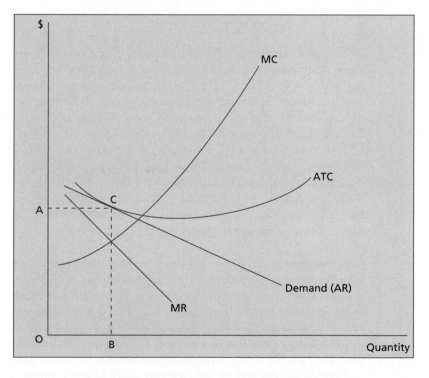

demand—moving the demand curve downward to the left—or making demand more price sensitive—flattening the demand curve. The result is to bring AR and ATC closer to tangential. Of course, this shrinks the once substantial profits, because when average revenue equals average total costs, as in Exhibit 14–8, there are no profits. Perhaps better

14–1

BUSINESS 2 BUSINESS

Same Sticker, New Price

A local computer dealer advertises a state-of-the-art desktop system for $2,395, delivered and set up for use. Can you think of at least three ways the dealer could effectively raise price without editing the ad?

than any other perspective, this framework underscores the importance of a market orientation, a focus on innovation, and constant striving to maintain and extend distinctive competencies in order to be able to price for profits.

Economic Theory and Financial Rudiments

These abstractions from economics underlie a number of tools used in marketing and financial management every day. The equality of average revenue and average cost in Exhibit 14–8 is the basis for break-even analysis. At the **break-even quantity**, we realize a sales level—at a specified price—at which total revenue equals total cost. Similarly, we can speak about a **break-even price**, the average revenue needed to cover costs, given a particular sales level.

Of course, most marketing decisions are not made with an aim to break even, but with a goal to improve from the current position. In this case when we speak of breaking even, we mean attaining a situation that does no harm to our current profit level. Marginal analysis is the name frequently given to this task of evaluating the incremental volume needed to cover incremental costs or the incremental loss of average revenue in the instance of price cuts. Exhibit 14–9 offers a series of examples of break-even and marginal analysis to reacquaint you with these essential financial rudiments of pricing.

Some Final Words on Models of Competitive Environments

These models of competitive environments require ambitious assumptions about the completeness of information about costs and customer demand. The oligopoly model is not too clear about how the equilibrium at the kink is obtained. Both models also mask the countless means by which competitors can challenge one's profitable position.

But they effectively simplify a complex interaction between demand and supply factors. They provide a structure for thinking about changes from the status quo. And they identify some normative prescriptions for pricing.

In the heat of battle, some managers have lost sight of these pricing fundamentals. For example, under pressure from its regional distributor one cutting tool manufacturer cut its prices by 10 percent. This effectively halved its gross profit margin. But there was no way on earth to double sales volume in the market, the critical expansion rate needed to avoid a profit decrease.

Exhibit 14–9 Financial Rudiments

At break-even, Total revenue = Total cost

Alternatively, Price × Q   = FC + VC = FC + (UVC × Q)

    Where   Q is quantity, FC is fixed costs, VC is variable costs, UVC is unit variable costs, and price is average revenue

We can solve for Q using algebra:

$$(\text{Price} \times Q) - (\text{UVC} \times Q) = FC$$
$$Q\,(\text{Price} - \text{UVC}) = FC$$
$$Q = FC/(\text{Price} - \text{UVC}) = FC/\text{Unit margin}$$

We can also solve for price, assuming a fixed Q

$$\text{Price} \times Q \quad = FC + (\text{UVC} \times Q)$$
$$\text{Price} = [FC + (\text{UVC} \times Q)]/Q = \text{Average cost}$$

When selling a mix of products, break-even is usually considered as a dollars-in-sales figure. We have unit costs typically expressed as a percentage of revenue. Thus, at break-even,

TR = FC + (C% × TR)

(1–C%) × TR = FC or TR = FC/(1-C%)

An income statement equivalent of break-even is: Gross profit = GS&A

Net sales	$60,000,000	100%
Cost of goods sold (COGs)	45,000,000	75
Gross profit	15,000,000	25
General, selling, administrative (GS&A)	15,000,000	25
Net profit before taxes	0	0

Consider the case of profits:

Net sales	$60,000,000	100%
Cost of goods sold	45,000,000	75
Gross profit	15,000,000	25
General, selling, administrative	12,000,000	20
Net profit before taxes	3,000,000	5%

Marginal analysis scenario: What sales increase is needed to cover a $1.2 million increase in marketing expenditures? We "break-even" on the expenditure if new revenue (NR) covers $1.2 million and the new COGS

NR = $1.2 million + COGS

NR = $1.2 million + .75NR

.25 NR = $1.2 million

NR = $1.2 million/.25

NR = $4.8 million

Another company in the food service industry thought its selection and delivery service justified a 5 percent price premium with its institutional customers. Unfortunately, purchasers didn't place such a high regard for the service because they were measured on acquisition costs. The firm's market share and profits dropped through the floor.

Issues in Price Management

This section reviews a number of key concepts and tools for the effective management of price. We begin with a look at pricing objectives. Then we address pricing through the channel and the indirect means of channel margin management. We take up several issues involving pricing a line of products, including the knotty legal and tactical challenge of pricing for different market segments. The chapter offers a succinct discussion of bid pricing and negotiation, with related material on leasing. We conclude with an overview of the qualities and benefits of a pricing system.

The Pricing Strategy

The formulation of a sound pricing strategy requires consideration of demand and cost factors in a competitive environment approximating one of these market structures. A price strategy consists of a specific approach to achieve the pricing objective. Pricing objectives might be

- To increase profitability by 12 percent over the next year.
- To thwart the efforts by competitors to gain a foothold in the market.
- To get competitors to accept us as a price leader.
- To restore order in a chaotic market.
- To increase market share to 17 percent.
- To smooth the seasonality of purchases.

To achieve these outcomes, a pricing strategy capitalizes on the unique strengths of the enterprise and the opportunities in the market. Here are examples of price strategies:

- To gain market share by concentrating on small users served by our full-line distributors.
- To build customer trust by reducing prices on products having highly visible cost reductions.
- To win customers from competitors by bundling items at a low total price, including items not carried by our rivals.

Clearly, the execution of a sound price strategy involves effective product management, careful formulation of the communication mix, and apt collaboration with channel partners. As the program is formulated, it is important to subject it to various tests of financial soundness, such as those in the previous section. In order to be able to develop sound pricing strategies, let's explore some of the managerial issues to be handled.

Channel Pricing

We explained in Chapter 9 that channel intermediaries should be compensated for the work they do. That requires that we incorporate channel intermediary prices, costs, and margins into our pricing strategy. In this section we describe how prices and costs ripple through the channel. We show how organizations are connected using sets of unit cost breakdowns. We apply the mechanism in a new product scenario.

Exhibit 14–10   Channel Margin Chain

When stated that margins in the channel are 15, 25, and 20 percent for manufacturers, wholesalers, and dealers, respectively, these are the product-level income statements implied.

Manufacturer		Wholesaler		Dealer	
Net sales	100%	Net sales	100%	Net sales	100%
COGS	85	COGS	75	COGS	80
Gross profit	15	Gross profit	25	Gross profit	20

For managerial purposes it is useful to equate the net sales of the firm on the left to the COGS of its neighbor on the right. Below we do this for a single item so think of net sales as price.

Manufacturer		Wholesaler		Dealer	
Net sales	$100	Net sales	133	Net sales	167
COGS	85	COGS	100	COGS	133
Gross profit	15	Gross profit	33	Gross profit	34

Because gross profit and COGS are complements and we connect net sales to COGS on the right, any dollar figure known in the channel allows us to complete the chain. Use the same margin chain to complete the income statements below.

Manufacturer		Wholesaler		Dealer	
Net sales		Net sales		Net sales	
COGS	—	COGS	—	COGS	$48
Gross profit		Gross profit		Gross profit	

We highlight the tendency to enlarge the set of functions expected from channel partners when new products are introduced. With this backdrop we explore avenues for managing price to ensure channel margins that match up to the functions needed to be performed by the channel. Importantly, reseller prices cannot be specified directly for legal reasons we will discuss shortly. We have to manage price *indirectly*.

Prices through the Channel

Pro Spot is a California manufacturer of welding equipment especially useful for automotive body shops. Body shop owners and other buyers purchase Pro Spot equipment from distributors. Hence, Pro Spot's factory price is different from what Ray's Auto Body pays for a welder. Nevertheless, Pro Spot and Ray are connected in the unit cost breakdowns of the channel participants. When we analyze purchase volume or assorted products, we can follow the same procedures with simple pro forma income statements instead of unit costs.

Follow the example in Exhibit 14–10. The left-hand box shows manufacturer's net sales to distributors, the direct costs involved, and resulting gross profit. Practically speaking, the factory price represents the distributor's cost of goods sold (COGs)—actually nearly all of its direct costs. If the distributor follows a discount structure that's negotiated with the manufacturer or that's simply typical of the product category, its price to dealers can be determined. The boxes below apply to unit prices and costs. We see the same connection between factory net sales and distributor costs of goods and gross profit; likewise for distributor sales and dealer costs of goods sold.

Exhibit 14–11

Margin Chain
Solution

Wholesaler		Dealer	
Net sales	100%	Net sales	100%
COGS	85	COGS	70
Gross profit	15	Gross profit	30
Apply the chain to work from a $10 dealer price			
Net sales	$7.00	Net sales	$10
COGS	5.95	COGS	7
Gross profit	1.05	Gross profit	3

Exhibit 14–12

New Product
Pricing
throughout the
Channel

Here we price a product through the channel that costs $4.50 to produce and a 25 percent factory margin is expected. First, $4.50 = .75 factory price. Therefore, factory price = $6.00.

Wholesaler		Dealer	
Net sales	$7.06 because 6.00 =.85 net sales	Net sales	$10.08 because 7.06 = .7 net sales
COGS	6.00	COGS	7.06
Gross profit	1.05	Gross profit	3.02

Finally, in the third set of boxes, we invite you to apply the percentage terms to complete the picture of connected prices, costs, and margins of channel partners. Unit profits or margins are often used in conversation that connects to income statement gross margins. When income statements are summarized line by line in percentages, the base is conventionally the net sales or net revenue line. That is, costs and gross profits are percentages of net sales. The same convention holds true at the unit level. Thus, *unless stated otherwise, gross profits or unit margins at any level of the channel are expressed as percentages of that organization's unit price or net sales.*

Margin Chains

It is not uncommon for channel margins to be expressed as a string of percentages. For example, construction sealants are marked up 15 percent and 30 percent by wholesalers and dealers. Given factory or end user price, and using the framework from Exhibit 14–10, we can easily determine prices and costs throughout the distribution channel. The algebra of channel pricing looks a bit tedious. But with regular involvement in a particular product setting, the mechanics become second nature.

Consider some of the pricing issues that involve the channel. Say marketing research has identified a new segment that would pay $9 to $11 for a sealant delivering certain new benefits. The pricing problem is what is the maximum factory price that will play out in the channel as a $10 price to users? Exhibit 14–11 works the numbers. The analysis could go the other way after the cost analysts reveal that it will cost $4.50 to make the product and a 25 percent gross profit is expected. Exhibit 14–12 works the numbers from the factory costs.

Channel Margin Management

Especially with a new product, the promotional tasks of channel intermediaries may be quite significant. Manufacturers may advertise and cultivate leads in order to support their channel partners, but there remains an important role for resellers. They must stock sufficient levels of inventory of a product whose demand has not yet been proven. Also, the selling tasks may require extensive demonstration and contact with multiple parties in a customer organization.

What are the prospects of obtaining such important channel functions if reseller margins are inadequate? Right, the prospects are dim. Our channel intermediaries can cut back on the roles they perform for our product or reallocate their effort to products and activities that may be more profitable.

A key part of our pricing strategy will be to manage the margins of our intermediaries. This has to be done indirectly because the Supreme Court has not seen to distinguish between price fixing by competitors and "price fixing" between channel partners. (Thus, it is just as illegal for Monsanto to tell its wholesalers to sell its herbicides at no less than $X as it is for Monsanto and Scott to conspire to fix their factory prices at $Y.)[8]

Manufacturers can affect reseller margins by several indirect means: exclusivity, territories, location restrictions, customer assignments, and advertising. Each method aims to control the pressure on a reseller's price. Sheltered from price pressures, channel members will then have margins sufficient to compensate for intensive selling effort, stocking, or other channel services.

Vertical Restrictions

When a manufacturer promises a reseller **exclusivity**, a pledge to supply no other resellers in the trade area, the supplier aims to bridle **intrabrand competition**, price pressure from sellers of the same brand. This enables relatively high reseller margins and thus motivates extra selling effort and other channel services. Usually, this manufacturer pledge is reciprocated by the reseller, which promises not to carry directly competing products. As we have mentioned elsewhere, bilateral pledging provides a structure for refining and deepening a business relationship.

Another way to manage intrabrand competition is to judiciously space resellers or, more realistically, use resellers that serve different market areas. This can be done by **territorial restrictions**, confining the reseller's activities to a particular geographic zone, or by **location restrictions**, specifying the site or sites from which the product may be sold. Obviously, each approach brings a measure of exclusivity. The explicit territorial clause is more exclusive than the location clause because the former forbids activities outside one's territory, while the latter has a range limited only by the efficiency and inventiveness of the fixed site reseller.

Customer restrictions specify the type of business the reseller may or may not serve. If distributors can resell to other distributors, all the above mechanisms for rationalizing the distribution network may be jeopardized. Therefore, it is common to prohibit wholesalers from selling to other types of wholesalers. In addition, a manufacturer may make certain large accounts explicitly off-limits to its resellers.

Advertising

What about advertising's effects on channel margins? In the evolution of markets it sometimes happens that the marketing channel is not the best way to differentiate the product. If buyer sophistication increases or new advertising can effectively communicate product benefits, why not use it to do so? The results may be a positive brand image and strong customer preferences. The secondary effect of highly effective advertising is to intensify price competition *among resellers*. Think about it. Imagine you're purchasing a large quantity of ink jet printers. You know the product performance advantages of Hewlett-Packard machines from reliable test issues in computer magazines, and HP advertising outlines benefits you appreciate in terms you can understand. You don't need a distributor salesperson to school you on how or what to purchase; you're looking for a good price. Distributors soon recognize this character of the marketplace and begin to discount the HP printers.

Push versus Pull

If we take this idea a little bit further, we see that advertising and other promotions to differentiate the brand effectively among end users can essentially pull the product through the channel. This is the fundamental aim of the **pull strategy**, direct communication with end users to differentiate the product through the media. This contrasts with some of the ideas presented earlier in this section that preserved reseller margins and otherwise enabled their performance of key promotion activities. The **push strategy** is the label attached to the general approach to support and reward reseller activities to differentiate the brand among customers.

To Classify Promotion Mixes   In some marketing texts, push and pull strategies are discussed as polar options that compete for resources in a firm's marketing communication efforts. True, these strategies do manifest themselves in the communication mix: push strategies reflecting trade promotions, selling aids for the channel, healthy margins, and low levels of advertising aimed principally at supporting the claims of salespeople; pull strategies showing high levels of advertising, a strong brand image, and broad distribution of 800 numbers for presale support from the manufacturer. In the field of abrasives, most of you know 3M because of its advertising, but you may not have heard of the world's leader, Norton, because it stresses a push strategy. We want you to see, however, that the two strategies are much more than a simple dichotomy of promotion emphasis.

To Manage Channel Effectiveness—via Prices!   Recognize push and pull in Exhibit 14–13 for their roles in channel coordination and price management—and *recognize their roots in careful analysis of market behavior.* Can customers and prospects use media-provided information to form strong preferences? Or is product evaluation and use so difficult that it takes personal selling or a close look at an array of options or special help with installation and training, and so on to differentiate?

In the former case of media-provided data, a business marketer should develop a strong advertising campaign and commit to high spending to build and maintain the brand image. Sales gains and declining end user prices prove the aptness of the strategy. One business marketer described this situation as "heaven," noting that he was able to raise factory prices, though distributors continued to cut prices to end users—who touched a bit of heaven themselves. In essence, the manufacturer was able to use effective advertising to capture a larger share of total margin (value) in the channel. The advertising heightened reseller competition on price, increasing the quantity demanded—total channel throughput.

In the latter case, when customers depend on the channel to differentiate products, upstream business marketers must apply their resources to enable, support, and reward reseller activities. High reseller margins—perhaps protected from intrabrand competition—are the rule.

Final Words on Channel Pricing

Business products sold through intermediaries must be priced to account for the margins earned by those intermediaries. This section demonstrated the connection of unit costs, margins, and prices in the channel. We showed how the margin chain percentages and any dollar measure of price, cost, or margin can be used to determine the remaining dollar elements in the channel. Facility with the margin chain is critical for costing to price and proper price positioning.

Exhibit 14–13
Push versus Pull Strategies

Push: Product is differentiated by personal selling, channel service, and so on.

Pull: Product is differentiated through the media.

Manufacturers have a significant stake in the management of resale prices of their products. Clearly, if reseller margins—and therefore prices—are too high, users forgo the benefits of the product and factory sales suffer. But if reseller margins are too low, grave consequences may occur also: Intermediary selling effort, service, stocking, and so on may deteriorate, causing end user frustration and eventually a switch to products of another manufacturer. Although it is not legal for manufacturers to specify resale prices, there are a number of nonprice restraints that work to control intrabrand competition and thereby preserve margins. We identified exclusive territories, location clauses, and customer restrictions as means to limit intrabrand competition on price but encourage reseller service.

Finally we noted that markets evolve or creative breakthroughs occur in communications that result in viable alternatives to reliance on resellers to differentiate the brand. As reseller participation in promotion and other channel functions declines, intrabrand competition can greatly intensify, thereby reducing prices and reseller margins. A real key to the decision to push or pull is determining how customers process information. They call the shots: If differentiation can occur through media, a pull strategy will squeeze reseller margins and users will benefit from low prices. When the preponderance of differentiation can only be performed by the channel, we opt for a push strategy that must support and rightly compensate the differentiation efforts of our channel partners. Users gain from fitting reseller services.

Product Line Pricing

To this point in the chapter our discussion has presumed the price management of a single product. But many companies offer a line of products. To some extent the products may be substitutes. An example is the array of high-speed personal computers from Compaq or the overnight and second-day delivery options from UPS. Or the products in the line may be complements: Loctite adhesives for Loctite applicator systems, books authored by a well-regarded seminar leader on setting priorities and achievement. This section briefly discusses some of the managerial issues involved in pricing related products.

UPS has a service at a fitting price for a spectrum of shipper needs.

© 1997 United Parcel Service of America, Inc.

(In other words, whatever you need to move your business.)

You already know that UPS offers more guaranteed, on-time delivery options than anyone.* We'd like to remind you why. Your business demands it. And nobody is more committed to your business than UPS. Every truck, every plane — indeed, every UPS person — is fully dedicated to getting whatever you need, wherever you need it, whenever you need it there. Consider the range of delivery options only UPS can offer. Same day? Overnight by 8 A.M.? 10:30 A.M.? How about 2nd Day A.M., or Worldwide Express? Even Saturday delivery. Whatever your business demands, we will deliver. Just say the word.

UPS

MOVING at the SPEED of BUSINESS.

www.ups.com · 1-800-PICK-UPS

*Call for guarantee details. ©1997 United Parcel Service of America, Inc.

Pricing Substitute Products

When substitute products differ in size, the pricing task tends to be driven largely by cost factors. Following this line, a 6′ × 10′ tarp carries a price twice as high as the 10′ × 12′, and a 20′ × 20′ goes for 6.67 times the price. There is something to be said for the simplicity of this approach, but it clearly neglects the demand side of the equation. Small-size buyers may be triers who might be induced in greater numbers with a discount price. Are 10′ × 12′ tarp buyers looking for the same benefits as 20′ × 20′ buyers? Do they have the same range of alternatives? Can the large size encourage use and repeat purchases?

Similarly, when products differ in quality, we find a tendency to use cost or input formulas too. This, of course, neglects to consider the value of the quality differences to customers. Often the cost associated with a quality-enhancing component, design, or ingredient is far less than the value it provides the user. An overpowered starter on trucks used in Manitoba is vital for machine performance in winter because the cost of downtime is so monumental. This can work the other way too: a large incremental cost for small gains in performance or value. Scrubbers that remove 90 percent of emissions may cost $X to produce; those that remove 95 percent may cost $2X. Clearly, both cost and benefit sides must be examined in pricing any product. Some firms tend to forget the benefit side when cost differences in the line are so handy. The reason a firm carries multiple products in a line is to appeal to different market segments. Examine the price sensitivity of each segment—as well as the differences in production and selling costs to each.

Pricing Complementary Products

We know that the demand for many business products is derived from demand for other goods and services. This section looks at the situation involving a single firm selling the products used in combination. For example, many commercial buildings feature washroom soap dispensers sold by firms that also supply soap. The sale of a materials testing system brings follow-up sales of replacement parts and service.

The popular approach is to price the "driver" product relatively low in order to penetrate the market, and then make high margins on the follow-up business of parts, consumables, or service. But most buyers are weary of such "traps" and will try to evaluate alternative supply arrangements on a system basis. Indeed, they may avoid the driver product for fear of being locked into a vulnerable supply position. When the driver product represents a specific investment on the buyer's part, the seller may wish to provide some assurances to the buyer that it won't be "held up" by exploitative prices on complementary products or services over the life of the asset.

A relationship management approach to pricing would enable the parties to consider a structure for adjusting prices in a long-term supply contract. Current prices could be adjusted at a programmed annual rate to reflect the likelihood of changing input costs. Then we might add a clause that provided exceptions. A company in the Northwest pegged its price in a long-run supply contract to fluctuations in the market price of gold because gold was a costly material for one component. Costs were hard to forecast and a slight rise in the price of gold meant the supplier's profit margin evaporated, unless some price adjustment were made.

Recall from Chapter 2 that contracts represent just one set of ways that firms might organize for ongoing exchange. The selling firm could make matching investments to service the buyer's specific investments, perhaps locating a supply facility near the customer. Alternatively, the seller might license proprietary products to enable customers to purchase from another source in the event the seller ever gouged the customer on price—or shirked other obligations in the relationship.

Segmentation Pricing

Throughout the chapter we have instructed you to price according to both supply and demand factors. We consider costs to the extent that they must be covered, but we attend to the value customers can expect from the product. Now, if different customer segments derive different value from the product, we should thoroughly explore the opportunity to charge them different prices. Indeed, the entire motivation for segmenting markets is to reap greater financial rewards by customizing a marketing mix for a group of customers.

It may or may not be easy to isolate different markets in order to charge different prices. When segments are defined geographically, it may be possible to charge different prices in different regions. When segments are accustomed to service by distinct channels (e.g., adhesives via catalog versus bearings distributor versus plastics wholesaler), different prices are possible. But it may take a great deal of creativity and remarkable integration with other elements of the marketing program—especially channels and advertising—when purchasing habits are fluid. Bootlegging and "gray markets" attest to inevitability that buyers from one locale, channel, or industry find out when there are better deals given in another.

Different Prices to Competitors   The **Robinson–Patman Act** (1936) prohibits some types of **price discrimination**. When sellers charge different prices on similar products to customers that are in competition—and the effect is likely to lessen competition substantially—they violate U.S. pricing statutes. Most litigation involves alleged price discrimination by sellers, but buyer initiatives for a obtaining price advantages over their competitors buying the same product also are illegal.

Understand all key ingredients here. If a railroad charges one rate for 10 boxcars to a company shipping scrap metal and another rate for a company shipping air compressors, is that illegal? The answer is no because the scrap metal shipper does not compete with the air compressor shipper. And managerially, it makes good sense to charge different rates to groups of customers with different price sensitivities: Scrap metal could go by barge or truck, compressors realistically only by truck.

What if a company sells processed beer brewing by-products to a large pet food company in St. Louis for $X per ton and to a small pet food company in Rochester, New York, for $1.2X per ton? First off, it may be that the St. Louis market is more competitive than Rochester's. Thus, $X is what it takes to meet competition in St. Louis. If Rochester and other markets are not "subsidizing" predatory (below-market) prices in St. Louis, then there is no legal difficulty here.

Alternatively, the law allows for price differences based on quantity purchased, when the associated cost differences are evident. Compared to a small order, often a large purchase has more economical shipping and handling costs per unit, and equivalent administrative costs (e.g., order processing and billing) are distributed over more units.

Illegal price discrimination must be reasonably expected to have an adverse impact on competition. Adverse impact does not mean one of our competitors is unhappy or has slumping sales. We distinguish *injury to a competitor* from *injury to competition*. When competition suffers, we might see firms going out of business because of losses attributable to price discrimination or we could expect a small number of firms to increase their already high market shares. This tends toward a monopoly and restricted purchasing options for buyers.

Finally, we need to note that *price discrimination to resellers that participate in different channel functions appears to be legal.* In today's business environment we see all kinds of purchasing strategies by end users. Some buy direct and receive shipments centrally in order to route to the plants. Other users will rely on wholesalers to ship to plants and set up parts and materials for use on the shop floors. We see similar variation in functions performed by different wholesalers. For example, some will exclusively serve end users, others will do substantial business with another level in the channel: dealers or resellers. It seems silly in such an environment to apply a simplistic trade discount scheme such as end users pay list price, Y, wholesalers pay $.7Y$, and dealers $.8Y$.

Instead, manufacturers can charge different prices, based on customer performance of the different channel functions. The Supreme Court has stated that functional discounts do not violate the Robinson–Patman Act.

> In general, a supplier's **functional discount** is said to be a discount given to a purchaser based on the purchaser's role in the supplier's distributive system, reflecting, at least in a generalized sense, the services performed by the purchaser for the supplier.[9]

Bidding and Negotiating

Up to now, our discussion of price has implicitly emphasized **administered prices**; that is, prices established by a seller as impersonal, take-it-or-leave-it offers to prospective buyers. This type of pricing dominates the consumer marketplace and is common in business markets. Nevertheless, many transactions between firms involve competitive bidding or negotiation.

Bid Pricing
In a publication called *Commerce Business Daily*, an undergraduate intern at PPG Industries might notice that the U.S. Department of Energy has asked for proposals to construct and evaluate a solar-powered post office in Utah. The city of Centerville advertises

for bids from highway construction companies to repair a stretch of U.S. 42. A metropolitan hospital asks three waste disposal companies to bid for the task of properly managing medical wastes.

As you can see from these examples, buyers take a proactive role in making market forces work to satisfy organizational needs. Competitive bidding is very common in government and quasi-public institutions (schools, hospitals, social service agencies) largely to satisfy external constituencies that otherwise have difficulty auditing performance. Competitive bids provide some assurance of input efficiency.

Goals and Constraints   Not every bidding occasion is a business opportunity. The potential bidder must carefully examine the request for proposals or bids. A successful bid is one that meets the goals of both buyer and bidder. Begin by taking stock of your firm's mission and strategy. Do we have experience in this area? Do we want to build on this experience? If so, with this type of account? Will we have the capacity to complete the project if we get it? Is this a contract that can develop our company's reputation in a new field connected to important follow-on business? What level of effort is involved in preparing the proposal?

Next, and certainly as part of preparing a proposal, consider the buyer's objectives. Frequently price is not the ultimate criterion. For a Department of Defense communication system, the first criterion might be security, for aircraft landing gear, reliability; for highway repair, speed.

With an informed appreciation of your competitors' abilities, realistically assess your firm's capacity to measure up on buyer criteria. Not every competitor is in a position to bid. They may have capacity tied up in previously won jobs. They may have key personnel assigned elsewhere. They may have let it be known that they are no longer interested in a particular line of business.

We should bid for the job if we want the business and have a reasonable chance of competing favorably for the contract. The bid price should reflect consideration of costs and competitive action.

Many firms prepare bids according to a standard formula built from experience. A marketing consultant calculated a bid for one project by estimating the hours of telephone interviewing, analytical services, and report writing using standard rates of $14, $50, and $75, respectively. A building contractor summed 1.2 × materials cost + 1.5 estimated labor.

These standards are fine as starting points, but the final bid should reflect current operating realities. For example, why bid the telephone interviewing at $14 if the call center is already at full use? Why price to recoup $20,000 of warehouse rent if the space will be idle otherwise? And why bid $15,000 if you are confident that no competitor can deliver for under $20,000.

Exhibit 14–14 shows how decision theory can help in the evaluation of bid options in uncertain situations. In this example, IROD's knowledge of its rival's scant ability to prepare a low-price bid leads it to submit a high price, $12. Although there is a slight chance of losing the contract at the high price, the expected payoffs are superior to the expected profits from a bid that's sure to win.

Protocol   Buyers opt for one of two general formats for soliciting proposals. **Open bidding** means that any organization can vie for the business. Open bids tend to be sought in two polar situations: (1) when needs are tightly defined for simple products or services—for example, 400 yards of pea gravel or printing political handbills—and (2) when needs are vaguely defined, perhaps only specifying a solution—for example, extinguish wellhead fires or transport earth moving equipment from Peoria to Siberia. In

Exhibit 14–14

Bidding: Applied Decision Theory

In this simple illustration, IROD is considering two bid levels: one high and one low. If IROD wins at the high level, its profits will be about $150,000. If IROD wins at the low level, its profits will be around $100,000.

A rival firm, Doro, has a realistic chance of winning the contract too. Although it cannot match IROD's cost structure to prepare a bid better than IROD's low bid, Doro could edge IROD's higher bid level. Finally, with its current labor problems, Doro is far behind on three other projects. IROD executives think it is unlikely that Doro will pursue the job except at a high profit level.

The accompanying table summarizes the situation and the expected payoffs from each possible bid by IROD.

IROD's Options	Possible Actions by Doro (probability)		Expected profits
	Bid $13/unit (.8)	**Bid $10/unit** (.2)	
Bid $12/unit	IROD wins, Profit = $150K	IROD loses, Profit = 0	.8 × $150K = $120K
Bid $9/unit	IROD wins, Profit = $100K	IROD wins Profit = $100K	$100K

the former case, open bidding energizes market pressures on commodity-like products. Price is the only criterion.

In the latter case, open bidding enables the broadest set of creative solutions to address the problem. The buyer may ask to negotiate price with the vendor whose proposal reflected the best thinking and promise.

Closed bidding features the solicitation of proposals from an exclusive set of potential suppliers. For example, American Express may ask three marketing research companies to submit proposals to conduct a concept evaluation for a new type of corporate credit card. The closed bidding format reflects the buyer's ability to identify capable suppliers. Closed bidding also recognizes the significant costs of bid preparation. Imagine five companies spending $5,000 each preparing bids on a research project that yields $20,000 in profit. The industry risks self-destruction if the costs of bids outrun the profits from projects.

Negotiated Prices

Unlike the bidding process, in which the buyer essentially asks potential suppliers to "give us your best shot," **negotiation** involves two-way communication and problem solving to come to mutually agreeable terms. Recall our discussions of negotiation in Chapter 7 and conflict management in Chapter 9. Of course, the parties have conflicting interests: Seller wants a high price, buyer a low price. But seldom does the entire transaction pivot on the number to the right of the dollar sign.

Often negotiation over price spills over into other issues. The buyer makes a concession on price if buyer inventories are trimmed by JIT. The seller makes a concession on price if the buyer will agree to share production schedule information, enabling more efficient seller production and distribution. Sometimes payment timing solves what initially appeared to be a price issue.

Negotiation Strategy   Business marketers cannot approach every business bargaining situation in the same way. Some exchange parties are long-term, others are brand new. And haggling over a lease is apt to be more significant than customer late payment fees.

Two fundamental questions are key to selecting an initial negotiation strategy: (1) Is the relationship with the other party important? (2) Are the material outcomes important?[10]

Avoidance is a common course when the party doesn't really need the deal or the partner. A small supplier may find a potentially large account that fails to read proposals or even return phone calls. **Accommodation** is sacrifice to build or sustain a relationship. **Compromise** is a hybrid of competition and accommodation. It is often an easy solution, bringing a premature end to the negotiations. **Competitive negotiation** has a winner and a loser; it is the right course when it is critical to win *this* deal. Little regard is given to the prospects for subsequent exchange with the party. **Collaboration** is joint problem solving, searching for creative win–win solutions.

The real negotiation strategy options are then competition, collaboration, and accommodation.[11] The characteristics are summarized in Exhibit 14–15. Think carefully of the stakes of the issue and the relationship as you prepare to pursue one of these strategies.

Leasing   Related to the issue of negotiation over price is the matter of who owns the product. Companies in the capital equipment business often lease more items than they sell outright. **Leasing** involves a contract for the temporary use of a product or premises in exchange for payment or rent. The seller can use its own cash to finance a lease. More commonly, leasing is arranged by the credit subsidiaries of large companies or by financial firms specializing in the field. CIT Financial, General Finance Corporation, and Commercial Credit Corp. are leading lease specialists.

Two types of lease arrangements are used in business. A **full-payout lease** or **financial lease** is a contract that cannot be canceled and is fully amortized over the term of the lease. Lease payments on a Mita 6500 copier might total $12,600 over five years, surpassing the purchase price of $10,800. The financial lease usually includes a purchase option at the end of the term. An **operating lease** is a short-term contract that can be canceled. Usually, operating expenses are covered by the lease payment.

Let's try to understand the buyer's interest in leasing by asking you to imagine yourself going into the commercial painting business after you complete this class. To preserve your limited capital and credit, you might lease scaffolding on a full-payout basis. You realize that by not purchasing scaffolding you cannot claim its depreciation from your taxes or claim any salvage value. Nevertheless, for a tax-deductible expense of $600 per month, you get the equipment you need for many low-rise jobs over the next four years. Alternatively, you could lease scaffolding as needed for particular jobs. On a monthly basis, the operating lease would run closer to $900, but if an estimated three-month job only took two, the operating lease payments would only total $1,800.

Strategically the seller can use lease terms to control the mix of leases and purchases. A low imputed interest rate on a lease may be just the spark needed to induce customers to acquire the latest model. Broader market penetration may bring additional exposure and perhaps additional demand for service or accessories.

Final Words on Bid Pricing and Negotiation

Many companies price their products and services by means other than a single administered schedule. Sales to government agencies often involve bid pricing. Capital goods sales in private industry also involve bidding, but proposals are complex. Negotiation may occur after proposals are evaluated. And a variety of leasing options may be considered in light of the objectives of both buyer and seller.

Negotiation strategy is best determined by the importance of the outcome and the exchange relationship. In a partnership, the temptation to split the difference is the lazy way out. It forgoes the opportunity to look at price negotiation as a collaborative

Exhibit 14–15 Characteristics of Different Negotiation Strategies

Aspect	Competition (Distributive Bargaining)	Collaboration (Integrative Negotiation)	Accommodative Negotiation
Payoff structure	Usually a fixed amount of resources to be divided	Usually a variable amount of resources to be divided	Usually a fixed amount of resources to be divided
Goal pursuit	Pursuit of own goals at the expense of those of others	Pursuit of goals held jointly with others	Subordination of own goals in favor of those of others
Relationships	Short-term focus; parties do not expect to work together in the future	Long-term focus; parties expect to work together in the future	May be short-term (let the other win to keep them happy) or long-term (let the other win to encourage reciprocity in the future)
Primary motivation	Maximize own outcome	Maximize joint outcome	Maximize others' outcome or let them gain to enhance relationship
Trust and openness	Secrecy and defensiveness; high trust in self, low trust in others	Trust and openness, active listening, joint exploration of alternatives	One party relatively open, exposing own vulnerabilities to the other
Knowledge of needs	Parties know own needs, but conceal or misrepresent them; neither party lets the other know real needs	Parties know and convey real needs while seeking and responding to needs of the other	One party is overresponsive to other's needs so as to repress own needs
Predictability	Parties use unpredictability and surprise to confuse other side	Parties are predictable and flexible when appropriate, trying not to surprise	One party's actions totally predictable, always catering to other side
Aggressiveness	Parties use threats and bluffs, trying to keep the upper hand	Parties share information honestly, treat each other with understanding and respect	One party gives up on own position to mollify the other
Solution search behavior	Parties make effort to appear committed to position, using argumentation and manipulation of the other	Parties make effort to find mutually satisfying solutions, using logic, creativity, and constructiveness	One party makes effort to find ways to accommodate the other
Success measures	Success enhanced by creating bad image of the other; increased levels of hostility and strong in-group loyalty	Success demands abandonment of bad images and consideration of ideas on their merit	Success determined by minimizing or avoiding conflict and soothing all hostility; own feelings ignored in favor of harmony
Evidence of unhealthy extreme	Unhealthy extreme reached when one party assumes total–zero-sum game; defeating the other becomes a goal in itself	Unhealthy extreme reached when one subsumes all self-interest in the common good, losing self-identity and self-responsibility	Unhealthy extreme reached when abdication to other is complete, at expense of personal and/or constituent goals
Key attitude	Key attitude is "I win, you lose"	Key attitude is "What's the best way to address the needs of all parties?"	Key attitude is "You win, I lose"
Remedy for breakdown	If impasse occurs, mediator or arbitrator may be needed.	If difficulties occur, a group dynamics facilitator may be needed	If behavior becomes chronic, party becomes negotiationally bankrupt

14–2

BUSINESS 2 BUSINESS

The Importance of Price

Sales reps often press for lower prices or more pricing authority, thinking that their offerings are not competitive with their accounts. This bias for lower and lower prices is not simply a customer advocacy position. It might well reflect an incomplete understanding of buyer needs or their selling roles.

What do these data on the importance of different attributes in the customer-supplier relationship reveal about this phenomenon and what do they suggest for sales force management and pricing?

	Purchasing Managers		Sales Reps	
Product Attributes	**Rank**	**Mean**	**Rank**	**Mean**
Reliability	1	1.31	1	1.36
Quality	2	1.37	2	1.42
Durability	3	1.39	8	2.03
Engineering	4	1.48	7	1.83
Workmanship	5	1.63	10	2.21
Service Attributes				
Delivery	6	1.73	6	1.76
Service	7	1.80	5	1.53
Reputation	8	2.01	3	1.45
Marketing	9	2.17	11	2.44
Monetary Attributes				
Financial Terms	10	2.25	9	2.18
Price	11	2.63	4	1.51

SOURCE: Data used with permission from Ramon A. Avila, William B. Dodds, Joseph D. Chapman, O. Karl Mann, and Russell G. Wahlers, "Importance of Price in Industrial Buying: Sales versus Purchasing Perspectives," *Review of Business* 15 (Winter 1993), pp. 34–38.

problem solving process—a process that looks at the entire exchange and the roles performed by the partner. New roles—stocking, promoting, ordering, exchanging—and new means of coordination—forecasting, producing, shipping, holding—could emerge.

A Pricing System

Price is a critical element of marketing strategy. It belongs under the purview of the marketing manager. But she must be equipped with the right tools. These pricing tools include information on costs, customers, and competitors as well as familiarity with channel policy and the law.

Accurate and timely information on internal operating costs and channel margins are critical. Supplier assistance in cost containment, design efficiency, and related facets of supply chain coordination should be reflected in the cost data as well. Finally, realistic cost forecasts should reflect consideration of experience effects, global supply factors, and government action.

Unless our products provide value to customers, we are out of business. Our capital goods must be reliable and durable, efficiently producing quality output and enabling customers to realize cash flows sufficient to pay the price (lease) on our equipment. Similarly, supplies and MRO items must provide value to the customer in excess of our price. We need careful analysis of customer requirements, supported by empathic dialogue and sound feedback from the sales force. We must train and reward the sales force for its critical role in this system.

Competitor price data are also needed in the pricing system. Again, we want to encourage our salespeople to bring good information to the process. Another component here is a bid tracking system that records the bids tendered, by account, and allows score keeping. Are we winning 25 percent of bids or 35 percent? How does this compare to year-ago rates? What are the batting averages of different managers making pricing decisions?

Can a pricing system pay off? Of course! Elliot Ross of the McKinsey Company tells of a firm that revised its accounting system to better sort fixed and variable costs by product and market. Then, with the help of its sales force, it compiled buying profiles and pricing histories for major customers by product type and key competitor. Finally, it loaded the new cost, customer, and competitor databases on personal computers for each pricing manager, provided guidelines, and issued periodic feedback on personal performance. Margins improved in a slumping business cycle and profits increased $25 million in the first year.[12]

Summary

Price is the dollar amount exchanged for a particular product-and-service configuration. It captures the focus of accountants, market managers, operations managers, sales staff, and pricing specialist on the seller side. It's the aim of buyers seeking value on the customer side.

The factors of supply and demand have been formally analyzed by economists. Their models of competitive structure give important insights into the dynamics of pricing in different competitive situations. We reviewed the fragile equilibrium status of prices in oligopolistic settings and reviewed the profit maximization axioms of monopolistic competition. The latter supported a refresher treatment of the financial rudiments of simple pro forma income statements as well as break-even and marginal analysis, enabling us to evaluate candidate pricing strategies.

The key managerial topics of pricing involve channel margin chains and margin management. Because reseller margins should generally compensate for performance of channel functions, it is vital to manage price in order to insure adequate reseller rewards and fitting channel services to end users. Reseller prices can only be managed indirectly through vertical restrictions—territory, location, and customers—and advertising.

In a critical discussion of the strategies of push and pull marketing, we examined how they best fit customer buying processes and work to manage channel margins and functions. Essentially, if products can be differentiated via the media, we should follow a pull strategy and allow reseller margins to erode. If personal selling and logistical excellence are needed to differentiate the product, the supplier should push—that is, work to support the margins of channel partners who provide the key differentiating functions.

The chapter developed key ideas for managing prices of related products. Substitutes should be priced for different segments. Complements should be viewed as a system, recognizing the possibility of specific investments by buyers. When buyers seek to safeguard their specific investments, sellers should recognize their ability to make pledges or otherwise reduce buyer perceptions of vulnerability.

When companies charge different prices to customers in different market segments, they must pay careful attention to Robinson–Patman Act provisions against price discrimination. Violations occur when (1) different prices are charged to competitors, (2) the differences are not attributable to cost differences, (3) the product is essentially the same for each, and (4) the effects are damaging to competition. Fortunately, in the face of channel systems in flux, the Supreme Court has said that functional discounts appear to be contractually fitting and legal.

Before concluding the chapter with a brief discussion of a system for pricing, we covered the topics of bid pricing, negotiation, and leasing.

Key Terms

accommodation	exclusivity	negotiation
administered prices	financial lease	oligopoly
avoidance	full-payout lease	open bidding
break-even price	functional discount	operating lease
break-even quantity	inelastic demand	price
closed bidding	intrabrand competition	price discrimination
collaboration	learning curve	pull strategy
competitive negotiation	leasing	push strategy
compromise	location restrictions	Robinson–Patman Act
customer restrictions	monopolistic	territorial restriction
elastic demand	competition	

Discussion Questions

1. Price is a means of allocating scarce resources in a society. Are there any other ways? Identify strengths and weaknesses of one or two other means of allocating scarce resources in a society.

2. As a budding business marketer you have been advised in this chapter to price products according to the value they provide customers. But customers seldom come right out and say, "If I could get a good custodial service (or MRO supplier or parts source or manufacturers' rep, etc.), I'd gladly pay $X." Identify two or three marketing research tools that could help define the dollar value of product benefits for a business customer.

3. Select members of the class to call at least four local businesses to obtain prices on the following specific items. (Try to find someone in the market to actually buy each of these products or services.) Record each quote and speculate about the aptness of a kinked demand curve in the product market.

   One hundred pounds of dry ice.

   Close cracks and seal a specific blacktop parking lot.

   Paint a specific building.

   40 4′ × 16′ × 1/2″ sheets of drywall, delivered.

   A copy machine that makes 35 to 45 copies per minute.

4. For a copy machine that makes 35 to 44 copies per minute, identify one or two market segmentation bases that would capitalize on different price sensitivities among prospects.

5. Wexford Bearings sold casters and ball bearings through a network of industrial distributors throughout North America. Although margins could be as high as 35 percent on specialty bearings, most products were priced to afford distributors 25 percent margins. Recently Buskin, a distributor in Erie, Pennsylvania, gave a 5 percent discount to Midland Motors on a large order of standard bearings. Buskin took the order for the whole year's anticipated volume and promised up to three deliveries per month within 48 hours of reorder. What's Buskin's gross profit on the Midland account if its purchases run to $46,000?

6. Continuing from question 5, Gustav Himmelfarb, marketing vice president at Wexford, took a call from Hank Buskin, owner of Buskin Distributing. Hank asked for a price break on the volume he did with Wexford to service Midland. "Look, we've engineered a good supply contract and they've made a commitment to us. This is probably 20 percent of Wexford's volume in western Pennsylvania. And it's predictable! Steady! But I've got to let you know that it's really a stretch for me to make money on Midland. We've cut our margin 20 percent and have eaten what's left with the blue ribbon service Midland has come to expect. We need a 2.5 percent price break from Wexford on the Midland business if this thing is going to hold together." How should Himmelfarb respond?

7. The commercial painting business you set up last year has been a remarkable success. Now your company is one of four invited to submit proposals and prices for painting and glazing West Fork's community conservatory. What are the factors to be considered as you evaluate this opportunity and prepare a proposal?

8. Some of the hard-hitting hurricanes of the 1990s have embarrassed some of the largest builders and tool makers. It seems that the roofs that stayed on were hand-hammered. The power-nailed roofs blew apart. If Senco or Bosch were to develop new power hammers in response, would you recommend that they make the "guns" for proprietary fasteners or general purpose? How would you price and "package" these complementary elements?

9. Is it possible to bid on the job of finishing the interior passenger compartment of a Boeing airliner in the design stage? Explain.

10. Many business marketers strive to keep prices a secret from their competitors. Price lists are closely guarded and quotes to customers are so often customized it is difficult to back figure to a list price. What are the advantages and disadvantages to such a pricing approach?

Internet Exercise

Cellophane was a breakthrough packaging material in the middle of this century. Although new materials such as bubble wraps and Cryovac have been developed, giving many more packaging options, cellophane is still widely used. Use the web to find two or three possible suppliers of cellophane in 36″ × 500′ rolls. How much do prices differ? Based on information available on their web sites, how do suppliers differentiate? Are there other potential dimensions for differentiation on customer service? What economic model of market structure seems to apply best?

Cases

Case 14.1   Benchtru

Benchtru (a large, multiproduct company) was analyzing pricing options for a new anti-static flooring. Market research had determined a potential of 500,000 square yards per year in research and computer labs, even if priced at $40 per yard. Profit targets and fixed costs were $2.4 million per year. Direct costs per yard were hard to estimate. Estimators figured $22 per square yard at volumes less than 100,000 and $16 per square yard at greater volumes.

Develop a schedule for Benchtru showing break-even yardage and market share at prices of $30 to $40 per yard, in $2 increments.

Case 14.2   Medicus Major

Medicus Major uses overseas manufacturers to supply small medical instruments and supplies. Among several channels to distribute its products, Medicus uses a national distributor, Galax, which does half its Medicus business selling directly to large hospitals and the other half to small local dealers that supply small hospitals and clinics. Margins are conveyed through a suggested discount off "list." Small hospitals and labs pay about list. Large hospitals typically buy at list less 12 percent. Wholesalers buy at list less 40 percent. Dealers pay, on average, list less 20 percent. What are the prices paid by all resellers and users for examination lenses sold by Medicus for $4? What is the average gross profit earned by the wholesaler on Medicus products? A small clinic pays the $11 list price on a water-activated fiber glass splint.

1. What are the prices paid by the dealer and Galax on the splint? Why should the intermediaries receive different discounts?

2. What increase in sales must Galax produce to cover the new debt service costs of $185,000 per year for its truck fleet expansion?

3. Medicus is a little disappointed with the account coverage Galax has provided it in the South. One solution up for discussion is to try to line up Dixie Supply (a leading distributor in the South), which has made several acquisitions in the past two years in trying to establish a national presence. What are the possible consequences on prices, channel margins, and channel functions if Medicus adds Dixie to its distribution system?

Additional Readings

Avila, Ramon A., William B. Dodds, Joseph D. Chapman, O. Karl Mann, and Russell G. Wahlers, "Importance of Price in Industrial Buying: Sales versus Purchasing Perspectives," *Review of Business* 15 (Winter 1993), p. 34–38.

Dolan, Robert J. "How Do You Know when Your Price Is Right?" *Harvard Business Review* 73 (September–October 1995), pp. 174–6+.

Holmlund, Maria, and Soren Kock, "Buyer Perceived Quality in Industrial Networks," *Industrial Marketing Management* 24 (Summer 1995), pp. 195–205.

Journal of Business Research, special issue on pricing, vol. 33 (July 1995).

Kaplan, A.D.H., Joel Dirlam, and Robert Lanzillotti, *Pricing in Big Business.* Washington, DC: The Brookings Institution, 1958.

Lewicki, Roy, David Saunders, and John Minton, *Essentials of Negotiation.* Burr Ridge, IL: Richard D. Irwin, 1997.

Monroe, Kent B., *Pricing: Making Profitable Decisions.* New York: McGraw-Hill, 1990.

Monroe, Kent, and Tridib Mazumdar, "Pricing Decision Models: Recent Developments and Research Opportunities," in *Issues in Pricing Theory and Research,* Timothy Devinney, ed. Lexington, MA: Lexington Books, 1988, pp. 361–88.

Seymour, David, *The Pricing Decision.* Chicago: Probus Publishing Company, 1989.

Smith, Gerald, "Managerial Pricing Orientation: The Process of Making Pricing Decisions," *Pricing Strategy & Practice* 3, no. 3 (1995), pp. 28–39.

Woodside, Arch, "Making Better Pricing Decisions in Business Marketing," in *Advances in Business Marketing and Purchasing,* Arch Woodside, ed. Greenwich, CT: JAI Press, 1994, pp. 139–83.

Part IV

Investing for Value in Customers and Yourself

L ike the finale to a week at summer camp, Part IV aims to conclude the text with the boldest material for you to take away. We introduced Part I saying, "This is what business marketing is about." The same overture can play for Part IV. But now we're looking at the essentials of business marketing with a new level of sophistication. In fact, the term *sophistication* comes from the Greek word *sophist,* or "learned man."

Chapter 15 is all about control—gauging success or failure and making adjustments. Accountability impels this. The learning organization demands this. Throughout this text we've spotlighted innovation and touted the creative and quick-footed organization. You can soon join the game. But let's be ready to assess new systems and arenas with apt measures and models.

Looking at the table of contents for this book, a colleague told us that Chapter 16 seemed like Mom's departing admonition: "Don't forget your coat!" or "Be careful!" Granted, you've heard in marketing class that the customer is a firm's most important asset, but here we describe different types of customer relationships and vividly highlight the profit sensitivities to increasing retention rates. With a heightened motivation to retain customers, we examine some imperatives for managing relationships.

We close the book with a look at the fast-moving trends of globalization, information technology, and careers in the field. Chapter 17 provides a platform for considering a variety of futures in business marketing. We hope you will choose to be in it. Better still, shape it!

Chapter 15

Evaluating Marketing Efforts

ROCKWELL INTERNATIONAL

Rockwell International has been NASA's primary contractor since the beginning of America's space program. As a government contractor, Rockwell has built bombers and other aircraft since World War II. But Rockwell is not just an aviation and aeronautics company; the company also manufactures military communication systems, truck axles, power tools, telephone switching systems, and a host of other products. Keeping track of all of the businesses Rockwell is in is a monumental task, but it's important in order to know where to invest and where to pull back. ●

Primarily a defense and space contractor in the 1980s, the company was faced with a smaller post–Cold War market when the 90s began. A declining NASA budget also boded for a difficult future, and during the summer of 1996, NASA announced that Rockwell would not win the contract to build the replacement for the Space Shuttle. ●

Yet, in the past decade, Rockwell has carried out what its management describes as a "quiet revolution." In 1985 military contracts accounted for 50 percent of the company's revenues; now they amount to less than one-sixth. And electronics and other commercial ventures have grown at annual rates greater than 15 percent. By dropping some product lines, selling the aerospace and defense businesses, and focusing on specific electronics markets, Rockwell has changed. As one financial analyst put it, "Rockwell was aggressive, and they decided to seek growth instead of a kind of comfort." ●

These decisions required information, particularly information about marketing performance and capability. Rockwell's ability to gather and share that information across divisions enabled the company to make the hard decisions, like selling off major divisions. Without those effective information and control processes, though, the company itself would have ultimately faced demise. Instead, the company is growing at a faster-than-average rate.●

Visit its home page: **www.rockwell.com.**

Learning Objectives

Throughout the book, we've discussed how to evaluate specific marketing actions, such as how to evaluate the success of a direct mail campaign. In this chapter, we'll tie those evaluations together into part of an overall marketing evaluation system.

After reading this chapter, you should be able to

● Describe the importance and dimensions of control systems.

● Select appropriate tools of control for specific situations.

● Calculate tolerance ranges for marketing performance.

● Describe how control processes contribute to other organizational processes such as reengineering and strategic planning.

For learning to occur from experience, there must be some judgment of success and failure. There must be some notion of what worked and what didn't; being able to identify what works and what doesn't is dependent upon a system that spots success.

Source: William Miller, "Don Beall: Conglomerator," *Industry Week* (January 22, 1996), p. 12; Norton Paley, "All for One," *Sales & Marketing Management* (January 1996), pp. 22–23; *Rockwell Annual Report,* 1994; "What's Hot—Rockwell on CNBC December 7," Rockwell International home page, www.rockwell.com, December 3, 1997.

The Importance of Evaluating Marketing Efforts

Not too long ago, a company (one that asked to remain nameless) set a goal for a particular product of selling 100,000 units. It dropped two products that were similar and increased sales for the preferred product from 70,000 units to three times the goal, or 300,000 units. The sales force had their best year ever, making more money per rep than ever before. Yet, every unit sold cost an average $2 in losses. How could this happen?

It happened because information concerning performance wasn't gathered and shared on a timely basis. Costs were higher than expected; prices were lower than expected as more buyers took advantage of quantity discounts, and, worse, the information didn't reach decision makers in time.

Rockwell International, on the other hand, has been profitable because its management has been able to maintain close control over costs. Furthermore, with access to marketing information, they've made the right expansion decisions, too.

This is a chapter about evaluation of performance, but it is also as much about the use of information as about the creation of information. An important element of successful learning in learning organizations is that information is shared and then acted upon. Successful marketing requires understanding the impact of one's decisions on the organization's profit, which means recognizing costs as well as projecting revenue. First, though, we will discuss control systems in general, and then move on to cost recognition.

Control Systems

Rockwell, using marketing research, identifies a segment of the market whose needs have not been well met and for whom competition is soft. It designs a product and strategy, launches the product, and then what? Does it turn its back in order to focus on the next product? Scan the research data looking for another market opportunity? Of course, someone at Rockwell does.

Someone else, though, is responsible for seeing that the first product is successful. As the strategy is implemented, the product manager must sift through the data from the field in order to learn what works and what doesn't. The **marketing control system** is the system that measures actual performance against planned performance, measures productivity and profit by types of products, customers, or territories, and measures other key marketing variables such as customer satisfaction. A sound marketing control system is not just an income statement, totaling revenue and subtracting costs. A sound marketing control system is balanced and includes—in addition to financial information—**operational measures**, measures of productivity, process (or operations) effectiveness, and other elements that impact customer satisfaction.

The process of control, illustrated in Exhibit 15–1, is measuring performance, comparing performance against a standard, and then examining why performance was either above or below standard. If performance was above standard, management would like to duplicate those circumstances that led to greater performance. If performance was below standard, then whatever barriers prevented standard performance should be identified and eliminated.

Two important elements of a control process are the **sensor**, or measuring tool, and the **standard**, or the goal against which performance is compared.[1] Standards can be absolute, such as a budget. Significant deviation under budget can be just as bad as deviation over budget if it means that opportunities are lost. For example, the marketing manager can decide to bring salary expenses well under budget by reducing everyone's

Exhibit 15–1
Process of Control

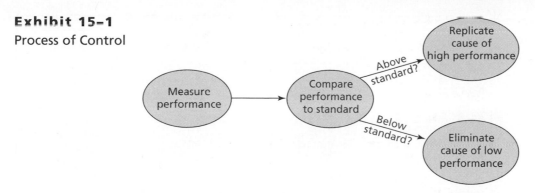

pay, but if all the employees left, there would be trouble. Standards can also be a range of acceptable performance, called a **tolerance** range. For example, if management decides that no action will be taken against salespeople who achieve 95 percent of their quota, nor will significant bonuses be paid until reaching 150 percent, then 95 to 150 percent of quota is the tolerance range.

Dimensions of Control

The processes of control are universal and can be applied to any level of marketing analysis. The marketing executive has to develop a strategy for the firm's marketing efforts and then analyze results and make the necessary changes; a salesperson has to develop a sales strategy for a territory and analyze results in order to adapt. There are, however, two dimensions of analysis and control that help us categorize and understand control processes. These dimensions are macro versus micro levels of control, and inputs versus outputs. Exhibit 15–2 illustrates the two dimensions of control systems.

Macro versus Micro Control

The macro versus micro dimension of control is the level of the organization that is being evaluated. When the total organization is undergoing evaluation, the level of control is macro. For some organizations, a macro control system may include divisional control or strategic business unit (SBU) control if those operate as virtually stand-alone units; 3M, for example, operates its 40+ divisions as independent companies. Anything less than that would be micro control, including analysis of a product line, a market segment, or functional area such as sales or marcomm.

Exhibit 15–2
Dimensions of Control

	Micro	Macro
Input	Regional Sales Office Expense	Total Selling Expenses
	Trade Show Budget	Promotion Budget
	Product X Development Cost	Total R & D Budget
Output	Regional Sales Office Revenue	Total Revenue
	Leads from Trade Shows	Corporate Position
	Sales for Product X	Total Division Revenue

Exhibit 15–3
Control of Input and Output Variables in Marketing

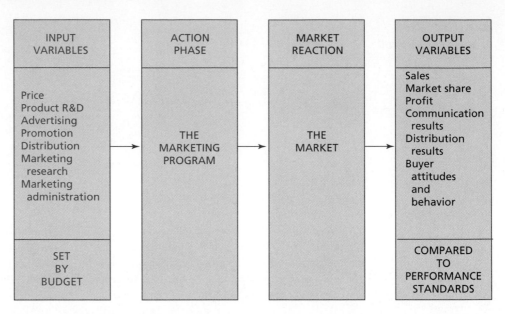

INPUT VARIABLES	ACTION PHASE	MARKET REACTION	OUTPUT VARIABLES
Price Product R&D Advertising Promotion Distribution Marketing research Marketing administration	THE MARKETING PROGRAM	THE MARKET	Sales Market share Profit Communication results Distribution results Buyer attitudes and behavior
SET BY BUDGET			COMPARED TO PERFORMANCE STANDARDS

Macro Control   Learning organizations do not create strategy and then set it afloat until the next time to develop a strategy. One of your authors was in the strategic planning office of a division of Rockwell International; each year we developed a seven-year plan. The reason we rewrote the plan each year was that the situation changed every year. While the plan would be formalized as the seven-year plan, in reality we were simply recognizing the changes that had already taken place in our plan since that document was written. As a learning organization, we were constantly taking current performance and market realities and looking ahead in order to be strategically positioned to capitalize on any market changes. For us, macro control was an ongoing process of forecasting the future and adjusting strategy based on current performance.

Contrast this to the organization that conducts a complete marketing audit every seven years without strategic adjustment in the interim. While students may think it unlikely that a firm would operate for several years without much thought given to strategy, it does happen. The challenges of day-to-day operations can consume an executive's time and thoughts, leaving no room for macro, or strategic, control. That is why some companies have designated macro control as the primary responsibility of one executive, someone who can focus on the big picture and not get lost in the daily management issues.

Micro Control   Micro control is an evaluation of a subset of the macro control system. Micro control processes can include evaluations of product lines, market segments, or functional areas. Micro control is also necessarily short-term–oriented. At this level of control, for example, managers would compare annual or monthly performance of specific areas such as a sales office, the trade show program, and other areas against standards.

Input–Output Analysis

An income statement is probably the ultimate input–output analysis. The company puts money in (expenses) and hopes to take money out (revenue). What happens in between is the marketing program, as illustrated in Exhibit 15–3. In recent years, however, input–output analyses have gotten more sophisticated as business marketers have recognized that income statements do not measure all of the inputs that go into delivering value, nor does revenue provide adequate output analysis when examining the total

15–1

FROM THE FIELD

Implementing the Balanced Scorecard

Business marketers evaluate the results of their marketing programs within the context of the broader corporate strategy. These marketing results, as Rockwater, an undersea construction division of Brown & Root/ Haliburton learned, are just one element in the Balanced Scorecard.

The Balanced Scorecard is a total company measurement system comprised of four components: measures of learning and growth, internal business process, financial results, and customer results, all centered around the vision and strategy of the organization. When Rockwater attempted to create a vision and mission for the company, management quickly learned that measures for all four components were required in order to provide employees with direction.

For example, Rockwater determined that there are two stages between the customer recognizing a need and having that need met. The first stage involves the sales process, while the second stage is the supply process. The sales process is further broken down into two steps: (1) identifying customers with needs and understanding those needs and (2) then winning the business. In order to evaluate performance for winning the business, for example, Rockwater uses conversion ratios, looking at the success rate for proposals.

But Rockwater doesn't just analyze outputs; Rockwater also examines inputs, such as the amount of time spent with customers. The management team believed that spending quality time with key customers is a prerequisite for influencing vendor choice.

The results for Rockwater have been tremendous. For example, the company was able to recognize that the most satisfied customers were those served by the most satisfied employees. This finding led to the development of measures and processes designed to enhance employee satisfaction so that customer satisfaction would be improved. The Balanced Scorecard approach also allows management to identify the relationship between satisfaction and financial performance; for example, more satisfied customers pay in 10 days versus 120 for dissatisfied customers. Just the impact of customer satisfaction on the bottom line in terms of paying faster is $15 million annually!

Source: Robert S. Kaplan and David P. Norton, "Putting the Balanced Scorecard to Work," *Harvard Business Review* (September–October 1993), pp. 134–142; Robert S. Kaplan, "Devising a Balanced Scorecard Matched to Business Strategy," *Planning Review* (September–October 1994), pp. 15–19, 48; Robert S. Kaplan and David P. Norton, "Using the Balanced Scorecard as a Strategic Management System," *Harvard Business Review* (September–October 1993), pp. 75–85.

marketing health of the organization. As you can see in From the Field 15–1, Rockwater, a global undersea construction company, is using a sophisticated approach called the Balanced Scorecard to analyze inputs and outputs.

Input Analysis   For a long time, business marketers were most concerned with managing costs as the key input variable. The reasoning for such concern goes something like this: There is a cost associated with every action, thus the best way to manage inputs (to control actions) is to manage costs.

A value-based approach, though, challenges the fundamental assumption that costs represent the best way to manage inputs. At times, the best way to manage inputs may be to consider the value of the input rather than its cost. For example, **cycle time**, or the time it takes to complete an action such as to develop a product, is rapidly gaining recognition as having a value that cannot be adequately represented by cost. EIS, a company that prints pricing labels for grocery stores, has gained a significant competitive advantage by reducing

Federal Express has created a competitive advantage by reducing the cycle time required for delivering packages.
Courtesy Federal Express.

cycle time. Grocery stores want to put new pricing labels on the shelves as soon as they make the decision to change a price; hence, the company like EIS that can most quickly print and ship these labels to all stores in a particular chain is most likely to get the business as long as costs are reasonable.

Cycle time is a core competency for Federal Express (which we profiled at the start of Chapter 5), as it has to get some packages to their destination by 9:30 the next morning. As mentioned in Chapter 8, Mitsubishi gained a significant competitive advantage by reducing the cycle time associated with product development. JIT (just-in-time) delivery is another example of how cycle time is reduced. Cycle time is becoming a significant factor in success, and not just for companies like EIS or Federal Express.

Other inputs include price, marketing activities, and the costs associated with those activities. Price is considered an input variable because it is an input into the marketing process and must be managed, as discussed in Chapter 14. Budgets are a key element in the control of marketing activities; pricing plans operate much the same way in controlling pricing. We'll discuss these more later in the chapter when we address using control systems.

Output Analysis   In the previous few chapters, we've examined performance evaluations for marcomm activities, including performance evaluation for trade shows, the sales force, and other marketing areas. These are forms of output analysis. Output analysis, therefore, includes more than just revenue; for a particular marketing activity, output analysis can include the number of leads gathered, or the number of demonstrations, or the number of displays set up in distributors' locations. For example, Rockwell exhibit managers tally the number of leads generated at each trade show as a measure of the show's success.

Another important output of the marketing program should be customer satisfaction. We will discuss how to measure customer satisfaction when we discuss customer retention strategies in Chapter 16, but it is important to recognize here that customer satisfaction can be viewed as a surrogate for future sales. While customer satisfaction cannot predict competitive action or leap-frogging technology that can hurt sales, without customer satisfaction, there can be no repeat sales. Hence, customer satisfaction is not just a measure of performance but also a measure of the market health of the organization.

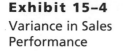

Exhibit 15–4

Variance in Sales
Performance

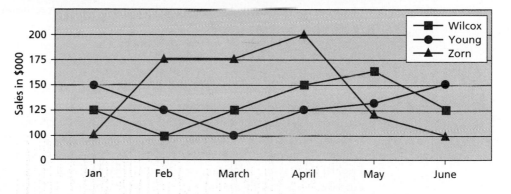

Efficiency Analysis Combining input and output figures gives the marketing manager an indication of the efficiency with which those inputs were managed. For example, you may have learned about return on assets managed (ROAM = net income divided by assets) or return on investment (ROI = net income divided by investment) in an accounting class. These are both measures of how efficiently inputs are managed—in this case, inputs being assets or investment. Similar marketing combinations are conversion ratios (the input being the number of sales calls and output being the number of sales), return on advertising, and other measures that combine the cost of an input and the associated sales or output. Dividing outputs by inputs results in measures of how efficiently the marketing manager used those inputs to generate the outputs.

For example, one input into the sales process is free samples. A measure of how efficiently samples are used could be to divide the number of samples given away by the number of sales closed. Similarly, one Rockwell division divides dollars spent on trade shows by the number of leads generated in order to evaluate the cost per lead. It uses this information to compare the cost effectiveness of various shows.

Control and the Nature of Data

Marketing control is the gathering, evaluation, and use of information regarding marketing processes. The first step is to gather information, or to collect data. As you may recall from a marketing research or statistics class, data have several important properties or characteristics. These characteristics are that data vary, and that the variance is likely to remain within a range. Understanding the causes of variance is important in order to know how to secure the desired results.

Data Vary

First, performance data vary. For example, if we are examining the performance of a sales office with 10 salespeople, it is likely that we will find 10 different revenue figures, a different revenue figure for each salesperson. If we examine each salesperson, we will find that revenue will vary for that salesperson over time. In Exhibit 15–4, we have the performance of three salespeople plotted over time. As you can see, Young starts and ends with the best sales performance but is not the best rep for any other month. Zorn has three great months and three so-so months. Thus, sales performance varies both across reps and for any rep over time.

Sales, as with any marketing results, will vary for any combination of reasons. Zorn could have been sick in May and June or spent two weeks in a training seminar. Wilcox may have learned a new method of prospecting that accounts for the three-month rise. Or Wilcox's territory may have had several new businesses start operations. The process of selling is imperfect, and variance will result from month to month. But sales may vary for no known reason. To expect that sales should always go up is unrealistic because variance can be positive or negative.

Observations Fall within a Range

A second important characteristic is that the data will fall within a range. As long as the process is held steady, the outcome will vary but within a set of boundaries. If the observation is outside that boundary, then something is different with the system. In a well-understood system, this natural range of performance is the same as the tolerance. For example, a manufacturing system may allow a gap of .5 millicrons between two parts. From 0 to .5 is the tolerance, or allowed range of the gap. In sales, tolerance is usually described in terms of a minimum standard of performance, or quota. (Note, though, that quota can sometimes be set higher than tolerance. See Chapter 13 for quota-setting methods.) Going back to Exhibit 15–4, the observed tolerance would be $100,000 to $200,000, with $100,000 being quota.

Sales above the tolerance range (in this case, greater than $200,000) would certainly be accepted, but management would want to examine the situation closely. Is the territory too large? Does this salesperson use a strategy better than the company's suggested strategy?

At the same time, however, that plant management wants its manufacturing line to operate at capacity, sales management wants each salesperson to sell to the potential (or capacity) of the market. If 10 buying decisions are made in January in Zorn's territory, then capacity would be 10 sales (the equivalent of those 10 decisions). The control process should provide information regarding the salesperson's output relative to potential. The challenge in marketing control is knowing what potential is, because potential varies. (It is a function of the number and type of buying decisions that could be made that month and is beyond the salesperson's control.)

Marketing control systems are not just interested in sales performance. Marketing managers must also consider a number of internal processes that support sales and marketing efforts and impact customer satisfaction. For example, how quickly the credit department assesses the creditworthiness of a potential customer impacts shipping because the product can't be shipped until the sale is accepted, and the sale can't be accepted until the account's credit has been qualified and approved. Management must control cycle time in the credit department.

AT&T, for example, significantly improved cash flow by redesigning a new sales installation process, reducing the number of steps from 12 to 3. The new system increased the number of invoices paid in the first 30 days from 31 to 71 percent. More importantly, customer readiness to repurchase increased from 53 to 82 percent.[2] Thus, internal systems, like how quickly products are delivered and installed, can impact customer satisfaction and sales performance.

Four Causes of Variance

A marketing control system can identify variance, but more important than simply identifying variance is understanding the cause of variance so that something can be done about it. There are four causes of variance: tinkering, systematic, external, and random. Systematic and tinkering causes of variance occur because of changes to the process. For example, deciding to use a particular selling strategy over another strategy may represent a change to the selling process. Random and external causes of variance are not due to the process but due to other factors.

Exhibit 15–5

An Example of Systematic Variance

Each dot represents a salesperson's performance. With the introduction of a new product, a higher tolerance range is achieved.

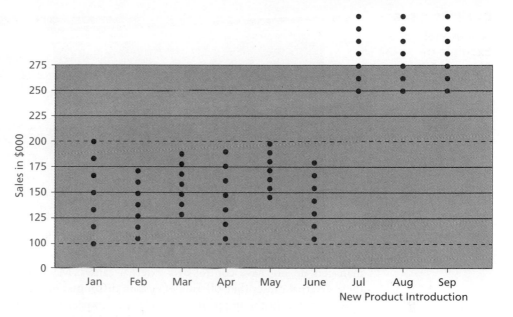

Tinkering Variance

Tinkering is making changes within a process in order to make the process more productive, by either reducing defects or increasing volume. The purpose of tinkering is to narrow the range of variance. If the upper boundary of the tolerance range represents the system in perfect working condition, then tinkering should raise the bottom boundary. Referring back to Exhibit 15–4, tinkering may account for the overall rise from March through May. Note, though, that performance fell in June; tinkering does not always work to improve sales performance.

Tinkering might include such activities as reviewing objection-handling skills among the salespeople, changing the media schedule for advertising, changing the graphics in the booth for the next trade show, or adjusting the price. Tinkering is making minor adjustments within the marketing process that are intended to improve performance.

Systematic Sources of Variance

Systematic change is changing systems and creating a new tolerance. If a new selling strategy is used, for example, then a new range of performance should be expected. The new strategy is successful if the new range is higher than the old range. Tinkering is changing within a system; systematic variance is change due to the implementation of a new system.

For example, in Exhibit 15–5, we see the effects of a new product introduction on sales. For the first six months of the year, sales performance stayed within $100,000 to $200,000 for each of the seven salespeople. With the introduction of the new product, however, sales were immediately no lower than $250,000. As the sales team gained experience and learned more about how to sell the new product, sales continued to climb. This climb will continue until a point at which the system is stable and a new tolerance is established.

External Causes of Variance

The marketing system operates in an environment that has an impact on the system's effectiveness. For example, there may be seasonality in purchasing habits. There are also economic cycles that must be contended with. Like random variance, marketing

Exhibit 15–6

A Seasonal Example of External Source of Variance
Each dot represents a salesperson's performance. The range of performance across the sales team varies due to seasonality in purchasing.

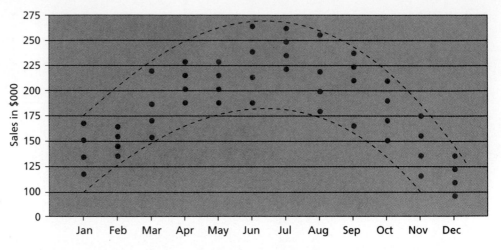

managers do not have control over external causes. Marketing managers can react to those external causes (like offering off-season discounts) or seek to influence the external causes (such as furthering political agendas that impact the organization), but only when external causes and their impact are identified. Exhibit 15–6 illustrates the tolerance for a sales office with seasonal sales.

Random Causes of Variance

Random variance is that variance caused by uncontrollable and unidentified causes. We must recognize a certain degree of randomness in every system. The important thing for managers is to be able to recognize random variance. Managers often try to fix random variance with tinkering. Since tinkering can't affect random variance, however, money and energy spent on such tinkering are wasted. Hence, recognizing random variance is important.

For example, suppose a salesperson's performance varies by 15 percent over time; one month she is 5 percent below quota, the next she is 10 percent over quota, and her performance is almost always within that range. After a year, she gets a new manager who doesn't understand the concept of random variance, so every time her performance is below quota, he makes her come straight into the office at 8:00 every morning and return by 5:00 every night. Her territory being 30 minutes away from the office, she was in the habit of going straight from home to her first appointment and home after her last call, enabling her to begin with an appointment at 8:00. Thanks to this new manager's plan, she loses at least one sales call each day, or 20 per month. As a result, her sales fall further, she gets frustrated, and considers quitting before she will get fired. Tinkering to fix random variance can be fatal.

In the chart showing systematic increase in performance, there is also variance within the first six months of performance. The key for the sales manager is to identify how much of that variance is random and how much is due to salesperson actions, or tinkering. Similarly, marcomm managers have to consider how much of the changes in advertising, direct mail, and trade show exhibit performance are due to random variance, just as pricing managers have to recognize random variance in response to price changes. The potential for tinkering inappropriately can be just as great and just as dangerous in all aspects of marketing as in sales.

Understanding the nature of data is important so that management can recognize controllable and uncontrollable sources of variance. Tinkering and systematic sources of variance are within the manager's control, whereas random and external sources are not.

Xerox bench-
marked its
distribution system
against the world's
best, L.L. Bean.
Courtesy Xerox
Corporation.

Management can, however, respond to external sources of variance, turning them into competitive advantage. For example, Rockwell has had to contend with the end of the Cold War, which reduced the need for military equipment by the United States. By anticipating the change and planning for it, Rockwell has been able to remain profitable.

Tools of Control

Having the right tool for any job makes the job much easier. Whether you are working on your car, on a computer, or on the kitchen sink, knowing what needs to be done is not enough. Being able to finish the job requires the right tools.

The same is true in business. Getting the job done right requires both the knowledge of what should be done and the knowledge and tools to complete the job. Controlling marketing programs requires knowing what to do and choosing among an array of tools. There are three types of tools in control systems: standard setting processes, measurement tools, and tools used to search for causes of variance.

Standard Setting Processes

The first type of tool used in any control process is the process for setting a standard of performance. As mentioned earlier, the process of control begins with setting standards and then observing performance. In marketing, output standards are often goals for performance, such as desired market share, sales quota, delivery time, product development cycle time, and other marketing processes. Budgets are input standards.

Benchmarking

One type of standard is a **benchmark**, or the performance level of the best organization for that particular task. For example, when Xerox wanted to set standards for distribution performance, it went to L.L. Bean, the catalog company. Xerox studied L.L. Bean's warehousing system, learning the distribution processes used by L.L. Bean. It then took L.L. Bean's performance as a benchmark, the standard of performance for

---

15-1

BUSINESS 2 BUSINESS

Benchmarking Bean

Entire books have been written on the process of benchmarking. One problem is getting permission to benchmark a company. Why would L.L. Bean, for example, want to allow a company to benchmark against it? If you wanted to benchmark against a company like L.L. Bean, what would you offer in return?

---

distribution, and measured its own performance against L.L. Bean's. Benchmarks can be found by examining the best at a particular activity, and not necessarily the best in your own industry.

A couple of points should be recognized about benchmarks. Xerox did more than simply identify L.L. Bean's performance level and then set that as a goal. Xerox also audited L.L. Bean's processes in order to learn what could be used by Xerox in reengineering its own distribution processes. Benchmarking includes learning the processes of the benchmarked organization.

A second point about benchmarking that the example illustrates is that a benchmark can come from any industry. What you are looking for is the best in the world at a particular function; in this case, an office equipment company examined the distribution systems of a mail order clothing merchant.

Benchmarks are just one type of standard; other standards are set by trade associations (such as quality standards) or reflect goals that management desires. L.L. Bean, for example, may be the best in distribution, but Bean management sets goals for improving distribution nonetheless.

Quota and Target Setting

Quotas are minimum acceptable levels of performance, usually associated with sales performance. (See Chapter 13.) As minimum levels of performance, quotas can represent the bottom of the tolerance range in sales performance. Sales quotas are often determined by estimating market potential for a particular product and then estimating the market share or penetration for the product based on historical performance and estimated impact of marketing plans. For example, if Rockwell Engineering held 20 percent of the market for the previous year, all things being equal, the division should expect 20 percent next year. All things are rarely equal, however, and if the company expected a new product launch to significantly increase sales, estimated market share may rise to 24 percent. Applied to a market of $100 million, Rockwell Engineering's total sales quota would be $24 million. Individual salesperson quotas are then a function of the overall quota. One such method would be to divide total sales quota by the number of salespeople to determine individual quotas.

Quotas are also determined for each activity deemed important. (See Chapter 13.) If management wants to increase the amount of business coming from current customers, they may impose a customer call quota. The number of calls to be made on current customers would be determined by setting a customer sales target and then using conversion ratios to determine a call quota.

Performance targets can be set for all marketing activities, such as setting a new product development cycle target of 18 months, or a billing cycle time of three days. Quotas can also be set for the number of credit applications or orders processed by the credit or order entry department. Using past performance as a guide and accounting for future plans, quotas and performance targets can be used as standards for performance.

Budgets and Pricing Plans

Budgets and pricing plans are tools of control systems that act as limits on marketing activities. For example, the pricing plan in the first example of this chapter did not limit discounts appropriately and the company ended up losing money on each product it sold. A good pricing plan, as you know from Chapter 14, optimizes sales while also maximizing profit. A sound pricing plan also provides guidance for salespeople when responding to customer requests.

Budgets are like benchmarks and other standards, but in this case, budgets are used to provide limitations and guidance on what can be spent rather than a goal to be achieved. Budgets are determined for personnel (how many people and at what cost), equipment, advertising, trade show activity, and so forth. We've already discussed budgeting procedures for personnel decisions about sales (Chapter 13), advertising and other promotional activity (Chapter 10), and other marketing activities. These procedures for setting marketing budgets are important tools for controlling marketing decisions.

Measurement Tools

Another set of important tools for controlling marketing decisions are measurement tools. Measurement tools used in marketing include marketing audits and customer satisfaction measures. Accounting systems are also important marketing measurement tools, and marketing managers can choose from among several.

Marketing Audits

Most students who think of audits first think of the IRS. An audit, however, can be any close examination of any part of the business. One particular type of audit that can be a useful control tool is the marketing audit.

A **marketing audit** is a comprehensive and systematic evaluation of the firm's marketing operation and the environment in which it operates. The audit gives marketing management the opportunity to step back and view the big picture, and then re-examine the details in order to make sure that all of the internal processes are contributing to strategic objectives. The audit also enables management to examine the environment to determine if the strategic objectives are most appropriate.

One question that many students have is how does a marketing audit differ from the SWOT analysis discussed in Chapter 6. A SWOT analysis is necessarily a macro analysis, and can contribute that big-picture view to the marketing audit. The marketing audit, however, will examine all of the internal processes that are part of the marketing function. For example, we discussed earlier how marketing control processes would monitor such elements as the cycle time of processing credit applications. The process of evaluating credit applications would be one of those internal processes that an audit would examine.

There are six areas audited as part of the marketing audit:

- *The environment:* customers and competitors, government regulations, and other macro-level factors: this is similar to the opportunity–threat analysis of a SWOT.

- *Marketing strategy:* goals, strategy; this is similar to the strengths–weaknesses analysis of a SWOT.

- *Marketing orientation:* an examination of the marketing culture; determining the company's attitude toward the customer. Understanding the orientation is important as it can be the basis for how processes are carried out and the resulting customer satisfaction.

- *Marketing systems:* an evaluation of the systems for marketing analysis, planning, and control; seeks answers to questions such as "How does information flow from the market to decision makers?" and "Who is involved in planning for new products or new markets?"

- *Marketing functions:* an examination of the marketing practices, such as product development, sales force management, bidding, invoicing, shipping, promotion, and others, on the basis of financial and customer performance.

- *Marketing productivity:* seeks to answer questions concerning how well each functional area uses resources, such as people, money, and facilities.

A periodic marketing audit is good practice, regardless of the degree of learning orientation. Some students (and some businesspeople) think that if a company has embraced and practices learning, with appropriate information-sharing mechanisms and empowered managers to act on information, then audits are not necessary. The thinking goes that what would be learned in an audit would already be known from the course of daily operations. The reality is, though, that even members of learning organizations need to step back and look at how each of the minute parts contributes to the overall organization's effectiveness. An audit may not be necessary annually, but regular audits do provide management an opportunity to examine how well each part fits into the overall scheme of the organization.

Customer Satisfaction Measurement

An area of growing importance is the measurement of customer satisfaction. The area of customer satisfaction is so important that we've devoted an entire chapter to the retention of customers in which we discuss customer satisfaction measurement in detail.

At this point, though, remember that just as there are multiple determinants in choosing products, there are also multiple determinants of customer satisfaction and that these are not always the same. Peterbilt Trucks may choose Rockwell axles because of the ease in installing these axles, but poor delivery may cause dissatisfaction. Measuring satisfaction at the macro level can tell the company something about the overall marketing orientation of the firm and its performance relative to customer expectations. From a diagnostic perspective, though, management must find out what each of those determinants of satisfaction are and gather information about the company's performance so that they can manage the processes that result in satisfied customers.

Customer satisfaction can be measured by surveys. Moore Business Forms measures customer satisfaction through surveys, but has found that these surveys have to include people throughout the customer organization. If only the top-level buyer is surveyed, indication of dissatisfaction usually reflects lower-level dissatisfaction that has festered for some time. By surveying people directly involved with the purchase, use, and disposition of the product, Moore has been able to use the results to improve performance.

Some customers create their own satisfaction indices. Rockwell, for example, regularly reviews vendor performance, giving each vendor a grade as well as specific performance feedback. Vendors who are willing to participate in this process learn how to improve their service in ways that they can then translate to other customers, increasing overall business, not just business with Rockwell. At the same time, Rockwell asks these vendors

Exhibit 15–7

Income
Statement Using
Full Cost

Revenue (after returns)	$1,050
Less cost of goods sold	400
Less selling expenses	158
Less administrative expenses	285
Less research & development	110
Income before taxes	$ 97

to rate Rockwell as a customer. Rockwell learns important lessons on how to work with the vendors to improve their own operations, perhaps cutting Rockwell's cost but certainly increasing the vendors' commitment to the partnership.

Accounting Systems

Accounting systems measure financial performance: costs and revenue. For a marketing manager, the key is to understand how costs are allocated so that the true profitability of any particular area, product, or market can be determined. The issue is how fixed costs and overhead are allocated. Any accounting system can take the direct cost of supplies and components and add those together to come up with the cost of a product. The challenge is adding into the cost of that product costs for management, office supplies, warehousing, and so forth. There are three approaches to cost allocation: full costing, contribution analysis, and activity-based costing (ABC). Choice of a costing approach is very important to marketing managers; products have been mistakenly harvested, for example, because the accounting information used by managers didn't allocate costs appropriately.

Full Costing   Assume that a sales office sells two products. In the sales office are two sales teams: one responsible for selling product A and another that sells product B. In this example, we can directly allocate the cost of team A to the sales of product A to calculate the profit generated by product A. The challenge is what to do with overhead costs associated with running the sales office. Rent, for example, could be split between the two teams on the basis of space allocated to each team. The sales office would have to keep track of who made how many copies in order to allocate copying charges.

As much as possible, each cost would have to be directly related to one product or the other in order to truly understand the profitability of each product. Otherwise, fixed costs are allocated on the basis of the number of units sold, sales revenue, or other arbitrary amount. Unfortunately, costs are not always that easy to allocate accurately. At some point, a rule has to be established that allocates fixed costs to one product or the other. For example, assume one sales team sold both product A and product B and each represented 50 percent of the office's sales. To determine the profitability of each product, as illustrated in Exhibit 15–7, sales costs would be divided by two and then subtracted from the revenue of each product.

Contribution Analysis   Contribution analysis allocates costs based on incremental costs along each step of the marketing process. For example, the costs of a sales office are added to manufacturing and distribution costs in order to determine the profit, or contribution, of that sales office. Fixed costs associated with headquarters management is not added until it is time to calculate the overall profit. Contribution costing is a form of value added, in that costs are added as they occur along the supply chain and profit (or contribution) can be calculated at any given point in the supply chain, as illustrated in

Exhibit 15–8

Income Statement: Contribution Margins With Three Sales Offices

	Sales Office A	Sales Office B	Sales Office C	Total
Sales	$350	$320	$380	$1,050
Less variable costs	170	160	175	
Contribution margin	$180	$160	$205	
Fixed costs controllable by sales manager	53	52	54	
Sales manager's contribution margin	$127	$108	$151	
Fixed costs identified with but not controlled by sales manager	19	19	19	
Sales office contribution	$108	$ 89	$132	$328
Common costs				$231
Income before taxes				$97

Exhibit 15-8. Note that net income remains the same after all costs are accounted for, as we are simply allocating costs. The additional information learned is the profit for each sales office, which doesn't affect total profit.

Contribution costing works well in evaluating the overall cost containment practices and revenue generation of the sales office, but it does not allow management to examine issues within the office. For example, if several products are sold and the incremental costs associated with selling each product are not readily identifiable, contribution costing does not provide a mechanism for allocating the costs of running the sales office to each of the various products.

Activity-Based Cost Accounting   ABC allocates fixed costs to products or other units (such as a sales office) according to the activity that creates or drives the cost. For example, suppose a sales office is responsible for selling two products and has only one team of salespeople selling both products. Each product represents 50 percent of the office's sales. The important activity in this situation would be the number of sales calls per product. If digital wamometers (DWs) take three sales calls to close and tricometers take two sales calls to close, then the total calls to close two sales (one of each product) is five. The DW is allocated 60 percent of the office's costs because it is more difficult to sell, and the tricometer gets 40 percent. Contribution or full-costing approaches would allocate 50 percent of fixed costs to each product on the basis of sales volume as illustrated earlier. Note the difference in income in Exhibit 15–9; would management decisions be the same using ABC versus contribution?

As another example, suppose 20 percent of leads generated from advertising are in the Atlanta region. If so, then 20 percent of the national advertising costs would be allocated to the Atlanta sales office. At the same time, however, we would like to allocate revenue to the advertising in order to determine the direct effectiveness of the advertising. In order to judge each method of lead generation fully, we must know both costs and revenue.

One method, if the company does not have the ability to track leads all the way to the sale, is to examine conversion ratios and then estimate revenues. For example, if mar-comm could tell us how many hot leads were sent to the field, then we could forecast sales on the basis of the conversion ratio. We should know where a hot lead is in the buying cycle (if you remember from Chapter 10, a hot lead is defined as someone near a decision in the buying cycle), and the sales force should have the data that tell us the

Exhibit 15–9

Comparison of
Contribution and
ABC Methods

	Digital Wamometer			Tricometer
Sales	$545			$545
Less variable costs[1]	320			335
Contribution margin	$225			$210
		Contribution Method		
Less fixed mfg. costs[2]	85	50	50	15
Less fixed selling costs[3]	30	25	25	20
Income using ABC	$110			$185
Income using contribution		$150	$135	

[1]Includes commission paid to salespeople as well as direct manufacturing and shipping costs.
[2]Total fixed mfg. costs=$100 but allocated based on complexity of set up and other activities in mfg. process in ABC.
[3]Total fixed selling costs (administrative overhead and sales office expenses) = $50, but allocated on the basis of digital wamometer requiring six calls to every four for the tricometer using ABC.

conversion ratio at that point in the buying cycle. If the conversion rate is 50 percent and average order size is $1,000, then for every 100 leads, we should generate $50,000 in revenue. Allocating revenue to the show program enables the manager to estimate the profit (or contribution) of the program, information needed to make decisions concerning future marketing activity investments.

Which Accounting System Is Better?   As usual, the answer to the question of which accounting system is better is "It depends." If the objective is to evaluate the overall sales office and treat that office as a profit center, then the contribution approach is appropriate. In that situation, an income statement is created that indicates how well the office manager did in generating revenue and controlling costs in order to contribute to the company's profitability. Contribution costing is also used to make decisions about adding, keeping, or eliminating products and works fine when costs are directly attributable to the entity (e.g., sales office or product) being examined. If there are shared resources that have to be allocated, ABC may be more useful. The final objective, though, is always to create an income statement that accurately reflects the use of resources (costs) in order to generate value (revenue).

Search Tools

Search tools are those tools that management uses to search for variance and causes of variance. Reporting systems and information systems enable management to accumulate data in a way that can be used to search for variance. These tools provide mechanisms for data analysis.

While these tools can be used to identify variance, they do not always identify the cause for the variance. Other tools, such as case analysis and experimentation, are used to examine the data for causes of variance.

Reporting Systems

In marketing, as in many areas of business management, information flows in many directions. **Reporting systems** are formal mechanisms for creating and sharing information, and generally involve the flow of information either up or down the organization.

For example, each week each salesperson tallies the number of sales calls made for each type of account and about each type of product. Also tallied are the number of new prospects, the number and amount of new sales, customer service calls, total sales, and other sales information. This information is given to the sales manager, who tallies it for the sales team. The district manager sums it up for the district, and so forth. For example, Richard Langlotz, branch manager for Minolta Business Systems, has identified time with customers as a key variable. By tracking the amount of time his salespeople spend with customers, Langlotz can estimate sales for the next four weeks, make decisions regarding training needs, evaluate individual salesperson performance, and handle other marketing decisions.

Reporting systems, therefore, serve several functions: They provide information used in forecasting, performance evaluation, and problem identification. At the macro level, reporting systems enable management to spot general trends, potential threats, and opportunities whereas at the micro level, reporting systems enable managers to identify and implement successful tactics and strategies or identify problem causes and eliminate them. Reporting systems are important for learning to occur because these are one set of mechanisms by which information is carried that enables such learning.

Information Systems

A reporting system represents the creation of information by gathering data, assembling them in a meaningful way, and then sharing them. An **information system** is the mechanism for storing information, providing access to the information, and manipulating that information. Part of the access–manipulation function is the ability to aggregate data from various sources and combine them in meaningful ways. For example, suppose Rockwell decided to enter the forklift market. Would it be a profitable market? Forecasts would have to be generated concerning expected revenues and expected costs. Revenue information would have to come from external sources and would be a function of the number of warehouses in a geographic area, the number of forklifts used, the frequency of purchase, and so on. Costs, on the other hand, would have to be determined from a number of internal sources, such as procurement, manufacturing, and sales. An information system would enable the manager to pull this information together and create income statements representing net income under various market conditions.

As another example, we've discussed the use of decile analysis in Chapter 11 and other chapters. In the industrial paper–plastics industry, profitability is a function of customer share, or the percentage of the customer's purchases that we sell. So if Johnson Packaging buys 30 percent of its paper from Mead, Mead has a 30 percent share of that Johnson Packaging's business. By examining customer records, management can identify customer share break-even points (what customer share do we need to break even?), identify profitable and unprofitable accounts, and then develop specific account strategies to turn unprofitable accounts into profitable ones. This type of analysis requires an information system that stores information in the form needed and then allows access to the appropriate manager.

Let's take a global account example from Rockwell International. The minimum required annual revenue potential is $1 million, so we'll start with sales equal to that. (The average should be higher, as most global accounts will have greater potential.) Suppose that the salesperson's compensation is $100,000 per year, with a travel-and-entertainment budget of an additional $60,000. If the contribution margin is less than 16 percent (or $160,000), then even when selling 100 percent of potential Rockwell will lose money.

Rockwell International's success in managing so many different businesses is partly due to its ability to evaluate information from many different sources and use it in strategic planning.
All photos courtesy Rockwell International.

The example sounds easy and seems obvious. Yet that analysis requires an income statement for each account, plus an estimate of customer share. A financial statement is the responsibility of the accounting department; estimates of share come from the sales force. We have two very different functions in the organization who probably collect and store information to meet their own needs. Accounting may not have the ability, for example, to create independent financial statements for each account, especially in situations where we may want to know profitability for smaller accounts. Creating a reporting system that feeds into an information system capable of providing this type of analysis is challenging.

Case Analysis

Probably every marketing major will conduct case analyses before graduation. Certainly, students using this book will engage in some case analysis. The question for consideration now is when is case analysis used in business?

Case analysis is used as a method of explaining success or failure after the fact. When a new product is launched and is successful beyond expectations or fails miserably, a case analysis should be conducted to examine potential causes. The hope is that successes can be replicated and failures avoided. Case analyses are also used by exhibit managers, advertising managers, and other marketing managers to understand performance. What these examples illustrate is that case analysis methods that you use to learn from cases in this book are appropriate for conducting an examination of marketing projects.

Case analysis can also be used as a method of stepping back and examining an ongoing marketing system. Sound case analysis involves the gathering of relevant facts, an examination of assumptions underlying decisions, identification of causes and possible solutions for problems, and making recommendations, just as a student does when writing up a case from this text. Such case analyses are used by learning organizations to further learning by having managers from other areas conduct case analyses on ongoing operations.

Experimentation

Experimentation is one method used to identify causes of variance. An experiment is research to measure causality by changing one or more variables in order to see the effects on another variable.[3] Some experts consider tinkering, where the manager changes things such as prices until the desired results occur, as a form of experimentation. Experimentation, however, is properly used to isolate sources of variance.

Experimentation differs from tinkering in two important ways. First, the intention of experimentation is to determine the cause of an outcome, and then affect the outcome by manipulating the cause. Of course, the ultimate desire of any manager is to manipulate causes in order to influence the outcome, but the initial intention of experimentation is to find the cause. The only goal when tinkering is to improve performance and the manager does not care how or why it works.

The second difference is that other causes are controlled for. In order to isolate a cause, other potential causes must be identified and ruled out or controlled for (meaning that we can identify how much variance is due to each cause, so that we can see just how much variance is due to the potential cause being examined). Tinkering does not contain any control for other possible causes, which can lead to imperfect understanding of cause and effect. Without controlling for competitive action, for example, a manager may think that a price reduction will always result in a gain in sales if a gain in sales is observed the first time the manager lowers prices. If the manager lowers prices again and competition does the same, the result is likely to be no change in sales but a lower profit. Experimentation should control for the impact of competitive action.

Firms using experimentation often create a reality tree, an example of which can be found in Exhibit 15–10. A reality tree begins with an outcome, usually an undesired effect. (While experimentation can be used to determine causes of positive variance, more often it is used to determine sources of negative variance.) All possible causes are hypothesized and other effects of each cause are also listed. For example, if low sales are hypothesized to be due to either low quality or poor sales effort, possible other outcomes of each potential cause would be listed. Low quality would also result in more complaints about product performance whereas poor sales effort would show up in conversion ratios and other sales factors. The list of possible causes can be narrowed down to one or a few by examining other outcomes of those causes. Then an experiment can be designed to isolate the impact of each cause. Exhibit 15–10 illustrates the reality tree that Moore Business Forms created concerning an invoicing problem.

Statistical Analysis

As mentioned earlier in this chapter, data vary. Management uses a tolerance range when evaluating variance to determine if it is due to tinkering, random, systematic, or external sources of variance. Statistical analysis is being used at a greater rate in order to understand variance.

For example, a quota may be set that determines the bottom of the tolerance range. (Quota is usually set without thought given to tolerance range, but quota is the minimum accepted performance or, by definition, the bottom of the tolerance range. See Chapter 13 for more details on quota setting.) At the same time, however, management must identify at what point above quota is a salesperson's performance high enough to represent a systematic improvement in performance. Similarly, a marcomm manager may use statistical process control methods to examine advertising and trade show performance.

Variance is calculated by first calculating an average. If there were 10 salespeople who sold a total of $20 million, then the average would be $2 million. Then subtract the average from each individual observation and square the result. So if one salesperson sold $2.5 million and another sold $1.5 million, the squared difference in both cases would be .25 (i.e. 2.5–2=.5; .5×.5=.25; 1.5–2=–.5; –.5x[–.5]=.25). Then calculate the average squared difference. (Add all of the squared differences and divide by the number of observations, in this case salespeople.) The average squared difference is called the variance

Exhibit 15–10
Current Reality
Tree

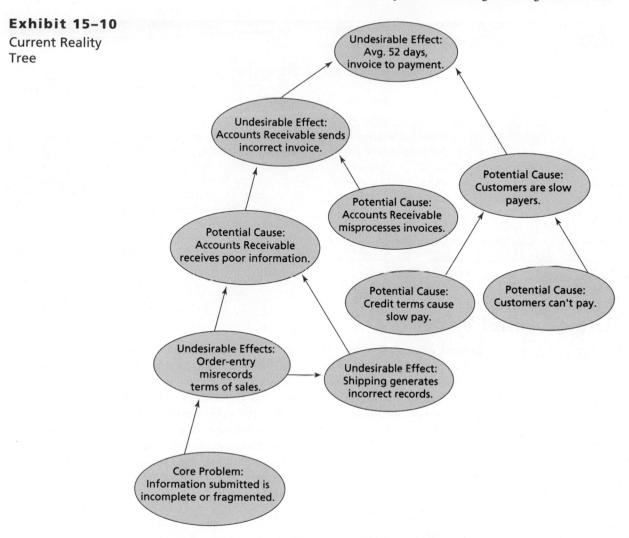

SOURCE: Adapted from J. F. Tanner and E. Honeycutt, "Re-Engineering the Sales Force Using the Theory of Constraints," *Industrial Marketing Management* 25 (1996), pp. 1–9.

but is not the statistic we want to use. Take the square root of the average squared difference and you have the standard deviation, which is the statistic that is used to examine variance in performance.

Any performance greater than two standard deviations above or below the mean, or average, performance would be considered significantly different; causes of that performance should be explored. Thus, the usual performance range is two standard deviations in either direction from the mean. Anything more than that represents systems-level variance. If we are talking salesperson performance, then anyone below the mean by more than two standard deviations may need significant training or the opportunity to look for another line of work, for example. On the other hand, check the salesperson more than two standard deviations above the mean and see if there is anything that can be copied by others.

15–2

BUSINESS 2 BUSINESS

Partnering within Rockwell

In Chapter 7, we discussed the importance of building internal partnerships. Rockwell International, with so many divisions spread out over the world, has as tough a challenge as any organization in creating internal partnerships. Think for a moment about just the need for partnerships within marketing. When Rockwell exhibits at a defense show, who is in charge: the division that sells planes, the division that sells military communications, the radar division, or someone else? And when advertising is created, how can Rockwell develop advertising across all of the various divisions that still has a Rockwell look? What processes have to be engineered to make sure that these internal partnerships develop?

Using Control Systems

Control systems allow for the control of daily activities and investment decisions. Control systems are an integral part of the business marketing manager's existence, but control systems also have roles in special situations, too.

For example, Rockwell International is essentially a manufacturer and marketer of transportation equipment. It is just that the equipment varies from truck axles to the space shuttle, a fact that makes for many challenges in evaluating performance and allocating investments. In addition to daily management decisions, control systems play an important role in enabling Rockwell to determine what strategies are working among their wide variety of products and markets. Control systems are also important contributors to reengineering and organizational learning.

Strategic Planning

Control at the macro level is an important element in the strategic planning process. A firm's control processes, as discussed earlier, should contribute information concerning the firm's performance in various areas in order to assist in making strategic decisions. Control tools, such as the marketing audit, can also contribute information to aid in the identification of opportunities and threats in the environment.

For example, the government is still a primary customer of Rockwell International. Not only did Rockwell manufacture the space shuttle and other aeronautical transportation systems, the company is the primary contractor for several military aircraft and more mundane transportation systems like trucks and other vehicles. Rockwell also manufactures communication systems to support these transportation systems as well as communications products such as microwave, radio, and satellite systems. The company has acquired and divested a number of communications operations over the past 25 years. These strategic decisions were made incorporating information from marketing audits, performance evaluations, financial analyses, and customer satisfaction studies, as well as keeping track of Department of Defense and NASA expenditures in the federal budget, and other sources of information.

Reengineering and Process Design

In order to increase output, one of two things must occur. Either greater inputs must be placed into the process or the process must be made more efficient. For example, the number of salespeople could be considered an input into the selling process. In order to sell more, more salespeople could be hired or each salesperson could be asked to sell more. Just asking them to sell more, though, won't see that it happens. Neither will paying more per sale lead to the quantum levels of productivity improvement that firms seek. In many cases, the selling process itself will have to be improved in order to achieve greater sales. **Reengineering**—the designing of work processes in order to achieve objectives—reflects the fact that most processes have evolved over time, serving objectives that may no longer be considered relevant. Reengineering the sales process, in this example, is a viable alternative to simply hiring more salespeople.

Organizational Learning and Control

As you recall from Chapter 7, there are two types of organizational learning: single- and double-loop. Control systems should contribute to both types of learning. Single-loop learning involves finding variance and seeking to minimize it in the next operating period. Variance can be from either revenue projections or expense budgets; controlling for revenue and costs can lead to a stronger profit picture. For example, Andrea Wharton (marcomm director for Alcatel, a French telecommunications company), reviews the performance of each trade show by comparing actual costs with the budget, and number of leads identified with the objectives, among other things. Her careful analysis means that after six shows, she still has enough money to do what is needed to attract enough qualified buyers to her company's booth in the six remaining shows for the year.

A challenge for all managers is complacency, particularly when things seem to be going well. Advertising managers who are comfortable with an advertising theme may not recognize when it is time for change. Focusing on single-loop learning is a form of complacency, for when the market does change, the firm's ability to make a profit can be in danger.

Sometimes, the need to manage for profit leads to double-loop learning. For example, if a firm is nearing or in bankruptcy, whatever mental models it was using before may not be worth repeating. Out of such crises come the most dramatic examples of double-loop learning.[4]

Managing for Quality

We've discussed methods for financial analyses, but marketing control systems must control for more than just revenues and expenses. The quality of marketing processes must be controlled as well. Again, control systems provide input into both single- and double-loop learning, learning that influences process design.

For example, Moore Business Forms had an invoicing system that generated an average of two wrong invoices for every correct invoice. Customers, as one can well imagine, were very dissatisfied with Moore's billing system. When would they know which bill to pay? A completely new system of billing was designed, a result of double-loop learning. Single-loop learning improved performance within the new system, resulting in even greater gains than before. Results include

- Improved customer satisfaction.

- Shorter billing cycle.

15–2

FROM THE FIELD

Measuring Quality: Quality Is in the Eye of the Beholder

The Total Quality Management movement has rejuvenated the careers of many business consultants, but has it really had any impact on how American business is conducted? One study, conducted by the University of Michigan, indicates that TQM has raised quality expectations among buyers without a corresponding real increase in quality. As a result, buyers are more dissatisfied than ever with the quality of products their businesses are receiving.

In a study conducted by the Quality Research Institute, only 15 percent of customers surveyed believed their vendors had adequate quality management procedures. At the same time, however, 73 percent of executives believe their companies have instituted effective quality management procedures. Why is there such a huge difference?

One reason may be how quality is measured. Too many executives rely on internal measures of quality, only comparing actual performance to performance targets. What is ignored is that customers are setting different performance targets, based on their needs.

The Diagnostic Imaging division of Berlex Laboratories in Wayne, New Jersey, is different from most companies. At Berlex, customers, both internal and external, write the performance specifications. Satisfied internal customers are able to then deliver higher-quality output because they have higher-quality inputs. One result is highly satisfied external customers; another is financial success. Berlex has enjoyed growth faster than the industry's due to its ability to improve customer satisfaction.

Source: Mary Azzolini and James Shillaber, "Internal Service Quality: Winning from the Inside Out," *Quality Progress* (November 1993), p. 75; Jacques Murphy and J. A. Taylor, "Taking Quality as Seriously as Profits," *Industrial Engineering* (January 1995), p. 28; Thomas Stewart, "After All You've Done for Your Customers, Why Are They Still Not Happy?" *Fortune* (December 11, 1995), p. 178.

- Faster payment cycle.
- Reduction in bad-debt write-offs.

While the financial results were important, the improvement in customer satisfaction should also result in greater sales in the future.

Managing for quality is important because quality is defined by the customer, as you can see in From the Field 15–2. Customers may be getting tired, however, of responding to customer satisfaction surveys. In one instance, satisfaction cards asking only five questions were sent to 500 customers. Not one was returned.[5] Companies must find other ways to measure customer satisfaction, and then use that information to evaluate the performance of their marketing systems.

Summary

Marketing control systems are important elements in organizational learning. The control process consists of measuring performance, comparing performance against a standard, and then examining performance to determine causes of variance, or deviation from the standard. Learning occurs when the manager recognizes the cause of variance and then eliminates negative causes or repeats positive causes.

Control occurs at both the macro, or system, level and the micro, or subsystem, level. Control processes also exist for inputs and outputs. Combining input and output anlysis is useful for examining efficiency.

The data used to evaluate performance vary from one observation to the next due to changes in the system, tinkering with the system, external causes, or random variance. The tolerance range is the amount that the measurements can vary without cause for alarm.

Tools for controlling marketing performance include the standards used to compare with performance. Types of standards include budgets and quotas, benchmarks, and pricing plans. Measurement tools include marketing audits, customer satisfaction measurement, and different types of accounting systems, such as cost accounting and activity-based costing. Causes of variance can be determined through experimentation, reporting and information systems, case analysis, and statistical analysis.

Control systems are used to support strategic planning, reengineering, and organizational learning. With proper control systems, organizations can learn to repeat successful performance and avoid the causes of poor performance.

Key Terms

benchmark	operational measure	standard
cycle time	random variance	systematic change
information system	reengineering	tinkering
marketing audit	reporting system	tolerance
marketing control system	sensor	

Discussion Questions

1. Each Wednesday, Jon Archer holds a meeting with his salespeople. Those who aren't reaching quota get yelled at; those who are get cheers. "We set our quotas a little high because it gives each person something to shoot for. Then, with encouragement or a kick in the pants, we motivate them to achieve it." Is Jon's plan a good one? Why or why not? Utilize the sources of variance information in your answer.

2. Classify the following sources of variance:
   a. An advertising manager observes that three new publications have been introduced in one industry, fragmenting readership of the magazines that have carried the company's advertising.
   b. A company trains every salesperson on partnering skills, changing the company's selling strategy from needs satisfaction to partnering.
   c. A manager encourages a salesperson to spend more time getting to know each buyer more personally.
   d. An exhibit manager observes downsizing in corporate purchasing departments, fewer visitors to the booth, and an increase in time spent by each visitor in the booth.
   e. An exhibit manager observes greater attendance at shows in the spring than for shows in the fall.

3. When is cycle time an important consideration? Explain the value created by a reduction in cycle time in the following instances:
   a. The sales cycle.
   b. Product development process.

   c. The process of creating and placing advertising.

   d. The credit approval process.

4. Is customer satisfaction measurement micro analysis or macro analysis? Justify your choice.

5. Explain the relationship of quota to the tolerance range. Consider how each is determined in your answer. Also consider the performance range discussed in the chapter. Is it a tolerance range or something else?

6. Visitors to the booth ranged in number between 270 and 330 per day for every show the previous year. In the current year, the exhibit manager used direct mail and specialty advertising premiums to invite prospects to the booth. The first show resulted in 320 visitors. Is the direct mail worth doing? What information do you need to make that decision?

7. Can the contribution method be combined with the ABC method? If so, how? If not, why not?

8. Three different industries buy the same motor from Anderson Electric, using the motors for different applications. The same salespeople sell to all three industries, but because the applications are different, different advertising campaigns have to be created. The same booth is used for trade shows in each industry, with different graphics that illustrate the different applications. Advertising is designed to support both field sales and trade show efforts. The manager of marketing for Anderson's line of motors wants to evaluate the performance of the marketing program. What information is needed? Where would you go to find it? What analyses would you conduct with the information?

9. What are some indications that a marketing audit may be needed?

10. Illustrate with examples (two each) when a marketing manager would want ABC-based information and when contribution-based information would be appropriate. Be sure to illustrate how the information would be used and why that method is the preferred method.

Internet Exercise

Open Rockwell's home page (**www.rockwell.com**). Interact with the site as you think a potential buyer for avionics and communications might when looking for a product from Rockwell.

   a. Keep a log of what you do (what sites you view and how much of the site you read).

   b. Compare and contrast how Rockwell would evaluate your use of the site with how a user would evaluate the site's effectiveness. Why would it be important for Rockwell's marketing manager to recognize the user's perspective when evaluating Rockwell's site?

WWWW
I N T E R N E T

Cases

Case 15.1   Megalith Tool Company

Chelsea Swanson slammed the door to her office and reflected upon the meeting with the new division president that had just concluded. "Either prove to me that your program is working or face the fact that you'll need another job," was how the president ended the conversation.

Exhibit 1
Exhibit Budget
Data

Salary	$42,000
Benefits	13,000
Travel	25,000
Booth shipment/storage	95,000
Booth refurbishing/building	200,000
Direct mail pre- and postshow	100,000
Booth giveaways	30,000
Total	$505,000

Exhibit 2
Hot Leads from
Trade Shows

	Last Year	Current Year
National Shows		
NTC	1,300	1,725
ICC/Pro-Form	1,870	1,480
ToolCon	1,525	1,775
Con-Squared	1,760	1,640
Global Tool Expo	1,820	1,890
Regional Shows		
Northwest region	420	540
	380	460
	620	480
	320	330
	455	610
Central region	390	520
	545	415
	610	530
	480	760
	675	480
	370	520
Southern region	490	540
	510	580
	485	525
	395	490
Southwest region	495	475
	395	520
	510	425
	430	540
Northeast region	670	580
	630	655
	540	510
	470	545
	535	690

Exhibit 3
Additional Marketing and Sales Information

Regional Sales Office	Sales	
	Last Year	Current Year
Northwest	$10.50 million	$10.75 million
Central	12.20	13.45
Southern	9.25	10.70
Southwest	9.35	11.65
Northeast	10.60	12.10
Average order size = $10,000		
Conversion ratio of hot leads = 10%		
Contribution margins for each regional sales office		
Northwest region	20%	
Central	22	
Southern	24	
Southwest	18	
Northeast	21	

Chelsea thought angrily, Prove it! I've never had to prove my performance before!

As exhibit manager for Megalith Tool Company, Chelsea was responsible for managing the trade show program that included five national shows and 24 regional events. The company manufactures tools and controls, selling in three different industries. Chelsea's first thought, after she calmed down a little, was the budget for the program, which we see in Exhibit 1. Perhaps the president would be satisfied if I just cut the budget, she thought.

But she did ask for performance, Chelsea remembered. She pulled out a series of reports that she creates after each show and began compiling performance data. Selected results for show performance are in Exhibit 2. Additional sales and marketing data can be found in Exhibit 3.

Analyze the results. Create a tolerance range that she can use to predict future performance given current investment and strategy. Is the program profitable?

Case 15.2   Polk Performance Products

Chad Polk stood before all 50 employees and their families at the annual company Christmas dinner, reviewing the company's performance for that year. "Sales were up 15 percent this year, meaning that every employee will receive a bonus equal to 15 percent of his or her annual pay!" A loud cheer rose up, and Polk smiled.

Polk Performance Products (PPP) manufactured chemicals sold to machine shops and other small contract manufacturers. The company sells three product lines, including maintenance chemicals such as cleansers and lubricants, caustics or chemicals used in the etching process, and plating chemicals (such as chrome). The company's six salespeople sold to distributors, who then sold to manufacturers.

Polk may have smiled as he announced the bonus, but two weeks later, in a meeting with employees to announce the new year's bonus plan, Polk did not appear to be as happy. "Folks, we can't have a bonus program on the basis of sales only." He pointed to his secretary, who dimmed the lights in the small auditorium and turned on a slide projector. "Each salesperson has one account that represents 10 percent of our volume; the remaining

40 percent of our sales volume is divided among 30 other distributors. Yet among those six large accounts, we average only 35 percent of their total chemical business. In other words, 65 percent of the business that should be ours is going to someone else."

Polk changed slides, showing a picture of a railroad tank car. "Now our quantity discount program gives each of these distributors 10 percent of the shipping costs back as a rebate for each carload they purchase, which really means that all we do is pass along our savings from the railroad to the customer." The next slide was a bar chart. "In talking with our customers, I've found that we're still 10 percent higher on costs to our largest customers but 5 percent lower on prices to our smaller customers. I could just raise and lower prices to be competitive, but I don't know now if we'll make any money that way."

At this point, Bill Stacy, the plant manager, stepped forward and said, "According to our accountants, the plant has a contribution margin of 29 percent. I've pledged to Chad that we'll have that up to 35 percent by the end of the year. That means we have to cut our operating costs by more than 7 percent."

Polk continued, "Our shipping costs reduce our profit by 5 percent, administrative expenses by another 5 percent, and selling costs by 20 percent, meaning that we lost a little money last year. As I am in charge of sales, I am committed to reducing selling expenses to 15 percent." He heard but did not acknowledge the mutterings of one rep, who wondered which salesperson would be fired in order to reduce expenses. "At the same time, however, I am looking for ways to increase our share of the business in our largest distributors, in addition to making that business more profitable. That is why the employee bonus program, mine included, will be 10 percent of net profit before taxes rather than sales for this year."

Polk asked his old friend, your professor, for help in finding ways to improve the contribution margin as well as increase revenue. Your professor then assigned the project to your class. First, list all of the information you want to receive from Polk. Then describe the analysis you would perform with that information. (It might be helpful to create a chart, with each variable listed in the first column and analysis in the second.)

What are some methods of increasing sales and reducing selling costs that Polk may want to consider? What are some other potential decisions that the analysis may point to?

Additional Readings

Jaworski, Bernard, Vlasis Stathakopoulos, and Shanker Krishan "Control Combinations in Marketing: Conceptual Framework and Empirical Evidence," *Journal of Marketing* 57 (January 1993), pp. 57–69.

Kaplan, Robert S., "Devising a Balanced Scorecard Matched to Business Strategy," *Planning Review* (September–October 1994), pp. 15–19, 48.

Kaplan, Robert S., and David P. Norton "Putting the Balanced Scorecard to Work," *Harvard Business Review* (September–October 1993), pp. 134–42.

Kaplan, Robert S., and David P. Norton, "Using the Balanced Scorecard as a Strategic Management System," *Harvard Business Review* (September–October 1993), pp. 75–85.

Koehler, Robert W. "Triple-Threat Strategy," *Management Accounting* (October 1991), pp. 30–34.

Reed, Richard, David J. Lemak, and Joseph C. Montgomery "Beyond Process: TQM Content and Firm Performance," *Academy of Management Review* 21, no. 1 (1996), pp. 173–202.

Chapter 16

Customer Retention and Maximization

SOCCER V

There is probably no more important task in marketing than keeping good customers. Here is a disguised tale of how one nimble supplier "related" to its market's largest customer. Realistically, setbacks occur in some transaction environments despite sound marketing efforts. ●

In 1994 Soccer V won the contract to supply uniforms, warm-ups, and bags to all players for the new City Soccer Club (CSC). The package was valued at about $39,000 in direct revenue, but Soccer V estimated another $8,000 in sales would result from replacement purchases and incremental business from players stopping at one of the stores to get fitted. Not all teams or players would replace their uniforms each year, but at least three new teams would be formed annually and follow-up business was expected to be about half the original contract. ●

Although Soccer V supplied many high schools, colleges, and other clubs in the region and was hard pressed to deliver all uniforms before the season, all deadlines were met and very few orders had to be corrected or adjusted. A couple of the principals at Soccer V were hired as coaches for CSC and adequate inventories were maintained all season. CSC voiced no complaints to Soccer V. ●

In 1995 CSC merged with the Eastern Hills Futbol Club and reconstituted its board of directors. CSC awarded a new uniform contract to Soccer Crazed, a single-site supplier whose bid was less than 1 percent lower than Soccer V's. One of the partners at Soccer Crazed sat on the CSC board. ●

In 1996, Soccer Crazed went out of business and the CSC contract went back to Soccer V. Inflation-adjusted prices are nearly equivalent to those in the 1994 contract.●

For a sense of the Soccer V operation, visit the web site of a competitor: **http://www.tsisoccer.com**●

Learning Objectives

In a number of ways, this chapter is a companion to Chapter 5's discussion of opportunity. That chapter began with attention to current customers as a basis for growth, new product ideas, and accesses to other markets. We think we've established the importance of keeping good customers in subsequent chapters on strategy, product development, communications, channels, and more. As one of our final lessons in business marketing, of course, we echo some of those key concepts. In a systematic and vivid fashion, Chapter 16 addresses the managerial challenge of retaining—that is, keeping—good customers. We can think of no more important topic for you to take away from the class.

We need to evaluate the makings of a good customer and sharpen attention to what it takes to satisfy customers. The financial implications of customer retention are detailed and complemented by emerging measures for tracking customer satisfaction. Imperatives for marketing strategy and action will be discussed.

At the end of the chapter you should be able to

● Classify different customer relationships on a continuum from always-a-share to lost-for-good.

● Identify the structural characteristics of the transaction environment that make for the above classification.

● Graph the profit implications over a range of customer retention probabilities.

● Identify the points of emphasis for retention efforts—strong or marginal customers.

● Describe some of the key avenues for bonding exchange parties in a relationship.

● Apply a basic satisfaction measurement system in the management of relationships.

● Discuss three avenues for strengthening good relationships.

Conquest and Aftermarketing

Marketing strategy and action frequently pivot on military metaphors and jargon. Managers talk about battlefields, penetration, flanking, reinforced positions, combative advertising, retaliation, and more. Perhaps such activities reflect the warrior archetype that resides in the heart of many striving professionals.

At the same time let's recognize the broad array of participants in marketing planning and execution. Many hands play a role in the effort: corporate image makers, advertisers and telephone professionals, engineers and general managers, sales reps and distributors, installers and service personnel. The successes of Microsoft, Magna Corporation, Boeing, Grainger, and other corporate giants reinforce lessons from the history of nations: A "battle cry" knits zealous cooperation, remarkable effort, and sacrifice for the supragoal of the organization. The spirit of conquest pervades the enterprise.

From *MicroNews,* the in-house newsletter at Microsoft, we have the "Battle Hymn of the Reorg":

> *Oh, our eyes have seen the glory of the coming of the Net,*
> *We are ramping up our market share, objectives will be met,*
> *Soon our browser will be everywhere, you ain't seen nothin' yet,*
> *We embrace and we extend!*
> *Our competitors were laughing, said our network was a fake,*
> *Saw the Internet economy as simply theirs to take.*
> *They'll regret the fateful day the sleeping giant did awake,*
>
> . . .
>
> *Glory , glory to the vision,*
> *Though Netscape treats us with derision,*
> *But soon will come the hour*
> *When their stock price starts to sour;*
> *We embrace and we extend![1]*

But what happens after the victory? In the history of business and the history of nations, conquest is an enigma. Sometimes the machinery of conquest is reapplied in new territories. Alexander the Great moved his armies ever eastward. Hitler's machine ground up nations on every compass point. Indeed, the past two centuries are replete with now-scorned expansion-minded dictators. Do we stretch the metaphor to note that many of 1970's Fortune 500 firms are no longer on the roster?

Frankly, as Wang found out in the field of office automation, conquest is a much smaller piece of marketing than the jargon and jingles convey. In military parlance, if one cannot hold and secure conquered territory, the conquest is for naught. Indeed, much as thousands of Napoleon's troops retreated from the Russian winter without coats or shoes, Wang lost account after account as its service deteriorated.

Good news! The lost art of customer retention has been rediscovered in business. In almost every sector of commerce we see a renewed interest in recognizing and keeping best customers and in improving the value of average and below-average accounts. Interestingly, these efforts are guided largely by another metaphor, marriage, and motivated by new market measures and financial tools.

In contrast to the military symbols, many observers see marketing in terms of courtship, betrothal, and permanent union. For example, Theodore Levitt notes that

> *"the sale merely consummates the courtship. Then the marriage begins. How well the marriage is depends on how well the relationship is managed by the seller."[2]*

Recall the relationship development model presented in Chapter 2. This model proposed a gradual deepening of dependence between buyer and seller, propelled by positive reinforcements of trusting behaviors.

In this chapter we want to build upon the background of Chapters 2 and 5 to examine the financial impact of lasting customers. In order to do this, let's revisit and examine more closely the types of customer relationships we are apt to find in business markets.

The Nature of a Customer

The behaviors of buyers and sellers interact with fundamental characteristics of the exchange environment to define the nature of their relationship. This section will use some basic elements of each sphere to describe a continuum of trading relations.

Always-a-Share Relationships

Almost every organization needs printing services. It might be menus, training manuals, product literature, catalogs, company newsletters, or newspaper inserts. Given the technical specifications of a printing job, usually a buyer can choose from several capable printers. Price and credible delivery date are prime selection criteria. The buyer can award a printer in the set of candidates almost any share of its printing business.

Furthermore, this share of business can fluctuate from year to year, largely depending on the competitive environment and the printer's aggressiveness in pricing and scheduling. Lone Star Web may do 40 percent of a customer's printing in one period, none in the next, and 60 percent in the period after that. Notice that even though the printing customer did not use Lone Star Web for a period, the buyer can and often will make purchases in subsequent periods. This type of account is called an **always-a-share** customer because the buyer can taper or augment purchases in increments, and multiple suppliers can have a share of a customer's business in either the current period or future periods.

Like printing services, other products frequently purchased on an always-a-share basis include standard trucking services, catering, consulting, supplies, basic chemicals, and materials. Multiple suppliers typically vie for an increasing percentage of the customer's business. And buyers can rely on a mix of suppliers without incurring significant additional variance that jeopardizes product performance. In the opening vignette, despite its initial contract, Soccer V had an always-a-share relationship with CSC. Indeed, CSC switched three times—to Soccer V, to Soccer Crazed, and back to Soccer V—in just over two years.

The situation is very much akin to your use of several stores, catalogs, and garage sales for your wardrobe. Even if you buy almost all of your clothing from The Limited or L.L. Bean, it is always easy to spend a portion—always-a-share—of your budget at the Gap or the new consignment shop near campus.

Lost-for-Good Customers

When Ford or Toyota select a supplier of exterior mirrors for one or more of their models, the styling and assembly process tend to cement this relationship for long periods. It will be difficult to switch from a metal mirror to an injection-molded plastic mirror except at model change periods.

On the face of it, almost any trucking company or UPS could deliver, but Ryder Integrated Logistics coordinates the delivery of components, such as these purifier units, to Whirlpool's appliance plants, JIT.
© Steve Jones

The situation is similar in the field of telecommunications and computer systems. When a school district decides its computer labs will be Macintosh, the software and accessories will necessarily be Mac-based. The faculty will be trained on Macs and the instructional materials will build upon Macs. Consider the barriers to switching to Windows machines. Indeed, the investments in software, accessories, learning systems, and human resources are largely scrapped when the switch occurs. Perhaps the lab consultants must all attend retooling seminars and the maintenance contract must be terminated with penalty.

Thus, **switching costs** are the forgone value of investments plus economic penalties and other expenses associated with finding, evaluating, and using a new supplier. To further illustrate, many tool makers will rely on a JIT relationship with a regional metal service center. To switch to a new supplier means finding another well qualified one, bringing it up to speed on the specialty metals and fabrications needed, and testing the new PC to PC order system. There may be additional costs associated with learning the language of each other's firm and ironing out miscommunications. Sometimes legal costs are incurred for litigation or the voidance of contracts.

When a customer willingly incurs these costs to use a different supplier, it is because the incumbent is no longer regarded as viable. There's a better alternative out there that the customer, in essence, must pay to deal with. And is it likely that the customer would "pay" the switching costs again to return to the incumbent? Usually the answer is no. Relationships cemented by switching costs are called **lost-for-good relationships** because the prospects of a customer making a costly switch to a competitor followed by a costly return to the incumbent are remote—probably weaker than a cold call prospect.

The lost-for-good label on these types of exchange motivate retention by accentuating the "dark side." That is, a customer is lost when it grows disenchanted with our performance and finds an alternative that promises sufficient advantages to overcome the associated switching costs. Reacquiring such a customer is practically hopeless. Apply the model in your own purchasing sphere. Will you return to a bank where you closed your accounts? Will you rejoin a Greek organization that you quit in protest last spring? Indeed, cold calls probably yield better prospects for these organizations than you yield.

Notice that these types of accounts can have excellent staying power. Because the customer incurs costs to switch suppliers, we might expect frequent communication, joint planning, and requests for adjustment in these durable associations. *Consistent high performance* is required to retain these accounts. And structural features of the exchange support its continuity.

Implications of Exchange Type

Always-a-share and lost-for-good represent polar ends of a continuum of exchange situations. Sellers will retain customers by giving good service and responding to customer needs. Differentiating the offering on dimensions that forge structural ties and create exit barriers will tend to move the relationship toward the lost-for-good variety. For example, an always-a-share supplier might move from a fill-in role to become a major supplier by meeting customer criteria for becoming a preferred supplier. The standards for preferred supplier vary from firm to firm, but often include quality programs, employee safety and training efforts, and delivery specifications. Like Soccer V in the opening vignette, sellers can seek long-run supply contracts, build interpersonal linkages, and attempt to forge technical ties in an effort to move the account toward the lost-for-good type. We will develop these ideas below.

Of course, supplier action and market evolution can move the exchange the other way too. For example, plug compatibility and software standards have dramatically lowered exit barriers in the field of computer mainframes, moving the exchange from lost-for-good toward always-a-share.

Exhibit 16–1 summarizes the characteristics of each type of exchange. The classification is quite simple, but it puts a valuable focus on the nature of the customer relationship. The classification also illuminates the durability of any exchange and prompts management to consider the value of key accounts or customer groups.

Retention Probability and Customer Value

The marketing concept has always emphasized the satisfaction of customers to keep them coming back. But only in the past decade or two has information technology helped us put a dollar value on this highly strategic asset, the satisfied customer. Exhibit 16–2 depicts the expected food service purchases from a growing key institutional cafeteria account at a food wholesaler. The volume figures are rough forecasts, but represent the best estimates available, based on historical data, industry analysis, and revealed company strategy. If we also connect our expectations of slimming margins over the life of the account (reflecting shared economies in purchasing and servicing), we can forecast gross profits from the account.[3] These profit forecasts are discounted at 10 and 20 percent and summed to give the two NPV estimates at the bottom right.

Of course, we must not bank on these boxed NPV figures because *they are realized only if we retain the account.* Therefore, Exhibit 16–3 plots NPV against different retention rates. Understand what a retention rate is. With just a 20 percent chance of continuing a lost-for-good business relationship each year, the probability of holding the account through the sixth year is tiny ($.2^6 = .000064$). Even at .6 retention, the chance of serving the account in year 6 is less than 5 percent.

The story is different with an always-a-share account. In this analysis, retention probabilities equate to expected share of purchases. You may recall that in Chapter 5 we modeled customer lifetime value accounting for the probability of purchase as a function of

Exhibit 16–1
Lost-for-Good
and Always-a-
Share Customers

Permaglide conveyance systems—
integrated materials handling products

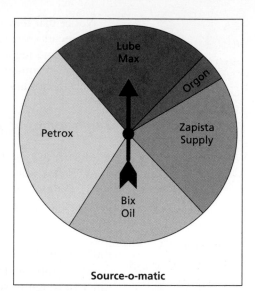

Source-o-matic

Lost-for-Good	Always-a-Share
Customers are tied to a system. They face significant switching costs. Switching costs may include	Customers can allocate their purchases to several vendors. A period of no purchases can be followed by a period of high purchases.
Specific investments	
Cancelation penalties	Suppliers are largely interchangeable.
Setup costs for a new supplier	
Retraining	
Finding and evaluating a new supplier	

Examples

Telecommunications systems	Lubricating oils
Franchises	Printing services
Warehouse rackings	Office supplies
Computer systems	Bulk chemicals

Exhibit 16–2
Food Service Key
Customer
Purchase and
Profit Forecasts

Year	Expected Purchases	Estimated Margin	Gross Profit	NPV @ 10%	NPV @ 20%
1	$1,000,000	15.0%	$150,000	$136,364	$125,000
2	1,080,000	14.4	155,520	128,529	108,000
3	1,166,400	13.4	156,204	117,359	90,396
4	1,259,712	12.5	156,892	107,159	75,661
5	1,360,489	11.6	157,582	97,846	63,329
6	1,469,328	10.8	158,275	89,342	53,006
				$676,598	$515,392

Exhibit 16–3

Customer NPV as a Function of Retention Rate: Lost-for-Good Customers

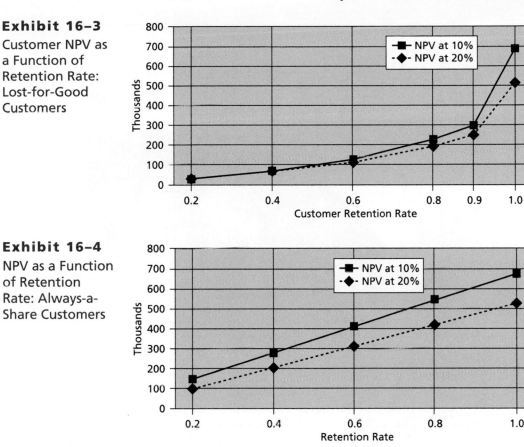

Exhibit 16–4

NPV as a Function of Retention Rate: Always-a-Share Customers

recency, the time since their last purchase. Regardless of approach, purchase probabilities do not drop precipitously as in the lost-for-good situation. Thus, Exhibit 16–4 shows NPV as a function of retention rates which remain at the same level in each buying period.

Compare the simple graphs in Exhibits 16–3 and 16–4. First note that a .8 retention rate with a lost-for-good customer brings less profit than a .4 retention (share-of-purchase) rate with an always-a-share customer. Although these simple models ignore the promotion and account service expenses, the retention imperative for lost-for-good customers comes through quite clearly. Do not doubt: What's lost is lost. A 20 percent defection rate is a serious problem.

Another insight from the graphs concerns the payoffs from efforts to improve retention. Exhibit 16–4 shows that with a linear relationship between retention and net present value, efforts to boost retention yield the same incremental profits at various retention levels for always-a-share relationships. Thus, whether we boost retention (share-of-purchases) from .2 to .3 or .8 to .9, Exhibit 16–4 shows the same incremental profits. In contrast, at lost-for-good accounts, with the curvilinear relationship between retention and NPV, retention gains at the high end tend to dwarf gains obtained on the low end. For example, at the 10 percent discount rate, improving retention rates from .4 to .6 brings a $57,000 gain in profits. Meanwhile, moving from .8 to .9—half the other increment in retention—nets an additional $75,000! Therefore, marketing expenditures to cement business with an already good account will typically yield a better payoff than those same expenditures aimed at making a marginal customer an average customer.

Exhibit 16–5
Relationship
Benefits to Sellers

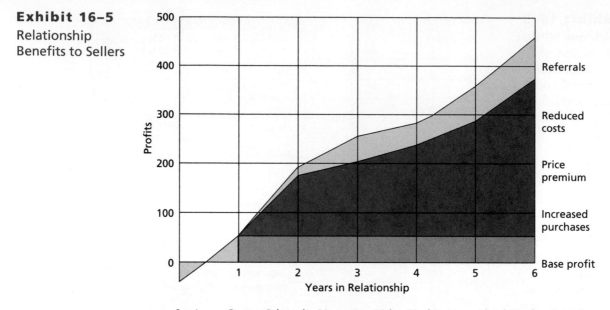

SOURCE: Jon Anton, *Customer Relationship Management: Making Hard Decisions with Soft Numbers,* © 1996. Reprinted by permission of Prentice-Hall, Inc., Upper Saddle River, NJ.

Additional Payoffs

The simple models in the previous section don't tell the whole story. They show only mysteriously expanded purchases. They aptly demonstrate the payoffs of retention and the distinction between always-a-share and lost-for-good accounts. But they skirt the detail that can reveal the source of additional payoffs in long-term relationships. Exhibit 16–5 is a powerful graphic depicting the "stack" of benefits that can result.[4] A good buyer–seller relationship will grow additional business opportunities: new products, increased purchases. When supported by first-rate service and product quality, premium prices can be charged. Selling costs can be better managed, and because of tighter coordination between buyer and seller, the benefits of production and logistical efficiencies are shared. Finally, we should explicitly recognize the "spillover" from one relationship to others. Customer referrals, joint demonstrations at trade shows or at new prospective customers, and articles in the trade press connect the relationship to other business. Indeed, long-standing relations represent implicit endorsements.

Customer Relationship Management

Now that we have underscored their financial impact and provided a scheme for classifying relations, it is time to address systematically the challenges of building, running, and strengthening relationships. The challenge of "building" will pivot upon the relationship development process from Chapter 2 and emphasize the strategy of forging relational ties through role performance, social ties, technical linkages, investments, and contracts. Are there product positioning options, pricing mechanisms, and other strategic measures that can build relationships? We show that there are indeed.

"Running" a relationship involves the values, personnel, and systems dedicated to maintaining a high-performance relationship. The topical distinction is a bit artificial because some maintenance is needed in the building phase, and building or expansion may

16–1

BUSINESS 2 BUSINESS
Hindsight at Soccer V

Customers are dynamic, of course. But when customers are involved in mergers and acquisitions, downsizing, and political infighting, it can create havoc for suppliers. In the opening vignette, for example, Soccer V did many things right, attempting to bond with a key account: It did the ordering, fitting, and silkscreening jobs well; personnel penetrated the customer's organization at the coaching level; and its prices were competitive. Are there other means by which its relationship with CSC could have been cemented to withstand the merger and the new board composition?

be a phenomenon in an established relation. Nevertheless, we use this organizational device to focus on a fitting capstone set of concepts. Commitment to customers is shaped by leadership and corporate culture. Customer service and product quality is not just a marketing job. It requires "all hands" working with empathy, efficiency, and empowerment toward the goal of customer satisfaction. Naturally, reward systems and information systems are needed to control the process.

Similarly, we carve out a separate discussion for "strengthening" relationships. "Strengthening" uses the themes introduced in the "building" phase to fortify and maximize the value of a strong buyer–seller relationship. The realm of possibilities for deepening dependence and expanding the scope of joint action in an established relationship is quite different from those we see in the fragile associations that promise someday to evolve into strong working partnerships.

Building Relationships

Companies remain in business relationships for two basic reasons: (1) because they have to and (2) because they want to. Firms have to stay in a relationship when there are no alternatives or when technical features of the exchange bind the parties for extended periods. Firms want to stay in relationships that are satisfying; they meet financial objectives, they evidence cooperation, and they can be projected into the future with confidence.

A happily married couple doesn't really care if their state's divorce laws are strict. Likewise, parties to a mutually satisfying business relationship are not apt to fret about switching costs. Thus, let's begin this section with a discussion of quality performance as a relational tie.

Performance and Exclusivity

Time and again business buyers tell us they are looking for performance at a good price. They call this value. Value is often described as the ratio of quality and service to price. In many markets, however, customers respond to service improvements as if the value equation has an exponential function in the numerator. That is, instead of

$$V = Q/P \tag{1}$$

it seems more accurate to posit

$$V=Q^2/P \qquad \qquad (2)$$

In Equation 1, a 9 percent price cut or a 10 percent quality boost yield the same impact on customer value:

$$V=Q/P \ . \ . \ . \ 1.00/(1.00-.09) = 1.1 \sim 1.10/1.00 = 1.1$$

In Equation 2, the impact of quality on value dwarfs the cut:

$$V=Q^2/P \ . \ . \ . \ 1.10^2/1.00 = 1.21$$

Thus, 10 percent increase in quality nets a 21 percent gain in value. The model formalizes what we see in the marketplace routinely: Superior performance, quality, and distinctive and reliable service are sources of competitive advantage that build customer loyalty. Customer retention is a logical and empirical reality for high-performance firms, organizations that do their job better than the rest.

Of course, quality and service expectations are shaped by the market. What begins as a unique service—a distinction that gains market share or enables a price premium—often becomes widely mimicked. In a short time it becomes the industry standard. The business travel industry is replete with examples of breakthroughs that are now common: frequent flier programs, express checkout, fax service, in-room data transmission lines, and more.

So where is the glamour in business travel? Sadly, the promise of a service does not correspond to fulfillment. Exhibit 16–6 is a composite of some of the service breakdowns recounted by business travelers.[5]

The impact of quality and service in building a relationship comes from actually delivering it . . . every time. Consistent execution of what counts with the customer distinguishes your offering from the offering of your competitors. This gets you repeat business. This gets you requests to tackle special needs. This gets you invitations to propose new means of conducting business. This is the critical prerequisite for relationship development.

Social Ties

The importance of social ties in business relationships is evident all around us. Business relationships are built on friendships, and friendships are built upon a variety of social interactions. Consider these examples. The mayor and the school superintendent sit in the university president's box at Saturday night's basketball game. An account executive at a midsized ad agency heads the local direct marketing association. An air conditioning manufacturer hosts heating, ventilating, and air conditioning (HVAC) engineers for a Toronto harbor cruise and cocktails. The sales rep asks about the CFO's family and community chest activities before taking up the new leasing options. The hospital purchasing agent receives three hams, 22 greeting cards, and four cans of nuts at Christmastime.

Although we don't doubt that many gifts and outings are intended to bring quid pro quo, the "strings-attached" variety are apt to be resented and eschewed for the complexity they bring buyers. If 18 holes is intended to bribe, what purchasing agent can enjoy the round? And how can it weigh against the slightly lower bid from the supplier who hosted a small group at the symphony? Marketing professionals regard gifts and social

Exhibit 16–6
Service Quality
Breakdowns

Most of us encounter poor service with distressing regularity. On a typical business trip, the only thing worse than the service may be the response to your complaints.

What You Experience	What the Service Provider Says
Your radio alarm fails.	We only sell it. Read your warranty.
The trunk of your airport limo is full of water and greasy tools, so your garment bag and its contents get soaked.	Did you buy our optional personal-property insurance?
You try to check in to claim your assigned seat on the plane.	Sorry, this line is closed. Please move on.
You pick up your rental car at your destination.	We're all out of compacts, but we can rent you a minivan once the mechanic is through with it.
You check into your hotel with a supposedly guaranteed reservation.	Sorry, but we have no record of your reservation, and we're full.
Breakfast is a half-hour late.	Sorry, it went to the wrong room.
Your secretary calls. Back at the office, the photocopier is down.	We'll need a few days to get it fixed.
The hotel telephone is making funny noises.	We'll have to schedule a service rep, but I can't say for sure when he'll be out.
Your answering service abruptly says, "Oops, hold on," and you get cut off from a long-distance call.	This happens all the time. It's nothing to worry about.
You order a hot sandwich for lunch, but it arrives cold and greasy.	Our chef is out sick today, so an assistant is cooking.
You check out of the hotel—or try to. Your bill is wrong; the breakfast charge was not included.	I'll fix it for you as soon as I track down my supervisor.
When you finally pick up your baggage after the flight home, it's torn and broken.	Fill out a claim form, but I'll warn you: Our liability limit is low.

SOURCE: Robert Desatnick, and Denis Detzel, *Managing to Keep the Customer,* © 1993. Reprinted by permission of Jossey–Bass Publishers, San Francisco, CA.

affairs as a means of thanking customers and building personal relationships in a world of e-mail and faxes.[6] One purchasing expert summed up this tradition from the customer's vantage point:

> *Business lunches—and other reasonable forms of entertainment—are old, pleasant, and respectable parts of buyer–seller relationships. . . . A good buyer knows, for example, that a supplier is not trying to subvert him by taking him out to lunch. But he also realizes that the supplier has sound business, as well as personal reasons for his largesse.*[7]

Exhibit 16–7 details how buyers and sales reps view luncheon meetings.[8]

Indeed, often (and more effectively than tacit bribery), these social exchanges occur to support the candid disclosures, frank feedback, and high-risk proposals inherent in problem solving as well as the inevitable requests for flexibility and adjustment that commercial trading involves. Considerable research shows how communication, concern for one's partner, fairness, honesty, and shared values enable trust, which fosters a long-term orientation and commitment to a relationship.[9] Exhibit 16–8 shows an empirically supported model of the precursors and consequences of trust and commitment.

Exhibit 16–7   Buyer's and Seller's Views of the Business Lunch

Exhibit A

The objectives and reasons for business luncheon meetings, as perceived by buyers and sales representatives.

Statement to Evaluate

1. Buyer–seller business is the purpose of the business lunch.
2. The business lunch provides an opportunity for buyer and seller to get to know each other better.
3. A function of the business lunch is to "sell something."
4. The business lunch gives the buyer (seller) a chance to get away from the office and all its distractions to discuss buyer–seller business.
5. Business lunches help solve some kind of business problem.
6. Buyer–seller business talk on a business lunch is valuable.
7. Personal talk on a business lunch is valuable.
8. Buyers expect to be taken out to lunch.

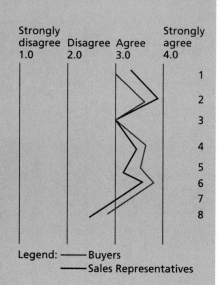

Exhibit B

Appropriate topics for discussion at business luncheon meetings and effects on personal relationships and order placement, as seen by buyers and sales representatives.

1. Conversations on the business lunch are typically buyer–seller business oriented.
2. Price negotiation occurs on the business lunch.
3. Delivery problems are discussed on the business lunch.
4. Quality issues arise and are discussed on business lunches.
5. Personal relationships do develop between buyer and seller as a result of the business lunch.
6. The personal relationships that do develop help the buyer (seller) get his job done more efficiently.
7. The more a buyer gets taken out to lunch by a particular supplier, the more likely it is that that supplier will receive orders from that buyer.
8. Salespeople who develop personal relationships with buyers get more orders, assuming *all* other things are equal, than those salespeople who don't develop personal relationships.
9. Very few orders are ever given (or received) as a result of the business lunch.

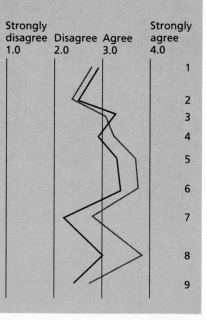

Exhibit 16–7   Continued

Exhibit C

Reactions of buyers and sales
representatives to various suggestions for
making business luncheon meetings more
effective.

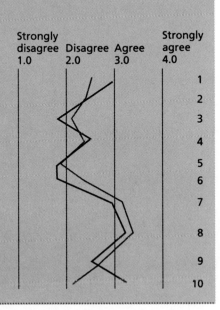

1. There should be more buyer–seller business discussed on the business lunch.
2. There should be more personal talk on the business lunch.
3. The business lunch should follow prearranged lines of discussion.
4. There should be more prelunch preparation by both buyer and seller on business topics that are going to be discussed on the business lunch.
5. The amount of time allowed for the business lunch should be decreased.
6. Alcohol should be forbidden on the business lunch.
7. The best business lunch results when just buyer and seller go out to lunch together.
8. The best business lunch results when buyer and seller and a person from a support group (engineering, quality control, etc.) go out to lunch together.
9. The best business lunch results when an additional buyer or seller—besides the original one buyer and one seller—go out to lunch together.
10. Managers (or principals) should participate in the business lunch often.

SOURCE: Adapted from Paul Halvorson and William Rudelius, "Is There a Free Lunch." Reprinted with permission from *Journal of Marketing* 41 (January 1977), pp. 44–49, published by the American Marketing Association.

16–2

BUSINESS 2 BUSINESS

The Fairway

You have landed a part-time job in the county purchasing department. After looking at proposals from three suppliers, you recommended purchasing all the golf course herbicides from GreenBlade. It's been six weeks since your recommendation went forward. Now you receive a small package with a note from Bernie Tassmer at Green Blade: "Thanks for picking a winner, GreenBlade. And next time we go out, I get two strokes a side. Best regards, Bern" The package contains four all-week passes to the PGA tournament up-state next month and two dozen tour-quality golf balls. What should you do?

In the evolution of business relationships it's common for parties to interact at equivalent organizational levels: sales rep to buyer, installer to user, engineer to general manager, director of purchasing to VP of marketing. But as a relationship matures, interactions cut across levels. Account managers and customer teams interface with

Exhibit 16–8

The Foundation and Payoffs of Trust and Commitment in Business Relationships

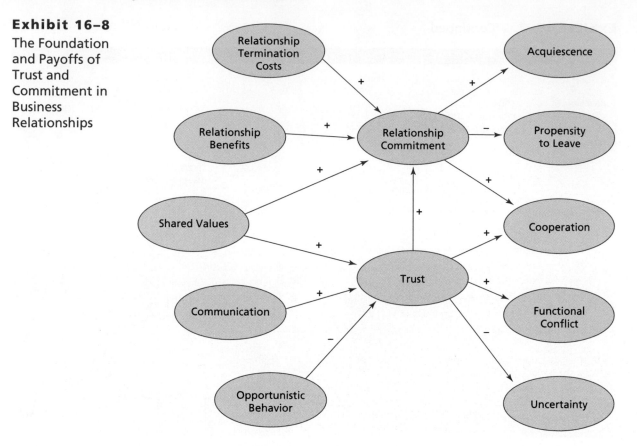

SOURCE: Adapted from Robert Morgan and Shelby Hunt, "The Commitment–Trust Theory of Relationship Marketing." Reprinted with permission from *Journal of Marketing* 58 (July 1994), pp. 20–38, published by the American Marketing Association.

cross-functional high-performance work teams on the buyer side. How effective can the partnership be without courtesy, professionalism, empathy, and justice? Do you think business friendships support or impair communication, shared visions, problem solving, and adjustment? Would a customer switch to another supplier without giving the people its managers like at the supplier organization a chance to amend service breakdowns or explore new means of working together? Indeed, it's hard to overemphasize the role of social ties in business relationships.

Technical and Formal Ties

We can sometimes get caught up in the feel-good aspects of buyer–seller relationships to the neglect of critical structural ties. An aluminum casting company that locates in proximity of the aluminum supplier, so that molten aluminum can be conveyed by pipeline, is structurally committed to the supplier. A telemarketing agency that uses IBM computers and call distributors is technically tied to that operating system. Likewise, a supermarket chain that adopts Advanced Promotion Technology's interactive point-of-purchase and satellite communication system cannot easily change systems or suppliers.

Selling a "system"—whether offering computational power, medical and disability insurance, telecommunications, MRO supplies, or food service—is a double-edged sword. On the one hand, by coupling formerly separable elements, it increases the complexity of changing any element. A switch to another system or product configuration means a high dollar outlay, new learning, insuring compatibility, and sustaining efficient work flow. These are switching costs that tend to move the exchange toward the lost-for-good variety. On the other hand, the lack of system divisibility can be an impediment to trial, making new account acquisition difficult.

Systems and Mods

Thus, a customer adopting our system becomes locked in to a degree. But the system itself can be an impediment to adoption. This double-edged character of systems demands that firms give careful attention to the modularity of their system. **Modularity** means the system is comprised of distinct subsystems or components. If a module can be tested to "sample" the performance of the full system, market penetration possibilities are enhanced. For example, a dockable laptop computer can lead a user to purchase an entire workstation. A keyless door lock may lead a hotel to adopt the supplier's complete security system.

Modularity is also a factor to consider for account retention. Current customers don't want to be using obsolete systems when technology and innovation bring improvements. Software companies routinely provide free or low-cost upgrades to current users. This can regain competitive advantage over rival suppliers' innovations and nip sources of current user frustration, extending the relationship. Thus, many accounts can be retained if the possibility exists to swap elements of the fading system for new and improved modules.

Of course, if competitors' modules can connect to your system, the relationship begins to take on the character of always-a-share. But the upside risk is that such openness reduces perceived risk among potential adopters. They see less possibility of being "held up" by the system provider. In essence, this serves as a pledge to provide exemplary quality and service. A seller recognizes the buyer's apprehensions about being locked in to one supplier, but is so confident it can do the best job, that it welcomes the presence of rivals to keep it on its toes.

Investments

Another avenue for establishing relationships that last involves **specific investments**, the dedication of assets that have sharply reduced value outside the relationship. Think of the scope of investments that companies make—in people, locations, procedures, equipment, and more—that have real value only within a relationship. For example, an industrial distributor may send its people to a week-long seminar to learn how 3M wants distributors to connect to its new order systems and conform to new standards of reporting distributor activities, performance, and quality control. Little of this investment in man-hours, talent, and know-how carries over to relationships with other suppliers. The distributor stays in the relationship to reap the return on the training investment.

Similar effects result from investments in specific locations (a steel mill locates near a coal depot), specific supplier qualification standards (ISO 9000), or specific equipment (a customer designs an assembly process utilizing a supplier's proprietary technology built into unique components). These are technical and structural commitments that bind the parties. From the Field 16–1 discusses the structural ties at Volkswagen's new factory of factories.

You probably have enough relational scar tissue to recognize the instability of one-way commitments. (But you don't have to tell us you forked out $220 for the security guard uniform in the job you kept one week, or took a French course to talk to the cute

---

16–1

FROM THE FIELD

Structural Ties at VW

Outside of Rio de Janeiro a radical experiment is underway. Volkswagen is building trucks in modules at a plant that involves seven different assemblers. The $250 million plant has main suppliers using their own workers and equipment to put together about 100 trucks and buses per day. More than a new way of manufacturing, it's a new type of lost-for-good relationship.

VW is led by Jose Lopez, a former General Motors executive who left GM to try his ideas for the superefficient factory. For nearly a decade, other automakers such as Ford and Chrysler have contracted with suppliers for complete modules on such parts as brakes and suspensions. In the Lopez system, hundreds of suppliers are reduced to seven final assemblers, each accountable for a single module:

- Iochpe–Maxion (Brazil)   Chassis
- Rockwell (U.S.)   Axles, brakes, suspension
- Iochpe–Maxion, Bridgestone (U.S.), Borlen (Brazil)   Wheels and tires

- Motoren–Werke Mannheim (Germany), Cummins (U.S.)   Engine and transmission
- Tamet (Brazil)   Cab
- VDO Kienzle (Germany)   Steering and instruments
- Eisenmann (Germany)   Painting

In the new plant, VDO Kienzle, the German instrument manufacturer, installs seats, instrument panels, and interiors on cabs moving down the line. Yellow lines on the factory floor mark the area where 200 VDO workers assemble the interiors.

This approach, says VW, has cut work hours by 12 percent compared to a typical plant. It also reduces investment—VDO put $10 million into the plant—and trims inventories. Because the plant's employees represent eight different work forces, it may be hard for unions to gain leverage. The challenges for suppliers in this lost-for-good relationship: ensuring quality in each module, getting teamwork in the whole, and managing the logistics of JIT delivery.[10]

---

exchange student across the hall.) A relationship is apt to last when both parties commit. Indeed, many business relationships are supported by *mutual* investments or pledges. This has the effect of building exit barriers or switching costs for both parties, motivating the parties to resolve differences.

Consider how suppliers may pledge or signal their commitment to the relationship by making reciprocal investments. For the shipper who locates at the railroad spur, the carrier designs a railroad car for the special transport of its industrial valves and controls. Distributors who attend manufacturer training may receive special displays and promotion assistance from their supplier, and know the training costs often exceed the small fees—if any—charged by the manufacturer.

Contracts

We would be remiss in our discussion of customer retention if we neglected the topic of contracts. A **contract** is a promise to perform some act in exchange for a payment or some other consideration. A contract has the force of law, but when used to cement a relationship, a contract typically specifies means of adjustment other than litigation. Indeed, in classical contracting, the parties try to foresee every contingency and specify adjustments and outcomes.[11] Of course, when the contract is for 3, 5, or 10 years or more, the relevant future is quite cloudy. Uncertainty pervades. Hurricanes, strikes, wars, power failures, acquisitions, supply shortages, technology, new regulations, adverse publicity, bridge collapse, and other calamities may impact the exchange. It is impossible to anticipate every event.

The parties try to forge contractual terms that preserve the relationship in the face of these and other unknown contingencies. An account can be retained through even the worst circumstances if the contract gives guidelines for joint action and adjustment. Better yet are mechanisms that look forward in the relationship. These involve information sharing for *structural planning*.

To illustrate, consider Beta, a company shipping automobile parts with carrier Gamma. Beta holds very low inventories at its different assembly plants, so it is vital that Gamma provide reliable, on-time delivery. Accordingly, Beta and Gamma hold formal meetings to discuss the most troublesome routes and set goals for service improvement. After 30 days if targets are still being missed on a significant percentage of shipments, other routes might be tested.

A Beta representative summed up, "We will make every effort to help them correct their problems. Usually the problem is legitimate and usually they fix it. If they can't, I want them to know that I don't like having to switch [carriers] on them, but that I have to. We can't afford to have a plant close down."[12]

The Mix of Relationship Ties

We have discussed five basic means of cementing relationships: superior performance, social ties, systems, specific investments, and contracts. Our treating each bond in a separate subsection should not suggest that the bonds are used on an either–or basis. They interact with each other—sometimes positively, but also sometimes negatively.[13]

For example, firms making specific investments in people, sites, or equipment need to protect the value of those assets. Although we talked about reciprocated investments serving as pledges of continuity, contractual provisions or social ties may also provide assurances. This is a positive interaction.

On the negative side, detailed contractual elements can blemish a relationship. Imagine, over lunch and a hand shake, a vendor says, "we'll send a testing truck right away if ever the boiler shows signs of stress." How many billable hours can the customer's attorney rack up defining the "signs of stress," specifying what testing truck and the qualifications of the testing crew, and pinpointing the clock time equivalent of "right away"? Most professionals recognize the risks to a relationship from such legalism and know that because the vendor's reputation is on the line, an earnest effort at performance is apt to result.

Running Relationships

Recently at a beautiful wedding before a standing-room–only congregation of family and friends, the presider told the bride and groom that the strength of their marriage would depend on three things: accepting each other as they are, communication, and help from Above. We needn't stretch the metaphor: These success factors hold for buyer–seller relationships too.

Exhibit 16–9
Communication
Channels and
Objectives

Telephone	Confirm appointment.
	Answer a question about delivery.
Fax	Summarize yesterday's meeting.
	FYI: an article in a trade magazine.
E-mail	Request the name of a former consultant.
	Give congratulations on a story in the press.
	Request easy-to-find data in a planning document.
Business letter	Formally introduce a new account representative.
	Summarize reasons for next quarter's price increase.
	Thank you for the order.
Face to face	Negotiate production commitments.
	Resolve dispute about marketing effort.

Organizational Character

It is folly to plan to remake a business partner into the organization yours wants to deal with. Certainly it is fitting to consider the prospects for mutual learning and skill development. And over the long run, trading is a means to affect change. We expect trading partners to discover new means of doing business and become more efficient as a result. But don't pretend that you can make a strong working relationship with a late-paying customer with corruption in its purchasing department. Chances are very slim that the customer can be straightened out by your culture of integrity at the supply firm. The same goes for buyers: Don't believe your zeal in a relationship is enough to reform a low-price supplier with delivery and quality problems.

Communication

Communication has been called the "glue that holds together" a relationship.[14] Between buyer and seller in a durable association, communication includes meetings between top executives (e.g., director of purchasing and VP of marketing) to forge the goals and principles of the relationship, as well as the interactions over transactions and operations between sales and purchasing reps. Furthermore, when buyer and seller partner, interfirm contact occurs in many positions: between engineers, among financial and production planners, between operators and delivery and service personnel, and so on.

Managerial attention is given to a number of aspects of these communications. Recalling concepts from Chapters 9 through 12, communication objectives and message requirements will determine the channels used and formality. Exhibit 16–9 summarizes the options and gives illustrative examples of objectives.

Formal Structures Efficiency considerations must be weighed, not only in each discrete communication episode, but in the establishment of a system for coordinating the relationship. Electronic data interchange (EDI) mechanizes ordering and information sharing on inventories and deliveries. Biweekly vendor review meetings formalize a process for identifying snags in current operations, detailing plans that might indirectly affect the partner, introducing new systems and products, and spotting new opportunities in markets and technologies. These are just a few of the possibilities for structuring communication opportunities.

Productive and lasting relationships often hinge on buyer and seller personnel assigned the responsibility of managing the relationship.
© Chuck Keeler/Tony Stone Images.

Specialists   Successful companies apply creative means to get customers to talk. Consultant Carla Furlong tells of an external contractor hired by the U.S. Department of Defense to work with an in-house technical expert to develop a series of training modules on the safe operation of agency motor vehicles. After a long period of no progress, a new team of customer contact specialists was assigned and the first module was delivered in just three months. In the next two years another 17 rolled off the presses.

   Why the great turnaround? One visit by the new team uncovered the initial snag. It turned out, the contractor was keen on in-depth training, but the customer wanted less. "Operating a nuclear-powered airship might need that kind of detail," laughs program manager Bernard Lukco. "But we were looking at a pallet jack. You weren't going to fly it, just push it across the floor." Looking back, the customer let things drag with the contractor because dealing with an array of experts intimidated client people and tied their tongues. They simply couldn't articulate concerns properly. The relationship support team solved a key linkage breakdown.[15]

Forums   Sometimes it can be quite productive to bring customers together to interact. Together they just might disclose how you might be able to serve them better. For example, Service Master invited CEOs from the health care industry to attend a seminar featuring famed management consultant Peter Drucker. Service Master President Chuck Stair explained; "This was another way to listen to [our] customers as they interacted with a respected source of leadership [Drucker]."[16]

Customer Satisfaction Surveys

Many companies have instituted customer satisfaction measures, a distinct communication tool with remarkable potential to impact retention. Satisfaction surveys assess performance on many elements from many levels in the customer organization and even other downstream customers. To presume that no news from customers is good news puts the firm in a precarious position. Proactive satisfaction measures are necessary because many customers don't take the time to register complaints with a supplier and allow problems to be addressed; *they simply switch suppliers.*

Exhibit 16–10
Satisfaction
Survey Design

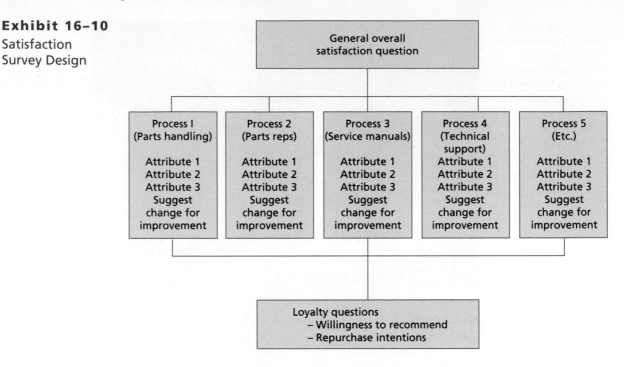

SOURCE: Jon Anton, *Customer Relationship Management: Making Hard Decisions with Soft Numbers,* © 1996. Reprinted by permission of Prentice-Hall, Inc., Upper Saddle River, NJ.

Types of Information

Satisfaction studies can be done by telephone or mail, but the typical high level of detail favors mail. Summarized in Exhibit 16–10, there are four major types of information to capture in a satisfaction study.[17]

1. Ascertain satisfaction with the overall relationship. These relationship-defining questions include
   a. Overall satisfaction: "Overall, we are very satisfied with our relationship with the Sigma Company." (Customer personnel indicate their degree of agreement or disagreement with the statement.)
   b. Intention to repurchase: "My company is very likely to make additional purchases from Sigma."
   c. Willingness to recommend: "I would certainly recommend the Sigma Company to a friend at another firm."
   d. Likelihood of a sustained relationship: "We expect to be doing business with Beta for the next three years or more."

   Willingness to recommend has been a good predictor of the durability of relationships. The other overall satisfaction measures work well as criterion variables in models that statistically estimate the factors that best explain variation in customer satisfaction.

2. Measure satisfaction with specific aspects of the relationship using a battery of questions. For example, a parts supplier might be evaluated on several key facets or processes of the relationship (its sales representative, its product manuals, its order process, product performances, technical support, etc.). A company that performs

several very different functions for its customers—say, parts supply, applications engineering, and product reconditioning—will need to evaluate facets in each arena. Parts supply, for example, might be evaluated on facets unlike the facets of product reconditioning. Each facet is reflected on several attributes. Thus, satisfaction with the sales rep is gauged in terms of customer reports of rep knowledge, courtesy, follow-through, availability, and so on.

3. Use open-ended questions to invite customers to express issues not covered in the structured portion of the survey. Many times, we can find out the number one source of frustration in a relationship by asking the customer to identify "the one thing our company could do to improve XXX."

4. Finally, the survey will need to ask for important classification data: customer firm characteristics, product types, complaint experience, and so on.

What Gets Measured?

Sometimes it is difficult for a supplier to know just how far to cast the net in a satisfaction survey. Does it matter if the inside salesperson has a nasal tone? Should we fret if customers don't really like the multilingual service manuals? Do customers really want three-day turnaround on payment confirmations?

In this regard we think Anton's acronym, **TERRA,** provides a useful template for thinking about the domain of customer expectations.[18]

Tangibles	Physical plant: appearance of sales reps, service technicians, and other personnel; equipment.	Shipping cartons are sturdy enough to withstand the stresses of transit and warehousing.
Empathy	Identification with the customer's needs; caring and individualized attention.	We receive patient instruction on self-service and repair by telephone, when we seek to get equipment up and running again without a service call.
Reliability	Fulfillment of promises, consistency.	Deliveries are always within the scheduled three-hour window.
Responsiveness	Customer assistance and redress are provided promptly.	Repair parts are shipped within 24 hours of a customer call.
Assurance	Seller's personnel and agents are knowledgeable; they inspire trust and confidence.	We have full confidence in your rep's advice on installation.

Analysis and Meaning

What would you do with performance ratings for eight relationship processes on a total of 61 product and service attributes from informants at 450 customer organizations? Indeed, take shelter when you see an avalanche coming. If you can overcome the anxiety and trepidation, there's a good chance you'll see beyond the avalanche to the gold mine of customer retention avenues.

A good starting place with the data is a look at the overall satisfaction scores. Note the percentage of customers rating your company in the top one or two categories on the scale. Compare these "top-box" scores to previous measures, perhaps graphing the history of quarterly top-box scores over the past several years, as in Exhibit 16–11.

Exhibit 16–11

History of Top-Box Satisfaction Scores

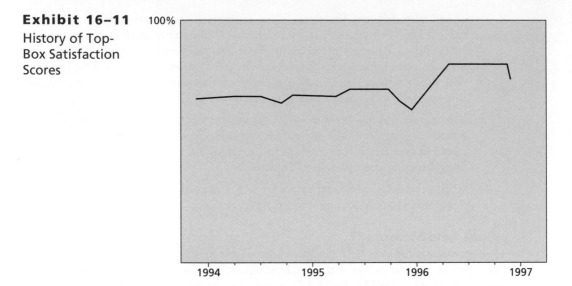

Whether the overall score is stable or trending up or down, to manage customer relationships it is vital to understand how different facets of the relationship affect the level of satisfaction. Remember that each facet (e.g., sales reps, warranty claims, product literature, technical support, logistical services) is measured on several attributes. By calculating an average performance score for the attributes of each facet, we obtain a relationship facet performance score (RFP score).

The RFP scores can then be used as independent variables in a regression analysis of overall satisfaction. That is, we suspect that

> Overall satisfaction = f(customer reports of sales reps, warranty claims, product literature, and other facets)

Statistical output from a regression analysis might read like this:

$$\text{Overall satisfaction} = 3.2 + .82 \, (\text{RFP}_{\text{warranty}}) + .53 \, (\text{RFP}_{\text{rep}}) + .12 \, (\text{RFP}_{\text{technical support}}) + .06 \, (\text{RFP}_{\text{product literature}}) + e$$

If we have taken care to standardize the RFP scores, the regression coefficients on each score indicate the relative importance of each facet in "explaining" variation in overall satisfaction. In this situation, based on the highest regression coefficient, how the supplier handles warranty claims is the key determinant of overall satisfaction, followed by sales rep performance. Supplier performance on technical support and product literature play relatively minor roles in overall satisfaction. Exhibit 16–12 shows the strong and weak statistical associations graphically.

A Closer Look

Now that we know that handling warranty claims and sales rep behaviors dramatically impact overall satisfaction, we can more closely examine the effect of specific attributes of these two facets. Again, regression analysis helps us in this regard.

This time we suspect that

> Overall satisfaction = f(attributes of the facet warranty claims service) and
> Overall satisfaction = f(attributes of the facet sales rep behaviors)

Exhibit 16–12

Strong and Weak Statistical Models of Customer Satisfaction

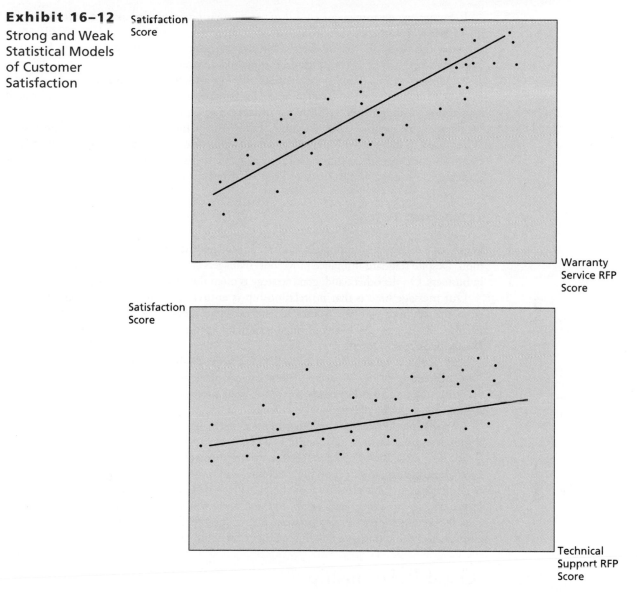

Illustrative statistical output shows that some attributes of warranty claims handling have large effects on satisfaction while other attributes have minimal impact:

$$\text{Overall satisfaction} = 2.9 + .73 \text{ (helpful operators)} + .46 \text{ (fairness)} + .28 \text{ (minimal paperwork)} + .09 \text{ (prompt payment)}$$

These statistical estimates help us to work on the most important attributes to provide good warranty service. The subject of much company attention of late, streamlining paperwork builds customer satisfaction in the preceding example. But take a look at the regression weights. Having operators who can solve customer problems has nearly three times the impact as paperwork reduction. Another key attribute is fairness. Perhaps our customers need some clarification on warranty service standards. If we can properly manage their expectations so that we can match their standards of fairness, we stand to improve customer satisfaction.

In summary, customer satisfaction measurement has exploded as a commercial activity in parallel with the dissemination of relationship marketing and the harder data showing the costs of winning versus keeping customers. Satisfaction surveys have become standard means of tracking and tuning business relationships.

No doubt, there are many companies offering a plethora of statistical and graphical models. Most work on this basic premise that one or more key criterion variables (overall satisfaction, willingness to recommend, intention to continue buying) can be statistically "explained" by specific seller activities arranged in a hierarchy of facets and processes. When used in concert with person-to-person, group-to-group, and other less structured means of customer interaction, the satisfaction survey is part of a valuable system of relationship communication. It helps to keep relationships running.

Forces from Beyond

This final subsection on running relationships matches the final element in the wedding sermon. Despite standard insurance provisions, managers seldom are allowed "act of God" alibis in business. On the other hand, good strategy is often the preferred label for good fortune.

Our message here is that no relationship is entirely governable by the parties. Recall from the opening vignette, Soccer V gave excellent service and had a number of social ties to CSC. Yet as CSC went through a difficult merger-and-growth phase, the relationship with Soccer V suffered.

Any business relationship may well face similar trials. Key personnel get reassigned. New ownership brings an array of new expectations and supply connections. And key accounts relocate to other lands. Let's not even pretend that every facet of relationship management can be planned and controlled.

Consolation derives from periodic attention to the upside—some of the fortuitous breakthroughs in one's business relationships. We have seen partnerships born out of calamities—a cash flow crisis staved off by a supplier willing to share risk, a plant safety concern solved by engineering expertise met on the touchline, and more. One of the authors invited a panel of professionals to his class. Two of the panelists—who were total strangers beforehand—forged a strong working relationship. In the months following their classroom presentations they orchestrated a partnership between their respective firms to serve a large client with a complicated marketing program that neither firm could have executed by itself.

Strengthening Good Relationships

It could well be argued that effectively managing a good relationship implicitly consists of strengthening it. *Nolo contendere.*

This section gives explicit and separate attention to the task of strengthening good relationships. We can regard the previous section as presenting the fundamental building blocks for relationships—they are akin to the security, nutrition, and physical and mental exercise we need to be healthy. But one does not live to be healthy. One maintains a healthy lifestyle as a means to higher things: intellectual accomplishment; service to family, business, and community; artistic expression and aesthetic enrichment of the culture.

Along these lines, we want to borrow the school motto, *Semper altius* (always higher), from Gateway Academy in St. Louis. It is a powerful theme for the challenge of strengthening business relationships. There is no pinnacle in a business relationship. Complacency can spoil the best relationships—it must be fought at every level. Effective management is ever striving.

16–2

FROM THE FIELD

Vacancies atop Frequent Guest Programs?

Hyatt hotels president Darryl Hartley-Leonard told *Advertising Age* in a January 1993 interview that he would "love to" terminate its frequent-guest program, if only the other major hotel chains would do likewise. As of 1997, no major hotel chains have abandoned their programs and Hyatt Gold Passport continues. Maybe these frequency programs are vital marketing efforts in the business travel market, but even a quick look at most of their programs is a sorry revelation.

Although many point to Holiday Inn as the pioneer in the frequent-guest arena, Marriott's Honored Guest program captured the heart of the market—and a larger portion of its wallet—in the mid-1980s. Marriott awarded points for every dollar spent at its hotels, not just overnight stays. Points could be redeemed for free stays and discounts. Membership was free and broad enrollment was sought as a preemption to competitor programs. The response was dramatic: Marriott stole share from the other hotels, while customers spent more in its restaurants and lounges—thus taking pressure off room rates.

Sheraton and Hyatt followed with similar programs, rewarding total spending. Although Sheraton was able to charge a membership fee and soon innovated with awards that included frequent-flyer miles, no one seemed able to cut into Marriott's lead.

The Westin Hotels have put some splash into the design of their mailers to Westin Premier members, but most of the others are stodgy. One observer dubbed Westin's value propositions "simplistic" and its approaches— which could and should be highly individualized and interactive—"superficial." A case in point is Rick Barlow's 1995 travel pattern.[19]

DO THEY EVEN KNOW I'M HERE?
by Rick Barlow, publisher, *Colloquy*

Remarkably, all the major hotel brands below failed to acknowledge in any way the radical change in my lodging patterns in 1995. Since 1986, 85% of my hotel stays have been at ITT Sheraton hotels. Beginning in early 1995, I intentionally spread my activity around. With 49 hotel nights during the year, I qualified as a legitimate high-value hotel guest, even without considering my ability to set travel policy for my employees, thereby affecting thousands of hotel nights annually. At no time since I changed my lodging pattern have I received from any of the brands an individualized message attempting to influence my behavior. While, remarkably, ITT Sheraton has not inquired regarding my diminished activity, neither has any other brand thanked me for my increased activity, welcomed me back or invited me to advise them on how to consolidate or improve upon their gains. Had any of them made even the slightest effort to acknowledge my potential, a significant share-of-customer gain was there for the taking. Surely my example is not unique. What a waste!

1995 Hotel Nights

Marriott	19	39%	(42%*)
Sheraton	9	18	
Hilton	7	14	
Harrah's	8	16	(25%**)
Fairmont	2	4	
Hyatt	2	4	
Four Seasons	1	2	
Westin	1	2	
Total	49		

*Includes Courtyard and Ritz Carlton stays.
**Includes Homewood stays.

Supragoals

Relationships last to the extent that they satisfy the goals of the partners. When joint stakes are high, we expect close collaboration and durability. To strengthen relationships, one or both of the partners may need to work hard to keep these shared goals in focus.

Research in countless different settings has shown that members of a group tend to put aside differences and work intensively and cooperatively in the face of a threat from outside the group. Although the impact of a potential calamity is stronger than the impact of potential gain, a good relationship manager can rightly cast the prospect of a missed opportunity as a calamity or threat.

When companies attend to the entire value-added chain, it becomes a bit easier to perceive opportunities and threats to relationships with their immediate or primary exchange partners. For example, Chrysler engages its suppliers in a cost-cutting program called SCORE (Supplier COst and Reduction Effort). Geiger Technic (Kalamazoo, Michigan) suggested changes to the engine cooling system in the 1998 Intrepid and Concord. By combining coolant pressure bottle, overflow bottle, and bottle bracket into a single injection-molded part, Geiger reduced cost, weight, and space—an eventual savings of nearly $1 million.[20] Similarly, look for safety engineers and air bag suppliers to work with auto manufacturers to rethink current air bag designs that seem to put small passengers at risk in low-impact collisions. Attending to upstream partnerships, Microsoft rallied its suppliers and reemphasized its commitment to PC workstations when the prospects of simpler, network-linked machines started to glimmer.

Needs Anticipation

While superordinate goals typically derive from forces outside the relationship, ongoing vigilance and creativity must be applied to the internal workings of the relationship itself. From the Field 16–2 reveals a case of underachievement, but there are brighter possibilities. For example, a supplier who notes high turnover among customer personnel can count on some role in retraining each newcomer on its equipment. Perhaps the supplier's ad agency can redesign manuals and operating instructions to include better graphics and make them easier to follow.

Another alternative for the supplier is to detail tactfully to the customer the costs of turnover in terms such as reduced productivity, training costs, and machine repair attributed to inexperienced operators. With a good understanding of the impact, some strategic joint action can be undertaken to develop a better recruiting and hiring policy, design a career path or a job rotation plan, or establish an apprentice program for high schoolers.

Does the supplier usually know a better way to run its customer's business? We doubt it. But the supplier who knows the customer well and examines the root causes of operational inefficiencies can be an important resource of ideas, skills, and linkages to other resources.

Let's look at one more example. A customer that makes frequent order changes and requests for emergency shipments seems to have inventory management problems. In this situation it is quite common for the customer to pressure the supplier to carry higher inventories or relocate a distribution center nearer the customer. If the relationship is strong enough, however, the supplier might propose a look at the entire process. A new demand forecasting model and a "sensor" in the production process—providing a lead indicator of the need for extraordinary shipments—have solved several perceived "delivery and inventory problems."

Lagniappe

Pronounced lan-yapp and rooted in Louisiana's Creole dialect, this word **lagniappe** means anything given beyond strict obligation, a surprise or surplus benefit from an exchange. We think you have seen the power of lagniappe in personal or family relations. Recall your sweetheart's reaction to the card or flowers you sent on "no special occasion." Maybe predawn on the day of the big game, your dad knocked off the mud and polished your soccer shoes. The grins and gratitude from these simple actions can take a relationship to a higher plane.

Business marketing relationships work similarly. Hugh Hart Pollard, who heads a consulting firm in Little Rock, Arkansas, sends a handwritten, personal note to his clients at their homes, thanking them for their business. Moreover, with each note he sends a book matching the personal interests of the client: sports, history, travel, gardening. Pollard says his letters and books are intended to say, "You are very important to me, not only professionally, but personally." In the short run, customers typically call Pollard to thank him. But in the longer run, Pollard believes the "higher plane" his relationships attain makes it more likely his clients will approach him with problems. The relationship becomes more robust to inevitable and unnoticed slip-ups. Pollard gets an extra chance to make things right.[21]

In another instance, a travel agent ordered too many theater tickets for a summertime tour group. By the terms of sale, the theater company did not have to reimburse the agent. But with empathy for what the agent was trying to set up and with an eye toward future business, the theater waived all charges but a $25 cancellation fee.

In a corporation with many employees, this orientation toward the customer must pervade. Furthermore, it must be matched with empowerment. A Marriott bellman called a cab for a departing guest and casually asked about the man's stay. When he grunted that his breakfast was a little late and cold, the bellman confidently stated, "I don't think you should pay for that." He took the man to the front desk and quickly voided the breakfast charges.[22]

Had the bellman gotten any static from the desk manager or the cashier, or if he had needed a manager to sign off, none of the hotel's empowerment seminars would have been worth the scratch pads provided. We are reminded of a quip from Lou Holtz, former coach at Notre Dame: "When all is said and done, a lot more is said than done." The polemics of service in excess of expectations are puny; but *practice* produces payoffs.

Summary

Despite a tradition and vocabulary of conquest, marketing has embraced the renewed priority of customer retention. Newly assembled data at many firms has shocked managers by detailing the astronomical cost of acquiring one customer. At the same time, fresh looks at the lifetime value of customer's purchases reveal the huge opportunity loss when a customer "defects."

Our analysis of this marketing challenge profiled two basic types of business relationships: (1) lost-for-good and (2) always-a-share. Lost-for-good could be dubbed stuck-for-a-while because they are cemented by significant switching costs. The buyer cannot easily switch to another supplier because personnel might have to be retrained, product designs would need reworking, downstream customers would be let down, or some aspect of setup would be costly.

Always-a-share customers can taper and restart their purchases. They may be responsive to promotions or price incentives, but lost-for-good customers are cemented by quality service and reliability. Simple NPV models of each type of customer dramatize the retention imperatives of lost-for-good accounts. Furthermore, they point to an emphasis on best customers. If a supplier's retention efforts can realize a 10 percent gain in retention probability, the efforts have a much higher payoff on accounts with a .8 retention likelihood than on accounts with a .5 retention rate.

Beyond the NPV models, lasting customer relationships can provide additional business opportunities through new products, increased purchases, premium prices, and selling efficiency. We can also expect positive reputational spillover from relationships that last.

The overall challenge of customer relationship management was broken down into three processes: building, running, and strengthening. The process of building relationships consists of several interacting devices for bonding. First is the bond attained by superior performance. Customers might ask their best supplier for a price break, but they will seldom ask a cut-rate supplier for blue ribbon service. The latter just can't do it. Plain and simple, superior performance is a powerful means of securing repeat business.

Social ties also play a key role in business relationships. To cooperate in commercial exchange, parties must comfortably disclose needs and dissatisfaction. A common language, some shared expectations, and reciprocated confidence in other's abilities and motives are critical to a productive exchange relationship. Thus, social affairs, gifts, and personal interaction can be an important relational bond.

We must also consider technical and formal ties between trading parties. If XYZ's video and graphics editing system is built around an Apple computer, Apple and XYZ are cemented by the technical design of the system. Similarly, where I choose to locate my factory to process bauxite into aluminum fairly well settles my limited slate of potential suppliers of electricity.

Finally, contracts can be forged on mutual pledges that bind the trading parties for long-run exchange. The contracting parties know they cannot specify every contingency held in the future. So they establish mechanisms for joint planning and flexibility. They aim to allow dispute resolution and adjustment to occur within the relationship.

The process of running relationships pivots on the presumption of good partner selection, effective communication, and outside help. Trading partners should not expect their counterpart to change. Effective communication includes formal structures for interaction, such as EDI and regularly scheduled meetings; specialists, such as relationship support teams; and professional forums, such as user groups and conferences.

Customer satisfaction surveys have emerged as a widely used tool of customer retention. Typically, criterion measures such as satisfaction and intention to repurchase are modeled statistically as a function of a hierarchy of service attributes, facets, and roles.

Relationships should never be taken for granted. To avoid complacency we proposed business marketers adopt the motto "always higher." Attention to external opportunities and threats as well as to the root cause of internal inefficiencies and underachievements can uncover new avenues for bonding. Furthermore, companywide commitment to and empowerment for delivering lagniappe is a true manifestation of a customer retention priority.

Key Terms

always-a-share relationship	lost-for-good relationship	switching costs
contract	modularity	TERRA
lagniappe	specific investments	

Discussion Questions

1. Find out the retention rate in your college. Be sure you understand how it is defined or calculated in the local administrative offices. Now, develop a model that documents this attrition's financial consequences for the school.

2. For many years the Chicago Marriott Hotel has been a site of the American Marketing Association's Summer Educators' Conference. The AMA conference locale follows a three-year cycle: East Coast, West Coast, Chicago (headquarters of the AMA). Is this an always-a-share or lost-for-good relationship? What sort of ties do you think bond the AMA and the Marriott? How can the Marriott maintain those ties?

3. The Market Rex consulting firm hosted a brunch for several of its key clients at the Tavern on the Green in Manhattan when the major trade show was held at the New York Hilton. Outline three reasons why such an apparent extravagance might be good business practice. Describe three special cautions or hazards in this type of hospitality.

4. Examine two or three suppliers to your college or university, perhaps a food service, a forms supplier, engineering, or maintenance. What are the bonds in the relationship? How secure is the university or college account?

5. List the switching costs for the following situations:
   a. Executive offices of a large bank switch caterers.
   b. An auto manufacturer switches to a new sound system supplier.
   c. A land grant university shelves its own power plant for a commercial utility.
   d. A large steel door manufacturer switches from a direct sales force to distributors.

6. Outline a customer satisfaction survey for your college. First, who are the customers? What arenas and facets will be measured? What are three to five attributes of two of these facets?

7. Outline a customer satisfaction survey for a copier company.

8. Computer chip manufacturers strive to get computer companies to design machines around their chips. But to get adopted into a design, the chip must typically be licensed to other chip makers. Computer makers are afraid of "hold-up" by the chip supplier. How does licensing solve this problem? What can the chip maker do to cement a relationship in the absence of a strict technical tie.

9. Professor Gary Frazier at the University of Southern California is one of the world's experts on relationships between firms. Time and again he has shown that a company's track record of performing key functions in a superior fashion is a source of power or bargaining leverage. For example, key roles for cutting tool manufacturers selling through industrial distributors in India are (1) product quality, (2) allocation and delivery of goods, (3) reimbursement for damaged products, (4) distributor assistances (training programs, operation manuals), and (5) a cooperative representative. A manufacturer doing these things well is less

likely to coerce its distributors or disagree over key issues than a similar manufacturer doing its job poorly. Indeed, superior role performance correlates very highly with distributor satisfaction with the supplier relationship.

What are the key roles for a bank, marketing research firm, rental car company, or commercial laundry? Ask two or three professionals who purchase such products to rate the suppliers on these roles and describe how they allocate their purchases to the possible suppliers in one of these areas.

10. Lagniappe means exceeding expectations. But what are the origins of customer expectations? Are expectations an important facet of relationship management?

Internet Exercise

Especially in the business travel market, many companies have implemented frequency marketing programs. Frequent-flier programs are one example, but the firm that wears the name Frequency Marketing, Inc., defines frequency marketing as "the strategy whose objective is to identify, maintain, and increase the yield from best customers through long-term, interactive, value-added relationships."

The company magazine *Colloquy* is available on line. Check out the site at **http://www.colloquy.org** and, if you like, others that come up in a frequency marketing search, to examine the role of rewards for best customers. In essence, is it better to give "trophies" or "funny money"?

WWW
I N T E R N E T

Cases

Case 16.1   Has the Fat Lady Sung?

You know that when your *Consumer Reports* subscription is about to expire, the publisher sends appeal after appeal—even beyond expiration—to get your renewal. Such behaviors beg the question, When is a lost customer lost?

Ben Barclay, owner of Barclay Business Products, follows a five-step process that many companies in business markets have employed:

1. *Spot the flagging account.* Key accounts are fairly easy to track through personnel changes and restructuring. But smaller customers may fall through the cracks if not routinely tracked in the customer database.

2. *Find out why the account left.* This may take some digging. Talk to associates with recent or frequent contact with the customer. A face-to-face meeting is a chance to uncover difficulties and missteps. Sometimes a solution can be found.

3. *Request another chance.* An apology and request for another try gets a better response than not asking.

4. *Offer an inducement.* Sometimes the seller needs to buy back the account with a special deal—a customized service or discount.

5. *Mechanize follow-up.* When the face-to-face contact fails, continue goodwill communications and assign the account to a telemarketer to call the account periodically.[23]

At a business where you've worked or by conducting a convenience interview with a friend or family member, describe the particular steps taken with "lost" accounts.

Case 16.2   Paper, Scissors, Rock

Rocky's World of Soccer is Centerberg's top retailer of soccer gear and fashions. Rocky Cantino has used a variety of data capture techniques—a newsletter, clinics, and events—to build a file of 15,000 soccer players, parents, and coaches in Centerberg. He bought a Power Mac and PageMaker and in the past three months has run two very successful mail promotions. He spent about $9,000 on each of these mailings and "found" the money for this venture by reducing his newspaper ad budget.

Ron Wilson is advertising rep for the *Centerberg Courier.* He learned of Rocky's newfound interest in direct mail in a recent call to pick up an ad if it was ready. Indeed, noting that Rocky's spending with the paper was running about $16,000 behind last year's pace, Ron took Rocky to breakfast last Friday. Before they went out, Rocky took Ron to the back to show him his Mac and laser printer. Copies of the last letter and minicatalog were on the desk. Ron was surprised and impressed by the quality of work and marketing savvy of Centerberg's former soccer all-star.

At breakfast Wilson praised Rocky's efforts to stay in closer touch with his customers by mail, but cautioned against borrowing against newspaper advertising to get it done.

Is Wilson a fast-talking, self-serving salesman trying to bleed a dying relationship? Or is he onto a new role for the newspaper to play in Rocky's communication mix? What should Ron Wilson do?

Additional Readings

Anton, Jon, *Customer Relationship Management: Making Hard Decisions with Soft Numbers.* Upper Saddle River, NJ: Prentice-Hall, 1996. p. 12.

Bradach, Jeffrey, and Robert Eccles, "Price, Authority and Trust: From Ideal Types to Plural Forms," *Annual Review of Sociology* 15 (1989), pp. 97–118.

Colloquy, the on-line magazine of Frequency Marketing, Inc. *http://www.colloquy.org.*

Crosby, Lawrence A., Kenneth R. Evans, and Deborah Cowles, "Relationship Quality in Services Selling: An Interpersonal Influence Perspective," *Journal of Marketing* 54 (July 1990), pp. 68–81.

Desatnick, Robert, and Denis Detzel, *Managing to Keep the Customer.* San Francisco, CA: Jossey–Bass Publishers, 1993.

Fernandez, Ricardo R., *Total Quality in Purchasing and Supplier Management.* Delray Beach, FL: St. Lucie Press, 1995.

Furlong, Carla, *Marketing for Keeps.* New York: John Wiley & Sons, Inc., 1993.

Gundlach, Greg, and Patrick Murphy, "Ethical and Legal Foundations of Relational Marketing Exchanges," *Journal of Marketing* 57 (October 1993), pp. 35–46.

Halvorson, Paul, and William Rudelius, "Is There a Free Lunch," *Journal of Marketing* 41 (January 1977), pp. 44–49.

Horovitz, Jacques, and Michele Jurgens Panak, *Total Customer Satisfaction: Putting the World's Best Programs to Work.* Burr Ridge, IL: Irwin Professional Publishing, 1994.

Jackson, Barbara B., *Winning and Keeping Industrial Customers.* Lexington, MA: Lexington Books, 1985.

Levitt, Theodore, *The Marketing Imagination.* New York: The Free Press, 1983.

Mohr, Jakki, and John R. Nevin, "Communication Strategies in Marketing Channels: A Theoretical Perspective," *Journal of Marketing* 54 (October 1990), pp. 36–51.

Morgan, Robert, and Shelby Hunt, "The Commitment–Trust Theory of Relationship Marketing," *Journal of Marketing* 58 (July 1994), pp. 20–38.

Palay, Thomas, "Comparative Institutional Economics: The Governance of Rail Freight Contracting," *Journal of Legal Studies* 13 (June 1984), pp. 265–87.

Pepper, Don, and Martha Rogers, *Enterprise One to One: Tools for Competing in the Interactive Age.* New York: Currency Doubleday, 1997.

Schonberger, Richard J., and Edward M. Knod, Jr., *Synchroservice! The Innovative Way to Build a Dynasty of Customers.* Burr Ridge, IL: Irwin Professional Publishing, 1994.

Smith, J. Brock, and Donald W. Barclay, "The Effects of Organizational Differences and Trust on the Effectiveness of Selling Partner Relationships," *Journal of Marketing* 61 (January 1997), pp. 3–21.

Thomas, Richard, and David Ford, "Technology and Networks," in *Business Marketing: An Interaction and Network Perspective,* Kristian Moller and David Wilson, eds. Boston: Kluwer Academic Publishers, 1995, pp. 263–90.

Vavra, Terry G. *Aftermarketing: How to Keep Customers for Life through Relationship Marketing.* Chicago: Irwin Professional Publishing, 1995.

Zeithaml, Valerie, A. Parusuraman, and Leonard Berry, *Delivering Quality Service.* New York: The Free Press, 1995.

Chapter 17

The Future of Business Marketing

Globalization, Technology, and Career Trends

APPLIED MATERIALS

Applied Materials is a manufacturer of semiconductor manufacturing equipment whose purpose is "To enable the Information Age." Its mission statement outlines eight strategy areas: quality, customers, people, products, management, suppliers, profit, and citizenship. Through these strategies, one can quickly see that this company seeks to understand and serve customers', employees', and suppliers' needs worldwide. As its citizenship statement says, its commitment is global: "Through our example and actions, continue to break down the social, cultural, racial, and national boundaries which can unproductively separate our world. To make a positive contribution to each society in which we operate."●

An old adage states that the cobbler's children go without shoes, but that isn't the case with Applied Materials. As a company whose purpose is to enable the Information Age, it has implemented as much of the Information Age as is possible. As the firm sees it, the only way to succeed globally is to empower employees everywhere with sophisticated communication and decision-making tools.●

While Applied Materials' customers (companies like Intel and Motorola) are probably more familiar, Applied Materials has grown to over $4 billion in annual sales. Future growth looks bright, as the company has become significantly more efficient, as evidenced by profits increasing at a faster rate than sales. As we enter the Information Age, expect Applied Materials to lead the way.●

Check out its home page: **www.appliedmaterials.com**●

Learning Objectives

Business marketing is an ever changing and evolving set of practices that make for a challenging and exciting career. In this closing chapter, we examine a number of factors that will shape business marketing in the years to come.

After reading this chapter, you should be able to

- Recognize the state of globalization for any given company.
- Articulate the importance of globalization to business marketers.
- Outline some of the challenges to building relationships with people from other cultures.
- Identify changes in technology that will have a significant impact on marketing practice.
- Compare and contrast different career options in the future of business marketing.

The future of business marketing is intertwined with career opportunities. It wasn't too long ago that few companies had web pages, for example, but now many companies have marketing staff that do nothing but manage web sites and net marketing. Such communication has globalized operations at a rapid pace, changing much of the way that marketing happens.

Source: Applied Materials 1996 Annual Report; Mission Statement page, Applied Materials home page, **www.appliedmaterials.com**, June 5, 1997.

499

Exhibit 17–1

Key Issues in the Future of Business Marketing

Named by Marketing Leaders Panel	Named by Marketing Academics
1. Establishing new forms of work linkages between marketing, product management, and sales	1. Developing real product and service innovations faster
2. Improving global marketing management knowledge and skills	2. Searching for new markets by going global
3. Increasing the actionable value of customer databases	3. Finding partners that add to the mix of competencies and strengths—firms will buy other firms' competencies, not products
4. Increasing the marketing value of new technology such as the Internet, the web, and extranets	4. Integrating marketing into all functions of the organization
5. Reaching customers on a one-to-one basis through mass customization	5. Increasing dispersion of information and decision making
6. Linking marketing decisions to cash flow and results through activity-based cost (ABC) accounting	
7. Selecting business partners and managing strategic alliances	

SOURCE: Ralph Oliva, "Marketing's Agenda 2000," *Marketplace: The ISBM Review* (Spring 1997), pp. 1–2; Donald Lehmann and Katherine E. Jocz, *Reflections on the Futures of Marketing* (Cambridge, MA: Marketing Science Institute, 1997).

Marketing and the New Millennium

One of the challenges of studying and practicing marketing is dealing with change. To be sure, advances in technology have caused countless things to change; for example, many college students below age 22 may not recall life without VCRs or personal computers, yet companies like Blockbuster and Microsoft did not exist until those technologies were commercially feasible. The impact of those technologies on companies in all industries has also been tremendous; just consider the impact that VCRs and PCs have had on training, for example.

The practice of marketing is also changing. Throughout this book, we've attempted to emphasize cutting-edge marketing practice and theory so that you might cope with change; however, to assume that all businesses have implemented state-of-the-art marketing practices would be foolish. While we've also tried throughout the book to identify factors that cause change, this chapter is devoted to change and a look ahead.

Recently, the Institute for the Study of Business Markets (ISBM) hosted a panel of nine leading marketing thinkers, who identified seven challenges and changes for business marketing listed in Exhibit 17–1. The exhibit also lists a summary of key issues from *Reflections on the Futures of Marketing,* a book published by the Marketing Science Institute. Notice the consistency between the two groups.

As you can see, we've already discussed a number of these challenges and changes. For example, when reading Chapter 15, you might have asked why ABC accounting methods were in a marketing book; the answer is that it is a tool that marketing managers use, just like regression analysis when conducting marketing research. As the marketing leaders on the ISBM panel believe, ABC is one of the important tools for future business marketers.

Exhibit 17–2
Globalization of
Business
Marketers

Stage 1: No direct foreign marketing
Stage 2: Infrequent foreign marketing
Stage 3: Regular foreign marketing
Stage 4: International marketing
Stage 5: Global marketing
Stage 6: Global partnering

SOURCE: Adapted from Philip Cateora, *International Marketing,* 9th ed. (Burr Ridge IL: Richard D. Irwin, 1996), p. 18.

Another challenge is how to respond to growing needs for partnerships, both with suppliers and with customers. Both leadership groups indicate the importance that business relationships will have in the next century. Relationships have also been a major theme of this book, and we've illustrated their importance in areas such as developing products and growing sales.

Several of the challenges and changes, though, bear further discussion because prior chapters have not explicitly dealt with those topics. Specifically, we'll examine the issues of globalization and technology change in more detail—in particular, in the context of business relationships.

Globalization of Business Marketing

It is fun to read all of the mistakes that companies make when going into new markets, but the reality is that companies that operate globally grow faster and are more profitable than those that stay domestic.[1] Du Pont, for example, earns almost all of its profits outside the United States, even though foreign sales account for only 51 percent of total sales.[2]

Stages to Globalization

One author has developed a five-stage model of globalization, to which we will add a sixth stage. The stages, outlined in Exhibit 17–2, illustrate the degree to which a company has committed to serving global markets.[3] Companies do not necessarily go through each stage; they may skip stages or even back up and repeat a stage. But the model is useful in understanding how companies typically approach globalization.

No Direct Foreign Marketing
Companies rarely begin with global markets in mind, and they may stay domestic for some time. There is no active marketing in foreign markets, although products may find their way into other countries through distributors and foreign customers that come to the selling organization. Often, it is the unsolicited sale to a foreign company that causes the seller to explore other markets.

Infrequent Foreign Marketing
Infrequent foreign marketing may be caused by the need to reduce temporary surpluses of inventory or by the occasional sale to a foreign buyer which gets followed up with a brief marketing effort. For example, Northwest Metals, an American contract manufacturer, has sold to foreign customers at trade shows in the United States. For companies

in this stage, foreign marketing activity is halted when domestic demand increases and takes up the surplus or when the occasional account decides to purchase elsewhere. Because the effort is viewed as temporary, there is no change in organizational structure or adaptation of the product.

Regular Foreign Marketing

At this stage, the company has committed production capacity and marketing dollars to the foreign market. The commitment may take the form of foreign manufacturing capacity, and marketing may be done through foreign distributors or agents or through company personnel. Products may be adapted to fit the needs of the foreign market, but the company's attention is still on the domestic market. For example, Aquatics Unlimited received an unsolicited order from the Japanese government. The company turned attention to international markets because of the interest expressed by the Japanese. When the Korean government passed requirements to clean up its waterways, Aquatics was already there and able to grab a large share of the business.[4]

In this stage, companies may have their own sales and marketing operations but are more likely to have international partners (outsourcing their marketing). These partners might include distributors, manufacturers representatives, or licensees, who have paid a fee to license and market the product. It is unlikely that any company in this stage has much invested in foreign markets, investments such as joint ventures, or sales offices.

International Marketing

The company now begins to actively seek new markets throughout the world, and products are planned and produced with specific foreign markets in mind. The company is fully committed to an international or multinational strategy. For example, Brady and Associates is a landscape contractor that began its international marketing with a trip to Vietnam, the success of which led to a focus on the Pacific Rim. In two years, the company was able to land contracts with government agencies in China and Vietnam.[5]

Brady and other international companies will develop partnerships with companies to comarket products, partnerships often structured as joint ventures. Fuji–Xerox, for example, is a joint venture between Fuji (we know it here for its film) and Xerox; the company (Fuji–Xerox) develops and manufactures products that other Xerox companies (Xerox USA and Rank Xerox, the European company) market. Rockwell International, on the other hand, has sales and marketing offices around the world that develop sales and marketing strategies for each of the countries in which it operates.

Global Marketing

In contrast to the many-markets view of the previous stage, the world is seen as one market. A global company seeks unified strategies that reflect the commonalities of market needs across countries in order to maximize returns through global standardization. For example, Compaq is seeking a global advertising agency in order to standardize its advertising approach in all markets.[6] Standardization doesn't imply that cultural differences are ignored; rather, the standard approach is adapted to fit specific cultural needs.

Global Partnering

Searching for lead users and other significant global partners represents an advanced stage of global marketing. At this stage, companies truly treat the world as one market, but with varying opportunities based on individual companies or accounts, rather than individual countries. Grafo Regia, a Mexican packaging manufacturer, has developed partnerships with companies such as U.S.-based Kellogg's. More than half of the company's business comes from a select group of global partners.

Note, though, that global partnering is more than just having partners in other countries. Grafo Regia, for example, partners with Kellogg's around the world, not just in developing joint business in the United States or Mexico. Just as in domestic markets, there are different types of relationships in global markets. Some are transactional and others are partnerships. There are, however, different culturally based perspectives on relationships in other countries, including *keiretsus* in Japan and networks in Europe.

Relationships in Other Cultures

To businesspeople from other cultures, the United States is a Johnny-come-lately when building relationships in business. Cultures such as Japan are built on the quality and quantity of personal relationships in which business is only one element. Latin cultures, such as in Mexico, emphasize personal relationships. Even in staid Britain, a BBC commentator discussed how consumers practice socialistic capitalism, as they base their purchase decisions on which shopkeeper they like best rather than on economic criteria like price or quality of merchandise. The point is that personal relationships and partnerships are not unique to the United States; on the contrary, business based on relationships is a concept that has been practiced for centuries elsewhere with differing cultural twists.

Networks and *Keiretsus*

Americans tend to think of relationships as **dyadic**; there are only two parties: one buyer and one seller. In much of the rest of the world, the perspective is more toward a **network** of relationships, recognizing that companies share relationships with many other companies and that these relationships are governed by reciprocity of ties and shared values.[7] While the formalization of such networks is not as great in Europe as in Asian countries, the concept is similar. We will examine Asian networks in greater detail as these differ the most from the dyadic view of relationships.

Almost as a form of social security, relationships develop in Asian countries on the basis of quid pro quo. Gifts and favors are extended in order that gifts and favors will be received later (particularly when needed), but *later* may mean years or even generations later. The basis of exchange, though, is personal relationships built through what is called *amae,* or indulgent dependency, in Japan. (*Guan xi* is a similar concept in China.) *Amae* is the feeling of nurturing concern for, and dependence upon, another. Reciprocity is an important element, to be sure, but the personal element should not be overlooked.

Another important concept influencing relationships is harmony, or *wa* in Japan, and can be defined as the quality of human relationships involving cooperation, trust, sharing, and warmth.[8] Maintaining *wa* is a central point of Japanese culture.

In Japan, relationships between companies can develop into a **keiretsu**, or family of companies. Executives may sit on the boards of their customers or their suppliers; companies form strong alliances for product development, marketing, and finance; and there is much dealing among the companies within a *keiretsu.*[9] Toyota, for example, defines the Toyota Group *keiretsu* as 14 core companies (most of which were spun off from Toyota Motor Corp.) and another 170 that receive preferential treatment. In many of these 170, Toyota holds an equity position and exchanges managers or has seats on the board of directors.[10] The Sumitomo Group, a steel industry *keiretsu,* is very formalized and run by a council.

Note, though, that *keiretsu* are not universal in Japan. Nippon Steel, for example, competes with Sumitomo Metal Industries and has diversified alliances across a number of groups (*keiretsu*). Nippon, however, is not a formal member of any group's council.[11] What is universal is the presence of alliances, based on personal relationships and the practice of *amae*.

In other Asian cultures, similar cultural concepts drive business relationships; in China, for example, personal relationships are also necessary for sufficient trust to develop. Without that trust, as in Japan, buyers believe sales pitches to be exaggerated.

Can American companies find a place in the tight networks and *keiretsu* of Japan and other Asian countries? While no U.S. companies sit on the councils of any *keiretsu,* they are able to build relationships. For example, Fuji and Xerox co-own Fuji–Xerox, a copier and business products company that operates in Asia. Texas Instruments, finding that doing business in Korea is similar to doing it in Japan, has developed several partnerships with Korean companies.[12]

Relationships and Social Structure

Another important element in non-U.S. parts of the world is rank. The United States is not a classless society, but rank is much more important in the rest of the world. In Asia, for example, the customer is king as in the United States, but even more so. This means that the seller must do as much as possible to meet a buyer's wishes. Buyers expect and receive deferential treatment from sellers.

One translation of this difference in rank is that buyers often receive more service in Asia than in the United States. For example, Hyundai Motor Company purchased two multimillion-dollar pieces of equipment from an American company but turned to an Asian vendor for later pieces because the American company was late in delivery, took too long to get the machines up and running, and charged extra for engineering support in order to make the equipment run as promised.[13] Failing to recognize the importance of the buyer, the company forfeited all future business with Hyundai.

Such service provided by Japanese companies extends to their global customers. Thus, not only do we find unique challenges when doing business in Japan, companies competing against the Japanese for business in other countries have to match or exceed those levels of service in order to earn a share of the business.

Relationships and Time

Not only do Americans tend to see relationships as dyadic and both parties as having equal status, Americans tend to focus on transactions and look at relationships as series of transactions. As mentioned earlier, relationships in Asia are built and expected to extend over generations. This difference is due to a difference in perspectives of time.

In some cultures, time is viewed as **monochronic** or linear. Americans (and Swiss, Germans, and Scandinavians) divide time into small units and are obsessed with promptness. Using **polychronic** perspectives, other cultures view time in terms of the simultaneous occurrence of many things and with more involvement with people.[14] Latin America is more polychronic, which results in the *mañana* stereotype of lateness. But to someone from Mexico, arriving half an hour after an appointed time is not being either late or rude.

Further, time and relationships are often viewed in cyclical terms in Eastern cultures. Relationships do not necessarily begin and end, but ebb and flow. Westerners tend to view relationships as either "on" or "off," which reflects a short-term perspective. Such a view may be fine when the relationship is on, but no investment is made in a relationship that is currently off. Read on about the difficulty Compaq has had managing relationships in From the Field 17–1.

17–1

FROM THE FIELD
Compaq: The Quest for Global Growth

Compaq is the world's leading supplier of PCs but the fifth largest computer company overall. In a quest to achieve the number 3 position in the next three years, Compaq has attempted to globalize its marketing strategy. Visit the web site (**www.compaq.com**), for example, and you'll find the ability to jump to web sites for every country in which Compaq has an office. You'll also find consistent graphics across all sites, indicating a global approach to business (but be prepared to read the text in the language of the country whose site you are visiting).

On the other hand, Compaq is just now exploring the use of a global advertising agency. As Kathleen Harrington, Compaq's director of advertising says, "Clearly . . ., it does make sense to speak to Fortune 500 worldwide companies . . . in one voice."

And Compaq has alienated channel partners, those who resell Compaq computers to users. In April 1997, the company let it slip out that it might purchase either Micron Electronics or Gateway 2000, direct sellers of PCs and clear competitors to Compaq's reseller partners. When those sales failed, Compaq announced that it would create a 2,000-member direct sales force, but "This does not mean Compaq's taking the business direct," says Compaq's new VP of marketing communications, David Middleton. "It's an account coverage model not unlike our major competitors," such as Hewlett–Packard and IBM. Of course, Compaq's reseller partners are not so sure.

With 50 percent of sales coming from outside the United States (Asia alone represents over $1 billion in sales and European sales are nearly twice that), the stakes are high. It will take more than global advertising to keep all of Compaq's partners working together to achieve the goal of being number 3 in the overall computer market.

SOURCE: Bradley Johnson, "Compaq, Digital Mull Global Shop Consolidation," *Business Marketing* (May 1997), p. 3; Dana Blankenhorn, "Balancing Act," *Business Marketing* (June 1997), pp. 1, 43; Compaq 1996 Annual Report.

Challenges in Global Marketing

The differences in types of relationships, social structures, and perspectives of time reflect past and contemporary challenges in global marketing today. What makes globalization such a challenge for the future? The challenge is not that global marketing will be any tougher than it was in the past (with the exception of increased competition for global markets), but rather that for most companies in industrialized nations, the domestic market is not going to be the growth market.

Competition for Growth

As one respected marketing professor wrote, "Many firms will focus attention away from markets that are just big and towards markets that promise higher-than-average growth."[15] While he was talking about the United States as the "big" market with no growth, the statement could have been made about Europe and the growth markets to which he referred are those in industrializing countries. For example, GNP growth for the world is expected to average 3 percent per year into the next century but more than twice that for southeast Asia and 35 percent more than that for Africa.[16]

Yet, in spite of the increasing importance of world markets, we continue to make the same poor assumptions which lead to the same dumb mistakes. During the Depression, for example, Carl Crow published a book arguing that America could pull itself out of

Many developing countries are investing in infrastructure (highways, water and sewage, utilities, etc.) improvements, creating new global competitors out of potential suppliers. Courtesy 3M.

the Depression by selling one product to each person in China—which was dubbed "Chinese marketing." Crow assumed that if something sells here, it will sell in China, and also assumed that the Chinese had enough purchasing power to each buy an American product.[17] Both are poor assumptions. Yet in 1994, an American CEO was quoted as saying, "If we could sell one piece every year to every Chinese . . . ."[18]

Competition for People

Similarly, we recently held a conference for our students on global marketing issues. One marketing manager told us it was a waste of time as none of our students would be involved with global marketing early in their career, but then we reminded him that he worked for Cable & Wireless, a British telecommunications company. Surely, global issues meant something to the performance of his company. With the increasing importance of world markets, business marketers will face the challenge of finding globally minded and globally qualified management.

Competition between Countries

In addition to the competition between companies, governments of various countries work to tilt the playing field in favor of their own companies. Airbus, for example, is a European airplane manufacturer that competes against Boeing for commercial jetliner sales. Airbus, unlike Boeing, was started with capital provided by several European governments and continues to enjoy government support. Government **subsidies** like those provided Airbus lower the cost of operating, as costs are paid by the government.

The United States likes to position itself as a bastion of free trade when, in reality, the government subsidizes a number of industries. Wheat, for example, is heavily subsidized by the government although farm subsidies seem to be drying up. Technology is subsidized through the use of research grants for developing new technologies. Furthermore, **tariffs** (taxes on imported goods) and **import quotas** (import limits on the amount of product types) are regularly applied by the U.S. government in order to protect U.S. interests. Tariffs and quotas heavily restrict a company's ability to compete in any given market.

Free markets and trading areas such as those created by the North American Free Trade Agreement (NAFTA) or the European Common Market are the result of countries seeking open markets for their products. Tariffs and quotas are not imposed on goods exchanged between trading block countries so it should be just as easy to do business within the trading area as it would be within the company's home country. The hope is that increased trade between the countries will mean increased business overall.

Poorly officiated markets can also wreak havoc to a company's marketing plans. Software piracy in China, for example, is a problem that many Americans are aware of only because of the impact on video games and other popular forms of software. But piracy also happens to business marketers. Unlicensed copies of business software can ruin a company's market, but the government of the country in which the piracy occurs may not care since the affected company is not one of its own.

Technology and Marketing

Just as with the globalization of markets, change due to advances in technology is not new to business marketing. Yet, technology change is expected to create new ways of marketing that haven't existed. In this book, we've already discussed the impact of the Web, electronic systems such as EDI, and other technology-driven changes. Here, we'd like to step back from the microlevel examination of technology (such as how technology impacts ordering) and take a macrolevel perspective of technology. (Of course, it will be fun to look back in 20 years and see what turned out to be true.)

The technology that is likely to have the greatest impact on marketing is that which enables decision makers to make better decisions or enhances communications. Marketing is becoming defined more in terms of creating value than creating exchange or transactions,[19] and it is the creative use of data gained through stronger communication with customers that enables marketing to live up to that definition.

Decision Making and Communicating

Du Pont, for example, has developed a Rapid Market Assessment technology that enables the company to determine if a market (usually a country or region previously not served) warrants development.[20] The result of the analysis is a customer-focused understanding of the foreign market, no matter what the level of economic development. Such an understanding is key to not only assessing the opportunity but also creating value in order to capitalize on the opportunity. The technology is a conglomeration of both data-gathering tools and analysis models—in other words, software that includes the way data are gathered as well as analyzed.

In order to have information in order to make better decisions, communications have to be faster and better. Thus decision making and communicating go hand in hand. While we've talked about the need for improved communication between buyer and seller, internal communication is also important. For example, Scientific-Atlanta's new KnowledgeNet communication system organizes product, customer, and market information from a wide variety of sources in order to provide the worldwide sales force with the data they need to create value for their customers.

17–2

FROM THE FIELD
Mapping New Markets

Larry Brophy, president of GeoDemX Corp., states that creating a national (or global) model of your customers and "using it to identify prospects in Dallas is like trying to produce a Picasso painting with a paint roller— you lose all detail." What Brophy's company does is create software that enables businesses to use geodemographics , or demographic profiles of geographic areas, to profile customers and then generate lists of prospects who also look like those customers.

First applied to consumer marketing, geodemographics is now being used to reach the SOHO (small office, home office) market with direct marketing. By recognizing that people like to live near people who are like them, SOHO marketers (companies like Xerox and Dell) assume that other SOHO buyers are in the same neighborhoods.

Other business marketing applications include using geodemographics of businesses (rather than consumers) for commercial real estate projects and to determine trading areas of industrial distributorships. At the heart of these applications is a geographic information system, or GIS.

GIS integrates data from a number of sources and then overlays the data with maps. Combining the result with sophisticated display technology and database technology, business marketers are able to make better informed decisions. These decisions can then be acted on by a sales force using contact management software like GoldMine or ACT, with relevant data about the prospect (including instructions on how to get to the area) downloaded to the rep. Then when you get ready to call someone in Dallas, you'll know quite a bit about her before ever picking up the phone or knocking on her door.

SOURCE: The Larry Brophy quote is from Larry Brophy, "The Art of Prospecting for Customers," *Business Geographics* (May 1997), pp. 22–25. The rest of this article is original to this book.

At the same time, companies are using information technology to better understand their own businesses. Emerson Electric, for example, has developed models and systems of tracking expenses that make it much more efficient in purchasing. Furthermore, these systems interact with information systems of their partners, both suppliers and customers. This shared information drives inefficiencies out of the supply chain, increasing the value created.

What this means to today's business marketing student is that it is not enough to know the basics of operating a computer. Technology is the application of science to commercial needs, which includes being able to take models of how to store and manipulate information in order to make decisions. Geography is one area of science that is helping businesses manipulate information in order to make decisions. Mapping technology, as you can see in From the Field 17–2, is aiding many companies in developing better marketing and sales plans for micromarkets.

We mentioned earlier that today's traditional-age college student (one below age 22) may not remember a world without VCRs. It may not be too long before virtual reality is similarly taken for granted. What will happen to trade shows and sales calls if virtual reality can be used to demonstrate even the largest or most complex equipment? Can we just send a disk instead of a salesperson? As one consultant said, "Because of the use of on-line services and CD-ROMs, there's not as much need for armies of sales folks anymore."[21] Canon USA, for example, used virtual reality to sell and educate dealers when

17–1

BUSINESS 2 BUSINESS
Local Culture vs. Global Technology

Information and communication technology can mean instant global communication, increasing the globalization of business. At the same time, global partnerships require personal relationships. Is there a conflict between cultures and technology, and if so, how would the conflict impede change? How might this conflict be exploited by a company like Applied Materials, whose customers are truly global marketers and global buyers?

it introduced a high-volume copier.[22] Dealers could simply load the disk into their PC. In the near future, we may not even need a disk, instead sending the virtual reality images over the net. (If so, will we need as many airlines?)

The Future for Business Marketing Careers

The current strong economy has made college campuses a favorite place for companies to look for the next generation of sales and marketing leaders. Unisys, for example, has experienced such worldwide growth in information services sales that it found the need to begin recruiting on college campuses.[23] According to the U.S. Bureau of Labor Statistics, the impact of the strong economy has been felt in marketing, as marketing managers represent one of the fastest growing positions.[24] Nationally, almost 40 percent of all firms plan to increase their marketing hiring.[25] In this section, we'll briefly describe the many types of jobs available, the skills necessary, and the importance of lifelong learning in order to manage a successful career.

Types of Business Marketing Jobs

At this point in the book, many students have probably already read one or more chapters with great interest, thinking "This is something I'd like to do." Business marketers can focus their talents on areas such as exhibit management or can seek broader application of their talents as product or market managers. Sales is also a great way to get started because you have to learn the product inside and out, the customer's business, and how your own company operates. Sales can also be a lucrative career; for example, of the five highest paid employees at Wallace Computer Services, four are salespeople and the fifth is the CEO.

Business marketing jobs can first be categorized in terms of marketing or sales, yet in many companies, careers often include a lot of switching between sales and marketing positions. Sales is one area with many entry-level opportunities that can lead into marketing, as illustrated by the career path at Wallace Computer Services we see in Exhibit 17–3. On the other hand, Stephanie Stewart began her career in trade show marketing with Ericsson and then moved into sales.

Stephanie found an entry-level job in marketing communications with Ericsson (a Swedish telecommunications company) immediately upon graduating from college. Her duties included developing sales brochures, graphics design for trade show booths, and other general marketing responsibilities. She believed that the next step in growing her

Exhibit 17–3
Career Path at
Wallace
Computer
Services

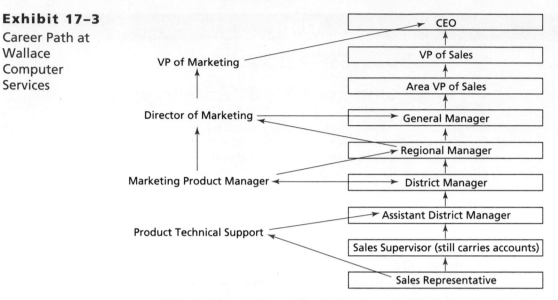

SOURCE: Weitz, Castleberry & Tanner, *Selling: Building Partnerships.* Third edition. Burr Ridge, IL: Irwin/McGraw-Hill, 1998.

career should include more direct customer contact. In the telecommunications equipment business, sales positions usually require some industry experience so she was able to get the position she wanted.

Richard Langlotz, after a stint in retailing, entered a sales position with Lanier selling dictation equipment. He quickly moved to Minolta Business Systems in sales, then into sales management; he now runs a branch office. His responsibilities include managing the technical service staff, inventory management, and managing salespeople. Richard has no interest in pursuing a marketing position, but finds his career has moved more into general management.

Moni Cantu also found an entry-level marketing position, working for an import–export company in south Texas. Her job involves buying products in Mexico for resale in the United States. Is this a marketing job? She thinks so. After all, she is responsible for marketing the products to companies in the United States. Sometimes she acts as a broker, other times as a distributor—it depends on the situation.

Necessary Skills

"When you sell (business) services, you need to know a lot about cost–benefit ratios and all that quantitative stuff," says Shireen Wedlock, sales and marketing manager for Britcom Telemarketing.[26] Understanding financial ratios and being able to determine return on investment are so important that these skills are the focus of training for senior salespeople at Moore Business Forms. But even those who are engaged in the management of marketing activities have to calculate return on their marketing investment.

Computer literacy is another important set of skills no matter what your area of marketing. As Ted Urpens believes (head of sales training for Caradon Everest, a British window manufacturer) quality and depth of knowledge about customers increase with the application of computers. One application involves taking digital pictures of the building to be retrofitted with Caradon Everest windows, which are then superimposed with

17–2

BUSINESS 2 BUSINESS
You Against the World

Assume you plan to enter a career with a company like Applied Materials, along with 12 other new college graduates from top schools in your region. How would your college education help you compete against them for top spots in the company? What should you do to fill gaps in your knowledge and skill set?

the recommended windows. Information can then be used to configure customized products and calculate prices.[27] So sales and marketing personnel with Caradon Everest must not only know windows and construction, they also have to know the computer.

One futurist believes that job performance will be based less on an ability to coordinate work functions and more on improving key work processes.[28] In marketing, this means being able to serve customers more quickly, effectively, and efficiently. For example, we discussed cycle time and its importance to product development in Chapter 8. The faster a company can get a product to market, the faster it can take advantage of the market opportunity. The same is true, though, for all marketing activities. The faster one can prepare a trade show program, the more flexible one is, and the more able to take advantage of new opportunities. What good is it to develop a product and then be unable to launch it effectively because the marketing plan isn't ready? Or what good is it, six weeks before a trade show opens, to identify it as a means to reach a new market, if it takes 10 weeks to plan for the show? Thus all business marketers will need to build skills and knowledge involving work processes.

All of these skills are in addition to the traditionally crucial qualities such as enthusiasm, general business knowledge, and strong marketing knowledge. Just as importantly, businesses need ethically developed marketers. Think of the negative attention Nike gets for underpaying workers in other countries. Business marketing organizations are responsible for being good corporate citizens wherever they do business.

Importance of Lifelong Learning

AT&T spends over $1 billion annually educating its work force. On any given day, over 6,000 AT&T employees are learning new skills. Who is in charge of this training and education? "We try to impress upon our associates [that] we'll help you, but you should manage yourselves," says Anne Fritz, AT&T's VP for human resources.[29] She continues with this credo, "Make time for education."

These are not idle statements or the comments of someone promoting training for her own department's benefit, but rather the beliefs of someone who has just been through a 40,000-person layoff and saw who stayed and who left. Managing a career requires constant investment in that career. In the kids' soccer movie, *The Big Green,* one youth says, "We may not be the sharpest tools in the shed . . .", which is an accurate statement about learning. To be effective, the mind must be continually sharpened through lifelong learning.

Learning doesn't stop once you get your degree; here at the Motorola training facility, employees are continuing to develop their knowledge and skills.
© 1998 Michael Abramson.

One vice president told us that when he wanted someone with 10 years of experience, he wanted someone who had 10 years of new experiences, not one year repeated 10 times. On-the-job training is not enough; to create more effective theories of how things work and how to create technology by applying those theories, lifelong learning has to be a priority.

Monsanto's Protiva division (which makes a hormone product that stimulates milk production in cows) provides each salesperson with an annual self-development budget.[30] With $3,000, he can choose internal or external training, depending on what he sees as his biggest needs. One rep spent some of the budget on a visit to the Chicago Board of Trade to learn about agricultural commodities trading while another spent $800 attending a three-day course called "Changing to a Team-Based Organization" at Cornell University.

Career development will be as much about skills and knowledge development as it will be about positions. As globalization and technology change the business marketer's job, new skills and knowledge will have to be acquired. With these skills and knowledge, effective marketing processes can be developed to capture the opportunity in global markets.

Summary

Here we've discussed two of the important factors that will impact a career in business marketing. You must recognize that change will be a reality in any business marketing career. Jobs to which a student aspires now may not exist as such in 5 or 10 years. On the other hand, how jobs change should provide challenge and satisfaction, too.

Companies that participate in global markets are often growing faster and making more money than those staying at home. We listed six stages through which companies tend to go: no foreign marketing, infrequent foreign marketing, regular foreign marketing, international marketing, global marketing, and global partnering. When a company desires to practice global partnering, it should recognize that network perspectives dominate in much of the world. Further, differences in relationship status and perceptions of time influence how relationships are formed.

Global marketers face challenges such as increased competition for customers and qualified personnel. Global marketers, and those who stay domestic but fight global competitors, must also recognize that their competition may have unfair advantages when supported by their country's government. Such support can be in the form of subsidies (such as Airbus receives) or tariffs and import quotas.

Information and communication technology are also changing the nature of business marketing. Both forms of technology have increased the globalization of business. Because marketing is more about creating value than creating exchange, information and communication technology enable marketers and buyers to make decisions that increase the value provided by a value chain.

These changes and others will have a significant impact on the career of the business marketer. Skills and knowledge regarding global markets, information and communication technology, and marketing processes will be critical to the success of tomorrow's business marketer. Yet, these skills involve technologies and practices that have yet to be developed. That is why lifelong learning will be so important for tomorrow's business marketing leader.

Key Terms

dyadic relationship	**monochronic time**	**subsidies**
import quotas	**networks**	**tariffs**
keiretsu	**polychronic time**	

Discussion Questions

1. Many universities no longer require a foreign language for business school graduates. Assume your school's dean recently stated, "Every student should have a foreign language; it should be required of all of our students." Do you agree with that statement? Why or why not?

2. One of your peers was complaining, "I hate taking these principles courses in other business areas. I'll never use any of this stuff—I just want to do marketing! Why should I have to take it?" Tell your friend why.

3. Do you practice socialistic capitalism? What about *amae*—do you practice a form of *amae*? Is it something you could do or should do? Why or why not?

4. An article in the June 1997 issue of *Business Marketing* suggested that networking is the most important method of job hunting ("Searching for a Job? Network First" by Martha Stone, p. 23). How does this personal form of networking compare to the *keiretsu* concept, if at all, and how does it compare to *amae*?

5. Choose either Mexico, Germany, or Japan, then write down five stereotypes that you feel are commonly held about people from that country. Then write down five stereotypes that you feel are held about people from your country. Assuming that there is a grain of truth to these perceptions, discuss how these two lists represent culture clash. Then discuss how holding those stereotypes limits the ability to interact well. How can businesspeople overcome these stereotypes?

6. U.S. laws prohibit banks from owning stock in other companies. Does this law restrict U.S. companies from access to capital that Japanese competitors have through their *keiretsus?* Why or why not?

7. A recent forecast stated that business buyer's web site usage will double in the next few years. What advantages and disadvantages to purchasing does the web offer? Will the web and Internet replace salespeople? Why or why not?

8. We've argued that personal learning doesn't stop after college—at least not for careers on the move. First, write down your desired postgraduation job. Then state the skills you think will need regular updating and why. Also, state the skills you feel you still need to develop and how you plan to develop those skills.

9. A stock market drop in Asia causes a drop in the U.S. market. Iraq is sanctioned by the U.S. government, which won't allow any U.S. business to trade with Iraq, yet the French and Russians refuse to honor the sanctions and still do business with Iraq. How might these global political and financial incidents influence Applied Materials, General Electric, and Hewlett–Packard?

10. What are impediments to adoption of technology? Write about your own use of technology and how your life as a college student is different from college students' lives 25 years ago. What is different about how you learn versus how they learn? How do you expect it to change for your children?

Internet Exercise

INTERNET

Open any home page from any of the companies profiled in this book; then visit its Employment Opportunities site. It may take you awhile, but find a job announcement for a marketing position that requires three or more years of experience. What type of experience is it looking for? Be specific in your description of that experience and write about how you would go about getting that experience. E-mail the company and ask for its input as to where (like what companies or types of companies) you can go to get that experience.

Cases

Case 17.1 Digital Copiers

Copiers seem like a mundane product. After all, every office has at least one. Digital copiers, though, are different, combining computer printing capability with a raft of sophisticated copying options such as image manipulation and stapling. Sales of these super–high-tech copiers, which cost from $75,000 to $235,000, are expected to double in the United States to 155,000 units over the next four years. With such an opportunity, competition from all over the globe is entering the fray.

Xerox's strategy is to leverage existing relationships into new areas of key accounts. According to Xerox VP Joe McGrath, sales of the $235,000 DocuTech and $130,000 DocuColor are stimulated when different departments in the company see other departments using them. To leverage the relationships, Xerox has launched its own traveling show called DocuWorld.

Pitney–Bowes is also attempting to leverage existing relationships, with plans to improve interdivision lead exchanges. Pitney–Bowes is best known for its postage meter equipment. If interdivisional processes can be strengthened, the company hopes to gain access to buyers through existing meter accounts.

Sharp, the Japanese copier company, has to attract new customers because its digital copier is its first sale requiring senior corporate management approval. Best known for small to midsize copiers, Sharp is trying to reach a new market beginning with print ads. Similarly Oce-USA, the U.S. marketing arm of European office equipment manufacturer OCE, is trying to reach that same audience (which is also new to Oce) through television advertising.

1. Who do you think has the best opportunity right now in the U.S. market? Why?
2. How and why would you change your answer if you knew which vendor had the technically superior product?
3. Look each company up on the Web (**xerox.com; pitneybowes.com; oce.com**; and **sharp-usa.com**). Assuming you were a global customer, which company would you think would be able to provide you hassle-free global service? Which would you think would be the most difficult? Why?

SOURCE: Russell Shaw, "The Digital Copier Copycats," *Business Marketing* (June 1997), pp. 2, 45.

Case 17.2   Zerf Technology

Bill Doors wondered what he was going to do now. His company, Zerf Technology, knew it had to have a web page in order to stay in step with the high tech industry that bought his products. What he hadn't counted on was orders pouring in from countries he hadn't ever heard of. On which continent is Equatorial Guinea?

Zerf Technology began in a miniwarehouse storage facility rather than Bill Doors' garage because Bill lived in a condo without individual garages. His primary product is a battery for portable computers that lasts for 8 to 10 hours without recharging. Now Zerf uses the services of 30 sales agents across North America to sell the product to large end users (companies with laptops for all salespeople, for example) and OEMs. With the product available for only a year and a half, Bill has long outgrown the miniwarehouse and now utilizes a full-scale production facility. Sales have been good, but market penetration in the United States has been slower than Bill believes it has to be. Production could be increased by 50 percent easily. Once a battery is sold, there is little postsale service required. The batteries weigh less than a pound and can be shipped via any overnight delivery service.

At Comdex, the large computer show, several European distributors approached Bill about the possibility of entering Europe. Looking in the geographical section of his dictionary, Bill learned that Equatorial Guinea is on the west coast of Africa. A mining company with mines around the world wants 50 units shipped to Equatorial Guinea.

1. In what stage of globalization is Zerf Technology?
2. The case illustrates one unintended consequence of web advertising. What might others be?
3. Bill Doors was talking with one of the sales agents and realized that his products were already going out all over the world. Virtually every OEM to whom these products were sold has global customers. Outline what Bill should do to plan for a comprehensive global strategy.

Additional Readings

Campbell, Alexandra, and David Wilson, "Managed Networks: Creating Strategic Advantage." Institute for the Study of Business Markets, report 22–1995, 1995.

Donath, Bob, "Global Marketing Management—Plus." Institute for the Study of Business Markets, report 20–1996, 1996.

Lehmann, Donald, and Katherine E. Jocz, eds., *Reflections on the Future of Marketing.* Cambridge, MA: Marketing Science Institute, 1997.

Oliva, Ralph, "Marketing's Agenda 2000," *Marketplace: The ISBM Review* (Spring 1997), pp. 1–2.

AgriChem's Specialty Chemicals Division

Introduction

"We need to know more about the end-user of our products . . . the American farmer," stated Mita Strian, director of marketing research for AgriChem's Specialty Chemicals Division. "The farmer is the most critical link in the supply chain for our specialty agricultural products. We spend too much time with distributors, dealers, and retailers. And with extension agents. Our real customer is the American farmer. Life on the farm is different today. Farmers are different. We need to study farmers as our primary customer. Once we understand farmers, then we can decide which channels are best for distributing our products. Otherwise, we allow the middleman to control our destiny."

"Let's adopt some of the best practices of the consumer companies like Procter & Gamble. Let's study our end-user first," Mita finished with a flourish. She paused to reset the videotape and check her performance.

Background

This debate had been continuing since Mita Strian was hired from the marketing research group at Procter &

This case was prepared by Thomas W. Leigh for discussion purposes only; the company described is fictitious and any similarity between AgriChem and actual business firms is coincidental. Reprinted by permission of the author.

Gamble industrial products division. Mita and one other marketing research director had been hired after a year-long "best practices" study concerning market-driven firms shook up mind-sets at the parent firm. Among other things, this best practice study concluded that market-driven firms intensely researched and shared knowledge concerning the motives and requirements of the entire value chain involving their product. They looked beyond the immediate customer (i.e., the dealer, distributor, or retailer) to the customer's customer and, in many cases, all the way to the end-user. This immediately sparked debate among the marketing executives, market researchers, and field sales personnel concerning who the customer really is.

This debate was further fueled by the report's emphasis on branding, including brand awareness and brand equity, and the fact that marketing research was highly valued by decision makers at leading firms. As an executive at one "best practices" firm explained, "The marketing team must find out what the end-user or customer wants, starting with the voice of the customer . . . marketing research is how we hear the voice of the customer. Marketing researchers are a valued part of our decision-making team."

Historically, marketing research (MR) at AgriChem was a centralized department. The benefit of a centralized department was the development of a professional staff of experienced researchers who could work on a variety of products as needed. Marketing researchers were sourced internally through job postings. Of the 22 MR staffers, 17 were engineers in their prior work life. Many of them gravitated toward research because of its disciplined thinking and scientific methods. Of the remaining five marketing researchers, three were hired from marketing research suppliers. Mita Strian and George Cannon were recent hires from "progressive" companies. While they were housed in the marketing research center, most of their time was specifically assigned and billed to their respective SBUs: AgriChem and AgriFiber. These two divisions were central to the longer-term future of the parent firm; they were also subject to increasing technological advances and intensified competition from such agriculture giants as Monsanto, Calgene, and DuPont. The pressures of globalization and global competition were also intense in recent years. As Chairman William Stardinsky put it, "AgriChem and AgriFiber will provide the road map for the future of our other 16 divisions. . . . We need enhanced performance, but we also need to be a leader in organizational learning and knowledge application processes. We must be a leader in understanding our customers."

Marketing Research at AgriChem

The AgriChem Division had traditionally relied on the marketing research department to recommend and implement research studies. Marketing researchers typically did a lot of different studies—as James Meyer stated, "We are eclectic. We like to do a variety of research studies. It keeps the mind sharp and diversifies our skill base. Lately, we have been playing around with some perceptual mapping methods, conjoint analysis, discrete choice, and stated attribute versus derived attribute importance. We've had a couple of people attend seminars in correspondence analysis and cohort analysis. We like to be up to speed on the latest methods."

Most marketing researchers at the firm await the day when they can apply these advanced tools. Marketing research has historically emphasized (1) secondary research concerning trends in agriculture that affect "how we sell" or "how farmers buy"; (2) competitive analysis, especially the relative strength and weaknesses of the top two competitors in each product/market; (3) resource commitments of leading competitors in distributor, agent, and retailer channels; (4) relative sales force size and deployment to channels; (5) market share of competitors in key customer channels (i.e., dealer, distributor, retailer channels); (6) tracking field studies of product applications and

the new product initiatives of competitors; and (7) the relative growth rate of the various customer channels and the requirements to achieve "preferred supplier" status.

In recent years, the marketing research department had been asked to develop three new research capabilities. Top management had requested an industry structure analysis to fit the Michael Porter model. They had also requested an annual portfolio analysis by product/market for each division. Finally, annual customer satisfaction studies for tracking end-user (i.e., farmer) satisfaction with products and dealer/distributor customer services were commissioned for all divisions in 1995. A considerable amount of the available marketing research resources had been devoted to developing the customer satisfaction tracking system.

The results of the customer satisfaction study for the AgriChem Division had hardly been earthshaking. Overall levels of satisfaction with AgriChem's pesticides and herbicides had been very high among farmers across the country in early 1995. In the first full-scale research study in 1996, farmer satisfaction had again been quite high. However, the missionary sales force that works with dealers, distributors, and retailers is very concerned about the sales potential of new genetically engineered seed products that are immune to herbicides. Various companies such as Monsanto and Calgene are introducing such products in 1997. As one salesperson put it, "This could revolutionize how the American farmer raises corn. . . . Why don't we know more about this? Satisfaction studies don't tell us a thing about how farmers may react to really new products such as these."

The AgriChem Planning Session

Channel-back marketing was the phrase that kept ringing in Mita Strian's head. "It makes sense," she said to herself aloud. "Instead of peering down the channel, we need to understand farmers first. Then, we can design the right marketing mix, including product/applications solutions, promotional and selling approaches, and pricing and financing options, and select the appropriate channels and retailer intermediaries. It's obvious—understand the farmer first . . ."

Preliminary analysis of farmers in an informal planning session had concluded that "there was no simple description of the American farmer." In fact, it appeared that the American farmer might be usefully segmented on a variety of bases, in addition to the traditional terms of demographics, farm acreage, crop intensity levels, and usage rates of pesticides and herbicides. Research suggestions at the planning session concerned the need for psychographic studies, benefit (or value) segmentation, brand awareness and loyalty patterns, buying processes and key influences, and channel preferences and loyalty.

The AgriChem planning team, based strictly on personal observation and experience, had reached several tentative conclusions. First, farmers differ considerably psychographically. As one sales manager put it, "To some farmers, it is strictly a business; to others, it is family and cross-generational emotion. Like my Uncle Pete, it's working the land . . . and leaving the farm to his sons and grandsons."

Second, farmers differ considerably in their degree of business sophistication. Some are very knowledgeable about their region, their farm, and local conditions. Others are more sophisticated in terms of global and national trends, technology, and new farming processes. Some are astute business managers, with accounting systems and sophisticated planting software.

Third, farmers differ in terms of how they make their buying decisions. Some are very traditional in that they rely heavily on relationships they have established with local dealers, distributors, and retailers. They make their own decisions, but listen closely to the advice of channel intermediaries and agents. Others make their own decisions, but are well informed and sophisticated about new products, applications, yields, and prices. They want a lot of information, but don't want anyone drawing a conclusion for them. Then, there is the "corporate" farmer with large acreage, many employees, multiple farms, and many decision makers. These are the farmers who want

partnerships and solutions. Of course, there is always the price-shopper—the farmer who shops for the best deal and is willing to switch products or suppliers for a penny or two an application.

The planning group had agreed in general that (1) more research concerning farmers and end-users is needed if "we are to be more market-driven" and (2) the general observations developed at the planning meeting must be validated before AgriChem's strategy can be more fully developed.

The Current Situation

Mita Strian's marketing research plan was due at the end of the month. In particular, she needed to identify the research priorities and budgets necessary to support AgriChem's dual objectives of establishing a leadership position among farmers in the pesticide and herbicide businesses and serving as a model division for others to follow. While she was convinced that understanding farmers was the key to her marketing research plan, her recent discussion with George Cannon at AgriFiber had indicated that he was taking a slightly different approach—he was building his research plan around a detailed analysis of intermediary customers, their shares, and end-user segment access. As he put it, "I don't need to know much about my end-users, just which channels control their purchasing. I think the same thing applies in the AgriChem business."

Mita mused, "What are the marketing research priorities for AgriChem? What types of marketing research projects are best for getting the information I need? How am I going to get the marketing research staff to pay attention to these research needs?" She resumed preparing for her presentation to the AgriChem business team and marketing research staff on Thursday.

AmeriServe

Introduction

In October 1997, Jeffrey Raltz, logistics analyst for AmeriServe/PFS, was researching information on the possible partnership between AmeriServe, Miller Brewing Company, and J. B. Hunt. Miller had 500 carriers and numerous distributors in its network, but was considering J. B. Hunt for a role as its primary carrier. Raltz realized Miller needed to reorganize its distribution network for continuous growth and logistical value. He also realized that in order to increase economic value and density, J. B. Hunt needed to put in place a dedicated lanes transportation system to keep its trucks full to and from sites of distribution. (Load density simply means full truckloads of products.) AmeriServe stood to gain revenue through more efficient shipping of its products, but was concerned about the role it would play in the partnership.

Raltz was preparing to make recommendations for the future. He had just completed a market analysis of the beer industry including Anheuser-Busch, Coors, Stroh's, and numerous regional beers. Miller was strongest in the Midwest, southeast, and Texas, but weakest in New England, a region replete with microbreweries, and California, which was saturated with Mexican imports like Corona. Miller had networks effectively in place in the northeastern, southeastern, and southwestern United States, but their efficiency could be improved. The northwestern United States had to receive Miller products from Erwindale, California or Milwaukee, Wisconsin. The great distance created extensive uncertainty among retailers attempting to provide time and place utility.

Raltz wondered if the question was not more complex than just re-engineering a distribution channel. Miller wanted control over its product. It also wanted to dissolve its relationships with approximately 420 regional carriers, which was in itself a complex issue. J. B. Hunt was willing to take on the enormous responsibility of being Miller's primary carrier as long as it got increased economic value and density out of the partnership. Raltz and Ameri-

Serve/PFS were slowly evaluating how much involvement they should have with Miller and J. B. Hunt. To make the partnership work, Raltz knew he had to show his manager and executives from Miller and J. B. Hunt how AmeriServe/PFS would be able to add value to the supply chain. Raltz would present his recommendations and plan of action to executives of the three companies at the next executive meeting, in just 30 days.

The Players

AmeriServe/PFS

AmeriServe/PFS, which is a subsidiary of Holberg Industries Inc., procures and distributes food, supplies, and equipment to 14 major restaurant chains (including Wendy's, Burger King, Arby's, Dairy Queen, and nearly 800 KFC restaurants), and over 600 beverage distribution centers throughout North America. AmeriServe/PFS's mission is to provide custom-tailored distribution and related services that deliver a competitive advantage to the customer. As the largest food service and restaurant equipment supplier in the U.S., AmeriServe/PFS manages the distribution of over 4 billion pounds of goods annually.

AmeriServe/PFS's integrated Logistics Management Group manages over 12,000 beverage shipments for PepsiCo. At an annual transportation expense of over $30,000,000, this group delivers yearly savings in excess of $2,000,000 at a service level of 99 percent. The Logistics Management Group, formerly part of the PFS division of PepsiCo, was originally limited to the distribution of food, supplies, and equipment to the PepsiCo restaurants, but grew to incorporate the distribution of PepsiCo beverages. In July 1997, AmeriServe purchased PFS, creating opportunities to distribute goods to a variety of clients nationwide. Its scope now includes AmeriServe/PFS's incumbent business, and will soon incorporate inbound movements from their suppliers. The merging of PFS's customer service culture with AmeriServe's expertise in selling services to diverse groups of franchisees created a synergy that translated into the largest food and supply distributor in the nation.

J. B. Hunt

J. B. Hunt Transport Services Inc. is a diversified transportation services and logistics company.

This case was prepared by Lauren Daniels, Chris Jarrard, and Muniu Muiruri under the direction of Dr. Lou Pelton (University of North Texas) for the purposes of class discussion, and is not intended to illustrate effective or ineffective management practices.

Exhibit 1
Miller Brewing
Facilities, 1996
Assigned Ship
Plant Areas
(Headquarters:
Milwaukee, WI.)

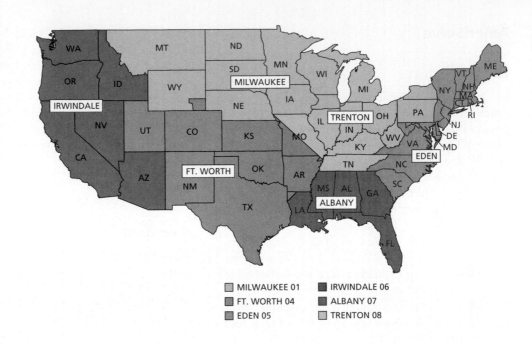

☐ MILWAUKEE 01	■ IRWINDALE 06
■ FT. WORTH 04	■ ALBANY 07
■ EDEN 05	☐ TRENTON 08

Through its subsidiaries, J. B. Hunt transports primarily full-load containerized freight throughout the continental U.S. and portions of Canada and Mexico. The company also provides logistics and transportation-related services that may use either J. B. Hunt equipment and employees, or equipment and services provided by unrelated third parties in the industry.

Miller Brewing Company

In June of 1969, Phillip Morris acquired 53 percent interest in Miller Brewing Company for $130,000,000. In 1970, Phillip Morris acquired the remaining outstanding shares, 47 percent, for $25,000,000 and $72,000,000 in notes due in 1982. Miller is the second largest brewing company in the U.S. It owns and operates Molson Breweries, the second largest beer importer in the United States. Internationally, Miller has formed a number of alliances with brewers from Japan, Brazil, China, and England. Miller owns eight breweries (see Exhibit 1 for continental U.S. locations and distribution areas), and majority interests in the Celis Brewery in Austin, Texas and the Shipyard Brewery in Portland, Maine.

It also owns a beer distributorship in Oklahoma and a hops processing facility in Wisconsin.

Miller Products

Miller has 15 different beers in all. The most popular brands come from the premium segment comprised of Miller Lite, Miller Lite Ice, Miller Genuine Draft, Miller Genuine Draft Lite, Miller Beer, and Icehouse. Containers (bottles, cans, and kegs) for beer products are purchased from various suppliers.

In 1996, shipment volume for Miller, including imports, exports, and nonalcohol brew, decreased 2.7 percent from the previous year, while the U.S. industry was up 1.8 percent. Intense competition, combined with softness in most of Miller's brands, resulted in the lower shipment volume. Despite higher shipments of Miller Lite in 1996, shipments of other premium-price brands decreased. Yet Miller depended on its premium brands, which accounted for nearly 83 percent of its total shipments. Miller's share of the U.S. industry (based on shipments) was 21.6 percent, down 1.0 share point from 1995.

Miller had spoken with many firms, including J. B. Hunt, AmeriServe/PFS, and other companies

Exhibit 2   Sales of Leading U.S. Brewers (in millions of barrels)

Company	Shipments			Market Share		
	1990	1994	1995	1990	1994	1995
Anheuser-Busch	84.6	85.9	84.8	43.5%	45.4%	45.2%
Miller Brewing	42.8	43.7	43.3	22.0	23.1	23.1
Adolph Coors	19.2	18.6	18.7	9.9	9.8	10.0
Stroh Brewery	26.2	19.1	17.1	13.5	10.1	9.1
S&P Co.	8.0	7.6	7.0	4.1	4.0	3.7
Total—leading brewers	180.8	174.9	170.9	92.9	92.4	91.1
Others	13.8	15.0	15.1	7.1	7.9	8.0
Total	194.6	189.3	187.6	100	100	100

Exhibit 3   Top 10 Beer Brands Ranked by 1995 Unit Sales

Brand	Sales (Mil. Barrels)			Market Share		
	1990	1994	1995	1990	1994	1995
1. Budweiser	47.9	39.1	37.2	24.8%	20.9%	20.0%
2. Bud Light	11.8	16.3	17.9	6.1	8.7	9.6
3. Miller Lite	19.9	15.5	15.8	10.3	8.3	8.5
4. Coors Light	11.6	12.5	12.9	6.0	6.7	7.0
5. Busch	9.4	8.5	8.1	4.9	4.5	4.4
6. Natural Light	3.0	7.1	7.1	1.6	3.8	3.8
7. Miller Genuine Draft	5.8	6.1	5.8	3.0	3.3	3.1
8. Milwaukee's Best	6.6	5.0	4.7	3.4	2.7	2.5
9. Miller High Life	6.0	4.4	4.4	3.1	2.4	2.4
10. Bush Light Draft	1.9	4.0	4.2	1.0	2.1	2.3
Total top 10	123.9	118.5	118.1	64.2	63.3	63.6
All others	69.2	68.7	67.5	35.8	36.7	36.4
Total	193.1	187.2	185.6	100	100	100

about a proposed partnership. After evaluating its needs, J. B. Hunt considered partnering with Miller. AmeriServe/PFS analyzed its needs and had also considered being the third link.

The Beer Industry

According to *IMPACT,* a publication that tracks the United States alcoholic beverage industry, consumers spent about $90 million for 6.6 billion gallons of alcoholic beverages in 1995. Beer accounted for the largest portion of the industry dollar. Consumers

spent approximately $50 billion on 5.8 billion gallons of beer in 1995, accounting for an 87 percent share of the industry, as measured by volume.

The U.S. alcoholic beverage industry underwent a consolidation prompted by the combined challenges of declining U.S. consumption trends in the highly developed marketplace and the steady rise in legal and regulatory actions. The increased scale needed to compete established numerous barriers to entry for smaller competitors.

Three producers dominated the U.S. beer industry (see Exhibits 2 and 3), commanding a combined

78 percent market share of the nation's beer products. Anheuser-Busch had a leading 45 percent share, Miller Brewing had a 23 percent share, and Adolph Coors had a 10 percent share.

Pricing in this industry moves in concert; the industry leader hikes prices and the rest follow. This price leadership helped boost industry profit margins to healthy levels. But a decline in real disposable income tends to put downward pressure on the prices of consumer products, because consumers move away from premium-priced, brand-name products toward value-priced brands. The alcoholic beverage industry last experienced this scenario in the early 1990s, when value-priced brands such as Busch and Natural Light cut into the market shares of such premium-priced brands as Budweiser, Michelob, and Molson. One of the most distinguishing characteristics of the industry is how heavily it is regulated and taxed. In 1995, every barrel of beer was taxed $18 and every six-pack was taxed 32 cents. In 1995, the U.S. government collected $3.3 billion from the beer industry.

In addition to pricing, population also drives demand. With the U.S. population growing at an annual rate of only about 1%, the American market for all alcoholic beverages is quite mature. Demographic trends affect the industry as well. Studies show that the largest group of purchasers for these products is young adults, a post–baby-boom demographic group that is growing very slowly. The aging population does not favor brewers, and the baby boom generation, that group of 80 million consumers between the ages of 32 and 52, is demonstrating an increased interest in healthy living and has therefore cut back its beer consumption.

Miller's Distribution System

Distribution is one of the principal methods of competition in the beer industry. Miller was losing revenue and market share to its competition because of its distribution system.

Under that system, over 500 trucking companies delivered beer on a domestic scale, but Miller did not know when the carriers were coming to pick up beer for delivery. It had a general idea, but the trucks were never on time. Numerous independent distributors controlled the flow and distribution of the product in their own territories. If Distributor X controlled the North Texas region, it dictated what grocery stores, convenience stores, and restaurants would receive Miller products. Miller had no control over the distribution of its product. It did, however, have "deep pockets." Because Miller is owned by Phillip Morris, it had never (until recently) considered reengineering its supply chain. But with regional breweries competing for market share, Miller had to create a competitive advantage in distribution to stay alive.

The Partnership*

In the proposed distribution system, AmeriServe/PFS would provide loads for Hunt to carry when not carrying Miller loads. AmeriServe and J. B. Hunt would develop an in-house continuous-move software program that would inform Hunt's truckers where and when loads were ready to be shipped. If the software showed that a load from Miller leaving Dallas would arrive in Boston at the same time an AmeriServe/PFS load was leaving Boston for Fort Worth, then a continuous move could be accomplished. This creation of a just-in-time (JIT), point-to-point, "dense" distribution network would provide benefits for all companies involved. The dedicated lanes would allow continuous movement of Miller and AmeriServe/PFS products with minimal interruptions and downtime. Hunt would gain load density, thus creating economies of scale. Miller would achieve more control over its logistics, and its distributors would concentrate on New England, the northwestern U.S., and California to work on an intensive system within these markets. AmeriServe/PFS would gain another cost-reducing channel of distribution. J. B. Hunt would charge Miller or AmeriServe/PFS for each load the companies ordered, but if Hunt's trucks remained full at all times, it would give both Miller and AmeriServe a discount on their loads. The proposed partnership could be a win-win-win situation.

Decision Options

The first option that Raltz considered was to not get involved with the partnership at all. AmeriServe/PFS wanted to manage as much freight as possible,

---

*It's important to note that the proposed partnership is still being considered. The partnership has not been approved yet and may never be approved, so the information is all speculative.

but Miller and J. B. Hunt were dominating the program. Raltz was uneasy about the minor role that AmeriServe/PFS might have to take if they did commit to the partnership.

The second option that Raltz wanted to present was a limited role by AmeriServe/PFS, in which they used the partnership as one cost-effective channel of distribution among others. AmeriServe/PFS could build density into the system by having J. B. Hunt, as the primary carrier, distribute all of their products on the same trucks as Miller's.

The third option that Raltz was considering was an equal partnering agreement in which all decisions would be split equally between Miller, J. B. Hunt, and AmeriServe/PFS. AmeriServe could team with J. B. Hunt and integrate continuous-move software programs that would benefit both companies in their strategic planning processes. AmeriServe/PFS could also set up a long-term alliance with Phillip Morris to possibly work on other supply-chain issues in other strategic business units. AmeriServe/PFS would further benefit because it could control its freight when it was being moved with Miller products.

AmeriServe/PFS historically takes a slow, methodical approach to decision making when it involves a partnership. However, Raltz knew that Miller and J. B. Hunt would want a decision by their next executive meeting. Raltz and his team needed to spend the next couple of weeks evaluating all three options. As the team leader, he needed to present his ideas and options to his upper-level executives first, before the executive meeting in a few weeks. Raltz was confident that he would be prepared with the decision that most benefited AmeriServe/PFS at least a week before the meeting was scheduled to take place.

Conclusion

A successful partnership requires each partner to add value. Miller wanted to add value to its supply chain by decreasing its number of regional carriers and distributors. J. B. Hunt would be the primary carrier and, together with AmeriServe/PFS, would work on an integrated continuous-move software program that would create an effective transportation system of combined Miller and AmeriServe/PFS products. Raltz understood that Miller and J. B. Hunt had deep pockets. Phillip Morris owns Miller and doesn't have to spend the time evaluating and analyzing all decision options like AmeriServe/PFS does. Time may be the biggest factor against this partnership because Miller and J. B. Hunt are ready to go, and AmeriServe/PFS is still methodically evaluating its position. Raltz knew that a partnership had the opportunity to be successful from a strategic standpoint, but he was being very careful as to how far AmeriServe/PFS committed itself before he knew where they stood. If Raltz finds out that AmeriServe/PFS has to take a minor position in the partnership, then he may pull the plug. If Raltz sees that it is going to be an equal partnership, he may go in front of AmeriServe/PFS's executives and speak favorably of the proposed partnership. From AmeriServe/PFS's standpoint, it all comes down to control.

Bama Pie, Limited

Bama Pie, Limited's phenomenal growth over the past 24 years of its 65-year history was due directly to the growth of its major customer, McDonald's, and a fanatical commitment to quality. As the single-source supplier of pies to McDonald's' U.S. operations, Bama was testimony to how a small, aggressive, and creative company could succeed competing with much larger organizations. By providing top-quality pie products and "never missing an order," Bama had been able to expand its core pie business by landing 50 percent of McDonald's' oven-ready, prebaked frozen biscuit needs. Its new role as a supplier of McDonald's' breakfast biscuit requirements was expected to allow Bama to increase total sales to approximately $100 million in 1992. Bama Pie's actual financial information was closely guarded since it was a privately held, family-owned limited partnership; the company's CEO was 38-year-old Paula Marshall-Chapman, who had succeeded her father and grandfather as head of the business.

Bama Pie produced more than 1 million pies per day from facilities in Tulsa, Oklahoma, for McDonald's. In 1968, the firm was producing only 500 pies per day. In 1991, the company completed a $38 million facility in Tulsa to produce the biscuits for McDonald's, arranging the bank financing within about six weeks. The new facility, in early 1992, was producing more than 120,000 biscuits per hour.

Other major customers included Pizza Hut (for which Bama was producing approximately 25 percent of its bread stick requirements), TCBY, and Braum's (an Oklahoma-based ice cream chain).

The company, in an effort to lessen its dependence on McDonald's, had begun seeking business with other major fast-food and convenience food companies. In 1992, more than 70 percent of Bama's business was with McDonald's. Less than 10 percent of the company's revenues came from products carrying the Bama Pie brand, the best-known of which was a 3-inch pecan pie. Of the McDonald's business, about 4 percent was exported to McDonald's' operations in Hong Kong and Taiwan. In early 1992, Bama was working toward establishing a joint venture in Hong Kong to provide pies to McDonald's in

This case was prepared by Raymond E. Belford of Oklahoma City University.

Hong Kong, the People's Republic of China, and Taiwan. Bama also had a licensing arrangement in Canada with a Canadian baker that provided pies to McDonald's' Canadian operations.

The firm considered itself responsible for McDonald's' pies worldwide. Marshall-Chapman's father, Paul Marshall, began providing technical assistance to McDonald's in the early days as he, Ray Kroc (McDonald's' founder), and Fred Turner (early president of McDonald's) worked together. The technical assistance in helping establish local bakeries in McDonald's' global enterprise had always been provided at no cost to McDonald's. "We see it as part of our service," said Marshall-Chapman.

In 1991, Bama competed in the national Baldrige awards for quality and made the fourth cut. The companies that reached the fifth cut were chosen for the prestigious award. The company was under consideration in 1992 for the award. Marshall-Chapman was named Quality Fanatic of the Year in 1989 by Philip Crosby of the Quality College.

The word most often heard around Bama Pie headquarters in Tulsa was *quality*. Marshall-Chapman had attended numerous quality conferences and had spoken to international groups about commitment to quality. The company had dropped the traditional mission statement (see Exhibit 1) for "Bama's Quality Circle." According to Marshall-Chapman, "We had a very nice mission statement of a traditional nature—very wordy, very flowery, like most progressive companies. If you've read most mission statements, they tend to be written for Wall Street or people outside the organization. We felt the mission should be written for our employees. Our Quality Circle is very simple and keeps us focused." (See Exhibit 2 for a description of the Quality Circle.)

The company also had a values statement (Exhibit 3) that reinforced "quality as a way of life" at Bama. The company's quality statement was read before every meeting held in the company. "It helps keep us focused," Marshall-Chapman explained.

Company History

The history of Bama Pie dates to 1927 when Henry C. Marshall decided to utilize the pie-baking talents of his wife, Cornelia Alabama Marshall (who went by the name Bama), to provide employment for himself after a lengthy period of being out of work. Bama Marshall began baking pies for the lunch

Exhibit 1   Mission Statement of Bama Pie, Ltd.

Bama Pie, Ltd., is an international company in business to develop, produce, and market fresh, frozen, and ready-to-prepare food products generally described as convenience foods, snacks, and other bakery items. We shall serve our products to food service and retail customers and are dedicated to developing new markets as well as serving our major customer, McDonald's. All our products will conform to specific requirements which will ensure our name represents QUALITY to ourselves, our customers, and our suppliers. This will provide continued growth and a fair return to the partners on their investment.

We shall continue to operate as a privately held and fiscally responsible company, and shall be oriented to serving our customer's needs.

In support of this, we are committed to:

- Being flexible and responsive to our customers.
- Ensuring that product requirements are adhered to throughout our processes.
- Maintaining a high degree of employee motivation by providing an environment of equal opportunity, fair treatment, and growth opportunities. This includes fair and equitable compensation, involvement, recognition, and rewards.
- Operating and establishing "partnership relationships" with our suppliers.
- Providing management with information and controls which empowers the planning and decision-making process.
- Being a "Corporate Good Citizen" by active and responsible involvement in our community.

Exhibit 2
Bama's Quality
Circle

BUZZINGS

The Busy B's • Bama Pie Ltd. • BTC • Bama Pailet • Base Inc. • Bama Sweets • Bama Foods • January 1992

BAMA'S QUALITY CIRCLE

OUR QUALITY FUTURE

1991 was a transition year for our Quality culture. You may have not been aware it was because "Quality" is a way of life at Bama—but subtle changes have been occurring. As a company, in our sixth year involved with the Quality Process, our needs are very different. We have matured with Crosby's principles and now is the time to adopt our own values. In 1992 we will be building a solid quality foundation based on these principles.

➤ People
➤ Products
➤ Services
➤ Profits
➤ Continuous Improvement

Our mission is to consistently strive to improve all processes, through continuous improvement, to ensure total customer satisfaction.

—Paula Marshall-Chapman

counter at the Woolworth's in Dallas. Her talents created a market for her pies that topped 75 per day (including take-home purchases), and the local owner of Woolworth's expanded his lunch counter to 75 stools to handle customer volume.

Bama was soon baking up to 300 pies per day for Woolworth's, and business at the lunch counter was

booming. Bama was spending so much time at her work, Henry began to think she was being unfaithful to him and was "carrying on" with the owner of the Woolworth's. He sent his son, Paul, down to "spy" on Bama. When Paul reported back that the reason the owner "liked Mama so much is because of the pies she was making," Henry came up with an idea.

Exhibit 3   The Bama Pie Values Statement

Customers

Bama will provide our customers with products and services that conform to their requirements and deliver them on time, at a competitive price.

Suppliers

Bama will encourage open and honest communication with our "partners" and reward those who have adopted and demonstrated use of the continuous improvement process. We will also encourage the sharing of ideas.

Passion

Bama will conduct our business with integrity and professionalism and with a strategy of continuous improvement. This will provide increased profits and create worldwide awareness of our products. We will continue to focus on being a "Corporate Good Citizen" by being active in our community.

Quality

Products and Services

Product quality and product safety will be the responsibility of every employee. We will sell quality products and services at a fair value. We will anticipate and react to our customers' needs. We will take pride in all products and services which we perform.

People

Bama will attract result-oriented people, provide a safe work environment, operate as an equal opportunity employer, focus on employee development and retention, develop mutual trust and respect for each other, and support promotion from within. We will inspire new ideas and innovation by creating the environment whereby we create employee satisfaction.

Through continuous improvement our name will represent QUALITY to our customers, our suppliers, and ourselves. We believe that if we live by these values we will establish the Bama Companies as world class and will achieve our long-range objectives.

The following passage from *A Piece of the Pie* by Paul Marshall describes the event.[1]

I heard Papa ask Mama something that made me cringe.

"Blanchie, how are things at Woolworth's?"

That question sounded innocent enough, but I knew Papa was fishing for an answer that would drive him into the rage which he had been holding in for weeks. (Paul still thought his father believed his mother was having an affair.) I looked over at Mama and saw her relaxed manner. She had no idea what was happening with Papa.

"I'm working harder these days, that's for sure. A man from the head office came down this week."

She stopped talking there. I guess she wanted to see if Papa was interested in her news or just making conversation.

Papa looked over at Mama and said, "So?"

"So he told me what a good job I was doing and how he wished more employees worked as well as I

did. Then he asked me if I would be willing to move to Amarillo and be in charge of the lunch counter at the new store there."

I got even more worried right then. Papa didn't say anything right at first. I must have held my breath for at least 10 minutes waiting for Papa to blow.

But he never did. When he finally broke the silence, he spoke in a soft voice. "Blanchie, if you can make pies for Mr. Tanner to sell, why can't you make pies for me to sell?"

Mama looked over at him, surprised like.

"What do you mean?" she asked.

"Just that. If Mr. Tanner can make money on your pies, why can't we? I've been thinking about this for weeks now. I'm not talking foolishness. You make some pies and I'll carry them around the area here and sell them."

Mama just rolled her head back, shut her eyes, and moaned a sigh. It was more like she was tired than anything else.

Papa didn't pay her any mind. He just kept on talking. "I've been looking at those Hubig pies in the stores. They make the smaller seven-inch pies thin so they look larger. They could cost a quarter of what

[1]Paul Marshall with Brian and Sandy Miller, *A Piece of the Pie* (Tulsa: Walsworth Press, 1987).

the big nine-inch family pies cost," Papa's voice was getting stronger. He wasn't looking at Mama anymore, but looking out above the rooftops across the street.

"I've checked on prices. Dried fruit runs about 5 cents a pounds and that's the most expensive part of the pie. How many pies could you make with a pound of dried fruit?"

Mama didn't answer. Papa didn't seem to be expecting an answer, either, because he just kept talking and even started gesturing with his arms, swinging this way and that.

"Your pies taste a hundred times better than Hubig's. Why, before long we'll be selling pies all over Dallas, then the whole country."

Papa stopped suddenly and turned to Mama who was wilted next to him. I think she must have been wishing he'd calm down and start talking about the smell of fresh cut grass or something.

"I've even come up with a name for the company." It was too dark to tell, but his voice sounded like there must have been a gleam in his eyes.

"Now you know I've always called you Blanchie because I didn't like Cornelia Alabama, or even 'Bama' like your family called you. But for a company, 'Bama' is just fine. In fact, I like it real good. 'The Bama Pie Company,' how does that sound Blanchie?"

I couldn't see Mama right then, but hearing the swing squeaking, I figured she sat up in her seat before she answered Papa.

"Well, I . . ."

I think Mama was surprised at how excited Papa was at the idea of starting a business selling her pies. From hearing her hesitate, I knew Papa would be selling Mama's pies before long.

"The idea sounds all right. But we don't have much of a place to make pies or enough pans and equipment. We . . ."

"Don't worry about a thing, Blanchie. Tell me what you need and I'll get it for you."

"Well, I'll have to think about it for a while. I . . ."

"Fine," Papa said. "We'll start tomorrow."

Thus, the Bama Pie Company was born, according to Paul Marshall's recounting of the event. The next day, Henry took $1.67 and went out to obtain what was needed. He talked a bakery goods supplier into granting credit with the $1.67 paid down on an order that totaled more than $25. He obtained the rest of what was needed on credit from the grocery store where the family had shopped and was known. That evening, the family pitched in to make pies, and the following day, Henry set out to sell the first Bama Pies. The first day's sales far exceeded expectations, and the company began to grow.

Soon the sales route had expanded to the delivery of two baskets of pies per day. When sales were slow, Henry Marshall would walk farther and extend the route until all the pies were sold each day. One day, as evening was approaching and he had a few pies left, he spotted a grocery store across the street from where he was. He approached the grocer and asked if he could leave the pies on consignment, promising to service the store daily with fresh products. The grocer agreed and thus began a new phase; Bama Pie became a wholesale distributor.

Soon a car was purchased and modified to carry the pies; and the company established routes in the Dallas area. All the Marshall children became involved in the business, including Paul. The company tried to expand into Waco in 1931, but was unsuccessful because of the Depression.

In the mid-1930s, Paul Marshall observed the operation of Bama's major competitor, Hubig Pies. He was overwhelmed with the modern, high-volume, machine-aided production. Seeing the operation made him aware of how small and old-fashioned Bama was. He attempted to convince his father of the need to purchase new equipment, but to no avail. The company continued to produce pies in a highly labor-intensive process. Paul's dream had become bigger than his father's; he saw the need to change to high-volume, machine-production methods as the way to expand the company. This conflict became a source of disagreement over the years between Paul and his father.

During the next few years, the older Marshall children opened other Bama Pie operations, including one in Oklahoma City started by Paul's sister Grace and her husband. In a move for independence, Paul moved to Oklahoma City and began working for his sister as a route salesman. It was in Oklahoma City that Paul met and eventually married Lilah

Drake, who worked in the kitchen of the pie company. Both had the dream of opening their own Bama Pie shop and looked toward Tulsa as a potential market; they began saving for the future.

In the meantime, Paul's brother, Henry, who had reopened the Bama Pie store in Waco, decided to leave the Waco operation and move to Tulsa. While Paul understood his dad's rule that whoever established a territory first had rights to it, he was disappointed that Tulsa would be taken. When Paul and Lilah discovered Henry was simply going to walk away from the Waco business, they decided to take over the Waco operation. Within a year, Waco was profitable and expanding. In January 1937, Paul's father told him his brother would like to return to Waco, which was closer to his wife's family. Paul and his brother agreed to trade operations, and on February 6, 1937, Paul and Lilah, with their new son John, arrived in Tulsa.

The company struggled through 1937, and a decision to buy a large quantity of new "soft wheat flour" from General Mills nearly did the company in. The new flour was developed for pies, but the formula worked best with baked pies, not the fried pies that made up the bulk of Bama's sales. After discovering the problem and restoring lost customer confidence, the company had grown to six drivers and 14 women assisting Lilah in the bakery by the spring of 1938.

The company continued to prosper as the United States entered World War II, and Paul was given a draft classification of 4-F (which exempted him from being called to duty) since the company was a major supplier to the military.

In December 1943, the owner of Mrs. Marshall's Pies offered to sell his company to Paul Marshall. Paul recounted the meeting in his book:

> *"Paul, I just wanted to meet another damned fool named Marshall who was in the pie business."*
>
> *I laughed and decided I like Archie Marshall.*
>
> *We talked shop for a while, then Archie asked. "Would you like to buy my business?"*
>
> *My eyes popped wide open. Who did he think I was, Rockefeller or something? I was almost embarrassed to answer him. But I wanted him to know who he was dealing with from the beginning. I wasn't going to play the high roller. "Archie," I said, "I couldn't buy the spare tire off of your Cadillac."*

> *Archie didn't look at me right then. He just swung his feet back and forth under the table and stared out the window for a few seconds. Then he turned to me and said, "I didn't ask you if you could buy my business. I asked you if you would like to buy my business."*
>
> *Well, it was a fact that I would love to have his business, but I didn't understand what he was talking about. "Sure, Archie, I'd like to have your business, but I don't have the kind of money you're looking for. I can tell you that right now."*
>
> *"I'll work that out," Archie said.*

They worked out a deal, and Bama Pie Company acquired Mrs. Marshall's Pies. One of the major contributions of the acquisition was an understanding of quality. Paul Marshall said, "The most valuable asset we acquired was a 10-cent calendar advertising Karo syrup. On that calendar was a phrase that became our slogan, 'Keep your eye on the key to success, QUALITY.' "

By the end of 1945, Bama Pie was a well-established and profitable operation. But over the next few years, the company was beset with major union organizing problems that left Paul Marshall with a bitter resentment of unions. He fought the union's attempt to unionize his company despite threats on his life and the members of his family. He endured beatings of his drivers, threatening calls at 2 AM, stink bombs that ruined products, smashed pies in the grocery stores, boycotts, and other forms of harassment.

He called national attention to his plight when he had a welder friend create a rotating track with a department store manikin fitted to it to put on the front of his bakery as a "counter-picket." He dressed the manikin in a suit and placed an American flag in its hands. The manikin moved continuously back and forth on a track above the street while the union's live picket walked back and forth below. Since the bakery was on heavily traveled U.S. Route 66, the counter-picket attracted national attention with photos appearing in *Life* and other magazines. One day a group of kids who had gathered to watch Duke (as the manikin was called) started calling the live union picket a "dummy." The union picket picked up a rock and threw it at one of the kids. This brought a barrage of rocks from the kids and he was driven off. That ended the picketing, but not the harassment.

As the union eroded Bama Pie's markets among grocery stores and hotel restaurants, Paul Marshall began to look for new markets immune from union pressures. At a Chicago bakery equipment auction in 1951, he encountered a refrigerated truck carrying frozen pies. In May 1953, he got into the frozen pie business when he contracted to provide pies for five new Howard Johnson's restaurants being constructed on the new Turner Turnpike linking Tulsa with Oklahoma City. Once in the frozen pie business, he quickly saw that the future of Bama Pie was in frozen pies—with frozen pies there were no stale pies to pick up, no more waste.

Bama supplied the Howard Johnson's restaurants until mid-1955, when Marshall was informed by the head office that Howard Johnson's was going to begin making its own pies. Bama Pie then trained its effort on large supermarkets. By the late 1950s, the company was working on a frozen turnover fried pie that could be sold in restaurants. By the beginning of 1960, all the other Bama Pie operations owned and operated by Paul's brothers and sisters had gone out of business, leaving only the Tulsa operation.

Another major turning point for Bama Pie occurred in 1965 when Paul Marshall landed the account of Sandy's restaurant chain (later purchased by Hardee's). In his book, Paul describes the event as follows:

I couldn't wait to get back to Tulsa so I could tell our employees about the orders we'd have coming in.

For 30 miles I nearly broke my arm patting myself on the back for landing the Sandy's account. I thought over what we had said in our meeting and grinned to myself. Then suddenly the sobering truth of our agreement hit home.

During my chat with Mr. Andres (president of Sandy's) he had pointed out all of the Sandy's locations on a wall map. And like some dunce, I was only thinking of the pies we would be selling to all those locations. The little red pins on the map were spread out over the midwest, from Arizona to Ohio. But I only saw inches between pins.

The reality of what those pins meant hadn't registered on me at the time, but now it was hitting me full force. Our trucks would have to drive 100 to 500 miles between stops! There wouldn't be any way my company could survive with shipping costs gobbling our profits.

By the time I was on the outskirts of Bloomington, I had come up with a plan to make it all work. I decided the only way to justify delivering pies to such spread-out markets was to acquire more fast-food customers and establish distribution points. The thought never occurred to me to call off the deal with Sandy's.

It was 11 o'clock when I reached Bloomington. The McDonald's hamburger store had just opened so, after I parked in their lot, I grabbed one of our sample frozen pies out of the dry-ice cooler in the trunk and then walked in and ordered coffee.

"You got any pie?" I asked the manager as he served my coffee.

"No, but I wish we did," he said.

Marshall discovered that individual McDonald's units were not allowed to make menu decisions and was told he needed to go to McDonald's headquarters in Chicago. He decided to make a cold call immediately and headed his car toward Chicago with his remaining frozen pies. Surprisingly, he was able to see the frozen-food buyer and arranged to leave some samples for a dinner of McDonald's executives that evening. He then headed back to Tulsa.

When he called to see how the pies fared, he was told they weren't bad, but were not what McDonald's was looking for. He convinced Al Bernardin, the McDonald's buyer, to allow him to attempt to develop a pie that McDonald's would want.

Bernardin told Marshall, "Well, Paul, we'd be willing to work with you on developing a good pie. But I'm certainly not going to promise anything. And I'll warn you, if you work for 10 years trying to come up with a pie that fits our needs, you still might not get the order."

The next attempt to make a pie that McDonald's would accept brought an unexpected response. The quality wasn't good enough. He was told the crust needed to be lighter and the apples needed to be sliced, rather than chipped.

"We want a quality product, not a cheap one. I promise you that we will pay the price for quality," Bernardin told him. Marshall was surprised that a low-priced, high-volume restaurant chain would be more interested in quality than price, but he was happy for the opportunity to develop the high-quality product McDonald's demanded.

For more than a year, Marshall traveled almost weekly between Tulsa and Chicago until he finally produced a product that McDonald's was satisfied with.

The pies were test-marketed in Joplin and Springfield, Missouri, and soon amounted to nearly 7 percent of each store's sales. Soon, Marshall was called to Chicago to meet with the top executives of McDonald's. To supply McDonald's' more than 600 restaurants on a national basis would require a significant investment for Bama Pie, and Marshall was concerned about coming up with the $250,000 he estimated would be needed.

When Fred Turner, McDonald's president, asked him if he was ready to begin supplying McDonald's on a national basis, Marshall had to tell the truth and admit he probably couldn't.

In his book, he describes the event:

> *"How much money would you need to get ready to supply McDonald's?" Turner asked.*
>
> *I was glad I had done some figuring on that question already. "It would cost us $250,000 to build a line that would produce 20,000 pies an hour."*
>
> *"Can you get that kind of money?" he asked, his eyes never wavering from mine.*
>
> *Mr. Turner was questioning me like a judge who wanted to know if I was guilty or not—there was no discussion called for.*
>
> *"I don't know," I said, feeling weak in the pit of my stomach. I figured Mr. Turner was wondering why we Oklahoma hicks were wasting his time. I had hoped our meeting would be real casual, just friends sitting down to talk over what would be needed to make McDonald's pies. I wasn't prepared for the rapid-fire questions and piercing eyes of Mr. Turner.*
>
> *"How long have you been doing business at your bank?" Mr. Turner asked.*
>
> *"Probably 25 years or so," I replied, hoping he wasn't going to ask our credit limit.*
>
> *"Do you owe them anything?"*
>
> *"Not much. Our mortgage is paid down quite a bit."*
>
> *"Fine," he said. "I'll send a couple of men down to Tulsa to talk with your banker and see if we can make this pie business work."*

> *"Thank you, sir."*
>
> *"What kind of contract would you like?" Mr. Turner asked.*
>
> *"If we can't give you the quality and service you need, Mr. Turner, a contract won't help either of us. But if we can, we won't need one."*
>
> *"I like your way of thinking, Paul," Mr. Turner said. He reached out and shook my hand, then Johnny's hand and marched out the door.*

A couple of days later, two McDonald's executives visited Marshall's bank, and the next day one of the bank's officers called and said, "Paul, I understand you could use a quarter of a million dollars?"

Thus began a long-term relationship with McDonald's that allowed Bama Pie to grow along with McDonald's as one of its key suppliers. During the 1970s and 1980s, Paul and Lilah traveled worldwide with McDonald's officials as consultants to assist local bakers in supplying fruit pies for McDonald's' far-flung global enterprise. In 1987, Bama Pie received an award for being a 20-year vendor to McDonald's.

Paula Marshall-Chapman

Paula Marshall-Chapman succeeded her father in 1985 as chief executive officer of the company and immediately made quality her top priority. "To be honest, we almost lost the account in the mid-80s because we had let our quality fall a bit as we struggled to keep up with our growth," Marshall-Chapman said. She said her father was ready to retire and was almost becoming a problem. "Someone would call from McDonald's about a problem, and he might tell them just what they could do with it. He really didn't relate to the younger technical staff that McDonald's was sending around. He might tell one of them that they didn't know anything about the pie business and that he was 'buddies with Ray Kroc and had been making pies since before they were in diapers.'

"When I took over, I spent a lot of time just listening," she said.

Taking over the company was not an automatic thing for Marshall-Chapman—she had to earn her way to the top. Paula first joined the company in 1970; she recalled: "My ideas of going off to college were sidetracked when I was a senior in high school.

I got pregnant. I first went to work in the thrift stores (Bama Pie's retail operation for picked up and damaged products) and began learning about the business. I learned how to meet and talk to customers, how to display merchandise, how I could increase sales by providing samples, and I also learned how much poor quality costs. We were selling pies for a nickel in the thrift store that could be sold for 50 cents if the product had not been damaged."

After a few years, Paula moved to the central office and learned how to manage the company's fleet of 35 trailer trucks. (The company in 1992 operated more than 90 trucks through Bama Pie Trucking, a subsidiary.) She said that job provided a learning experience in the areas of government regulation, fuel costs, and record keeping and generally broadened her view of the company.

In the mid-1970s, Bama decided to computerize, and Paula was selected to make the purchase. As a result, she was the person trained to run the new system, and in that capacity she learned the value of training people and helping people solve problems. Since she also had to set up the company's systems on the computer, she learned about costs, payables, and invoicing, and again expanded her knowledge about the company. "In my position, I got to be known as Bama's problem solver," she recalled.

Her father noticed her management talents but had been grooming her older brother, Johnny, to take over the company. Paula remembered, "Dad began to say things to me like: 'You really like this business, don't you?' 'Why don't you want to do more?' 'Women probably don't need to be in a CEO role.' Like most kids, when a parent says you can't do something, that's what you decide you want to do just to show them they are wrong."

Paula began her college education during this time, attending Tulsa Junior College and working full time. In 1982, her older brother had a serious illness and her other brother "got into a fight" with her father, so her father came to her and said, "You're going to have to be the one, or we're going to have to sell the company."

For the next three years, she traveled with her father everywhere. She said when her father first presented her as the future CEO to some of the McDonald's officials, they laughed. "During that time I learned a lot," she says. Some of the best advice her father gave her included: "Always have a good work ethic. Be committed to what you are doing. Commitment is what gets through hard times and there will always be hard times."

In 1985, Paul Marshall handed over the reins of the company to Paula and retired to Naples, Florida. According to other Bama executives, when he left, he left. He let her run the company and stayed out of the way. The company, which had been incorporated, was reorganized as a partnership in 1985 to allow Paula's parents to cash out their equity. Paula then became a general partner.

Between 1985 and 1992, Paula reshaped the company. She recruited a young, professional executive staff. She also completed a bachelor's degree through Oklahoma City University's Competency Based Degree Program and was recognized as a distinguished alumna of that program in 1989.

Employees described Paula as a "unique chief executive." One marketing representative who had previously worked for Pizza Hut in the PepsiCo organization was asked to compare what it was like at Pizza Hut and Bama. He said:

> At PepsiCo, everything was numbers driven. You either made the numbers, or you were gone. You didn't feel like you were treated as a person. Big companies are like that. You worked for an organization. Here you work for a human being who treats you as a human being. Paula is more concerned about long term. She doesn't look for someone to blame when a problem arises, she only wants to look for what caused the problem and find a way to fix the problem. I've never seen her blame anyone for anything.

Management in 1992

Marshall-Chapman reshaped the management team significantly after she took control of the company and assembled a highly professional staff with an average age under 40.

John Davsco, 45, was vice president of operations. He joined Bama Pie in 1989 after 19 years of high-level operations management with Pillsbury. A graduate of St. Louis University in 1968, he also had a brief career as a major league baseball pitcher with the St. Louis Cardinals and Cincinnati Reds.

William L. Chew, 35, vice president of finance, joined the firm in 1987 after two years as controller

Exhibit 4

Bama Pie, Ltd., Corporate Organization as of September 1990

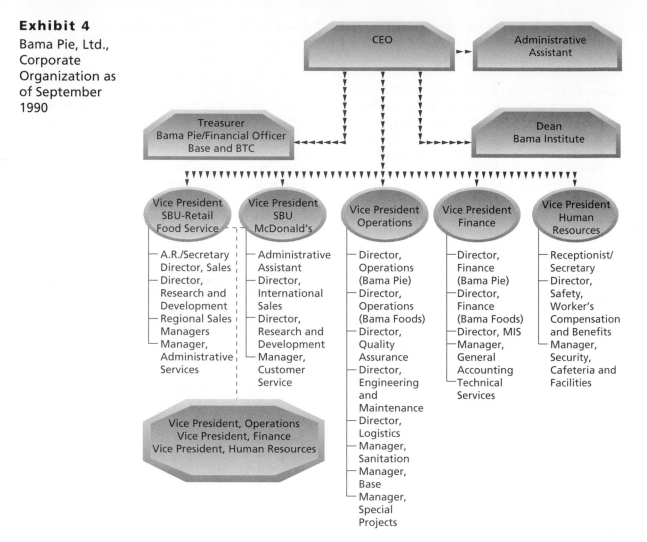

of a real estate management and development company and seven years with Price Waterhouse in Chicago. He was a 1978 graduate of the University of Illinois and a certified public accountant.

Kay White, 46, vice president of human resources, joined Bama Pie in 1976 as a line worker in production. She was promoted to supervisor and then plant manager and served 2½ years as operations director.

Brenda Rice, 31, vice president for quality assurance systems, joined the company in 1989. She previously was employed in McDonald's' R & D Division and worked with Bama Pie in developing the biscuit for McDonald's. She also worked as product development technologist with Magic Pantry Foods (Canada). She received an associate degree in food science from Humber College, Toronto, Canada, in 1981.

With more than 70 percent of the company's business coming from McDonald's, Bama had never developed a fully functioning marketing department. During 1991, the company began establishing a marketing strategy and hired Lynn Dickson, previously associated with Pizza Hut, to begin developing a professional marketing function within the company. Exhibit 4 presents an organization chart for the company.

Products

The products Bama Pie produced included 3-ounce pies and 3-inch biscuits for McDonald's, bread sticks for Pizza Hut, 9-inch graham cracker pie shells, 3-inch and 9-inch pecan pies, and soft cookies.

Exhibit 5

Bama Pie's Use of Ingredients in Its Products, 1984 versus 1991

Description	1984 Pounds (in Millions)	1991 Pounds (in Millions)
Frozen apples	3.5	9.2
Frozen cherries	3.0	1.6
Flour	2.0	11.0
Shelled pecans	2.0	0.3
Shortening	1.5	4.2
Sugar	1.0	2.6
Shelled eggs	0.9	0.4

NOTE: Reduction in cherries is because the cherry pie is now optional at McDonald's restaurants. In 1984, it was a required menu item. Reduction in pecans and eggs is due to reduced number of pecan pies being sold, an outcome attributed to increased weight and health concerns.

The 3-ounce pies supplied to McDonald's were provided frozen as either ready to fry or bake, with the bulk of the volume having apple or cherry fillings. The company could also produce pies with lemon, peach, and apricot fillings. The original pies supplied to McDonald's were fried turnovers. The baked product was an optional choice in the restaurants in the McDonald's organization and had been increasing in popularity.

The 3-inch biscuit was processed in the new 135,000-square-foot facility in Tulsa and was pre-baked to a ready-to-bake stage, frozen, and then baked off in the individual restaurant. The product took several years to develop, with McDonald's, Bama Pie, and Quaker Oats (the other 50 percent supplier) jointly working on the project. Currently, Bama supplied operations west of the Mississippi, and Quaker supplied restaurants east of the Mississippi. During the development of the product, the group experimented with more than 200 recipes.

According to Marshall-Chapman, the reason McDonald's wanted a ready-to-bake product was to ensure a consistent product at all its units. When biscuits first began appearing in restaurants, they were made from mixes. "Our customer has 8,000 domestic restaurants and, thus 8,000 biscuit bakers. That means a lot of variation is possible," Marshall-Chapman said.

The long development time resulted from McDonald's' insistence that the frozen product be equal in quality to fresh-baked, made-from-scratch products. To provide the product, a carefully controlled process was developed. The biscuits were essentially 90 percent baked, frozen, and then shipped to distribution centers for delivery to the restaurants. The product, packaged in a baking bag, was then finished off in convection ovens at the local restaurant to give that "just baked" appearance, taste, and texture.

The bread sticks were produced in the 11th Street plant of Bama Pie and were a frozen dough product, made under a confidential agreement with Pizza Hut with the recipe kept secret. The dough was processed, rolled to a specific thickness, and shipped frozen in flat pieces about 9 inches by 12 inches. The dough was thawed and the sticks cut at the restaurant before baking.

The 3-inch and 9-inch pecan pies were a mainstay of Bama Pie and had been produced for almost the entire 65 years of operation. The recipe was virtually unchanged from the original developed by Marshall-Chapman's grandmother. The pies were fully baked, packaged in single wraps, and then boxed in a variety of quantities. Customers included Wal-Mart and Sam's Wholesale Clubs.

The 9-inch graham cracker shells were produced for retail sale and were also provided to TCBY and Braum's. The shells came in a metal pie pan ready to be filled with a customer's own filling. The shells were often used for cheesecake and ice box pies or could be filled with ice cream or yogurt to provide an ice cream pie product.

The cookies were soft products that competed directly with the large soft cookies produced under the Grandma's label by Frito-Lay, a PepsiCo subsidiary. The cookies were packaged individually and boxed for retail sale. See Exhibit 5 for a comparison of the ingredients used in these products.

Operations

McDonald's Pies

The 3-ounce pies for McDonald's were processed in the 11th Street plant. Ingredients were mixed in two different areas. The dough was prepared in large mixers that fed a moving conveyor system that rolled the dough out on two separate belts approximately 24 inches wide. The filling was prepared in large, heated mixing bowls with real fruit added. This mixture was pumped through seven separate hoses that streamed filling on the bottom conveyor of dough. The top layer was then placed on top of the filling, and the pies were then cut and sealed in a two-step operation. The pies were sent to a spiral freezer where they were frozen. The process was basically the same whether the pie was a fried product or a baked product. The dough mixture was different for each product, and the baked product had slits cut in the top of each pie.

After freezing, the pies were processed slightly differently. The fried product was dipped in a liquid that immediately froze to the pie and caused the finished pie to have a bubbly, flaky texture. The pies were then hand-packed 12 to a tray, with six trays then boxed in an automated operation. Four boxes were packaged with shrink-wrap before moving into the storage freezer. The baked pies were processed similarly, but instead of being dipped when exiting the freezer, they were sprayed with water and dusted with cinnamon before packaging.

Each hour, samples were taken from the production process to the test kitchen where the same ovens and fryers used by McDonald's were installed. The product was finished off and tested to ensure specifications were being met. Each line was capable of producing 40,000 pies per hour, and more than 1 million pies were produced daily at the plant.

McDonald's Biscuits

The McDonald's biscuit was produced in a new facility that *Baking & Snack* magazine called "world class."[2] The facility contained two parallel production lines that included 250-foot ovens. The dough

[2]Laurie Gorton, "World Class: Bama Creates a Flexible Plant Dedicated to Making Ready-to-Bake Biscuits," *Baking & Snack,* November 1991.

was mixed and laid down on a flour-dusted conveyor belt that transferred the dough through a series of rollers until it was a 50-inch-wide sheet. The dough was then cut and passed through a metal detector before dropping into the baking pans. The biscuit pans passed three wide through the oven where modular construction and nine heating zones transformed the dough into a biscuit ready for freezing in about 15 minutes. The highly automated line removed the pans, cleaned them, re-oiled them, and returned them for reuse. The biscuits were then cartoned and put through a spiral freezer after cooling to 90 degrees. After freezing, the biscuits were wrapped and passed through another metal detector before being boxed for shipment and moved into the storage freezer.

Graham Shells

The graham shells were produced on a highly automated line that was installed in 1991 and put into operation in early 1992. The graham meal was mixed and fed into a hopper that dumped an exact measurement of meal into an aluminum pie pan and was then automatically pressed and formed. The shell moved through a process where the clear plastic cover was pressed into place and sealed to the pan. Next, the shells were automatically stacked and boxed for shipment.

Pizza Hut Bread Sticks

Using the secret recipe from Pizza Hut, the dough was mixed and fed onto a conveyor belt into a series of rollers that reduced the sheet of dough to the proper thickness and width. The dough was then run through a cutter that produced sheets of dough approximately 9 inches by 12 inches. These sheets were then frozen in a spiral freezer before packaging and boxing. The bread stick line was located in the 11th Street plant.

Pecan Pies

The 3-inch and 9-inch pecan pies were also produced in the 11th Street plant. The dough was prepared and rolled and fed onto a conveyor line where it was cut and dropped into the aluminum pie shell. The dough was then automatically formed inside the shell. The pies continued on and were filled with pecans and pie filling before entering an oven approximately 200 feet long. Once the pies were baked, they were conveyed back to packaging by passing through a cooling tunnel where they went through automated packaging machines and were hand-packed and boxed.

Cookies

The soft-batch cookies were processed in much the same manner as the pecan pies. The batter was measured and dropped onto a conveyor belt that took the cookies through the oven and returned them through a cooling tunnel for packaging.

The McDonald's Relationship

The relationship with McDonald's was unusual in that Bama had been the company's principal supplier of pies for 24 years and had never had a contract. Moreover, Bama did not sell directly to McDonald's. McDonald's selected and approved suppliers, but the actual sales were made to independently owned distribution centers that supplied the McDonald's restaurants around the country.

The company did not have a contract for the biscuit product either. "When a couple of banks heard we wanted to borrow $40 million to build a biscuit plant and didn't have a contract to even buy one biscuit, they ran away," Marshall-Chapman said. McDonald's put the company in touch with Texas Commerce Bank in Houston, and Bama found a bank that was actively seeking to develop a business relationship with McDonald's. In fact, the bank had formed a special group of McDonald's specialists. The bank understood that McDonald's developed "partnership arrangements" with suppliers and that contracts were not a part of the business. "They [both the bank and McDonald's] were eager to help, and we completed the deal at extremely favorable rates," Marshall-Chapman said.

Commitment to Quality and Staying Private

Favorable lending rates were extremely important to Bama Pie, since the company and Marshall-Chapman were committed to remaining private. Marshall-Chapman believed going public would ruin the company: "Public companies have to run the business for

Wall Street. They have to think quarterly. I want to run our business for my customers and my employees. I want to concentrate on developing the business, not worrying about what is happening to my stock price."

Decisions were made based on what the management team thought was best. A commitment to quality was evident in everything the company did. Marshall-Chapman believed that not having to answer to stockholders allowed the company to focus on quality; she indicated the company was ahead of the people who were teaching total quality management: "They [the Quality College and others] are now calling us and asking us what we've done new and what we're currently working on."

Bama insisted on quality from its suppliers. Suppliers were expected to ship random samples of product runs due for Bama in advance so they could be pretested. "We want to know if there is a problem before the shipment leaves their plant," Marshall-Chapman said. Vendors were willing to cooperate because it was much less expensive to provide the samples and get preapproval for shipment than to risk having a whole order rejected after shipment and returned.

The company had instilled a total quality management discipline in its approximately 600 employees through extensive training and educational programs offered through the in-house Bama Institute. Getting employees involved in all aspects of quality permeated everything, including internal record keeping. Within a year's time, inventory adjustments based on physical counts had dropped from between $50,000 and $70,000 per month to less than $3,000 per month and was still improving. "One month we'd have a negative adjustment, the next a positive adjustment," William Chew, vice president of finance said. At a time when the company was attempting to refine its cost system and implement standard costs under an activity-based cost system, the inventory problem was major. Chew commented, "Even our fork truck operators have gotten involved in helping solve the inventory adjustments problem."

To support the quality program and refine data for decision making, the company purchased a new computer system using Prism software on an IBM AS/400 mainframe. The conversion was implemented within one year. "We were able to do it because Paula released people from some of their regular jobs and put them on the project," Chew said. According to the consultants working with Bama, no company had ever been able to accomplish such a conversion in such a short period. The result was a system with world-class manufacturing software that supported an activity-based standard cost accounting system and electronic data interchange transactions.

Drug Policies

Bama was a "drug-free" workplace; all applicants for employment were screened for drugs. According to company officials, approximately one in five applicants tested positive. In addition, all employees (including Paula) had been drug tested and random drug testing was administered within the company. The random sampling for drug tests was determined by a computer program. Urine samples were taken and tested in a lab. A positive result was grounds for immediate dismissal.

According to Marshall-Chapman, the company's drug policy was mainly aimed at reducing accidents. Since the program had been implemented, accidents had declined significantly. Any employee involved in an accident at work was automatically drug tested.

BEBOPP

In 1990, Bama instituted the Bama Employees' Bonus on Profit Plan (BEBOPP) to provide bonus incentives to all employees in the company. The plan was based on an annual return on sales objective that was established by Marshall-Chapman. The goal was expressed as a percentage, and for each 0.5 percent above the target all employees shared in a bonus pool. The pool began at 2 percent of payroll and increased for each 0.5 percent above the target. For example, if Bama's return on sales topped the goal by 2 percent, the bonus pool would equal 3.5 percent of payroll. Even though the program was based on annual sales, quarterly payments were made to employees. All eligible employees received equal amounts from the pool.

Future Prospects

The company was attempting to decrease its reliance on McDonald's. The biscuit plant, which was also capable of producing cookies and other bread-type products, had underutilized capacity plus room for expansion. The main plant also had open capacity.

Opportunities for new business were coming in faster than the company could deal with them. John Davsko, vice president of operations, said, "We have people calling us all the time asking if we are interested in developing a product for them. Our reputation is bringing business. We had one potential customer referred to us by one of our suppliers."

However, there were problems with expansion. Management believed any expansion had to come mainly from new product development. Bama believed it could not seek additional customers for its fast-food pie product without putting its McDonald's account at risk. Likewise, it would be unwise to seek another customer for biscuits or bread sticks. According to Marshall-Chapman, about the only negative thing Paul Marshall had said regarding how Paula had handled the business since he left is, "He thinks we're expanding too fast, and he doesn't like us borrowing money."

BGH–Motorola: Radius Connects Business Relationships

Introduction

Laura Bidone, the marketing manager of Radius, had barely settled into her Buenos Aires office when she began to recount the Spanish proverb, "Tomorrow is often the busiest day of the week." Tomorrow promised to be busy. In October 1994, Bidone was hired to develop and implement a dealer relationship program for Radius, the newly formed communications division of Argentina's energy and technology giant, BGH.

It had been just eight months prior to her appointment as marketing manager that Radius's parent company, BGH, had negotiated an exclusive distribution contract with U.S.-based Motorola for the sales and marketing of two-way commercial radio systems in Argentina. The exclusive distribution agreement was unprecedented: Motorola had no exclusive contracts anywhere else in the world. In exchange for territorial exclusivity, BGH agreed to attain market share, dealer development, and profitability benchmarks that were established at the outset of the distribution agreement.

BGH is a traditional Argentine firm, having been in the local market since 1910. BGH originally entered the market as a household appliance producer, and it expanded into the communications industry in 1948. BGH products have always been imported or licensed for local production from multinational firms such as Motorola, Moulinex, Feders, General Electric, and Fujitsu. When Bidone took office, BGH had over 700 employees and its turnover was near $150 million. BGH is organized into five divisions (see Exhibit 1).

The culmination of the agreement between BGH and Motorola would be the May 1995 launch of a new dealer network plan, dubbed the "MSI Plan" (Motorola Shared Investment Plan) for Radius's dealers in Argentina.

Motorola demonstrated its commitment to BGH's marketing efforts by opening a local office in Buenos Aires. Motorola appointed Rodrigo Hebard, an experienced international marketing manager, as

the "point man" in the Buenos Aires office. As the point man, Hebard focused solely on Motorola's relationship with BGH, providing support and training to Radius's dealership network. Bidone was responsible for working with Hebard to organize a successful dealership network that would take full advantage of the two-way commercial radio market in Argentina. Bidone was excited about the working partnership with Hebard, but she was also anxious. Was Hebard aware of the state of the existing dealer relationships?

Bidone's uneasiness started to build. She knew that dealers currently viewed BGH–Motorola (the ascendant to Radius) as their main competitor, and they had little trust in or commitment to BGH–Motorola as their supplier. Bidone was equally concerned about the economic turbulence that pervaded the Argentine marketplace. She sat back in her leather executive chair and mulled over the impending launch of the MSI Plan.

Market Environment

Will the Economic Miracle Sizzle or Fizzle?

When Bidone was hired in October 1994, Argentina's economy was soaring, and top economists were predicting over 5 percent annual growth for 1995. Bidone's appointment as marketing manager coincided with the signing of the Bilateral Investment Treaty between Argentina and the U.S., triggering a surge in portfolio investment, direct investment and import financing. The economic turnaround was considered nothing less than miraculous.

When President Carlos Saul Menem took office, the Argentine economy was in total disarray. High inflation, a bloated public sector, and a stifling tax regime crippled its fiscal structure. Buenos Aires had financed deficits by heavy borrowing from the nation's financial system, and Argentina had been forced to suspend payments to international creditors. However, a series of fiscal and trade liberalization reforms restored fiscal confidence. Since Menem opened the historically closed Argentine market in 1991, gross domestic product growth climbed to nearly 25 percent. Inflation was slashed from 3,000 percent to just 8 percent between 1989 and 1993.

The economic turnaround championed by Menem and his economy minister, Domingo Cavallo, was impressive. Menem's trade liberalization caught the attention of the industrialized world. Between 1990 and

This case was prepared by Jacqueline Pels (University of Toronto) and Lou Pelton (University of North Texas) for the purposes of class discussion only, and is not intended to illustrate effective or ineffective management practices.

Exhibit 1
BGH
Organizational
Design

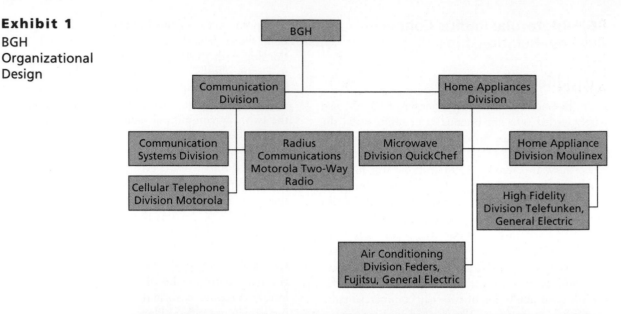

Exhibit 2
Argentine
Economic Capsule
(1989–95)
(Figures in
centavos)

	1989–91	1992–94	1995
Inflation rate (%)	2,218%	9.6%	1.6%
Growth rate (%)	0.7%	7.2%	–4.4%
Imports (000)	16,555	53,246	19,696
average	55,518	17,748	
Exports (000)	33,910	41,839	20,893
average	11,303	13,730	

SOURCE: Indec & Ministry of Economy, Argentina.

1993, U.S. investment in Argentina alone doubled, and goods trade with the U.S. reached $6 billion. U.S. companies, together with leading firms in Canada, Chile, Europe, and Japan, invested nearly $16 billion in the Argentine economy, largely in the high technology, energy and capital markets. As Exhibit 2 illustrates, there was good reason for Bidone to feel confident about the Argentine economy when she embarked on her new position in 1994.

However, as May 1995 approached, Bidone's confidence began to wane. Argentina's economic fire began to fizzle as a result of the Mexican peso crisis. The spillover from the Mexican peso devaluation—known as the "tequila effect"—hung over the decision environment for Radius. In fact, one leading Latin American economist declared Argentina "in rough shape" in early 1995. A surge in unemployment coupled with weak domestic demand signaled

a recession. Bidone wondered whether the timing was right for launching the MSI Plan.

Early polls suggested that Menem would be reelected for a second term of four years, and that popular support for Menem's economic policies would continue. Despite the stagnant economy in early 1995, leading economists remained confident about the future of Argentina. Despite recessionary indicators, economic forecasters expected five percent growth annually through 1998. Bidone read the economic forecasts with guarded optimism.

Motorola's Role in the Telecommunications Industry

By comparison to neighboring Brazil, Argentina was a small market for telecommunications equipment. Nevertheless, Bidone recognized that the market in

Exhibit 3
Two-Way
Commercial
Radio Competitor
Analysis

	BGH–Motorola	Kenwood	Yaesu
Mobile Radio	flexible frequencies	two frequencies	two frequencies
	variable power	two powers	programmable
	8/16 channels	16 channels	12/24 channels
	PL/DPL, TT	scan, DTSS	LED, T-out-T
	priority scan	CNT rating	priority scan
	rapid call	guarantee: 1 year	MIL-STD rating
	MIL-STD	price range: $590/650	guarantee: six months
	guarantee: two years		price: $550
	price range: $800/900		
Portable Radio	variable power	5 W power	variable power
	two/six channels	32/160 channels	six channels
	PC programmable	PC programmable	PC programmable
	touch code, PL/DPL	price: $480	MIL-STD rating
	quick call, MIL-STD		price: $400
	price: $700		

Argentina was projected to top $1.8 billion in 1995 and approach the $2.5 billion mark within 10 years. The telecommunications industry was the fastest growing sector in Argentina's information technology industry, outpacing oil and gas field machinery, computers and peripherals, and food processing equipment. The presence of many original equipment manufacturers (OEMs) such as Motorola, GTE, and AT&T was evidence that the Argentine telecommunications industry was coming of age. U.S. exports of telecommunications equipment accounted for about 18% of the total imports in the Argentine telecommunications equipment industry, and Motorola was a major supplier of the $450 million in equipment. Bidone was excited about being a part of a growth industry, and she carefully studied the market (see Exhibit 3).

At the same time, Bidone witnessed the uneven regulatory practices that had dampened market entry enthusiasm by leading U.S. firms in the early 1990s. When ENTEL, Argentina's state-owned telecommunications operator, was privatized in 1990, telecommunications firms in France, Italy, and Spain were granted five-year monopolies for basic service. ENTEL was divided into two regional providers: Telecom (North) owned by France Telecom and Italy's STET, and Telefonica (South) owned by Telefonica de Espana. The pioneering advantage of these European firms weighed heavily on Bidone's mind. Bidone was aware that Telecom and Telefonica—the two monopolies—were the key buyers of most

telephone equipment. She was concerned that these monopolies might extend their market control to other areas of telecommunications services, such as cellular and two-way radio communications.

So she was encouraged by the consortium led by GTE and AT&T, who were granted private regional cellular rights in Argentina in 1994, the first major competition to the European-owned network operators. Motorola was a supplier to these firms, and she believed that Radius would ultimately benefit from Motorola's relationship with them. But the dominance of GTE and AT&T in the cellular network industry also posed a competitive threat to Motorola, who was vying for the spectrum allocation for personal communications services (PCS). If Motorola was granted PCS development rights in Argentina, the Motorola trade name would be strengthened. Bidone believed that the brand equity of Motorola was paramount to the launch of the MSI program.

The Two-Way Commercial Radio Market

The mass marketing of cellular technology, coupled with the impending introduction of PCS in Argentina, seemed to position two-way radio as a dinosaur in the communications industry. Just when all indications pointed to the demise of two-way radio, there was a tremendous resurgence in North America and Europe for two-way communications equipment. Bidone thumbed through several trade journals. The journals reported an unexpected increase in the demand for two-way commercial radios in the U.S., Europe, and (most important) Latin America.

Why use two-way radios in an era of more sophisticated wireless communications? Two-way radios were created for commercial use. They provided instant communications using designated frequencies reserved for business use. Two-way radio communications were crisp and highly intelligible, and often far superior to public frequencies via cellular networks. Bidone was optimistic about the demand for two-way radio. In Argentina, it was increasingly being used as a tool to manage customer satisfaction:

- In retailing, service representatives used two-way radio communications to get customers instant answers or merchandise on the spot.

- Rapid price checks were possible by linking personnel in stores, offices, and warehouses.

- Stock rooms communicated instantly with sales representatives on the floor or in the field.

- Employees queried information to improve the efficiency and effectiveness of order fulfillment.

- Security and safety concerns were alerted immediately to the appropriate authorities.

A new generation of two-way commercial radio technology using iDEN (Integrated Dispatch Enhanced Network) made it possible to fold services such as voice dispatch, full duplex telephone interconnect and text messaging into a single network. In Europe, the TETRA system was developed to achieve the same type of integrated communications technology through two-way radio communications.

Bidone was particularly interested in an article about Motorola's development of a high-tech two-way radio network that promised to keep nearly 70,000 people connected during the Centennial Games in Atlanta, Georgia. The high-profile involvement of Motorola in the Olympics would certainly strengthen Radius's positioning in the marketplace.

Bidone recalled the fervor over two-way commercial radio at the Latin American Cellular Association's "Wireless '93 America" conference. Motorola's Visar two-way unit was the "gold standard" introduced at the conference, and Bidone remembered how well the Visar was reviewed by industry analysts.

Motorola was clearly viewed as the technology leader in two-way commercial radio. It had a rich history in two-way radio development, having been the supplier of two-way radios during World War II. The radios had come a long way since British Prime Minister Winston Churchill used the portable, 35-pound version in the battlefields. The latest generation of radios was lighter, sleeker, and extremely powerful.

The Competitive Environment

In Argentina, the two-way communications market was partitioned into amateur radio users and commercial users. The lucrative segment of the market was clearly the commercial users. The commercial user market was segmented into trunking (or big systems); BLU (long-distance radios); and conventional. The conventional segment consisted of portable two-way radios (like those used in retail stores) and mobile radios.

Despite its leadership in two-way radio technology, Motorola had some formidable competition: most notably, Yaesu and Kenwood. Until 1987, Motorola was the only brand of two-way commercial radios in the Argentine market, and BGH was the sole importer of the Motorola two-way radios.

In 1980, BGH controlled two firms in the communications industry: SICOM and Radio Mensaje. SICOM concentrated on the sales and service of complex communication systems, trunking, microwave communications and rural communication infrastructure development. SICOM sold two-way commercial radios to various public and private institutions, and it was the chief supplier of two-way radio communications to the Argentine police. Radio Mensaje primarily offered paging services.

In 1987, some importers brought Japanese-produced Yaesu amateur radios into the Argentine marketplace. Yaesu initially targeted the amateur radio user as a market entry strategy, offering a much less expensive two-way radio that satisfied local market standards. Yaesu positioned itself as a low-price leader, and it was successful enough to extend its market reach to the commercial user segment two years later. The Yaesu radio immediately captured market share from BGH–Motorola, carving out a prominent niche in the low-end segment. However, the Yaesu equipment was perceived as complex, and primarily for experienced users. Yaesu had no customer service representatives in Argentina, and it distributed primarily through import agencies.

The main Motorola competitor was Kenwood. Kenwood was considered a high-quality, two-way commercial radio. It was positioned in the premium price segment. Kenwood slowly won the premium segment of the commercial market, and BGH–Motorola was perceived as the "middle market" provider. Kenwood had customer service representatives in Argentina, but it also had a network of independent importers that dictated their own pricing policies.

BGH–Motorola's two-way radio was designed exclusively for the commercial market. It was targeted to workers who had little experience using two-way radio communications. The design was very user-friendly, and it simplified the communications process. Although Kenwood eroded BGH–Motorola's market share in the premium segment, BGH–Motorola was able to retain the large institutional users in the police and military because the Motorola radios were the only market offering that met military standards.

BGH was the local representative for Motorola's line of two-way commercial radios until 1994, when Motorola opened a local office to fortify its dealer support.

Motorola's Radius: A New Line for BGH

By 1990, competition intensified in the two-way commercial radio market, so Motorola launched Radius, a new generation of two-way portable and mobile radios. BGH opted to incorporate the new line in its existing line of Motorola two-way commercial radios. The Radius line was purported to be the best in the world, advancing two-way radio communications technology to an unprecedented level. The Radius offered several exclusive features, ranging from rapid call to touch codes. BGH wanted to recover much of the market share that eroded since Kenwood's introduction into the Argentine marketplace, and the Radius line seemed to offer an opportunity to recapture many premium segment users. BGH had a great deal of confidence in the Radius line, and it opted to spin Radius off as a separate business unit.

Jorge Rodriguez was appointed as sales manager of Radius. His first decision was to hire two direct sales representatives who would be charged with servicing current accounts and developing new accounts in the end-user market. The sales representatives, Ballesteros and Amoroso, were given a guaranteed salary for three months after which their compensation plan was fully incentive-based. Territories were assigned by dividing postal codes between them. After six months, Ballesteros and Amoroso recorded only one sale.

Amoroso justified the poor sales performance to Rodriguez. "Jorge, prospective end-users may take a long time to decide on the two-way radio system that best meets their needs. But once they make a decision, they want the radio immediately." Rodriguez knew that the actual order fulfillment time was between 90 and 120 days. Ballesteros also indicated the need for service and installation support for customers. Radius offered the apparatus with no technical assistance. These service gaps made it difficult to sell the Radius line to prospective customers. It was equally difficult selling the Radius line to current two-way commercial radio users because the price was nearly twice as much as the competition's.

Yet Rodriguez enjoyed some success selling equipment to some SICOM dealers that were already buying other communications equipment from BGH. It did not take long for Amoroso to recognize the sales potential for Radius, and he asked to join Rodriguez in identifying new dealers in the provinces. Amoroso's first attempt at selling to dealers was a success: He sold 30 radios and established one new dealer. Amoroso abandoned the end-user market and concentrated solely on developing new dealers. Ballesteros soon followed suit. In the absence of Radius sales support, SICOM serviced current end users of all two-way radio communications.

By 1992, Radius started to blossom. Sales climbed from 30 units to 300 units per month, and another sales representative was added to help develop a dealer network. BGH–Motorola was the market leader in the gas and oil extraction, government and public enforcement segments of the two-way radio market. Other segments like private security companies, taxis, and truck drivers did not perceive the benefit of the premium-priced Radius line. BGH reacted to the market growth of Radius in several ways:

• BGH began to build inventories of Radius products to serve dealers better. The inventory investment afforded BGH better pricing from

Exhibit 4
Radius Objectives

Long-Term Objectives	1.	Achieve a national distribution system
	2.	Obtain a 45% market share
	3.	Add a service dimension to the present market offerings
	4.	Increase the product mix offered in Argentina
Short-Term Objectives	1.	Try to make dealers sign exclusive distribution contracts
	2.	Improve the administrative procedures and control systems
	3.	Improve delivery times
	4.	Develop pre/post sales support to increase customer satisfaction
	5.	Design a sales and marketing training program for BGH's staff

Motorola, and it helped decrease the selling price gap between Radius and the competition.

- An administrative assistant was hired to provide office and sales support for Rodriguez and the three sales representatives. The assistant also helped process sales and purchase orders to satisfy dealers' product needs.

- Software was developed and implemented to improve the efficiency of sales and inventory management.

Rodriguez organized two annual dealer seminars to introduce new Radius products and offer marketing advice to motivate dealers' selling efforts. Yet there was no dealer database maintained by Radius.

Radius Goes "Over & Out"

By 1994, Radius's unit sales reached 450 units per month, and Radius became a very small business unit within BGH. Consequently, BGH invested few resources in Radius. BGH Chief Executive Officer Alberto Hojman felt that there was great potential for Radius if sound management practices could be employed. He recruited Juan Waehener, a senior marketing executive from Siemens Spain, to become general manager of the BGH Communications Division. Waehener became solely responsible for Radius. Upon taking office, Waehener invited Rodriguez to leave the company and promoted Amoroso to manage dealer sales. Three regional managers were appointed in the north, south, and central regions of Argentina. They were responsible for managing dealers in their respective territories. Waehener immediately recognized that his personnel lacked the professionalism necessary to manage dealer relationships, so he began distributing articles and books on

professional selling, and he sent his personnel to seminars and professional education courses. He conducted regular meetings to monitor his personnel's professional development. Collectively, they adopted several long-term and short-term objectives for the Radius group (see Exhibit 4).

In August 1994, Waehener confronted the problem of competitors' undercutting Radius pricing, and he introduced the *Cambio y Fuera* (Over & Out) promotion. The Over & Out promotion was designed to motivate nontraditional end-users to try the Radius radios by eliminating the price differential between Radius and its premium-line competitors. The one-month promotion allowed end-users to trade in their old two-way radios to any dealer for brand new Radius units at a low cost of only $400—about the same price as the leading competition—up to a total of 1,000 units. It took BGH three months to reach the 1,000-unit benchmark, and the Over & Out promotion was considered a failure.

Waehener evaluated the failure of Over & Out, and concluded that there were three major problems with the promotion. First, Radius had not inventoried sufficient units, so, order fulfillment took nearly 60 days. If an end-user traded in its old two-way radio, it would be without any two-way communications for nearly two months. Another problem was the failure to communicate the Over & Out program with dealers before launching the promotion. Dealers saw little value in the promotion. Consequently, the relationship between Radius and its dealers sunk to an all-time low. Instead of supporting Over & Out, the dealers capitalized on the service revenues of repairing the old radios.

The fundamental problem was that pricing was not the source of the deteriorating relationship between Radius and its dealers. The dealer relationship itself was the problem. Waehener learned that the dealers' commitment to BGH–Motorola and Radius had truly degenerated. Many large dealers were buying directly from Motorola's wholesalers in Miami, receiving the same 5 percent discount that Radius afforded to them. Miami wholesalers sold the same Motorola radios at $442 that Radius was selling for $535. The Over & Out promotion illuminated several problems in Radius's dealer relationships:

- Dealers saw Radius as their main competitor since the BGH Communications Division still sold equipment directly to end-users. BGH sold directly to end-users and to dealers at $535, but the dealer price to end-users was about $704.

- Radius had consistently poor order fulfillment, and promises of improved delivery times never were kept.

- BGH had only tried to sell two-way radios to the dealers, and it did not afford them other complementary lines of communications equipment. Dealers maintained that their profitability was largely predicated on the sales and service of a full line of communications equipment.

As a result of the declining dealer relationship, Radius had a difficult time obtaining information from its dealers. Radius dealers had little trust in Radius or BGH. When Bidone took office, sales were flat at 450 units per month, representing a meager 14 percent market share.

Developing Dealer Relationships

Upon her appointment as marketing manager, Laura Bidone was responsible for supporting Hebard's training program to regional managers and dealers. She was also responsible for developing the dealer database and a promotional plan. She had to pursue various market research plans to identify various market segments, to create an end-user database and to organize a telemarketing program. Bidone quickly recognized that the first order of business was to focus on dealer relationships. She felt the other marketing tasks would be futile in the absence of a dealer relationship program. With Waehener's guidance, Bidone sought to instill a sense of loyalty and commitment to Radius's dealers. To convey Radius's commitment to its dealers, a series of actions were introduced to offer technical and marketing support for Radius dealers:

- Dealers were given information about current and prospective end-users in their markets, and prospective end-users were sent a list of the nearest Radius dealers.

- Dealers were taught how to conduct market research mini-studies to improve their sales and promotional effectiveness. Radius also developed sales support materials for dealers.

- A customized training track was designed for each dealer and conducted by its regional manager. These seminars included topics such as sales forecasting, segmentation, database management, and direct marketing. Video segments were distributed to dealers' sales forces and other personnel.

- Dealers were invited to seminars designed to foster cooperation and coordination between Radius and its dealers' sales and marketing efforts.

- In order to support dealer activities, each regional manager conducted workshops in his province that included dealers, end-users, and the Radius management. The commercial strategy was presented and discussed.

- An inventory management software program was implemented by the communications division to ensure timely deliveries. Dealers were requested to keep safety stock of about 15 percent of forecasted sales to prevent stock-outs.

Bidone wanted to be sure that dealers knew that they were the priority in Radius's marketing strategy. She implemented a dealer classification plan designed to reward dealer performance. The total number of Radius dealers was reduced from 110 to 70, and dealers were given discount points based on sales performance benchmarks. Waehener supported Bidone's efforts by stopping all direct selling between Radius and end-users. This would transfer many customers to existing dealers.

The MSI Program Launch

Laura Bidone was pleased with the relationship-building actions enacted over the past year. Radius's average dealer started to increase sales by over 30% in just the first quarter after enacting the relationship program. As a result, dealers were increasingly cooperative. BGH (through Radius) contracted most of its dealers to reinforce a long-term commitment. The dealer commitment allowed Radius to obtain greater control over its distribution process and improve delivery times significantly.

The approach adopted by Bidone and Waehener was a relationship approach. However, Motorola's Hebard sought to implement a more traditional marketing approach through the MSI Program. The advantage of the MSI Plan was to afford Radius an additional 8% discount on all future purchases. In order to receive the special pricing, Radius would have to accomplish the following tasks:

- Establish a dealer in any city with a population exceeding 500,000 people or 120,000 workers that was not currently serviced by a dealer.

- Define an end-user market for marketing development (i.e., the transportation segment). This would involve a formalized program, through dealers, to attract new customers in a segment that had largely bought from Motorola's competition.

- Implement a communications policy with dealers to ensure co-alignment in sales, marketing, and distribution of the Motorola two-way commercial radio line.

Most important, Radius was expected to meet sales and marketing performance benchmarks. Bidone had a great deal of confidence in her dealer relationships. She was convinced that the success of the MSI program depended on Radius's ability to maintain and grow the dealership network. But the MSI program posed a dilemma. After pruning the dealers to 70 to strengthen relationships, the MSI program was designed to increase the number of dealers. Cast against the backdrop of economic uncertainty, the MSI program launch could potentially reverse the relationship-building efforts with dealers that Bidone and Radius had worked so hard to achieve.

Questions

1. Can the MSI program coexist with Bidone's dealer-relationship-building program? Will the newly committed dealers feel threatened by Motorola's initiative to increase the number of dealers?

2. Can Radius move from an unstructured and negative dealer relationship to a long-term partnership with dealers?

3. Recognizing that in 1995 the Argentine economy entered its worst recession in five years and many industries experienced sales declines over 50 percent, should the "tequila effect" impact Bidone's sales and marketing plans?

Calox Machinery Corporation (A)

Mike Brown, international sales manager, tapped his pencil on the notepad and contemplated his upcoming discussion with Calox's executive committee concerning the distributor situation in New Zealand. The Labor Day weekend break had not been especially conducive to his sorting out the conflicting information and varied opinions concerning the New Zealand predicament. After only 3 months on the job Mike had not expected to be involved in a decision that would have such far-reaching consequences.

On paper the decision looked simple: whether or not to adhere to his earlier decision to replace the original New Zealand distributor, Glade Industries, with a newly formed company, Calox New Zealand, Ltd. Despite his newness to the company, Mike was confident that Calox's executive committee would agree with whatever recommendations he made in this situation, since he had been charged with "solidifying" the International Sales Division. If he decided to reverse his decision to terminate Glade Industries, could he "undo" any damage done so far?

Three previous faxes were spread on his desk along with the brief notes that he had jotted down during Thursday's conference call between Calox's executives and the company's legal counsel. Mike swung back to the PC behind his desk and began to draft what he hoped would be the definitive Calox policy for New Zealand.

The Company

Calox Machinery Company began in 1946 as a partnership between John Caliguri and William Oxley. The two engineers met during World War II and discovered mutual interests in mechanical engineering and construction. Both were natives of Kansas City, and at the end of the war they established a partnership with the expressed purpose of developing high-quality excavation equipment and accessories. Their first product was an innovative hydraulically operated replacement blade for a light-duty scraper.

Calox's principal customers were independent contractors engaged in excavation of building sites, and airport and highway construction and maintenance. Calox's products were primarily replacement items for OEM (original equipment manufacturer) parts and accessories. Some OEM sales were achieved; that is, contractors could order new equipment from OEMs with Calox blades and accessories already installed. Growth over the years was slow, but steady.

The product line expanded to include payloader buckets, a number of dozer and scraper blades, and parts for aerial equipment including construction forklifts and snorkels. A key to the company's success was their specialty status; their products were used to enhance the performance of expensive equipment produced by Caterpillar, Eaton, International Harvester, Case, and other OEMs. Calox's strategy was simply to provide a better part, often at a premium price, and to have it readily available in the field through a network of strong distributors. Direct competitors in the United States included small specialty producers such as Bobcat, Dresser, and Gradall, as well as the parts divisions of the large OEM manufacturers. Primary competitors in international markets included Terex, Deutsch, Takeuchi, and Hitachi. William Oxley compared Calox to the Cummins Engine Company, which had achieved a superior position in the diesel engine market through a similar strategy.

The partnership was replaced by an incorporated structure in 1970, when Bill Oxley, Jr., became CEO. Despite slow growth of the U.S. economy, both 1990 and 1991 were very good years for Calox; annual sales increases of 12 percent were achieved, and the company set profit records each year. Sales for the 1991 fiscal year broke the $70 million barrier for the first time in the company's history. That year, approximately 280 people were employed at the single location in Kansas City, of which three-fourths were hourly workers engaged in fabrication.

International Sales

Calox's first international sale occurred in 1971, when the company responded to an unsolicited inquiry and shipped a small order to Canada. International sales

By Lester A. Neidell of the University of Tulsa. This case was written with the cooperation of management, solely for the purpose of stimulating student discussion. Data are based on field research in the organization. All events and individuals are real, but names have been disguised at the company's request. Faculty members in nonprofit institutions are encouraged to reproduce this case for distribution to their own students without charge or written permission. All other rights reserved jointly to the author and the North American Case Research Association (NACRA). Copyright © 1993 by the *Case Research Journal* and Lester A. Neidell.

languished throughout the 1970s, when a great deal of construction was put on hold due to the "energy crisis." Channels of distribution for international sales were much the same as for domestic sales. Independent distributors were given nonexclusive rights, although in practice most countries had only one distributor. Forty of Calox's 110 distributors were located outside the United States. In 1991 almost 25 percent of Calox's sales were generated internationally. In the 1988 to 1991 period, aided by the relative decline of the U.S. dollar against most other currencies, international sales grew at an annual rate of 16 percent.

Prior to Mike's arrival, there was no uniform procedure by which Calox investigated foreign markets and appointed distributors outside the United States. Bill Lawrence, Mike Brown's predecessor, essentially ran export sales as a one-man operation. Since Calox had very limited international experience, and most international markets were relatively small compared to the United States, primary market research was considered to be an unnecessary expense. In those countries guesstimated to have large enough markets, Bill obtained a list of potential distributors by advertising in that country's construction journal(s) (if available) and principal newspapers. He then made a personal visit to interview and select distributors. In smaller markets, distributors were appointed through one of two methods. Most commonly, Bill appointed a distributor after receiving an unsolicited request. In a very few cases, distributor applications were solicited via advertisements as in "large" markets, which were then reviewed in Kansas City. In all cases in which personal visits were not made, distributor applicants had to submit financial statements. Efforts to interview distributor applicants by telephone were not always successful, due to time constraints and the lack of a suitable translation service.

The New Zealand Distributorship

In 1986 Calox appointed G.W. Diggers, Ltd., as its agent for New Zealand. This arrangement was a novel one, for G.W. Diggers was also a producer of excavating equipment. Because of some earlier poor experiences in certain foreign markets, Calox had instituted a policy of not distributing through any company that also manufactured excavating equipment. This policy was not followed in New Zealand because of the limited distributorship options available. At the time of the appointment, the owner of

G.W. Diggers, Geoffrey Wiggins, assured Calox that the two lines were complementary rather than competitive, and that he intended to keep it that way. During 1989, G.W. Diggers purchased $800,000 of equipment and supplies from Calox.

In 1990 an abrupt change occurred in what had been a very successful, if short, relationship. G.W. Diggers was purchased by a large New Zealand conglomerate, Excel Ltd., which gave a new name, Glade Industries, to its excavating facility. The former owner of G.W. Diggers, Geoff Wiggins, was not associated with Glade Industries. Mike Brown's predecessor felt that the acquisition by Glade could only help Calox's position in New Zealand, because the resources available through Excel, Glade's parent company, were so much greater than what had been available to G.W. Diggers.

However, it soon became apparent that working with Glade was going to be very challenging. Glade raised prices on all Calox products in stock. Then they complained that Calox products were not selling well and that a "rebate" was needed to make Calox's products competitive in the New Zealand market. Simultaneously, Glade began production of a line of products competitive with Calox, but of a substantially poorer quality. During 1991 sales to Glade were virtually zero, and market information obtained by Calox indicated that Calox's former position in the New Zealand market was being occupied by Wescot Industries, with products imported from Great Britain. Exhibit 1 gives annual sales of Calox products to G.W. Diggers and to its successor, Glade Industries.

Mike Brown began his new job as international sales manager for Calox in June 1992. A few weeks after arriving at Calox, Mike received a long letter from Geoff Wiggins. Geoff suggested that the situation in New Zealand was critical, and that he would be willing and able to establish a new distributorship, Calox New Zealand, Ltd., to the exclusive distributors of the Calox product line. Mike then invited Geoff to come to Kansas City the last week of July to discuss the proposal. Mike found Geoff to be very affable, technically knowledgeable, and an excellent marketing person. In the time period since selling his business to Excel Ltd. Geoff had been working as a general contractor. The 24-month "no-compete" clause Geoff had signed when he sold G.W. Diggers had expired. Geoff provided figures that indicated New Zealand's 1991 imports

Exhibit 1

Annual Sales to
G.W. Diggers and
Glade Industries
(in Thousands of
U.S. Dollars)

Sales to G.W. Diggers				Sales to Glade		
1986	**1987**	**1988**	**1989**	**1990**	**1991**	**1992 (6 months)**
21	310	535	801	105	70	10

of excavating equipment were roughly NZ$2 million, out of a total domestic market of nearly NZ$3 million. (In 1991, US$1 equaled NZ$0.62.) He claimed that G.W. Diggers had achieved, at the height of its success, almost a 50 percent share of the New Zealand market. Geoff argued persuasively that with his personal knowledge of New Zealand's needs, Calox could once again achieve a dominant market position. With the blessing of the vice president of marketing, Mike and Geoff shook hands on a deal, with the exact details to be worked out by mail and faxed over the next few weeks. Geoff urged that time was of the essence if Wescot's market advances were to be slowed, and left a $100,000 order for 75 units to be shipped in 120 days, but not later than November 15, 1992.

Communications with Glade

Mike began to prepare a letter of termination to Glade. However, before this was completed, Calox received three mailed orders from Glade, totaling $81,000. This was the first contact Mike had with Glade and the first order received from Glade in 5 months. Because the standard distributor's agreement required a 60-day termination notice, Mike felt the Glade orders had to be honored.

A short time later Calox received a letter in the mail from Glade stating that they had heard rumors that another company was going to supply Calox products to Glade's customers and that delivery had been promised within 150 days. The letter continued by saying that this information could not possibly be true because Glade had an exclusive distributor agreement. This was news to Mike as well as to others at Calox headquarters because it was against company policy to grant exclusive distributorships. A search of Bill Lawrence's files turned up a copy of the initial correspondence to Geoff Wiggins, in which Geoff was thanked for his hospitality and a sole distributorship arrangement was mentioned. However,

the distributorship agreement signed with Wiggins was the standard one, giving either party the ability to cancel the agreement with 60 days' notice.

Mike and the other senior Calox executives assessed the situation at length. The letter mentioning the "sole distributor agreement" was in a file separate from all other New Zealand correspondence. It was nothing more than a statement of intent and probably not legally binding in the United States. However, New Zealand courts might not agree. Further, the distributorship agreement should have been renegotiated when Excel purchased G.W. Diggers, but this had not happened. Glade could make a case that the distributorship had endured for 2 years under the existing agreements, which included the letter in which exclusivity was mentioned.

Mike determined that the "sole distributorship" letter also contained "extenuating circumstances" language which Calox could use to justify supplying the new New Zealand distributorship:

> [T]here may be occasions in the future, when, due to unforeseen circumstances, some entity in your nation refuses to purchase any other way than direct from our factory. We do not want to lose any potential sales, however we pledge our best efforts to cooperate with you for any such possible sales should they present themselves and provided there is a reasonable profit to be made on such sales by us and cooperation can be worked out.

The letter also specifically stated that all agreements between Calox and G.W. Diggers were subject to the laws of Missouri. Furthermore, Mike felt that Glade had not lived up to the actual signed distributorship agreement in that Glade had not promoted Calox products, had not maintained adequate inventory, and had engaged in activities and trade practices that were injurious to Calox's good name.

Armed with this information, Mike sought legal counsel, both in the United States and New Zealand.

After a week, Calox's U.S. attorney, based on their own investigations and those of a law firm in Christchurch, New Zealand, offered four "unofficial" observations:

1. New Zealand is a "common law" nation, whose commercial law is similar to that of the United States.

2. It was possible to argue that because G.W. Diggers had changed ownership, previous agreements might not be binding. However, the most likely court finding would be that there was an implied contract between Calox and Glade on the same terms as with G.W. Diggers, because numerous business dealings between Calox and Glade had occurred after the takeover.

3. Calox was required to give Glade 60 days' termination notice.

4. There was a possibility that a New Zealand court would agree to assume jurisdiction of the case.

After reviewing the above issues Mike suggested to Calox senior management that Glade be terminated. Mike reasoned that Glade would react in one of two ways. One possibility was that they would accept termination, perhaps suggesting some minor compensation. A second scenario was that Glade would attempt to renegotiate the distributorship agreement. Mike was instructed to draft and fax a termination letter to Glade. This letter, sent by fax on August 20, is reproduced in Exhibit 2. The next day the first order for the new distributorship was shipped; the expected arrival date in New Zealand was October 10, 1992.

Glade's faxed reply, dated August 24, was not encouraging (see Exhibit 3). It appeared that Mike and the rest of the Calox management team had miscalculated. Despite the tone of the Glade letter, and the expressed request to ship order #52557, Mike suggested to the executive committee that no additional product be shipped to Glade.

While Mike and the rest of Calox management was deciding how to respond to Glade's initial rejection of the termination letter, a longer fax, one with a more conciliatory tone, dated August 31, was received from Glade (see Exhibit 4). In this letter Glade argued that Calox's best interests were served by working with Glade and mentioned an order for approximately 10 times the "normal" amount of product. However, the order was not transmitted with the fax letter. Glade offered (for the first time) to come to Kansas City for a visit.

Glade's conciliatory letter created a great deal of consternation at Calox headquarters. Its arrival the week before Labor Day meant that holiday plans would have to be placed on the back burner while a suitable response was formulated. Two distinct camps developed within Calox.

One set of managers, whose position was supported by Mike Brown, felt strongly that despite potential legal risks, retaining Glade as a distributor would be a bad business decision. Although Glade had made promises and was offering to renegotiate, it was still producing a competitive line. Also, Glade's historical performance did not augur well for Calox's long-term competitive situation in New Zealand. The "extraordinary" order was viewed as a ploy to entice Calox into continuing the relationship. It was likely to take upwards of two years for all that machinery to clear the New Zealand market. Cognizant of Glade's earlier price manipulations, many of this group felt that Glade might resort to "fire sale" prices when confronted with a large inventory, further damaging Calox's reputation as a premier supplier.

This camp considered that Calox's long-term interests would best be served by terminating the Glade distributorship and completing a formal agreement with Geoff Wiggins. However, there was concern that outright rejection of the Glade order would add to potential legal problems.

These managers also suggested that any further correspondence with Glade should emphasize that Calox could and would exercise a unique product repurchase option upon termination of the distributorship. This provision in the distributorship contract provided that Calox, upon proper termination of the distributorship by either party, could repurchase all remaining Calox inventory from the distributor at 80 percent of its net sales price to the distributor. Thus, if Calox did produce and ship the large Glade order, Calox would, if the order were shipped normally via sea freight, be able to buy it back for 80 percent of the price paid by Glade before it ever reached New Zealand.

The alternative camp wanted to forestall any legal battles. Headed by the U.S. sales manager and the comptroller, they argued that Glade had finally

Exhibit 2

Fax from Calox to Glade, August 20, 1992

Calox Company, Inc.
P.O. Box 21110
Kansas City, MO 64002
U.S.A.

August 20, 1992

Mr. Ian Wells
Group General Manager
Glade Industries
39 Ames Road
Christchurch, New Zealand 2221

Dear Mr. Wells:

This letter is to inform you that Calox Company terminates any International Distributor's Sales Agreement or other Distribution Agreement that you may have or be a party to as Distributor expressly or impliedly with Calox Co. as Manufacturer. Said termination is effective 60 days from the date of this letter.

During the past year the following have gravely concerned us and effectively shut off our sales to the New Zealand market.

Reorganization of G.W. Diggers under Glade leading to continuous loss of personnel knowledgeable of the excavation business and difficulty for Calox's understanding with whom we are doing business. In June 1990, we were advised by telex that we were dealing with Excel Ltd., not G.W. Diggers or Glade.

Only $10,000 purchases for an eight-month long period from us, which we clearly found led to major loss of Calox sales to the marketplace and a complete domination of the excavation business by Wescot Industries, a major competitor.

Lack of effort on the part of Glade in promoting our product and maintaining effective selling facilities.

Numerous complaints to us from Customers in New Zealand about Glade continually changing policies, lack of stock, and wildly increasing prices have clearly pointed out that our reputation, as well as G.W. Diggers', has been badly hurt and will impair sales for some time to come.

No progress has been made in introducing our heavy industrial line to the New Zealand market despite assurances from Glade personnel that progress would be made.

We have thoroughly investigated the New Zealand Market and now have firmly decided that it is time for Calox to make a change in its distribution of products.

For the long term, this will allow us to best carve out a full niche in a market we and you have allowed competitors to dominate for too long. We must guarantee ourselves a consistent, aggressive sales effort in the market, which will not be subject to the effects of major policy changes such as those we have seen from Glade.

While two shipments are already en route to you, order number 52557 has not yet been completed for shipment. Since it will be ready imminently, please let us know immediately whether you wish, under the circumstances, to receive shipment or to cancel this order.

Sincerely,

Michael Brown
International Sales Manager

Exhibit 3

Fax from Glade to Calox, August 24, 1992

Glade Industries   24 August 1992
39 Ames Road
Christchurch, New Zealand 2221

Mr. Michael Brown
International Sales Manager
Calox Company, Inc.
P.O. Box 21110
Kansas City, MO 64002
U.S.A.

Dear Sir:

We acknowledge receipt of your letter dated 20 August 1992.

We are currently discussing its contents with our solicitors. They are also reviewing the distribution agreement.

Please proceed with the shipment of order #52557.

Yours faithfully,

GLADE INDUSTRIES LTD.
Ian Wells
Group General Manager

"gotten its act together" and that the new Glade team of three sales executives would provide greater market coverage than Geoff Wiggins's "one man show." This group introduced the possibility of re-opening negotiations with Glade, supplying Glade by diverting the order already shipped to Geoff Wiggins, and producing the (yet unreceived) large Glade order.

By Wednesday, September 2, the two sides had hardened their positions. Mike was determined to break with Glade and begin anew in New Zealand. However, he was concerned about legal ramifications, and, on Thursday, September 3, Calox's executive committee and Mike conferred with their Kansas City attorneys via a conference call.

The lawyers agreed that any further business conducted with Glade would be detrimental to a termination decision. They warned that despite the termination letter (Exhibit 2) any further shipments to Glade would likely yield a court ruling that the distributorship was still in effect and, furthermore, that the buyback provision could not be enacted. They also said that if all business with Glade were terminated, and Glade did come to the United States to file, the most they would be likely to receive if they won the court case were the profits on the new sales to Geoff Wiggins, which amounted to $10,000. This sum was probably not large enough to warrant legal action by Glade, especially considering the apparently poor financial situation at Glade and the expense of initiating legal action in the United States.

At the end of this conference call, which lasted about 30 minutes, Bill Oxley, Jr., turned to Mike and said, "Mike, I'm off to the lake now for the holiday. I'd like your recommendation Tuesday morning on this Glade thing."

Exhibit 4

Fax from Glade to Calox, August 31, 1992

Glade Industries   31 August 1992
39 Ames Road
Christchurch, New Zealand 2221

Mr. Michael Brown
International Sales Manager
Calox Company, Inc.
P.O.Box 21110
Kansas City, MO 64002
U.S.A.

Dear Sir:

I refer to your letter dated 20 August 1992, terminating our agreement which was executed on 28 February 1986.

In accordance with this agreement and attached to this letter is our order #A1036, for 600 products and parts. We would be pleased if you would confirm this order in due course.

We respectfully ask that you reconsider your termination decision as we believe that it is not in your best interests for the following reasons:

1. G.W. Diggers/Glade were not achieving an adequate return on investment until June 1991. An unprofitable distributor certainly is not in your best interests as principal.

2. The individuals that contributed to that unprofitable performance are no longer working for our company. Incidentally I understand that you have appointed Mr. Geoffrey Wiggins to a position as distributor in New Zealand. How can you justify appointing the person responsible for your market share decline over the past three years?

3. Our purchases certainly have been reduced the last nine months due to our need to get inventory down to lift overall return on investment. That situation has now been corrected with the order attached to this letter.

4. We now have a young aggressive marketing team, all highly experienced in marketing products of a similar nature to yours. When Bill Lawrence was in New Zealand, I advised him that I was restructuring our marketing group. A resume on our three senior marketing men is attached. These men have all commenced in the last four months. I am confident that this team will achieve market leadership in New Zealand and selected export markets with or without Calox's involvement. We have already commenced targeting Wescot's customers. Our recommendation is that you renegotiate your distribution agreement with us, with the inclusion of mutually agreed performance targets which will satisfy your objectives in terms of profitability and market share from the New Zealand market. I would like you to advise me a time which is convenient to you, for me to meet with you in Kansas City to commence negotiation of this distributor agreement.

Yours faithfully,

GLADE INDUSTRIES LTD
Ian Wells
Group General Manager

These are the three new men who have commenced to work for us:

Sean Cox, Sales Manager
35 years old. Formerly CEO of Sean Cox Industries of Christchurch. SCI was the chief contractor for the Auckland airport, but sold its business to Midland Industries. Mr. Cox has fifteen years experience in the construction industry.

Joshua Dunn, Sales Representative, North Island
46 years old. Formerly an independent sales representative for various equipment manufacturers, including Hitachi and Ford New Holland.

Brian Muldoon, Sales Representative, South Island
23 years old. Construction engineering degree from New South Wales Institute of Technology (Sydney, Australia). Formerly a management trainee with our parent company, Excel Ltd.

Calox Machinery Corporation (B)

Mike Brown decided that, despite the potential legal risks, sound business practice dictated that he follow through with the termination of Glade's distributorship, and his recommendation to that effect was accepted by the Calox executive committee. Mike's letter fax of September 9 (Exhibit 1) was very specific. First, he restated that it was in the best interests of both parties to terminate the distributorship. Second, since there was no prospect that the Glade order could be completed and delivered prior to the termination date of October 20, 1992 (60 days from the first letter; see Case A, Exhibit 2), he made it known that Calox would exercise its buyback option if Glade did indeed forward the missing order. Following legal advice, Mike added the caveat, "We are open to your comments, of course." The legal reasoning behind this was that if Calox did begin producing the large Glade order, and then bought it back while it was on the open seas, it could be interpreted by the courts that Calox was deliberately attempting to damage Glade financially.

Glade's "hardball" reply (Exhibit 2) was discouraging. In it Glade requested an accounting of sales to other distributors, claiming that they (Glade) were legally entitled to recover all Calox profits from these sales. Several Calox executives began to waffle, and proposed again the solution of diverting the order

already shipped to Geoff Wiggins, producing the (still unreceived) large Glade order, and renegotiating with Glade (see Case A).

Before an acceptable response could be agreed upon, another fax (Exhibit 3) was received from Glade. In this conciliatory letter, Glade offered to forgo any claims if their large order was completed and if Calox agreed not to exercise their buyback right.

Calox management breathed a huge sigh of relief and instructed Mike to inquire about the specifics of the order, complete it, ship it to Glade, and be done with them! Mike, however, felt it was necessary to obtain additional legal counsel before doing this.

The lawyers were emphatically negative. They felt quite strongly that if Calox shipped the large order, the courts would rule the original agreement binding, despite all the communication about termination. The courts would interpret the correspondence as a ploy by Calox designed to coerce Glade into placing a large order. They reiterated their previous advice that at the current time, Glade could only obtain minimal damages in U.S. courts; it would hardly be worth Glade's time and energy.

Mike and the company's legal counsel agreed that a final letter had to be written to Glade that would summarize the communications between Calox and Glade and make perfectly clear Calox's position. This letter had to clearly impart that Calox, with the advice of legal counsel, did not recognize as valid Glade's claim that any agreement had been breached. Glade, in fact, had violated the previous distributorship agreement by failing to market Calox's products. Due to Glade's negligence, Calox had sustained damage to their reputation and good name, so that any legal recompense would be forthcoming to Calox. Calox's intent in the New Zealand market was to repair the damage that Glade had done to Calox's reputation by forging ahead with an aggressive new distributor.

By Lester A. Neidell. This case was written with the cooperation of management, solely for the purpose of stimulating student discussion. Data are based on field research in the organization. All events and individuals are real, but names have been disguised at the company's request. Faculty members in nonprofit institutions are encouraged to reproduce this case for distribution to their own students without charge or written permission. All other rights reserved jointly to the author and the North American Case Research Association (NACRA). Copyright © 1993 by the *Case Research Journal* and Lester A. Neidell.

Exhibit 1

Fax from Calox to Glade, September 9, 1992

Calox Company, Inc.   September 9, 1992
P.O. 21110
Kansas City, MO 64002
U.S.A.

Mr. Ian Wells
Group General Manager
Glade Industries
39 Ames Road
Christchurch, New Zealand 2221

Dear Mr. Wells:

Reference your 31 August letter, we must regretfully advise that we feel it is in our best interest to continue with our termination of sales to Glade Ltd. as we explained. We appreciate the points you made in your letter, but nevertheless remain convinced that working with Glade Industries Ltd. is not the best way for Calox to achieve its goals in New Zealand.

While we have not yet received your order number A1036 for 600 items referenced in your letter, I should point out that first, Calox is not able to complete an order for all 600 items prior to the termination date, and second, we would want to exercise our option to purchase back all good outstanding products at 80% of our net selling price.

In consideration of these factors, we do not believe it advisable to accept your offer. We feel that this would only affect your situation and we do not seek to take advantage of you in this regard. We are open to your comments, of course.

Sincerely,

Michael Brown
International Sales Manager

Exhibit 2

Fax from Glade to Calox, September 14, 1992

Glade Industries   14 September 1992
39 Ames Road
Christchurch, New Zealand 2221

Mr. Michael Brown
International Sales Manager
Calox Company, Inc.
P.O. Box 21110
Kansas City, MO 64002
U.S.A.

Dear Sir:

I acknowledge receipt of your letter of 9 September 1992.

I am very concerned at the position in which Calox Co. has been selling direct into New Zealand to Glade's customers. This is in direct contravention of your obligations and undertakings under the Distributor Agreement between us and in particular in breach of the undertaking contained in your letter of 27th January 1986.

We have clearly suffered loss and damage as a result of these actions on your part in breach of the Distributor Agreement which we would be entitled to recover in legal proceedings.

We therefore seek from you a full account of all sales made by you direct into New Zealand in breach of the agreement and payment to us of all profits made by you in respect of those sales.

Yours faithfully

Glade Industries, Ltd.
Ian Wells
Group General Manager

Exhibit 3

Fax from Glade to Calox, September 17, 1992

Glade Industries
39 Ames Road
Christchurch, New Zealand 2221

17 September, 1992

Mr. Michael Brown
International Sales Manager
Calox Company, Inc.
P.O. Box 21110
Kansas City, MO 64002
U.S.A.

Dear Sir:

I refer to my open letter of 14 September 1992.

As indicated in that letter we are most concerned at the loss and damage we have suffered by your acting contrary to the terms of the existing Distributor Agreement.

We are, however, prepared to forgo our rights in relation to those breaches in return for your agreeing to supply the 600 items referred to in our order #A1036 and not to seek to exercise any rights of repurchase in relation to those items upon termination of the agreement.

Yours faithfully,

Glade Industries Ltd.
Ian Wells
Group General Manager

Carlsberg United Breweries Ltd.

It was the second week of October. Niels Mikkelsen, vice president of marketing at Carlsberg, the old Danish beer producer, was thinking about the upcoming year. The company was about to launch its second expansion wave in South East Asia. Singapore and Vietnam were already part of Carlsberg's distribution network, and next was Thailand, with Malaysia to follow.

Thailand, formerly known as Siam, is a kingdom with 56 million people. It has been open to influences from the West since the mid 19th century. However, communist infiltration and different military governments have made the progression to a free market economy rather bumpy. The country encourages foreign investments in the form of joint ventures, but requires that the voting majority in these ventures remains in Thai hands. This has not impeded the tremendous economic growth experienced over the last few years, though. Thailand's rate of unemployment is decreasing and taxes paid from these ventures are naturally appreciated by the government.

Carlsberg, to attract Thai investors and to add distributors and licensed breweries to its network, plans to go on an extensive, nine-location road show with corporate presentations. The first road show is scheduled for February 4 in Bangkok, followed by shows in Chiang Mai in the north, Udon Thani and Ubon Ratchathani on the border to Laos, then Khon Kaen, Phitsahulok, and Nakhon Ratchasima in central Thailand, and finally Chon Buri and Phuket in the south.

These presentations have to take the competition, mainly the Bhirombhakdis family, with surprise. The Bhirombhakdis' Boon Rawd Brewery Company controls about 75 percent of the Thai beer market. The company was granted Thailand's first beer license in 1933, and has since established a network of over 1,000 distributors selling their local Singha label. Besides beer, the Thai brewer controls almost 40% of the bottled water market, and, to Carlsberg's dismay (since Carlsberg also produces and sells soda waters) the Boon Rawd Brewer Company has a staggering 90% of the soda water market.

Sven L. Gibson wrote this case as the basis for class discussion rather than to illustrate either effective or ineffective handling of an administrative situation. Certain names and data have been disguised. Special thanks to Professor John F. Tanner for his support.

Mikkelsen, well aware of how crucial it was to match personalities and corporate cultures between his marketing and public relations team with those of the presentation partner, pondered how these teams together could overcome the difficulties of the local culture, language, and communication, which he, from his previous experience in the South East Asia, knew existed. Which company should he choose as partner to handle the important road show presentations?

Background

Most Danish corporations, and Carlsberg among them, used to use an advertising agency for all external, and also some internal, communication needs. Over time it became obvious that some of these needs could be handled directly, either because time could be saved, or because as few people as possible were to be involved, thus minimizing leakage of company classified information.

A major part of the company's communication needs are corporate presentations; the corporation as a whole, collectively or through its sales personnel, presents its views or products according to set guidelines in line with the company's mission. Such presentations may be tailored to a range of audiences: large audiences such as a company's shareholders, or smaller ones like the board of directors of a potential distributor.

Carlsberg's advertising agency had contracted out the Carlsberg presentations and road shows—common practice among agencies due to the specific knowledge and experience required to perform these tasks—to the corporate presentation company ST Studios. ST Studios had proven to be the presentations partner Carlsberg needed, so Carlsberg began to bypass its agency in most presentations matters. ST Studios and Carlsberg had worked together in this fashion for the better part of a decade.

ST Studios was started some 20 years ago by three, then rebellious, photographers who believed that advertising should be aesthetic as well as selling; it was important to keep the "bean counters" a safe distance from the artists.

The founders were all strong willed, but managed to stay together for seven years before one of them left to start his own agency. Co-founders Tom Olsen and Jim Stewart remained. Together they built a company with a reputation for high creative standards, on-time delivery, and personal integrity. If Olsen or Stewart thought that the customer's ideas were wrong or could be improved upon, he told the customer so. No customer could remain indifferent to the duo; customers either loved them or hated them. This approach had, however, produced mostly good relations with the customers, and in the long run it proved positive for the balance sheet also.

ST Studios had always had the latest in equipment. By the mid-1980s the company was a highly specialized presentations company dedicated to corporate image programs. These presentations involved video productions, 3-D animations, and multiprojector presentations, along with all the still-image presentations that the business graphics competition provided. On top of this, ST Studios composed and produced all the music and sound effects for the presentations using the company's latest investment: a brand new digital recording studio.

ST Studios was in numbers a small business, with less than 30 employees in its one office. However, small meant being flexible, and the company cooperated with many freelancers. The customer base was most of the Danish blue-chip companies, especially shipbuilders, financial organizations, and agricultural/chemical companies. ST Studios had acquired a vast experience from producing shows and presentations all around the world due to the fact that 95 percent of everything produced in Denmark is exported.

At ST Studios the customer interface was made up as follows; a sales manager in charge of general PR and four account executives, who in turn were assisted by four producers, each with specific knowledge of still-image presentations, 3-D computer animation, multiple projector presentations, and digital sound production. ST Studios utilized computer graphics artists who were brought in on projects as early as possible to provide technical input.

Nothing lasts forever, though, and when Carlsberg employed a new marketing director, Marts Hansson, ST Studios was no longer the beer brewer's corporate presentations supplier. Marts Hansson, due to previous ties with DeeGraphics, closed Carlsberg's doors for ST Studios, and DeeGraphics, ST Studios' fiercest competitor in Denmark, could take over as Carlsberg's presentations partner. DeeGraphics had tried for a long time to get a foot in Carlsberg's door, managing to establish some ties with a few of its department managers. Now, under the wings of Marts Hansson, DeeGraphics moved in with full force.

DeeGraphics' history starts with a Swedish advertising agency called Kreate, which at the end of the seventies realized an increasing need among its customers for presentation graphics, overheads, and slides. Producing such material was time consuming and involved many creative people better needed elsewhere in Kreate's organization.

A search for a less labor-intensive system was begun, and the solution turned out to be a computerized work station constructed by Genigraphics, a Syracuse, New York, company started by a group of laid-off NASA engineers who used and commercialized knowledge of flight simulation techniques, creating the business graphics industry. Kreate bought one of the first Genigraphics systems and started DeeGraphics to produce their highly needed presentation graphics.

DeeGraphics, led by Per Ledin, a very dynamic lawyer, started serving Kreate and its customers, but there was a growing market for business graphics and DeeGraphics expanded further. In spite of the economic downturn in Europe in the beginning of the eighties DeeGraphics' expansion continued. It established offices in all of the Scandinavian capitals: Stockholm, Copenhagen, Oslo, and Helsinki.

Part of DeeGraphics' growth came from large corporations outsourcing their presentation needs. By placing graphic workstations inside corporations, DeeGraphics managed to stay close to the customer, providing almost instant service: the customer proofreads the presentation; then the job is digitally transmitted to DeeGraphics' closest office where the job is received, developed and processed, and returned by courier to the customer.

DeeGraphics' customers include most of the Scandinavian multinational corporations, including telecommunications, pharmaceuticals, and financial services. DeeGraphics, however, provided still-image presentations only. If video or multiple-projector slide shows were asked for, DeeGraphics would turn those projects over to Kreate, its parent company.

The customer interface at each DeeGraphics office was made up of three parts: a regional manager in charge of staff, operations, and PR; a direct sales function executed by account executives also acting as art directors; and, assisting them, computer graphics artists brought in on projects as early as possible. DeeGraphics had chosen this short line of command to emphasize flexibility vis-à-vis the customer.

Lars Quist was DeeGraphics' account executive and main liaison with Carlsberg. His children, incidentally, attended the same middle school as Marts Hansson's children; moreover, the Carlsberg production manager also lived in the same neighborhood as Quist and his family. This was not by design, but Lars Quist did not deny that "proximity and frequency are on my side."

For almost a year Carlsberg did not use ST Studios' services, mainly because Marts Hansson, the main decision maker at Carlsberg in these matters, held the view that "We don't need that fancy stuff [3-D animations and digital sound] to sell beer—beer is a commodity."

ST Studios did not give up hope of regaining its former position as Carlsberg's presentations partner. The brewer was continually informed on the technical and administrative advances that were made at ST Studios. Ellen Jacobsen, Marts Hansson's secretary, once noted: "This month I think Sven Lorentz has called me six times to set up a meeting with Mr. Hansson." Lorentz was eager to show how ST Studios could be Carlsberg's total presentations partner, be it a single still-frame, a multiprojector slide show, or a vivid 3-D animation with digital sound. The founders of ST Studios, Tom Olsen and Jim Stewart, had also been active and had, at several trade shows, presented how corporations could benefit from ST Studios' fresh approaches to presentations.

The Present

It wasn't, however, until Carlsberg employed its new vice president of marketing, Niels Mikkelsen, that ST Studios managed to regain Carlsberg as a customer. Mikkelsen, age 46, with a degree in chemistry from the University of Copenhagen and an MBA from INSEAD, France, had taken over from Marts Hansson as vice president of marketing at Carlsberg.

He had been head-hunted five months earlier from the car maker Volvo's Malaysian subsidiary, where he had been the director of marketing. Mikkelsen and his family had enjoyed the climate and exotic culture of Malaysia for five years. The stay had profited the whole family, but they wanted to return to Denmark. Now Mikkelsen was to test his experience in marketing communication in South East Asia at Carlsberg's Copenhagen headquarters.

Carlsberg had been present on the South East Asian beer market for several years, with no sudden breakthroughs. Patience, well known to Mikkelsen, is the key to progress in this part of the world.

The next target in South East Asia was well known by both DeeGraphics and ST Studios, the latter one repeatedly approaching Carlsberg. In Mikkelsen's first week at Carlsberg, the marketing director exclaimed: "There are people from ST Studios everywhere." ST Studios was well prepared. Tom Olsen expressed that "We've been planning to regain [the account] ever since the day we lost it." Jim Stewart added, "Losing a customer is one thing, but losing it to DeeGraphics was particularly disturbing, since [DeeGraphics] is the archenemy."

The process of ousting DeeGraphics had not taken off until Sven Lorentz, account executive at ST Studios, while on vacation, had happened to meet Anne Linnet, Mikkelsen's new secretary. Lorentz had emphasized the two companies' mutual history, he had been adamant on Carlsberg returning as a customer to ST Studios. "With Marts Hansson gone, it is time for Carlsberg to profit from the investments in technology that [ST Studios] has undertaken." Evidently quicker turnaround was ensured using all-digital equipment for both picture and sound.

As fortune had it, Anne Linnet knew about a small presentation that her superior, Mikkelsen, needed rather quickly, and she thought that ST Studios ought to get a chance. Carlsberg could also benefit from using ST Studios' services since Carlsberg did not have to pay royalties for music used in its presentations and road shows—ST Studios could compose the music and Carlsberg would own it.

Quicker turnaround was like music in Mikkelsen's ears. However, his interest was also in supplier dependability. Whichever supplier he chose, it should be flexible and solid. Over the course of the coming year Mikkelsen foresaw more than 40 corporate presentations together with numerous smaller events. In South East Asia alone, Carlsberg had 43 salespeople who all needed up-to-date sales promotion material. Much of the material built on previous presentations, but with a great need for upgrades. All in all this called for a solid, dependable supplier with quick turnaround.

If Anne Linnet, who had had a good relationship with ST Studios before, recommended Mikkelsen try ST Studios, he would do so for two reasons. First, the presentation was small, and if ST Studios did not do well Mikkelsen could continue working with DeeGraphics. Second, Mikkelsen was intrigued by the new digital technology that ST Studios utilized. Mikkelsen saw a possibility of sending manuscripts and proofs over the Internet. Could a presentation be edited in Copenhagen at the same time it was "on the air" in Bangkok, he wondered.

Decisional Hierarchy

Once a week the well-liked Mikkelsen handled contacts with the department heads and their PR and information needs. At Carlsberg weekly interdepartmental meetings were held on Tuesday afternoons. Historically this had proved to be the most quiet time of the week at the Copenhagen office. The meetings used to be dominated by a male hierarchy where the chain of command was not to be broken. This had gradually changed, though, with the exception of two departments referred to as "the old guards" by Mikkelsen: the manufacturing department, led by production manager Bowe Smulsen, and the accounting department managed by the accountant Peter Possel. These two department managers still expected the "old rules" to be adhered to.

Consequently, it was highly disturbing to Bowe Smulsen and Peter Possel that Niels Mikkelsen allowed not only his secretary Anne Linnet but also the confident Rita Leibert from the sales department to speak their minds at the weekly meeting, especially since their preferences differed. Smulsen had had a very good relationship with DeeGraphics' account executive Ole Botter, and argued ST Studios to be "less technically knowledgeable" than DeeGraphics. A similar case was presented by Peter Possel, who declared that what he received from ST Studios was never "good enough." Rita Leibert, on the other hand, had just received part of a presentation for the fall kick off for Carlsberg's sales force for the European large consumer sales which she was very pleased with; to work with ST Studios and their reps "makes the whole difference—they know what I want," she said.

Among Rita Leibert's new responsibilities, as assistant to Robert Andersen, the sales department manager, was the fall kickoff. It was customary for the department to get far away from the office, hiking, skiing, or doing "something different" before charging up for the coming season. Rita Leibert had talked about this with Anne Linnet, who suggested she talk with ST Studios' producer Jacob Frank or the account executive Sven Lorentz. Rita Leibert had done that and praised ST Studios' employees.

Jacob Frank had also made a good impression on Anne Linnet. The two had met at a marketing congress with local Copenhagen businesses when she was the guest speaker. ST Studios was responsible for the presentations, and Sven Lorentz had involved producer Jacob Frank.

At the latest meeting the previous Tuesday afternoon there had been talk about technical differences between ST Studios and DeeGraphics. In these discussions ST Studios turned out to have a slight edge, however, "I do not see why the whole company needs to go with ST Studios," Smulsen had said. "Our product doesn't improve simply because we use 3-D animations in our presentations." Robert Andersen, the pragmatic manager of the sales department, tried to solve the dilemma, saying, "We should use the company that knows our market best, technicalities aside, and that is ST Studios because of our mutual history." He was referring to the 10 years when ST Studios was traveling around the world on behalf of Carlsberg.

Carlsberg United Breweries Ltd.

Carlsberg, founded in 1847 and awarded Sole Supplier to the Royal Danish Court, became Denmark's largest beer producer with annual sales of $2.3 billion. Advertising expenditures were $17 million, with more on marketing and PR. Company headquarters is in Copenhagen, from where operations on all continents are supervised. Carlsberg uses wholly owned plants, part-owned subsidiaries, joint ventures, partnerships, and licensed breweries, depending on the laws and customs of the country in which the company is operating. One-half of its sales are generated in Europe, one-fourth are in the Western hemisphere, and the rest are equally divided between Africa and Asia.

Several personnel at Carlsberg's headquarters in Copenhagen influence buying decisions concerning presentation materials, shows, and exhibitions. However, depending on the specific cost of a project—ranging from a few hundred dollars up to over a million dollars—and depending on the urgency of a project (an urgent project requires relatively less consensus on supplier), the relative influence on a project varies greatly between gatekeepers, influencers, deciders, users, and purchasers.

The Thai road shows were extremely important for Carlsberg's future. The results would affect the whole company. This was highly evident when the CEO, P. J. Swanholm, one day called Mikkelsen to point out the importance of market knowledge and flexibility in any presentations supplier. Swanholm was a man who was used to getting his way, a man "of the old guards." However, the people he had promoted were people quite independent in nature, and the people he had hired were always "people that could do what I cannot," he had remarked. The discussion made Mikkelsen compare DeeGraphics with ST Studios in his mind, wondering what other presentation companies might meet Swanholm's requirements.

Mikkelsen had in the last few weeks often consulted with the new Thailand general manager, Matthias Ritterband. Like Mikkelsen, Ritterband had experience from that part of the world. Ritterband pointed out the importance of applying a culture-specific tone to the presentations, and recommended that whomever Mikkelsen chose to produce the shows should cooperate with Rittapanat Tchongthai, a Thai communications consultant whom Ritterband had worked with in Singapore and Vietnam. Furthermore, Ritterband did not see the technology used as providing a competitive advantage. "The message is more important than the actual execution," he said, continuing, "Thailand is less technologically developed than Scandinavia and may not appreciate something too advanced."

Mikkelsen knew that he was ultimately responsible for the Thai road shows. However, it could be seen as a trickle-down effect. Could he subdivide the presentations? If so, he could portion out projects where responsibility would be dependent on importance of a given part and the costs involved.

Carlsberg's organization is typical for a large corporation. There is an executive board with a CEO, a CFO, and the vice presidents of the corporate departments of accounting, marketing, sales, manufacturing, and R&D, along with representatives from the major shareholders. Further, Carlsberg has a supervisory board consisting of people representing the county, local and national politics, and Danish industrialists.

Moreover, since the company operates on all continents, there are region managers responsible for Europe, North America, South America, South East Asia, the Middle East, and Africa. In each country where Carlsberg keeps a business venture, the brewer has, depending on ownership share, either a president, a vice president, or one or more board members in place to protect Carlsberg's interests.

Questions

1. What presentations partner should Carlsberg choose and why?

2. What could DeeGraphics and ST Studios do to increase their chances of winning Carlsberg's Thai project?

3. Is there anything within the Carlsberg organization that could be improved upon in order to make the presentations purchases more effective? More efficient?

Dirigo Industries

The Agri-bio Division of Dirigo was primarily involved in the large-scale production of "plantlets" for distributing to commercial greenhouses and large-scale corporate farms and in technical consultancy to its clients. Technically, the production procedures were referred to as plant propagation by genetic engineering. A major application was the development of fruits and vegetables that would have genetic characteristics to resist disease and damage from severe climatic conditions. Other applications dealt with "engineering" the aesthetic qualities (e.g., taste, texture, colour) of plants.

Agri-bio was a market leader in the industry, largely because of its mass production technology to which it had held a patent for three years. Its largest selling product was a resilient variety of ornamental fern, with which it controlled about 25 percent of the 15 million-unit fern market in North America.

In January 1983, Agri-bio established European operations in Evry, France as a result of an outside consultant's report that there appeared to be an enormous potential demand in Western Europe for a new variety of asparagus that Agri-bio laboratories had developed. The asparagus plantlets were marketed in trays of 80–120 plantlets and sold under the brand name SAGA. Though not widely known among potential buyers in the European market, plantlets produced in such laboratory environments as those of Agri-bio could easily qualify for unrestricted shipment across national frontiers within the EEC. Agri-bio France operations were intended to supply all of Western Europe.

In addition to the SAGA brand, Agri-bio marketed a resilient variety of fir trees (plantlets) throughout Europe under the brand name SAFR. Though Agri-bio management were convinced that the market for biotechnically produced fir trees had a vast potential, they were uncertain as to how quickly Agri-bio would be able to penetrate the market.

Based on estimates of 50% annual growth in the European plantlet market, Agri-bio had committed itself to a programme of rapid expansion. Additional

This case was prepared by David Guatschi, professor at INSEAD. It is intended to be used as a basis for class discussion rather than to illustrate either effective or ineffective handling of an administrative situation. Any resemblance of the persons or firms in this case to real persons or firms is purely accidental and unintentional. Copyright © 1984 INSEAD Fontainebleau, France. Revised 1987.

products were under development. A summary of the key elements of the first-year plan for Agri-bio France is presented in Exhibit 1.

In terms of its development, the European market was estimated to be about eighteen months behind the U.S. market. The early stage of market development was commonly acknowledged as the principal reason for higher operating costs in Europe, as compared to the U.S. European unit prices for Agri-bio products were kept within a 10 percent "safety zone" around corresponding U.S. prices, for which unit gross contribution margins are about 250 percent of unit variable costs.

As a part of the general annual review, the Director of Sales for Agri-bio France submitted a summary of the activities of the sales force, as well as a summary of marketing intelligence data pertaining to competitors and collected by field sales personnel. Certain aspects of the report appeared to have a direct bearing on the variance between planned and actual levels of activity for 1983, as summarised in Exhibit 1.

First, the sales force reported that a new competitor, Tech-gro, began operations in France during the second quarter of 1983. Tech-gro was a subsidiary of a large U.S. seed company which, it had been rumoured for several years, was investing heavily in biotechnology applications in agriculture. Tech-gro's market entry had not been incorporated into Agri-bio's 1983 plan. Though Tech-gro did not produce fir tree plantlets, Tech-gro France marketed a wider line of products than Agri-bio France and had used an aggressive promotional campaign and a low price to induce purchase by large-scale greenhouses.

Agri-bio salesmen reported that Tech-gro's average selling price was 15.00 FF per unit for its competing variety of asparagus. This compared with Agri-bio marketing research forecasts of an industry average of 15.75 FF per market unit (100 plantlet equivalent) and an average forecasted price for the Tech-gro product of 15.50 FF per market unit. (Agri-bio market analysts included in the calculation of the industry average price relevant production costs incurred in conventional production.) The actual industry average price was 15.20 FF per market unit.

Assuming an analogous production technology, the Agri-bio production manager had estimated that Tech-gro France had the capacity to deliver to the market approximately 10 thousand units in any given three-month period. However, a recent article in the *Nouvel Economiste* reported that Tech-gro had applied

Exhibit 1

	Plan (1983)		Operating Results (Jan.–Dec. 1983)	
	SAGA	SAFR	SAGA	SAFR
Revenues				
Sales (units)	50,000	65,000	53,000	59,000
Price per unit (FF)	16.0	20.0	15.25	23.50
Revenues (FF)	800,000	1,300,000	808,250	1,386,500
Total market (units)	200,000	500,000	230,000	600,000
Market share (units)	25%	13%	23%	9.8%
Unit variable costs				
Production (FF)	3.0	3.0	3.0	3.79
Distribution (FF)	2.0	2.0	2.57	2.71
Marketing (FF)	1.0	1.0	1.43	1.0
Contribution				
Per unit (FF)	10.0	14.0	8.25	16.0
Total (FF)	500,000	910,000	437,250	944,000
Loss in unit sales due to				
Production attrition	1,000	1,300	2,900	1,500
Distribution loss	250	250	750	375
Product mix	43.48%	54.52%	48.25%	51.75%
Production (units)	55,000	70,000	57,000	61,250
Inventory units as of 31.12.83	3,750	3,450	350	375

NOTE: A unit for Agri-bio is a small aluminum tray containing 80–120 plantlets growing in a nutrient solution. Units corresponding to the total market are lots of 100 "marketable plants."

for a patent on its production process which produced units of 120–180 plantlets growing in a nutrient composition and encased in a clear, durable plastic box.

A second aspect of interest in the sales manager's year-end report was documentation of a four-month strike at a large asparagus grower's facility in Poitiers. This had apparently led to a totally unforeseeable demand for approximately 2 thousand units of the Agri-bio product.

Investigation into the higher than expected distribution loss for asparagus revealed that in-transit delays by certain carriers had resulted in shipment times that in many cases far exceeded the expected shelf-life of the Agri-bio product. Under normal conditions (temperatures between 5 and 25 degrees Celsius) plantlets could remain unattended in trays for a maximum of six days. Furthermore, the product required some special handling as trays could not be turned on their sides.

For the fir trees operation, a large brush fire in Norway during July 1983 depleted the stock of conventional seedlings. However, this potentially favourable influence on the demand for SAFR was blunted somewhat by a seven-week truck and rail strike in Norway. A large petroleum company announced in August 1983 that it was investing in the propagation of fir tree plantlets by biotechnical means.

The Agri-bio production manager reported that 1983 production levels were not as high as anticipated because of labour and materials supply problems. As labour productivity had increased only slightly during the course of the year, inexperience among the workers was responsible for relatively high levels of attrition in production and distribution loss. Moreover, the sole supplier of trays used in production had been unable to assure timely delivery throughout the year.

Given the information in Exhibit 1, assess how well Agri-bio France has done. Considering the results of the first twelve months of operations, is the original plan still appropriate? If not, how might it be adapted to the current environment?

ExhibitsPlus: A Change in a Customer's Paradigm for Buying

ExhibitsPlus is a supplier of custom-built exhibit booths for companies to exhibit their products and services at trade shows. Pat Nelson, senior account executive, is working with Data Telecom (DT), a company whose North American operations are based in Toronto but has significant operations located across the United States and Mexico. Data Telecom's primary business is selling telephone switching systems to companies for internal phone systems. The switches range in cost from $500,000 to $5 million.

Data Telecom

Data Telecom is a well-established company, having been in business for over 70 years. Conservative, the company only entered the U.S. and Mexican markets 20 years ago, and is often referred to as the IBM of telecommunications for its blue-suits–and–white-shirts image. This carefully cultivated image is believed to lower the perceived risk among buyers when choosing Data Telecom. On the other hand, the company has experienced severe competition over the last 10 years and actually lost money in domestic (Canadian) operations last year. The U.S. business barely breaks even and the Mexican operations carry the profit ball for DT.

At the end of last year, the company announced a 10 percent reduction in work force, along with a significant restructuring. One area that has been restructured is corporate marketing and the company, which was known as a leader in manufacturing quality, is now applying TQM principles to marketing.

Jack Truitt is the marcom director for DT. His job is to manage all marketing communication in North America, so he manages advertising, trade shows, sales collateral (brochures, pamphlets, etc.), direct mail, web sites, and public relations. He told Pat that he is the strategist; his primary job is to work with Sales and upper management to determine marketing strategy, and then oversee the groups who carry out the strategy in the specific areas just mentioned. Pat has

This case was prepared by J. F. Tanner Jr. for the purposes of class discussion, based on general industry information and trends. Data Telecom and ExhibitsPlus have been disguised.

labeled Jack as a driver, and he has been the subject of a lot of press in the trade show industry as a maverick who likes to be innovative for the sake of being innovative. Jack came to DT's North American Operations from Europe, where he headed marketing and was very successful. Company pundits predict he will be the next VP of marketing and sales.

Jack wants to own no booths, which is opposite of the DT policy in the past. DT has always purchased custom-built booths, usually one per year at a price of about $150,000 to $175,000. Each booth has a life of about five years, and since the company does about 150 shows each year (each show equates to about one week of booth use), the booths rotate from show to show. Each old booth also has to be refurbished whenever corporate marketing strategy dictates, usually about every other year at a cost of about $50,000 per booth. Now Jack wants his exhibit vendor to buy the existing booths back at book value (except for the one that needs replacing, which will be trashed) and then rent them to him when he wants them. ExhibitsPlus would have to cover any refurb costs, but could rent the booths to companies that do not compete with DT. Custom graphics and other adaptations could be made for any customer who wanted to use the booths at a price of about $25,000—a one-time-per-booth charge. His belief is that this will lower his costs substantially. DT pays ExhibitsPlus about $100,000 to store exhibits between shows plus costs to ship the exhibits to various destinations. The storage fees would no longer be applicable because DT would not own the booths. Shipping would still be a separate item and not included in the rent. Truitt expects the rent to be about 40% of current costs of building, refurbing, and storing.

Betty Franklin is the trade shows manager. She has worked her way up to the North American Corporate office over a 20-year career, in which she began as a secretary while in her midthirties and a single mom. She earned her college degree while with DT, and Pat classifies her as an expressive. Pat has sensed some tension between Betty and Jack, which she has put down to the fact that Betty may feel passed over by Jack's promotion. Betty has very strong relations with the field sales force, which has always made booth design very effective. She can express the company's communication strategy in the same terms as the customer and the salesperson, which is useful when creating a new booth look, graphics, a show theme, etc. Jack, being new to NA Ops, doesn't have the same type of relationship with Sales.

Jack reports to the VP of sales and marketing, a man who is nearing retirement. The VP came out of sales, so he focuses more time on sales than on marketing. He is entirely responsible for the allocation of budget to the various marketing areas, including new product development, customer service, and marcom. All marketing research is outsourced. Pat has met this man several times, and feels that he is very conservative, particularly in terms of graphic design. Pat also feels that he patronizes women, and a quick glance at the management of the sales force would indicate that women have a tough time getting promoted at DT.

There are four exhibit managers (EMs) who each manage one of the displays. They are responsible for shipping the booth to the next show and making sure it is set up properly and then taken down at the end of the show. They are also responsible for coordinating all aspects of each show they manage. They work closely with the sales force to plan the right atmosphere for each show, targeting the right types of accounts, and saying the right things so that many leads can be generated. Each EM also manages the follow-up to each lead, tracking what each salesperson does with leads and if they close. This is so DT will know if the show was worthwhile.

Bill Bradley is the most senior of the EMs. He is also an expressive, and has been with DT for about 12 years. His background is advertising, and he is very strong with graphics. He is the least detail-oriented person, which always causes Betty problems because he'll forget stuff at shows and depend on Betty to take care of him.

Toniqua Davis has been with DT for eight years, beginning right out of college. She has a bachelor's degree in marketing and wants to move into sales. Pat figures Toniqua is a driver, but she hasn't worked much with her.

Shawn Gale is the youngest of the exhibit managers, at 27, and has been with DT five years. Shawn is an analytical, has the firmest grasp on how to evaluate a show's success, and probably has the dullest eye for graphics. Senior management always likes the results of Shawn's shows because it is so obvious if the show was successful, and Shawn never needs to be bailed out at a show by Betty, but the salespeople don't think much of her.

Gerry MacDonald is the newest member of the DT show staff, having joined the company from Giltspur, a competitor of ExhibitsPlus. She has been with DT for about six months, and has been in the show industry for over 10 years. Pat hasn't classified Gerry's personality yet. Gerry doesn't have a college degree, but seems to make up for it with her experience.

The RFP

Each year, DT puts out an RFP (request for proposals). In this RFP, the needs for a new booth and any refurbishing of old booths are spelled out. Companies such as ExhibitsPlus are expected to create speculative designs (called spec designs for short), building scale models of their designs. These are then presented to DT, who selects a supplier. Pat has argued that this drives up DT's costs because spec designs are very expensive (a company may have as much as $20,000 invested), and the costs have to be covered for designs that are bid and lost. DT hasn't paid any attention to that argument in the past, but then again, most buyers in the industry request spec designs.

For a spec design, Pat schedules meetings with the buyer and her design staff. The design staff includes architects and graphic designers. Sometimes, she includes the buyer's advertising agency if they aren't also bidding on the job. Sometimes, the buyer's sales department is involved and in some organizations, trade shows are managed by a sales manager or director of sales. These meetings are designed to give the staff the greatest amount of information possible, but some companies don't allow these meetings. Some buyers also cherry-pick, taking the best ideas out of each spec design and including them in the final design. DT has been known to do that.

Jack has mentioned to Pat that this year's RFP will be for a custom-designed booth with modular design so that the booth can function as a 10'×10' up to a 40'×40'. If purchased, it would be about a $200,000 sale. Jack also expects the RFP to require the winning company to buy the four old booths and refurbish them to fit the same specifications. Length of the rental agreement has not been determined. The RFP, though, will be sent to several advertising firms who are encouraged to bid in the hopes of winning other advertising business. They would then subcontract the building of the booth to someone else.

ExhibitsPlus

Pat managed to win the DT business two out of the last three years, but two years ago, it was won by Freeman Exhibit Company out of Dallas. Before that, the business was held exclusively by Southern Designs, a company that is no longer in business.

ExhibitsPlus has two sister companies: a shipping company that ships the booths (all competitors except Freeman have to ship using a major carrier like Mayflower or Allied, who have special trade show divisions) and a drayage company (*drayage* is the term used to describe unloading the booth at the shipping dock of a convention center, then moving it to the appropriate point on the exhibit floor, then moving it out, and loading it up at the end of the show). Drayage, though, is usually sold to the show organizer, who then requires all exhibitors to use the same drayage company. The only advantage to ExhibitsPlus's customers is that for those shows where ExhibitsPlus is the drayage provider, the unloading and loading process is much smoother and faster. This is, however, a significant advantage because it means more time for installing and dismantling the booth. Saving time is a critical advantage in the eyes of most exhibit managers because it means more time to fix any problems (and there are always problems) and greater likelihood of getting the exhibit installed on time.

ExhibitsPlus also has its own install-and-dismantle (I&D) team to set up and take down the booth if the customer wants. Only Freeman has this complete set of offerings. The RFP is really cloudy on who will provide these services and Pat, in talking with Jack, believes that it is because Jack hasn't really thought these things through. The contract with ExhibitsPlus expires in four months, and the new RFP will probably be issued in one month to six weeks.

ExhibitsPlus is a family-owned business founded in 1920 by a young WWI veteran, Ted Ruch (pronounced *roosh*). Ted's daughter, Sally R. Massy, took the company over in 1960 and is about to retire, passing the reins on to her two children: Gil, who runs the transportation side, and Nancy, who runs the exhibit building and I&D business.

The transportation business was acquired in 1948. Most custom booths are built of plywood and laminate materials; therefore, they can be quite heavy. The life of the booth is also a function of how well the booth is cared for when it is shipped and stored. For those reasons, Sally Massy realized that she could save her customers money and provide better service by doing the shipping, so she bought a struggling home-moving company and turned it into an exhibit-shipping company. Then she purchased an Army surplus warehouse and used it to store exhibits.

The business, though, has changed. Companies like Nimlok provide lower-cost and shorter-life booths by using newer materials, fabrics, and special structural and fastening technologies. These technologies make it easier to snap pieces together to create a nice look with materials that are lighter (and therefore less expensive to ship and store). Shorter booth life is not a problem when a company wants to change the look year after year. For that reason, ExhibitsPlus also developed its own line of low-cost customizable but standard booth designs, called the ExhibitPro line. These sell for about half the price of a custom booth, and are customized through the use of special graphics. In addition, ExhibitPro booths don't necessarily require special I&D, so the exhibit manager can save money by installing and dismantling the booth personally. In terms of units sold, ExhibitsPlus sells twice the number of ExhibitPro booths as it does custom booths, but revenue is about equal and profits are greater on the custom booth sales. Currently, ExhibitsPlus does not rent any booths.

Competition

As mentioned earlier, Freeman Exhibit Co. is the only competitor that offers comparable services. Freeman, based in Dallas, offers one advantage that ExhibitsPlus does not—it also provides show services to the show organizer. (Show services include carpeting the exhibit hall, setting up the drapes that separate the booths, putting up signs, providing cleaning services, and offering other services to exhibitors sold through the show organizer.) That results in about a 2:1 market share advantage for drayage between Freeman and ExhibitsPlus. Freeman also has a reputation as an industry leader because of the Freeman family's participation in many of the industry associations and its donations to industry causes. Freeman is the industry's largest exhibit builder.

Most exhibit builders are small, serving a limited geographic area, meaning that while they may ship exhibits anywhere in the world, their customers come from a limited area. While it is unlikely that

Data Telecom will send the RFP to any of these companies, Pat does know that DT's advertising agency is planning to bid on the job. Usually an advertising agency will farm the work out to one of the small exhibit builders. Ad agencies also usually cost 5 to 10% more than ExhibitsPlus because they add their profit to all charges. In addition, ad agencies have to find shippers and storage facilities.

Champion Communications is a rapidly growing competitor that has acquired a number of the smaller custom shops around the country. Its strategy has been to go into a large city like Atlanta or Dallas and buy two exhibit builders: one known for creativity and one with an established customer base. The company is run by Marjorie McGaslin, who left ExhibitsPlus because she wasn't one of the family and couldn't expect to be CEO. She has partnered with a financier in Denver. The firm is expected to continue to grow through acquisition until she has locations in 10 cities; currently Champion covers six cities and is already probably one of the top five companies in terms of annual revenue. Champion does offer storage but contracts all shipping through Mayflower.

Giltspur, in the process of changing the name to GES, is another large competitor but does little exhibit building. It specializes in providing show services, I&D, shipping, drayage, and everything but exhibit building, but it does a little of that when needed. Pat believes that Gerry will get GES an invitation to bid, and if GES does, it will sub the building of the booth out, and try to make its money on the other aspects of the deal (shipping, storage, etc.).

Develop an account plan for Data Telecom. In your plan, you need to consider issues such as the stage of the relationship between DT and ExhibitsPlus, the risks associated with this change in buying strategy for both sides, and relative merits of the various vendors.

Fearless Eye: Where Do We Go From Here?

Brad Mathison sat at his desk, pondering his future and the future of his company. Brad founded Fearless Eye in 1992 to provide multimedia services to the Kansas City business community. The company grew quickly, with customers throughout the United States and projected revenues in 1997 of $460,000, a 90 percent increase over 1996. He knew that his employees were counting on him to make the right decisions to continue growing the company, while maintaining the relaxed atmosphere that had encouraged creative, artistic thinking thus far.

The Multimedia Industry

Multimedia can be defined as media (software and associated equipment) that combine text, sound, video, animation, and/or graphics into a single presentation. Multimedia began with computer animation products, and advances in computer technology have led to an explosion in the market for multimedia products. Exhibit 1 provides an overview of the computer animation industry.

In 1994 the computer animation industry represented 19.4 percent of the total computer graphics industry, with an annual growth rate of 32 percent. If this trend continues, the computer animation industry is projected to produce worldwide revenues of $21.2 billion in 1998. The North American market is estimated to be $11.9 in 1998. Exhibits 2 and 3 provide an overview of revenues for the industry.

Despite the size of the market, industry profitability often has been inconsistent for a number of reasons. Human capital is scarce and expensive, capital costs are relatively high, and production costs are difficult to project. Expansion of operations requires talented, cross-trained employees. In 1996 14,000 animators graduated from art school, while 34,000 positions opened up. Fifty percent of California's Rowland High School graduates go to work for Disney at starting salaries of $40,000. Entry-level salaries quickly escalate to over $80,000.

Because technology drives the industry, capital requirements are substantial. A complete workstation can

This case was prepared by Faye McIntyre, Merle E. Frey, and Randolph E. Schwering for the purpose of class discussion only and is not intended to represent effective or ineffective marketing decision making.

range from $40,000 to $100,000. And rapid advancements can render existing and nondepreciated equipment obsolete. Capital costs have declined, however. Windows NT animation systems are now available for $30,000 to $40,000 and serve as an alternative to Silicon Graphics Unix systems, which cost $70,000 and up.

Added to these factors is the long development cycle typical of the industry. Movies can take years to make and require a huge, and many times temporary, influx of employees and equipment. Production of video games can take a year or more with average start-up costs ranging from $50,000 to $250,000 and high end costs reaching $2,000,000.

Customer Needs

Both the customers for the multimedia industry and their needs are diverse. Professional presentations are in high demand among corporate clients, who request interactive training and marketing tools ranging in cost from $400 to $500,000.

There is an ever increasing demand for special effects among video and movie production companies. The movie *The Titanic,* released in 1997, illustrates one application. Though filmed in a warm location, the movie was set in much colder temperatures. Compositing, the merging of film and animation, allowed the producers to add the effect of colder air by animating actors' "breath."

Game animation and interactive web page development are also growing, but the "bread and butter" for many firms is forensic animation products. Though this segment is a relatively small portion of the overall multimedia market, revenues from these customers are key to Fearless Eye. There are few competitors for forensic animation and growing demand for quality work by experienced firms. However, forensic engineering projects require technical expertise that most animators often lack. Thus, Fearless Eye often subcontracts for this expertise, adding to costs and complicating product delivery schedules.

For all customers, two factors are essential: time and costs. Improved technology has greatly reduced the time required to develop multimedia products. In such a hardware-intensive industry, faster rendering speed (the ability to have the computer develop animated models from information provided by the worker) of workstations on the market today allows for quick creative refinements to animation. A 30-second video that once took weeks to render can now be created overnight.

Exhibit 1

History of the
Computer
Animation
Industry

- On April 20, 1951, MIT engineer Jay Forrester gave the first live demonstration of computer graphics.
- In 1959 the first computer drawing system, DAC-1, was created by General Motors and IBM, enabling the user to input 3-D descriptions and rotate the object.
- In November 1960 Digital Equipment introduced the first small interactive computer, PDP-1.
- In 1961 MIT student Steve Russell created that first video game, "Spacewar."
- During the mid-1960s IBM responded to corporate interest in computer graphics by releasing the first commercially available graphics computer, IBM2250.
- In 1968 the University of Utah formed a world-class computer science program led by Dave Evans.
- In the 1970s CBS Sports and Bell Labs used computer graphics on television to create movement and rotation of company labels.
- Star Wars was released in 1975, displaying the first use of computer-aided modeling in the movie industry.
- In 1982 Lucas Films and Atari created the first film studio/video game production company, LucasArts.
- In 1985 the multimedia industry is created as compact discs with read-only memory (CD-ROMs) were created, allowing digitized music and full-motion video to be used more effectively than they could be on floppy disks.
- In 1986 a new venue was created for computer graphics, the courtroom, as Forensic Technologies used forensic animation to help jurors visualize events relative to the case.
- Also in 1986 Disney used computer graphics in place of hand-drawn cell animation for the first time during creation of the movie, *The Great Mouse Detective*.
- In March 1989 Pixar Animation Group won an Academy Award for the fully animated short film *Tin Toy*.
- In 1991 Disney and Pixar agreed to create the first computer-animated, full-length feature film, *Toy Story*.
- In 1992 computer animation was used for the first time in a criminal trial as forensic animation was used to trace the path of eight bullets.
- In 1993 *Jurassic Park* was released, introducing the movie industry to its 3-D dinosaurs.
- In 1995 *Toy Story*, the world's first feature film created solely with the use of computers, was released.
- By 1995 nearly 50% of all films made in Hollywood contained digitally enhanced images.
- In 1995 the Department of Defense conducted its largest military excursion ever as over 300 sites were simultaneously linked, thanks to the use of 3-D computing.

Reduced production costs allow customers to spend money elsewhere. Compositing created the feel of the desired location for *The Titanic* without the expense of being there. Ralph Maiers, visual effects supervisor for Digital Magic in Santa Monica, California, said, "Without these tools, the fight sequence on the wall [of *The Long Kiss Goodnight*] probably would have cost a little over $1.5 million, but it was done with them for about $250,000."

Competition

Local competition in the Midwest region is relatively young and consists mostly of small firms. Most companies in the industry operate as owner/operators. There is strong competition for the local animation, interactive media, and video productions segments and weaker competition for forensic animation. Exhibit 4 provides a list of local and regional competition for these four products.

Though Internet site developers are abundant, many do not have the expertise to develop 3-D graphics, animation, and interactive sites. This may change in the future as customers expect more of their Internet sites.

Other potential changes in the competitive structure include the possibility of more start-up firms with the reduction in hardware and software

Exhibit 2

Computer Graphics Industry Revenues (in billions), by Application, 1993, 1998

	1993	1998 (Projected)
CAD/CAM	$10.8	$13.8
Art/animation	2.5	5.6
Multimedia	10.0	24.2
Real-time simulation	0.5	1.0
Scientific visualization	2.1	4.9
Graphic arts	2.6	6.5
Virtual reality	0.1	1.3
Other	7.4	11.6
Total	36.0	68.9

Exhibit 3

Computer Animation Industry Revenues (in billions) by Application, 1994

Film and video production	$2.17
Advertising	.98
Broadcast	.97
Corporate communications	.87
Games	.21

costs, an increase in the capability of in-house corporate departments, and increased overlap between multimedia firms and other business-to-business service providers (e.g., video production companies developing animation and advertising agencies building multimedia capabilities). Some in the industry have suggested that advanced artificial intelligence may one day obviate the need for animators altogether. At this point, the industry remains "relaxed" with most firms serving as specialty service providers.

Fearless Eye

In spite of heavy capital investment, Fearless Eye has a strong balance sheet and low debt ratio. Exhibit 5 provides a breakdown of how revenues are allocated. With a pretax profit of 27 percent, the firm should be in good shape to reinvest for future growth.

Fearless Eye currently has eight employees (including Brad): six full-time and two part-time. All are young, in their early to midtwenties, with a strong desire to work in a "fun" atmosphere where they can maximize their creative talents. This has contributed to a reputation for providing high-quality products. The firm has high credibility with an impressive client list, including Sprint. This has led to Fearless Eye's ability to charge a price of $125 per man hour for its services, compared with $75 to $120 charged by local competitors. Unfortunately, the atmosphere has also led to problems with the business side of the operations. Employees prefer the creative part of the job and many times fail to accurately track hours spent for particular clients, making it difficult for Brad to price a finished product and project profitability accurately.

The Current Situation

Because multimedia is a young, fast-growing industry, Fearless Eye is well positioned to build its business in a number of ways. Fearless Eye could continue to be a generalist in multimedia products, or the firm could choose to specialize by concentrating its efforts on one or two segments of the market. Another option is to align with advertising agencies and/or production companies.

A second, but equally important, issue is that of pricing. In addition to problems with employees accurately tracking time spent on projects, Brad questions how to measure the time required for "creativity." Personal experience indicates that many creative ideas are not generated while sitting at the workstation or even at the office.

Exhibit 4
Competitive Firms

Competition for Interactive
- Digital Lagoon
- Forcade & Associates
- Propeller Creative
- Metro Productions
- Macvideo Interactive
- Image Group New Media
- Look & Fell Newmedia
- Media 5
- Trinity
- Deepwater
- Media Farm
- Designlab Corp.
- Rick Herman Design

Competition for Video Production
- Digital Lagoon
- Metro Productions
- Macvideo Interactive
- Paddock Productions
- Flagler Productions
- Video University Productions
- American Media Group
- Video Post
- Take 2 Productions
- Great Plains Television
- The Animation Studio
- On Location Video

Competition for Animation
- Media 5
- Forcade & Associates
- The Animation Studio
- Metro Productions
- Macvideo Interactive
- Video University Productions
- Trinity
- Digital Lagoon
- Forensic Media
- Media Farm Video Post
- RSI

Competition for Forensic Animation
- The Animation Studio
- Video Production University
- RSI
- Forensic Media
- Engineering Animation

Exhibit 5
Net Revenue
Allocation, YTD
July 1997

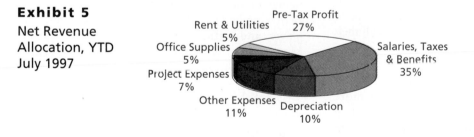

Pre-Tax Profit 27%
Rent & Utilities 5%
Office Supplies 5%
Project Expenses 7%
Other Expenses 11%
Depreciation 10%
Salaries, Taxes & Benefits 35%

Another complication in the pricing decision is how to price products that include graphic objects already developed by Fearless Eye. A software graphic object refers to programming that combines data and procedures into a miniature stand-alone program. This software object can be developed once, then reused in other applications. More than graphic "clip art," these objects can incorporate complex properties depicting movement, dynamic response to external parameters, etc. As Fearless Eye produces new products, its library of graphic objects is growing, as is the question of how to price the use of the objects beyond the product in which they were developed.

Brad is unsure about what to do, but he realizes these decisions will impact the long-term viability of the firm.

Fruit of the Loom® Activewear

Fruit of the Loom® Activewear is a line of high-quality unembellished wearables produced and marketed by Fruit of the Loom. This outerwear line consists primarily of shirts, sweats (fleece), and sport shirts, as well as some jackets, pants, and shorts. These products are made of jersey and fleece knit, pique, denim, nylon, and other types of cotton and cotton–polyester blend fabrics.

Currently, Fruit of the Loom (FTL) Activewear products generate in excess of $500 million in sales through the company's direct activewear customer base. Ninety percent of these revenues are from sales to wholesalers and large screen printers, with the remaining 10 percent of sales coming from special accounts, which are private label customers and other direct sales. More than 100 multi- and single-brand wholesalers nationwide service the imprinted activewear market by reselling blank activewear primarily to embellishers (screenprinters and embroiderers) of which there are between 40,000 and 50,000 in the United States.

An important segment of the market for Fruit of the Loom's Activewear is the promotional products market, consisting of about 15,000 independent promotional products distributors (PPDs). After purchasing the items from wholesalers or embellishers, these distributors sell imprinted items to "end users," who consist of a variety of corporate and organizational buyers. End users then incorporate the items—which are imprinted with their logo, name, and/or message—into their marketing, advertising, and other promotional programs to achieve objectives with their customers, employees, and stakeholders.

Fruit of the Loom would like to position itself as *the* educational source for information about wearables, assisting distributors in becoming more comfortable with and knowledgeable about selling wearables, especially the Fruit of the Loom brand, to end users. FTL's management wishes to create top-of-the-mind awareness among distributors for Fruit of the Loom as well as stimulate demand for the Fruit of the Loom brand. Fruit of the Loom's goal is that distributors specify the FTL brand when ordering wearables from wholesalers or embellishers.

This case was prepared by Marjorie J. Cooper, PhD (Baylor University), for the Promotional Products Association International (PPAI) annual collegiate competition, and is used with PPAI's permission. The case was adapted for class discussion purposes; data may have been disguised.

A Brief History

In 1926, Jacob Goldfarb, a Polish immigrant, purchased the Union Underwear Company in Indianapolis, Indiana. At that time Union Underwear produced only one undergarment, the so-called unionsuit. Today, Fruit of the Loom is publicly held and listed on the New York Stock Exchange (as FTL), and its operating headquarters are in Bowling Green, Kentucky.

Over the years, Fruit of the Loom has consistently focused on developing its vertical manufacturing structure, its ownership of its manufacturing entities. Today, the company not only produces a number of lines of clothing but also owns and operates the plants that produce many of the fabrics from which the clothing is made.

In 1992, Fruit of the Loom experienced one of the greatest expansion years in the history of the company. Seven new manufacturing facilities were added, and the company sold more than one billion garments in a single year.

Today, Fruit of the Loom employs 33,000 people in more than 50 locations around the world. Fruit of the Loom manufactures and markets basic family apparel, including printable activewear, casualwear, sportswear, infant and children's wear, socks, and underwear for men, boys, ladies, and girls. Brand names include Fruit of the Loom, BVD, Gitano, Best, Cumberland Bay, Screen Stars, Lofteez, Proplayer, and Official Fan. Licensed brands include Munsingwear, Wilson, Botany 500, and John Henry.

Product Description

Fruit of the Loom Activewear includes garments made primarily from jersey, fleece, denim, pique, knit, nylon, and other materials. Jersey is the fabric used in the manufacture of almost all basic T-shirts. The fabric consists of a variable weight, circular (flat) knit with a plain stitch in which the loops (courses and wails) intermesh in only one direction. Fleece is a circular knit fabric consisting of a thick, smooth, heavy face and a soft "napped" backing with a surface that resembles sheep's wool. Used in many better-quality golf or sports shirts, pique knit fabric is a medium- to heavy-weight circular fabric where the courses are raised in the warp direction, giving the appearance of a honeycomb texture. These three fabrics are made into jackets, shirts, pants, shorts, and other "outerwear" in many different colors and styles.

How the Promotional Products Industry Works

Promotional products are imprinted items that are given away (1) without obligation (in which case they are called specialty advertising) on the part of the recipient or (2) as a reward (premium) for the recipient's having done something to earn the product, such as making a purchase, opening an account, or fulfilling the stipulations of a loyalty program. Promotional products, however, are not only given to customers. These useful items are given for employee recognition and productivity, as "thank-you" gifts by charity organizations to valued donors, and as incentives to stimulate sales force productivity. In fact, the uses for promotional products in a variety of organizational settings are virtually limitless.

The types of items that are used range from inexpensive key tags, pens, and magnets to expensive leather accessories, crystal, and original artwork. At least 17,000 different items have been identified as having been used as promotional products in the past, and the list continues to grow.

Wearables—caps, jackets, shirts, shorts, gloves, and other clothing items—make up approximately 24% of the volume in promotional products. Thus, wearables are an important category of promotional products and account for more than $2 billion in promotional product sales annually. It is the wearables segment of the promotional products market that is of interest to Fruit of the Loom.

A central issue for this case is the structure and functionality of the distribution channels within the promotional products industry. The most common distribution channel in the promotional products industry looks something like this:

Manufacturer → Embellisher → Promotional Products Distributor (PPD) → End User → Recipient

In general, embellishers order blank products from manufacturers and imprint them with an end user's name, logo, and/or message, depending on the directions supplied by PPDs. Embellishers are usually called "suppliers" in the promotional products

industry, and they imprint using such processes as screen printing and embroidery.

Promotional products distributors perform a function for clients analogous to that performed by advertising agencies for advertisers. In fact, ad agencies often work with PPDs as they assist clients in putting together a total promotional program that includes promotional products as one of the selected media.

Either as part of a larger advertising program or independently, PPDs meet with clients (end users) and determine their promotional needs. For example, a client may plan to introduce a new product or wish to increase store traffic. The client may be interested in doing an internal marketing program to increase productivity among employees or in conducting a sales force contest. Some end users are businesses, and some are nonprofit organizations that use promotional products for fundraising or increasing their pool of donors.

PPDs help end users determine their promotional objectives, and then distributors design a program that will help the end user meet those objectives. Because distributors are experts in the application of promotional products, these useful imprinted items always carry out an important role in the execution of the client's marketing communications programs.

Recipients are those toward whom promotional products programs are targeted. They may be customers, employees, stockholders, the media, or some other group in which the organization has an interest.

FTL emphasizes that it does not wish to challenge or change this channel of distribution. It would be difficult, as well as cost-prohibitive, to physically reach and properly service PPDs using a field sales force. Rather, the company's objective is to better educate distributors about the use of wearables as promotional products in general and to stimulate preference among distributors for FTL brand apparel.

It should be noted that many PPDs use salespeople to call on end users. These salespeople are sometimes distributors' employees and sometimes independent contractors to distributors. Since end users look on these salespeople as experts in the promotional products area, the influence of the sales force cannot be overstated. Promotional products salespeople are in a position to guide end users in their selection of wearables products and brands.

Fruit of the Loom's Distribution Channels

The distribution channel described above is a generic channel used by many distributors in the promotional products industry. However, Fruit of the Loom's distribution channels are many and varied, even within the promotional products industry. Following are the different channels used by FTL:

1. *FTL → wholesaler → PPD → corporation*

   FTL bills the wholesaler for blank goods. The PPD purchases blanks from the wholesaler and has the wholesaler drop ship to an embellisher. The embellisher bills the PPD for embellishment and ships the finished product to the corporation or its fulfillment house. (A fulfillment house is a company that is paid by the end user to warehouse products and ship them when the end user needs them.) The PPD bills the corporation for the finished product.

2. *FTL → wholesaler → embellisher → PPD → corporation (end user)*

   This is the standard distribution channel for the promotional products industry. FTL bills the wholesaler for blank goods. The wholesaler bills the embellisher for blank goods. The embellisher imprints the blank goods and bills the PPD for the finished product. The PPD bills the corporation for the finished product. In some cases, however, the wholesaler may bill the PPD for the blank goods with the embellisher being paid separately for embellishment by the PPD.

3. *FTL → embellisher → corporation*

   Fruit of the Loom bills the embellisher for the cost of the garments. The embellisher in turn bills the corporation for the finished product.

4. *FTL → wholesaler → embellisher → corporation*

   FTL bills the wholesaler for blank goods. The wholesaler bills the embellisher for blank goods, and the embellisher bills the corporation for finished goods.

5. *FTL → integrated wholesaler/embellisher → corporation*

   FTL bills the integrated wholesaler/embellisher for the blank garment. The wholesaler/embellisher bills the corporation for the garment and the embellishment.

6. *FTL → PPD → corporation*

   FTL bills the PPD for blank goods. The PPD arranges for embellishment/delivery and bills the corporation.

There are several issues to note concerning the distribution of FTL wearables in each of these channels. First, in some cases the PPD is bypassed, which is a sensitive issue within the promotional products industry. Second, the embellisher may be a screenprinter or embroiderer. Third, the PPD may assume the role of a fulfillment house. And, finally, some wholesalers and PPDs have internal embellishment capabilities. FTL has little ability to influence these distribution channels and choices.

Remember that PPDs, regardless of how they purchase wearables, control a large percentage of corporate markets. Since PPDs are often the brand decision makers for wearables, FTL needs to achieve high levels of recognition and preference among PPDs and their salespeople.

Objectives

Fruit of the Loom's goal is to increase sales of FTL Activewear products to PPDs through wholesalers/embellishers. Yet it is currently impossible to measure these sales or sales variances because most of FTL's sales volume is done through wholesalers/embellishers. Therefore, FTL management believes that the best way to establish a benchmark and to measure progress is through "top-of-mind" survey data.

In a recent research project, PPDs were asked, "When considering T-shirts, what brand comes to mind first?" Fruit of the Loom ranked number 2 with 33 percent of respondents citing the FTL brand first. Hanes ranked number 1 with 42 percent of respondents. The next leading competitor was Russell with 8 percent.

FTL then asked, "When considering fleece, what brand comes to mind first?" FTL ranked number 1 with 22 percent of respondents. Hanes ranked number 2 with 20 percent, and Russell was third with 18 percent.

Finally, respondents were asked, "When considering sport shirts (golf shirts), what brand comes to mind first?" FTL ranked number 4, tied with Anvil brand, with 4 percent of respondents saying that FTL came to mind first. Outer Banks was number 1 with 23.6 percent, Hanes was number 2 with 9.8 percent, and Jonathan Corey was number 3 with 6.2 percent. The next leading competitors were Crystal Springs and Russell/Jerzeez, tied at 3.8 percent.

With this data in mind, FTL's two-year marketing communications goal is to achieve the following "top-of-mind" recognition in annual iterations of this same study:

- *T-shirts.* Rank number 1 with at least a 4 percent point gain.

- *Fleece.* Gain at least 3 percentage points and maintain the number 1 ranking.

- *Sport shirts.* Secure a solid number 2 position and a minimum 7 percentage point gain.

Target Market

The promotional products apparel market constitutes a substantial opportunity for FTL to market its Activewear line. As indicated above, most promotional products distributors (PPDs) purchase promotional apparel from wholesalers and embellishers. Most distributors, particularly if they are ordering in large volume, order directly from wholesalers, preferring to do the embellishing themselves or to contract directly with an embellisher.

There are approximately 15,000 distributors in the promotional products industry, accounting for more than $9 billion in industry sales annually. They are located throughout the United States and in many foreign countries. However, for this case, you should concentrate your efforts on the U.S. market.

Many distributors are small, with only one to five employees. There are, however, about 373 distributors with sales volume of $2.5 million or larger. These distributors, who account for approximately 44 percent of the annual $9 billion+ in promotional products sales, are of keen interest to FTL.

FTL's research indicates that PPDs significantly influence promotional product apparel purchasing decisions, particularly the brand purchased. Other research among PPDs indicates that they and their end users are looking for some key benefits from manufacturers and embellishers:

- *Quality product.* Because the products that the end user gives out to customers, employees, and other constituencies are so closely tied to the end user's company or organization, it is imperative that the quality reflect the image that the end user wishes to portray. Distributors, as well as end users and recipients, appreciate a well-made product.

- *Product consistency.* It is especially important to end users that all products they include in their programs be of a consistent quality and workmanship.

- *Good value.* End users like to give away promotional items that have a perceived value higher than the actual cost. Thus the end user appears generous, and recipients believe they are getting more value than the actual cost of the item.

- *Fast turnaround.* When end users order wearables, they are often operating under tight deadlines. Thus, the ability of the wholesaler and embellisher to produce and deliver the item quickly becomes an important criterion in the PPD's supplier selection.

- *Known and trusted brand names.* Both end users and recipients look for familiar brands that they recognize. A nationally known and respected brand adds perceived value to the imprinted item.

- *Choice of style.* Not all end users want to give the same T-shirt or jacket. They want to select new, updated styles with which recipients will be impressed.

End users tend to rely on distributors' expertise in deciding which brand of wearables will be best for a program. For example, if an end user wants an order of T-shirts, he or she will usually defer to the distributor's judgment as to which brand of T-shirt to order. It is for this reason that FTL's objective is to establish closer ties with distributors.

Competition

Fruit of the Loom identifies three sets of competitors in the promotional wearables marketplace:

1. *First and second tier apparel mills.* Examples are Hanes, Russell/Jerzeez, Anvil, Oneita, and Lee. This category of competitor competes head-to-head with FTL for the floor space of wholesalers of blank merchandise, such as Staton

Wholesale and Broder Brothers. Which products wholesalers select to carry and how much product they purchase for resale to their customers depends on demand for a particular style and brand, wholesalers' ability to "turn" (merchandise "turns" are how many times in a given period the merchandise can be sold) the product, price, and promotional activity. This category of competitor would be the most negatively affected by increased brand awareness and sell-through by FTL.

2. *Manufacturers of promotional wearables.* Examples include Swingster, W.E.K., Dunbrook, and K-Products. These competitors rarely sell to blank wholesalers. Rather, they sell to PPDs as well as directly to corporate clients. They tend to specialize in a particular product niche or have custom capabilities. Additionally, they will frequently sell a finished, embellished product rather than a blank product.

3. *All other manufacturers of promotional products.* Examples of these include Cross Writing Instruments, Hazel (notebooks and leather products), phone card manufacturers, and anyone else who manufacturers products that compete for end users' promotional products dollars. However, since wearables is the single largest category of promotional products (24 percent), and since FTL's research indicates that PPDs and corporate purchasers understand the value of imprinted wearables versus other promotional products, FTL does not spend a lot of resources trying to convince PPDs to buy wearables rather than other promotional product items.

In addition to competition from other well-known brands, Fruit of the Loom is experiencing competition from global economic factors that impact the wearables industry. With the rapidly changing tariff structure in the United States, imports, including reduced-duty programs such as 9802, have increased. (A 9802 program is a case in which the fabric is knitted and cut to shape in the United States and sent offshore for assembly. The finished product is then shipped back to the United States for sale.) This situation has resulted in a commoditization of wearables such that brand importance along with brand equity has declined.

Promotion and Advertising

In the past, Fruit of the Loom has used a variety of means to communicate with distributors. The company has a program that provides samples and sales tool kits to distributors, along with Activewear catalogs. FTL has used trade shows, a rebate program, and educational seminars to better reach distributors. Advertising in industry trade publications has also been part of FTL's communication program.

Currently, FTL offers its blank Activewear wholesalers co-op reimbursement for qualifying advertisements and nonadvertising activities that promote the FTL brand. Reimbursement is made to direct customers up to a maximum of 1 percent of their total dollar purchases from Fruit of the Loom on a calendar-year accrual basis. The program applies to all advertising of Activewear first-quality products with the various FTL garment label trademarks. Reimbursements per claimed advertising expense are made on an 80 percent/20 percent basis (with FTL paying 80 percent) or, in some cases, on a 50 percent/50 percent basis. FTL also offers wholesalers who participate in certain FTL promotional programs an additional 0.5 percent of annual dollar purchases for advertising specifically to the promotional products distributor market.

Assignment

Fruit of the Loom's objective is to increase sales of Fruit of the Loom Activewear styles through its existing network of wholesalers. More specifically, FTL wants to expand and strengthen its relationships with distributors, creating a pull-through demand that includes the present network of wholesalers in its distribution channel. That is, FTL wants distributors to purchase FTL from wholesalers and/or ask their embellishers to order Fruit of the Loom from wholesalers.

FTL believes that it is essential to create a greater link between FTL and the existing network of distributors. The company desires to play a more personal and engaged role in PPDs' businesses. The company believes that by communicating its brand message effectively and by providing PPDs with education and tools to assist them in selling wearables, it will engender brand and product awareness as well as brand loyalty, thus "pulling" the FTL product through the wholesale network to distributors.

The assignment is to develop a business to business advertising and promotional campaign/ program to assist Fruit of the Loom in successfully reaching its stated target market, promotional products distributors. Your role is that of a promotional products distributor, whose client is Fruit of the Loom and whose target market on behalf of your client is other promotional products distributors.

This campaign must specify the specific target audience(s) and provide ideas, promotions, tools, and communication tactics (including events, if applicable) for stimulating distributor interest in the FTL brand apparel. Please note that your target market is not wholesalers, embellishers, or end users but specifically promotional products distributors.

This project is intended to be a comprehensive, integrated marketing communications campaign. This means that the campaign you develop should include any of the following that you deem advisable: direct mail, trade advertising, special event sponsorships, and/or educational programs. The decision about what to include is up to you.

The total annual budget for the advertising/ promotion campaign is $500,000 to cover all media costs, including promotional products. This budget does not cover sales force or publicity expenses.

The program that you recommend should contain a plan for prioritizing target audiences. You may find that your budget will limit this campaign to only certain prospects. In this case, your plan should also include a rationale for which target segment you have elected to reach.

It will also be necessary to develop messages and incentives that will produce results. Some marketing avenues yield a greater return than others; and with a limited budget for a complete national campaign, you will need to plan carefully to maximize the efficiency and effectiveness of your plan. Consider also how you will measure those results.

Again, your plan must include promotional products marketing—that is, the use of advertising specialties and/or premiums—and it may include targeted media, such as direct mail. Your plan may also include industry trade publications and trade show promotions. Messages should be high-impact, positive, and exciting for your target audience. Most of all, you should keep in mind the unique structure of the promotional products distribution channel.

You are expected to do your own research, rounding out the information given in this case with data that you compile on your own from either primary or secondary sources. One source of information can be found at the online Promotion Clinic sponsored by the Promotional Products Association International. The address is **http://www.promotion-clinic.ppa.org.** Additional information can be found at Fruit of the Loom's Activewear site at **www.FruitActivewear.com** and Fruit of the Loom's site at **www.Fruit.com.**

MacTec Control AB

Georg Carlsson is president of MacTec Control AB, a Swedish firm located in Kristianstad. Georg began MacTec in 1980 with his wife, Jessie. MacTec grew rapidly and now boasts of 30 employees and annual revenues of about $2.8 million. Since 1985, MacTec has been partly owned by the Perstorp Corporation whose headquarters are located nearby. Perstorp is a large manufacturer of chemicals and chemical products, with operations in 18 countries and annual revenues of about $600 million. Perstorp has provided MacTec with capital and managerial advice, as well as chemical analysis technology.

MacTec's Aqualex System

MacTec's product line centers around its Aqualex system: computer hardware and software designed to monitor and control pressurized water flow. The water flow consists mostly of potable water or sewage effluent as these liquids are stored, moved, or treated by municipal water departments.

The system employs MacTec's MPDII microcomputer, installed at individual pumping stations where liquids are stored and moved. Often these stations are located quite far apart, linking geographically dispersed water users (households, businesses, etc.) to water and sewer systems. The microcomputer performs a number of important functions. It controls the starts, stops, and alarms of up to four pumps, monitors levels and available capacities of storage reservoirs, checks pump capacities and power consumptions, and records pump flows. It even measures the amount of rainfall entering reservoirs and adjusts pump operations or activates an alarm as needed. Each microcomputer can also easily be connected to a main computer to allow remote control of pumping stations and produce a variety of charts and graphs useful in evaluating pump performance and scheduling needed maintenance.

The Aqualex system provides a monitoring function that human operators cannot match in terms of sophistication, immediacy, and cost. The system per-

This case was written by Professor James E. Nelson, University of Colorado. © 1989 by the Business Research Division, College of Business and Administration and the Graduate School of Business Administration, University of Colorado, Boulder, CO 80309-0419.

mits each individual substation to: control its own pumping operations; collect, analyze, and store data; forecast trends; transmit data and alarms to a central computer; and receive remote commands. Alarms can also be transmitted directly to a pocket-size receiver carried by one or more operators on call. A supervisor can continually monitor pumping operations in a large system entirely via a computer terminal at a central location and send commands to individual pumps, thereby saving costly service calls and time. The system also reduces the possibility of overflows that could produce disastrous flooding in nearby communities.

MacTec personnel work with water and sewage engineers to design and install the Aqualex system. Personnel also train engineers and operators to work with the system and are available 24 hours a day for consultation. If needed, a MacTec engineer can personally assist engineers and operators if major problems arise. MacTec also offers its clients the option of purchasing a complete service contract whereby MacTec personnel provide periodic testing and maintenance of installed systems.

An Aqualex system has several versions. In its most basic form, the system is little more than a small "black box" that monitors two or three lift station activities and, when necessary, transmits an alarm to one or more remote receivers. An intermediate system monitors additional activities, sends data to a central computer via telephone lines and receives remote commands. An advanced system provides the same monitoring capabilities but has forecasting features, maintenance management, auxiliary power back-up, and data transmission and reception via radio. Prices for the three different types in early 1989 are $1,200, $2,400, and $4,200.

Aqualex Customers

Aqualex customers can be divided into two groups—governmental units and industrial companies. The typical application in the first group is a sewage treatment plant having 4 to 12 pumping stations, each station containing one or more pumps. Pumps operate intermittently and, unless an Aqualex or similar system is in place, are monitored by one or more operators who visit each station once or twice each day for about half an hour. Operators take reservoir measurements, record running times of pumps, and sometimes perform limited maintenance and repairs. The sewage plant and stations are typically located in flat or rolling terrain, where gravity cannot be used in lieu of pumping. If any monitoring equipment is present at all, it typically consists of a crude, on-site alarm that activates when fluid levels rise or fall beyond a preset level. Sometimes the alarm activates a telephone dialing function that alerts an operator away from the station.

Numerous industrial companies also store, move, and process large quantities of water or sewage. These applications usually differ very little from those in governmental plants except for their smaller size. On the other hand, there are considerably more industrial companies with pumping stations and so, Georg thinks, the two markets often offer close to identical market potentials in many countries.

The two markets desire essentially the same products, although industrial applications often use smaller, simpler equipment. Both markets want their monitoring equipment to be accurate and reliable, the two dominant concerns. Equipment should also be easy to use, economical to operate, and require little regular service or maintenance. Purchase price often is not a major consideration. As long as the price is in an appropriate range, customers seem more interested in actual product performance than in initial cost outlays.

Georg thinks worldwide demand for Aqualex systems and competing products will continue to be strong for at least the next 10 years. While some of this demand represents construction of new pumping stations, many applications are replacements of crude monitoring and alarm systems at existing sites. These existing systems depend greatly on regular visits by operators, visits that often continue even after new equipment is installed. Most such trips are probably not necessary. However, many managers find it difficult to dismiss or reassign monitoring personnel that are no longer needed; many are also quite cautious and conservative, desiring some human monitoring of the new equipment "just in case." Once replacement of existing systems is complete, market growth is limited to new construction and, of course, replacements with more sophisticated systems.

Most customers (and noncustomers) consider the Aqualex system the best on the market. Those knowledgeable in the industry feel that competing products seldom match Aqualex's reliability and accuracy. Experts also believe that many competing products lack the sophistication and flexibility present in Aqualex's design. Beyond these product features, customers also appreciate MacTec's knowledge about water and sanitation engineering. Competing firms often lack this expertise, offering products somewhat as a sideline and considering the market too small for an intensive marketing effort.

The market is clearly not too small for MacTec. While Georg has no hard data on market potential for Western Europe, he thinks annual demand could be as much as $9 million. About 40 percent of this figure represents potential; the rest is demand for replacing existing systems. Industry sales in the latter category could be increased by more aggressive marketing efforts on the part of MacTec and its competitors. Eastern European economies represent additional potential. However, the water and sewer industries in these countries seem less interested in high-technology equipment to monitor pumping operations than do their Western counterparts. Additionally, business is often more difficult to conduct in these countries. In contrast, the U.S. market looks very attractive.

MacTec Strategy

MacTec currently markets its Aqualex system primarily to sewage treatment plants in Scandinavia and other countries in northern and central Europe. The company's strategy could be described as providing technologically superior equipment to monitor pumping operations at these plants. The strategy stresses frequent contacts with customers and potential customers to design, supply, and service Aqualex systems. Superior knowledge of water and sanitation engineering with up-to-date electronics and computer technology is also important. The result is a line of highly specialized sensors, computers, and methods for process controls in water treatment plants.

The essence of MacTec's strategy is demonstrating a special competence that no firm in the world can easily match. MacTec also prides itself on being a young, creative company, without an entrenched bureaucracy. Company employees generally work with enthusiasm and dedication; they talk with each other regularly and openly. Most importantly, customers—as well as technology—seem to drive all areas of the company.

MacTec's strategy in its European markets seems fairly well-decided. That is, Georg thinks that a continuation of present strategies and tactics should continue to produce good results. However, one change is the planned creation of a branch office conducting sales and manufacturing activities somewhere in the European Community (EC), most likely the Netherlands. The plan is to have such an office in operation well before 1992, when the 12 countries in the EC (Belgium, Denmark, France, Greece, Ireland, Italy, Luxembourg, the Netherlands, Portugal, Spain, United Kingdom, and West Germany) would mutually eliminate national barriers to the flow of capital, goods, and services. Having a MacTec office located in the EC would greatly simplify sales to these member countries. Moreover, MacTec's presence should also avoid problems with any protective barriers the EC itself might raise to limit or discourage market access by outsiders.

Notwithstanding activities related to this branch office, George is considering a major strategic decision to enter the U.S. market. His two recent visits to the United States have led him to conclude that the market represents potential beyond that for western Europe and that the United States seems perfect for expansion. Industry experts in the United States agree with Georg that the Aqualex system outperforms anything used in the U.S. market. Experts think many water and sewage engineers would welcome MacTec's products and knowledge. Moreover, Georg thinks U.S. transportation systems and payment arrangements would present few problems. The system would be imported under U.S. Tariff Regulation 71249 and pay a duty of 4.9 percent.

Entry would most likely occur in the form of a sales and service office located in Philadelphia. The Pennsylvania and New York state markets seem representative of the United States and appear to offer a good test of the Aqualex system. The two states together probably represent about 18 percent of total U.S. market potential for the system. The office would require an investment of $200,000 for inventory and other balance sheet items. Annual fixed costs would total close to $250,000 for salaries and other operating expenses; Georg plans to employ only a general manager, two sales technicians, and a secretary for at least the first year or two. Each Aqualex system sold in the United States would be priced to provide a contribution of about 30 percent. Georg wants a 35 percent annual return before taxes on any MacTec investment, beginning no later than the

second year. The issue is whether Georg can realistically expect to achieve this goal in the United States.

Marketing Research

Georg had commissioned the Browning Group in Philadelphia to conduct some limited marketing research with selected personnel in the water and sewage industries in the city and surrounding areas. The research had two purposes: to obtain a sense of market needs and market reactions to MacTec's products, and to calculate a rough estimate of market potential in Pennsylvania and New York. Results were intended to help Georg interpret his earlier conversations with industry experts and perhaps facilitate a decision on market entry.

The research design employed two phases of data collection. The first consisted of five one-hour, tape-recorded interviews with water and sewage engineers employed by local city and municipal governments. Questions included:

1. What procedures do you use to monitor your pumping stations?

2. Is your current monitoring system effective? Costly?

3. What are the costs of a monitoring malfunction?

4. What features would you like to see in a monitoring system?

5. Who decides on the selection of a monitoring system?

6. What is your reaction to the Aqualex system?

Interviewers listened closely to the engineers' responses and probed for additional detail and clarification.

Tapes of the personal interviews were transcribed and then analyzed by the project manager at Browning. The report noted that these results described typical industry practices and viewpoints. A partial summary from the report appears below:

> The picture that emerges is one of fairly sophisticated personnel making decisions about monitoring equipment that is relatively simple in design. Still, some engineers would appear distrustful of this equipment because they persist in sending operators to pumping stations on a daily basis. The

distrust may be justified because potential costs of a malfunction were identified as expensive repairs and cleanups, fines of $10,000 per day of violation, lawsuits, harassment by the Health department, and public embarrassment. The five engineers identified themselves as key individuals in the decision to purchase new equipment. Without exception, they considered MacTec features innovative, highly desirable, and worth the price.

The summary also noted that the primary purpose of the interview results was for construction of a questionnaire to be administered by telephone.

The questionnaire was used in the second phase of data collection, as part of a telephone survey that contacted 65 utility managers, water and sewage engineers, and pumping station operators in Philadelphia and surrounding areas. All respondents were employed by governmental units. Each interview took about 10 minutes to complete, covering topics identified in questions 1, 2, and 4 above. The Browning Group's research report stated that most respondents were quite cooperative, although 15 people refused to participate at all.

The telephone interviews produced results that could be considered more representative of the market because of the larger sample size. The report organized these results under the topics of monitoring procedures, system effectiveness and costs, and features desired in a monitoring system:

All monitoring systems under the responsibility of the 50 respondents were considered to require manual checking. The frequency of operator visits to pumping stations ranged from monthly to twice daily, depending on flow rates, pumping station history, proximity of nearby communities, monitoring equipment in operation, and other factors. Even the most sophisticated automatic systems were checked because respondents "just don't trust the machine." Each operator was responsible for some 10 to 20 stations.

Despite the perceived need for double-checking, all respondents considered their current monitoring system to be quite effective. Not one reported a serious pumping malfunction in the past three years that had escaped detection. However, this reliability came at considerable cost—the annual wages and other expenses associated with each monitoring operator averaged about $40,000.

Respondents were about evenly divided between those wishing a simple alarm system and those desiring a sophisticated, versatile microprocessor. Managers and engineers in the former category often said that the only feature they really needed was an emergency signal such as a siren, horn, or light. Sometimes they would add a telephone dialer that would be automatically activated at the same time as the signal. Most agreed that a price of around $2,000 would be reasonable for such a system. The latter category of individuals contained engineers desiring many of the Aqualex System's features, once they knew such equipment was available. A price of $4,000 per system seemed acceptable. Some of these respondents were quite knowledgeable about computers and computer programming while others were not. Only four respondents voiced any strong concerns about the cost to purchase and install more sophisticated monitoring equipment. Everyone demanded that the equipment by reliable and accurate.

Georg found the report quite helpful. Much of the information, of course, simply confirmed his own view of the U.S. market. However, it was good to have this knowledge from an independent, objective organization. In addition, to learn that the market consisted of two, apparently equal-size segments—of simple and sophisticated applications—was quite worthwhile. In particular, knowledge of system prices considered acceptable by each segment would make the entry decision easier. Meeting these prices would not be a major problem.

An important section of the report contained an estimate of market potential for Pennsylvania and New York. The estimate was based on an analysis of discharge permits on file in governmental offices in the two states. These permits are required before any city, municipality, water or sewage district, or industrial company can release sewage or other contaminated water to another system or to a lake or river. Each permit showed the number of pumping stations in operation. Based on a 10 percent sample of permits, the report estimated that governmental units in Pennsylvania and New York contain approximately 3,000 and 5,000 pumping stations for waste water, respectively. Industrial companies in the two states were estimated to add 3,000 and 9,000 more pumping stations, respectively. The total number of pumping stations in the two states (20,000) seemed to be growing at about 2 percent per year.

Finally, a brief section of the report dealt with the study's limitations. Georg agreed that sample was quite small, that it contained no utility managers or engineers from New York, and that it probably concentrated too heavily on individuals in larger urban areas. In addition, the research told him nothing about competitors and their marketing strategies and tactics. Nor did he learn anything about any state regulations for monitoring equipment, if indeed any

existed. However, these shortcomings came as no surprise, representing a consequence of the research design proposed to Georg by the Browning Group six weeks ago, before the study began.

The Decision

Georg's decision seems difficult. The most risky option is to enter the U.S. market as soon as possible; the most conservative is to stay in Europe. The option also exists of conducting additional marketing research.

Majšperk (A)

The topic of the Wednesday, May 20th, 1992 meeting had been debt: about DM1.6 millon and growing. In fact, so much debt sat on Majšperk's (pronounced MYSH-burg) balance sheet that the cash requirements for the payment of interest left nothing for the day-to-day operation of the textile mill itself. The size of the debt to Kreditna Banka Maribor and to Meilinger AG, Majšperk's main supplier of raw material, had finally spurred the bank to intervene. If some arrangement could not be worked out, a liquidation of Majšperk could put 500 textile workers in rural Slovenia permanently out of work.

The atmosphere at the meeting, conducted in German, English, and Slovenian, had been less than congenial. The bank representative, the bank's appointed consultants (FINEA), Majšperk senior management, and Herr Meilinger himself had discussed the immediate future of the company. The presence of the Western Business School MBA student, Bernd Petak, and of Olga Božič, graduate of the International Executive Development Center, was clearly not appreciated by FINEA's self-appointed meeting chairman.[1] Although officially only observers, Olga and Bernd had been asked to assist Majšperk's 29-year-old acting managing director, Nataša Vuk, to help develop a rescue plan.

On the following Friday evening, Bernd Petak and Olga Božič found themselves sitting around Nataša's conference table with Majšperk's young team of executives. Company management faced a hard deadline. At Wednesday's meeting, FINEA had notified Majšperk that it intended to submit its recommendation to Kreditna Banka Maribor by June 18th. For all practical purposes, any reorganization plan or other attempt at self-help would have to be accomplished before this deadline.

As Nataša's assistant delivered the first of many rounds of powerful Balkan coffee, Bernd wondered how he could contribute to the deliberations. He had only three more days in Slovenia before he would return to Canada. He hoped that in those three days he could help Majšperk's management assess their situation and formulate a concrete action plan. He wondered if Majšperk was worth saving? Did the company have any potential to make profit? No one seemed to have answers to these questions. However, Olga Božič, whose EMBA policy project group had analyzed Majšperk, was quite familiar with the people and the situation. To assist with the analysis, one of Majšperk's MIS analysts had installed a local area network-connected PC at the end of the long conference table. As other employees began to leave the mill for the weekend, the small group around the table got down to work.

Majšperk and the Yugoslav Textile Industry

The world market for fine wool textiles, such as those used in the manufacturing of men's suits, had long been dominated by the northern Italians. Surprisingly, the key ingredient for the production of top-quality fabric is water. Crystal clear water enables the wool, imported from Australia and New Zealand, to be dyed effectively. From their high mountain valleys, companies such as Cerruti and Zegna distributed their prestigious wares to premium clothing manufacturers around the world, building multimillion dollar family empires in the process.

Early this century, it was discovered that an area near the ancient city of Ptuj, now in Slovenia, was blessed with the pure, clean water so essential for quality textile production. A textile mill built in the tiny agricultural town of Majšperk immediately became the area's only major industrial employer. For the families in the Majšperk area, wages from the textile mill became an important supplement to the local agricultural economy. Often several members of a family worked at the mill in addition to operating their small farms. Over time, the Majšperk mill became far more than a place of work. The mill

By Bernd Petak of Deloitte & Touche Management Consultants, Nenad Filipovič of the International Executive Development Center, and Tony Dimnik of McGill University. The authors gratefully acknowledge the support of the Western Business School and the International Executive Development Center. Management cooperated in the field research for this case, which was written solely for the purpose of stimulating student discussion. All events and individuals are real. Faculty members in nonprofit institutions are encouraged to reproduce this case for distribution to their own students without charge or written permission. All other rights reserved jointly to the authors and the North American Case Research Association (NACRA). Copyright © 1994 by the *Case Research Journal*, Bernd Petak, Nenad Filipovič, and Tony Dimnik.

[1]The Western Business School is located in London, Canada. The International Executive Development Center (IEDC) is a Slovenian-based institution that offers an Executive MBA (EMBA) program to East-Central European managers.

workers organized sports activities in the community and even staged musical productions in the mill's large auditorium. As a result, the mill became an integral part of the local culture.

Under the Yugoslav brand of communism, Majšperk existed as a "socially owned" enterprise. This meant that neither the state nor any private group of investors had any claim on the owner's equity portion of the balance sheet. The management "voice" normally associated with a firm's ownership instead sat with an elected council of workers. Officially, the council had the final say in all matters relating to the operation of the mill, including the appointment of management. Although profitable operations were a desirable goal, the worker's council found itself mostly concerned with the welfare of workers. This meant that issues of safety, benefits, and full employment were of primary importance. The managing directors of socially owned enterprises were ultimately responsible to the workers they managed for all actions and company performance. Under the charter of many firms, the worker's council actively approved major policy and spending decisions, much as a board of directors would in a conventional North American corporation. By the end of 1992, controversial privatization legislation was expected to be enacted by the Slovenian parliament, clearing the way for many socially owned enterprises such as Majšperk to be placed into private hands.

Slovenian Independence

Throughout the post–World War II period, and up to his death in 1980, Yugoslavia's charismatic leader, Marshal Tito, engineered an apparent economic miracle. A clever social architecture, reinforced by the carefully applied threat of force, kept ancient ethnic rivalries subdued. Hybrid communist/capitalist economic policies then allowed Tito to generate one of the highest standards of living in Central Europe. Traditionally open borders permitted the free flow of goods in and out of the country. The heavily export-oriented economy allowed individual Yugoslavs to amass tidy sums of hard foreign currency. These were often spent on consumer goods via shopping expeditions to neighbouring countries such as Austria. In 1980, the death of Tito heralded the end of relative harmony in Yugoslav politics. Inspired by the fall of communism in other East-Central European coun-

tries, and fuelled by regional nationalism, ethnic unrest reappeared. Throughout the 1980s, great stress was placed on the Yugoslav economy and, consequently, on companies such as Majšperk. The ability of individual Yugoslavs to afford luxuries was drastically reduced, and it became clear that Yugoslavia's economic success had come with a price tag. A multibillion U.S. dollar foreign debt and a high percentage of bad loans held by domestic banks pushed the Yugoslav economy to the point of collapse. Inflation rates rose to astronomical levels, peaking in 1989 with annual percentage rates in the thousands.

When Slovenia, Yugoslavia's northernmost republic, declared independence in 1991, Majšperk suffered a further blow. Overnight, Majšperk lost access to the critical Yugoslav market. The company had to develop new international markets in order to survive.

Majšperk in Crisis

In late 1991, Olga Božič and a group of her IEDC classmates were given permission to study Majšperk for a policy project. The group found Majšperk to be in poor shape. Technically bankrupt, the company had shown a loss in two of the last three years (see Exhibit 1), and had experienced monthly cash shortages. Starting in the late 1980s, the occasional inability to meet the payroll forced Majšperk's managing director to request a substantial series of loans from Kreditna Banka Maribor, the local state-owned bank. The high interest rates associated with these loans saddled Majšperk's income statement with large payments, which increased losses and further exacerbated the cash shortages. By October 1991, Majšperk was no longer able to meet its debt obligations. Taking on additional debt was not expedient, since monthly inflation rates in Slovenia were over 5 percent and interest rates remained very high. The debt crisis was accentuated by the unusually liberal trade credit (net 90 days) offered to Majšperk by Meilinger AG of Germany. Majšperk had come to depend on Herr Meilinger's generous credit terms as a source of short-term financing. The deteriorating situation is what had led Herr Meilinger and his bookkeeper to attend the May 20th meeting in person.

Olga Božič and her IEDC policy project group had made a number of sweeping recommendations at the conclusion of their study in 1991. One of their key recommendations was the removal of the

Exhibit 1
Majšperk Three-Year Income Summary*

	1989	1990	1991
Net sales	12,074,171	17,986,428	8,774,700
Total expenses	6,020,131	14,707,430	6,482,513
Operating profit	6,054,040	3,278,998	2,292,187
Interest expenses	7,161,115	1,725,714	3,770,260
Provision for taxes	91,555	619,286	0
Net income	–1,198,630	933,998	–1,468,073

*All figures are converted to DM from either Yugoslav dinar (1989, 1990) or Slovenian tolar (1991), at yearly average exchange rates.
SOURCE: Company records.

managing director. The worker's council concurred, appointing Nataša Vuk as acting managing director. Other key retirements resulted in new, younger management in all key positions.

Despite the change in management, many of the problems identified by the policy group continued to plague Majšperk. The company still had a very complicated costing system that provided little information for decision making because costs were arbitrarily allocated to production. Management had no way of accurately determining which products or orders contributed positively to profits and which did not. Since they did not have accurate cost information, management could not focus their marketing efforts on the most profitable products. The accounting system was good at generating reports required by law but it did not provide management with regular, accurate, and timely financial information on company performance.

Another continuing problem was excess personnel. Reduced sales had made some of the company's work force redundant. Workers had been sent home for months at a time due to reduced production schedules, but these workers continued to receive full salaries.

Despite the problems, the situation at Majšperk was not entirely hopeless. The IEDC policy group identified a number of positive elements in the operations of the firm. Majšperk was recognized as a quality producer. It was even suggested in one customer interview that product quality was "higher than necessary." Majšperk's spinning and weaving equipment consisted primarily of older, fully depreciated machines. Over the years these machines had been fine-tuned for optimum performance. Majšperk's young, new management team was another positive element. They were dedicated, extremely well educated, and intimately familiar with all aspects of their company's operations.

Products

The Majšperk textile mill produced two types of products: wool fabric and knitting wool. Wool fabric was produced in a weaving process and sold to manufacturers of men's suits and other clothing. Wool fabric production was measured in meters, and product lines were identified numerically. Knitting wool was packaged in banded balls and sold by the kilogram, and product lines were identified alphabetically. The two types of wool products were further subdivided into domestic and export, and pure wool and blended wool, categories. Blended wools contained both wool and artificial fibres such as polyesters and acrylics.

Historically, Majšperk had sold all its products through distributors, but the company's management intended to expand its marketing efforts directly to clothing manufacturers and knitting wool retailers. In addition to providing raw materials, Meilinger AG had been a major international distributor of Majšperk products. To be competitive, Majšperk offered its customers minimum trade terms of net 60 days.

Friday Night

In preparation for the weekend, Branko Purg, Head of Marketing and Sales, had summarized the sales results for the first quarter of 1992 (see Exhibit 2). He thought that sales levels would be similar for each of the subsequent quarters of 1992.

Exhibit 2 Majšperk Record of Sales, 1st Quarter of 1992

Product Line	Where Sold	Quantity Sold	Unit (Meters or Kilograms)	Average Unit Price (DM)
2104a	Export	24,000	M	11.80
	Domestic	3,000	M	21.20
70295	Export	12,000	M	12.75
1535	Export	8,000	M	14.50
	Domestic	5,000	M	20.50
1907	Export	8,000	M	11.50
	Domestic	2,000	M	17.50
2239	Domestic	2,000	M	18.80
2103	Domestic	16,000	M	28.00
1093	Export	4,000	M	13.70
	Domestic	1,000	M	19.20
TFDK	Export	10,000	Kg	9.00
	Domestic	1,000	Kg	15.00
Jelka	Export	3,000	Kg	12.60
	Domestic	10,000	Kg	21.00
Sport	Domestic	2,000	Kg	30.00
Belgi	Export	64,000	Kg	2.70

SOURCE: Company records.

As the sun went down outside, Bernd Petak and Olga Božič discussed the situation. In the next few days they would have to develop some arguments to justify the existence of Majšperk. The intentions of Kreditna Banka Maribor were unknown. The following week, the bank's consultants, FINEA, would begin their investigations. Had FINEA been instructed to formulate a liquidation plan? At the very least, on June 18th it would be up to Majšperk's management to present their case in the most positive light.

Majšperk (B)

Majšperk employed six individuals to calculate product costs on an ongoing basis, but their system involved a complicated and arbitrary method of cost allocation. At the request of Bernd Petak, Branko Purg, Head of Marketing and Sales, and Darinka Fakin, Head of Operations, analyzed the costs for each product. They had a good idea of what the material and labour costs were for each product but they had to make judgement calls for other costs. They examined each cost item and tried to determine to which product it belonged and if it was variable with the volume of that product. Their estimates of the variable costs of each product are presented in Exhibit 1. These figures include labour, material, and other costs that were thought to actually vary with

production volume. Costs thought to be fixed for the first quarter of 1992 were documented separately (see Exhibit 2), and were expected to be representative of the rest of the year.

Darinka indicated that Majšperk's normal policy was to manufacture to order. This meant that inventory levels were usually comparable between years.

Majšperk's Acting Managing Director, Nataša Vuk, estimated that interest expenses for the first quarter were DM586,865 and would stay at that level for each of the following quarters in 1992. Due to its losses, Majšperk did not incur any corporate income tax expense in the first quarter.

To minimize the distortions caused by inflation and exchange rate fluctuations, it was collectively decided that all analysis would be done in German marks, as was often done in Slovenian business.

Exhibit 1   Majšperk Variable Costs by Product Line

Product Line	Cost (DM), by Meter or Kilogram
2104a	8.10
70295	8.40
1535	8.82
1907	5.73
2239	5.15
2103	8.76
1093	6.43
TFDK	7.67
Jelka	10.16
Sport	17.50
Belgi	0.92

SOURCE: Company records.

Exhibit 2   Majšperk Summary of Fixed Costs for 1st Quarter of 1992

Fixed Cost Area	Cost (DM)
Maintenance	205,728
Energy	102,211
Transport	11,423
Communications	3,807
Change in inventory	90,135
Office expenses	229,576
Other	180,491
Depreciation	45,462
Total	868,833

SOURCE: Company records.

By Bernd Petak of Deloitte & Touche Management Consultants, Nenad Filipovič of the International Executive Development Center, and Tony Dimnik of McGill University. The authors gratefully acknowledge the support of the Western Business School and the International Executive Development Center. Management cooperated in the field research for this case, which was written solely for the purpose of stimulating student discussion. All events and individuals are real. Faculty members in nonprofit institutions are encouraged to reproduce this case for distribution to their own students without charge or written permission. All other rights reserved jointly to the authors and the North American Case Research Association (NACRA). Copyright © 1994 by the *Case Research Journal,* Bernd Petak, Nenad Filipovič, and Tony Dimnik.

Majšperk (C)

After studying the data presented in the Majšperk (B) case, Nataša Vuk and her team turned their attention to cash flows.

Exhibits 1 and 2 indicate Majšperk's expected net sales and raw material deliveries for the balance of 1992. Exhibit 3 outlines additional cash expenditures from the first quarter of the year. These were expected to be typical of the remaining quarters, except for the value-added tax (VAT). It was expected that the VAT would drop to DM500 per month for April through September and would rise to approximately DM2000 per month in the final quarter. Majšperk also planned to purchase a new dyeing machine at a cost of DM75,000. Payments for the new machine would start in October 1992, extend for 12 months, and include interest of 12 percent per year. The DM18,750 import duty for the machine could be deferred until 1993.

Exhibit 1 Majšperk Expected Net Sales for the Balance of 1992

Month	Sales (DM)
April	403,001
May	488,978
June	404,111
July	702,117
August	899,776
September	1,046,835
October	901,116
November	712,113
December	700,706

SOURCE: Company records.

By Bernd Petak of Deloitte & Touche Management Consultants, Nenad Filipovič of the International Executive Development Center, and Tony Dimnik of McGill University. The authors gratefully acknowledge the support of the Western Business School and the International Executive Development Center. Management cooperated in the field research for this case, which was written solely for the purpose of stimulating student discussion. All events and individuals are real. Faculty members in nonprofit institutions are encouraged to reproduce this case for distribution to their own students without charge or written permission. All other rights reserved jointly to the authors and the North American Case Research Association (NACRA). Copyright © 1994 by the *Case Research Journal*, Bernd Petak, Nenad Filipovič, and Tony Dimnik.

Exhibit 2 Majšperk Raw Materials Shipments for 1992

Month	Amount (DM)	Status
	*Wool/Polyester**	
Jan.	464,000	Already received
Mar.	696,000	Already received
June	696,000	Scheduled
Oct.	464,000	Scheduled
	Acrylic†	
Feb.	16,500	Already received
May	40,400	Scheduled
Sept.	40,400	Scheduled
Nov.	16,500	Scheduled

*Wool/polyester was purchased from Meilinger GmbH on 90-day terms. A 3.24% financing charge was added to each payment.
†Acrylic was purchased from other suppliers and had to be paid for in full 30 days PRIOR to receipt of shipment.
NOTE: Each month Majšperk paid DM4500 for additional materials such as those used in packaging.
SOURCE: Company records.

Exhibit 3 Majšperk Summary of Other Cash Expenditures in 1st Quarter of 1992

	January	February	March
Labour	258,000	270,000	260,000
Energy	44,145	44,000	35,000
VAT*	20,000	20,000	20,000
Miscellaneous	10,000	10,000	10,000

*The VAT was collected by vendors in Slovenia as part of the selling price of many goods and was paid to the government according to a specified schedule.
SOURCE: Company records.

Marketing in the Hardwood Industry

Logs cut from hardwood forests are an important raw material used by many domestic and foreign producers. Unlike pine and other softwoods, which are used mostly for general construction, the demand for oak, black walnut, black cherry, white ash, maple, and other hardwoods derives from consumer demand for high-value products such as hardwood furniture, cabinets, flooring, millwork, and moldings. When properly finished, hardwoods offer a finish that is both durable and beautiful. The wood is also very strong, so even pieces that do not have a perfect appearance are well suited for making frames of chairs, sofas, and other furniture covered with various upholstery materials.

Hardwood forests cover many of the rural areas of the eastern United States—areas where there is often little other industry. Thus, the forest products industry is important to economic development—and to the employment and quality of life of people who live and work in these areas.

Unfortunately, that potential for economic development is not always achieved. A key reason for this is that many of the firms that harvest logs do not focus on any particular target market or specific customers. Rather, they just see the market opportunity in terms of the products they have always produced: hardwood logs or perhaps "green" rough-sawn lumber cut from the logs. As a result, they sell a commodity product to distant customers who view logs from one supplier as like all of the others on the market and simply purchase logs at the lowest price.

Under this production-oriented, commodity approach, the hardwood produced in rural regions of the U.S. has usually been shipped to other regions—including foreign countries—before the wood is processed into intermediate and finished products. But when the wood is sold and shipped out of the region as an unfinished commodity, the profit opportunities—and associated employment—relevant to the secondary processing are exported as well.

This case was prepared by Thomas Ponzurick and James P. Armstrong, PhD/Associate, both of West Virginia University. Selected material courtesy of the Appalachian Export Center for Hardwoods, West Virginia University; Dr. Jack Coster, professor of forestry, West Virginia University; Dr. David W. Patterson, professor of wood science, University of Arkansas-Monticello; and executive producer and senior editor, Professor Judy Wilkinson.

Historically, in this commodity-market environment, successful producers were those who could operate with the lowest total cost. The major cost areas are raw material (lumber), labor, any processing that is done, transportation, and, of course, any marketing-related expenses. Small and medium-sized producers are at an inherent disadvantage in this competitive, cost-oriented environment. They cannot achieve economies of scale because they can't spread their overhead expenses over a large number of units produced. As a result, there is little way for them to obtain a competitive advantage in production or distribution.

Some hardwood producers, including some smaller ones, were able to improve sales and profits—in both the U.S. and international markets—by differentiating their offerings with higher-quality products and service. For example, firms that worked to keep lumber dry and clean were better able to meet the needs of some customers. Further, some customers appreciated supplier firms that did a good job of sorting and grading different types of woods. And some suppliers focused on supplying species of wood that were desirable but less readily available.

In spite of such efforts, in the past most hardwood from U.S. producers was just sold as a commodity in a very competitive market. However, some people in the hardwood industry are applying marketing concepts to help change this situation. They are focusing attention on ways to expand the market for existing hardwood products and also trying to identify markets with specific needs so that they can increase the value added to the hardwood lumber—by producing finished or semiprocessed products—before it is shipped out of the region where the trees are cut.

These efforts are having an effect. For example, some companies have found markets for hardwood-based composite materials for use as beams, columns, or rafters in building construction. Traditional materials for structural framing include softwood lumber and nonrenewable resources such as steel and aluminum. These structural hardwood composites are manufactured by breaking lower-quality hardwood logs into small pieces such as strands, flakes, or thin sheets of wood (veneer) and reforming the pieces into large members with names like "parallel-strand lumber" or "laminated veneer lumber" for the construction market. By finding market opportunities for structural hardwood composites, companies add value by using small or poorly formed logs, less desirable hardwood species, and sometimes even the hardwood waste from other industrial processes. Development of value-added markets for structural hardwood composites also has resulted in job creation and economic development in rural, forested areas.

However, producing structural hardwood composites is just one way to meet customer needs that were not previously being satisfied. An increasing number of customers want to buy kiln-dried boards rather than green lumber that isn't immediately ready to use for their own production purposes. So, many firms that cut and sell hardwood are taking the step of adding value to their product by doing the kiln-drying process. But numerous other opportunities to add value still exist. To uncover them, U.S. hardwood suppliers are asking basic questions like: What are the needs of different customers in the broad product market for hardwood? Who are these customers and where are they located? What kind of hardwood products—beyond the commodity lumber we've sold in the past—do they want? What are the opportunities to differentiate what we sell and add more value to our product through additional processing that meets the needs of specific target segments? How do we go about finding the answers to these questions?

One opportunity for expanding both the market and value-added product opportunities lies in the area of international exports. Prior to 1980, many firms that supplied hardwood ignored the export market. Domestic demand was sufficiently large to sustain growth and profitability. However, as domestic demand softened and competition grew more intense, U.S. suppliers began to rethink entry into the international marketplace. In the last decade, efforts to market hardwood products to foreign markets have expanded significantly and the value of exported hardwood products has increased substantially.

Despite some recent success, there is still a vital need for more U.S. suppliers to adopt the marketing concept, especially in targeting the export marketplace. Currently, international buyers focus most of their attention on the higher-grade hardwood products. But growth of sales and profits from exporting will depend on the U.S. industry's ability to find markets for more of their available product inventory—including lower grades and species of hardwood. In fact, finding markets for value-added products may be the best way to improve sales of the lower grades and species. This would not only result in more efficient and profitable use of hardwood resources, but it could also reduce costs by improving economies of scale in production.

However, the question that should be uppermost in marketers' minds is what these customers want in the way of hardwood products. To answer this question, one must first determine the needs of these international buyers. In the case of U.S. hardwood suppliers, Canadian buyers are currently the largest market for these products.

Most of the Canadian firms that import U.S. hardwood to Canada are concentrated in a few geographic areas: over 75 percent are located in either Ontario or Quebec. Much of the imported lumber is purchased by Canadian manufacturers who use it to produce their own products—including furniture, cabinets, hardwood flooring, and molding and millwork for the construction industry. However, these customers account for only about 31 percent of U.S. imports. Canadian wholesalers—especially brokers and agents—account for more than half of the Canadian hardwood lumber purchased from U.S. sources. Many of these middlemen specialize in international sales. In fact, nearly 20 percent of all U.S. hardwood lumber imported by Canada is subsequently resold and exported to Europe—usually after some value-adding activities such as grading, sorting, repackaging, or additional product processing.

Red oak, hard maple, and white oak are the principal hardwood species that Canadian customers import from the United States. However, there are also markets for some species of lesser value—including soft maple and yellow poplar.

All types of lumber are graded according to quality, and this grading is important to Canadian buyers who have different hardwood needs. About 70 percent of the total volume of hardwood lumber purchased by Canadian firms is the higher-quality Number 1 Common grade or better. The other 30 percent of lumber imported is graded as Number 2 Common or lower. Firms that purchase the lower grades of lumber are mostly flooring manufacturers, furniture manufacturers, and brokers.

Marketing research studies indicate that Canadian hardwood lumber buyers are relatively satisfied with the quality of products and services now being provided by U.S. suppliers. However, the research reveals that suppliers could enhance customer satisfaction and their competitive advantage by improving their product quality through more accurate grading and reporting of moisture content as well as by providing cleaner and straighter lumber. Buyers would also like to see better distribution customer service from U.S. suppliers. This includes improving the reliability of lumber supplies and reducing order cycle time—that is, the time from when a customer orders lumber until it is delivered. And of course, organizational buyers are always interested in competitive pricing.

Importantly, the research also shows that over one-third of the firms that import hardwood lumber from the United States are potentially interested in purchasing finished hardwood parts from U.S. suppliers. Examples in the area of finished hardwood parts include parts for making furniture, doors, stairways, and railings. Organizations showing an interest in these finished products include importers, export brokers, and manufacturers of various hardwood products. These results indicate that there may be a good opportunity for U.S. suppliers of hardwood products to custom produce such parts for specific customers. Yet, it is still unknown how substantial this opportunity might be, how eager Canadian buyers might be to purchase value-added finished hardwood products, and at what prices. To begin to answer these questions, U.S. suppliers need to determine the types and specifications of the finished hardwood products desired by individual buyers. That will require that supplier firms do more marketing research or have more direct personal selling contact with buyers for specific firms than has been typical in the past. Alternatively, working with these customers may require closer relationships— partnerships—with middlemen who can help producers with some of the required marketing functions.

It appears that U.S. hardwood firms face a variety of possible opportunities to expand sales and improve profits. Export markets, including Canada, appear to offer greater potential than has been captured. Further, some of the opportunities are ones that focus on the value-added products that have the potential to foster economic development in rural areas of the U.S. where such activities have in the past been limited. However, just having access to hardwood forests alone isn't enough to turn these opportunities into profitable business. Developing international markets for value-added hardwood products requires that individual supplier firms adapt their marketing strategies to marketplace needs. Producers need to identify specific target markets and understand the unique needs and buying behavior of these markets. They also need to get beyond production-oriented thinking and develop whole marketing mixes to serve their target customers. That means figuring out what type of products and services to offer. It also means making decisions about how to price specific offerings—because a firm that is doing something unique for its customers won't just face perfect competition and a price that is set by the market. A firm that does a good job with this marketing strategy planning has the potential to satisfy some target customers very well—and in the process gain a sustainable competitive advantage. And, of course, as more firms do that, they will not only make better profits but also will contribute to the economic development of the areas in which they operate.

Questions

1. Why is it important for firms that produce and supply hardwood to adopt the marketing concept?

2. What are some of the ways hardwood products can be adapted to meet value-added market needs?

3. In what ways does the marketing mix strategy need to be different for hardwood suppliers who focus on a specific target market than for firms that just sell rough-sawn logs or green lumber in the commodity market?

4. What are some of the potential target markets for U.S. hardwood suppliers selling to the Canadian market? Which marketing mix variables are likely to be most important to the target markets you have identified?

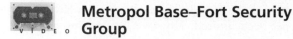

Metropol Base–Fort Security Group

Pat Haney, president of Metropol Base–Fort Security Group (Metropol), was sitting in his office contemplating the future direction of his company. Metropol, a leading Canadian security firm whose services included the provision of uniformed security guards, mobile security patrols, polygraph testing, insurance and criminal investigations and a broad range of specialized services, was faced with a number of challenges which threatened its future profitability. "Increasing competition, especially from large multinationals such as Pinkertons, is further reducing already low industry margins," offered Pat. He was also concerned about Metropol's reliance on the commodity-like security guard business for 90 percent of its revenue. "We have to find some way to meaningfully differentiate our services from those of our competitors," Pat observed. "That is essential if we are to achieve the kind of growth we desire."

Company Background

Metropol was founded in Winnipeg, Manitoba, in 1952 by George Whitbread, a former RCMP officer. He perceived the need and profit potential in providing security services to the business sector, particularly at large industrial sites such as hydro installations and mines in northwestern Ontario. At the time most businesses security needs were not being met.

By 1970 the company had grown to such an extent that Mr. Whitbread could not run and control the operation on his own, so he hired a couple of assistants. That turned out to be a big mistake, as the assistants proved to be relatively ineffective.

In 1975, Mr. Whitbread had become so frustrated trying to manage the business on his own that he hired former Manitoba Premier Duff Roblin to act as a consultant to the firm. Mr. Roblin ended up purchasing the company.

Pat Haney joined the firm in 1976. He was hired to run the Winnipeg operation, which at the time

This case was written by Stephen S. Tax, MBA, under the supervision of Professor W. S. Good, as a basis for classroom discussion rather than to illustrate either effective or ineffective handling of an administrative situation. Copyright by the Case Development Program, Faculty of Management, University of Manitoba. Support for the development of this case was provided by the Canadian Studies Program, Secretary of State, Government of Canada.

was 80 percent of the firm's business. It was also expected that Pat would develop an overall marketing program for the company. "My experience was in the computer field," declared Pat. "When I first heard about Metropol Security I thought it was a stocks and bonds company."

In the late 1970s and early 80s Metropol expanded into Saskatchewan and Alberta and was aggressively seeking acquisitions. Finally, in 1984 it merged with Base–Fort Security, the leading security firm in Alberta and a major competitor in B.C. and a number of other areas in Canada. Pat believed this move offered economies of scale as well as other benefits and was an important step toward making Metropol a national company.

Sales topped $30 million in 1985 making Metropol the third largest security company in Canada. Offices were maintained in B.C., Alberta, Saskatchewan, Manitoba, Quebec, the N.W.T., and Newfoundland with 70 percent of their business coming from western Canada.

The Security Industry

Security products and services were purchased by individuals and businesses as a means of reducing the risk of loss or damage to their assets. The amount of security purchased depended upon individual risk preferences, their perception of the degree of risk involved, and the value of the assets to be protected. Security, therefore, was very much an intangible product subject to individual evaluation.

The industry offered such services as unarmed uniformed security guards, mobile patrols, investigations, consulting and education as well as "hardware" products such as alarms, fences, locks, safes, and electronic surveillance devices (ESDs) and monitoring equipment. Most companies purchased a package combining various services and hardware systems. "It would not make much sense to have 50 television monitors and only one person watching them," Pat pointed out, "nor would it be wise to have 50 security guards roaming around a building which had no locks on the doors."

There were a number of factors which contributed to the competitive nature of the security industry. All a firm needed to enter the business was to open an office. Start-up costs were minimal and no accreditation was required by the company or its employees. Clients considered the cost of switching

Exhibit 1

Forecast Market Growth for Security Guard and Private Investigation Services, Electronic Security Devices (ESDs) and Hardware Products in the United States, 1985–1995*

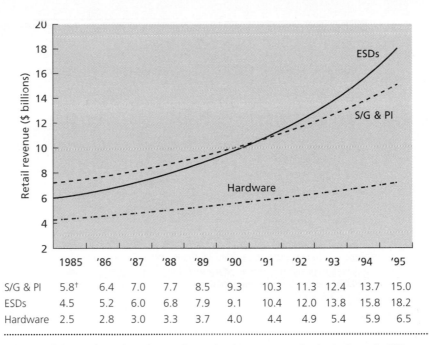

	1985	'86	'87	'88	'89	'90	'91	'92	'93	'94	'95
S/G & PI	5.8†	6.4	7.0	7.7	8.5	9.3	10.3	11.3	12.4	13.7	15.0
ESDs	4.5	5.2	6.0	6.8	7.9	9.1	10.4	12.0	13.8	15.8	18.2
Hardware	2.5	2.8	3.0	3.3	3.7	4.0	4.4	4.9	5.4	5.9	6.5

*The Canadian growth rate for each type of service/product was expected to be similar to the U.S. pattern.
†All figures are in $ billions.
SOURCE: Metropol research.

from one firm to another quite low, so the business often went to the lowest-cost provider. Most customers really did not understand the difference in services provided by the various competitors in the security business, which made differentiation very difficult. Pat found in studying the financial statements of the large multinational security firms that most security companies earned pretax profit margins of about 4 percent on gross sales.

The 1985 security guard and private investigation markets in Canada were worth about $400 million retail. ESDs and other types of hardware added close to another $400 million to this figure at retail prices.

Growth was expected to continue in the security field for a variety of reasons including a general increase in the level of risk around the world, the rising cost of insurance, economic growth, technological innovation which created new security problems, and an increasing sophistication among security system purchasers. The ESD and security guard segments were expected to outpace basic hardware sales growth (Exhibit 1).

On the negative side was the industry's poor reputation for the quality and reliability of its services. This perception threatened to limit growth

and provide an opportunity for new competitors to enter the market.

Competition

Metropol's competition came in both a direct and indirect form from a variety of competitors. "We compete with other firms who primarily offer security guard services as well as a number of companies that provide substitute products and services," observed Pat.

There were literally hundreds of security guard businesses in Canada ranging in size from one or two expolicemen operating out of a basement to large multinational firms like Pinkertons, Burns, and Wackenhut. Metropol was the third largest firm in the country with a 7.0 percent market share (Exhibit 2). It was the leading firm in western Canada with a 25 percent share of that market.

Hardware products served as the foundation of a good security system. While items such as fencing, lighting, alarms, safes and locks were to some extent complementary to the security guard business, they also competed with it—firms could substitute some proportion of either their security guard or hardware expenditures for the other.

Exhibit 2

The Largest
Security Guard
Companies
Operating in
Canada, Ranked
by Market Share

Company Name	Canadian Revenue ($ Millions)	Employees	Market Share (%)
1. Pinkertons	50	4,600	12.5%
2. Burns	30	4,500	7.5
3. Metropol Base–Fort	30	2,000	7.0
4. Wackenhut	12	2,000	3.0
5. Canadian Protection	12	1,700	3.0
6. Barnes	12	1,500	3.0
7. Phillips	10	1,200	2.5
Canada	400	40,000*	100%

*In-house guards could raise this figure by as much as 100 percent. However a better estimate would be 50–60 percent, as in-house accounts use more full-time staff. This means that there are more than 60,000 people working as guards or private investigators at any time. Further, with turnover at close to 100 percent annually, there are over 100,000 people working in this field over the course of a year.
SOURCE: Metropol research.

Insurance had long been a favorite substitute for security and other loss prevention services. Business spent more on insurance than all forms of security products combined. However, falling interest rates, a series of major disasters around the world, and a trend to more generous damage awards by the courts were making insurance a more expensive alternative. Faced with higher premiums, lower limits and higher deductibles, businesses were likely to consider spending more on loss prevention products and services.

The various levels of government also provided some basic protection services to companies (fire, police, etc.). However, their services were geared more to personal than business protection. These government services tend to set the base level of risk in a community. Tight budgets were not permitting these services to keep pace with the growth in crime and the increase in the value of corporate assets. This provided the private security business with an opportunity to fill the void.

Businesses were spending almost as much on ESDs and related services as for security guard services. There were a number of different ESD products ranging from small electronic gadgets to the very popular central station monitoring systems. ESDs were the fastest growing segment of the security industry. The principal attribute of these products was that they provided accurate and reliable information to whoever was responsible for responding to a problem situation. Thus, to a large extent, these products

were really productivity tools that enhanced the performance of security guards, the fire department and/or the police force. They did tend to reduce the amount of security guard service needed. Some security-conscious firms with large-scale security needs hired their own internal (in-house) specialists. In most cases they would also hire guards from companies like Metropol to do the actual patrolling.

The primary basis of competition in the security business was price. However, this was as much the fault of small, poorly managed firms and large multinationals trying to purchase market share as it was a fundamental characteristic of the industry. "I've seen companies bid under cost," observed Pat, "and they did not necessarily know they were doing it. It is a very unprofessional business in that sense. If you offer superior service and give a customer what he wants, in most cases you don't have to offer the lowest price. Just recently the Air Canada Data Centre job went to the highest bidder. Lowering your price is very easy, but not the way to succeed in this business." However, since price was a key factor in getting jobs, cost control became crucial if profits were to be made. Pretax margins of 4–8 percent quickly disappeared if unanticipated costs occurred.

Market Segments

The market for security products and services could be segmented in a variety of ways such as by type of

Exhibit 3

Security Guard
Service Market
Segmentation by
Gross Margins
and Guard Wages

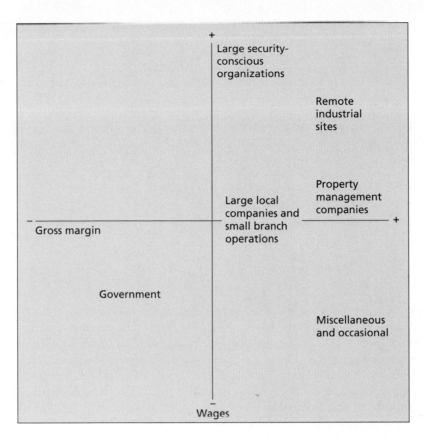

service, type of business, geographic location, sensitivity to security needs, government versus private companies, and occasional versus continuous needs. Metropol segmented their customers and the rest of the market using a combination of the above bases as outlined below and in Exhibit 3.

- *Large security-conscious organizations (private and public).* The common feature among these companies was that they had the potential for heavy losses if security was breached. They typically had high-value assets, such as computers or other high-tech equipment, or valuable proprietary information as in the case of research and development firms. These buyers were usually quite knowledgeable about security and rated quality over price. This group included firms in both local urban and remote, rural locations.

- *Organizations for whom security was a low priority.* This group was dominated by local companies, commercial property management companies, and branches of firms which were headquartered elsewhere. They were less knowledgeable about

security and tended to have limited security programs. They were price sensitive and principally utilized low-cost security guards.

- *Government organizations.* Government organizations (nonhospital) typically awarded contracts based on a tendered price for a predetermined period of time, usually 1–2 years. The price for these contracts was commonly in the vicinity of the minimum wage plus 5 percent.

- *Occasional services.* These included anything from sporting or entertainment events to social or emergency services. Contracts were seasonal, as with a C.F.L. or N.H.L. sports team, or one-time affairs. Wages paid to the security personnel were usually quite low but profit margins to the firm were above average.

Buyer Behavior

The buyer of security services was commonly in the stronger position. This resulted from a multitude of firms offering what buyers perceived to be largely

Exhibit 4

Customer Decision-Making Criteria—Survey Results: How Important Are the Following Attributes to You when Making a Decision on Security Services?

	Not Important			Very Important		Average Score
	1	2	3	4	5	
Consistency and reliability	—	—	—	3	14	4.824
Quality of service representatives	—	—	—	5	12	4.706
Price competitiveness	—	—	3	8	6	4.176
Company reputation	1	1	—	7	8	4.176
Emergency services	—	2	4	7	4	3.765
Full range of products and services	—	4	2	6	5	3.706
Consulting services	—	6	6	3	2	3.059
National coverage	4	4	6	2	—	2.375

*The survey was a convenience sample of Metropol customers.
SOURCE: Metropol research.

undifferentiated products and services and sellers trying to "win" business by providing the lowest price. Further the cost of switching suppliers was low because of the customer's perceived similarity of their services. It was also quite simple for firms to bring the security function in-house if they believed they could achieve substantial cost savings or other improvements in their security programs. In addition, some buyers tended to give security considerations a low priority in their budgeting.

Firms purchasing security products and services had three levels of decisions to make: (1) a general policy on the role and risk–cost framework security would play in their firm, (2) a decision regarding the types of products and services to be purchased, and (3) the selection of suppliers.

Each decision level involved new groups or individuals within the organization. Policy decisions were generally made at the senior executive level, while the product/service and supplier decisions tended to be made at the local level.

Most purchases were straight tender purchases based on a sealed bidding process. Firms with whom security was a low priority and most government agencies tended to choose the lowest bidder. Companies who took a greater interest in the quality of their security program considered attributes other than price when deciding upon their security supplier.

As part of a study on the security industry, Metropol surveyed buyers' ratings of the importance of several factors in choosing a security firm. They also had buyers rate Metropol's performance on those performance factors. Among the most significant decision-making criteria identified were consistency and reliability, availability of service representatives, and price. Metropol scored highest on the quality of their representatives and the customers' view of the firm's reputation (Exhibits 4 and 5).

Metropol

Metropol organized its operations on a regional (provincial) basis. The Manitoba headquarters developed a centralized policy and operating guidelines procedure which was instituted in all offices. While sales representatives dealt with the day-to-day needs of customers, top management was involved in making sales presentations to large accounts.

Services

Despite Metropol's variety of services, supplying unarmed, uniformed security guards accounted for most of their revenue. Their sales revenue breakdown by service type was:

Security guards	90%
Mobile security checks	8
Other (investigation, polygraph testing, retail services, consulting, and education)	2
	100%

Providing security guard services involved more than just sending guards to industrial or office sites.

Exhibit 5
Customer
Decision-Making
Criteria—Survey
Results: How
Would You Rate
Metropol Security
on the Following
Attributes?

	Poor	Fair	Sat.	Good	Excellent	Average Score
	1	**2**	**3**	**4**	**5**	
Consistency and reliability	1	1	5	7	3	3.588
Quality of service reps.	—	2	—	11	4	4.000
Price competitiveness	—	1	4	10	2	3.765
Company reputation	—	—	2	10	5	4.176
Emergency services	1	1	6	7	3	3.556
Full range of products and services	1	2	7	6	1	3.235
Consulting services	—	4	5	5	2	2.944
National coverage	1	—	7	3	—	3.091

Metropol had to train, pay, uniform and insure the guards. They also had to supervise and dispatch their people as well as provide reports to their clients.

"We have attempted to provide greater value to our customers than our competitors have," stated Pat. "For example, we have a 24-hour dispatch service, while all the other firms use an answering service. There is a $100,000 (annual) difference in cost, but we can respond much faster to any situation. Some customers will say they just consider price in their purchase decision but end up linking and buying the extra service."

Metropol also gave their guards special training on the procedures to follow in the case of such emergencies as bomb threats, hostage takings, and fire evacuations. Again, this was an attempt to differentiate their services from those of other security guard companies.

The mobile security business was contracted out to local firms. This market was not considered to be a growth area, and Metropol did not invest a great deal of resources in it.

Investigative and polygraph services were contracted out to a couple of ex-RCMP officers. Metropol had maintained these investigators on its staff at one time but found that demand for these services was not great enough to justify having the high-salaried people as full-time employees.

Education programs were another means Metropol used to create added value and increase switching costs for their customers. Pat explained, "We give seminars on such topics as 'The Protection of Proprietary Information' for our clients and even invite some companies we don't currently serve. We

want our clients to realize that if they switch security firms they will be losing something of value."

Metropol did not sell hardware products such as fences, alarms and locks. However, it could arrange the purchase of such equipment for its clients. It was presently considering working in conjunction with a systems engineer so the company would be able to provide a total security package to its customers.

Costs

Metropol divided its costs into two groups: direct and administrative. A "typical" job had the following cost characteristics:

Direct costs	83–86%
Selling and administrative costs	8–9
Pretax profit margin	4–7

Given the above figures, cost control was a key success factor for Metropol and the security industry in general. Metropol's margins were, in fact, higher than the industry average of approximately 4 percent. "We use a job-costing process," volunteered Pat. "Every pay period (two weeks) we look at what we made on each job. We consider and analyze every expense item very closely to see if there was any deviation from what was budgeted."

Direct costs included wages, uniforms, bonding, transportation and supervision. Metropol did a good job of keeping its costs as low or lower than its competitors' despite offering a higher level of service. Some of this was a result of economies of scale in purchasing such items as uniforms, and was achieved because of their comparatively large size. The company also did a superior job in collecting their outstanding receivables within a two-week period.

Pricing

Prices were determined by identifying the direct costs associated with a job, allowing for a contribution to selling and administrative overhead, and providing for a profit margin. Consideration was also given to any particular reason there may be for pricing a bid either particularly high or low. "We once bid at very close to our direct cost for a job in a town where we had no competition in order to discourage other firms from entering that market," noted Pat. He also suggested that it was important to anticipate competitors' likely pricing strategy when bidding on a job as well as recognizing that some projects had greater potential for cost overruns.

Promotion

Metropol individually identified the companies in each of their trading areas that were potential clients and concentrated their promotional efforts on that group. In Manitoba this "club" amounted to about 500 firms.

Once these firms were identified, strategies were developed either to sell to those potential accounts which presently had no security service or to become the logical alternative for those businesses who were using competitive services. "We want to put pressure on these incumbent firms to perform," explained Pat.

Metropol used, among other things, their educational seminars to stress to their clients that they offered superior services. At times firms using competing security companies were invited as a means of encouraging them to switch to Metropol.

Employees

Metropol employed about 2000 people, 1900 of whom were security guards and 100 who were selling, administrative or management personnel.

Security guards came principally from three backgrounds: (1) young people [18–25] who could not find other work, (2) older people [50–65] looking for a second career, or (3) ex-military or police personnel who liked the quasi-military nature of the job.

Annual employee turnover in the security guard industry was very high, estimated to be in the vicinity of 100 percent. Metropol's turnover rate was in the same range. Reasons for the high level included a combination of low wages, generally boring work, and a lack of motivation or support from senior management.

"We have some employees who have been with the company for 15 years," Pat pointed out. "However, the wages we pay are based on our billing rate, which often only allows for minimum wages to be paid to our employees." Intense competition and clients who wanted to pay a bare minimum for security guard services forced companies to pay their guards the legal minimum wage. This caused high turnover rates which, evidently, did not bother some clients. Other customers, concerned with employee turnover, specified a higher minimum wage rate which the security company had to pay its guards. Pat liked this attitude because it allowed him to pay his people a higher wage and still be competitive.

Metropol's supervisors and customer service representatives (salespeople) did a good job servicing their accounts and handling any crisis that arose. They helped maintain Metropol's reputation as a competent and reliable security company despite the generally poor reputation of the industry.

The Future

Pat turned his attention to the future. He believed that the way business was conducted in the security guard industry would not significantly change in the near future. He did expect the business to become somewhat more professional with guards being trained in formal, standardized programs. The pressure on profit margins was expected to continue and perhaps even intensity as the larger, multinational firms fought for market share and smaller independents struggled for survival. Pat was thinking about how he could use Metropol's present position and reputation in the security guard sector to expand into more profitable segments of the industry or improve the company's general standing within the guard sector. Some of the opportunities he was considering included

- Geographic expansion.
- Focused strategy.
- Expanding the range of security products and services offered by the company.

- Diversification into other service areas outside the security field.
- Serving the consumer home security market.

Geographic Expansion

"To be a national company in Canada you need a presence in southern Ontario," observed Pat. Even though many companies' security needs were handled at the local level, there was considerable potential for a national accounts program. To be involved in providing a national service, a company had to be active in the Toronto area, where most national companies' security decisions were made. In addition the Ontario market offered substantial local business. Pat explained, "We handle Northern Telcom's security guard needs throughout western Canada, but not in Ontario. Northern Telcom has three times the business volume there as it does in all of the western provinces combined."

There were three ways Metropol could enter the Ontario market: (1) by purchasing a local security firm, (2) through merging with another company, or (3) by bidding on contracts in Ontario and opening up an office once a contract was obtained.

Pat believed that the "merger method" was the most appealing since it offered the potential for increased profits with virtually no additional cash investment. He had discussed the possibility with two firms that had head offices in Ontario and were also minor competitors in the Winnipeg, Edmonton, Calgary, and Vancouver markets. The western offices of the merged firm could be closed down and the business operated under the Metropol name. "The gross margin on their western contracts would go right to the bottom line," suggested Pat. "Because all the current Metropol offices could meet their administrative needs and absorb any incremental expenses."

A restricting factor in this strategy was Metropol's limited product/service line. To provide a complete security package for any company on a national basis, it was necessary to offer the hardware and ESD packages in addition to the security guards.

Focused Strategy

This alternative was really a continuation of Metropol's current strategy. Following this approach Metropol's principal objective would be to become the fastest growing security guard firm in western Canada, with the highest profit margin and return on equity, the lowest employee turnover, and the most satisfied customers in the business of providing contract, unarmed security personnel. This strategy required an increased emphasis on developing a formal marketing program and increasing the value added to Metropol's security guard and support services. Tighter control of costs and employee motivation would be critical success factors, as would be the need to carefully segment the market and identify the most profitable clients.

The strategy would be designed to match the distinct competencies and resources of Metropol with the needs of the marketplace. Pat believed that while the strategy "sounded good," it would be very difficult to implement. "Even if you offer the highest quality service, you might not get the job," he offered. "Too many contracts, particularly those involving the government sector and crown corporations, are based solely on price, and simply supplying a higher service level in the provision of security guards is not likely to change that."

Expansion of Security Products and Services

From the customer's point of view there was an advantage to having one firm coordinate and provide the complete security coverage required by his business; the security system was more effective and efficient. If the customer had to contract with different firms for guards, fences, locks, lights, alarms, and ESDs, there was likely to be a lot of overlap and, in some cases, gaps in the overall system. Also, it was likely to be more expensive. Pat considered an investment in the production of hardware equipment much too costly given his firm's limited resources, but he was investigating the possibility of arranging a deal with a large multinational distributor of security hardware and ESD products.

Pat explained, "We would like to have an exclusive relationship whereby they (large multinationals) would provide us, at wholesale, with all the hardware and ESD equipment we needed on a private label basis (Metropol brand) and they would train our people. We could offer them our monitoring services and access to new markets." Metropol would package the system, which would include hardware, software, and people in whatever mix its clients needed. The products would be sold to the client or leased on a five-year arrangement.

The expanded product line strategy would deliver significant benefits to Metropol. Hardware and ESD equipment offered better margins than security guard services and in some cases were subject to becoming obsolete. This provided opportunities to sell upgraded systems. For example, television monitoring devices had already gone through several generations of change despite their relatively recent entry into the security product mix. Service contracts to maintain the equipment would provide another source of additional revenue. Finally, the need of these systems for close monitoring and servicing increased the dependence of the customer on Metropol. This higher dependence meant that switching costs for the customer were much higher than with security guard services. This would be especially true if the equipment was leased for a five-year period.

Diversification into Other Service Areas

This alternative would capitalize on Metropol's skills in hiring people for contract-type jobs and administering a payroll. Their current product line would be expanded to include one or all of the following additional services which could be provided on a contractual basis: secretarial services, nursing care, janitorial services, or landscaping services. The commercial sector would continue to be their primary target market.

Several years ago Metropol got into the dry cleaning business with poor results. "Businesses like janitorial and landscaping services are beyond our particular expertise," revealed Pat. "However, we are looking at providing people and handling the payroll for temporary clerical or nursing services. In those cases, we would be taking our established skills to another market."

Pat sited Drake International's experience as evidence that the strategy could work. That company went from providing temporary help to the provision of security guards.

The Consumer Market

Another alternative for Metropol would be to expand into the consumer market for security products and services. The major products of interest to residential customers were locks, supplementary lighting, fences, mobile home checks, house sitting, and alarm systems. This segment was growing slower than the business sector, but still offered substantial opportunity.

Pat was currently exploring Metropol's opportunities as a franchisor of home alarm systems to the numerous small Canadian alarm system dealers. "We would become the Century 21 of the alarm business," Pat suggested.

The alarm business in Canada was made up of a large number of small independent dealers and a few large multinationals. The "small guys" would buy their alarms from wholesalers in small lots which precluded much discounting. They also had to contract out their alarm monitoring to their competition, the large multinationals, because they could not afford the central station monitoring equipment. In most cases advertising and financing of installations for customers was too expensive to be carried out on a significant basis.

Pat thought a Metropol alarm franchise offered a number of important strategic advantages to independent alarm dealers: (1) by arranging with a large alarm manufacturer to produce a private label Metropol brand alarm line they could pass on volume discounts to their dealers, (2) franchisees would have the Metropol name behind them, (3) co-op advertising would provide greater exposure, (4) an arrangement for consumer financing could be established, and (5) Metropol would set up a central monitoring system.

Consideration was also being given to making locksmiths subdealers of Metropol alarm systems. "Normally a customer must call a locksmith and an alarm specialist to secure his home," suggested Pat. "It would be more effective, especially from a selling perspective, if the locksmith could do both."

Conclusion

Pat realized that the alternatives he was considering were not merely incremental changes in Metropol's strategy. In fact, each option represented a distinct direction for the firm's future development. "We have to define our business's mission more specifically," Pat thought to himself. "Then we can choose and implement the strategy that best suits that mission."

Northcrest Salmon

NAFTA promised great opportunities, or so the senior management at Northcrest Salmon believed. As a small ($70 million in annual sales) salmon processor located in Portland, Oregon, the company has experienced very slow growth for nearly 10 years and was looking to expand. NAFTA seemed to offer an opportunity to expand into a new geographic market, Mexico.

Northcrest is owned by two families: the Rardins and the Petersons. Even though NAFTA was passed several years ago, it wasn't until the senior executives (the elder Rardin, who is CEO, and the elder Peterson, who is chair of the board) realized that the company's lack of growth meant less opportunity for their children to find a place in the business that they began to look south for growth. Their only other international experience was Canada, where the company has marketed products since its origins back in 1920. In the northwest United States and nearby parts of Canada, Northcrest ships in its own trucks direct to large grocery chains, but uses fish wholesalers for reaching institutional (restaurant and food service) customers. In the rest of the United States, the company uses a specialized freight company that can bring other loads back to the Northwest, thus cutting costs. Otherwise, Northcrest's trucks would return empty, raising costs.

Northcrest believes its strengths lie in managing processing costs. Because the company is completely vertically integrated, even doing its own catching and smoking, the company can control costs better than many competitors such as Putnam Sound. Vertical integration also means making adjustments in how fish are prepared, as there are some regional differences in taste preferences. For example, a heavily smoked fish is more popular in some parts of the country whereas other areas seem to prefer a lighter smoked taste. Salmon, though, is the only product produced by Northcrest, and it prepares almost 400 tons total of smoked (about 50 tons per year), fresh (almost 70 tons), and canned salmon for distribution across the United States and Canada.

This case was prepared by John F. Tanner Jr. (Baylor University) and Mauricio G. Gonzalez (Monterrey Tech, Mexico) for the purposes of class discussion. Some names and data have been disguised.

The company's first sales stop in Mexico was Expo Alimiento, a food show in Monterrey, in October 1997. At the show, Greg Benesh, Northcrest's sales vice president and son-in-law to the Rardins, met several representatives of Fjiord Supply Co. (FSC), a Mexican fish distributor. Impressed by the FSC distribution system, Northcrest signed a deal for FSC to distribute smoked and fresh salmon in Mexico, as FSC was uninterested in the canned products. FSC's customer list includes the largest and best-known restaurants and hotels in Monterrey. In addition, FSC is the leader of a consortium of five major fish distributors that distribute fish products throughout Mexico, each taking a geographic area. By signing with FSC, Northcrest is assured of nationwide distribution through the consortium.

FSC is located in Monterrey, an industrial city in northern Mexico. It distributes fish products such as shrimp, lobster, crab, whitefish, pollock, and haddock to institutional users and retailers. These products are purchased directly from ships that fish both the Gulf of Mexico and the Pacific Ocean, and from other processors like Northcrest. Institutional users include restaurants, cafeterias in schools and plants, airline food service companies, and hospitals. Major retailers served include Gigante and Walmart/Sam's. FSC does not distribute any canned fish products; these are usually distributed directly to retailers by the canners.

In many ways, Monterrey is very much like the United States. Many parts of the city could easily be mistaken for parts of Houston or San Antonio, Texas. The rest of Mexico, though, is very traditional and slow to embrace change. Even Mexico City, with one of the world's largest populations, is somewhat conservative. Eating out, though, is very common in Mexico and many restaurants of all cuisines can be found in the larger cities.

Shipments began to FSC in November, a month after signing the deal. In March, Molly Wagner was named head of Latin America Sales for Northcrest. Prior to the position, Molly was account manager selling to Kroger and several other major grocery chains. She met with her new boss, Greg Benesh, to discuss the situation.

Benesh told her, "Molly, there are two things you need to work on right away. As you know, we signed FSC as a distributor for Mexico last October and began shipping products to them in November. Frankly, sales have been disappointing. So one objective you have is to turn that around. The second is to find ways to distribute the product beyond Mexico."

"What do you think the problem is with FSC?" she asked.

"I'd rather let you nose around and see what you come up with," he replied. "I've got my own ideas but I don't want them to bias you at this point." He handed her a folder. "Those are the sales figures for the FSC account. Plus, all of my notes from conversations with Jaime Hernandez, head of FSC. Look those over, meet with Jaime if you want, and come up with a plan. I'd like to get it implemented May 1."

"That's not much time, Greg."

"I know. But I don't think it will take much time to turn FSC around. At the same time, you can begin looking at ways to expand. But you need to realize that, while the opportunity here is terrific, the risk is that if FSC doesn't turn around, we may pull out of Mexico. If we do that, there won't be a Latin America Sales Division."

Molly took the notes back to her office and reviewed them. She identified several issues and put together some ideas on possible solutions to discuss with Jaime Hernandez.

Notes from Benesh

9/23. Met with Jaime Hernandez and Cesar Sepulveda of FSC, at Alimiento Expo at the Cintermex in Monterrey. Company located in Monterrey, appears to have controlling market share for fish sales in northeast Mex. Also distribute some beef products. No smoked products now (didn't see any at the show; looks like we would be first—in fact, there is very little salmon of any kind in Mexico). JH liked fresh salmon better than smoked but wanted to learn more about it. They also asked about the U.S. market for pink trout—I think it is like a rainbow trout.

9/30. Followed up with JH of FSC via phone. Secretary doesn't speak English. He wants to visit our facilities with an eye to signing a distribution contract. Has also talked with Putnam Sound (a Northcrest competitor) and is expecting a proposal from them. Wants exclusive distribution. Told him we could give him a protected territory but that wasn't what he wanted. Likes the Dallas Cowboys. Faxed us a market share report that indicates they

have 50% of their market in most categories but there is no independent verification service in Mexico for fish sales. Their total consumption figure was estimated based on a study by a Monterrey Tech professor.

10/5. Notes from visit of FSC to Northcrest. Jaime brought Cesar Sepulveda, who is their shipping director, and Fermin Garza who is the marketing director. JH is the CEO. They were suitably impressed but still wanted to see Putnam Sound. They left us and went straight to Putnam. Key issues appear to be market acceptance since salmon is new to the market. They currently offer pink rainbow trout (fresh only), which is similar in flavor and texture, but they do not offer any smoked products. Price may be problem considering transportation difficulties. They provided forecasts for market (see Exhibits 1, 2, and 3) and it looks attractive. They asked about our distribution channels across the Southwest.

10/7. Spoke with JH—he called. They were unimpressed with Putnam, I think, but unwilling to admit it. Wants me to come down and work out a deal. Set it up for 10/12.

10/12. Monterrey: Signed deal. Because they work with four other distributors, this gives us all of Mexico. (Is that legal in the U.S.?) Price is going to be an issue because of delivery costs. Their margin will be the same as with the pink rainbow trout (30%) but our retail price will be about 5% higher. Ours will retail for about $7.00 per pound. Pink rainbow is $6.50 to $6.90. But this is their first smoked product. We will pay $1.00 per pound advertising support for the first six months, plus 10% overage for samples.

10/28. Received first shipment of 1 ton each product.

11/15. Checked with JH to see how sales are doing. Fresh is doing better than smoked. Penetration appears to be at 15%, so off to a fast start.

11/30. Checked with JH to recap first month. One ton shipment of fresh arrived spoiled; apparently the truck overheated while awaiting a check at the border (I thought NAFTA meant open borders) and was returned today. We will expedite another shipment and have it there in two days. Fortunately they caught it before too much went out. Orders are up for December. We have not received any copies of

Exhibit 1   Actual and Forecast Sales in Tons, Monterrey, Mexico

Month	Fresh Salmon		Smoked Salmon		Shrimp		Lobster		Whitefish		Pink Rainbow Trout	
	Act.	Fore.	Act.	Fore.	Act.	Fore.	Act.	Fore.	Act.	Fore.	Act.	Fore.*
Oct.		1.2		0.8	4.0	6.0	.07	1.5	5.0	6.5	3.3	4.0
Nov.	1.0	1.2	0.6	1.0	4.5	7.0	0.7	1.5	5.0	6.5	2.9	3.5
Dec.	1.2	1.4	0.8	1.0	4.5	7.0	1.0	2.0	4.0	5.5	3.4	4.5
Jan.	0.5	1.2	0.7	1.0	4.0	6.0	0.5	1.2	3.5	5.0	2.6	3.5
Feb.	0.4	1.0	0.6	0.8	3.5	5.0	0.5	1.2	3.0	5.0	2.4	3.3
Mar.	0.4	1.2	0.6	1.2	4.0	5.5	0.7	1.5	7.0	9.5	1.9	3.1
Apr.		1.2		0.8		6.0		1.5		9.5		2.9
May		1.0		0.8		5.0		1.2		6.5		2.9
June		1.0		0.7		5.0		1.0		5.5		2.8
July		1.0		0.7		4.5		1.0		5.5		2.8
Aug.		1.2		0.7		4.5		1.2		3.5		2.9
Sept.		1.3		0.9		5.0		1.5		5.5		3.2

Forecasts are for total market, not just FSC.
* Includes forecasted effects of salmon sales.

Exhibit 2   Actual and Forecast Sales in Tons, Rest of Mexico

Month	Fresh Salmon		Smoked Salmon		Shrimp		Lobster		Whitefish		Pink Rainbow Trout	
	Act.	Fore.	Act.	Fore.	Act.	Fore.	Act.	Fore.	Act.	Fore.	Act.	Fore.*
Oct.		3.5		3.5	4.0	6.0	1.0	2.5	4.0	5.5	4.2	5.6
Nov.	1.5	3.5	2.0	3.5	4.5	7.0	1.0	2.5	4.0	5.5	3.6	5.9
Dec.	1.0	5.8	3.8	6.0	4.5	7.0	1.5	3.0	3.5	4.9	3.9	7.2
Jan.	-0-	3.5	2.7	3.5	4.0	6.0	1.2	2.7	3.5	4.7	2.9	5.7
Feb.	-0-	2.7	2.0	3.5	4.0	6.0	1.0	2.5	4.0	5.5	2.8	5.4
Mar.	-0-	4.5	1.7	3.5	4.5	7.0	1.0	2.5	7.0	9.5	3.0	5.2
Apr.		3.5		3.5		7.0		2.0		11.0		4.9
May		3.5		3.5		5.5		1.8		9.0		4.8
June		3.5		4.5		5.5		1.8		8.5		4.8
July		3.5		4.5		5.0		1.5		7.5		4.6
Aug.		3.5		4.5		4.5		1.5		6.5		4.9
Sept.		4.4		6.0		6.0		2.0		7.5		5.4

Forecasts are for total market, not just the FSC consortium.
* Includes forecasted effects of salmon sales.

their advertising yet. JH says hasn't run any yet, but will in December. Fish a big Christmas seller.

12/12. Called JH after receiving fax on advertisement. Running a print ad in Mexico's version of *Progressive Grocer.* Running same ad in magazine for institutional food uses. 1/4 page, B&W emphasizing salmon but mentioning full product line. He tells me the headline means something about salmon for gracious living, and the copy is about using smoked salmon for parties.

Exhibit 3

Composition by Segment for Salmon Sales

Overall Market	
Institutional	85%
Consumer	15
Institutional Market Composition	
Hotels	35%
Clubs	10%
Restaurants	55%
Consumer Market Composition	
Sam's/Walmart	65%
Gigante (grocery)	35

NOTE: Salmon accounts for most of FSC's volume to Sam's, Walmart, and Gigante

12/15. Call from JH. Two orders canceled because of shipping problem in November. Has not affected smoked sales at all. One distributor has cut his order in half for fresh, saying it doesn't sell. Don't know if related to distribution problem or pink rainbow trout sales.

1/10. Call from JH. Smoked is hard to sell; he says they don't have anything else like it so buyers don't know what to do with it. Fresh is cannibalizing pink rainbow trout when it sells, if at all. I asked for faxes of ads in current magazine issues. He halted the ads for January, saying they wouldn't be effective. He says the salmon products are hurting his overall sales, too. Asked him for fax of all sales figures to compare with forecast. Said he'd think about it.

2/1. JH finally sent fax on sales. Sales seem to be steady at about 50 percent of potential for smoked, fresh down around 30 percent. Shipments under 1 ton are costing us 10 percent more on delivery and told JH he'd have to eat that. He didn't like it but I told him if sales were to reach his forecast, we'd hit 1 ton no problem once a week. Problem is shelf life of fresh is only 1 week. Another spoiled shipment would ruin us, even if it was his fault for not selling it fast enough. Maybe we should pull out. NAFTA's not all it was cracked up to be.

3/3. Talked with JH. He says sales will go down during summer because whitefish is plentiful and cheap and has high summer sales. Wants to find a new way to ship product to get costs down. We could airfreight it since the cost differential is not as big for shipments under 1,000 pounds. I suggested that to him, saying we could split the cost difference. It would lower our margin by 3 percent but raise his since he was paying the 10 percent overage on shipping. This would make his margin 27 percent, which is less than for trout but better than the 24 percent he was getting using trucks. He said that was fine. When I asked him about the summer sales forecasts and how we were doing with product acceptance, he seemed indifferent. Asked if he wanted to work with us to open distribution into other Latin American countries and he said he'd think about it. Asked if he was doing any shipping back to the States and he said no, hadn't really thought of it. Said he might look into it. Asked if he wanted us to work with him and he said he'd think about it. I wonder what he's thinking about.

Questions

1. Evaluate Northcrest's decision to enter Mexico. What factors should have been considered in selecting a distributor for Mexico? For other Latin countries?

2. What are some possible solutions to increasing penetration in Mexico?

3. How should Molly go about implementing those solutions? Be specific. What should she do next? If that is successful, then what? You may want to create a flow chart showing the steps.

4. What are some cultural differences that may have affected Northcrest's success in Mexico?

Outdoor Sporting Products, Inc.

The annual sales volume of Outdoor Sporting Products, Inc., for the past six years had ranged between $6.2 million and $6.8 million. Although profits continued to be satisfactory, Mr. Hudson McDonald, president and chief operating officer, was concerned because sales had not increased appreciably from year to year. Consequently, he asked a consultant in New York City and the officers of the company to submit proposals for improving the salespeople's compensation plan, which he believed was the basic weakness in the firm's marketing operations.

Outdoor's factory and warehouse were located in Albany, New York, where the company manufactured and distributed sporting equipment, clothing, and accessories. Mr. Hudson McDonald, who managed the company, organized it in 1956 when he envisioned a growing market for sporting goods resulting from the predicted increase in leisure time and the rising levels of income in the United States.

Products of the company, numbering approximately 700 items, were grouped into three lines: (1) fishing supplies, (2) hunting supplies, and (3) accessories. The fishing supplies line, which accounted for approximately 40 percent of the company's annual sales, included nearly every item a fisherman would need such as fishing jackets, vests, caps, rods and reels of all types, lines, flies, lures, landing nets, and creels. Thirty percent of annual sales were in the hunting supplies line, which consisted of hunting clothing of all types including insulated and thermal underwear, safety garments, shell holders, whistles, calls, and gun cases. The accessories line, which made up the balance of the company's annual sales volume, included items such as compasses, cooking kits, lanterns, hunting and fishing knives, hand warmers, and novelty gifts.

While the sales of the hunting and fishing lines were very seasonal, they tended to complement one another. The January–April period accounted for the bulk of the company's annual volume in fishing items, and most sales of hunting supplies were made during the months of May through August. Typically, the company's sales of all products reached their lows for the year during the month of December.

Adapted from a case written by Zarrel V. Lambert, Auburn University, and Fred W. Kniffin, University of Connecticut, Stamford. Used with permission.

Outdoor's sales volume was $6.57 million in the current year with self-manufactured products accounting for 35 percent of this total. Fifty percent of the company's volume consisted of imported products, which came principally from Japan. Items manufactured by other domestic producers and distributed by Outdoor accounted for the remaining 15 percent of total sales.

Mr. McDonald reported that wholesale prices to retailers were established by adding a markup of 50 to 100 percent to Outdoor's cost for the item. This rule was followed on self-manufactured products as well as for items purchased from other manufacturers. The resulting average markup across all products was 70 percent on cost.

Outdoor's market area consisted of the New England states, New York, Pennsylvania, Ohio, Michigan, Wisconsin, Indiana, Illinois, Kentucky, Tennessee, West Virginia, Virginia, Maryland, Delaware, and New Jersey. The area over which Outdoor could effectively compete was limited to some extent by shipping costs, since all orders were shipped from the factory and warehouse in Albany.

Outdoor's salespeople sold to approximately 6,000 retail stores in small- and medium-sized cities in its market area. Analysis of sales records showed that the firm's customer coverage was very poor in the large metropolitan areas. Typically, each account was a one- or two-store operation. Mr. McDonald stated that he knew for a fact that Outdoor's share of the market was very low, perhaps 2 to 3 percent; and for all practical purposes, he felt the company's sales potential was unlimited.

Mr. McDonald believed that with few exceptions, Outdoor's customers had little or no brand preference and in the vast majority of cases they bought hunting and fishing supplies from several suppliers.

It was McDonald's opinion that the pattern of retail distribution for hunting and fishing products had been changing during the past 10 years as a result of the growth of discount stores. He thought that the proportion of retail sales for hunting and fishing supplies made by small- and medium-sized sporting goods outlets had been declining compared to the percent sold by discounters and chain stores. An analysis of company records revealed Outdoor had not developed business among the discounters with the exception of a few small discount stores. Some of Outdoor's executives felt that the lack of business with discounters might have been due in part to the company's pricing policy and in part to the pressures which current customers had exerted on company salespeople to keep them from calling on the discounters.

Outdoor's Sales Force

The company's sales force played the major role in its marketing efforts since Outdoor did not use magazine, newspaper, or radio advertising to reach either the retail trade or consumers. One advertising piece that supplemented the work of the salespeople was Outdoor's merchandise catalog. It contained a complete listing of all the company's products and was mailed to all retailers who were either current accounts or prospective accounts. Typically, store buyers used the catalog for purposes of reordering.

Most accounts were contacted by a salesperson two or three times a year. The salespeople planned their activities so that each store would be called upon at the beginning of the fishing season and again prior to the hunting season. Certain key accounts of some salespeople were contacted more often than two or three times a year.

Management believed that product knowledge was the major ingredient of a successful sales call. Consequently, Mr. McDonald had developed a "selling formula," which each salesperson was required to learn before taking over a territory. The "formula" contained five parts: (1) the name and catalog number of each item sold by the company; (2) the sizes and colors in which each item was available; (3) the wholesale price of each item; (4) the suggested retail price of each item; and (5) the primary selling features of each item. After a new salesperson had mastered the product knowledge specified by this "formula" he or she began working in the assigned territory and was usually accompanied by Mr. McDonald for several weeks.

Managing the sales force consumed approximately one third of Mr. McDonald's efforts. The remaining two thirds of his time was spent purchasing products for resale and in general administrative duties as the company's chief operating officer.

Mr. McDonald held semiannual sales meetings, had weekly telephone conversations with each salesperson, and had mimeographed bulletins containing information on products, prices, and special promotional deals mailed to all salespeople each week. Daily call reports and attendance at the semiannual

sales meetings were required of all salespeople. One meeting was held the first week in January to introduce the spring line of fishing supplies. The hunting line was presented at the second meeting, which was scheduled in May. Each of these sales meetings spanned four to five days so the salespeople were able to study the new products being introduced and any changes in sales and company policies. The production manager and comptroller attended these sales meetings to answer questions and to discuss problems which the salespeople might have concerning deliveries and credit.

On a predetermined schedule each salesperson telephoned Mr. McDonald every Monday morning to learn of changes in prices, special promotional offers, and delivery schedules of unshipped orders. At this time the salesperson's activities for the week were discussed, and sometimes the salesperson was asked by Mr. McDonald to collect past due accounts in the territory. In addition, the salespeople submitted daily call reports, which listed the name of each account contacted and the results of the call. Generally, the salespeople planned their own itineraries in terms of the accounts and prospects that were to be contacted and the amount of time to be spent on each call.

Outdoor's sales force during the current year totaled 11 full-time employees. Their ages ranged from 23 to 67 years, and their tenure with the company ranged from 1 to 10 years. Salespeople, territories, and sales volumes for the previous year and the current year are shown in Exhibit 1.

Compensation of Salespeople

The salespeople were paid straight commissions on their dollar sales volume for the calendar year. The commission rate was 5 percent on the first $300,000, 6 percent on the next $200,000 in volume, and 7 percent on all sales over $500,000 for the year. Each week a salesperson could draw all or a portion of his or her accumulated commissions. McDonald encouraged the salespeople to draw commissions as they accumulated since he felt that they were motivated to work harder when they had a very small or zero balance in their commission accounts. These accounts were closed at the end of the year so each salesperson began the new year with nothing in the account.

The salespeople provided their own automobiles and paid their traveling expenses, of which all or a

Exhibit 1   Salespeople: Age, Years of Service, Territory, and Sales

Salespeople	Age	Years of Service	Territory	Sales Previous Year	Sales Current Year
Allen	45	2	Illinois and Indiana	$330,264	$329,216
Campbell	62	10	Pennsylvania	1,192,192	1,380,240
Duvall	23	1	New England	—	414,656
Edwards	39	1	Michigan	—	419,416
Gatewood	63	5	West Virginia	358,528	358,552
Hammond	54	2	Virginia	414,936	414,728
Logan	37	1	Kentucky and Tennessee	—	447,720
Mason	57	2	Delaware and Maryland	645,032	825,088
O'Bryan	59	4	Ohio	343,928	372,392
Samuels	42	3	New York and New Jersey	737,024	824,472
Wates	67	5	Wisconsin	370,712	342,200
Salespeople terminated in previous year				1,828,816	—
House account				257,384	244,480
Total				$6,478,816	$6,374,816

portion were reimbursed by per diem. Under the per diem plan, each salesperson received $70 per day for Monday through Thursday and $42 for Friday, or a total of $322 for the normal workweek. No per diem was paid for Saturday, but a salesperson received an additional $70 if he or she spent Saturday and Sunday nights in the territory.

In addition to the commission and per diem, a salesperson could earn cash awards under two sales incentive plans that were installed two years ago. Under the Annual Sales Increase Awards Plan, a total of $10,400 was paid to the five salespeople having the largest percentage increase in dollar sales volume over the previous year. To be eligible for these awards, a salesperson had to show a sales increase over the previous year. These awards were made at the January sales meeting, and the winners were determined by dividing the dollar amount of each salesperson's increase by his or her volume for the previous year with the percentage increases ranked in descending order. The salespeople's earnings under this plan for the current year are shown in Exhibit 2.

Under the second incentive plan, each salesperson could win a Weekly Sales Increase Award for each week in which his or her dollar volume in the cur-

rent year exceeded sales for the corresponding week in the previous year. Beginning with an award of $4 for the first week, the amount of the award increased by $4 for each week in which the salesperson surpassed his or her sales for the comparable week in the previous year. If a salesperson produced higher sales during each of the 50 weeks in the current year, he or she received $4 for the 1st week, $8 for the 2d week, and $200 for the 50th week, or a total of $4,100 for the year. The salesperson had to be employed by the company during the previous year to be eligible for these awards. A check for the total amount of the awards accrued during the year was presented to the salesperson at the sales meeting held in January. Earnings of the salespeople under this plan for the current year are shown in Exhibit 2.

The company frequently used "spiffs" to promote the sales of special items. The salesperson was paid a spiff, which usually was $4, for each order obtained for the designated items in the promotion.

For the past three years in recruiting salespeople, Mr. McDonald had guaranteed the more qualified applicants a weekly income while they learned the business and developed their respective territories. During the current year five salespeople, Allen,

Exhibit 2 Salespeople's Earnings and Incentive Awards in the Current Year

Salespeople	Sales Previous Year	Sales Current Year	Annual Sales Increase Awards Increase in Sales (Percent)	Annual Sales Increase Awards Award	Weekly Sales Increase Awards (Total Accrued)	Earnings*
Allen	$330,264	$329,216	(0.3%)	—	$1,012	$30,000†
Campbell	1,192,192	1,380,240	15.8	$3,000 (2d)	2,244	88,617
Duvall	—	414,656	—	—	—	30,000†
Edwards	—	419,416	—	—	—	30,000†
Gatewood	358,528	358,552	(0.1)	400 (5th)	1,104	18,513
Hammond	414,936	414,728	—	—	420	30,000†
Logan	—	447,720	—	—	—	30,000†
Mason	645,032	825,088	27.9	4,000 (1st)	3,444	49,756
O'Bryan	343,928	372,392	8.3	1,000 (4th)	1,512	19,344
Samuels	737,024	824,472	11.9	2,000 (3d)	1,300	49,713
Wates	370,712	342,200	(7.7)	—	612	17,532

*Exclusive of incentive awards and per diem.
†Guarantee of $600 per week or $30,000 per year.

Duvall, Edwards, Hammond, and Logan, had a guarantee of $600 a week, which they drew against their commissions. If the year's cumulative commissions for any of these salespeople were less than their cumulative weekly drawing accounts, they received no commissions. The commission and drawing accounts were closed on December 31 so each salesperson began the new year with a zero balance in each account.

The company did not have a stated or written policy specifying the maximum length of time a salesperson could receive a guarantee if commissions continued to be less than his or her draw. Mr. McDonald held the opinion that the five salespeople who currently had guarantees would quit if these guarantees were withdrawn before their commissions reached $30,000 per year.

Mr. McDonald stated that he was convinced the annual earnings of Outdoor's salespeople had fallen behind earnings for comparable selling positions, particularly in the past six years. As a result, he felt that the company's ability to attract and hold high-caliber professional salespeople was being adversely affected. He strongly expressed the opinion that each salesperson should be earning $50,000 annually.

Compensation Plan Proposals

In December of the current year, Mr. McDonald met with his comptroller and production manager, who were the only other executives of the company, and solicited their ideas concerning changes in the company's compensation plan for salespeople.

The comptroller pointed out that the salespeople having guarantees were not producing the sales that had been expected from their territories. He was concerned that the annual commissions earned by four of the five salespeople on guarantees were approximately half or less than their drawing accounts.

Furthermore, according to the comptroller, several of the salespeople who did not have guarantees were producing a relatively low volume of sales year after year. For example, annual sales remained at relatively low levels for Gatewood, O'Bryan, and Wates, who had been working four to five years in their respective territories.

The comptroller proposed that guarantees be reduced to $250 per week plus commissions at the regular rate on all sales. The $250 would not be drawn against commissions as was the case under the existing plan but would be in addition to any commissions earned. In the comptroller's opinion,

Exhibit 3   Comparison of Earnings in Current Year under Existing Guarantee Plan with Earnings under the Comptroller's Plan*

| Salespeople | Sales | Existing Plan | | | Comptroller's Plan | | |
		Commissions	Guarantee	Earnings	Commissions	Guarantee	Earnings
Allen	$329,216	$16,753	$30,000	$30,000	$16,753	$12,500	$29,253
Duvall	414,656	21,879	30,000	30,000	21,879	12,500	34,379
Edwards	419,416	22,165	30,000	30,000	22,165	12,500	34,665
Hammond	358,552	18,513	30,000	30,000	18,513	12,500	31,013
Logan	447,720	23,863	30,000	30,000	23,863	12,500	36,363

*Exclusive of incentive awards and per diem.

this plan would motivate the salespeople to increase sales rapidly since their incomes would rise directly with their sales. The comptroller presented Exhibit 3, which showed the incomes of the five salespeople having guarantees in the current year as compared with the incomes they would have received under his plan.

From a sample check of recent shipments, the production manager had concluded that the salespeople tended to overwork accounts located within a 50-mile radius of their homes. Sales coverage was extremely light in a 60- to 100-mile radius of the salespeople's homes with somewhat better coverage beyond 100 miles. He argued that this pattern of sales coverage seemed to result from a desire by the salespeople to spend most evenings during the week at home with their families.

He proposed that the per diem be increased from $70 to $90 per day for Monday through Thursday, $42 for Friday, and $90 for Sunday if the salesperson spent Sunday evening away from home. He reasoned that the per diem of $90 for Sunday would act as a strong incentive for the salespeople to drive to the perimeters of their territories on Sunday evenings rather than use Monday morning for traveling. Further, he believed that the increase in per diem would encourage the salespeople to spend more evenings away from their homes, which would result in a more uniform coverage of the sales territories and an overall increase in sales volume.

The consultant from New York City recommended that the guarantees and per diem be retained on the present basis and proposed that Outdoor adopt what he called a "Ten Percent Self-Improvement Plan." Under the consultant's plan each salesperson would be paid, in addition to the regular commission, a monthly bonus commission of 10 percent on all dollar volume over his or her sales in the comparable month of the previous year. For example, if a salesperson sold $40,000 worth of merchandise in January of the current year and $36,000 in January of the previous year, he or she would receive a $400 bonus check in February. For salespeople on guarantees, bonuses would be in addition to earnings. The consultant reasoned that the bonus commission would motivate the salespeople, both those with and without guarantees, to increase their sales.

He further recommended the discontinuation of the two sales incentive plans currently in effect. He felt the savings from these plans would nearly cover the costs of his proposal.

Following a discussion of these proposals with the management group, Mr. McDonald was undecided on which proposal to adopt, if any. Further, he wondered if any change in the compensation of salespeople would alleviate all of the present problems.

SAP/Microsoft: Dancing with the Bear

To provide enterprise business solutions for sustained competitive advantage.
—Mission Statement

On an American Airline flight from Pittsburgh to Atlanta, in seat 4B, Stephen Rietzke (alliance director for Systems, Applications and Products in Data Processing, Inc. [SAP]) looked over the slides of a PowerPoint presentation. Stephen must present an hour-long overview at SAP's meeting in Atlanta. The presentation consists of the highlights of the recent performance and forecasts of SAP's alliance with software leader Microsoft. As Stephen sat planning his presentation, he thought back to the start of the alliance and how it all began.

In 1992, Stephen received a phone call from SAP corporate headquarters in Waldorf, Germany. The phone call instructed Stephen to analyze an expansive list of prospective alliance partners in order to instigate a change in direction for one of the largest business software application vendors in the world, SAP. Stephen hung up the phone and proceeded to compile a brief list of prospective alliance partners.

This call initiated a defining moment in the business software industry. The software market consists of numerous large and small business software companies. Many of these software vendors focused on niche markets or limited their markets to either mainframe or microcomputer formats. The crossover from mainframe to microcomputer had yet to be conquered. The phone call from Waldorf, Germany, was to change this.

Background

In Mannheim, Germany, in 1972, three engineers had an idea: to create a company that produces and markets standard software for integrated business solutions. The company they started, Systemanalyse and Programmentwicklung @, is now called Systems, Applications, and Products in Data Processing Inc. or SAP AG for short.

This case was prepared by Rick Rasor, Robert Taylor, and Amy Ward under the direction of Lou Pelton (University of North Texas) for the purpose of class discussion and is not intended to illustrate effective or ineffective management practices.

From the beginning, SAP approached application software from a business viewpoint. By collaborating with business and information technology (IT) executives and partners worldwide, SAP developed a unique understanding of the challenges faced in implementing technology solutions for business users. SAP developed software that could help companies link their business processes, tying together disparate functions and helping their whole enterprise run more smoothly. The versatile, modular software could be quickly and easily adapted to new business processes, too, so as business grew, so did its capabilities.

SAP's innovative thinking soon made it the top software vendor in Germany. Today, SAP is the largest supplier of business application software in the world and the world's fourth largest independent software supplier, overall. Led by the continued technological leadership of SAP's flagship R/3 System, sales in the last three months of 1996 were the best in the company's history.

The company's headquarters are located in Waldorf, Germany, with regional offices located in more than 40 countries worldwide. SAP currently employs 1,250 employees around the globe. And, so far, SAP has helped more than 7,500 companies in 85 countries receive better returns on information. A better return on information means meeting customers needs faster. It means making the most of changes in the marketplace.

To make sure that customers get a better return on information, SAP has created the SAP Partner Program. The Partner Program helps SAP provide an end-to-end service for customers. The Partner Program combines leading resources, products, and services from companies worldwide. Partners provide expertise in hardware, complementary software, industry and business practices, information technology and implementation support. The Partner Program allows SAP to focus on what it does best by developing leading-edge business application software solutions.

Microsoft

Background

Microsoft was founded as a partnership on April 4, 1975, by William "Bill" H. Gates III and Paul G. Allen and was incorporated on June 25, 1981. Since its creation, Microsoft's mission has been "to create software for the personal computer that empowers and enriches people in the workplace, at school, and at home." Over the years, Microsoft, best known for the development of the Windows platform, has grown to become an international company with offices in more than 50 countries and with products in over 30 languages. As a global company, Microsoft strives to develop products that meet the needs of consumers worldwide. Microsoft pursues this challenge through its partnering strategy.

Partnering Programs

Microsoft currently has 12 partnering programs in which prospective partners may become involved. Each partnering program aims to utilize the unique strengths of each channel member. By analyzing a prospective business partner's business focus, primary business, customer base, and technology focus, Microsoft determines which program best suits the prospective partner. For example, a business that resells software and whose information and resources include Microsoft Intercom and Microsoft Direct Access would qualify for the Microsoft Certified Solution Provider partnering program. By categorizing prospective business partners, Microsoft can optimize the results of the partnership and ensure that its customers' needs continue to be met.

Microsoft's partnering mission statement is as follows: "Microsoft's core business model fosters growth and opportunity for the firms that partner with us to deliver compelling customer solutions based on Microsoft platform products and tools. To respond to the diverse needs of all of our channel partners, we offer many different partnering programs and resource offerings to you to help you succeed with Microsoft products."

Microsoft chooses to pursue a *keiretsu* partnering strategy. Microsoft organizes its enterprise *keiretsus,* such as the SAP project, around value-added products and service chains.

Microsoft enterprise *keiretsus* provide customers with:

- Better enterprise operating systems, optimized for multiple hardware platforms.

- Integrated enterprise management solutions for improved centralized administration of disparate systems, as well as reduced computing costs.

- Integrated line-of-business and packaged client–server applications, optimized for Microsoft's operating systems and server applications.

- Comprehensive partner services complement Microsoft's direct services and focusing on global, multivendor services and support.

- The opportunity to leverage the core competencies of providers at every level of the supply chain to receive the best services.

According to Deborah Willingham, vice president of Microsoft's Enterprise Customer Unit, "Collaborating with industry partners is not just practical; it is critical to meeting Microsoft's goals. By partnering, we can get closer to achieving [our] goals while maintaining our focus on core products and technology."

How Partners Benefit

Microsoft's investment in partners allows them to focus on their core competencies. Also, as demand for Microsoft products such as Windows NT and BackOffice expands worldwide, so too does the market for complementary services, solutions, and systems. As the market continues to grow, Microsoft's partners will be able to increase their business substantially. In addition to increased business, Microsoft's partners will also be able to collaborate with Microsoft on new technology, which will maintain their integration with Microsoft products. This integration of products and services will ensure the continued growth of the partnership and will ensure that the products remain compatible through upgrades.

R/3 Technology Overview

SAP's R/3 System presents a standard business software application for client–server computing. R/3 optimally supports all business activities by allowing easy adjustment and high flexibility to change and progress. At the core (see Exhibit 1) R/3 contains powerful programs for accounting and controlling, production and materials management, quality management and plant maintenance, sales and distribution, human resources management, and project management. R/3 also allows integration of banks and other business partners into intercompany communications.

Alliance Overview

With the R/3 System, SAP possesses a product with multi-tier management capability. SAP wants to obtain worldwide acceptance for R/3 by interfacing the product with current management information technology systems. Integrating R/3 with existing IT systems would not only create a competitive advantage for SAP; it would also reduce costs to the customer in both time and money.

In 1993 SAP entered into a technology-based alliance with the Microsoft Corporation which allowed SAP access to Microsoft's vast technology infrastructure. SAP and Microsoft jointly integrated R/3 with a variety of Microsoft's existing software and hardware applications. In return SAP offered Microsoft access to its industry-leading advances in the client–server arena. Together SAP and Microsoft now offer fully integrated R/3 System solutions. R/3 easily integrates with Windows NT, Windows 3.1, Windows 95, and Windows for Workgroups, Microsoft Excel, Access, Word, and Microsoft SQL Server platforms.

Another major factor of consideration for the alliance is the increasing business reliance on electronic commerce and the Internet. By integrating R/3 with the Microsoft Internet Information Server companies now have the capability of sending faxes, e-mail, and Internet e-mail directly from the Microsoft Exchange while working within the R/3 System.

Microsoft (as well as other alliance partners) allows SAP simplified system consultation and provision of installations and ongoing support worldwide. To assure this, both SAP and Microsoft have opened competency centers. Competency centers provide training and customer support for the R/3–Microsoft system. Alliances such as this allow SAP access to new technologies. This gives SAP the ability to keep R/3 compatible with the latest developments in the industry.

Several factors make the SAP–Microsoft alliance a good marriage. Both SAP and Microsoft have one common goal, the co-development of the R/3 business application system and Microsoft platforms into a worldwide industry standard. Microsoft sells platforms, personal productivity software products and tools for Windows- and Intel-based systems. SAP sells enterprise business solutions (R/3 system and other products). Microsoft can provide customers with the network operating system, database, Internet and programming development products and tools, while SAP can provide the business application software that sits on top of it.

Traditionally Microsoft focused mainly on distributing its products through channels, and SAP marketed its products through a direct sales force. Recently both companies have broken these traditions. SAP now focuses on "down market" initiatives and Microsoft is trying to sell "up enterprise." In other words, both companies want to meet in the middle.

Both SAP and Microsoft now focus their attention in all business software markets, regardless of customer size, with focus on both horizontal cross-industry solutions and vertical industry solutions. This brings a common goal of "enabling the total supply chain through business software automation." Both companies possess the products and the desire necessary, making this "extended supply chain" a reality.

Another interesting factor is that SAP practices an open door policy with its competitors. SAP works with numerous horizontal and vertical information technology companies, forming marketing partnerships. On the other hand, Microsoft does not traditionally work well with others, especially companies such as IBM, Oracle, and Computer Associates. By partnering with SAP, Microsoft maintains a "back door" to the other companies in the industry.

"When you dance with the bear, you let the bear lead," is a common phrase used among SAP employees. In this case the bear represents Microsoft. Microsoft is definitely the leader in this partnership (see Exhibit 2). More and more organizations turn to the Microsoft NT Server Platform today because of its strong, integrated security, scalable performance, and broad choice of hardware platforms. This makes Microsoft the perfect alliance partner for SAP, but Microsoft also needs SAP. Microsoft wants to provide mission critical platforms that rival mainframe and beyond computing requirements; therefore Microsoft desires access to SAP's marketplace. At this point Microsoft and SAP do not compete with one another; this gives them a truly symbiotic alliance. Since R/3's integration into the Windows NT Server platform, more than 45 percent of all new R/3 installations have been on the Windows NT Server. Microsoft and SAP continue to expand their horizons and enjoy a successful business relationship.

Exhibit 1

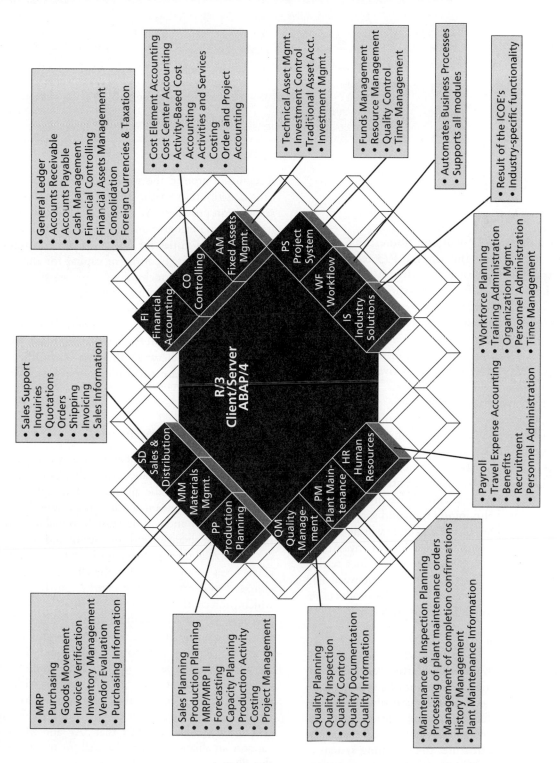

- General Ledger
- Accounts Receivable
- Accounts Payable
- Cash Management
- Financial Controlling
- Financial Assets Management
- Consolidation
- Foreign Currencies & Taxation

- Cost Element Accounting
- Cost Center Accounting
- Activity-Based Cost Accounting
- Activities and Services
- Costing
- Order and Project Accounting

- Technical Asset Mgmt.
- Investment Control
- Traditional Asset Acct.
- Investment Mgmt.

- Funds Management
- Resource Management
- Quality Control
- Time Management

- Automates Business Processes
- Supports all modules

- Result of the ICOE's
- Industry-specific functionality

- Sales Support
- Inquiries
- Quotations
- Orders
- Shipping
- Invoicing
- Sales Information

- Workforce Planning
- Training Administration
- Organization Mgmt.
- Personnel Administration
- Time Management

- Payroll
- Travel Expense Accounting
- Benefits
- Recruitment
- Personnel Administration

- MRP
- Purchasing
- Goods Movement
- Invoice Verification
- Inventory Management
- Vendor Evaluation
- Purchasing Information

- Sales Planning
- Production Planning
- MRP/MRP II
- Forecasting
- Capacity Planning
- Production Activity
- Costing
- Project Management

- Quality Planning
- Quality Inspection
- Quality Control
- Quality Documentation
- Quality Information

- Maintenance & Inspection Planning
- Processing of plant maintenance orders
- Management of completion confirmations
- History Management
- Plant Maintenance Information

Modules (central cube):
FI Financial Accounting · CO Controlling · AM Fixed Assets Mgmt. · PS Project System · WF Workflow · IS Industry Solutions · SD Sales & Distribution · MM Materials Mgmt. · PP Production Planning · QM Quality Management · PM Plant Maintenance · HR Human Resources

R/3 Client/Server ABAP/4

Exhibit 2

SAP/Microsoft Relationship History

Apr. 1993	Joint development agreement between SAP and Microsoft.
Apr. 1994	First release of R/3 on Windows NT Server.
Oct. 1995	SAP availability of R/3 on Microsoft SQL Server.
Oct. 1995	First customer goes online.
Mar. 1997	R/3 gains Microsoft BackOffice Logo certification.
Sept. 1997	More than 45% of all new R/3 installations are currently installed on Windows NT Server.
Sept. 1996	More than 3,200 R/3 installations on Windows NT Server.

Partner Contributions

SAP Contributions

For this alliance, SAP will contribute the business software applications (mainly the R/3 technology) for the technology infrastructure that Microsoft provides. The business software applications allow mid-market and small-enterprise customers to increase the productivity of their current systems while reducing the cost of maintaining their core systems. SAP also contributes name recognition to the alliance. In Germany, SAP's name recognition rivals Microsoft's name recognition in the United States. SAP currently ranks fourth worldwide in software providers and controls 30 percent of the business software applications market while its closest competitor controls only 10 percent of the business software applications market. Capital contributions from SAP will consist of capital for the introduction of current technology, user assistance programs, and future product development. SAP will also jointly fund and support competency centers. One of these centers will be located at SAP headquarters in Waldorf, Germany. At the competency centers, extensive joint product testing will take place to improve integration between R/3 and BackOffice and to ensure that the products remain symbiotic through future upgrades.

Microsoft Contributions

Microsoft, although the larger partner, does not contribute a disproportionate amount of resources. Each of the partners in this alliance contributes equally, ensuring that the foundation for a true alliance exists. For this alliance Microsoft will contribute the technological infrastructure, the operating system in which R/3 works. Microsoft's tremendous name recognition around the world will also be a significant contribution to the alliance. Microsoft's name recognition provides SAP the opportunity to increase its own name recognition and provides for immense growth opportunities for SAP. Capital contributions from Microsoft will consist of capital for the introduction of current technology, user assistance programs, and future product development. A jointly funded competency center will be located at Microsoft headquarters in Redmond, Washington, where joint product testing will take place to improve integration between R/3 and BackOffice and to ensure that the products remain symbiotic through upgrades.

Decision Environment

Alliance teams signify one hallmark of a true alliance. The SAP–Microsoft alliance has such a hallmark. Part of the formation of the alliance included the formation of an alliance team. Each partner contributes an alliance director and additional staff to make decisions regarding the alliance. With the health and survival of the alliance as their primary goals and concerns, the alliance team can ensure that the alliance remains on course. Problems that arise can be jointly resolved, which protects the interests of the alliance and of the partners. Given Microsoft's keiretsu philosophy of partnerships, the alliance team enables this to be a long-term alliance with no impending end. Without the alliance, team people would handle conflicts that arose at the corporate level of each company with their own company's agenda as their primary concern. This type of decision environment would impede the success of an alliance. The fact that SAP and Microsoft support an alliance team bodes well for the success of this alliance.

Future Concerns

Alliances are like marriages—for success, each partner must have an enormous amount of trust for the other. Currently SAP and Microsoft seem to possess this critical trust; perhaps this stems from the lack of direct competition with one another. The "traveling companion" relationship shared by SAP and Microsoft bodes well for the continued success of the alliance. History shows us, though, that many more alliances fail than succeed.

Recently, Microsoft has been under investigation by the U.S. Department of Justice. Charged with unfair practices such as bundling (making buyers purchase unnecessary products in order to receive the desired product by bundling the products together), the company has responded by fighting back with advertising and in court. Microsoft also agreed to unbundle its web browser in an effort to reduce Department of Justice concerns. This brings up a few questions:

- What threats exist to the relationship between SAP and Microsoft?

- Will the litigation against Microsoft affect the future of the relationship? If so, in what way?

- What would stop either partner from forming alliances with the other partner's competitor? And if this happened, how would it affect the current relationship?

- How should Rietzke evaluate the quality and success of the relationship? Be specific. What measures should be used?

- Finally, what possible problems could arise from the partners' exchange of technology? How should the alliance influence product development processes? Why?

Sources of information:

http://www.sap.com/partner

http://www.microsoft.com/germany/partner/sap/us

http://www.microsoft.com

Texas Instruments: Digital Signal Processors

Texas Instruments (TI) is a large ($12 billion sales in 1995) global, technology-based corporation with R&D manufacturing operations throughout the world. Although it is well known for its consumer products (calculators and laptop computers), these products represent a relatively small part of TI's business worldwide.

The central business (and core technologies) of Texas Instruments are

Semiconductor components: This represents over half of TI's annual sales volume worldwide. This business designs, develops, manufactures, and delivers integrated circuit chips for a wide variety of applications to original equipment manufacturers (OEMs) worldwide. These components are the heart of the intelligent products from computers and industrial equipment to high-end TVs and stereos.

Defense systems: TI is a world-leading supplier of tactical, defensive products for the U.S. and allied military services.

Materials and controls: Texas Instruments has a proprietary "clad metal" process, which enables the molecular bonding of two dissimilar materials. This technology is at the core of a large business in thermostatic controls and protectors, automotive trim and coinage metal, and other specialty material products.

Information technology: TI is developing and marketing a variety of "client–server" software applications for use in a spectrum of business situations.

Personal productivity products: This TI line includes calculators, mostly sold in large sets to schools for classroom use, as well as laptop computers and other "personal" digital products.

With manufacturing facilities in over 40 countries and nearly 50,000 employees worldwide, Texas Instruments represents a major force in most of the markets it serves. The general public throughout the globe knows TI for its consumer products, but

This case was prepared by Ralph A. Oliva, Institute for the Study of Business Markets, Penn State University, for illustrative purposes only, but is based on a real-world business situation. Certain numbers, names, and elements of the situation have been altered. Reprinted by permission of the author.

individual target segments know the products TI produces for that specific segment. Texas Instruments sells everything from ordnance to the military, to calculators for classroom use, under the parent "Texas Instruments" brand name.

Texas Instruments Semiconductors

The core of Texas Instruments' business, representing the bulk of its annual revenues and the largest share of its employee base, are semiconductor integrated circuit products. As mentioned, these products are the working chips which power everything from today's computers, to intelligent products such as answering machines, stereos, and medical technologies—anything with logic and memory. Texas Instruments manufactures one of the broadest lines of semiconductor product families.

One element of the Texas Instruments business mix is the dynamic random access memory (DRAM) business. Dynamic random access memories—the heart of the working memory of many computer systems—are especially in demand when the desktop personal computer business is on the upswing. Because of the entry of manufacturers around the world, DRAM pricing is largely market driven.

The price for building a new factory to produce DRAMs is quite high ($500 million per factory). The inherent volatility in this business, coupled with its commoditylike pricing, makes it a difficult business to be in over the long haul.

Texas Instruments has significant capacity in DRAMs, but over the past few years has moved most of its DRAM capacity into joint venture arrangements with customers having a large and stable demand such as Acer Computer, Hitachi, Cannon, and Hewlett-Packard.

Digital Signal Processors (DSPs)

Over quite a few years, Texas Instruments had developed core technologies and competencies in the processing of electronic signals. Learning to understand and process signals from various sorts, very rapidly as well as to compress, store, manipulate, and retrieve signals is a core competency of Texas Instruments. Building on this competency, Texas Instruments was working to develop a lead in the more custom-oriented, less volatile, digital signal processing (DSP) market.

DSPs enable many exciting features in the electronic products of which they are a part. Digital answering machines, high-end stereophonic receivers, computer workstations processing video signals, and special color displays—all rely on digital signal processing technology. DSPs enable electronic design engineers to put much more "sizzle" into the products they design at low cost. However, since DSPs are more of a custom than a commodity product, DSP designers need to be cautious about their source of supply. If they commit to a DSP in a piece of equipment they are designing, such as a stereo, they need to be absolutely certain that the supplier can meet their demand with the right parts at the right price at the right time. In addition, developments in DSP technology are very rapid, so staying at the state of the art can be difficult in this area.

Because of its critical competencies in this area, the opportunity for better profitability and less volatility, Texas Instruments has decided to focus its semiconductor business around digital signal processing.

Digital signal processors are finding their way into a wide variety of products including

- High-end TVs.
- Stereos.
- TV cameras.
- Video recorders.
- Answering machines.
- Automobiles (in braking systems, engine control, traction control, entertainment, and heating and cooling systems).
- Digital cellular telephones.
- Digital pagers.

The DSP Market

Texas Instruments sells its DSP and other semiconductor products largely through a direct sales force who are typically focused on larger national accounts, where a full profile of "silicon, software, service, and support" can be provided. In addition, such manufacturers, once a Texas Instruments IC is "designed in," often require very strict (JIT) delivery ground rules and a direct electronic connection (electronic data interface [EDI]) to their manufacturing operation.

The remainder of the customers for these products are treated through a two-tier distribution scheme, working through large, value-added distributors and a variety of smaller value-added resellers who develop specific "solutions" which incorporate TI digital signal processors. The value-added resellers produce full printed circuit boards that accomplish a specific application, which are then sold to companies who incorporate them in their products.

Because of their importance to the OEM using the DSPs, the decision to buy and use digital signal processors is an important one. First of all, not all companies are aware of digital signal processing technology and what it can bring to their products. Some would rather utilize a standard off-the-shelf microprocessor, such as Intel's Pentium processor, and build the application that they require using software solutions that run on a more general-purpose chip. The digital signal processor has advantages over the general-purpose processor for many applications, because it's more customized to the sorts of end equipment solutions that are required. DSPs are faster, more versatile, and more economical in many applications than the general-purpose processor or other approaches to a solution. The "value-in-use" of the DSP in many design solutions can be three to five times higher than alternatives. To some leading-edge companies this is well-known fact; to many companies who have not yet explored the use of DSPs, this was not fully known.

Perceptions of TI in the Marketplace

TI was investigating the possibility of repositioning itself in the marketplace around becoming the leading supplier of digital signal processing solutions. Before beginning to do this, TI market research was conducted in major regions of the world in 1993. At that time the current perceptions of the company were as follows:

> Sixty-seven percent of design engineering managers think of TI as an "off-the-shelf–oriented" company.

> Only 31 percent believe that TI supplied the integrated circuits that allow customers to differentiate their design.

Focus groups consistently generated statements such as

"TI is all over the place. They don't seem to have a focus."

"They have a 1970s image."

"TI is a jigsaw puzzle that no one has put together."

This general perceptual pattern had resulted from the fact that up to this point, most of TI's market communications had been fairly diffuse and run on a division-by-division basis. So although TI had leadership products across many product categories in the semiconductor business, no one central unifying position had surfaced for Texas Instruments. As a result, the sales team was having trouble positioning TI in this emerging field of digital signal processing. It was not easy to convince engineers to design a product into their end equipment or to get purchasing agents to pay a price premium for TI DSPs.

Texas Instruments' "Total Integration"

TI had experimented with a theme of "Total Integration" for a couple of years, which essentially may be summarized as follows:

Satisfying the needs of today's electronic original equipment manufacturer (OEM) requires more than leading edge semiconductor components and solutions. It requires "Total Integration."

Total integration is TI's ability to bring together the best of

- *Silicon technologies*
- *Service*
- *Information*
- *Software application tools*

TI's approach to integration includes more than the ability to put more functions on a single integrated circuit silicon chip. Total integration brings together the necessary technologies, tools, information, and talents needed to help TI customers—designers of computers, stereos, TVs, cellphones, and so on—to move on to their next level of integration faster and with a better product.

A communications campaign based on this essential proposition was implemented and tested, but results were not as powerful in creating a position for TI as desired. There wasn't a single, focused benefit that could be associated with the name Texas Instruments that was crisp, clear, and tightly defined.

Texas Instruments' "Digital Signal Processing Solutions"

In 1994, Texas Instruments decided to focus its semiconductor market communications on a more concentrated proposition: Texas Instruments is the leading provider of "Digital Signal Processing Solutions." Basically, TI wanted to reach its more critical customers—design engineers in certain original equipment manufacturers—with the message that if their application was of a certain (very demanding) category, a special sort of integrated circuit called a digital signal processor (DSP) was the best solution, and TI DSPs were the easiest to use, state of the art, and overall best value.

The Role of the Design Engineer

The design engineer is the most critical component of the buying chain for TI digital signal processors. The design engineer inside a large company, such as Sony, is responsible for the overall design of a consumer electronic product, such as a TV, radio, or answering machine. As they're working their design, if they decide to "design in" an integrated circuit from Texas Instruments, Texas Instruments then has the chance to deliver many integrated circuits over the life of the manufacture of that product. Capturing the design engineer at the design-in phase of the product life cycle is crucial to the selling process.

Digital signal processors are not the easiest technology to use. To enable designers to simulate what DSPs will do as part of their product designs, a suite of software tools is necessary. Extensive documentation, applications information, and other technical support may be required as part of a design-in. Sometimes DSPs represent a more risky, although potentially much more cost-effective solution than more conventional means. Design engineers are not rewarded for taking great risks, especially manufacturing risks in OEM products. They want solutions that position their products as leading edge, get the product to market quickly at competitive prices, and assure them of never being held up because of lack of supply of parts they had specified in the design.

Because of the strategic nature of a DSP design-in, design engineers often could not make the decision to employ DSPs on their own. If they specified a specific part from a specific company, and that company—for any reason—couldn't live up to specifications, delivery, or just-in-time standards, the results could be disastrous for their product. Therefore, DSP design-ins often involved other "influentials" in the purchase chain, both up and down. Senior management, engineering management, and product managers were often involved in the process, although most lacked full knowledge of what this product family could do. In addition, the purchasing department inside the OEM often played a key role.

Design engineers tend to be sponges for information of use to them in doing their job. Recent surveys have shown that they gain information from wherever they can: the Internet, trade magazines, conferences, journals, peer networks, university contacts, and manufacturers representatives.

For a group of design engineers who had embraced the digital signal processing product family, the whole notion of DSPs as part of their solution was cool. They seemed to take great joy in pushing the envelope of what the DSP could do, which in turn enabled them to load their products with a wide variety of features and benefits beyond what was typically expected—at very reasonable prices.

Integrated Market Communications

At the beginning of 1994, Texas Instruments began the design and implementation of an integrated market communications program, targeted at building a leadership share of the market in the high-growth digital signal processing business. TI already had a significant share of this market, but TI's target was clear: to be number one in this market in less than a two-year period. Key competitors in this area could be viewed as quite formidable. Motorola, Analog Devices, and AT&T Microelectronics all were suppliers of DSPs.

Beyond that, a powerful force in the semiconductor industry, Intel, was beginning to discuss how its general-purpose processors were becoming so powerful and so cost-effective that it might be possible in the future to do what today's DSPs do, at a better price with more flexibility, by utilizing general-purpose processors such as Intel's Pentium. Intel has a great reputation and the enviable position of being the virtual standard in the industry for general-purpose microprocessors. Standards had not yet emerged for digital signal processors, although because of their use in a variety of special-purpose applications, it was unclear how standards could or should be established.

Questions

1. What questions would you need to ask further to begin building an integrated market communications program for TI digital signal processors?
2. What are the most important things you know now?
3. What would you need to know?
4. What are the key audiences who should be considered?
5. Build a behavioral timeline that begins to address the desired beliefs and behaviors of each of these audiences.
6. Outline a brief IMC plan to accomplish the tasks set down in your behavioral timeline.
7. How would you begin to compute the ROI on the program you're beginning to build?

Whole Tree Energy™

"I can see the whole project goin' south when we meet with the community groups," contended Jeb Boskirk, director of licensing and environmental affairs at a Midwest power utility. "These are school teachers, students, bankers, hunters, shopkeepers, machinists, and housewives. Very few economists or tech heads are gonna be there, Dave. And we'll be lucky if there's no orchestrated counterpoint by some citizen group—it could be tree huggers, no-growth reverts, or just a well-oiled NIMBY.[1] We've got to do our homework, sure. But we're going to need lots of help from you to make this fly."

David Ostlie, founder and president of Energy Performance Systems, Inc., knew that Jeb Boskirk was right. Jeb was skilled in the vital process of securing land, working with state licensing agencies and EPA approval boards, as well as surviving the local hearings and town meetings, all prerequisites to bringing a new power plant into being. Ostlie believed in the promise of electricity from burning wood, and more than two decades of tests and research had supported his theory. But now he was close to bringing his patented Whole Tree Energy (WTE) system on line in a real 100-megawatt (MW) power plant—power for nearly 100,000 people. He needed to review again the role he and his tiny company would have to play in this complex marketing environment to make WTE happen.

Background

Since Thomas Edison found carbon to be a suitable filament and invented the first practical light bulb, civilization's appetite for electric power has expanded relentlessly. Most of this demand has been answered by power plants that burn coal, oil, or natural gas. Although research continues to show advances, currently very little electric power is generated from solar, wind, and geothermal energy. The construction of nuclear power facilities in the United States has virtually ground to a halt.

Biomass fuels are immense, ubiquitous, clean, and, in most cases, cost-effective sources of energy. Utilities have substantial and—with further R&D—growing opportunities to exploit this resource.[2]

Biomass fuels are the energy resources in living things and their waste products. The greatest supply of biomass energy lies in natural forests. Other sources include wood residue and agricultural by-products. For example, wood chips are frequently burned at small power plants owned by paper companies and saw mills. Ethanol is economically produced from corn. The energy from animal waste and grasses has also been studied.

What we call fossil fuels—coal, oil and natural gas—are in essence prehistoric biomass. The difference is fossil fuel deposits are *depleted* by extraction; biomass fuels are *renewable*. In addition, biomass fuels yield fewer emissions. Burning trees, for example, emits carbon dioxide (CO_2), but no more than what the trees have absorbed from the environment during their growth. Fossil fuels emit CO_2 that hasn't been in the atmosphere for eons. Furthermore, while many coal-fired power plants require expensive equipment to control emissions of sulfur dioxide (SO_2), wood and grasses release very low levels of SO_2 that are sometimes barely measurable. Wood also has an advantage over coal in the release of very low levels of nitrogen oxides (NOx).

Despite the promise of biomass fuels, many obstacles currently limit their viability. Power plants are constrained to small-scale operations, thermal efficiencies need to be improved, fuel delivery systems need to be developed, overall economic viability needs to demonstrated, and the public needs significantly more education about both the promise and limits.

Whole-Tree Energy™

David Ostlie's inspiration for the WTE concept began in 1978 when he built his house in a new

This case was prepared by F. Robert Dwyer (University of Cincinnati) for the purposes of class discussion. Input from William Rudelius (professor of marketing at the University of Minnesota and a member of the board of directors at EPS, Inc.) and Thomas Osterhus (doctoral candidate at the University of Cincinnati and staff consultant at Cynergy) is gratefully acknowledged. Some of the case facts come from EPS literature and the case "Energy Performance Systems, Inc." in Eric Berkowitz, Roger Kerin, Steven Hartley, and William Rudelius *Marketing*, (Burr Ridge, IL: Irwin, 1997), pp. 119–21.

[1]NIMBY stands for "not in my back yard." It is a crude label for groups that might agree on the need for, say, a new power plant or jail or bus depot, but not be willing to accept it in their neighborhood.

[2]EPRI (Electric Power Research Institute), "Biomass State-of-the-Art Assessment," 1991. Abstract at **http://www.epriweb.com.**

woodland development in central Minnesota. On cold winter mornings the smoke from each new home's fireplace or wood-burning stove was sometimes enough to make one choke. Ostlie set out to build a high-energy, smokeless woodburner. A former iron worker then employed by Northern States Power (NSP), Oslie built a chest freezer-sized unit that he installed and tested in a storage area beneath his garage. He used the same wood cleared for the driveways throughout his neighborhood, but dried it more thoroughly than his neighbors' woodpiles. As a result, Ostlie's device generated such high temperatures that the wood burned completely and gave off a clear, virtually sootless exhaust.

In a 1993 interview, Ostlie recalled his thinking that led him to start a company and begin the long road of concept drawings, slide presentations, and component testing: "Having some knowledge of the electric power industry, I knew that the few existing wood-burning power plants used chipped or shredded wood. I was also aware that the process of breaking wood down to this size is expensive. Being able to avoid these costs would be a great advantage."[3]

The videotape companion to this case details the concept of WTE. To recap the key elements,

1. Tree plantations of fast-growing hybrid hardwoods provide a harvest in seven years. A 400-MW plant serving a 50-mile radius would require about 3 percent of this acreage for plantations—most likely marginal farmland, with some receiving subsidies to be taken from the production of food crops.

2. Trees are efficiently cut and transported to the plant site.

3. Within a large fiberglass dome whole trees are stacked in cross-hatch fashion upwards of 100 feet (30m) by a large crane.

4. Waste heat from the plant is piped into the dome to dry the stack for 30 days, removing over 65 percent of the trees' moisture and allowing a cleaner, more efficient burn.

5. Trees are conveyed from the dome to the nearby boiler wall, where they are cut to fit, approximately 28 feet (8.5m).

6. A ram pushes the pile of trees 12 to 16 feet high into a charge pit; then another ram pushes it into the furnace.

7. The slightly oversized boiler promotes high heat release and complete combustion.

The time line in Exhibit 1 summarizes the research that has gone into the WTE system. Ostlie sometimes wonders just how much more has to be demonstrated before a power utility will commence to build a commercial plant and he wonders at what stage of the purchase process and what constituency he should direct his limited marketing resources.

At most power companies, the decision process to bring a new plant on line is lengthy and complex. Capacity planners play a key initiating role in the process. Their job is to forecast energy demand for the market served and check the adequacy of current plant capacity. Demand is analyzed for base demand as well as peak demands, such as when air conditioners run flat out to cope with stifling summer temperatures. In these two areas, WTE is relatively attractive for base load service; natural gas plants serve peak loads.

Capacity planners typically evaluate the options by first specifying the resources for each alternative site, technology, and array of base loaders and peakers by calculating equivalent costs (e.g., dollars per kilowatt-hour). Optimization programs support the process of structuring the problem and allow sensitivity analysis on the sequencing of options, the impact of delays, input costs, and more.

An executive committee reviews the recommendations from capacity planning. Financial criteria and market service standards are tightly applied, and the environmental and political dimensions of the recommendation are fully considered. The utility's Licensing and Environmental Affairs staff will then seek to obtain EPA and state licensing agency approval, acquire the needed property, and interface with local governments and community groups.

[3]Leslie Lamarre, "Electricity from Trees," *Electric Power Research Institute EPRI Journal* (January/February 1994), p. 19.

Exhibit 1

WTE Time Line

Early 1980s	Ostlie tests a clean wood-burning unit beneath his garage. It leaves no cinders and provides a clear exhaust. Ostlie convinces NSP to scale up the design to explore its commercial viability.
1984	Osltie works in cooperation with St. John's University in Collegeville, MN. Using St. John's' 1.6-MW boiler and 4-foot-long sections of dried trees, Ostlie reaches 2,400° F, besting the temperatures typical of the superheat cycles at the largest coal-fired plants.
1986	Converting one of its coal-fired boilers for 10 MW, NSP tests the WTE output capacity and emissions over a 100-hour period. Output efficiency of 30 percent of capacity is the criterion for success at utility scale. Ostlie achieves a rate of 90 percent and maintains an average output of 6–7 MW over the test. EPA reports the lowest measures of NOx emissions of any solid fuel in the United States. SO_2 and particulate emissions are also very low—even without the removal systems common at coal-burning plants.
1988	NSP puts the WTE project on hold. Ostlie leaves the company, takes his patent, and forms a new company called Energy Performance Systems, Inc. (EPS).
1991	EPRI releases its own study of biomass fuel, which shows the attractiveness of combustion of fast-growing tree crops. In Aurora, MN (pop. 3,000), EPS and EPRI join in a demonstration project to harvest, transport, stack, dry, and combust 3,000 tons of whole trees. Standard logging trucks each bring about 25 tons to the site. A tower crane and remote control grapple pile the trees more than 100 feet high on a base 30 feet square. The pile is stable and the 30-day drying period reduces moisture content to 20 percent. Combustion tests are favorable, with one experiment producing a wood-burning world record of 4.2 million Btu per hour per square foot. (Compare to a coal-fired boiler's heat release rate of about 2 million Btu per hour per square foot.)
1992	NSP and Wisconsin Power & Light approach EPRI and EPS to explore the feasibility of building a WTE plant.
1995	EPRI releases computer models for evaluating biomass power technologies, saying WTE shows "the potential for improved cost and performance relative to the existing technologies." Cost and thermal efficiency estimates are provided, but the report states, "Since neither the advanced wood gasification nor the WTE technologies have reached maturity nor been commercialized, utilities should use the estimates for these advanced systems with caution."
1997	The Minnesota Department of Natural Resources continues to monitor a 1995 planting of 1,000 acres of fast-growing, hybrid poplar trees.

Wind Technology

Kevin Cage, general manager of Wind Technology, sat in his office on a Friday afternoon watching the snow fall outside his window. It was January 1991 and he knew that during the month ahead he would have to make some difficult decisions regarding the future of his firm, Wind Technology. The market for the wind profiling radar systems that his company designed had been developing at a much slower rate than he had anticipated.

During Wind Technology's 10-year history, the company had produced a variety of weather-related radar and instrumentation. In 1986, the company condensed its product mix to include only wind-profiling radar systems. Commonly referred to as wind profilers, these products measure wind and atmospheric turbulence for weather forecasting, detection of wind direction at NASA launch sites, and other meteorological applications (i.e., at universities and other scientific monitoring stations). Kevin had felt that this consolidation would position the company as a leader in what he anticipated to be a high-growth market with little competition.

Wind Technology's advantages over Unisys, the only other key player in the wind-profiling market, included the following: (1) The company adhered stringently to specifications and quality production; (2) Wind Technology had the technical expertise to provide full system integration. This allowed customers to order either basic components or a full system including software support; (3) Wind Technology's staff of meteorologists and atmospheric scientists provided the customer with sophisticated support, including operation and maintenance training and field assistance; (4) Finally, Wind Technology had devoted all of its resources to its wind-profiling business. Kevin believed that the market would perceive this as an advantage over a large conglomerate like Unisys.

Wind Technology customized each product for individual customers as the need arose; the total system could cost a customer from $400,000 to $5

This case was prepared by Ken Manning, University of South Carolina, and Jakki Mohr, University of Colorado. This case is intended for use as a basis for class discussion rather than to illustrate either effective or ineffective administrative decision making. Some data are disguised. © Copyright by Jakki Mohr 1990. All rights reserved.

million. Various governmental entities, such as the Department of Defense, NASA, and state universities had consistently accounted for about 90 percent of Wind Technology's sales. In lieu of a field sales force, Wind Technology relied on top management and a team of engineers to call on prospective and current customers. Approximately $105,000 of their annual salaries was charged to a direct selling expense.

The Problem

The consolidation strategy that the company had undertaken in 1986 was partly due to the company being purchased by Vaitra, a high-technology European firm. Wind Technology's ability to focus on the wind-profiling business had been made possible by Vaitra's financial support. However, since 1986 Wind Technology had shown little commercial success, and due to low sales levels, the company was experiencing severe cash-flow problems. Kevin knew that Wind Technology could not continue to meet payroll much longer. Also, he had been informed that Vaitra was not willing to pour more money into Wind Technology. Kevin estimated that he had from 9 to 12 months (until the end of 1991) in which to implement a new strategy with the potential to improve the company's cash flow. The new strategy was necessary to enable Wind Technology to survive until the wind-profiler market matured. Kevin and other industry experts anticipated that it would be two years until the wind-profiling market achieved the high growth levels that the company had initially anticipated.

One survival strategy that Kevin had in mind was to spin-off and market component parts used in making wind profilers. Initial research indicated that, of all the wind-profiling system's component parts, the high-voltage power supply (HVPS) had the greatest potential for commercial success. Furthermore, Kevin's staff on the HVPS product had demonstrated knowledge of the market. Kevin felt that by marketing the HVPS, Wind Technology could reap incremental revenues, with very little addition to fixed costs. (Variable costs would include the costs of making and marketing the HVPS. The accounting department had estimated that production costs would run approximately 70 percent of the selling price, and that 10 percent of other expenses—such as top management direct-selling expenses—should be charged to the HVPS.)

High-Voltage Power Supplies

For a vast number of consumer and industrial products that require electricity, the available voltage level must be transformed to different levels and types of output. The three primary types of power supplies include linears, switchers, and converters. Each type manipulates electrical current in terms of the type of current (AC or DC) and/or the level of output (voltage). Some HVPS manufacturers focus on producing a standardized line of power supplies, while others specialize in customizing power supplies to the user's specifications.

High-voltage power supplies vary significantly in size and level of output. Small power supplies with relatively low levels of output (under 3 kV[1]) are used in communications equipment. Medium-sized power supplies that produce an output between 3 and 10 kV are used in a wide range of products including radars and lasers. Power supplies that produce output greater than 10 kV are used in a variety of applications, such as high-powered X-rays and plasma-etching systems.

Background on Wind Technology's HVPS

One of Wind Technology's corporate strategies was to control the critical technology (major component parts) of its wind-profiling products. Management felt that this control was important since the company was part of a high-technology industry in which confidentiality and innovation were critical to each competitor's success. This strategy also gave Wind Technology a differential advantage over its major competitors, all of whom depended on a variety of manufacturers for component parts. Wind Technology had successfully developed almost all of the major component parts and the software for the wind profiler, yet the development of the power supply had been problematic.

To adhere to the policy of controlling critical technology in product design (rather than purchasing an HVPS from an outside supplier), Wind Technology management had hired Anne Ladwig and her staff of HVPS technicians to develop a power supply for the company's wind-profiling systems. Within six months

of joining Wind Technology, Anne and her staff had completed development of a versatile power supply which could be adapted for use with a wide variety of equipment. Some of the company's wind-profiling systems required up to ten power supplies, each modified slightly to carry out its role in the system.

Kevin Cage had delegated the responsibility of investigating the sales potential of the company's HVPS to Anne Ladwig since she was very familiar with the technical aspects of the product and had received formal business training while pursuing an MBA. Anne had determined that Wind Technology's HVPS could be modified to produce levels of output between 3 and 10 kV. Thus, it seemed natural that if the product was brought to market, Wind Technology should focus on applications in this range of output. Wind Technology also did not have the production capabilities to compete in the high-volume, low-voltage segment of the market, nor did the company have the resources and technical expertise to compete in the high-output (10 kV +) segment.

The Potential Customer

Power supplies in the 3–10 kV range could be used to conduct research, to produce other products, or to place as a component into other products such as lasers. Thus, potential customers could include research labs, large end-users, OEMs, or distributors. Research labs each used an average of three power supplies; other types of customers ordered a widely varying quantity.

HVPS users were demanding increasing levels of reliability, quality, customization, and system integration. *System integration* refers to the degree to which other parts of a system are dependent upon the HVPS for proper functioning, and the extent to which these parts are combined into a single unit or piece of machinery.

Anne had considered entering several HVPS market segments in which Wind Technology could reasonably compete. She had estimated the domestic market potential of these segments at $237 million. To evaluate these segments, Anne had compiled growth forecasts for the year ahead and had evaluated each segment in terms of the anticipated level of customization and system integration demanded by the market. Anne felt that the level of synergy between Wind Technology and the various segments was also an important consideration in selecting a

---

[1]kV (kilovolt): 1,000 volts.

Exhibit 1

HVPS Market
Segments in the
3–10 kV Range

Application	Forecasted Annual Growth (%)	Level of Customization/ Level of System Integration*	Synergy Rating**	Percent of $237 Million Power Supply Market***
General/univ. laboratory	5.40	Medium/medium	3	8
Lasers	11.00	Low/medium	4	10
Medical equipment	10.00	Medium/medium	3	5
Microwave	12.00	Medium/high	4	7
Power modulators	3.00	Low/low	4	25
Radar systems	11.70	Low/medium	5	12
Semiconductor	10.10	Low/low	3	23
X-ray systems	8.60	Medium/high	3	10

*The level of customization and system integration generally in demand within each of the applications is defined as low, medium, or high.

**Synergy ratings are based on a scale of 1 to 5; 1 is equivalent to a very low level of synergy and 5 is equivalent to a very high level of synergy. These subjective ratings are based on the amount of similarities between the wind-profiling industry and each application.

***Percentages total 100 percent of the $237 million market in which Wind Technology anticipated it could compete.

NOTE: This list of applications is not all-inclusive.

target market. Exhibit 1 summarizes this information. Anne believed that if the product was produced, Wind Technology's interests would be best served by selecting only one target market on which to concentrate initially.

Competition

To gather competitive information, Anne contacted five HVPS manufacturers. She found that the manufacturers varied significantly in terms of size and marketing strategy (see Exhibit 2). Each listed a price in the $5,500–$6,500 range on power supplies with the same features and output levels as the HVPS that had been developed for Wind Technology. After she spoke with these firms, Anne had the feeling that Wind Technology could offer the HVPS market superior levels of quality, reliability, technical expertise, and customer support. She optimistically believed that a one-half percent market share objective could be achieved the first year.

Promotion

If Wind Technology entered the HVPS market, they would require a hard-hitting, thorough promotional campaign to reach the selected target market. Three

factors made the selection of elements in the promotion mix especially important to Wind Technology: (1) Wind Technology's poor cash flow, (2) the lack of a well-developed marketing department, and (3) the need to generate incremental revenue from sales of the HVPS at a minimum cost. In fact, a rule of thumb used by Wind Technology was that all marketing expenditures should be about 9 to 10 percent of sales. Kevin and Anne were contemplating the use of the following elements:

1. Collateral Material

Sales literature, brochures, and data sheets are necessary to communicate the product benefits and features to potential customers. These materials are designed to be (1) mailed to customers as part of direct-mail campaigns or in response to customer requests, (2) given away at trade shows, and (3) left behind after sales presentations.

Because no one in Wind Technology was an experienced copywriter, Anne and Kevin considered hiring a marketing communications agency to write the copy and to design the layout of the brochures. This agency would also complete the graphics (photographs and artwork) for the collateral material. The cost for 5,000 pieces (including the 10 percent markup for the agency) was estimated to be $5.50 each.

Exhibit 2
Competitor Profile (3–10 kV Range)

Company	Gamma	Glassman	Kaiser	Maxwell*	Spellman
Approximate annual sales	$2 million	$7.5 million	$3 million		$7 million
Market share	1.00%	3.00%	1.50%		2.90%
Price**	$5,830	$5,590	$6,210	$5000–$6000	$6,360
Delivery	12 weeks	10 weeks	10 weeks	8 weeks	12 weeks
Product customization	No	Medium	Low	Medium	Low
System integration experience	Low	Low	Low	Medium	Low
Customer targets	Gen. lab.	Laser	Laser	Radar	Capacitors
	Space	Medical	Medical	Power mod.	Gen. lab.
	Univ. lab.	X-ray	Microwave	X-ray	Microwave
			Semiconductor	Medical equip.	X-ray

*Maxwell was in the final stages of product development and stated that the product would be available in the spring. Maxwell anticipated that the product would sell in the $5,000–$6,000 range.

**Price quoted for an HVPS with the same specifications as the "standard" model developed by Wind Technology.

2. Public Relations

Kevin and Anne realized that one very cost-efficient tool of promotion is publicity. They contemplated sending out new product announcements to a variety of trade journals whose readers were part of Wind Technology's new target market. By using this tool, interested readers could call or write to Wind Technology, and the company could then send the prospective customers collateral material. The draw-back of relying too heavily on this element was very obvious to Kevin and Anne—the editors of the trade journals could choose not to print Wind Technology's product announcements if their new product was not deemed newsworthy.

The cost of using this tool would include the time necessary to write the press release and the expense of mailing the release to the editors. Direct costs were estimated by Wind Technology to be $500.

3. Direct Mail

Kevin and Anne were also contemplating a direct-mail campaign. The major expenditure for this option would be buying a list of prospects to whom the collateral material would be mailed. Such lists usually cost around $5,000, depending upon the number of names and the list quality. Other costs would include postage and the materials mailed. These costs were estimated to be $7,500 for a mailing of 1,500.

4. Trade Shows

The electronics industry had several annual trade shows. If they chose to exhibit at one of these trade shows, Wind Technology would incur the cost of a booth, the space at the show, and the travel and incidental costs of the people attending the show to staff the booth. Kevin and Anne estimated these costs at approximately $50,000 for the exhibit, space, and materials, and $50,000 for a staff of five people to attend.

5. Trade journal advertising

Kevin and Anne also contemplated running a series of ads in trade journals. Several journals they considered are listed in Exhibit 3, along with circulation, readership, and cost information.

6. Personal selling

(a) *Telemarketing* (*Inbound/Inside Sales*).[2] Kevin and Anne also considered hiring a technical salesperson to respond to HVPS product inquiries generated by product announcements, direct mail, and advertising. This person's responsibilities would include answering phone calls, prospecting, sending out collateral material, and following up with potential

[2]"Inbound" refers to calls that potential customers make to Wind Technology, rather than "outbound," in which Wind Technology calls potential customers (i.e., solicits sales).

Exhibit 3 Trade Publications

Trade Publication	Editorial	Cost per Color Insertion (1 page)	Circulation
Electrical Manufacturing	For purchasers and users of power supplies, transformers, and other electrical products.	$4,077	35,168 nonpaid
Electronic Component News	For electronics OEMs. Products addressed include work stations, power sources, chips, etc.	$6,395	110,151 nonpaid
Electronic Manufacturing News	For OEMs in the industry of providing manufacturing and contracting of components, circuits, and systems.	$5,075	25,000 nonpaid
Design News	For design OEMs covering components, systems, and materials.	$8,120	170,033 nonpaid
Weatherwise	For meteorologists covering imaging, radar, etc.	$1,040	10,186 paid

NOTE: This is a partial list of applicable trade publications. Standard Rate and Data Service lists other possible publications.

customers. The salary and benefits for one individual would be about $50,000.

(b) *Field Sales.* The closing of sales for the HVPS might require some personal selling at the customer's location, especially if Wind Technology pursued the customized option. Kevin and Anne realized that potentially this would provide them with the most incremental revenue, but it also had the potential to be the most costly tool. Issues such as how many salespeople to hire, where to position them in the field (geographically), and so on, were major concerns. Salary plus expenses and benefits for an outside salesperson were estimated to be about $80,000.

Xerox DocuTech and DocuColor

At the 1994 IPEX trade fair in London, two start-up companies literally stole the show with new color printing products that replace offset presses for many applications. Indigo, an Israel-based company with a Japanese partner, and Xeikon, a Belgian company, introduced products that provided color print on demand from digital masters. Xerox and other major suppliers to the printing industry were surprised by these launches, as the products they had under development were years away from reaching the market.

The next year at DRUPA, (arguably the world's largest trade fair encompassing 18 buildings in Dusseldorf, Germany), Indigo and Xeikon, who had partnered with industry giant AGFA, were again the talk of the show. Heidelberg, the German printing press company, introduced a similar product and wrote over 100 orders at the show. On the other hand, people were asking "Where's Xerox—why don't they have a product?" It was a question that Xerox asked itself.

"The biggest limitation for us was the software front end," says Joe McGrath, VP–general manager for Xerox's Color Production Systems. "We had the printing capability through our Japanese partner, Fuji Xerox, but not the digital imaging software." That software, though, was the specialty of two companies: Scitex (another Israeli company) and Efi (based in Southern California). McGrath quickly signed these two companies on to the project. ColorBus, another vendor, added critical interfacing capabilities.

The tone of McGrath's voice is filled with both pride and awe. "Sometime in late summer of 1995, after DRUPA, we set May 1 of the next year [1996] as a new-product launch date and began developing a product. This meant that we had about nine months to develop and launch a product—almost no time compared to the usual product development cycle." Weekly PicTel (video telephone) meetings were held simultaneously between engineers in Israel, Japan, Southern California, and Rochester, New York; product performance data files were shipped

This case was prepared by J. F. Tanner Jr. (Baylor University) and Robert Dwyer (University of Cincinnati) for the purposes of class discussion and is not intended to illustrate effective or ineffective management practice. Some information has been disguised or created to fit teaching needs. Thanks to Joe McGrath and Xerox for the accompanying video and other information.

via e-mail, and all of this had to be coordinated through so many time zones that for some engineers, meetings took place in the middle of the night.

Concurrent marketing development meant that once the product was ready to launch, so were the marketing plans. On May 1, 1996, the DocuColor will be launched. A global video conference is planned during which the product will be demonstrated simultaneously in San Francisco, Chicago, Toronto, London, Zurich, and Sao Paulo, Brazil. Keeping in mind that software has to be written so that the user interface is in the local language, the DocuColor will be the first truly global launch for Xerox. DocuColor will be launched in all target countries faster than any other Xerox product, 10 years faster than for some products.

"Time to market and relative market share are key objectives for us," says McGrath. "We know Canon has something in the works, so we want to beat them to the market." At the same time that the product was being developed, the marketing plan was also in the works so no delays in launching the product would occur.

DocuColor represents a major improvement over the earlier black-and-white–only DocuTech system. DocuTech, however, still has strong market potential. One industry source expects the market for DocuTech-type products to total $8 billion by 2000, and DocuColor-type products should total $4 billion. DocuTech products cost between $350,000 and $500,000 each depending on the various features selected.

Both DocuColor and DocuTech deliver high-quality 600-dots-per-inch output at rates of 70 and 135 pages per minute, respectively. Because Xerox products are completely digital, image quality is better than with other systems that combine digital imaging with offset output. Service, reliability, and other factors related to uptime (the time that the machine is up and running) also play a role in the decision to select Xerox over competition.

This case's video portrays three key customers who use DocuTech. Their stories illustrate the benefits of demand printing to manufacturing organizations. The product can serve a variety of industries, but Xerox has organized by vertical markets and your focus is on the manufacturing environment epitomized by the companies profiled in the video. Marketing research indicates a complex buying process, detailed below.

Buying Process

Product manuals accompany the purchase of almost every product; the more complex the product, the more complex the manual. These manuals have to be constantly updated with every change to the product, every change to the law applying to the product (for example, warnings that may have to accompany the product), and every change concerning customer service options. Producing and storing these manuals is the function of a technical publications (tech pubs) department and/or a printing department.

The choice of black and white (B&W) or color depends on the nature of the print job. B&W is fine for most manuals; however, in situations involving color coding of products or parts, the color option is preferred. Thus, the printers serve the same basic market and the choice depends on the individual needs of the buyer.

DocuColor and DocuTech are products aimed at companies that have their own printing department and offset printing presses. Both products may be sold to the same department so that the B&W jobs can be accomplished on the lower-cost DocuTech. A key influencer or decision maker is the head of that department, who could be titled director or manager of printing. This person may also initiate the purchase. Such a change in technology represents a major change in the way the department operates, including a reduction in personnel (sometimes offset by increasing in-house volume by bringing in jobs formerly farmed out to third-party printers), a change in job design, and other similar factors. Thus, the purchase represents a major change in the way the center operates.

The product is a capital purchase and requires a capital budget, so the controller or chief financial officer of the corporation will also review the financials of the purchase. This person will be interested in issues such as payback (how long it takes for savings to offset the investment), purchase terms, whether leasing is available, and other options.

The tech pubs department may be run by director of documentation or documentation manager. This department writes the product manuals and other product materials, and then coordinates the production of the manuals with the printing department. Initiation of the purchase may come from this department. People from this department are interested in easy-to-use systems that mean less time spent on preparing a manuscript for production. If digital originals can be used, less time is spent copy editing and proofing manuscripts. With offset presses, someone must examine galleys or pages, special proofs that are printed and checked for accuracy of the printing plates. This process is tedious and expensive, but can be avoided with digital input because there is no retyping of the original manuscript.

The logistics department is another area impacted by the purchase. Storage space is devoted to manuals and other printed material that accompanies products—the space and items stored are managed by the logistics department. The manager of logistics is included in the process in order to assess the benefits gained by freeing up the space, as well as issues involved in printing on demand and managing lower levels of inventory.

Many large companies also have a document storage department, which is responsible for managing records of all types. Electronic storage and retrieval systems are often used by these departments to minimize the costs of space and labor required to locate documents. A representative of this department would also participate.

The purchase process may take several months, and would include demonstrations of the product using originals provided by the buying organization. Leads for the DocuTech or DocuColor may come from salespeople in other Xerox divisions, advertising in trade publications, or meetings at trade shows. Salespeople also work to identify their own leads. The salesperson for the account will survey the firm to determine the needs; this survey may involve several of the people listed above. Then a demonstration of the product is given to the individuals participating in the purchase. At that point, a proposal is also prepared that quantifies the benefits received, lists the costs, and spells out the implementation process.

Each salesperson works with a systems analyst, who provides technical support to the salesperson and to the account. Since each account may have its own software package from which it takes its documents, the analyst's job is to make the implementation of a system as easy as possible for the user. The analyst works with the salesperson and prospect through the entire sales process and continues to support the customer after the sale.

Marketing Communication Options

While the initial launch of the product involving the global video conference for DocuColor is already planned, communications plans specific to markets like manufacturing have not been developed. Launch for DocuColor is scheduled for May, but Jerri Tuso, the marketing manager tasked with the manufacturing market, knows a communications plan is needed through the end of the year. Up to this point in the year, very little has been spent on advertising and the communications campaigns of last year have been allowed to die out as the company readied for the launch of the new product line.

Jerri is relatively new to marketing management, having spent the previous four years in the field as a sales rep. She was one of the first DocuTech salespeople, handling a territory that included Amdahl, one of the accounts described on the video. Six months ago, she made the switch to marketing. At first, she was excited about DocuColor, but when she learned that she was assigned to manufacturing (which has little need for the color system), she was disappointed. One challenge, she thought, will be generating excitement about a black-and-white printer when everyone is touting the color system.

The video illustrates the themes of reengineering and documents on demand that have to be the focus of the campaign. Of course, the ability to print in color will be emphasized in all corporate campaigns (a corporate campaign is any campaign aimed at the general business audience, as opposed to a vertical market like manufacturing).

Advertising

The marketing communications plan should support the sales force, which plays the primary role in working with what are expected to be large buying centers to develop custom system solutions in order to win the sale. In an integrated fashion, the communication program should introduce the concept of documents on demand, establish Xerox's Docutech as the technological breakthrough in reliability and efficiency, and position Docutech as a key component in the next generation of the quality revolution for serving inside and outside "customers."

From experience and a bevy of media kits, the following options were under consideration for the communication program.

DBMS

A monthly magazine aimed at IS managers and others who design and build large-scale database applications. The magazine provides comprehensive current reviews of database tools and strategies, including relational and object-based systems, data warehousing, electronic commerce, and deploying corporate applications within the firm and beyond.

Circulation: 82,198 incl. 10,792 paid.

Reader mix (selected segments)

Manufacturer (all)	6,626
Computer-related manufacturer	4,746
Applications software development	9,751
VAR, VAD. system integration	4,579
Systems software development	3,382
Communications services	1,929
Healthcare, medical, legal	3,390

Ad rates:

1 pg. B&W	$10,400
1 pg. color	11,700

INFORMATIONWEEK

A weekly magazine giving news and commentary on products, technology, and suppliers. Emphasis is on the bottom-line business benefits of technology.

Circulation: 350,000 (all nonpaid)

Reader mix:

	Total	Corp. mgt.	Info Sys.
Manufacturing (all)	91,929	8,521	38,696
Manufacturing (computers, software, perif.)	33,151	4,503	10,893
Medical, dental, pharmaceutical	21,142	1,662	10,656
Computer/network consultant, VAR/VAD systems	42,756	12,818	10,822

Ad rates:

1 pg. B&W	$30,095
1 pg. color	35,375

INSIDE TECHNOLOGY TRAINING

Published 10 times a year. Examines computers and IT as the subjects of training and means of delivering training. Provides resources for trainers, new product information, enterprise computing, and more.

Circulation: 40,000 (nonpaid)

Ad rates:

1 pg. B&W	$4,450
1 pg. color	5,120

INTEGRATED DESIGN & MANUFACTURING

Published nine times per year. Covers advanced information technologies that link product design and production activities at large manufacturing firms. Features examine networking technologies, product data and document management, rapid prototyping, new technology updates, industry news.

Circulation: 85,000 (nonpaid)

Ad rates:

1 pg. B&W	$5,600
1 pg. color	7,150

STORAGE MANAGEMENT SOLUTIONS (SMS)

Published bimonthly. *SMS* examines storage technology information needs of end users, MIS and DP managers, network managers, and corporate information officers in large firms. Features on disaster recovery, network storage architecture, data accessibility and protection, and new products are common.

Circulation: 40,000 (nonpaid)

Ad rates:

1 pg B&W	$9,750
1 pg. color	12,500

DATA STORAGE

Published nine times per year. Covers technology and manufacture of data storage devices and systems. Product reviews; integration, design and assembly issues; technical information on media and software.

Circulation: 15,120 (nonpaid)

Ad rates:

1 pg. B&W	$3,265
1 pg. color	4,295

IN-PLANT GRAPHICS

Published monthly for managers and supervisors of in-house printing and reproduction operations in business, education, and government organizations. Addresses graphic communications, typesetting, electronic publishing, prepress, offset and specialty printing, bindery, and mailroom operations.

Circulation: 34,641 (nonpaid)

Subscriber mix:

	Total	Dept. mgt.	Corp. Admin or Purchasing
Internal printing dept.	32,851	14,590	17,226
Mfg. (excludes quick printers and comm. publishers)	15,058	4,158	10,700
Educational institutions	3,154	2,510	462
Professional service (legal, medical, arch.)	2,176	1,265	848
Government including military	1,885	1,387	351

Ad rates:

1 pg. B&W	$5,970
1 pg. color	7,850

IN-PLANT PRINTER

Published bimonthly for managers, supervisors and operators of reproduction and printing departments at business, education, government, and nonprofit organizations. Articles focus on increasing productivity, quality, justifying equipment, training, and job cost controls.

Circulation: 33,859 (nonpaid)

Subscriber mix:

	Total	Dept. Mgt. and Purs.	Corp. Admin
Internal printing dept.	30,819	20,428	7,627
Mfg. (excludes quick printers and comm. publishers)	5,303	3,239	1,525
Schools and universities	5,158	4,291	475
Construction, engineering, and arch. services	491	307	151
Government	2,538	1,926	374

Telemarketing

Three telemarketing firms have offered bids for prospecting calls. One, TeleConquest, claims up to 100 contacts per day at a cost of $6 per call if Xerox provides the list or $8 per call if Teleconquest provides the list. Contacts are defined as telephone calls where the caller reaches either the person on the list or the person who would make the decision (if the person on the list does not). This is a flat fee for any sales call intended to last less than five minutes. Jerri recognized the TeleConquest name, thinking she had heard good things about it, but had never used it herself. If Xerox provides the list and owns it (i.e., did not rent it from another source), TeleConquest will update it as it goes.

A second firm, TMT, charges based on the number of dials made. It estimates, in its proposal, that it would take 10 dials to make a contact with a person who would be involved in the decision. TMT charges $.40 per dial and $4 per contact, but does not offer a list. It will, however, update the list if Xerox owns it. When the firm was used for the DocuTech launch, a two-step process was employed of first asking for permission to send a brochure, with a follow-up telephone call setting up an appointment for the salesperson. While almost 8,000 brochures were sent, only 94 appointments were set at a cost of $60,000. But there were no figures available on how many of those appointments ultimately ended up as purchases.

The third firm is a division of a large database company, Data Source. Its costs are the highest per contact—$13—but it also expects a much higher contact rate and believes it offers a higher-quality list. Its costs include the list charge. Data Source uses a manufacturing database (which Jerri must utilize if she uses Data Source) that it has developed and already telequalified; it provides a report to the salesperson on each person contacted, what was discussed, and other information compiled through its existing data. This data bank already includes information concerning the contact's current equipment, whereas other lists are just name and a title, company name, phone number, and address. Data Source claims that its requests for literature range from 70 to 90 percent of calls completed and that it is able to close for appointments 25 percent of the time on the first call. It also provides free assistance in writing the telemarketing script.

All three companies offer fulfillment services at roughly the same price. A fulfillment service involves sending any brochure provided by Xerox and a personalized letter on Xerox letterhead. Costs vary depending on the volume, but are about $.50 a piece including postage. They can also offer an in-bound telemarketing service at a cost of $3 per call for Tele-Conquest, $2.50 per call for TMT, and $2.75 for Data Source.

Trade Shows

Corporate marketing exhibits in a number of trade shows per year, and provides exhibit support services to various divisions and product or market managers. Corporate will take care of any shows aimed at corporate financial officers, controllers, and other financial influencers; these shows will not affect the

Exhibit 1

Business Lists
(Telephone-
Verified Contacts)

Industrial and commercial machinery mfrs.	88,300
Machine tools–metal cutting	3,464
Electronic computer mfrs.	1,846
Office machines mfrs.	2,229
Electronic and industrial equip. mfrs.	24,585
Motors and generator mfrs.	1,485
Semiconductors and related devices	1,554
Measuring and analyzing instruments mfrs.	13,205
Search-and-detection sys. mfrs.	1,011
Industrial measuring/control mfrs.	1,273
Measuring-and-controlling devices	2,239

List prices (M=1,000)
$75/M on labels (one-time use) . . . add
$5/M for executive name and title
$35/M for diskette
$70/M for unlimited use for one year
$10/M for selections by firm size (e.g., within categories by number of employees; categories vary from list to list)

budget. Otherwise, Jerri will have to plan for any exposure in North American trade shows. On average, Jerri figures that a 40-foot–by–40-foot booth can be "rented" from corporate, shipped, and installed and dismantled for about $10,000 per show. Graphics would cost another $2,000. Staffing would be done out of another budget because mostly salespeople would staff the booth, so Jerri doesn't have to worry about that. The 40×40 booth is the minimum needed to display both the DocuTech and DocuColor machines; half is needed if DocuTech alone is shown.

The annual Graphics of Americas show is billed as an international trade show with the flavor of DRUPA. The show has about 15,000 attendees and 700 exhibitors, and runs for a week in early June. About 15 percent of attendees are from manufacturing. Show rental is $25 per foot and the show management company will make available the list of preregistrants, broken down by title, industry, or both.

Another show is the In-Plant Printing Management Association's annual meeting. This very small show, with about 600 attendees and only 50 exhibitors, is usually held in a hotel. Xerox has not shown here in the past, but the attendees are from the manufacturing market segment. This show runs in late July and costs about $2,400 to rent a 10×10 space.

Another show, Print®96, serves 900 exhibitors, covers 1 million square feet, lasts eight days.[1] The show attracts over 100,000 buyers, with 10 percent from outside the United States, and serves the printing industry. About 10 percent of the attendees are in-plant printing managers, and the show management company will sell a list of those in-plant attendees preregistered up until one month before the show. Heidelberg USA has already reserved 90,000 square feet for its booth, and print on demand (like DocuTech) is expected to cover over 230,000 square feet—almost a quarter of the total show floor. Show rental is about $20 per square foot, and the show is in September.

Direct Mail

Direct mail is another option. Data Source, for example, can provide mailing lists and also handle the mailing. Lists and mailing costs can be found in Exhibit 1.

Postal charges vary by weight and format:

Up to 1 oz.:	Regular, nonpresorted	$.32
	Presorted carrier route in flats	$.25
Not over 5 oz.:	Regular, nonpresorted	$1.24
	Presorted carrier route in flats	$1.13

[1]Print is a registered trademark of the Graphic Arts Show Company, Inc.

Printing and stationery are very sensitive to volume and materials. For example, a silk screener quoted the following prices to produce a 3″× 5″ vinyl sticker in three colors:

Quantity	Unit Price	Total
300	$2.13	$639
500	1.29	645
1000	.66	660

Promotional Products

Promotional products are often included with mailers or given away at trade shows. These items are some form of useful gift that includes the company's name and address, as well as advertising messages. Many items can be purchased, such as coffee cups, for less than a dollar. Several suppliers have home pages where current information is available, including **www.nelsonmarketing.com, www.promo-mart.com/exec,** and **www.imageworksmfg.com.**

Marketing Communication Plan

As the vertical market manager for the manufacturing market, Jerri must develop a communications plan. Realizing that she may not have all of the information she needs, Jerri thought the Internet might provide some additional solutions. However, she had to create a plan and develop a budget for up to $300,000 and then present it to the marketing team for approval. That meant justifying her choices.

As she thumbed through *Sales and Marketing Strategies & News* for some ideas, she thought about the work that lay ahead.

Sources of information used to prepare this case included Joe McGrath of Xerox Corporation, the Xerox home page, Business Publication Advertising Source, Standard Rate and Data Service, various trade publications, Graphics Art Show Company, Inc., the International Publishing Management Association, and the Electronic Documents Association.

Glossary

accessibility   means that members of a market can be reached or impacted by some directed marketing activity, a criterion of a good market segmentation approach

accessory equipment   hand tools, such as sanders, routers, portable saws, and other light tools, that are used in the manufacture of products

accommodation   a negotiation strategy of sacrifice to build or sustain a relationship

account retention   the percentage of accounts that continue doing business with the seller each year

account salesperson   a salesperson who has responsibility for specified accounts

action   the final stage of the hierarchy of effects model; the desired behavior that we want the audience of our marketing communications to do

action goals   goals that are intended to cause or bring about a desired response on the part of the receiver

activity quota   a type of quota that specifies the number and type of tasks or activities that salespeople should do; for example, a new business call quota would specify the number of noncustomers representing potential new business that should be visited in a period of time

adaptive learning   learning that occurs within a set of constraints or learning boundaries

administered channels   a form of channel relationship in which members recognize their participation in a larger system, but they interact without a formal chain of command or a set of rules. Coordination results from ad hoc division of labor and informal leadership

administered prices   prices established by a seller as impersonal, take-it-or-leave-it offers to prospective buyers

advantages   reasons for having features of a product or service

adversarial purchasing philosophy   to have several vendors for each product

aggression   a response to conflict that includes open or covert actions intended to injure the conflict party

always-a-share   a purchasing situation that allows the buyer to taper or augment purchases in increments, while multiple suppliers can have a share of a customer's business in either the current period or future periods

analyzer   an organization classified as a combination prospector–defender; less aggressive with innovation and change than a prospector, but not so attached to stability and efficiency as a defender; very selective in developing products and pursuing opportunities; seldom a first mover, but often a strong second or third, offering high quality and service

attraction   the degree to which the interaction between buyer and seller yields them net payoffs in excess of some minimum level. The payoffs are tangible and intangible rewards from the association, less economic and social costs

attraction efficiency a measure of trade show marketing efficiency, it compares the number of leads gathered at the booth with the number of prospects in the total show audience

augmented product that part of the offering that is somewhat customized for each particular customer

autonomous when a person makes a purchase decision alone for an organization

avoidance a common negotiation strategy when one party doesn't really need the deal or the partner

awareness a stage of the hierarchy of effects model, created when potential buyers become acquainted with the product or brand

awareness stage (of a developing relationship) buyer and seller independently consider the other as an exchange partner

barriers to entry obstacles a potential entrant must overcome in order to compete in a market

behavior choice theory states that buyers go through a choice process to arrive at decisions of *how* they will buy, as opposed to the choice process of *what* will be bought modeled as part of the buy-grid

benchmark the performance level of the best organization for a particular task

benefit how a product or service satisfies a need

beta testing (also called **field testing**) testing the product by letting customers use it in real-world conditions

bonus a lump sum payment for meeting a minimum standard of performance within a given period of time

breakdown budgeting methods of budgeting that begin with the manager setting a total budget, then allocating (breaking down) the budget to the various areas or functions, such as various forms of communication

break-even price the average revenue needed to cover costs, given a specific sales level

break-even quantity a sales level—at a specified price—at which total revenue equals total cost

brokers businesses that do not hold title, but bring buyers and sellers together, typically in environments where buyers and sellers lack the information needed to connect with one another

budget buildup (also called **objective and task**) a method of creating budgets that requires the decision maker to set the budget after determining the strategy and tasks; often used in creating communication budgets

buildup approach (to market size estimation) estimates come from calculating the value of various materials or parts units needed (building up) in a specific application or from specific accounts. Also called **factoring**

business marketing marketing products or services to other companies, government bodies, institutions (such as hospitals), and other organizations

business strength the strength of a company's offering relative to other companies' products

buy-class a type of buying decision, based on the experience of the buyer with a purchase of a particular product or service

buy-grid model describes how purchasing practices vary along a continuum representing the buyer's experience in buying that particular product or service

buy-phase model suggests that people go through a series of steps (or phases) when making a decision, beginning with problem recognition

buying center or **decision making unit (DMU)** when more than one person is involved, the group of participants in the company

cap a limit to how much a salesperson can make, no matter the amount of sales, even under a straight commission plan

capital equipment (also called **installations**) large equipment used in the production process that requires significant financial investment

cash-and-carry distributors channel intermediaries that hold title but provide no buyer financing or delivery

cash cows products that have high market share and strength in a steady market (no growth or shrinkage) and are those products that should contribute the most to the company's profit

catalog wholesaler a channel intermediary that holds title and relies exclusively on mail, phone, and fax orders from its catalog and does not have a field sales force

champions or **advocates** of a vendor; that is, someone who influences the decision in favor of a particular vendor

channel intermediaries organizations that facilitate the transfer of title between the producer and user of a product

circulation audit a study of the readers who get a particular magazine; used by marketers to determine if their ads are reaching the right buyers

closed bidding the solicitation of proposals from an exclusive set of potential suppliers

coercive power the ability of one channel member to mediate punishments to get another to do what it otherwise would not do

cognitive mapping a learning tool that is used to explore mental structures of beliefs and assumptions

collaboration a negotiation strategy characterized by joint problem solving, searching for creative win–win solutions

combination plan a sales force compensation plan that pays some combination of commission and/or bonus and a salary

commission base the item from which the commission is determined—usually unit sales, dollar sales, or gross margin

commission rate the amount paid per base item sold—usually a percentage

commitment stage (of a buyer–seller relationship) a lasting desire to maintain or preserve a valuable relationship. Thus, this commitment phase is

characterized by the parties exchanging significant resources. When the parties share a common belief in the effectiveness of future exchange, they dedicate resources to maintaining the relationship

company orientation the degree to which the individual works to achieve benefit for the company

competency trap any skill or technology that a company sticks with due to comfort with the familiar, in spite of evidence that better alternatives may exist

competitive advantage something that provides incremental value when compared to other offerings

competitive negotiation a negotiation strategy that has a winner and a loser; it is the right course when it is critical to win *this* deal but shows little regard to the prospects for subsequent exchange with the party

compiled lists database of names, addresses, and classification information assembled by companies that comb directories and public records and even make physical observations

compliance programs programs where purchasers must be in compliance with federal guidelines in order to be eligible to supply the government

component parts or **OEM parts** parts assembled into the final product without further transformation

compromise a hybrid of competition and accommodation strategies of negotiation; often an easy solution that brings an end to negotiations before creative solutions delivering win–win outcomes can be explored

conceptual map a picture of abstract ideas, options, persons, or companies based on two or three key variables

concurrent manufacturing a system in which suppliers schedule their own manufacturing based on the shipment needs of their customers

conflict felt or enacted tension between parties—in this situation, channel members

consultative selling a form of selling where the seller brings specialized expertise into a complex problem in order to create a somewhat customized solution

contract a promise to perform some act in exchange for a payment or some other consideration

contract manufacturers companies that make assemblies or components for OEMs

contractual channels channel relationship form in which members are tightly coordinated by formal procedures and pledges of ongoing exchange. Nonrefundable fees and 5- to 10-year agreements are common devices to ensure longevity

controlled circulation distribution of a magazine to only qualified readers; qualifications are usually based on the readers' influence over certain classes of purchases

controller person who controls or sets the budget for the purchase

conversion ratio a productivity index calculated by dividing outputs by specific antecedent efforts; for example, appointments booked/prospects contacted or sales made/appointments kept

core competencies what a company does best that gives it competitive advantage and provides the greatest value to the customer

core product the tangible item and/or the customary services offered

corporate channels a relationship structure in which we see the integration of most channel functions (delivery, selling, promoting, customer feedback, inventory, ordering, service, etc). What we tend to see are degrees of vertical integration in marketing channels. A firm that uses its own sales force and its own fleet of trucks from its own distribution centers is highly integrated

corporate relationship exchange safeguarded by ownership or vertical integration; represents the extreme of the contractual dimension

cost per thousand (CPM) a critical variable in selecting trade publications; can be calculated by dividing the cost of an ad's space by the number of readers (in thousands)

cost-plus contract the purchaser will reimburse the supplier for all of its costs, plus a certain percentage of those costs for profit

coverage ratio reports the percentage of product shipments accounted for by firms actually assigned the NAICS or SIC classification of the product. Thus, a high coverage ratio means that firms producing the bulk of this product or service actually are accounted for in the category

cross-functional sourcing teams purchasing teams that include members of various functional areas within the firm, and sometimes include personnel from suppliers and customers

cross-selling selling additional products after the first sale, but these products may not be related to the original sale

customer lifetime value (LTV) an estimate of the net present value of the stream of benefits from a customer, less the burdens of servicing the account or managing the relationship

customer restrictions contractual agreements in distribution that specify the type of business the reseller may or may not serve

cycle time the time it takes to complete an action such as developing a product

decile report a method of customer analysis that orders the firm's customers from best to smallest, on the basis of purchase volume for the period, summarized by *tenths*

decision maker the person who makes the final decision

decline stage that stage of the product life cycle when sales decline and products are removed from the market

defender an organization classified as one that aims to find and secure stable product market positions, offers a limited range of products, avoids the forefront of technology, ignores dynamic events on the outside of its core area of operation, and defends market position with low price, quality, and service

defensive strategies strategies designed to minimize loss

demand elasticity the percentage change in sales relative to the percentage change in price

dependence balancing a means of safeguarding a relationship by which one party reduces its dependence on the exchange partner by cultivating relationships with other exchange partners, perhaps making itself less replaceable in the exchange or giving itself new options to the current exchange relationship

dependent variables   the effects or outcomes of an experiment or statistical model

derived demand   situation in which demand for a firm's products and services is derived from the demand for its customers' products and services (whose demand may also be derived)

desire   the third stage of the hierarchy of effects model; the recognition by the buyer that when the needs occur, the advertised brand is the brand or product to buy (or the company to visit at the trade show, or the home page to visit, etc.)

desk jobber   a channel intermediary that takes title, buying products from a supplier, but never taking physical possession; instead products are delivered directly to the user. Also called a **drop shipper**

development stage   that stage in the product's life when it is being designed and readied for market

dimensional   the term mailers use for an enclosure that is something other than flat pieces of paper

direct marketing   an interactive form of marketing using one or more advertising media to effect a measurable response and/or transaction at any location, with this activity stored on database

direct response (communication)   communication delivered directly to the prospect to obtain an action outcome

dissolution   termination of an advanced relationship

diversification   a growth strategy by which a firm aims to serve new markets with new products

dogs   products with low share in a poor market

dormant accounts   accounts that have stopped buying

downsize   to lower the number of employees through early retirement and layoffs

draw   a loan paid to the salesperson to provide him with stable cash flow; it is repaid from the salesperson's commission

drop shipper   a channel intermediary that takes title, buying products from a supplier, but never taking physical possession; instead products are delivered directly to the user. Also called a **desk jobber.**

dyadic relationships   a concept of business relationships in which there are only two parties: one buyer and one seller

economic order quantity (EOQ)   the quantity that minimizes both ordering and storing costs

elastic demand   situation in which the quantity demanded of a product is highly sensitive to changes in its price

electronic data interchange (EDI)   the use of electronic transmission of data between buyer and seller to order and maintain product inventory

empathic dialogue   active listening and identification with customer concerns, resulting in customer-centered communication and problem solving

engineer to order   complete customization, with the product designed from scratch to meet the customer's needs

environmental factors   those characteristics of the world beyond the market level; includes the economy, technology, political factors, and social factors

ethics   moral codes of conduct; rules for how someone should operate that can be utilized as situations demand

evoked set   the products of which the buyer is aware

exclusivity   (e.g., distribution or territory exclusivity) a pledge to supply no other resellers in the trade area

exit   a means of managing conflict by leaving a relationship

expansion stage   (of a developing relationship) stage characterized by the association progressing from one of testing and probing to one of enlarging rewards and the scope of exchange

experiments   the systematic manipulation of variables to allow the detection of cause-and-effect relationships

expert power   the ability to gain a target firm's compliance based on that target's belief that the source is knowledgeable

exploration stage (of a developing relationship) we find the parties probing and testing each other. Initial purchases can take place in this stage, but they are part of a trial process. The relationship is very fragile. The parties have not significantly invested in the exchange. Neither party depends highly on the other. The association is easily terminated.

extrinsic rewards rewards given by the organization

f

facilitating supplies or **facilitating services** support company efforts but are not part of the final product

factoring approach to market size estimation in which estimates come from calculating the value of various materials or parts units needed (factors) in a specific application or from specific accounts. Also called **buildup approach**

faxback a way for readers to respond to trade publication advertising that is similar to bingo cards

features physical characteristics of the tangible item or service

field salespeople (also called **outside salespeople**) salespeople who visit accounts at the accounts' locations

field testing see **beta testing**

financial lease (also called a **full-payout lease**) a contract that cannot be canceled and is fully amortized over the term of the lease

financial risk (also called **economic risk**) risk associated with the cost of the new product and with the potential for lost revenue if the product breaks down or doesn't perform as advertised

first-mover advantage a significant competitive advantage gained by being the first in the market

five forces of competition industry rivals, powerful suppliers, powerful customers, threat of potential entrants, and substitutes

fixed-price agreement that means that if it costs more to build an item than thought, the supplier has to cover the higher costs

focus groups a method of qualitative marketing research that brings a small group of customers together to discuss a specific topic or issue, under the direction of a professional moderator

forward buying buying in larger quantities than are currently needed because the discount is greater than the carrying costs

frequency the number of times a potential buyer is exposed to an ad

full-function wholesalers intermediaries that hold title and provide a broad array of services for their suppliers and customers

full-line selling selling the entire line of associated products

full payout (**lease**) a contract that cannot be canceled and is fully amortized over the term of the lease. Also called a **financial lease**

functional discount a discount given to a purchaser based on the purchaser's role in the supplier's distributive system, reflecting, at least in a generalized sense, the services performed by the purchaser for the supplier

functional structure organization by marketing function

gap analysis a set of tools for comparing performance outcomes or expectations on specific criteria

gatekeepers control information into and out of the buying group, or between members of the group

generative, or double loop, learning the creation of knowledge that occurs when changing assumptions and beliefs

geographic salesperson the most basic sales force structure, giving each salesperson all accounts within a specified geographic area

global account manager (GAM)   a salesperson who calls on the headquarters of an account that buys centrally for implementation or delivery globally; the salesperson is responsible for developing account strategy for the entire account although local salespeople may call on offices around the world. See also **national account manager**

growth stage   that part of the product life cycle when sales and profits grow at a fast rate, following the introduction stage

hierarchy of effects   a model used by many companies when planning communication campaigns because it describes the successive stages through which the audience progresses when interacting with marketing communications

horizontal dimension   a dimension of the buying center or how many departments are involved

horizontal shows   trade shows that include many industries and professions

house account   an account handled by a sales executive in which the company does not pay anyone commission on sales from the account

identifiable   a criterion for a good segmentation approach; it means that members of market segments can be enumerated and evaluated

import quotas   limits on the amount of a product that may be imported

inbound telemarketing   calls initiated by the customer or potential customer

independent variables   the factors we manipulate in an experiment (price, headlines, telephone script, copy strategy, etc.) or control by selection in our marketing program (size of firms targeted, list source, time since last purchase, etc.)

individual factors   demographic and psychographic factors, or psychological factors that influence an individual's buying behavior

industrial distributors   merchant wholesalers, including a number of subtypes that differ in the functions they perform

inelastic demand   situation in which the quantity demanded is not very price sensitive

influencers   individuals who seek to affect the decision maker's final decision through recommendations of which vendors to include or which products are best suited to solve the organization's needs

information power   a source of potential influence residing in a channel member's reliance on facts and figures, models, and insights from its partner

information system   the mechanism for storing information, providing access to the information, and manipulating that information

infrastructure   transportation, communication, and other utilities

initiator   starts the purchase process by recognizing the need

inside salespeople   salespeople who sell at their company's location

in-suppliers   suppliers whose products are ordered automatically in a straight rebuy

integrated marketing communications (IMC)   strategic, two-way communication targeted to specific customers and their needs coordinated through a variety of media

interest   the second step of the hierarchy of effects model; reflects the buyer's desire to learn more about what (e.g. product, brand, company) is being discussed in the marketing communication

internal partnering   creating partnering relationships with other functional areas (customers and suppliers within the firm)

intrabrand competition   price pressure from sellers of the same brand

intrinsic rewards rewards people give themselves (feelings of satisfaction, for example)

introduction stage the second stage of the product life cycle; here the product is first introduced to the market and potential customers are learning what the product is and does

investment risk the risk that is present when a company decides to go ahead with the product and, should it fail, the company would lose some or all of the investment

JIT relationship a form of buyer–seller partnership that requires the supplier to produce and deliver to the OEM precisely the necessary quantities at the necessary time, with the objective that products produced by the supplier conform to performance specification every time

joint demand situations where two products are used together and are demanded together

just-in-time (JIT) the concept of shipping products such that they arrive at the customer's location exactly when needed

justice the rendering of what is merited or due

keiretsu in Japan, a family of companies (literally) in which members of companies sit on the boards of directors of their customers or suppliers

key account a large or high-volume customer, often assigned a specific sales representative

known requisites requirements for success that have been identified by the firm

lagniappe anything given beyond strict obligation; a surprise or surplus benefit from an exchange

lead users buyers or users who face needs that will be general in the marketplace, but they recognize these needs months or years before the market is aware, and/or they are able to generate solutions to needs independently of manufacturers or suppliers

leapfrog to introduce a product that is at least one step better technologically than other products already available

learning the connection of new information to what we already know

learning boundaries an organization's assumptions and beliefs that limit learning

learning curve the tendency of costs to decline with repetition or cumulative experience

learning laboratories environments set aside for learning

learning organization one that consistently creates and refines its capabilities by connecting new information and skills to known and remembered requisites for future success

leasing the use of a contract for the temporary use of a product or premises in exchange for payment or rent

legal legitimate power explicit authority over certain behaviors granted to the source in a sales agreement or contract

lifetime value (LTV) an estimate of the net present value of the stream of benefits from a customer, less the burdens of servicing the account or managing the relationship

limited function wholesalers channel intermediaries that take title but don't provide the full spectrum of services, perhaps stocking just a single line of products or extending no credit or no delivery

line and staff organization an organizational structure where those who conduct the primary tasks of the department are part of the line—their managers are called line managers—and all support personnel are staff

lobbying any attempt to persuade a government official or governing body to adopt policies, procedures, or legislation in favor of the lobbying group or organization

location restrictions contractual agreements in distribution channels specifying the site or sites from which the product may be sold by intermediaries

loose lead strategies attempt to generate as many leads as possible, relying on a qualifying process to sort out good leads from bad

lost-for-good a classification of customer relationships characterized by the prospects of a customer making a costly switch to a competitor followed by a costly return to the incumbent being remote—probably weaker prospects than a cold call prospect

loyalty steadfast perseverance in the face of conflict's felt tension or abuse

make to order manufacturing or production begins making the product after receiving an order

make to stock marketing supplies forecasts of demand, and manufacturing makes enough to handle that demand

manufactured material material that has been transformed from raw material and requires further processing before the user can use it

manufacturers' agents agents who do not take title but sell the lines of noncompeting principals for a commission

manufacturers' sales branches and offices wholesaling operations that a manufacturer owns and operates

market attractiveness a composite measure of the potential for sales and profits in a particular market segment for a particular company's portfolio of products

market development a growth strategy in which a firm markets its current products to new markets

market factors characteristics of the market that influence buyer behavior

market orientation superior skills of understanding and satisfying customers via (1) the systematic gathering of information on customers and competitors, both present and potential, (2) the systematic analysis of the information for the purpose of developing market knowledge, and (3) the systematic use of such knowledge to guide strategy recognition, understanding, creation, selection, implementation, and modification

market penetration an endeavor to gain a larger share of the market in which a firm currently competes using its existing products

market position the strength of the company relative to competitors; can be measured by market share, but should also reflect forecasts of future share; used in the sales resource allocation grid to determine sales force allocation

market sensing anticipating market requirements ahead of competition

marketing audit a comprehensive and systematic evaluation of the firm's marketing operation and the environment in which it operates

marketing channels systems organized to deliver products and related services

marketing control system the system that measures actual performance against planned performance, measures productivity and profit by types of products, customers, or territories, and measures other key marketing variables such as customer satisfaction

matrix sales team a form of team selling in which several product specialists work with several account managers

maturity stage the third stage of the product life cycle, when sales level off

media kit material to support staged events; contains information about the event and key information for publication in news stories; usually given to members of the press

merchant wholesalers channel intermediaries that take title to the merchandise

minority subcontracting programs that require general contractors and other major suppliers to allocate a certain percentage of the total contract to minority-owned subcontractors

mission statement a formal expression of why the organization exists

modified rebuys the process would include most or perhaps all of the steps in a new buy

modularity a system comprised of distinct subsystems or components

monochronic time a linear perspective of time that is part of the culture of Americans (and Swiss, Germans, and Scandinavians) in which they divide time into small units, with only one activity per unit, and are obsessed with promptness

monopolistic competition a market in which there are a large number of differentiated sellers, such as corporate training companies, custom marketing research firms, and industrial distributors. The actions of one firm have effects on others, but each seller brings some unique competency to the market and offers distinctively valued services and products. Each firm faces a downward-sloping demand curve

motivation the amount of effort that the buyer is willing to expend to engage in that set of tasks

MRO or **maintenance, repair, and operations products** products sold to users for use in the company's operations are often labeled MRO items

multi-attribute model model based on the idea that people view products as a collection of attributes or "bundle of benefits"; provides a picture of how alternatives are evaluated

multilevel selling where members of a selling organization at various levels call on their counterparts in the buying organization; a form of team selling

NAICS (pronounced "knacks") North American Industrial Classification System establishes a common code between the United States, Canada, and Mexico that is compatible with the United Nations' two-digit system of industry classification, ISIC

national account manager (NAM) a salesperson who calls on the headquarters of an account who buys centrally for implementation or delivery

nationwide; the salesperson is responsible for developing account strategy for the entire nation. See also **global account manager**

needs satisfaction selling a process of selling that involves identifying the buyer's needs and tailoring the sales pitch to fit those needs

neglect to leave the conflict untreated, perhaps allowing the relationship to atrophy or fade in significance

negotiation method of decision making by give-and-take bargaining that is used to resolve conflicts

net buying influences the percentage of a trade show audience that has influence in the buying process for the specific product exhibited

network a web of companies sharing relationships with many other companies; these relationships are governed by reciprocity of ties, dependencies, and shared values

new buys products or services never purchased before

news release (or **press release**) a brief memo or report containing news information, such as the announcement of a new product, an award, or changes in management

nondisclosure agreement an agreement that the parties involved will not share any information about the new products with anyone who has not also signed that agreement

norms standards of behavior for the parties in a relationship; the guidelines by which the parties interact

North American Industrial Classification System see **NAICS**

objective and task see **budget buildup**

offensive strategies strategies designed to maximize gain

oligopolies markets characterized by just a few sellers, each offering a product that is quite similar to the others. Entry barriers tend to be high and pricing latitude very limited.

open bidding any organization can submit a bid to vie for the business a buyer promises

operating lease a short-term contract that can be canceled

operational measures measures of productivity, process (or operations) effectiveness, and other elements that impact customer satisfaction

opportunity risk the risk that occurs when a company decides to kill a product and thereby lose all of the revenue that could have been gained if it had been a success

organizational culture the collectively held values, ideology, and social processes embedded in a firm

organizational factors characteristics of the organization that influence buying behavior; includes the size of the company, profitability, corporate culture, distribution of power, organizational policy, and other factors

original equipment manufacturer (OEM) a company that purchases a product or service to be included in its own final product

outbound telemarketing selling via telephone with the call made by the marketer (compare with **inbound telemarketing**)

outside salespeople see **field salespeople**

outsourcing the process of finding another organization to supply the buying organization with a product or service, usually one that was previously created in-house

out-suppliers suppliers whose products are not considered in a straight rebuy

partnership a relationship characterized by mutual commitment, high trust, and common goals

partnership purchasing or **preferred supplier system** system that seeks to maximize the benefits of collaboration between the buyer and a few suppliers

payback the amount of time needed for savings or revenues to equal costs or investments

perceived probability (usually just called **probability**) the perception that effort on a particular set of tasks will lead to accomplishment of performance outcomes that will, in turn, lead to the desired rewards

performance quota a quota that specifies levels of outcomes, or performance, such as revenue, gross margin, or unit sales in a period of time

performance risk the risk that the product will not perform as intended

personal selling interpersonal communication in which one person attempts to secure a purchase from another person

polychronic time a perspective in non-U.S. and non-European cultures in which time is viewed in terms of the simultaneous occurrence of many things and with more involvement with people

position a product's place in the mind of the buyer

positioning a loosely used term that generally refers to marketing efforts to secure a valued categorization in the mind of a customer

power an ability of one organization, Alpha, to get another organization, Beta, to do what it would not do otherwise; it derives from Beta's dependence on Alpha for valued resources that are not easily obtained elsewhere

preferred supplier a status conferred by a buyer that grants a supplier an assured (usually large) percentage of the buyer's business and first opportunity to earn any new business

press agentry the planning and staging of an event in order to generate publicity

press kit (or **media kit**) material to support staged events; contains information about the event and key information for publication in news stories; given to writers for trade and general business publications

price the amount of money paid by a buyer to a seller for a particular product or service

price discrimination sellers charge different prices on similar products

primary demand buyer demand for a type of product, rather than for a specific company's product

principal the manufacturer or other person or firm who contracts for the services of the agent in its own behalf

product a bundle of benefits; a collection of solutions to needs and wants

product development an effort to serve customers in markets where a firm already has a presence using a new array of products

product life cycle a cycle of stages that a product, technology platform, or product category goes through, from development, introduction, growth, and maturity to decline

product line a group of products that share a technology platform

product portfolio management methods of managing all products simultaneously as you would a financial portfolio, balancing risk and return among all product investments

prospect someone for whom we know needs, budget, and time frame for purchase

prospector an organization classified as likely to be a first mover, detect early signals of opportunity and move on them, compete in new markets or with new marketing methods, and operate in many product markets

prospector (telemarketing position) the telemarketer supports the efforts of one or several field reps in finding and qualifying prospective customers

public affairs the part of PR that deals with community groups; there are two types of public affairs: lobbying and community involvement

public relations the management function that focuses on the relationships and communications with individuals and groups in order to create mutual goodwill

publicity the generation of news about a person, product, or organization; appears in broadcast or electronic media

pull strategy direct communication with end users to differentiate the product through the media

purchasing agent the person who actually makes the purchase

push strategy the general approach of supporting and rewarding reseller activities to differentiate the brand among customers

quality function deployment (QFD) a process of linking customer needs to product attributes during the design process

question marks products in high growth markets that currently have low market share

quota a useful control mechanism for sales force management that represents a quantitative minimum level of acceptable performance for a specific time period

r

random variance that variance caused by uncontrollable and unidentified causes

raw materials materials processed only to the point required for economic handling and distribution

reach the total number of buyers that see an ad

reactor an organization classified as one that lacks a well-defined strategy, has an inconsistent product mix; is not a risk taker, and is not aggressive; generally takes action under environmental pressures

reader service cards cards sent to a magazine's publisher by a reader that indicates the reader's interest in products or companies who advertised in the magazine; the lead (or reader) information is then distributed to the appropriate companies

reciprocation a similar action returned by the other—for example, a seller's price concession in response to purchaser's commitment to an annual level of total purchases

reengineering the process of designing work processes in order to achieve objectives; reengineering reflects the fact that most processes have evolved over time, serving objectives that may no longer be considered relevant

referent power the potential to influence another based on the other's desire to identify with or be like the source firm

relational contracts contracts that don't try to bring every future contingency up for consideration in the present, but establish means of continuous planning, adjusting, and resolving conflicts; relational contracts can specify decision-making authority by issue (material standards, shutdowns, training, and maintenance) and establish procedures or structures for planning to assure ongoing effective exchange

reporting systems formal mechanisms for creating and sharing information, generally involving the flow of information either up or down the organization

response lists the house files (direct order customers and inquirers) of other companies

reverse marketing proactive management of the supply function

reward-measurement theory an expectancy theory of organizational buyer motivation; similar to expectancy theories you may have been introduced to in management class

reward power the ability to provide payoffs to a party for specified behaviors or outcomes

risk usually thought of in terms of the probability of an outcome and the importance or cost associated with the outcome

Robinson–Patman Act (1936) prohibits price discrimination when sellers charge different prices on like products to customers who are in competition and the effect is likely to lessen competition substantially

role theory suggests that people behave within a set of norms or expectations of others due to the role in which they have been placed

rolling launch to launch a new product in certain areas, rolling to (launching in) new areas as support personnel are trained and ready

safeguarded relationships relationships that are protected through contracts

sales potential the total forecasted sales for a product category in a single account or sales territory

sales resource allocation grid a method to determine workload that focuses on sales potential and market position to determine which accounts should be the focus of sales resources

sample survey a questionnaire administered to a representative group of a particular population

scenario a focused description of different futures presented in a coherent manner; a forecasting technique that requires managers to write explicit anticipated futures and articulate the chains of events that would need to occur to make the future happen; a method used for organizational learning

script-based selling using scripts or memorized sales pitches from which the salesperson does not deviate

secondary demand demand for a particular vendor's offering or product

self-efficacy a perception by a person in which she considers her own ability to carry out the tasks

self-orientation the degree to which the individual works to achieve personal benefit

sensor any measuring tool used in observing marketing performance

SIC Standard Industrial Classification codes were developed by the U.S. government to collect and disseminate meaningful information on different sectors of the economy

single-line wholesalers limited-function wholesalers that don't carry a full assortment of items

single sourcing occurs when a company selects one supplier to satisfy all needs in a given area

social relationship a trading association supported principally by social bonds and habit; this organic dimension is the degree to which social bonds are part of the business relationship

social risk (also called **ego risk**) risk that the purchase will not meet the approval of an important reference group

spanning processes processes that link internal processes with the customer

specialization ratio   the percentage of total shipments by firms in a NIACS or SIC classification accounted for by the particular product of that specific code. A tightly focused industry has a high specialization ratio; most of the total business done by firms in this code is in the field coded

specialty advertising   the use of products to advertise another product or company; for example, putting a company's name on pens and pencils, and then giving those away

specialty wholesaler   firm carrying a vary narrow line and supporting that with technical expertise and consultative selling

specific investments   the dedication of assets that have sharply reduced value outside the relationship, including investments in people, locations, procedures, equipment, and more that have real value only within a particular relationship

split premiums   a form of specialty advertising where half of the freebie is mailed to the prospect; the other half is given to the prospect after he listens to a sales pitch at a trade show booth or after a visit by a salesperson

spot exchanges   money traded for easily measured commodities. Communication content is quite narrow between transacting parties and their identity is hardly relevant. Trading terms are simple and clear. Performance is practically immediate

standard   the goal against which marketing performance is compared in a marketing performance evaluation system

Standard Industrial Classification codes   see **SIC**

stars   products whose market growth is high in a market in which the products also have high market share

statistical series   an estimation technique that uses the correlation between demand and some other set of economic activities to yield a forecast

straight commission   a compensation plan that pays a certain amount for each sale, but there is no salary; see **commission base** and **commission rate**

straight rebuy   a purchase made with the vendor of the previous purchase, without any shopping or examining of other vendors

straight salary   a compensation plan in which a salesperson is paid a fixed amount of money for work during a specified time

strategic goals   what a company wants an overall strategy to accomplish

strategic partner selling   a sales strategy in which both parties share expertise and resources to create customized solutions, and there is a commitment to joint planning for mutual benefit

strategic partnership   results when both parties have keen interests in maintaining an ongoing exchange relationship. The strategic essence of the partnership rests on the significance of the resources and long-run consequences of the efforts

strategy   the science and art of conducting a campaign—achieving some end—on a broad scale, involving significant resources and long-run implications

subsidies   payments by a government that lower operating costs in order to make the country's companies more competitive

substantial   a market segment promises sufficient business to justify the efforts to serve it, a criterion of a good segmentation approach

sugging   the unethical practice of using marketing research as a guise for selling

sunk cost   an irretrievable cost or investment

supplier verification   formal efforts to obtain evidence of supplier capabilities and commitment

supragoal   a goal against which other goals are aligned

switching costs   the forgone value of investments, the economic penalties, and the other expenses associated with finding, evaluating, and replacing a current supplier with a new one

SWOT analysis   a self-assessment framework for examining a firm's **S**trengths and **W**eaknesses, and **O**pportunities and **T**hreats

synergy   a situation in which the whole is greater than the sum of its parts

systematic variance   a change in performance outcomes due to changing systems and creating a new tolerance

t

tactic   decisions that have a narrow scope, involve limited resources, and have only short-run consequences, in contrast to **strategy**

tactical goals   desired outcomes for specific actions

tariffs   taxes on imported goods

team selling   the term for when a group of salespeople handle a single account and each salesperson brings a different area of expertise or handles different responsibilities

technology platform   the core technology that is often the basis for a product line or group of products

telemarketing   the systematic and continuous program of personally communicating with (potential) customers via telephone and/or other electronic media

telequalify   the telephonic process by which a list owner or compiler periodically verifies names, titles, addresses, and other data in the list, improving the quality of the list for direct marketers

territorial restriction   a contractual provision between supplier and reseller confining the reseller's activities to a particular geographic zone

tight lead strategies   direct marketing efforts seeking responses (especially inquiries) from individuals who are already highly qualified as potential customers

time fragmentation   one characteristic of buying centers is that members come and go

tinkering   making changes within a process in order to make the process more productive, by either reducing defects or increasing volume

tolerance   a range of acceptable performance, used when applying statistical process control to any work process, including marketing processes

total buying plans   the percentage of the audience planning to buy exhibited products within the next 12 months

total cost of ownership   the total amount expended in order to own a product or use a service

trade publications   magazines written for a specific profession, industry, or trade

trade shows   temporary exhibitions of products and services, somewhat like shopping malls for industrial products

traditional legitimate power   the ability of the source firm to influence the behavior of the target firm because cultural norms support the right of the source

transactional relationships   situations where buyers and sellers interact with only selfish consideration, without thought of the possibility of future interaction

truck jobber   a wholesaler that carries all its inventory on a truck and services customers on a frequent basis or a route

trust   the belief that a party's work or promise is reliable and a party will fulfill his or her obligations in an exchange relationship

u

upgrading   convincing the buyer to use a higher-quality product or newer product

user   the business equivalent of the final consumer

user   part of the buying center that tries to influence the decision; sometimes, other influencers will represent the users' perspective

v

valence   the degree of importance or value attached to a reward

value analysis   a thorough review of the costs and value associated with a component part

value chain system of value creation (each organization adds its value to whatever it is that the system is creating)

vertical dimension a dimension of the buying center or how many layers of management are involved

vertical integration bringing a function or technology within the boundary of the firm; assures continuity in the relationship because suppliers are now hierarchically connected employees. That is, employees work in an environment of formal rules, authority, reporting structures, and special responsibilities. Goals tend to be shared and, overall, control of activities is enhanced

vertical show a trade show that focuses on one industry or profession

volatility wide swings in demand that are caused by derived demand

work load all of the activities that a salesperson must do to cover a territory

Endnotes

Chapter 1

1. Salt Institute, 1995 statistics provided by McLean, VA

Chapter 2

1. Thornton, Emily, "McManaging Supplies," *Far Eastern Economic Review* 158 (November 23, 1995), p. 76.

2. *On Liberty* People's ed. (London: Longmans, Green & Co., 1865), summarized in Milton Friedman and Rose Friedman *Free to Choose* (New York: Harcourt, Brace, Jovanovich, 1980).

3. Murphy, Elana Epatko, and Clarissa Cruz, "Real Payoffs Result when Suppliers Join in VA Effort," *Purchasing* (November 23, 1995), pp. 22–23.

4. Dwyer, F. Robert, Paul H. Schurr, and Sejo Oh, "Developing Buyer-Seller Relationships," *Journal of Marketing* 52 (April 1987), pp. 11–27.

5. Baldrige Office, ADAC Laboratories. *1996 Award Winner, Malcolm Baldrige National Quality Award* (Milpitas, CA 95035, 1997).

6. Frazier, Gary, Robert Spekman, and Charles R. O'Neal, "Just-in-Time Exchange Relationships in Industrial Markets," *Journal of Marketing* 52 (October 1983), pp.52–67.

7. Helper, Susan, "How Much Has Really Changed between U.S. Automakers and Their Suppliers?" *Sloan Management Review* 32 (Summer 1991), pp. 15–28; Anil Kumar and Graham Sharman, "We Love Your Product, but Where Is It?" *Sloan Management Review* 33 (Winter 1992), pp. 93–99.

8. Wilson, Elizabeth J., and Richard P. Vlosky, "Partnering Relationship Activities: Building Theory from Case Study Research," *Journal of Business Research* 31 (May 1997), pp. 59–64.

9. Levitt, Theodore, "After the Sale Is Over . . . ," *Harvard Business Review* 61 (September-October 1983), pp. 87–93.

10. Comer, James, and B. J. Zirger, "Building a Supplier–Customer Relationship Using Joint New Product Development." Paper presented at the World Marketing Conference, Sydney Australia, 1995.

11. Scanzoni, J. "Social Exchange and Behavioral Interdependence," in *Social Exchange in Developing Relationships,* R. L. Burgess and T. L. Huston, eds. (New York: Academic Press, 1979), p. 72.

12. Leigh, Thomas and Arno Rethans, "A Script-Theoretic Analysis of Industrial Purchasing Behavior," *Journal of Marketing* 48 (Fall 1984), pp. 22–32.

13. Schurr, Paul and Julie Ozanne, "Influences on Exchange Processes: Buyers' Preconceptions of a Seller's Trustworthiness and Bargaining Toughness," *Journal of Consumer Research* 11 (March 1985), pp. 939–53.

14. See "Bose Corporation, JIT II Program," Case N9-694-001, Harvard Business School, 1994; Lance Dixon, "JIT II at Honeywell," *Purchasing* (February 17, 1994), p. 22; Minahan, Tim "JIT: How Buyers Changed It!" *Purchasing* (September 5, 1996), pp. 36–38.

15. Ping, Robert, and F. Robert Dwyer, "A Preliminary Model of Relationship Termination in Marketing Channels," in Gary Frazier, ed., *Advances in Distribution Channels Research* (Greenwich, CT: JAI Press, Inc., 1992), pp. 215–34.

16. For a good overview, see Robert M. March, "Managing Business Relationships with East Asia: Building and Pilot Testing a Model of Long-Term Asian/Western Business Relationships," Working paper 3/1997, University of Western Sidney, Nepean, 1997.

17. Dixon, Lance, "JIT II at Intel," *Purchasing* (May 19, 1994), p. 19.

18. Heide, Jan B., and George John, "The Role of Dependence Balancing in Safeguarding Transaction-Specific Assets in Conventional Channels," *Journal of Marketing* 52 (January 1988), pp. 20–37.

19. Anderson, Erin, and Barton Weitz, "The Use of Pledges to Build and Sustain Commitment in Distribution Channels," *Journal of Marketing Research* 29 (February 1992), pp. 18–34.

20. Macneil, Ian, "Economic Analysis of Contractual Relations: Its Shortfalls and the Need for a 'Rich Classificatory Apparatus,' *Northwestern University Law Review* 75 (February 1981), pp. 1018–63. Thomas Palay, "Comparative Institutional Economics: The Governance of Rail Freight Contracting," *Journal of Legal Studies* 13 (June 1984), pp. 265–87.

21. Buss, Dale, "Growing More by Doing Less," *Nation's Business* (December 1995), pp. 18–21.

22. Morales, Rebecca, "Product Development and Production Networks: The Case of the Mexican Automotive Industry," *Journal of Industry Studies* 1 (October 1993), pp. 30–42.

23. Moller, Kristian, and David Wilson, eds., *Business Marketing: An Interaction and Network Perspective* (Boston: Kluwer Academic Publishers, 1995), pp. 10–11.

Chapter 3

1. Fox, Harold W., and David R. Rink, "Coordination of Purchasing with Sales Trends," *Journal of Purchasing and Materials Management* (Winter 1977), pp. 10–18; Harold W. Fox, and David R. Rink, "Purchasing's Role across the Product Life Cycle," *Industrial Marketing Management* 7 (1978), pp. 186–92.

2. Hendrick, Thomas E., and William A. Ruch, "Determining Performance Appraisal Criteria for Buyers," *Journal of Purchasing and Materials Management* (Summer 1988), pp. 18–26.

3. Richeson, Leslie, Charles W. Lackey, and John W. Starner Jr., "The Effect of Communication on the Linkage between Manufacturers and Suppliers in a Just-in-Time Environment," *International Journal of Purchasing and Materials Management* (Winter 1995), pp. 21–29.

4. Mullich, Joe, and Mary Welch, "Government's Buying Power Remains Strong," *Business Marketing* (July 1995), pp. 21–22.

5. Sriram, Ven, and Snehamay Banerjee, "Electronic Data Interchange: Does Its Adoption Change Purchasing Policies and Procedures?" *International Journal of Purchasing and Materials Management* 30 (Winter 1994), pp. 31–40.

6. Foster, Thomas A., "It's about Time and Inventory," *Distribution* (July 1994), p. 6.

7. "Adopting Suppliers," *Purchasing Executive Bulletin* (May 25, 1994), pp. 1–3.

8. Ammer, Dean, *Materials Management and Purchasing* (Homewood IL: Richard D. Irwin, 1980).

9. Tanner, John F., Jr., and Earl D. Honeycutt, "Reengineering the Sales Force," *Industrial Marketing Management* (1996), pp. 65–70.

10. Klotz, Dorothy E., and Kalyan Chatterjee, "Dual Sourcing in Repeated Procurement Competitions," *Management Science* 41, no. 8 (August 1995), pp. 1317–27.

11. Gross, Andrew C., Peter M. Banting, Lindsay N. Meredith, and I. David Ford, *Business Marketing* (Boston: Houghton-Mifflin Co., 1993).

12. Akacum, A., and B.G. Dale, "Supplier Partnering: Case Study Experiences," *International Journal of Purchasing and Materials Management* (January 1995), pp. 38–44.

13. Fram, Eugene H., "Purchasing Partnerships: The Buyer's View," *Marketing Management* (Summer 1995), pp. 49–55.

14. Stump, Rodney L., "Antecedents of Purchasing Concentration: A Transaction Cost Explanation," *Journal of Business Research* 34 (1995), pp. 145–57.

15. Klotz and Chatterjee (1995).

16. Bunn, Michele D., "Information Search in Industrial Purchase Decisions," *Journal of Business to Business Marketing* 1, no. 2 (1993), pp. 67–102.

17. Graham, Jean, "A Simple Idea Saves $8 Million a Year," *Purchasing* (May 21, 1992), pp. 47–49; Barton A. Weitz, Stephen B. Castleberry, and John F. Tanner Jr., *Selling: Building Partnerships* 3d ed. (Burr Ridge IL: Irwin McGraw–Hill, 1997).

18. Ridnour, A., "Profile of a Purchasing Professional" *Purchasing* (July 13, 1995), pp. 56–72.

19. Nelton, Sharon, "Rising Hurdles for Vendors," *Nation's Business* (June 1996), pp. 46–47.

20. Heinritz, Stuart, Paul U. Farrel, Larry Guinpero, and Michael Kolchin, *Purchasing: Principles and Applications* (Englewood Cliffs, NJ: Prentice Hall, 1991).

21. Kaeter, Margaret, "An Outsourcing Primer," *Training and Development* (November 1995), pp. 20–25.

22. Apte, Uday M., and Richard O. Mason, "Global Disaggregation of Information-Intensive Services," *Management Science* 41 (July 1995), pp. 1250–62.

23. O'Reilly, B., "Your New Global Workforce," *Fortune* (December 14, 1992), pp. 52-66.

24. Buss, Dale D., "Growing More by Doing Less," *Nation's Business* (December 1995), pp. 18–24.

25. Fram (1995).

26. "Adopting Suppliers," *Purchasing Executive Bulletin* (May 25, 1994), pp. 1–3.

27. Trent, Robert J., and Robert M. Monczak, "Effective Cross-Functional Sourcing Teams: Critical Success Factors," *International Journal of Purchasing and Materials Management* (November 1994), pp. 3–11.

28. Mullich and Welch (1995).

29. Maynard, Roberta, "Trade Tide Rises across the Pacific" *Nation's Business* (November 1995), 18, pp. 53–55.

30. Janson, Robert L., *Purchasing Ethical Practices* (Tempe AZ: National Association of Purchasing Management, 1988).

31. Apte and Mason (1995).

32. Janson (1988).

33. Dorsch, Michael J., and Scott W. Kelley, "An Investigation into the Intentions of Purchasing Executives to Reciprocate Vendor Gifts," *Journal of the Academy of Marketing Science* 22 (Fall 1994), pp. 315–27.

Chapter 4

1. Day, Ellen, and Hiram C. Barksdale, Jr., "How Firms Select Professional Services," *Industrial Marketing Management* 21 (1992) pp. 85–91.

2. Anderson, Paul F., and Terry M. Chambers, "A Reward/Measurement Model of Organizational Buying Behavior," *Journal of Marketing* 49 (Spring 1985), pp. 7–23; Terry M. Chambers, Paul F. Anderson, and B.J. Dunlap, "Preferences, Intentions, and Behavior of Organizational Buyers under Different Reward Conditions," *Journal of Business Research* 14, (1986), pp. 533–47.

3. Hendrick, Thomas E., and William A. Ruch, "Determining Performance Appraisal Criteria for Buyers," *Journal of Purchasing and Materials Management* (Summer 1988), pp. 18–26.

4. Bandura, Albert, "The Explanatory and Predictive Scope of Self-Efficacy Theory," *Journal of Social and Clinical Psychology* 4, no. 3 (1986), pp. 359–73.

5. Tanner, John F., Jr., and Stephen B. Castleberry, "The Participation Model: Factors Related to Buying Decision Participation," *Journal of Business to Business Marketing* 1, no. 3, (1993), pp. 35–62.

6. Trent, Robert J., and Robert M. Monczak, "Effective Cross-Functional Sourcing Teams: Critical Success Factors," *International Journal of Purchasing and Materials Management* (November 1994), pp. 3–11.

7. Tanner, John F. Jr., "Predicting Organizational Buyer Behavior," *Journal of Business & Industrial Marketing* 5 (Summer/Fall 1990), pp. 57–64.

8. Tanner, John F., Jr., "Intel's Biggest Challenge," *IDEAS* (March 1995), pp. 1894–6.

9. Tanner and Castleberry (1993).

10. Berkowitz, Marvin, "New Product Adoption by the Buying Organization: Who Are the Real Influencers?" *Industrial Marketing Management* 15, (1986), pp. 33–43; Susan A. Lynn, "Identifying Buying Influences for a Professional Service: Implications for Marketing Efforts," *Industrial Marketing Management* 16 (1987), pp. 119–30.

11. Pettigrew, Andrew, "The Industrial Purchase Decision as a Political Process," *European Journal of Marketing* 9, no. 1 (1975), pp. 4–19.

12. Lynn (1987).

13. McWilliams, Robert D., Earl Naumann, and Stan Scott, "Determining Buying Center Size," *Industrial Marketing Management* 21 (1992), pp. 43–49.

14. Dholakia, Ruby Roy, Jean L. Johnson, Albert J. Della Bitta, and Nikhilesh Dholakia, "Decision-Making Time in Organizational Buying Behavior: An Investigation of Its Antecedents," *Journal of the Academy of Marketing Science* 21 (Fall 1993), pp. 281–92.

15. LaForge, Mary C., and Louis H. Stone, "An Analysis of the Industrial Buying Process by Means of Buying Center Communications," *Journal of Business and Industrial Marketing* 4 (Winter 1989), pp. 29–36.

16. Thomas, Robert J., "Industrial Market Segmentation on Buying Center Purchase Responsibilities," *Journal of the Academy of Marketing Science* 17, no. 3 (1989), pp. 243–52.

17. Tanner & Castleberry (1993).

18. Krapfel, Robert, "An Advocacy Choice Model of Organizational Buyers' Vendor Choice," *Journal of Marketing* 49 (Fall 1985), pp. 51–58.

19. Hawes, Jon M., Kenneth E. Mast, and Scott H. Barnhouse, "Perceived Personal Risk: An Examination across Demographic Groups of Purchasing Executives," *Proceedings* AMA Winter Educators' Conference, (1988), pp. 328–32; Tony L. Henthorne, Michael S. LaTour, and Alvin J. Williams, "How Organizational Buyers Reduce Risk," *Industrial Marketing Management* 22 (1993), pp. 41–48.

20. Henthorne, LaTour, and Williams (1993).

21. *The Power of Trade Shows,* research report (Trade Show Bureau, Bethesda, MD., 1995).

22. Bunn, Michele D., "Information Search in Industrial Purchase Decisions," *Journal of Business to Business Marketing* 1, no. 2 (1993), pp. 67–102.

23. Puto, Christopher, Wesley E. Patton III, and Ronald H. King, "Risk Handling Strategies in Industrial Vendor Selection Decisions," *Journal of Marketing* 49 (Winter 1985), pp. 85–98.

24. Kashani, Kamran, "Marketing Futures: Priorities for a Turbulent Environment," *Long Range Planning* 28 (1995), pp. 87–98.

Chapter 5

1. A good summary of Frederick Smith's breakthrough with Federal Express can be heard in George Smith, *Giants of Political Thought: The Audio Classics Series: Joseph Schumpeter and Dynamic Economic Change* (Nashville, TN: Knowledge Products, 1985).

2. Main, Ken, "Case Studies in Implementation," in *Manufacturer and Automation Protocol/ Technical and Office Protocol: Users Group Summary* (Dearborn, MI: MAPTOP Users Group of Society of Manufacturing Engineers (SME) 2, no. 3 (1987), pp. 141–47.

3. Guillart, Francis J., and Frederick D. Sturdivant, "Spend a Day in the Life of Your Customer," *Harvard Business Review* 72 (January-February 1994), pp. 116–25. Edward F. McQuarrie, "Taking a Road Trip: Customer Visits Help Companies Recharge Relationships and Pass Competitors," *Marketing Management* 3 (April 1995), pp. 8–21.

4. Slywotzky, Adrian, *Value Migration* (Boston: Harvard Business School Press, 1996).

5. Quelch, John, Robert Dolan, and Thomas Kosnik, *Marketing Management* (Homewood, IL: Richard D. Irwin, 1993).

6. Majaro, Simon, *International Marketing: A Strategic Approach to World Markets* (London: George Allen and Unwin, 1982, p. 42, cited in William Shanklin and John Ryans, *Essentials of Marketing High Technology* (Lexington, MA: Lexington Books, 1987), p. 154.

7. Bly, Robert, *Business to Business Direct Marketing* (Lincolnwood, IL: NTC Business Books, 1994).

8. Gensch, Dennis H., "Targeting the Switchable Industrial Customer," *Marketing Science* 3 (Winter 1984), pp. 41–54.

9. Slywotzky, Adrian, *Value Migration* (Boston: Harvard Business School Press, 1996).

Chapter 6

1. "Global Gamble," *Business Week* (February 12, 1996), pp. 63–72; Morgan Stanley web site **http://www.ms.com.**

2. Aaker, David, *Strategic Market Management* (New York: John Wiley & Sons, 1992).

3. Webster, Frederick, "The Changing Role of Marketing in the Corporation," *Journal of Marketing* 56 (October 1992), pp. 1–17.

4. HP, Intel Form Broad Alliance on Computers," *Wall Street Journal* (June 9, 1994), p. 3.

5. Waltner, Charles, "Computer Makers Shift Strategy: Growth of Networks Heightens Reseller Role," *Business Marketing* (June 1996), p. 1+.

6. Hamel, Gary, and C. K. Prahalad, *Competing for the Future* (Boston, MA: Harvard Business School Press, 1994).

7. Shapiro, Stanley, Robert Dolan, and John Quelch, *Marketing Management: Strategy, Planning and Implementation* (Homewood, IL: Richard D. Irwin, 1985).

8. Covey, Stephen R., A. Roger Merrill and Rebecca R. Merrill, *First Things First* (New York: Simon & Schuster, 1994).

9. Slywotzky, Adrian J., *Value Migration* (Boston: Harvard Business School Press, 1996), p. 73.

10. Porter, Michael, "How Competitive Forces Shape Strategy," *Harvard Business Review* 57 (March-April 1979), pp. 137–45. George S. Day, "Assessing Competitive Arenas: Who Are Your Competitors?" in Geroge S. Day and David J. Reibstein, eds., *Wharton on Dynamic Competitive Strategy* (New York: John Wiley & Sons, 1997); D. Sudharshan, *Marketing Strategy: Relationships, Offerings, Timing & Resource Allocation* (Englewood Cliffs, NJ: Prentice-Hall, Inc., 1995).

11. D'Aveni, Richard, *Hypercompetition: Managing the Dynamics of Strategic Maneuvering* (New York: The Free Press, 1994), p. 13.

12. D'Aveni (1994).

13. Miles, R. E., and C. C. Snow, *Organizational Strategy and Process* (New York: McGraw-Hill, 1979).

14. Hunt, Shelby, and Robert Morgan, "The Comparative Advantage Theory of Competition," *Journal of Marketing* 59 (April 1995), p. 11.

15. McGee, Tim, "How to Become a SuperStar Student," video course no. 140 (Springfield, VA: The Teaching Company, 1994).

16. Luecke, Richard, *Scuttle Your Ships before Advancing* (New York: Oxford University Press, 1994), pp. 13–33.

17. Wick, Calhoun, and Lu Stanton Leon, "From Ideas to Action: Creating a Learning Organization," *Human Resource Management* 34, no. 2 (1995), p. 302.

18. Rosenbloom, Judith, and Reed Keller, "Building a Learning Organization at Coopers & Lybrand," *Planning Review* (September-October 1994), pp. 28–29+; Coopers and Lybrand web site **http://colybrand.com.**

19. Jones, Susan, *Creative Strategies in Direct Marketing* (Lincolnwood, IL: NTC Business Books, 1991), p. 22.

20. Wick and Leon (1995), pp. 299–311.

21. D'Aveni (1994), p. 351.

22. Luecke (1994), p. 103.

23. Treacy, Michael, and Fred Wiersema, *The Discipline of Market Leaders* (Reading, MA: Addison-Wesley Publishing Company, 1995). Intel web site **http://www.intel.com.**

Chapter 7

1. Denison, Daniel R., "What Is the Difference between Organizational Culture and Organizational Climate? A Native's Point of View on a Decade of Paradigm Wars," *Academy of Management Review* 21, no. 3, (1996), pp. 619–54.

2. Van der Togt, Jorrit J. W., "Reorganizing for Growth in a High Technology Company," *Long Range Planning* 28, no. 5 (1995), pp. 93–100.

3. Huber, George, "Organizational Learning: The Contributing Processes and the Literatures," *Organizational Science* 2 (February 1991), pp. 88–115.

4. Hamel, Gary and C. K. Prahalad, "Corporate Imagination and Expeditionary Marketing," *Harvard Business Review* 69 (July/August 1991), pp. 81–92.

5. Locke, Edwin A., and Vinod K. Jain, "Organizational Learning and Continuous Improvement," *International Journal of Organizational Analysis* 3 (January 1995), pp. 45–68.

6. Schoemaker, P.J., "Multiple Scenario Development: Its Conceptual and Behavior Foundation," *Strategic Management Journal* 14 (1993), pp. 193–213.

7. Humble, John, David Jackson, and Alan Thomson, "The Strategic Power of Corporate Values," *Long Range Planning* 24 no. 6 (1994), pp. 28–42.

8. Day, George S., "The Capabilities of Market-Driven Organizations," *Journal of Marketing* 58 (October 1994), pp. 37–52.

9. Deshpande, Rohit, John Farley, and Frederick Webster, "Corporate Culture, Customer Orientation, and Innovativeness in Japanese Firms: A Quadrad Analysis," *Journal of Marketing* 57 (January 1993), pp. 23–37; Bernard Jaworski and Ajay Kohli, "Market Orientation: Antecedents and Consequences," *Journal of Marketing* 57 (July 1993), pp. 53–70; John C. Narver and Stanley Slater, "The Effects of a Marketing Orientation on Business Profitability," *Journal of Marketing* 54 (October 1990), pp. 20–35.

10. Slater, Stanley, and John C. Narver, "Market Orientation and the Learning Organization," *Journal of Marketing* 59 (July 1995), pp. 63–74.

11. Weitz, Barton A., Stephen B. Castleberry, and John F. Tanner Jr., *Selling: Building Partnerships,* 3 ed. (Burr Ridge, IL: Irwin McGraw-Hill, 1997).

12. Hutt, Michael D., "Cross-Functional Relationships in Marketing," *Journal of the Academy of Marketing Science* 23, no. 4, (1995), pp. 351–57.

13. Ingebretsen, Mark, "Mass Appeal: Ross Controls Builds Customers for Life with Mass Customization," *Business Marketing* (March 1997), pp. 1, 14, 52.

14. Konijnendijk, Paul A., "Dependence and Conflict Between Production and Sales," *Industrial Marketing Management* 22 (1993), pp. 161–67.

15. Sogomonian, Aram G., and Christopher Tang, "A Modeling Framework for Coordinating Promotion and Production Decisions within a Firm," *Management Science* 39 (February 1993), pp. 191–203.

16. Leigh, Thomas, "The Relationship between Marketing and Sales," presentation at the Transfiguring the Sales Force conference, Atlanta, GA, 1995.

17. Strahle, William, Rosann L. Spiro, and Frank Acito, "Marketing and Sales: Strategic Alignment and Functional Implementation," *Journal of Personal Selling and Sales Management* XVI (Winter 1996), pp. 1–20.

18. Ibid.; Hutt (1995).

19. Loro, Laura, "FedEx Mines Its Database to Drive New Sales," *Business Marketing* (March 1997), pp. 4, 32.

Chapter 8

1. Tanner, John F., Jr., and Lawrence B. Chonko, "Using Trade Shows throughout the Product Life Cycle," Center for Exhibition Industry Research Report, 1996.

2. Edgett, Scott, David Shipley, and Giles Forbes, "Japanese and British Companies Compared: Contributing Factors to Success and Failure in NPD," *Journal of Product Innovation Management* 9, (1992), pp. 3–10.

3. Murphy, William, and Linda Gorchels, "How to Improve Product Management Effectiveness," *Industrial Marketing Management* 25 (1996), pp. 47–58.

4. Edgett et al. (1992).

5. This section is based on James H. Flournoy, "Organizing and Getting New Product Ideas," in A. Edward Spitz, ed., *Product Planning* (Princeton NJ: Auerbach Publishers, 1972).

6. Liberatore, Matthew J., and Anthony C. Stylianou, "Expert Support Systems for New Product Development Decision Making: A Modeling Framework and Applications," *Management Science* 41, no. 8 (August 1995), pp. 1296–1314.

7. Kerin, Roger A., P. Rajan Varadarajan, and Robert A. Peterson, "First-Mover Advantage: A Synthesis, Conceptual Framework, and Research Propositions," *Journal of Marketing* 56 , no. 4 (1992), pp. 33–52.

8. Mizuno, Shigeru, and Yogi Akao, *QFD: The Customer Driven Approach to Quality Planning and Deployment,* translated to English by Glenn Mazur (Tokyo: Asian Productivity Organization, 1994).

9. von Hipple, Eric, *The Sources of Innovation* (New York: Oxford University Press, 1988).

10. Cooper, R. G., and E. J. Kleinschmidt, "Success Factors in Product Innovation," *Industrial Marketing Management* 16 (1987), pp. 215–23.

11. Atuahene-Gima, Kwaku, "Market Orientation and Innovation," *Journal of Business Research* 35 (1996), pp. 93–103.

12. Gupta, Ashok, Klaus Brockhoff, and Ursula Weisenfeld, "Making Trade-Offs in the New Product Development Process: A German/US Comparison," *Journal of Product Innovation Management* 9 (1992), pp. 11–18.

13. This section is based primarily on Simon J. Towner, "Four Ways to Accelerate New Product Development," *Long Range Planning* 27, no. 2 (1994), pp. 57–65.

14. Millson, Murray, SP Raj, and David Wilemon, "A Survey of Major Approaches for Accelerating New Product Development," *Journal of Product Innovation Management* 9 (1992), pp. 53–69.

15. Swink, Morgan, Christopher Sandvig, and Vincent Mabert, "Customizing Concurrent Engineering Processes: Five Case Studies," *Journal of Product Innovation Management* 13 (1996), pp. 229–44.

16. Kitchell, Susan, "Corporate Culture, Environmental Adaptation, and Innovation Adoption: A Qualitative/Quantitative Approach," *Journal of the Academy of Marketing Science* 23 (Summer 1995), pp. 159–205.

17. Link, Peter L., "Keys to New Product Success and Failure," *Industrial Marketing Management* 16 (1987), pp. 109–18.

18. Barrier, Michael, "Customers Need Training, Too," *Nation's Business* (December 1995), pp. 74R–75R.

Chapter 9

1. Bucklin, Louis P., *A Theory of Distribution Channel Structure.* (Berkeley, CA: IBER Special Publications, 1966).

2. "Outsourcing's Rising Tide," *Chemical Enginering* (April 1997), pp. 28–31.

3. Stern, Louis, and Adel El-Ansary, *Marketing Channels* (Upper Saddle River, NJ: Prentice-Hall, 1992).

4. Hlavacek, James, and Tommy McCuistion, "Industrial Distributors: When, Who, and How?" *Harvard Business Review* 61 (March-April 1983), pp. 96–101.

5. Dutta, Shantanu, Mark Bergen, Jan Heide, and George John, "Understanding Dual Distribution: The Case of Reps and House Accounts," *Journal of Law, Economics, & Organization* 11 (April 1995), pp. 189–204.

6. Anderson, Erin, and Barton Weitz, "Determinants of Continuity in Conventional Industrial Channel Dyads," *Marketing Science* 8 (Fall 1989), pp. 310–323. Jan Heide and George John, "The Role of Dependence Balancing in Safeguarding Transaction-Specific Assets in Conventional Channels," *Journal of Marketing* 52 (January 1988), pp. 20–37.

7. The MAC Group, now known as Gemeni Consulting, Inc., *The Planning Forum: Differentiation through Channel Strategy: Concepts and Practice* (May 1, 1990).

8. Fein, Adam J., and Erin Anderson, "Patterns of Credible Commitments: Territory and Brand Selectivity in Industrial Distribution Channels," *Journal of Marketing* 61 (April 1997), pp. 19–35.

9. Bergen, Mark, Shantanu Dutta, and Orville Walker, "Agency Relationships in Marketing: A Review of the Implications and Applications of Agency and Related Theories," *Journal of Marketing* 56 (July 1992), pp. 1–24.

10. Ping, Robert, "The Effects of Satisfaction and Structural Constraints on Retailer Exiting, Voice, Loyalty, Opportunism, and Neglect," *Journal of Retailing* 69 (Fall 1993), pp. 320–52.

11. Graham, John, "The Problem-Solving Approach to Negotiations in Industrial Marketing," *Journal of Business Research* 14, (1986), pp. 549–66. Harold H. Kelley, "A Classroom Study of the Dilemmas in Interpersonal Negotiations," in *Strategic Interaction and Conflict,* K. Archibald, ed. (Berkeley Institute of International Studies, University of California, Berkeley, 1966).

12. "Looking Back—1996 Was an Unusual Year: 1997 Doesn't Seem to Be Much Different," *Agency Sales Magazine* (May 1997), pp. 22–23.

13. Anderson, James, and James Narus, "Turn Your Distributors into Partners," *Harvard Business Review* 64 (March-April 1986), pp. 66–71.

14. Stern, Louis, Adel El-Ansary, and Anne Caughlin, *Marketing Channels* (Upper Saddle River, NJ: Prentice-Hall, 1996), p. 318.

15. Ibid., p. 252.

16. Boyle, Brett, F. Robert Dwyer, Robert Bobicheaux, and James Simpson, "Influence Strategies in Marketing Channels: Measures and Use in Different Relationship Structures," *Journal of Marketing Research* 29 (November 1992), pp. 462–71.

17. Stundza, Tom, "Service Centers Eye Processing Upgrades," *Purchasing* (May 1, 1997), pp. 32B1–B3.

18. Wisnia, Saul "Time Is of the ESSENCE," *Industrial Distribution* (April 1997), pp. 115–18. Marshall web site: **http//www.marshall.com**

Chapter 10

1. Arens, William F., and Courtland L. Bovée, *Contemporary Advertising,* 5th ed. (Burr Ridge IL: Richard D. Irwin Inc., 1994).

2. Welch, Mary, "Learning the Trade: Dentsu Gets Tips on b-to-b," *Business Marketing* (February 1995), p. 25.

3. Cleland, Kim, "A Lot of Talk, Little Action on IMC," *Business Marketing* (March 1995), pp. 1, 30; Tom Duncan, "Is Your Marketing Communications Integrated?" *Advertising Age* 65, no. 4 (January 27, 1977), p. 26.

4. Arens and Bovée (1994).

5. Center for Exhibition Industry Research, *The Power of Exhibitions,* Research Report, 1996.

6. Tanner, John F. Jr., Lawrence B. Chonko, and Joyce McKee, "Behind the Booth," *Marketing Management* 3, no. 1 (1994), pp. 40–43.

Chapter 11

1. Worsham, James, "A Global Reach for Small Firms," *Nation's Business* (October 1995), p. 40.

2. This section is based on William F. Arens and Courtland L. Bovée, *Contemporary Advertising,* 5th ed., (Burr Ridge IL: Richard D. Irwin Inc., 1994); and William Wells, John Burnett, and Sandra Moriarty, *Advertising: Principles and Practices,* 2nd ed. (Englewood Cliffs, NJ: Prentice Hall, 1992).

3. Tanner, John F. Jr., *Faculty Curriculum Guide to Trade Shows* (Center for Exhibition Industry Research, 1997). Any marketing or advertising professor can obtain a free copy of this book, which includes transparency masters, test bank, and lecture notes, by calling CEIR at (301)907-7626.

4. Tanner, John F. Jr., Thomas Ponzurick, and Lawrence B. Chonko, "Promotional Activities as Learning Activities: An Analysis of Trade Show Attendees," research monograph (Exhibit Management Educational Foundation of the Trade Show Exhibitors' Association, 1997).

5. DeLoitte & Touche Consulting Group, *The Role of Exhibitions in the Marketing Mix,* available from the Center for Exhibition Industry Research. (See note 3).

6. Gopalakrishna, Srinath, Gary L. Lilien, Jerome D. Williams, and Ian K. Sequeira, "Do Trade Shows Pay Off?" *Journal of Marketing* 59 (1995), pp. 75–83.

7. Tanner, Ponzurick, and Chonko (1997).

Chapter 12

1. Pasternack, Edward, "Scott Paper Company Achieves Growth with Innovative Marketing Campaign," *Direct Marketing* (May 1996), pp. 56–57; and Kimberly-Clark web site **http://www.kimberly-clark.com**

2. "Direct Marketing Flow Chart," *Direct Marketing* (May 1997), p. 3.

3. Dwyer, F. Robert, "Direct Marketing in the Quest for Competitive Advantage," *Journal of Direct Marketing* 1 (Winter 1987), pp. 15–22.

4. Harper, Rose, *Mailing List Strategies: A Guide to Mail Success* (New York: McGraw-Hill Book Company, 1986).

5. "The Business-to-Business Census: A Benchmark Study of Marketing Spending and Practices," *Business Marketing* (June 1996), Supplement.

6. Hodgson, Richard, *The Greatest Direct Mail Letters of All Time* (Chicago: Dartnell Corp., 1987), pp. 35–38; and Sargeant

House, *The Direct Mail Package* video from the Direct Marketing Educational Foundation, New York, 1986.

7. Joyce, Bernard, "Direct Marketing to Business," presentation at the University of Cincinnati, 1996.

8. The WEFA Group, *Executive Summary. Economic Impact: US Direct Marketing Today* (New York: Direct Marketing Educational Foundation, 1996.

9. Ray, Debra, "1996 Caples Award Winners," *Direct Marketing* (March 1997), pp. 13–17.

10. Locker, Kitty O., *Business and Administrative Communication* (Homewood, IL: Richard D. Irwin, Inc., 1992).

11. "The Business-to-Business Census: A Benchmark Study of Marketing Spending and Practices," *Business Marketing* (June 1996), Supplement.

12. Ibid.

13. Stone, Bob and John Wyman, *Successful Telemarketing* (Lincolnwood, IL: NTC Business Books, 1992), p. 183.

14. Ibid., p. 185.

15. Roman, Ernan, *Integrated Direct Marketing* (Lincolnwood, IL: NTC Business Books, 1995), pp. 46–47.

16. Eisenhart, Tom, "Telemarketing Takes Quantum Leap," *Business Marketing* (September 1993), pp. 75–76.

17. "NETmarketing 200 Best B-to-B Web Sites," *Business Marketing* (November 1997), p. 1.

18. *Best Practices in Interactive Marketing: A DMA Management Guide,* prepared by Price Waterhouse (New York: Direct Marketing Association, 1997).

19. Ibid., pp. 34–35; and Cisco web site **http://www.cisco.com.**

20. Frank, Malcom, "The Realities of Web-Based Electronic Commerce," *Strategy and Leadership* 25 (May/June 1997), pp. 30–37.

Chapter 13

1. DeConninck, J.B. and D.J. Good, "Perceptual Differences of Sales Practitioners and Students Concerning Ethical Behavior," *Journal of Business Ethics* (Fall 1989), pp. 667–86.

2. Sections of this chapter are based primarily upon Barton A. Weitz, Stephen B. Castleberry, and John F. Tanner Jr., *Selling: Building Partnerships,* 3rd ed. (Burr Ridge IL: Irwin McGraw–Hill, 1997), Chapters 13 and 17.

3. Vavra, Tony, *Aftermarketing* (Homewood, IL: BusinessOne Irwin, 1992).

4. Morgan, James P., "How the Top Ten Measure Up," *Purchasing* (June 4, 1992), pp. 62–63.

5. Davis, Dwight D., with Bill Sharp and Mark Schlack, "Can Digital Sustain Alpha's Edge?" *Datamation* (March 1, 1993), pp. 24–31.

6. Morgan, James P. and Shirley Cayer, "Working with World Class Suppliers: True Believers," *Purchasing* (August 13, 1992), pp. 50–52.

7. Carey, Robert, "Help-Wanted—Now!" *Sales & Marketing Management* (March 1997,) pp. 30–31.

8. Sager, Sue, Gary McWilliams, and Robert Hof, "IBM Leans on Its Sale Force," *Business Week* (February 7, 1994), p. 110.

Chapter 14

1. Kaplan, A.D.H., Joel Dirlam, and Robert Lanzillotti, *Pricing in Big Business* (Washington, DC: The Brookings Institution, 1958).

2. Smith, Gerald, "Managerial Pricing Orientation: The Process of Making Pricing Decisions," *Pricing Strategy & Practice* 3, no. 3 (1995), pp. 28–39.

3. Our model draws on Kent Monroe and Tridib Mazumdar, "Pricing Decision Models: Recent Developments and Research Opportunities," in Timothy Devinney, ed., *Issues in Pricing Theory and Research* (Lexington, MA: Lexington Books, 1988), pp. 361–88.

4. See Bill Richards, "Fishermen in Alaska, Awash in Salmon, Strive to Stay Afloat," *Wall Street Journal* (September 4, 1996), pp. 1, 6. Also see Alaska's site: **http://www.state.ak.us/local/akpages/FISH.GAME/geninfo/press/pressrel.htm**

5. Woodside, Arch, "Making Better Pricing Decisions in Business Marketing," in *Advances in Business Marketing and Purchasing,* Arch Woodside, ed. (Greenwich, CT: JAI Press, 1994), pp. 139–83.

6. Howard, J.A., and W.M. Morganroth, "Information Processing Model of Executive Decisions," *Management Science* 14 (1968), pp. 416–28.

7. Levitt, Theodore, *The Marketing Imagination* (New York, The Free Press, 1983).

8. *Monsanto Co. v. Spray-Rite Service Corp.*, 104 US 1464 (1984).

9. *Texaco, Inc. v. Ricky Hasbrouck, dba Rick's Texaco, et al.* 946 US 942 (1990), quoted in Louis Stern, Adel El-Ansary, and Anne Coughlan, *Marketing Channels* (Upper Saddle River, NJ: Prentice-Hall, 1996), p. 363.

10. Savage, G.T., J.D. Blair, and R.J. Sorenson, "Consider Both Relationship and Substance when Negotiating Strategically," *Academy of Management Executive* 3 (1989), pp. 37–48.

11. Lewicki, Roy, David Saunders, and John Minton, *Essentials of Negotiation* (Chicago: Irwin, 1997).

12. Ross, Elliot, "Making Money with Proactive Pricing," *Harvard Business Review* 62 (November-December 1984), pp. 145–55.

Chapter 15

1. Green, Stephen G., and M. Ann Welsh, "Cybernetics and Dependence: Reframing the Control Concept," *Academy of Management Review* 13, no. 2 (1988), pp. 287–301.

2. Keidel, Robert W., "Rethinking Organizational Design," *Academy of Management Executive* 8, no. 4 (1994), pp. 12–30.

3. McDaniel, Carl, and Roger Gates, *Contemporary Marketing Research* (Minneapolis: West Publishing, 1993).

4. van der Erve, Marc L.B., "Evolution Management: Planning for Corporate Development," *Long Range Planning* 28 (October 1995), pp. 101–8.

5. Luthans, Fred, Michael J. Rubach, and Paul Marsnik, "Going beyond Total Quality: The Characteristics, Techniques, and Measures of Learning Organizations," *International Journal of Organizational Analysis* 3 (January 1995), pp. 24–44.

Chapter 16

1. Rebello, Kathy, "Inside Microsoft," *Business Week* (July 15, 1996), pp. 56–70.

2. Levitt, Theodore, *The Marketing Imagination* (New York: The Free Press, 1983), p. 111.

3. Jackson, Barbara B., *Winning and Keeping Industrial Customers* (Lexington, MA: Lexington Books, 1985).

4. Anton, Jon, *Customer Relationship Management: Making Hard Decisions with Soft Numbers* (Upper Saddle River, NJ: Prentice-Hall, 1996), p. 12.

5. Desatnick, Robert, and Denis Detzel, *Managing to Keep the Customer* (San Francisco, CA: Jossey-Bass Publishers, 1993).

6. Kaydo, Chad, "Making an Impact," *Sales and Marketing Management* (September 1996), pp. 89–94+.

7. Ferrell, Paul, "Eats, Ethics and Economics," *Purchasing* (December 2, 1965), p. 5.

8. Halvorson, Paul, and William Rudelius, "Is There a Free Lunch," *Journal of Marketing* 41 (January 1977), pp. 44–49.

9. Morgan, Robert, and Shelby Hunt, "The Commitment-Trust Theory of Relationship Marketing," *Journal of Marketing* 58 (July 1994), pp. 20–38.

10. "VW's Factory of the Future," *Business Week* (October 7, 1996), pp. 52–56.

11. Gundlach, Greg, and Patrick Murphy, "Ethical and Legal Foundations of Relational Marketing Exchanges," *Journal of Marketing* 57 (October 1993), pp. 35–46.

12. Palay, Thomas, "Comparative Institutional Economics: The Governance of Rail Freight Contracting," *Journal of Legal Studies* 13 (June 1984), pp. 265–87.

13. Bradach, Jeffrey and Robert Eccles, "Price, Authority and Trust: From Ideal Types to Plural Forms," *Annual Review of Sociology* 15 (1989), pp. 97–118.

14. Mohr, Jakki, and John R. Nevin, "Communication Strategies in Marketing Channels: A Theoretical Perspective," *Journal of Marketing* 54 (October 1990), pp. 36–51.

15. Furlong, Carla, *Marketing for Keeps* (New York: John Wiley & Sons, Inc., 1993).

16. Furlong (1993), p. 51.

17. Anton, (1996), p. 12.

18. Zeithaml, Valerie, A. Parusuraman, and Leonard Berry, *Delivering Quality Service* (New York: The Free Press, 1990).

19. Adapted "Hotel Frequent-Guest Programs . . . A Slumbering Opportunity," *Colloquy* 5, and Rick Barlow, "Do They Even Know I'm Here?" *Colloquy* 5, no. 3 (1996), p. 15.

20. Kisel, Ralph, "Chrysler: Suppliers Hit Savings Goal Early," *Automotive News* (May 5, 1997), p. 6.

21. Kaydo, Chad, "Making an Impact," *Sales and Marketing Management* (September 1996), pp. 89–94+.

22. Furlong (1993), p. 90.

23. Adapted from Howard Scott, "Winning Back a Lost Account," *Nation's Business* (July 1996), p. 31R.

Chapter 17

1. "Things Go Better with Multinationals—Except Jobs," *Business Week* (May 2, 1994), p. 20.

2. "The 100 Largest Multinationals: Getting the Welcome Carpet," *Forbes* (July 18, 1994), pp. 276–79.

3. Cateora, Philip, *International Marketing,* 9th ed. (Burr Ridge, IL: Richard D. Irwin, 1996), p. 18.

4. Maynard, Roberta, "Trade Tide Rises across the Pacific," *Nation's Business* (November 1995), pp. 52–56.

5. Ibid.

6. Johnson, Bradley, "Compaq, Digital Mull Global Shop Consolidation," *Business Marketing* (May 1997), p. 3.

7. Achrol, Ravi, "Changes in the Theory of Interorganizational Relations in Marketing: Toward a Network Paradigm," *Journal of the Academy of Marketing Science* 25, no. 1 (1997), pp. 56–71.

8. Oikawa, Naoko, and John F. Tanner Jr., "The Influence of Japanese Culture on Business Relationships and Negotiations," *Journal of Business and Industrial Marketing* 7 (Fall 1992), pp. 55–62.

9. Ibid.

10. Gerlach, Michael, "Twilight of the Keiretsu? A Critical Assessment," *Journal of Japanese Studies* 18 (1992), pp. 79–118.

11. Ibid.

12. "Developing Suppliers in Korea," *Quality* (October 1990), pp. 28–32.

13. Cateora, 1996.

14. Ibid.

15. The quote is on p. 17 of John Farley, "Looking Ahead at the Marketplace: It's Global and It's Changing," in Donald Lehmann and Katherine E. Jocz, eds., *Reflections on the Futures of Marketing* (Cambridge, MA: Marketing Science Institute, 1997), pp. 15–35.

16. Ibid.

17. Tanner, John F. Jr., "Chinese Marketing: The Critical Culture Blunder," in *Marketing Channels: A Relationship Management Approach,* by Lou Pelton, David Strutton, and James Lumpkin (Chicago: Irwin, 1997), pp. 233–35.

18. Farley (1997), p. 23.

19. Webster, Frederick, "The Changing Role of Marketing in the Corporation," *Journal of Marketing* 56 (October 1992), pp. 1–17.

20. Donath, Bob, "Global Marketing Management: New Challenges Reshape Worldwide Competition," *ISBM Insights* 6, no. 4 (1996).

21. The quote is from p. 59 of Donna Cornachio, "How Not to Lose Your Job," *Sales & Marketing Management* (August 1996), pp. 58–63.

22. Maddox, Alice, "Sales Training Technology Goes the Distance," *Sales and Marketing Strategies & News* (September 1994), p. 58.

23. Leonard, Bill, "The Sell Gets Tough on College Campuses," *HRMagazine* (June 1994), pp. 61–63.

24. Allis, Sam, Marc Hequet, and David Jackson, "15 of the Hottest Fields," *Time* (January 20, 1997), pp. 58–61.

25. Miller, Cyndee, "Job Picture for Marketing, Sales Brightest in Years," *Marketing News* (August 29, 1994), pp. 1–2.

26. Wiesendanger, Betsy, "The MBA: Is It Relevant in Sales?" *Sales & Marketing Management* (May 1993), pp. 58–61.

27. Lancaster, Hal, "Managing Your Career: Technology Raises the Bar for Sales Jobs," *Wall Street Journal* (April 1, 1997), p. B1.

28. Barner, Robert, "Seven Changes That Will Challenge Managers—and Workers," *The Futurist* (March-April 1996), pp. 14–18.

29. Cornachio (1996).

30. Gelman, Jan "If You Had $3000 to Spend on Self-Improvement, What Would You Do?" *Selling* (September 1995), pp. 59–69.

Index

C

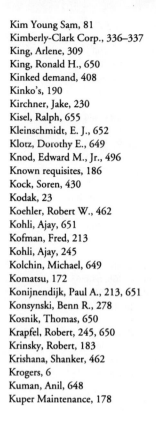

Jackson, Barbara B., 495, 654
Jackson, David, 651, 655
Jackson Timers & Controls, 398